GEDALYAHU ALON

JEWS, JUDAISM AND THE CLASSICAL WORLD

GEDALYAHU ALON

JEWS, JUDAISM AND THE CLASSICAL WORLD

Studies in Jewish History
in the Times of the Second Temple and Talmud

Translated from the Hebrew by

ISRAEL ABRAHAMS

JERUSALEM 1977

THE MAGNES PRESS, THE HEBREW UNIVERSITY

New ISBN 1-59045-958-X

Printed in Israel

at Central Press, Jerusalem

INTRODUCTION

by Shmuel Safrai

Gedalyahu Alon was born in 1901 in the town of Kobryn, Bielorussia; he died suddenly in Jerusalem in the year 1950, without having reached the age of fifty. In his youth he had attended the Slobodka Yeshivah in Lithuania, and had become known as a brilliant student. He immigrated to Eretz Israel, and was a member of the first graduating class of The Hebrew University (1931) taking his degree in Talmud and Classics. Later on, and until the day of his death, he taught Talmud and Jewish History at The Hebrew University.

During his lifetime he published a considerable number of scholarly articles in the various learned periodicals and similar publications that appeared in Eretz Israel in his time. After his death, his lectures on Jewish history were collected, edited, and published in two volumes under the (Hebrew) title "History of the Jews in the Land of Israel During the Period of the Mishnah and the Talmud" (1953–55). A few years later his published articles were gathered up between covers, in two more volumes entitled "Studies in the Jewish History of the Second Commonwealth and the Mishnaic-Talmudic Period" (1957–58).

In his teaching, as well as in his research, Alon's distinguishing characteristic was an extraordinary combination: mastery of Torah, that is, the whole compass of Jewish learning in the best tradition of the yeshivot, coupled with a profound scholarship in all branches of classical literature and history. He was at home in the Greek and Latin sources, from the epics of Homer to the codes of Justinian. He knew Roman law, and was at the same time familiar with the literature of Christian origins, from the New Testament to the last of the Church Fathers. Of course, he was equally in control of the whole gamut of Hellenistic Jewish literature.

Not only was he thoroughly familiar with all this material; he was also able to take passages relevant to his researches and analyze them, both linguistically and historically, so as to illuminate the picture he was trying to reconstruct. This is true of his various research articles and studies; it is true as well of his history of the Jewish people after the Destruction (his volumes on that subject are due to appear soon in English translation). Alon analyzed every detail of his source-material in depth, to the degree that such analysis was necessary for dealing with the problem he had under study. But this care for detail never obscured the broader view; in spite of his attention to the trees, the forest always remained visible.

His use of the text-critical method in handling the variegated Greek and Latin sources, by the application of philological and historical criteria, taught him to do the same with the Talmudic sources, always adjusting the method to the varying nature of the material. This combination of methodology with vast learning enabled him to clarify many important problems in the history of the Jewish people during the last few generations of the Second Commonwealth and the following period, the Mishnaic-Talmudic age. His researches centered on the nature and structure of Jewish society, as exemplified by the essay "Par'irtin" dealing with the High Priesthood during the last generations of its existence; or the study "Sons of the Sages," which concerns itself with the emergence of a social class of learned scholars during the second century and the beginning of the third.

A number of Alon's studies are devoted to the socio-political forms in which Jewish communities were structured during the Mishnaic-Talmudic period. Examples of this kind of investigation are: "The *Strategoi* in the Cities of Israel During the Roman Occupation" and "The Appointment of Judges in the Land of Israel During the Talmudic Period." In these studies the reader learns about the various kinds of social and religious leaders, and the levels of society from which they came; and he finds out how they exercised their leadership against the background of the prevailing governmental set-up; whether it was during the last days of the Temple, or later on, during the sunset years of classical civilization.

Some of these studies bring up questions that are central to the political and religious history of the Jews during the days of the Temple, like "The Attitude of the Pharisees to Roman Rule and the House of Herod," or the chapters that deal with Rabban Joḥanan ben Zakkai's exit from besieged Jerusalem, and his leadership at Jabneh. Others are dedicated to questions in the history of the *halakhah*, such as the essay dealing with Philo, and the studies that investigate the implications of the laws of ritual purity and impurity. In handling the complicated questions connected with these matters, the author is able to adduce much of the cultural history and religious practice of the age, and at the same time to illumine whole chapters in the relations between the Jewries of the dispersion and the Jewish people in its homeland, as well as between the various Jewish sects and parties. These relationships in their turn shed a great deal of light on the early years of Christianity and on the way in which some Jewish traditions passed over to the daughter religion and became Christian traditions.

Alon's studies were published in collected form some twenty to twenty-five years ago, so that it is only now that we can begin to measure his decisive influence on instruction and research at universities in Israel and elsewhere, in the many aspects of Jewish history and culture during the several centuries preceding the Christian era and during the first five or six centuries that stand at the beginning of that era. His researches opened up new areas of study, indeed wrote whole new chapters in the history of the Jews during those hundreds of years; but what is perhaps even more important, they set the tone for subsequent teaching and historical research. During the past few decades, anybody who has read any literature in English investigating the Jewish history of those centuries has been influenced by Gedalyahu Alon, whether the reader recognized the fact or not; whether Alon was specifically quoted by the author or not; whether Alon's influence on the methods and the conclusions was direct or indirect. Now at last, the reader of English can turn the pages of the present volume and confront a selection of the author's studies in their full stature. It is to be hoped that in so doing he will discover for himself the unique approach, the penetrating grasp and the broad perspective that were so characteristic of Alon.

Everyone interested in the field will surely be grateful to the late Prof. Israel Abrahams, who translated most of the essays but was unfortunately not spared to complete the task; and to Rabbi A. Oshery, who finished the translation. Thanks are also due to Mr. J. Schwartz who prepared the index, and to The Hebrew University Press and its directors, Mr. Hayyim Toren and Mr. Ben-Zion Yehoshua, as well as to Mrs. Janet Shvili and the Central Press printers, all of whom have spared no pains in the production of this book.

SHMUEL SAFRAI

The Hebrew University, Jerusalem
The Faculty of Jewish History
Menahem Av, 5736

CONTENTS

JEWS, JUDAISM AND THE CLASSICAL WORLD

DID THE JEWISH PEOPLE AND ITS SAGES CAUSE THE HASMONEANS TO BE FORGOTTEN?

It is a widely held view among scholars that the Sages and the people (who were with them) of the period preceding and following the fall of the Second Temple endeavoured to erase the Hasmoneans and all that they accomplished from the memory of the Jewish nation. This conception, which finds a place also in Jewish writings (see B. Katzenelson's foreword to *Sefer ha-Gevura* ['Book of Heroism']), attributes to Israel's Sages the intent to suppress the memory and deeds of the Hasmoneans by an 'internal censorship' (regarding the same viewpoint relative to other heroic chapters of the nation's history, the wars of the Zealots — the [First] War with Rome and the Bar Kokhba Uprising [Third War against Rome] — this is not the place to deal with the subject) and the minimization of the victories they achieved as the 'trivia' of miracles and wonders; since the Sages/scholars were unable to abolish the Festival of Hanukkah itself, they proceeded to invent legendary reasons for its observance, in order to obliterate the name and heroism of the Hasmoneans from the national memory. Prof. L. Ginzberg (*Ginze Schechter* [*Genizah Studies in Memory of Solomon Schechter*], I, p. 476) seeks to prove that Hanukkah was properly observed only in Babylon, where the Persian fire-worshippers wished to eradicate 'the Festival of Lights', and the Jews gave their lives for it, and consequently it struck root in their midst; but this was not the case in Eretz Israel, where its observance was not meticulously maintained.

Four arguments are advanced by this school of thought, as follows:

(a) No separate tractate is devoted in the Mishna to Hanukkah, and even the ritual rulings of the Tannaim and Amoraim of Eretz Israel in regard to the laws of Hanukkah generally are few.

(b) *I Maccabees*, which was originally written in Hebrew, was not preserved by the Jews.

(c) The Talmud (*T.B. Shabbat* 21b) enquires in all innocence: 'What is Hanukkah?' This shows that the Gemara did not know the origin and character of the festival.

(d) The fact that the miracle of the cruse of oil was made the focal point of the salvation.

When we examine the explanation offered by scholars for the desire of the Sages to expunge the memory of the Maccabees and their deeds, we find the cause to be in the struggle of the Pharisees (and the masses) against the last of the Hasmoneans — from John Hyrcanus onward. A case of 'The fathers have eaten sour grapes, and the children's teeth are set on edge' is presented. This general opposition to the latter Hasmoneans, which subsequently spread and embraced the entire House of the Maccabees in the opinion of these scholars, was brought about, according to prevailing view, by the following four factors (all or some of them):

(a) The opposition of the Pharisees, who made religion the sole basis of Judaism, and 'whose aim was a spiritual republic' (S. Dubnow, *Divre Yeme 'Am 'Olam* ['History of the People of the World'], II, p. 84), to the political character given to the nation by the Hasmoneans. The extension of the boundaries of Judea and the fact that the borders were secured by military power and a strong political regime — all this conflicted with the wish of the scholars and the people who were with them to preserve the distinct religio-spiritual character of the life of the community.

(b) The Pharisees were opposed to the monarchy generally, and especially because the throne belonged to the House of David. Hence, when the Hasmoneans proceeded to take the crown for themselves (and 'they ate the Messiah'), they became unfit to rule, being completely disqualified.

(c) Those high priests and kings of the House of the Hasmoneans, who waged many wars and shed much blood, were invalidated in the estimation of the Sages and the people from serving in the office of the high priesthood.

(d) The fact that the Hasmoneans joined the Sadducees and persecuted the Sages.

Now before we examine the arguments cited above to the effect that the memory of the Maccabees had been suppressed, let us first consider the facts quoted subsequently, which appear to explain and corroborate the entire phenomenon.

The categorical view inculcated by gentile scholars — theologians and historians — and even by Jewish savants (in part or as a whole) concerning the essential character of Pharisaism, namely, that, in contradistinction to the Sadducean outlook, it is a strictly religio-spiritual way of life that rejects and disqualifies the State, is groundless.[1] Firstly, the oldest sources provide us with no proof nor the slightest evidence for this assertion. Furthermore, it is refuted by the acts of a number of the great Sages who lived before and after the destruction of the Temple; for they wrought and fought, both physically and spiritually, in the political sphere. There are also basic laws, preserved in the tradition of the earliest Tannaim, testifying to the reverse (nor is the negation of the state to be deduced from particular ethical dicta, such as that of Shemaiah, 'Love work and hate lordship'; it is no more than advice offered to the individual not to strive for power). The Pharisees aided Queen Salome Alexandra all her life and even held power and controlled the government of the country (the distinction drawn between internal government and external policy — in other words, that the Pharisees were concerned only with internal affairs [see Klausner, *Historia Yisre'elit* ('Jewish History'), II, p. 142] appears to be without foundation). In the reign of this Queen, we know that the neighbouring peoples who had been subjugated by the Judeans and had given the latter hostages were in great fear, and that an army had even been sent to conquer Damascus (*Antiquities*, xiii, 16, 3; *Wars* i, 5, 3). Nay more, the Pharisees had not protested against the Queen's action in maintaining a force of gentile mercenaries (the hiring of mercenary armies, which at that period obtained also in other kingdoms, was connected with national-economic and social factors, and is not particularly significant for national-spiritual considerations). In a word, Pharisaism essentially — viewed from the aspect of its main and fundamental teachings — does not militate against the state, but seeks to perfect it, to purify and establish it on the basis of justice and religion, on 'that which is equitable and good', as the Sages understood those ideals. Most of the acts of many scholars testify to their association, before and after the destruction of the Temple, with the political and 'secular' affairs of the nation. A general impression and an historic-

1 It is customary to infer also from the attitude of the people and its leaders, who stood before and denounced both Aristobulus and Hyrcanus, seeking to restore the rule of the high priests in Judea (*Antiquities*, xiv, 3, 2; a similar statement is found in Diodor, see Reinach, *Textes*, etc., p. 76), that the Pharisees (we may assume that there were many Pharisees among the 'leaders of the people') were prepared to forgo political freedom. However, the people protested only against the usurptive monarchy of the aforementioned brothers, and sought autonomy for themselves (a governing Sanhedrin), for in any event it was quite evident that the Romans would rule over Judea in actual fact.

philosophical exegesis, based on few dicta, which are as a rule interpreted contrary to their simple meaning, are incapable of refuting the arguments alluded to at the beginning and of serving as counter-arguments for the purpose of grounding the basic conception, which is erroneous and without foundation.

The question of the attitude of the Sages and the people to the monarchy in general requires meticulous elucidation, and this cannot be done here. Broadly speaking it may be stated that we find in the Tannaitic tradition and in extraneous sources, in Temple times and later, conflicting views on the subject: there were those who favoured a limited, 'constitutional', monarchy, while others condemned it.[2] However, in the *Halakha* the former outlook prevails, and if we are to draw any inference from actual life, the conduct of the Pharisees in the time of Salome Alexandra proves that the Sages did not disqualify the monarchy (even though the Halakha in *Sifre Deuteronomy*, §157, rules: 'a king but not a queen'[3]). Likewise the instructions given by Jannai to his wife shortly before his death ('Fear not the Pharisees', etc., and similarly in Josephus, *Antiq.*, xiii, 16, 1) evidence the fact that the Pharisees did not object to the Hasmonean monarchy in principle. Otherwise, it was pointless for Salome to draw nearer to the Pharisees and become reconciled with them, if the very monarchy itself was invalid.

The attitude adopted by the Pharisees in the time of Salome (and at the beginning of Jannai's reign, before 'the evil broke forth' through him) also refutes the accepted assumption that all the Sages, as it were, negated a monarchy that did not stem from the House of David. But actually this is proven by explicit halakhic sources. For we have learnt in a Baraita (*Tosefta Horayot* ii 8; *T.B. ibid.*, 13a; *T.P. ibid.* 48a): 'A scholar takes precedence over a king, for if a scholar dies we have not his peer, but if a king dies, all Israel are fit to reign.' A similar exposition is given in *Midrash Tannaim* (p. 104): ' "Thou mayest not put a foreigner over thee" — this comes to exclude a proselyte. The implication is that a proselyte is excluded. Or does it mean that if there is no one from the tribe of Judah, a Benjamite may not become king? Therefore it is stated: Are not

2 See below, p. 31, note 34.

3 This is not the place to examine closely this ruling which apparently contradicts the earlier decision that formed the basis of the Pharisaic recognition of the monarchy of Salome Alexandra. I shall revert to it on another occasion.

all Israel fit to reign?', etc. Inevitably we must conclude that there is a distinction between everlasting kingship, which belongs to David, and temporary monarchy, which pertains to all Israel (this distinction is implicit, in essence, even in the *Testaments of the Twelve Patriarchs* and the *Book of Jubilees*, *q.v.*, in contradiction of the prevailing view, which seeks to infer from them that the Hasmoneans — and those circles for whom the authors of these books spoke — wished to take away the monarchy completely, even in 'the Messianic future', from the House of David). Undoubtedly, we have learnt in a Baraita (*T.P. Horayot* iii, 47a; *T.P. Soṭa* viii, 25c; although the Palestinian Talmud has not indicated this dictum as Tannaitic, it is nevertheless a Baraita): 'Priests may not be anointed kings.' Amoraim dispute the interpretation of the rule, for according to R. Judan of En-Todros the reason for it is to be found in the verse 'The sceptre shall not depart from Judah', while according to R. Ḥiyya bar Abba priests only are disqualified. In the view of R. Judan, therefore, kings can be appointed only from the tribe of Judah.

We find this view stated in a work — *The Psalms of Solomon* (xvii, 4–7) — written by a Pharisee at the end of the epoch of the Hasmoneans (the period of Hyrcanus II), and aimed reproachfully against their monarchy. However, these sources reveal to us the struggle within the school of the Sages themselves regarding non-Davidic sovereignty (even according to R. Ḥiyya bar Abba, a priest, at least, cannot be a king), for they do not wish to attribute to the majority of the scholars and the people complete opposition to the monarchy of the Hasmoneans, which was temporary; such an assertion would be refuted by the events and sources cited earlier. Furthermore, the laws relating to kings that we find in Tannaitic teaching but are not expressly recorded in Scripture, are probably to be regarded as products of the Hasmonean epoch (the concluding phase); in other words, the Sages instituted and corroborated these laws, which affirm in (and limit) the monarchy.

Also the *opposition of the Sages* and the people to the Hasmonean dynasty on account of the many wars that they waged and the bloodshed that invalidated them from the high priesthood is also a supposition without foundation. Without doubt, it is possible to explain thereby events that occurred in the reign of Jannai; but it cannot be substantiated as a fact. Did not Judah, Jonathan, Simon and John (to 'the end') shed much blood of gentiles and also of Jews from among the Hellenizers and their followers? Nevertheless we do not find any explicit reference to any protest made from among the scholars or the people against them.[4] It is true that Prof. Aptowitzer seeks to explain the silence of the author of *II Maccabees* (Jason of Cyrene, or of the abridger?) in regard to Judah's brethren for this reason; but this fact is to be explained by the nature of the book. For its purpose is not to narrate the exploits of the House of the Hasmoneans (like *I Maccabees*), but to answer the question 'What is Hanukkah?', that is, to set forth the series of events that were responsible for the institution of festive days in honour of the victories won at the beginning of the war of liberation. It will be noted that the book begins with the establishment of the Festival of Hanukkah, and ends with the commemoration of 'Nicanor Day'.[5]

However, the Halakhot relating to the laws of optional wars, which were apparently also taught in the period with which we are concerned, testify that the Sages did not forbid offensive wars intended to extend the boundaries of Judea and of Eretz Israel. Although the events related by Josephus, from the time of the Wars to the fall of the State, show that the ruling given by Shammai that the Biblical words, 'until it [the city] fall' means that it may be besieged 'even on the Sabbath', was not accepted by the entire people (and the Sages),[6] nevertheless it testifies to what extent the Pharisees permitted optional (i.e. non-mandatory — Tr.) wars, inasmuch as they overrode, at least in the view of some of them, the laws of the Sabbath. There is no basis, therefore, for explaining the opposition of the Pharisees to the Hasmonean kings and the fact that they disqualified them from the high priesthood on the ground of the general principle that they prohibited the wars that the Hasmoneans waged against their many neighbours, although the Sages of the Sanhedrin and those who were not members of it could withhold their consent from a demand that a given 'optional war should be embarked upon'. At

4 In *Tarbiz*, V, pp. 32 ff. (see below pp. 117–18) I endeavoured to prove that the Halakha in *M. Sanhedrin* ix 6, 'If a man stole a sacred vessel or cursed by *Qosem* or made an Aramaean woman his paramour, the zealots may fall upon him', was first taught in the period of the Hasmoneans, and was aimed at the transgressors (Hellenizers and their congeners), to whom it was permitted to apply the law of the 'zealots', without the normal, restrictive court procedures. We must also add here the tradition taught in the Talmud (*T.B. Sanhedrin* 46a) in the name of R. Eliezer b. Jacob, 'I have heard that the Bet Din beat and punish even if not enjoined in the Torah', etc., 'and it once happened that a man rode on a horse in the days of the Greeks', etc.

5 Those rabbinic dicta that Prof. Aptowitzer seeks to interpret and apply to our subject do not in reality deal with our theme, and constitute no evidence.

6 See, for instance, the speech of Agrippa before the First War with Rome broke out (*The Jewish War*, ii, 16, 4).

all events, the Baraita (*Qiddushin* 66a) that states that King Jannai 'went to Koḥalith in the wilderness and conquered sixty cities there, and on his return rejoiced exceedingly', etc., shows that the Sages shared in his joy and did not condemn him on account of the bloodshed.

The conflicts between the Pharisees and the kings of the Hasmonean dynasty, who sided with the Sadducees. Undoubtedly this is a corroborated fact, only first we must consider and clarify the facts that qualify and cast doubts upon it, in order to set it in its proven and assured framework. It is certain that Jannai fought and persecuted the Pharisees. But with regard to the other members of the House of the Hasmoneans the matter is extremely dubious. It is true that the Talmudic tradition testifies that John Hyrcanus became a Sadducee in the end, and likewise the Sages who put an unfavourable construction on the reforms attributed to him in the relative Mishna (*T.P. Ma'aser Sheni* v 56d; *Soṭa* ix 24a) apparently knew this or a similar tradition. It is also known that Josephus states the same explicitly and at length, namely, that John was in conflict with the Pharisees and oppressed them. But, on the other hand, we find a number of passages in rabbinic sources where John Hyrcanus is favourably mentioned, a fact that is difficult to reconcile with the tradition referred to. Furthermore, the statement of Josephus cited above, is referred to Jannai in the Baraita of *Tractate Qiddushin.* Even in the writings of Josephus there are indications that he was familiar with another tradition that attributed this episode to King Jannai, as did the Tannaitic tradition. Hence we must conclude that there were two conflicting traditions current among the people concerning the first 'king' of the Hasmonean dynasty, 'who slew the Sages'.[7] The Sadduceeism and evil deeds of John Hyrcanus are at any rate in doubt.

Even more so is the prevailing view concerning the (real) Sadduceeism of (the latter) Aristobulus and of the struggle of the Pharisees against him unproven. The fact that he wished in the last days of Queen Salome Alexandra's reign to gain the support of the Sadducean opposition, is no proof of his religious views, and even less of a conflict between him and the Pharisees when he ascended the throne.[8] On the contrary, when we examine our sources, we are able to find indications that the Pharisees did *not* side with his rival, Hyrcanus, and that some of them at least (like the circles for whom the author

7 See below, p. 26 and note 22.

8 Compare Elbogen, *MGWJ*, of the year 1926, p. 152.

of *The Psalms of Solomon* served as spokesman) objected to the tyranny and harsh rule of both brothers. Needless to say, Graetz's assumption that the episode reported in *T.B. Yoma* 71b concerning Shemaiah and Avṭalion's reprimand to a high priest refers to Antigonus, to whom the Sages were opposed because of his 'heathen acts', is without foundation. It seems likely that the incident occurred between Shemaiah and Avṭalion and one of the first 'ordinary' priests appointed by Herod. The conclusion to be drawn from all this is that we have no proven and confirmed tradition concerning the conflict between the Hasmonean dynasty and the Pharisees on account of the former's Sadducean tendencies, except with regard to one Hasmonean ruler only, namely, Jannai.

But the fact that even Jannai did not open 'war' till the middle of his reign and that the Baraita cited above puts the blame for his heresy and wicked deeds onto his Sadducean counsellors and the cantankerousness of a certain 'elder' from among the Pharisees but does not speak with disfavour of Jannai's own personality, throws light on our main thesis, to wit, that there is not general opposition here to Jannai's sovereignty and even less to the entire Hasmonean dynasty. Had the conflict between the Pharisees and Jannai conduced to the disqualification and depreciation of the Hasmoneans as a whole in the estimation and memory of the Sages, the tradition referred to would not have portrayed the king's early acts in that tranquil, dramatically objective spirit that it does.[9]

We must now examine the arguments cited above, which allegedly testify to the effacement of the memory of the Hasmoneans by the Sages and the people in the period of the Tannaim and Amoraim.

The suppression of I Maccabees (with regard to *II Maccabees* no surprise need, in fact, be felt, nor should any inferences be drawn, since it was originally written in Greek). This contention must be utterly refuted, for Jerome bears witness that he saw the book in the possession of Jews in Eretz Israel (at the end of the fourth century) written in Hebrew. Without doubt the Jews treated it as a work that carried the national *imprimatur*, even if they did not attribute the least sanctity to it. Origen, too, saw it in circulation among the

9 Both the Baraita cited above and the parallel account of Josephus (*Antiquities* xiii, 40, 5) show that John or Jannai did not join the Sadducees because of his leaning to the Sadducean *doctrines* but because the Pharisean Halakha would not grant the 'king' the extra privilege that he demanded; hence the religious-spiritual conflict was not the primary factor but only an internal political manoeuvre.

Jews in Eretz Israel at the beginning of the third century in a Hebrew (or Aramaic) version under the name σαβαναιέλ (or, Σαρβανηλ) Σαρβήθ (probably to be read: סרבת סרבני אל [10] — 'The War of the Fighters of God'). But it seems to me that also Epiphanius (end of the fourth century; he was born and spent most of his life in Eretz Israel), who refers in three passages to 'The Mishna of the Sons of the Hasmonean' (δευτέρωσις τῶν υἱῶν ʿΑσαμωναίου) actually refers to the *Book of the Maccabees*. However, there is certainly no decisive evidence for rejecting the accepted interpretation that the Mishna referred to is to be understood in the same sense as 'The Mishna of R. Akiba' or 'The Mishna of R. Judan' (= R. Judah ha-Nasi), mentioned by Epiphanius (together with *Mishne Torah*, 'Deuteronomy'), which signifies a Mishna of actual Halakha [a collection of laws]. But since we possess no reference to a halakhic Mishna of the Hasmoneans (the decree of 'the Hasmonean Court' in *T.B. Sanhedrin* 81a and *ʿAvoda Zara* 36b is irrelevant here), it therefore appears that the 'Mishna' in question connotes a *book* or *tradition*. For we definitely find 'Mishna' (*Matnita*) applied also to subjects that are neither *Halakha* nor *Haggada*, but any kind of tradition brought to the School House (in *Tractate Qiddushin*, too, the tradition concerning the beginning of Jannai's heresy is reported in the form *tanya*, 'it was taught'). It may well be, therefore, that Epiphanius in his exposition associated the *Book of the Maccabees* with the halakhic Mishnayot of the Tannaim (just as he included among them the Book of Deuteronomy under the name 'Mishne' Torah ['משנה' תורה]) in unwitting error (as is his wont when speaking of Jewish tradition and practices generally). Furthermore, the Baraita in *Qiddushin* is undoubtedly only a fragment from a general work (or what *approximates* to it) that was written by a Pharisee and dealt with activities of the Hasmonean dynasty (needless to say that this composition is not to be identified with *I Maccabees*). When we examine this Baraita we see that the confident assumption in regard to the 'internal censorship' that suppressed the heroic records of the Hasmoneans is completely refuted, for the tradition referred to speaks favourably of Jannai's conquests in Transjordania.

Likewise the tradition that we find in *Halakhot Gedolot* (ed. Warsaw, *Hilkhot Soferim*, p. 282 — ed. Berlin, p. 615) concerning 'the elders of Bet Shammai and the elders of Bet Hillel', who 'wrote *Megillat Bet Ḥashmonai*' ['the Scroll of the House of the Hasmonean'] (in

10 D. Hoffmann, *Magazin*, XV, 179.

Halakhot Gedolot, ed. Berlin, *Sefer Bet Ḥashmonai* ['the Book of the House of the Hasmonean'])—'but till now it has not been available to the generations *until there shall arise a priest to consult the Urim and Thummim*, and they [also] wrote *Megillat Ta'anit*' ['the Scroll of Fasting'], shows that the early Sages regarded the book as a halakhic work, as a kind of Tannaitic Mishna, like the *Scroll of Ta'anit*, and regretted its withdrawal from circulation and awaited its rediscovery when the Messiah came (it makes no difference whether we know the nature of this 'Scroll', or not; with the later works, *Midreshe Hanukkah* and the *Megillat Antiochus* we are not concerned here).

It will thus be seen that the assumption regarding the suppression of the 'Books of the Hasmoneans' in the days of the Tannaim and Amoraim is without any basis.

The fact that Rabbi did not devote a tractate in our Mishna to Hanukkah cannot serve as evidence that the festival was deliberately forgotten or its significance depreciated. For if we were to apply the *argumentum e silentio* to the Mishna, we should have to negate important precepts of the Torah, such as phylacteries, fringes, and *mezuza*, to which tractates were not assigned in our Mishna (even in the case of Purim, in respect of which it is customary to mention *Tractate Megilla*,[11] which deals with the festival, its laws are not taught in the Mishna. For only a part of the laws of this tractate are concerned with the subject and treat of *the reading of the Megilla only*; the rest deal with other matters unrelated to Purim, and omit the regulations referring to the Purim Meal, the Purim Fund, and the Sending of Portions, which are taught in the Tosefta, and the Baraitot of the Talmudim, and in the discussions of the Amoraim). In like fashion David Neumark concludes (*History of Jewish Philosophy*, I, p. 81) from the Mishna's silence with regard to angels that Rabbi was opposed to angelology, a proposition that is wholly improbable. In a word, the absence of tractates in the Mishna dealing with specific laws, and even the paucity of laws relative to a given subject in the Tannaitic tradition as a whole, has no bearing on these laws *themselves* or their importance in the time of the compilers of the traditions, or on the attitude of these scholars towards them. Thus, to begin with, we must interpret this fact only by purely historical-literary enquiry. For we cannot expect from the early Sages that complete methodicalness that we adopt in compiling collections of laws. Moreover, historical-literary factors obtaining prior to the

11 In contradistinction to Hanukkah, to which a tractate was not assigned.

period of these compilers were responsible, in ways that we are not in a position to examine, for the excessive detailing of some regulations and the diminution of others.

Ginzberg, however, states that 'the Palestinian Talmud contains almost no reference to the laws of Hanukkah', and deduces from this that in the days of the Amoraim Hanukkah was not kept properly in Eretz Israel. Needless to say that in the case of the Palestinian Talmud, too, the form of analysis referred to applies exactly as with regard to the Mishna. Only we must examine the fact itself presented by this great savant, as well as his aforementioned deduction, in the light of the laws and acts mentioned in our sources.

Undoubtedly the laws of Hanukkah cited in the Palestinian Talmud are few. But we find many laws (and legends) relating to the festival in *Pesiqta Rabbati*, which basically, at least, derives from the teaching of Eretz Israel (*Piskot*, ii, iii, iv, vi, viii) and the *Tanḥuma* (Naso) and in *Tractate Soferim* (ch. xx 1–8), which is also largely based on the learning of Eretz Israel (*ibid.* [halakha 3] we find the stringent regulation prohibiting the use of an old [earthenware] Hanukkah lamp). Nay more, even in the Babylonian Talmud, in the very primary passage that deals with the laws of Hanukkah, *T.B. Shabbat* 21b–24a, many of the regulations are cited by scholars of Eretz Israel, like R. Joḥanan, Ulla and R. Joshua b. Levi (particularly the last-mentioned sage). Thus we see that we have in our possession numerous Halakhot, relative to the laws of Hanukkah, that were taught in the Talmud of Eretz Israel (although only a few of them have been preserved in the Palestinian Talmud).

And did all of them, as L. Ginzberg thinks, make light of the observance of the precept of Hanukkah in the Land of Israel?

We know the dispute of the Amoraim — Babylonian and Palestinian (of the third century) — as to whether '*Megillat Taʿanit* has been annulled' or not, a dispute that we first find in the days of the Tannaim who were disciples of R. Akiba (*Tosefta Taʿanit* iv 6; *T.B. Rosh ha-Shana* 18b; the incident — 'It once happened that a fast was decreed on Hanukkah in Lod' — reported in Tosefta *ibid.*, ii, 5, *T.B. Eruvin* 41a; *T.P. Taʿanit* ii and parallels, have no direct bearing on our subject here).

Now both Talmuds arrive at the conclusion that although *Megillat Taʿanit* is no longer valid for all the other festivals ordained by the Sages and their observance ceased since the destruction of the Temple, nevertheless 'Hanukkah and Purim have not been annulled'. If so, in what respect was there a diminution of the significance of the

Festival in the days of the Amoraim of Eretz Israel? In truth the very source on which Ginzberg relies in order to deduce therefrom that the people continued to observe Hanukkah in *Babylon*, 'but not in the Land of Israel', actually proves the reverse. For the Baraita (*T.B. Shabbat* 21b; *Pesiqta Rabbati* No. 5, ed. Friedmann 5a) rules: 'In time of danger, it [the Hanukkah lamp] may be left on the table, and that is sufficient.' Thus, although on account of 'danger' the Rabbis no longer insisted on the Hanukkah lights being kindled publicly (*i.e.*, in the streets or windows), they nevertheless made no concession in regard to the observance of the precept itself. Only Ginzberg, who seeks support for his view in Tosafot, *T.B. Shabbat*, *ibid.*, s.v., ובשעת הסכנה, refers the Baraita to Babylon and the decree of the Guebers (Magi). However, not only is it entirely far-fetched to regard our Baraita as of Babylonian origin (like extremely few other Baraitot in the Babylonian Talmud), or to refer its obscurities, if it was taught in Eretz Israel, to Babylonian circumstances, and to date it as late as the period of the Sassanids (after 226), but, it must be borne in mind, that 'danger' in the Tannaitic tradition is always a stereotyped term for the edicts connected with the religious persecution following the War of Bar Kokhba.[12] Understood, therefore, in its simple connotation, the Baraita speaks of 'a generation subjected to religious persecution', when the ruling authorities sought to uproot the observance of the kindling of the Hanukkah lights among Jews, but the people were resolved to observe the precept with even greater devotion and kept the observance at the risk of their lives, even though the Halakha made a concession and exempted them from bringing forth the Hanukkah lamp into public view. But above all the position is made evident by the following source (5th century): in *Ekhah Rabba*, Parashah No. 1 (iv, 22; *Esther Rabba*, *Petiḥta* 2) it is narrated of Tarkinus (Trajan) 'that his wife gave birth to a child on the night of the Ninth of Av and all the Jews were in mourning; on Hanukkah the child fell silent. The Jews then asked: "Shall we kindle (the Hanukkah lights) or not?" and replied: "We shall kindle (the Hanukkah lamp) and whatever must come upon us shall come!"' (נדליק וכל מה דבעי לימטי עלן ימטי; ed. Buber, 45a: אמרו: נדליק, ומה דהיא היא). In the end the incident of the kindling of the lights of Hanukkah led to the Jews' offering their lives for the observance and to the massacre of thousands and

12 The word 'danger' used by R. Eliezer in *M. Shabbat* xix 1, which also refers to 'religious persecution', was apparently uttered in the period of decrees promulgated by Hadrian, which preceded the Bar Kokhba War.

myriads of the people. Undoubtedly, we are dealing only with Haggada, which 'is not to be relied upon' where history is concerned (in the parallel passage in *T.P. Sukka* v, 55b the story under discussion — 'We shall kindle' etc. — is missing); but the Haggada itself shows how meticulously the precept of the Hanukkah lights was observed, and how much the Sages and the people respected it.

With regard to the Diaspora, we may perhaps refer to John x 22, where he narrates the episode of the discussion between Jesus and 'the Jews' and notes that the incident occurred on Hanukkah (ἐγκαίνια), thus showing that in the place where this book was composed (at the beginning of the second century in Asia Minor) the festival with the observance of its primary precept was so well-known that events could be dated by it. With regard to Antioch, we learn this expressly from a statement by *Chrysostom* (end of the fourth century; he speaks, in a number of places, of the Jewish festivals and their precepts, as he knew them from the observance of the Jews of Antioch) in his 'Homilies' on John: Hanukkah is a great festival, which is observed in the presence of a large assembly.[13]

The proof adduced from the Talmudic question, 'What is Hanukkah?', namely, that the Sages wondered, because they did not know, what was the nature, significance or origin of the festival, is likewise without any basis. For what we have here is only a linguistic usage connected with the method of editing the themes discussed in the Babylonian Talmud. It is well known that sometimes, when the Talmud introduces into the main theme, based on its Mishna, statements from elsewhere, and intends at the end of this discussion to revert to the second tradition and cite it *in extenso*, so that it may be fully explained, the Gemara begins the citation of the said tradition with the words, 'What is such-and-such a subject?'. This, in our passage, too, is the usage of the words in question. For in the preceding discussion (*loc. cit.* 21a–21b) the Amoraim speak of the kindling of the Hanukkah lamp in relation to the ruling in the Mishna with regard to 'wicks and oils that the Rabbis declare may not be used for kindling the Sabbath lights', and state that they may also not be used for kindling the Hanukkah lights. Now although subsequently the Gemara cites, after the main subject of study, Baraitot dealing with Hanukkah and

13 Subsequently, indeed, Chrysostom states that the festival commemorates the rededication of the Temple by those who returned from exile. But such confusion is found in the writings of Chrysostom and other Church Fathers in the passages dealing with Jewish customs, and his erroneous 'explanation' does not invalidate the fact itself stated by him.

the observations of the Amoraim thereon, we nevertheless have here before us a kind of dual 'editing', that is to say, the Talmud reverts to the theme (of Hanukkah) and presents a lengthy discussion, the focal point of which is the Baraita in *Megillat Ta'anit*, and commences, as usual, with the two words mentioned above, as though the previous dicta, added at the end of the study of the main theme, had not been mentioned. At all events, the expression, 'What is Hanukkah?' is only a stylistic usage and manner of presentation, and not a question asked in ignorant surprise.

Let us return now to the last proof. First, it is well known that in our sources other reasons for the appointment of the eight days of Hanukkah and the kindling of the lights are given. Thus, in *Megillat Ta'anit*, apart from the miracle of the cruse of oil, another reason is stated: 'because they were occupied in the Temple eight days'. In *Pesiqta Rabbati*, No. 2 (ed. Friedmann, 5a) we read: Why are lights kindled on Hanukkah? — Because when the sons of the Hasmonean were victorious, 'they entered the Temple and found there eight iron spits (there is no need to emend the text and read 'seven spits' as in *Megillat Ta'anit*, because we have two variant traditions before us) and they fixed them (in the ground) and kindled lights in them'. From *Megillat Ta'anit* we learn that primarily the explanations cited above have as their purpose to answer the question: 'Why was it ordained that Hanukkah [so named because of the renewed *dedication* of the Temple after its defilement by the Graeco-Syrians] should be observed for eight days, whereas Moses' dedication [of the Tabernacle] lasted only seven days...and we likewise find that Solomon's dedication [of the Temple] was completed in seven days.' The ancients already found difficulty in answering this question. Thus the tradition reflected in *II Maccabees*, which seeks to interpret Hanukkah as though it served to compensate for the Festival of Tabernacles, which the Jews were unable to keep at the time of Antiochus's persecution, has as its primary aim the solution (in any case rather far-fetched) of the enigma of the observance of Hanukkah for eight days instead of seven, a riddle that puzzled the author of *Megillat Ta'anit* (of its 'Gemara'). The Haggada concerning the miracle of the cruse of oil is not intended, therefore, to provide a basis for the Festival of Hanukkah itself, but to explain the one puzzling feature — the observance of Hanukkah for eight days.[14] Thus we see

14 In the *Teshuvot ha-Geonim*, Lyck, No. 104 (cf. *Oṣar ha-Geonim*, Tractate Shabbat, Responsa, p. 23) the tradition adds the explanation: 'What is the

that this provides no basis for the inference that the Sages intended to uproot the memory of the heroic deeds of the Hasmoneans and to reduce the victory to a small cruse pertaining to the mysterious world of miracles.

But so far as our subject itself is concerned, there are a great number of references, relatively, to the House of the Hasmoneans and to the Hasmonean kings, and all of them — with the exception of the main acts perpetrated by Jannai in his conflict with the Sages of Israel, and the 'discredit' inferred from the statements relative to the reforms of John Hyrcanus, and the *one* tradition that presents him as a Sadducee — are favourable to them. We shall only indicate here a few sources by way of example, such as the Baraita in *T.B. Megilla* 11a: ' "I have not rejected them" — in the days of the Chaldeans; "neither did I abhor them" — in the days of the Graeco-Syrians, when I raised up for them (Simeon the Righteous) and Mattathias the Hasmonean and his sons;[15] "so as to destroy them utterly" — in the days of Haman when I raised up for them Mordecai and Esther; "to break My covenant with them" — in the days of the Romans, when I raised up for them the scions of the House of Rabbi and the Sages throughout the generations.' Akin to it is the tradition of *Mishnat Rabbi Eliezer*, p. 103 (written, apparently, in the Land of Israel, at the close of the Roman regime), which interprets the four species of plants used on Tabernacles to correspond to 'the four righteous men whom the Holy One blessed be He vouchsafed (to Israel) in every kingdom to save them and to spread Torah-knowledge in their midst. These are: in Babylon Daniel, Hananiah, Mishael and Azariah; in Persia Haggai, Zechariah, Malachi and Nehemiah; in the Graeco-Syrian kingdom the four sons of the Hasmonean, the eldest son, Judah, having been killed already; in Edom [i.e. the Roman Empire] Rabban Gamaliel, R. Joshua, R. Eleazar b. Azariah and R. Akiba.' Targum Pseudo-Jonathan to I Samuel, in Hannah's prayer, renders the verse, 'The bows of the

reason for the eight days of Hanukkah, neither less nor more? — Because the oils come from the portion of Asher... and there was a place there called Tekoa... and the return journey from there to Jerusalem takes eight days' (see Hame'iri, *T.B. Shabbat* 21b). This tradition is cited in *Eshkol*, II, p. 20 (ed. Auerbach) from the 'Yerushalmi'; so, too, in *Abudarham* (Pietrekow, p. 54a). Apparently, it primarily derives from the Midrash (sometimes called by the Earlier Authorities 'Yerushalmi').

15 According to the readings of MSS cited in *Dikduqe Soferim*.

mighty are broken, but the feeble gird on strength' [*ibid.*, ii 4], as follows: 'She prophesied concerning the Macedonian kingdom and said, "The bow of the people of Macedon shall be broken, and unto the Hasmoneans, who were feeble, miracles and mighty deeds shall be wrought" ' (there is no need to mention the prayer 'For the miracles'). Mention of John Hyrcanus's name occurs in the *Targum Yerushalmi* to Deuteronomy xxx 11: ' "and of those that hate him, that they rise not again" — and the enemies of John the High Priest shall not have a leg to stand on'.

These traditions and their like suffice to show that the Sages did not seek to eradicate the memory of the Hasmoneans and their great deeds from the heart of the nation. Confirmation of this is furnished by Jerome (who received, as we know, many traditions from the last of the Amoraim in the Land of Israel). In his commentary on Isaiah i 26 he writes: ' "And I will restore your judges as at the first, and your counsellors as at the beginning" — the Jews refer the verse to Zerubbabel, Ezra and Nehemiah and all the other princes who ruled over the people *till the time of Herod.*'

We thus see that in Jerome's time (the end of the fourth century) the people (and the Sages) included the kings of the Hasmonean dynasty among the great national leaders of the era of the Second Temple, and they did not discredit them on account of the evil of one or two of them.

The prevailing view, which we adumbrated at the outset, is not only not properly based on the sources and events, but is even negated by many testimonies, and therefore must be completely rejected, at least in its general and unqualified form. Essentially, the account of the relations between the Pharisees and the Hasmoneans in respect of individual members of this dynasty undoubtedly still requires careful examination.[16] But the Pharisaic attitude towards the entire dynasty

16 We know that the Sages and the people at the end of the epoch of the Hasmoneans were opposed to the latter's tyranny (see Josephus) and sought the restoration of the 'freedom' and the 'autonomy' they enjoyed prior to their regime. But it seems that the Pharisees fought for the rights of the Sanhedrin *vis-à-vis* the monarchy, which sought to restrict or annul them, and it is this opposition that was the primary factor leading to the affiliation of Jannai and John(?) to the Sadducean cult, not *vice versa*. See below, p. 24.

and its achievements is not negated by these facts *per se*. The latter days of the House of the Hasmoneans did not shame their earlier days in the estimation of the people.[17]

17 A number of important events prove that in Temple times the vast majority of the people were in favour of the descendants of the Hasmoneans and their monarchy, and sought to renew their rule (note Aristobulus's success in his rebellion in the year 56, and that of his son Alexander in 55, and that of Antigonus). But we learn from the Talmud, *T.B. Qiddushin* 70b (Nehardea, third century), that also after the destruction of the Temple, and in the Diaspora, men were honoured by, and gloried in, their descent from the Hasmoneans.

THE ATTITUDE OF THE PHARISEES TO ROMAN RULE AND THE HOUSE OF HEROD

I should like to preface my lecture proper with a few explanatory observations concerning its theme.

(a) It is not the purpose of this paper to present systematically the events relating to the subject, nor primarily to suggest solutions to the many problems connected with our topic. The object of the lecture is to question a number of fundamental premises that have been accepted by many scholars, and have paved a way for historic research in this field — a way that deviates at times in a marked degree from the right road — and to outline in general terms paths that, to my mind, are most likely to lead us to the truth. It will thus be seen that my intention is not to refute but to enquire.

(b) My lecture does not aim to set forth the views of the Pharisees on the regime of the Romans and of Herod and his offspring, but to explain their actual political attitude in the struggle between the Jewish people and the former for national freedom. It follows that the compass of this paper is necessarily confined to the period between Pompey's conquest of Judea (63 B.C.E.) and the end of the battle of Bethar (135 C.E.). For after this period the nation does not, in general, consider itself fit to fight for its independence militarily, and hopes, in a state of complete subjection, for redemption by Heaven.

(c) Seeing that the beginning of this epoch with which we are specially concerned goes back to the close of the Hasmonean period, and having regard to the fact that the actions of the Pharisees in those days are linked in the estimation of scholars — and this is largely true — with this chapter of Jewish history, and shed light on the Pharisaic approach also in the days of Herod and his descendants, it is first necessary for us to examine the policy of the Pharisees in their relationship with the last of the Hasmoneans.

Hence we shall submit our main investigation under five heads, as follows: (a) the beginning of Roman rule in Judea; (b) the period of Herod and Archelaus; (c) the days of Agrippa (I); (d) the time of the Great War; (c) the Bar Kokhba War. In addition, as a preamble, we shall also have to deal with the events of the reigns of Alexander Jannai and John Hyrcanus.

Let us now revert to the discussion of the theme proper.

The prevailing view among scholars, particularly among Christian savants (like Wellhausen, Eduard Meyer, Schürer, Herford and others[1]), and to a less degree among Jewish scholars,[2] concerning the attitude of the Pharisees towards the Hasmoneans and towards Rome and the Herodian dynasty is based on two erroneous premises: (a) that Pharisaism, unlike its opponent, Sadduceeism, was essentially a purely *religious movement*, whereas the rival movement was fundamentally political; (b) that the Pharisees, although it is generally accepted that they exercised the greatest influence on the nation, were only a *sect*, composed of 'professional' Scribes and Sages, who endeavoured to lead the people with or without their consent.[3]

These two premises, which have primarily been influenced by the particular light in which the Pharisees appear in the Christian sacred Scriptures,[4] have caused the non-Jewish scholars, and to a certain extent Jewish scholars, too, to fall into a third error, which is most detrimental to the examination of the events bearing on our subject, namely, the tendency to regard all the Pharisees from the angle of absolute *monism*.

It should be noted, however, that the Jewish scholars have largely

1 Wellhausen, *Die Pharisäer und die Sadducäer*, p. 93, *et passim*; idem, *Israelitische und jüdische Geschichte*, pp. 278 ff. (ed. Schoken, p. 7); Mommsen, *Römische Geschichte*, V; ed. Meyer, *Ursprung und Anfänge des Christentums*, II, pp. 284, 307; Schürer, *Geschichte des jüdischen Volkes* etc., I, p. 271; Herford, *The Pharisees*, p. 45.

2 Derenbourg, *Massa' 'Ereṣ Yisrael*, I, pp. 60–61 (see p. 60, n. 1; p. 85; II, p. 145); Dubnow, *Divre Yeme 'Am 'Olam*, I, pp. 3–12; 181; Klausner, *Historiyya Yisre'elit*, II, pp. 109, 117, *et passim*; Simḥoni, Introduction to *Milḥamot*, p. 5.

3 This view, however, is given particular emphasis by gentile savants.

4 Needless to say, even the rabbinic tradition of the Amoraic period presents the early generations of the epoch preceding the fall of the State from the aspect not of politics but only of religion and ethics; this lays us open to the error of anachronism. Furthermore, we must remember that the material preserved in the traditional works that were compiled at a late date throws no light on the range of thought and action of the earlier Sages, because the later generations possibly felt no need to preserve the teachings of their predecessors in the sphere of political affairs, as they preserved their dicta and the memory of their acts in matters of Halakha, ethics and religion, which by and large were the determining factors of the world of the later scholars.

been saved from all these pitfalls,[5] only they have not succeeded in achieving complete consistency,[6] and hence they have also at times deviated from the truth.

On the basis of these premises, scholars have built the following thesis: since essentially the Pharisees sought only to study and observe the Torah, hence they threw off the yoke of the Jewish kingdom and were indifferent to the political needs of the people. Moreover, they deliberately rejected the political freedom of the nation, because it was liable to undermine the ultimate foundation of Judaism, which, in their view, consisted of Torah and precepts only.

Consequently the Pharisees fought against the last representatives of the House of the Hasmoneans, who had built for themselves a dynasty and fashioned a state in Judea after the manner of 'all the nations'; and hence they willingly subjected themselves to the rule of the Romans and the House of Herod, provided it was granted them to lead the majority of the people in the way of the Torah, both Written and Oral.

More succinctly expressed: *the basic factor in the relationship of the Pharisees to the Hasmoneans and to the Romans was their opposi-*

5 Graetz, whose views were farthest removed from the prevailing conception, was the first to discern zealots and political fighters in the camp of the Pharisees. Yet, he, too, restricted them to the School of Bet Shammai, a restriction that is insufficiently grounded and is not proven to the point where we can infer that the others followed a different policy. Likewise Dubnow distinguishes between 'moderate' and 'extremist' Pharisees; and Klausner differentiates between 'quietists' and activists. But even among Jewish scholars (apart from Graetz) there is a marked tendency to identify the real Pharisees with those who retired from public life and sought to confine themselves to the Schoolhouse and leave the affairs of state to the Ruling Power (Klausner, *op. cit.*, p. 194). Credit is due to Kohler, who made clear the character of the zealots, showing that their movement emanated primarily from the religious sphere and loyalty to the Sages of the Torah (*Harkavy Jubilee Volume*, pp. 6–18).

6 Thus, for example, Graetz, despite the fact that he discerned among the Pharisees resolute opponents of the rule of foreigners (including that of Herod), who took up arms against them, nevertheless states, without producing evidence, that the Pharisees sided with Hyrcanus (and hence also with Antipater) against Aristobulus (Hebrew ed., I, p. 46); so, too, that Shemaiah and Avṭalion opposed Antigonus in his war against Herod (*ibid.*, p. 483). Similarly, we find that Dubnow, notwithstanding that he also recognized that many of the Pharisees used force against the foreign regime, states categorically that the Pharisees, as a whole, avoided taking part in external politics and eschewed political life, because they preferred the spiritual element in national life. Thus Klausner also was inconsistent in his interpretation of this chapter of Jewish history.

tion to the politicalization of the nation, emanating from the desire to conserve the religious-spiritual character of the life of the community.

This interpretation, although in the emphatic form outlined above is confined to Christian scholars, is nevertheless adopted, with some changes, also by Jewish scholars. Only the latter eliminate any antagonism in principle to Jewish political life from Pharisaic teaching and replace it with a doctrine that seeks to make statehood subordinate to the dominant element, which is religion; they also interpret the course of events in the light of this premise.[7]

Now before we examine this interpretation in the light of the *facts*, we must first consider the basic assumptions upon which it is founded, so as to expose the misleading exaggeration that they contain; it will then be found that the entire exposition is ill-founded.

For the premise that the Pharisees were merely pietists, who made the (whole) life of the nation an instrument in the service of the Torah, is disproved *ab initio* (even though there are to be found in the Haggada some observations redolent of this spirit), because the dicta of the early Sages who lived in Temple times, and also of those who lived after its destruction, both in the field of Halakha and Haggada, teach us the reverse. Likewise their acts, in so far as they are known to us from tradition, prove the same. The Halakha of the Pharisees is directed to the *welfare and improvement of society*, involving at times the *suppression of Torah*, and embraces, as we know, besides religious precepts, basic principles in the sphere of law — both civil and criminal — and even communal and state legislation, including ordinances affecting the monarchy.[8]

It need hardly be stressed that the Torah is certainly the *basis* of the Halakha, and that religion validates them both. But at times they provide only the form and framework; essentially the Halakha and its spirit are compounded of the element of piety and the aim to improve the civilized life, in all its aspects, of the nation as a whole. In point of fact, the latter element — 'the secular element' — is

7 Elbogen already observed (*MGWJ*, 1926, 146), against Dubnow, that the Pharisees did not fail, as the latter had stated, to intervene in the political affairs of the nation, as was evidenced by the help they gave to Salome, and by their aspiration to be in power in the days of Jannai.

8 The laws relating to kings that are incorporated in the Mishna and in Baraitot (and possibly also those cited by Philo, *De Specialibus Legibus*, VI, 157–169) are apparently, in so far as they are not mentioned in the Bible, actually laws observed in practice, and were presumably enacted in the days of the Hasmoneans (and of Agrippa I and Agrippa II). This also applies, it seems, to the laws regarding secular wars.

dominant. The same obtains also in the Haggada, which is composed (since earliest times) of many themes, relating to the nature and wisdom of life, to ethics and to history (and other 'sciences') and to *art* (poesy). The image, also, of the *Pharisee leaders* as they are known to us from tradition — from Josephus and the works of the apostles — men like Simeon b. Shetaḥ, Judah b. Tabbai, Shemaiah and Avṭalion, Rabban Gamaliel the Elder, R. Zechariah b. Eucolus, R. Joshua b. Ḥanania, R. Akiba and the like, likewise shows us men who are polarically different from 'pietists', which is how they should have been pictured on the basis of the aforementioned view of the Christian scholars.[9]

Equally erroneous is their conception of the Pharisees as a complete unit (excluding a minority of 'Scribes and teachers'), as a Jewish theological sect. It is a known fact that from the days of the Hasmoneans and onwards the Pharisees constituted the vast majority of the nation,[10] and hence, generally speaking, we have to regard the history of Jewry in our period, in all spheres, as also reflecting the history of the Pharisees.[11]

This confirms the initial premise that we may not expect *ab initio* unity of *outlook and action* among the Pharisees as a whole relative to the questions that concern us. Indeed, in the following pages we shall describe in outline the struggle within the Pharisaic camp itself and the changing views among them regarding the events relating to the question under discussion.

Let us revert to the happenings, and begin, first of all, with the war of the Pharisees against the Hasmoneans.

9 These distinguished personages are not at all 'holy men', who are isolated from the community and devote themselves to acts of piety, for they give instruction in state laws and also participate (together with their disciples, as did R. Akiba) in the political events of their time.

10 *Antiquities* xiii, 15, 5 *et al.*

11 Undoubtedly, there is no need to state that the 'Sages' were differentiated from the people and the disciples. But this fact does not necessitate our positing the existence of 'a sect of Pharisees' — as even Klausner seeks to do — in the days of Herod, when six thousand refrained from taking an oath of loyalty to Herod and Rome (*Historiyya Yisre'elit*, II, p. 100), since the episode occasions no surprise, for the majority of the people were incapable of rebellion, and only the greatest and most courageous among them were prepared to court danger; these, at that time, did not exceed the number cited above. And Klausner himself has modified his view; see *ibid.* At all events, 'the Sages of Israel' gave expression to the spirit and life of the nation, whose history mirrored the thoughts and deeds of the majority of the Pharisees.

The view of scholars that the Pharisees fought against King Jannai, or even against John Hyrcanus before him, because they were opposed to the process of excessive politicalization promoted by these rulers in Judea, *is supported by not a single fact*, explicit or implicit, in the sources. If we require evidence to disprove the above assumption, namely, that the Pharisees were opposed to the Hasmonean state, we need only recall that the Pharisees helped John Hyrcanus throughout his reign (till the end, and even their subsequent opposition is doubtful, as we shall see presently); nor did they combat Jannai at the outset, and they were supporters of Salome, who, as is well known, adopted a distinctly political attitude.

Similarly, we must reject the other premise (which is closely akin to the first), to wit, that all the Pharisees fought against the Hasmoneans, because they appointed themselves kings, whereas the monarchy belongs only to the members of the House of David. For we do not find that the Halakha invalidates monarchy in this world (except in the days of the Messiah, who, too, has been regarded by some as of priestly descent; see, for example, the *Testaments of the Twelve Patriarchs*, and so forth). Now if it is said that Herod slew the Sages for denying his right to the throne because he was not 'one from among thy brethren',[12] it follows that whoever is a Jew is fit for kingship; and to Agrippa the Sages said 'Thou art our brother', and confirmed him as king over them.[13] It is also expressly stated in a Baraita (*Midrash Tannaim*): ' "Thou mayest not put a foreigner over thee" — this excludes a proselyte. The implication (you say) is to exclude a proselyte, but perhaps (it means that) if there is no candidate from the tribe of Judah, no one from the tribe of Benjamin may be regarded as qualified? But can you say so, seeing that every Jew is fit to be king', etc.[14] Also the Tannaitic regulations appertaining to the laws relating to the king were, it seems, framed in the era of the Hasmoneans, whose monarchy they recognized.

However, it is evident from *The Psalms of Solomon* that there were certain Pharisees who disputed the right of the Hasmoneans to the throne on the ground that they were not descended from the House of David.[15] Only here we are primarily confronted with the differences

12 *T.B. Bava Batra*, 3b–4a.

13 *M. Sotah*, vii 8; *Sifre Deut.* §157; *Midrash Tannaim*, p. 104.

14 We find a similar statement in *T.B. Horayot* 13a: 'When a king of Israel dies, every Jew is qualified to become king.'

15 iv–vi; xxi. We find a similar statement made by one of the Amoraim in *T.P. Shekalim* vi, p. 49d (*T.P. Horayot* iii, p. 47c): 'Priests are not anointed

of opinion among the Pharisees themselves in regard to the monarchy, for there were some who excluded kingship from Israel in this world (for it is inconceivable that any family in the country, at the time with which we are concerned, had a valid genealogy proving that it was actually descended from the Davidic dynasty; see Aptowitzer, *MGWJ*, 1930, p. 120 ff.) and there were others — the majority — who gave it legal sanction.

Now since the question under discussion has many implications for the entire theme with which we are concerned, it is desirable to deal with it here in greater detail.

It appears that apart from certain other factors, we must interpret the struggle of the Pharisees against Alexander Jannai to centre on the rights of the Sanhedrin and its authority to rule *vis-à-vis* the monarchy. The Pharisees sought to protect them from being undermined by the king, for in this instance, too, the Pharisees were safeguarding the interests of the people, since the Sanhedrin was, in a sense, their representative. For we may learn from the coins struck by Jannai that in the middle of his reign he sought to abrogate the Sanhedrin (or to diminish its stature) since on some of the coins (apparently the earlier ones) he stamped in Hebrew only the words, 'Jonathan the High Priest and the Association (*ḥever*) of the Jews',[16]

as kings. R. Yudan of En-Todros said: This is based on the verse "The sceptre shall not depart from Judah."' But the simple meaning of the obscure Baraita is certainly in accordance with the following view of R. Ḥiyya b. Ba: ' "To the end that he may prolong his days in his kingdom, he and his children, in the midst of Israel". What is written thereafter? "The priests, the Levites... shall have no (portion),"' that is to say, that all the other tribes are qualified for the monarchy. At any rate we learn from this that there were some Sages who wished to separate the kingship from the priesthood. Only we must not connect these statements with that in the Baraita in *T.B. Qiddushin* 66a, made by Eleazar b. Poʿira, who said to Jannai: 'Let the royal crown suffice thee; leave the priestly crown to the descendants of Aaron', because not all the Sages agreed with these remarks, as is explicitly stated in the Baraita cited, and this apart, even Poʿira said what he did only on account of the suspicion that the king's mother had been taken captive in Modin.

16 However, it is still a moot point if 'the Association of the Jews' [*ḥever ha-yehudim*] means the Sanhedrin of all Israel, as stated, or signifies the entire nation. Nor do the sources of the period help us to decide the question; for sometimes Jannai and the Sanhedrin sign or are described as the representatives of the nation, namely, 'the High Priest and the Jewish People', and at other times the formula used is 'the High Priest and the Senate' (cf., for example, *I Maccabees*, 12:3–6). Nevertheless the interpretation given in the text appears more probable. Only, even if we adopt the other explanation,

implying that he and the Sanhedrin were joint rulers, and on other coins (the later ones) he engraved, 'Jonathan the King [in Hebrew]' and in Greek βασιλέως 'Αλεξάνδρου, without mentioning the Sanhedrin. From this it would seem that when the monarchy was firmly established, Jannai proceeded to take away the rights of the Sanhedrin, a view held also by Levy in his book on Jewish coins.[17]

Now this dyarchy, which finds expression in the earlier coins of Jannai, and in those minted by John before him, is embedded in the teaching of the early Tannaim in the laws relating to kings, which allocates to the king a sphere of his own and excludes it from the jurisdiction of the Sanhedrin, that is, *the law of the people* (the character of the Great Sanhedrin as the representative of the people requires clarification in a separate dissertation);[18] and, on the other hand, deprives the monarch of the right of absolute rule in given spheres, unless with the consent of the High Court of all Israel[19] (similarly we learn from the [Pharisaic] Halakha, which underlies the statements of Josephus in his *Antiquities*, where he sets out the Jewish 'Constitution' according to the Torah, 'that the king might

we have here at least an expression that implies the subjection of the High Priest's rule to the will of the people.

17 *Geschichte der jüdischen Münzen*; see also Graetz, *op. cit.*, p. 443, regarding John Hyrcanus, and *Dorot ha-Rishonim*, Part I, vol. iii, p. 222. Zucker (*Studien*, etc., pp. 44–49) also draws attention to the opposition between the Senate and the Hasmoneans, only he considers the basis of the conflict to lie in the fact that the 'Scribes' sought to impose the religious law upon the state, which was opposed by the Hasmoneans. He even asserts that the members of the Sanhedrin were then 'the professional Scribes', whose activity in the High Court was directed to supervising the life of the state and assuring that it should conform to the Torah and tradition. But both these assumptions are unproven; see below.

18 Needless to say, the matter depends to a large extent on the elucidation of the method of appointing the members of the Sanhedrin and the basis of the representation of the High Court 'of all Israel' relative to the Judean cities. But, this is not the place to discuss the subject. At any rate it can be said that although Josephus designates, as we know, the order of the Sanhedrin, together with the High Priest, as the 'aristocracy', yet the Great Sanhedrin, which took the place of 'the elders of the people' of old on a broad basis, served as the representative of the nation *vis-à-vis* those who stood at its head; see below, note 31.

19 *Sanhedrin* i 5, ii 4. However, on the question of the king's standing outside the jurisdiction of the courts, two alternating views are apparently to be discerned among the Tannaim, and likewise in the Halakha of Philo. I shall elucidate this on another occasion.

not do anything without the consent of the High Priest and the Sanhedrin').[20]

It seems to me that the clash between Jannai and the Pharisees in regard to the authority of the Sanhedrin can best be explained in the light of the numerous wars waged by the king against (distant) nations, and which the people — namely, the Pharisees — did not approve. For the Halakha rules that the king may not bring forth the people to fight an optional war except by permission of a court of seventy-one. Since the latter were opposed to these wars, therefore Jannai proceeded to abrogate the Sanhedrin (or to diminish its rights completely); in other words, he deprived the people of this right of partnership in the government.

Here I would point out that although the great majority of scholars are of opinion that the tradition found in Josephus concerning the conflict between John Hyrcanus and the Pharisees is true, its correctness is nevertheless open to considerable doubt. For we may learn, I believe, from a number of sources that there were differences of opinion among the Tannaim — and also after their time — regarding the commencement of the conflict between the Pharisees and the later Hasmoneans, some Sages assigning it to the period of John Hyrcanus and others to that of Alexander Jannai. It appears to me that in this case the historic truth rests with the view of an individual — Friedlander[21] — who holds that the tradition found in Josephus must be set aside before that of the Talmud (the Baraita in *T.B. Qiddushin* 66a), and we must posit that the Pharisees were never in conflict with John Hyrcanus — not even at the end of his reign.[22]

20 *Ant.* iv, 8, 17 — Πρασσέτω δὲ μηδὲν δίχα τοῦ ἀρχιερέως καὶ τῆς τῶν γερουσιαστῶν γνώμης. Now Josephus adds the High Priest to the Sanhedrin, contrary to the Halakha, and this accords with Josephus's view in other passages, too, where he joins the High Priest to the Sanhedrin, while the tradition of the Sages requires the Sanhedrin only. But as regards the king, it is possible to point to a few traditional sources that, like Josephus, require the High Priest to be associated with the monarch. I hope to discuss this subject in detail in a work that I am about to write on 'The Great Sanhedrin in the Days of the Second Temple'.

21 *JQR*, N.S., iv, pp. 443 ff.

22 Not only do we find a variant tradition in Josephus *vis-à-vis* the Baraita in *Qiddushin* 66a, the former attributing the beginning of the conflict between the Pharisees and the Hasmoneans to the reign of John Hyrcanus and the latter to that of Jannai, but we also find this divergence in Josephus's own tradition, and likewise in the case of the Sages. For Josephus states that when the people pelted Jannai with citrons and first rose up against him, they declared that he was disqualified for the priesthood because he was the

We come now to the beginning of the period that serves to determine our main theme, namely, to that of the conflict between the brothers Hyrcanus and Aristobulus, and the conquest of Jerusalem by Pompey. Scholars are of the opinion that all, or most of, the Pharisees sided with Hyrcanus, and the Sadducees with his adver-

son of a woman taken captive (in conformity with the statement of the Baraita cited above — 'his mother was captured in Modin'), a story that he relates in the name of Eleazar also of John Hyrcanus (Ant. xiii, 10, 5; *ibid.* 13, 5); this was noted with surprise by Zechariah Frankel, *Darkhe ha-Mishna*[2], p. 37, n. 34. It seems to me that we have here parallel, alternative accounts concerning a single episode. Similarly we may infer, to my mind, from another passage of Josephus, that the folk-tradition regarded the earlier Hasmoneans, including John Hyrcanus, as fit and proper rulers, and the later Hasmoneans, from Aristobulus and Jannai onwards, as wicked men. For we read in *Antiquities*, iii, 8, 9, that the Urim and Thummim ceased to function, according to Josephus's tradition (and contrary to the Tannaitic tradition, which testifies that there were no Urim and Thummim at all in the days of the Second Temple) — '*two hundred years* before I composed this work, because the Lord was wroth on account of the sins against the Torah'. This calculation brings us to a date shortly after the death of John Hyrcanus, since *The Antiquities of the Jews* was written in 93 C.E. We thus have evidence here that because of the abundance of transgressions (undoubtedly of those that carried the Urim, i.e., the high priests) the Divine Presence was exiled from Israel, showing that the Hasmonean kings from Aristobulus (and Jannai) onward were wicked, but this was not the case with their fathers before them. As for the tradition of the Sages, there existed, needless to say, a tradition that Joḥanan the high priest [John Hyrcanus] served in the high priesthood eighty years and in the end became a Sadducee (*T.B. Berakhot* 29a in a Baraita; only this "Baraita" appears to be late, since it is dependent on the Mishna of *Avot* ii 4, which is by Hillel the son of Rabban Gamaliel Berabbi). It also appears that this tradition was known to the Amoraim, who, in the Palestinian Talmud (*Ma'aser Sheni* v, p. 56d; *Soṭah* ix 10), put an unfavourable construction on the reforms of John Hyrcanus (or disapproved some of them and approved others). But, on the other hand, it can be shown that another tradition of the early Tannaim regarded John Hyrcanus as righteous from beginning to end. For such is the testimony of the Mishnayot that speak of his reforms, since according to the plain meaning of the Mishna these are mentioned with approval (*Ma'aser Sheni* v 15; *Soṭah* ix 10); while to say with Büchler, *Der galiläische 'Am ha-'Areṣ*, that the tradition refers only to the end of the Second Temple period is far-fetched. The Tannaitic tradition (with Josephus) likewise testifies that John Hyrcanus was vouchsafed a communication by a *Bat Kol* [Heavenly Voice] (or by prophecy, *Tos. Soṭah* iii 5; *T.B. ibid.*, 33a; *T.P. ibid.*, ix, p. 24b; *Ant.* xiii, 10, 7). The Baraita (*T.B. Rosh ha-Shana* 18b; *Megillat Ta'anit* vii), moreover, refers to him as Joḥanan, 'the high priest of God Most High'. Also Rabban Joḥanan b. Zakkai in his discussion with the Sadducees, when he wishes to point to an example of a great and righteous man, chooses

sary.[23] This view also emanates from the basic premise mentioned earlier, to wit, that the Pharisees were antagonistic to the Hasmonean monarchy, and it is logical to suppose that they would side with the one who lacked the character of a real ruler. Since Hyrcanus was only the shadow of Antipater, the Pharisees of those days paved the way for the rule of the House of Herod.

But this view finds absolutely no support in facts known to us. Nay more, we must assume the reverse, namely, that there were many Pharisees of whom some took no part in the conflict at all, and others who actively supported Aristobulus.[24] Halevy in *Dorot*

'Joḥanan the high priest' (*Yadayim* iv 6); nor can it be argued that the 'Pharisees' there 'answered them according to their own viewpoint', the view of the Sadducees, who cherished him greatly after he had joined them. In the Targum of Pseudo-Jonathan (Deut. xxx 11) it is stated: 'and let there not be to the enemies of Joḥanan the high priest a leg to stand on' (it is strange to assert that the reference here is to the father of Mattathias, as Aptowitzer holds, *Parteipolitik* xiii). Hence we must conclude that there were two divergent Jewish traditions: according to one the break between the Pharisees and the Hasmoneans occurred in the last day of Hyrcanus, according to the other in the reign of Jannai (Nahman Krochmal dealt with a number of these sources and sought to reconcile them by the assumption that John Hyrcanus had repented). But it would seem that we must accept the accuracy of the second tradition, being that according to both the testimony of Josephus and the tradition of the Sages (*T.P. Berakhot* vii, p. 11b) Jannai, too, was not hostile to the latter at the beginning of his reign (contrary to the statement of Rava in *T.B. Berakhot* 29a), for it is difficult to suppose that Jannai was at first more righteous than his father. Furthermore, Josephus declares that John, despite the fact that the Pharisees were in revolt against him, ruled at the end of his days in peace; now it is difficult to imagine that he could dwell in peace if the Pharisees, and the people with them, fought against him; this has already been pointed out by Friedlander.

23 There are historians, like Jawitz (cf. iv, pp. 185, 209), whose view approximates that given below, but they are inconsistent.

24 There is no evidence that the Pharisees were on the side of Hyrcanus and against Aristobulus all the time, even after the former had given up the throne and the high priesthood in favour of his younger brother, on account of Antipater, who was aided by the Arabs. For a distinction must be drawn between the preceding period, when Aristobulus sought to secure for himself the crown and the high priesthood *illegally*, by force and cunning, and conspired against his mother and joined the Sadducees, and the subsequent period, when Aristobulus rose to power with the consent of his brother and the people. Although at first Aristobulus joined forces with the Sadducees, this does not imply that his opinions and actions approximated to theirs, since his whole purpose in acting thus at the beginning was to gain the support of the country's opposition in order to attain to power. It may be assumed that after he had achieved his purpose by peaceful means he did

ha-Rishonim[25] has already drawn attention to Josephus's story about *Ḥoni ha-Me'aggel* who was slain by Hyrcanus's men because he refused to pray for the defeat of Aristobulus in the battle, declaring: 'These are Thy people and these are Thy priests.' Also the famous Baraita that relates that Hyrcanus's men sent up swine for the daily sacrifice[26] shows that the Pharisees did not regard Hyrcanus with affection. Similarly we learn from *The Psalms of Solomon* that when Judea was captured by Pompey, who made Hyrcanus the ruler, the Pharisees fled into the deserts to escape death.[27] But apart from this, if Aristobulus was able to make a stand against his brother, who was aided in the war by the powerful king of the Arabs, it is reasonable to suppose that many Pharisees supported him.[28]

However, at that period we are confronted to begin with by an event that apparently reflects most clearly the estrangement of the Pharisees from political independence, and which proves, as it were, that they deliberately wished to accept the yoke of Roman dominion. For Josephus relates that when Pompey was considering which of the rival brothers he should prefer, the people, represented on this occasion by the Pharisees, came to him and complained against both protagonists that they wished to enslave the people by means of the monarchy. They added that from of old the people were accustomed to be ruled by priests, and consequently they wished to restore the former position.[29]

Scholars are of opinion that the Pharisees wilfully sought to destroy the political freedom of the Jews and to subject them to Rome, just

not wish to anger the people and their leaders, the Pharisees, even though he did not, at the same time, estrange the Sadducees, his supporters.

25 Part I, Vol. iii, pp. 264–273.

26 *T.B. Soṭah* 49b and parallels; *T.P. Berakhot* iv, p. 7b.

27 xviii 16–18. Earlier, *ibid.* viii 16–18, he rebukes 'the princes of Jerusalem', who went forth joyfully to meet Pompey and 'opened the gates of Jerusalem and decorated its walls' in honour of his coming. Now this is more in keeping with the actions of Hyrcanus and Antipater than those of Aristobulus.

28 It is likewise inconceivable that the many wars that were fought in the fifties by Aristobulus and his son Alexander against Hyrcanus and the House of Herod and the Romans, when the ranks of the former were augmented by tremendous multitudes of the people, could have been waged by the Sadducees alone. If we suggest, in the context of our subject, that the people followed the Hasmoneans in spite of the Pharisees, we fail, to my mind, to examine and judge the facts objectively and are influenced by unproven postulates.

29 *Ant.* xiv, 3, 2.

as they had been subject to the Persians and the Greek kings.[30] But this is a distortion of the position; the request referred to does not imply the withdrawal of independence but the restoration of the dominion of the people. For the essence of the complaint of the Pharisees is not directed against freedom, but *against the state of subjection* that the Hasmoneans desired to impose on the nation, as is explicitly stated by Josephus. When the Pharisees demanded the restoration of the rule of the (high) priests, we must interpret the matter correctly, namely that we have here only an *official term* for the ancient *régime of the Sanhedrin*, because the high priest, in contradistinction to the king, did not enjoy, either in the Pharisaic Halakha or in actual fact, the status of an independent or *sovereign* ruler *vis-à-vis* the nation, but he was the head and representative of the Sanhedrin, and through it of the people, and his representative character stemmed primarily from the latter.[31] This fact is most clearly seen in the halakhic principle that the high priest judges and is judged, in contradistinction to the king, who could not be judged (by the Sanhedrin) nor could he join it in order to adjudicate. In truth, if the Pharisees had come to give up external *political* freedom in order to assure the internal dominion of the people, we should have the right to infer that national independence meant little to

30 Incidentally, the generally accepted premise of scholars in regard to the epoch of Persian and of Greek rule in Judea, namely, that the Jewish Community was at the time only a 'theocracy', and that the Jews were not concerned in those days with political matters, is also highly exaggerated. It seems that it can be shown from many records relating to that era that then, too, Jewry was not simply 'a church', and that the Jewish state in the Land of Israel contained quite a number of clear indications of political, and even military organization. It is my intention to demonstrate this in the projected work referred to earlier.

31 Without doubt the high priest was not considered the head of the Sanhedrin only, since he had personal power, too, and the phrase 'the High Priest and the Sanhedrin' or 'the High Priest and the People' is commonly found in the sources, showing that he exercised independent authority. But, unlike the monarchy, his authority was mostly interlinked with that of the Sanhedrin. Hence Josephus could write (*Ant.* xx, 10, 15) that the rule of the high priests in the days of the Persians and the Greeks, up to the time of Antiochus Epiphanus, was *democratic*. See *Wars* i, 8, 5, where we learn that the high priest (alone) was in charge of the Temple, and that in respect of all other public matters gubernatorial power was in the hands of 'the representatives of the people' [literally: 'the good men of the people'], i.e., the Sanhedrin.

them. But at the moment in question they did not have this choice,[32] for they knew full well that having brought her forces into Judea, Rome would never forgo her control over the country. Whether Aristobulus held the office of high priest, or was ostensibly king, or whether Hyrcanus secured these positions, the Jewish people could be in subjection to Rome. Consequently, since it was their fate to be subject to foreigners in either case, they sought to re-establish the rule of the Sanhedrin, which was in danger of being undermined by dictatorship.

I wish to point out once more that the Pharisaic Halakha not only does not oppose the *monarchy* as such, but even adopts a positive attitude towards it, although we find divergent views in Tannaitic teaching in regard to the *extent* of the king's authority,[33] and even though in the Halakha — that is, the Pharisaic — reflected in Josephus's *Antiquities* there is discernible a certain tendency to prefer the absolute rule of the Sanhedrin to that of "the constitutional monarchy".[34] Since, however, the stand taken by the Pharisees for

32 It should be noted here that Isaak Halevy (*Dorot ha-Rishonim*, Pt. I, *ibid.*, pp. 245–246) already observed that the action taken by the Pharisees, when they were at war with Jannai (88 B.C.E.), in inviting Demetrius Eucaerus to help them in their fight against the former, does not provide a sufficient basis to interpret it, as do the scholars, as though they wished to put the Land of Israel beneath the Graeco-Syrian yoke. For we can draw no analogy here for this period from the request made by the people to rid themselves of the rule of the Herods (or even of that of Aristobulus and Hyrcanus) by the Roman annexation of the country, because in those last days of the Jewish State Judea had in any case been conquered by the Romans, whereas in the reign of Jannai the Syrian kingdom had reached the nadir of its decline, and Judea was free and strong. At all events, it is not stated in the sources that the Pharisees made a promise of this kind to Demetrius. Although we read in Josephus, *Wars* (i, 4, 4) that the latter 'Ρᾳδίως υπακούσαντος κἀτ ἐλπίδα μειζόνων ('he readily complied with their request, in hopes of great advantages'); yet, it appears that it is actually from this passage that we may infer that the people had not promised him to accept him as their king, but that he himself hoped for 'great advantages' from the aid that he would give to the rebels. Only it does seem that the Pharisees were prepared to surrender to him, in recompense for his help, some of the Greek cities conquered by Jannai. The matter requires further investigation.

33 Tosefta *Sanhedrin* iv 6; *T.B. ibid.*, 48b; Tosefta *ibid.*, iv 5; *T.B. ibid.*, 20b.

34 *Ant.* iv, 8, 17, where according to Josephus (i.e. the tradition he had received), Moses charged the people to establish for themselves an aristocracy (i.e. the rule of the Sanhedrin and the high priest) but if they desired a monarchy, it should be subject to the high priest and the Sanhedrin. It is well known, that we also find divergent opinions among the Tannaim on the subject, some maintaining that it is a religious duty to appoint a king, others

holding that 'this section ('you may indeed set as king over you') was prescribed only to avoid complaints'. This is not the place to deal with this question in detail, namely, the attitude of Judaism to kingship. But briefly it may be stated that there are discernible differences of view on the subject within the nation in the era of the Second Temple. Thus we have seen that Josephus (and also in other passages) is opposed to monarchy, though not absolutely. We also find antagonism to the throne expressed in the *Book of Jubilees* (xi 2) and in *I Maccabees* viii 14–15 (this last source was overlooked by Heinemann, *Philons usw.*, p. 185; it should be noted, however, that there is no absolute proof regarding our subject to be deduced from the *Book of Jubilees,* since the ideas on this theme expressed there belong to the sphere of *ethico-political philosophy*). On the other hand Philo's attitude towards kingship is positive (we may infer this also from his attitude to Agrippa, as expressed in *De Legatione ad Caium*). The Halakha approximates most closely to that of Philo, as stated; hence it may not be maintained, in general, that the Pharisees were opposed to the Hasmoneans because they took the crown, but it can be said that they fought against the despots among them, who wished to negate the people's right to rule (needless to say, this is evidenced by the Pharisees' recognition of Salome as queen; only consideration should be given to the fact that the Halakha in *Sifre Deut.* §157 states that 'a king but not a queen' may be appointed. Apparently, it may be inferred that this principle was held valid at an early period from the statement of Josephus (*Ant.* xiii 16, 3), who asserts that Aristobulus and his associates objected to Salome's being queen, arguing that the Jewish people had acted improperly in allowing a weak woman to reign over them παρα τὸ εἰκός — 'unreasonably'. The question requires further investigation, for possibly the aforementioned halakhic ruling was not universally accepted).

Now we must also discuss the other reasons advanced by scholars in support of their premise concerning the basic opposition on the part of the Pharisees towards the Hasmoneans.

Some declare that the Pharisees were in conflict with the Hasmoneans because the latter waged many wars and shed much blood, and consequently were disqualified, in their estimation, for the priesthood. But John Hyrcanus (Simon and Jonathan) also did not tread the paths of peace (Aptowitzer's argument, *op. cit.*, pp. 4–5, that *II Maccabees* speaks only of Judah and not his brothers Jonathan and Simon, because the author was opposed to the latter since they shed blood, is unconvincing, for Aptowitzer's inference is from silence that is readily explicable. namely, that essentially *II Maccabees* in its present form was written with the sole purpose of describing the deeds of Judah alone in connection with the establishment of the festival of Hanukka, and the writer never intended to narrate the story of the entire House of the Hasmonean, see *ibid.* ii 19. Note also that the Book begins with a letter addressed to Egypt in connection with the observance of the festival, and ends with the celebration of the Day of Nicanor). Furthermore, we find a number of Halakhot in Tannaitic teaching, which seek to make the waging of optional wars easier (in respect of the observance of the precepts); see especially *'Eruvin* i 1; *Tosefta ibid.* iii (ii) 6; iv (iii) 7; *T.B. ibid.* 17a; *T.P. ibid.* i, p. 19c–d. Other scholars hold that religious differences were responsible for the conflict, but granted that these constituted factors in the struggle between the Pharisees and Jannai as time went on, yet they were not, at any rate, the initial causes, for we have no evidence of this at all. It is true that all the Jewish scholars are accustomed to interpret the story related by Josephus to the effect that Jannai was pelted by the people with citrons as identical with the episode mentioned in the Tannaitic tradition concerning 'a certain Boëthusian (or Sadducean) who poured the libation over his feet and they pelted him' as above. But we cannot but wonder as to what induced these scholars to adopt this conjecture. For it is clear that the Baraita and likewise the Mishna, *loc. cit.*, iv 9, certainly did not refer to Jannai, whom tradition always mentions by name. Have we then the right, because pelting with citrons is mentioned in both sources, to identify the incidents? It appears that it was a daily occurrence for the people to pelt with citrons anyone whom they wished to insult, as we read in the Talmud (*T.B. Qiddushin* 73a) concerning R. Zera, who was expounding in Maḥoza in Babylonia a Halakha that was not approved by his audience, 'and they all pelted him with their citrons'. Furthermore, Josephus declares that the people pelted him when 'he stood beside the altar and was preparing to sacrifice' — καὶ ἑστῶτος αὐτοῦ ἐπὶ τοῦ βωμοῦ καὶ θύειν μέλλοντος (*Ant.*, xiii, 13, 5) — thus he had not yet performed any act and could not, therefore, have 'poured the libation over his feet'. Moreover, Josephus offers another reason for the incident; in *Wars*, i, 4, 3, he stresses the tendency to insurrection at a festival, for at the festivals seditions usually broke out. Thus it was not the libation that was the cause of the trouble.

It should also be noted that the attempt of scholars to infer from the silence of the Mishna with regard to Hanukka (its regulations are mentioned there only incidentally) that the Mishnaic scholars did not fully accept this festival on account of their hostility to the Hasmoneans is not substantiated by any proof. Rather is this silence to be explained by recognition of the literary character of our Mishna and the manner of its compilation; for the Mishna does not contain the traditional material in full, nor is it entirely systematic in the arrangement of this material. Hence we find in it many halakhic rules mentioned only casually, even though it is generally agreed that no one ever objected to them (the same must be said relative to Louis Ginzberg's statement — *Ginze Schechter*, Pt. I, p. 476 — that since 'in the Palestinian Talmud the laws of Hanukka are hardly mentioned' we must therefore assume that this festival was preserved in the days of the Amoraim, especially in Babylonia, in defiance of the fire-worshippers, who sought to prevent the Jews from keeping it, but this was not the case in the Land of Israel, where they did not observe it properly. However, we find various ritual rules concerning Hanukka cited in the name of Palestinian Amoraim in the Babylonian Talmud and in the *Pesiqta Rabbati*, and even *Tractate Soferim* contains numerous Halakhot on this subject. Thus silence is no longer an argument in support of this contention).

Contrariwise, it should be noted that we find 'the House of the Hasmonean' and 'the kings of the House of Hasmonean' mentioned in a number of places in the rabbinic tradition, and nowhere are they spoken of with disfavour, except, of course, where opposition is expressed towards anyone, like Jannai, for example, who fought against them.

Finally, we must contradict the view of Aptowitzer (who in his afore-

the gubernatorial right of the Sanhedrin as the representative of the nation constitutes, to my mind, a decisive factor in the history of their relations not only with the Hasmoneans but also with the House of Herod, I consider it desirable to dwell here on the instructive fact, not stressed by scholars, that throughout the period from the time of the Hasmoneans to the destruction of the Temple, the Pharisees sat together with the Sadducees in the Sanhedrin,[35] and even jointly formed a government at the beginning of the war against the Romans. This shows that despite the radical differences between the Pharisees and the Sadducees in respect of basic religious laws and fundamental social questions, nevertheless since the latter came to participate in the national government because of their loyalty to the democratic order, the Pharisees did not oust them or dissociate themselves from them.[36]

mentioned book discusses the rabbinic sources opposed to the Hasmonean monarchy, but his arguments are not well grounded, being largely only daring attempts to misinterpret the sources) who endeavours to corroborate the tradition regarding the conflict of the Pharisees with John Hyrcanus, and he gives as the reason the fact that the latter regarded himself as king, whereas the Pharisees did not acknowledge his kingship. He sets out to prove (*ibid.*) by a careful examination of *Ant.*, xiii, 16, 1, that John was also regarded as king. But in one section of the same book (xiv, 9, 1–5) we find six references to Hyrcanus II as king, whereas we know that he was only high priest and ethnarch (see also Antiquities v, 10, 5). This is not the place, however, to deal with the main question.

35 Some scholars aver that the Pharisees eschewed sitting with the Sadducees on the Sanhedrin in the reign of Jannai, with the exception of Simeon b. Shetaḥ (*Dor Dor we-Doreshaw*[2], Pt. I, p. 127; Graetz, *op. cit.*, p. 488). They base their views on *Megillat Ta'anit* x; but actually this source proves the reverse, namely, that the Pharisees were forced out of the Bet Din against their will, save for Simeon b. Shetaḥ, who, on account of his close relationship to the monarchy, could not apparently be removed. From the conclusion of this tradition we learn that there were at any rate times when the Pharisees and Sadducees sat together, and even when the Sadducees were ousted, the reason was that their Torah-knowledge was considered too scanty (see *ibid.*). From the *Acts of the Apostles* we learn that Rabban Gamaliel the Elder sat on the Sanhedrin with Sadducees (v 34), and that the Sanhedrin which was due to judge Paul was composed of Sadducees and Pharisees (*ibid.* xxiii 6), and this was the position in the period immediately preceding the fall of the state.

36 It appears that we may also infer from the Talmudic tradition that Jannai enjoined Salome before his death not to fear the Pharisees but the hypocrites, and likewise from Josephus's statement that he told her to draw closer to the Pharisees and to appease them so that her sovereignty might be firmly established, that the Pharisees were not opposed *in principle* to the Hasmonean

The question of the Sanhedrin's authority *vis-à-vis* the rulers was also the cause of the Pharisees' first clash with Herod, when he served as Hyrcanus's governor in Galilee. The Pharisees charged him with illegally executing Hezekiah and his followers, since only the Sanhedrin had the power to judge capital cases.[37] And Shemaiah or Shammai, when he saw that the members of the Sanhedrin were afraid to punish Herod for undermining the authority of the Great Sanhedrin, rebuked them and prophesied to them that they would come to a bad end at the hands of Herod. At this point we reach the third chapter of our theme.

The scholars, including also Jews, incline to the view that initially, at least, the Pharisees' attitude to Herod was devoid of hostility. Some even say that they were pleased with him and supported him. This opinion,[38] which is primarily based on the general assumption that the Pharisees were opposed or indifferent to the political interests of the nation, the savants, both Jewish and gentile, seek to prove with the help of two arguments: (a) the statement of Josephus that Shemaiah and Avṭalion (or Shammai and Hillel) counselled that the gates of Jerusalem be opened before him and the Roman Sosius; (b) the hypothetical fact that in his reign Torah-knowledge increased in Israel through the activities of the academies of Hillel and Shammai, a phenomenon that is to be explained, in their view, by the fact that the Pharisees kept away from political life and accepted the yoke of Herod's sovereignty, provided they were able to dwell in peace and disseminate Torah among the masses.[39]

regime. I am inclined to think that the statement in *II Maccabees* (which was written by a Pharisee) that Judah the Maccabee urged his men to battle, with the words 'for the Torah, the Temple, the city, the land of the fathers and the *dominion of the people*'* (xiii 14) shows that Pharisees, at least in the days of the earlier Hasmoneans, considered the object of the wars against the Graeco-Syrians to be not only the achievement of the possibility to observe the Torah but also the liberation of the land and the people, and of the national πολιτεία, that is, the attainment of political independence. * This is the translation of the author's Hebrew version of the text; the Revised Standard Version reads: 'for the laws, temple, city, country and commonwealth' [Translator].

37 *Ant.* xiv, 9, 3; *Wars* i, 10, .

38 I have no hesitation in positing that this view took root among Christian scholars because of their aim to liken the Pharisees to the Herodians, who both receive unfavourable mention (and are even linked together) in the Gospels and in relation to Jesus and his early followers.

39 It seems that we cannot infer (as a reflection of the view of the Sages) from the words of Shemaiah in the Mishna (*Avot* i 10), 'Love work and hate

However, this entire conception is completely refuted by the facts. But first let us examine the two arguments just cited.

If there were Pharisees who favoured surrender to Herod and the Romans after a protracted siege and a war lasting three years, the explanation would be that they came to the clear realization that the people could no longer resist the Roman forces, which brought Herod to Judah. Since one of the factors that determined the attitude of most of the Pharisees of that epoch was their *realistic understanding* of events, we can in no way infer from the episode referred to the attitude of the Pharisees towards Herod and his masters apart from that crucial moment.

lordship', that the Pharisees wished at that time (the beginning of Herod's reign?) to give up their participation in the conduct of public affairs and to eschew taking part in matters of state. For this dictum is to be regarded only as good advice tendered to individuals, bidding them choose an upright and beneficial way of life, and not as a sort of *platform* of 'the Pharisaic sect' (had this been the intention of Shemaiah, he would not have failed to speak of the *Torah,* as though — according to the view of the Sages — the Pharisees regarded it as Israel's entire world). Moreover we find similar pronouncements even in other generations (like the statement 'Great is lordship, for it buries those that practice it') whose aim is to discourage people from seeking power; and Tannaim and Amoraim have been known to shun becoming administrators (in their area) of the community; hence we make no deduction from this saying regarding the attitude of the Pharisees to politics and the ruling authority. If Shemaiah said 'and seek no intimacy with the ruling power' (similarly Avṭalion in the next Mishna), we may undoubtedly infer that the Pharisees disliked the government of that time (of Herod and the Romans) on account of their wickedness and cruelty, but what evidence is there here of a *basic principle* held by the Pharisees prescribing passivity in affairs of state?

There is likewise no foundation for the assumption that the offensive remarks uttered by Shemaiah and Avṭalion to 'a certain high priest' after he had insulted them first were directed against Antigonus (*T.B. Yoma* 71b. This tradition is initially a Baraita, in the middle it is couched in Babylonian Aramaic, and at the end it uses Palestinian Aramaic; this shows that it has not been wholly preserved in its original form, and hence its value is impaired. But see *Dikduqe Soferim* and R. Ḥananel's recension), for he was both high priest and *king*. One is inclined to think that the person concerned was one of the early high priests appointed by Herod. It follows that Graetz's statement that the Pharisees held 'the last king of the Hasmonean dynasty' in contempt is groundless. It may also be added here that the fact that in the war of Antigonus against Herod and Hyrcanus the majority of the people supported the former (in Galilee 'all the inhabitants of the land rebelled against Hyrcanus and Herod', *Wars* i, 13, 4), proves that the Pharisees were not opposed to Antigonus.

In this connection, however, mention must be made of Josephus's statement in *Antiquities* that the *Běnē Bava* [sons of Bava], unlike the majority who counselled surrender to Herod when he fought against Antigonus for fear of retribution, continued to oppose him, and when Jerusalem was captured they fled to Edom and went into hiding there for many years.[40] Now it appears that these Bene Bava — that is to say, the family of Bava — are to be connected with Bava b. Buta, one of the early elders of the House of Shammai, who is mentioned in the Baraita,[41] and whom the Talmud (*T.B. Bava Batra*) brings into relationship with Herod.[42] Thus even at this hour of crisis we find divergent opinions among the Pharisees, some of whom (like the Zealots mentioned later) wished to fight against Herod to the end. With regard to the second argument, based on the fact that we have many Halakhot dating from that period, which apparently point to the increase of Torah at that period, we must bear in mind the well-known tradition cited in the name of R. Jose b. Ḥalafta, a Sage well versed in the history of the earlier generations, who testifies that in those days the established order of halakhic instruction, which had existed at an earlier period, had ceased to function, for at first the Halakha was decided in the Sanhedrin, so that there was no room for a multiplicity of views or for prolonged debate among the Sages.[43] On the basis of this tradition, we must therefore explain the increase of Torah-study not by the supposition that in Herod's reign in particular favourable conditions were created for the dissemination of Torah, but by the fact that in his days the norms of halakhic decision were changed and the basis of a fixed Halakha that was obligatory on the public was removed, whereas previously there was one Law for all Israel. Consequently the early halakhic rulings became submerged in a nameless tradition and only the heads of the generations (the Pairs) were mentioned.[44] Thus Herod's rule had evil consequences even in this sphere.

Similarly, the aforementioned view is not supported by the fact that Herod displayed clemency towards Shammai (and Hillel) and did not punish the Pharisees who refused to take the oath of allegiance

40 *Ant.* xv, 7, 9.

41 *Tosefta Ḥagiga* ii 11; *T.B. Beṣa* 20a–b; *T.P. ibid.* ii, p. 61c.

42 See Graetz, *op. cit.*, p. 487.

43 *Tosefta Ḥagiga* ii 9; *ibid. Sanhedrin* vii 1; *T.B. Sanhedrin* 88b; *T.P. ibid.* i, p. 21c.

44 See *Dorot ha-Rishonim*, p. 301 ff.; but the subject requires further study.

to him and to Rome.[45] Herod did all this out of fear, for at the beginning of his reign he was afraid of the people whose blood he had shed and whom he had enslaved.[46]

Against the above-mentioned view, on the other hand, it can be stated that the Pharisees were completely opposed to the Herodian rule throughout Herod's reign and that of Archelaus, his heir. This is shown (a) by the fact that as soon as his rule was established in Jerusalem, Herod slew forty-five men of the Sanhedrin, among whom there were undoubtedly many Pharisees;[47] (b) by the Talmudic tradition that declares that Herod killed all the Sages; (c) by the refusal of six thousand Pharisees to take the oath of allegiance;[48] (d) by the fact that at the end of his reign the Pharisees, Mattathias and Judah cast down the golden eagle that Herod had placed over the Temple gates, and in the end they were burned to death together with their disciples;[49] (e) by the disparaging observation concerning Herod that we read in Josephus as emanating from 'an anonymous Jewish source';[50] (f) by the statements of the Jews before Caesar at the beginning of Archelaus's reign and at the end, shortly before his banishment.[51]

With regard to the causes of the opposition to Herod's rule, we should note the following factors:

(a) The Pharisees disqualified him for the throne because he was not of Jewish descent, as the matter is explained in the Talmudic

45 *Ant.* xv, 10, 4.

46 A similar statement is made by Josephus relative to the period when Hyrcanus and Pompey besieged Aristobulus in Jerusalem, namely, that 'on account of the dread that seized the people when they saw the excellent deployment of the Romans', the number of people who favoured opening the gates of the city to the Romans grew ever more numerous. Regarding our own subject, see *Ant.* xv, 7, 9.

47 *Ant.* xiv, 9, 4; *ibid.* xv, 1, 2.

48 Josephus tells of two instances of refusal to take the oath of allegiance, and there is not sufficient reason for regarding them as only one; see Klausner, *op. cit.* Pt. III, p. 31, n. 3.

49 *Ant.* xvii, 6, 2–3. Compare also the episode of the ten who conspired to assassinate Herod on account of the theatre, amphitheatre and stadium that he built in Jerusalem, *ibid.* xv, 8, 3.

50 *Ant.* xv, 9, 5.

51 *Ant.* xvii, 1, 2; *Wars* ii, 6, 2. We must also add here what we learn from the testimony of Josephus (*Wars* i, 12, 4–5) with regard to 'the leading Jews' who came to meet Antony in Bithynia, then in Daphne, and a third time in Tyre, and demanded that he should remove Herod and his brothers from the government.

tradition,[52] and as we learn from the fact that Agrippa wept when he feared that the Pharisees did not recognize his sovereignty for the same reason.[53]

(b) We may assume that the Pharisees also opposed Herod because he completely abolished, or at least suppressed, the Sanhedrin, a fact that is most fully explained by Walter Otto in his book on Herod.[54] Akin to this is the latter's introduction of new laws that were contrary to the Halakha, and fundamentally appertained to the sphere of the Sanhedrin's authority, such as the statute relating to thieves that he enacted.[55]

(c) The fact that he deprived the high-priesthood of its glory and value by alternatively appointing and removing the high priests, in contradiction to the earlier tradition, which regarded the high-priesthood as a life-long office.[56] As we have already seen at the outset, the Pharisees looked upon the high-priesthood as but a *single element* of the Sanhedrin's regime. This fact, too, must therefore be added to the factor mentioned above, to wit, Herod's clash with the democratic order, which the Pharisees sought at all times to protect.

(d) The stamp of pagan-Greek culture that he imposed upon the Land of Israel and Jerusalem generally, such as the establishment of the stadium, theatre, hippodrome and the like.[57]

(e) The strengthening of the alien Hellenistic settlement in his kingdom to the detriment of the Jews in his spacious state, a trend that led to disastrous results for the Jewish population in the subsequent period. This policy, which finds particular expression in the establishment of the great city of Caesarea, which he formed into a gentile city,[58] brought the Jews to the realization that far more than he was

52 *T.B. Bava Batra* 3b.

53 *Soṭa* vii 8; *Sifre Deuteronomy* §157; *Midrash Tannaim* 104.

54 Otto, *Herodes*, pp. 117–118; Isaak Halevy, *Dorot ha-Rishonim*, p. 274; Klausner, *op. cit.*, Pt. III, pp. 1, 29.

55 See Gulak, *Sefer Klausner*, pp. 132–135. Compare *Ant.* xx, 9, 6, where we read that when Agrippa (II) wished to make a halakhic innovation in the Temple service, he could do nothing without the approval of the Great Sanhedrin.

56 See *T.B. Yoma* 8b–9; *T.P. ibid.* i, p. 38c. Compare also *Ant.* xv, 3, 1; so, too, *ibid.* 20, 6.

57 *Ant.* xv, 8, 1.

58 So, too, Samaria-Sebaste. Concerning both Josephus (*Ant.* xv, 8, 5) declares that he built them that they serve as 'evil wedges' against the Jews, that they should not rebel. The same applied to Geva in Galilee and Ḥeshbon in Transjordan (see *ibid.*, and also in *Wars*, iii, 3, 1). This apart, he also

king of his people, he sought to found his dominion upon the foreign population in the country, whom he greatly supported and aided at the expense of the Jews.[59]

(f) It may also be posited that the abject surrender of Herod to the Romans, and the cessation of all attempts by him to preserve any semblance of independent Jewish policy, also contributed to the negative attitude of many Pharisees to his rule.[60]

Now this attitude of absolute antagonism on the part of the Pharisees towards Herod,[61] remained unchanged also in the days of his

filled Jerusalem with Greek officials and 'guests', who played a large and important role in the government of the country.

59 In this regard note should be taken of the testimony of Nicholas of Damascus, in one of the fragments (Jacoby F., *Hist.*, II A, pp. 424–425), that after Herod's death the people rose up both against his sons and the Greeks. Only the nature of this episode — the conflict with the Greeks — is not sufficiently clear, for possibly it is identical with the event that we also encounter in the War with Rome [67 C.E.], when, at the outset, the Jews fought also against the Greek cities in the Land of Israel and the surrounding regions (so, too, in the time of the Hasmoneans).

We thus have two estimates of Herod's character as ruler, the one of Isaak Halevy in *Dorot ha-Rishonim*, who, on the basis of the aforementioned fact (see (e)], concluded that Herod preferred the Greek settlement in the Land of Israel to that of the Jews, and regarded Herod as 'king of the gentiles'; the other is that of Klausner, who rightly rejects this view, and endeavours to explain the fact that Herod supported the non-Jews, both those who were near and far (with Jewish money) for economic and also political purpose, by contending that he aimed at becoming 'the king Messiah' and supreme ruler (he fitted himself for this role *vis-à-vis* the gentiles by winning their hearts with lavish gifts). But there is nothing to prevent us from placing an entirely simple interpretation upon Herod's actions, namely, that he was neither 'king of the gentiles', nor 'king of the Jews', nor 'King Messiah', but just a despot, of the type of despotic rulers obtaining in the Hellenistic and Roman period, who had no ties — of race or spirit or of national aspirations — with the peoples over whom they ruled. Hence it was possible for Herod to be 'king of the Jews and the Greeks' without distinction (this is in essence actually what Josephus states in *Antiquities* xv, 5, 4), but it is nevertheless clear that Herod, out of fear of the Jews who hated him, strengthened the foreign element in the kingdom, since he relied upon them more than he did on 'his own people'.

60 The Pharisees' antagonism to Herod may also be deduced from the fact that some of them conspired with his brother Pheroras to assassinate him.

61 In essence the arguments presented in the text, whose purpose is to set forth the causes of the Pharisees' opposition to Herod's rule, have already been stated by several Jewish scholars (see especially the pellucid and methodical survey by Klausner, *op. cit.*, Pt. III, pp. 25–34). Only these historians are nevertheless of the opinion that the Pharisees refrained from being active

son, Archelaus, who was ultimately banished on account of the Jews. But at this point we must again rebut the view of the scholars who wish to infer from the request of the Jews (it appears that their chief spokesmen were also on this occasion Pharisees) to have Judea directly annexed to the governorship of Syria that the Pharisees were prepared to forgo political independence. For after we have enumerated above the characteristics of Herod's rule, it is obvious that the 'independence' that the Jews enjoyed in his reign was but twofold and threefold subjection, first to the Romans, then to Herod, and finally even to the Greeks, Israel's bad neighbours. Since the Pharisees were disposed to evaluate the facts realistically, they could not agree to the complete subjection of the people under the camouflage of ostensible sovereignty, and thus they sought to preserve the autonomy that the Romans vouchsafed the people until the fall of the state.

Now let us briefly clarify the Pharisaic attitude towards Agrippa. The tradition of Josephus,[62] that of the Tannaim,[63] and similarly the researches of modern scholars, lead us apparently to the conclusion that all the Pharisees took a completely positive stand relative to his rule. It seems, indeed, that the majority of the Pharisees accepted him and his sovereignty, as is evident from Josephus and many other sources of the Tannaitic tradition. The reasons for this attitude, as far as we can conjecture, were: (a) that he was descended on his mother's side from the Hasmoneans, and that he was halachically more eligible for the throne than his paternal grandfather; (b) that he acted as a Jew, from both the religious and political aspects,

in the affairs of the state and ineluctably gave way to the wicked despot. But we have already seen that there is no foundation for this assumption, which is apparently based on the fact that in Herod's reign the Pharisees did not perform any 'great exploit' in the conflict (such as they did in the days of Jannai). But it is not to be wondered at that scholars have not discerned in the nation, whose hands had become enfeebled after many bloody conflicts, those mighty forces it required in order to overcome the powerful despot, who had the unqualified assurance of Roman help (against the Jews, in contradistinction, for example, to the Arabs, for attacking whom he was nearly dethroned by Augustus). From Josephus we learn, in *Antiquities* xvi, 2, 4 (on the authority, it seems, of Nicholas of Damascus), that against Herod, the Pharisees, who were opposed to him openly and secretly, were prepared to fight with violence.

62 *Ant.* xix, 7, 3, etc.

63 In the passages where Agrippa is mentioned favourably by the Tannaim, it is reasonable to suppose that the reference is to Agrippa I, as is suggested by Hoffmann in *Mishna ha-Rishonim*, and by Naḥman Krochmal before him, although the matter is not proven.

preferring the Jews to the large gentile population that dwelt in his kingdom; (c) that to a large extent he sought to pursue an independent policy and was not completely subject to the Romans like his grandfather Herod. This is demonstrated by the well-known fact that he endeavoured to fortify the walls of Jerusalem and was forcibly prevented by the Roman governor in Syria and by Claudius, and also by the fact that he sought to make a covenant with the kings[64] who were under Roman suzerainty with a view, apparently, of strengthening his position against the wicked kingdom.

Nevertheless, it can be shown that some of the Pharisees were opposed to him, and for two reasons: (a) because these did not recognize his right to be king of Israel, since he was not 'from among thy brethren'; (b) because even he did not abandon, in adequate measure, the Greek idolatrous policy followed by Herod, but maintained it towards the non-Jewish areas, and even in the mixed settlements, like Caesarea, Tiberias and others. This is to be inferred from the Baraita in the Tosefta, the Talmud and the *Midrash Tannaim*,[65] where we read that exile was finally decreed upon Israel and they were doomed to destruction when they sycophantically said to Agrippa 'Thou art our brother', implying that he was fit to be king. Similarly, Josephus states that Simon the Pharisee preached in Jerusalem that Agrippa should be banned and excluded from the Temple because he builds theatres for the gentiles in non-Jewish territory and in Judea.[66]

We are thus again confronted by divergent views held by the Pharisees in regard to the subject under discussion.

We now come to the days of the great war against Rome in the years 66–70. It seems that the interval between this time and the death of Agrippa — twenty-two years — was the very period that gave rise to those new phenomena that we discern in the Pharisees' camp in the sphere of our subject and with which we shall deal at once.

In this intermediate epoch, the national movement in Judea grew stronger and more widespread. It suffered degeneration, however, at both ends: on the one hand it took the form of the advent of false Messiahs, and on the other the form of Sicarii, the well-known dagger-men. Nay more, even the ruling classes, the members of the

64 *Ant.* xix, 7, 2; *ibid.* 8, 1.

65 *Tosefta Sota* vii 16; *T.B. ibid.* 41b; *T.P. ibid.* vii, p. 22a; *Midrash Tannaim*, p. 104.

66 *Ant.* xix, 7, 14.

high-priesthood and the Sanhedrin, were at this juncture riddled by corruption, as we learn from Josephus[67] and from the Tannaitic tradition.[68] All these facts combined to cast the Jewish population into the abyss of anarchy.

This situation was inevitably conducive to the rise within the camp of the Pharisees of two new, and mutually opposed, movements, namely, a movement of zealots on the one hand, and, on the other, a policy of despair that sought to withdraw from the idea of a Jewish state and to cleave to the recognition of the advantage and necessity of Roman rule in Judea.

In truth, during the war against Rome and in the period immediately preceding it we find these two trends in Pharisaic circles alongside their classic and traditional policy, which was still dominant.

The personality of the Pharisee Zechariah b. Avqilus, whose actions at the time are known to us from the Talmud[69] and from Josephus,[70] may be regarded as typifying the Pharisee zealots, whose aim was to revolt against Rome with a view to casting off the yoke of her subjugation from the nation without giving due consideration to the actual factors of the movement. But we also have other evidence from this period concerning Pharisees who ruled, like the zealots, that it was prohibited by religious law to accept Roman dominion. Thus we read in *Canticles Zuṭa* on the verse 'Make haste, my beloved', 'The day that I made a covenant with Arḥumu (?), and two lambs were offered up, one on the north side of the altar on behalf of Arḥumu and one on the south side of the altar on behalf of Jerusalem.'[71] Now I have explained elsewhere[72] that Arḥumu denotes Rome, and the dictum comes to teach us that the Holy One blessed be He withdrew His *Shekhina* ["Divine Presence"] from Israel when they agreed to offer sacrifices on behalf of Rome, that is, on behalf of the emperors, a practice to which, as we know, Josephus and Philo testify. Since we learn from the *Wars* of Josephus and from the Talmudic Haggada that the cessation of the offering of sacrifices on behalf of the Roman emperor served as a signal for starting the great revolt, we have before us here an expression of the view of those Pharisees whose views approximated to those of

67 *Ibid.* xx, 8, 4.
68 *Tosefta Menaḥot*, iii 21; *T.B. Pesaḥim* 57a.
69 *T.B. Giṭṭin* 56a.
70 *Wars*, iv, 4, 1.
71 Schechter, p. 47; Buber 41.
72 *Sefer Klausner*, p. 165, n. 55.

the zealots, and who taught that it was fundamentally forbidden to accept the Roman yoke.

Contrariwise, we find R. Ḥanina, the Deputy High Priest, who was a contemporary, declaring about this time: 'Pray for the welfare of the government, (i.e. of Rome), since but for the fear thereof men would swallow each other alive.'[73] Thus there were Pharisees who despaired of the community's ability to govern itself in complete freedom, and realized the benefit of Roman rule in assuring law and order in the country. We find this view expressed also by another Sage, who, however, lived in the third century. For we read in Genesis Rabba (ch. ix): 'R. Simeon b. Laqish said: "And, behold, it was very good" — this is the Kingdom of Heaven; "And behold, it was very good" — this is the Earthly Kingdom. But is the Earthly Kingdom very good!? — Only it demands that people observe the law.' The meaning is that Rome evinces great ability in preserving public security.[74]

It seems that even Rabban Joḥanan b. Zakkai belonged to this school of Pharisees who advocated unqualified subjection to the Romans.[75]

The middle path between these two extremes was that followed by the Pharisees who continued the tradition of their early predecessors, and whose chief spokesman was, apparently, Rabban Simeon b. Gamaliel. It is known that he participated in the government of the Sanhedrin that was established after the defeat of Cestius Gallus, and he was faithful to those who charged him with the task of making the preparation for the war against the Romans in order to defend the liberty of the nation. Improbable is the view held by many scholars who imagine that Rabban Simeon b. Gamaliel and his colleagues were ineluctably swept into the revolt, or that he intended weakening the hands of the fighters by ostensibly joining them, as Josephus testifies, with deliberate untruth, about himself and his associates.[76] Rabban Simeon b. Gamaliel adopted the way of the

73 *Avot* iii 2.

74 A Tanna of the second century praises the Romans for the improvements they have effected in the sphere of material civilization (*T.B. Shabbat* 33b; cf. *T.B. 'Avoda Zara* 2b).

75 However, the matter is still a moot point.

76 *Life* v, 7; cf. *Wars* ii, 20, 3. But that the majority of the people (and the scholars) were on the side of the 'fighters' (at least at the beginning of the war) can be deduced even from the festive days appointed by Sages, which are enumerated in *Megillat Ta'anit*, see H. Lichtenstein, *HUCA*, VIII, pp. 299 ff.

earlier Pharisees, who were always opposed to Roman rule, only they chose to shut their eyes to the facts and avoided, unlike the Zealots, the shedding of Jewish blood in fruitless rebellions. Consequently, when he conceived that the moment was ripe for war and victory he did not hesitate to rebel against the government, nor did he yield before the extreme brutality of the Romans, whose aim at the time was total annihilation, but roused the nation to defend itself.

Now this classic policy of the Pharisees, who were realistic nationalists, survived even the fall of the state. For neither the destruction of Jerusalem nor the burning down of the Temple was able to destroy the spirit of the Pharisees, or to rob them of their longing for political freedom and their desire to fight for it when the opportunity occurred.[77]

The most reliable testimony to this fact is the War of Bar Kokhba. For, as is well known, Rabbi Akiba was one of the chief leaders of the people in this war, and although R. Joḥanan b. Torta said to R. Akiba: 'Grass will have grown out of thy jaws ere the Son of David appears',[78] the former only proves that there were some Pharisees who were opposed to the war. However, there is hardly

77 Scholars have already noted that the practical factor that, *inter alia*, induced the Zealots and the other rebels against Rome to rise up in revolt was the existence of a great and powerful Diaspora in the Roman empire, and particularly in the Parthian kingdom, which was prepared — at least many within it — to help 'the metropolitan country' in person and with substance; this information is given by Josephus for the period of this war. But attention should be paid to Philo's statement in *Legatio ad Caium* (XXXI) in explanation of the action of Petronius, who refrained from carrying out Caligula's edict to set up his image in the Temple, namely, that the Roman governor acted as he did not only for humanitarian reasons, as Josephus explains, but also (and chiefly) because firstly he feared the Jews in the country on account of their numbers and their courage and zeal for the Torah, and secondly because he knew that the Jews were dispersed in their multitudes throughout the Roman empire, and more especially because he had first-hand knowledge, as governor of Syria and commander of the Roman legions on the border of Parthia, that the Jews 'across the Euphrates', were numerous and strong, and he feared that if he went up against Judea he would have to fight in front and in the rear (where the Babylonian Jews would irrupt against him). Thus, in Philo's estimation, about thirty years prior to the period under consideration, there was a real prospect of the Jews' going forth against Rome with force.

78 *T.P. Ta'anit* iv, p. 68d. However, we learn from this Haggada that Bar Kokhba needed the Jewish Sages and acted according to their ruling.

any room for doubt that the majority of the Pharisees were in agreement with R. Akiba and Bar Kokhba, for otherwise this war, which lasted three and a half years, and in which myriads upon myriads of Jews took part, could not have been started at all, and at that time there were only Pharisees in Jewry.[79]

Only at that time we also find pacifist Pharisees, whose policy was based on a new idea of a credal nature, to wit, that there must be complete submission to Roman rule, because it was a Divine decree that this kingdom should endure upon earth until the Days of the Messiah. Thus we read in the Talmud that R. Jose b. Qisma reproved R. Ḥanina b. Teradion for organizing public assemblies, which he instructed in Torah, and thereby transgressed the government's edict, saying: 'This nation, which destroyed God's house and burnt His Temple, and still endures, was given sovereignty by Heaven.'[80] Indeed, this R. Jose was on intimate terms with the government, and when he died leading Romans attended the funeral. This credo was also held by Josephus, with change of form and adaptation to the situation, as we learn from his *Wars*;[81] and he, too, arrived at this belief only in the war against the Romans, or thereafter.

But this type of Pharisee represented a minority, as we have stated, until tyranny brought about the destruction of Bethar and the power of the Jews declined and they were no longer able to take up arms against Rome. At that period the Pharisees cease to contemplate rebellion against the government, and even forbid it for ever.[82] Their

79 Undoubtedly, even in those days there were to be found residual elements of the Sadducees among the Jews (see, for instance, *T.B. Shabbat* 108a), but, as a group they were no longer discernible within the nation.

80 *T.B. 'Avoda Zara* 18a.

81 For example, *Wars* iii, 8, 3.

82 The statement, it is true, emanates from Amoraim of the third century, *T.B. Ketubbot* 111a: 'What was the purpose of these three oaths? One, that Israel should not go up (in serried ranks) like a wall; the second, that they should not rebel against the gentile nations; the third, was the Holy One blessed be He's adjuration to the gentile nations not to oppress Israel too much' (compare *Canticles Rabba* on the verse, 'I adjure you'). But it appears that these views crystallized primarily shortly after the war of Bethar. In relation to this subject, we should, properly, deal with the attitude of the Halakha of the Tannaim — in the time of the Temple and after — and of the Amoraim towards the Roman regime from the aspect of the legal recognition inherent in their 'Bet Din decisions' of the Roman taxes and tolls, confiscation of property and jurisprudence. Because in this sphere, too, divergent views are to be found among the Sages, and it is even possible to trace the evolutionary courses in the Halakha from complete negation

former antagonism to 'Rome the guilty' and 'the Kingdom of Evil' turned to inveterate hatred in the heart and to prophecy and prayer regarding its downfall at the end of days.

I shall now sum up.

From the commencement of the Roman regime and that of the Herodian dynasty in Judea up to the time of Agrippa, the Pharisees as a whole were completely antagonistic to their rule. Although during his reign they did not oppose Herod openly out of fear, yet immediately upon his death they rose in armed revolt against his heir and also fought him politically, until he was dethroned. At the same time some of them even attacked the Romans in 'the War of Asvarus', that is, Varus.

In the reign of Agrippa the Pharisees were largely reconciled to his rule. But shortly after this period, a change came over the Pharisees: some of them wanted the Roman regime, because they despaired of the ability of the Jews to maintain peace, security and law in their country, and on the other hand, many Pharisees joined the Zealots and ruled that it was a religious duty to fight against the Romans by all means possible. After the fall of the state a new fundamental doctrine emerged among a number of pacifist Pharisees to the effect that the earthly dominion was given to Rome, and consequently it was incumbent upon them to submit to her without any reservation.

But the main path followed by the majority of the Pharisees remained unchanged, that is to say, they were opposed to Roman rule and longed for political freedom and democratic government, while acknowledging that a realistic appraisal of the circumstances must decide the choice of the opportune movement for action and determine the scope of its purpose.

to recognition resulting from adjustment to the realities of the situation and the acceptance of the Roman yoke. But this is not the place to deal with the matter in detail.

PAR'IRTIN

On the History of the High Priesthood at the End of the Second Temple Period

The Palestinian Talmud (*Yoma* i, 38c) relative to the Mishna *ibid.* i, 1, 'Seven days before the Day of Atonement the High Priest was removed from his house to the Chamber of the Palhedrin [פלהדרין]', cites the Baraita, 'Abba Saul used to call it the Chamber of the Bouleutin [בלווטין]. At first they used to call it the Chamber of the Bouleutin, but now they call it the Chamber of Palhedrin'. The Talmud adds: פראירתין מילא עבידה.[1]

Now the last three words are most obscure, and many scholars have sought to explain them in a variety of ways.[2] But not one of the explanations is satisfactory.

Before we deal with this difficult dictum, however, and examine, with a view to elucidating it, the parallel traditions in other sources (and in the Palestinian Talmud itself, below), we must first consider the last suggestion of Austersetzer (*Zion*, iv, pp. 294–306). To this end let us quote here the Baraita in *T.B. Yoma* 8b, on which the exposition of this scholar is based. But first of all we must note the following two points: (a) the statement under discussion in the Palestinian Talmud is certainly similar in meaning to 'the Chamber of the פלהדרין'; (b) it reflects unfavourably on the High Priests, as is shown by the passage in the Palestinian Talmud that follows immediately afterwards: 'In the First (Temple) where he and his son and his grandson ministered, there officiated eighteen (High) Priests; but in the Second (Temple), because they paid money (for their offices), and some say they killed one another by witchcraft, there officiated eighty (High) Priests', etc.

1 The reading פראידתין found in later editions is corrupt, and the interpretations based on it (see *Zion*, IV, p. 305) are erroneous.

2 Even Lieberman's suggestion (*Tarbiz*, III, p. 339) to regard פראירתין as the Greek word παρελθόντες, in the sense of 'a jest at the expense of the Palhedrin, who were not even πάρεδροι (παρεδρεύοντες) but only παρελθ, that is to say, they merely passed through the chamber without finding time to sit down', does not, in my opinion, warrant consideration.

Let us now return to the Babylonian Baraita.

'It has been taught: R. Judah [said]:[3] Was it the Chamber of the Parhedrin? Was it not rather the Chamber of the Bouleute! Originally, in truth, it was called the Chamber of the Bouleute, but because they used to pay money for the office of (High) Priest,[4] and they changed it[5] every twelve months like the Parhedrin who were changed every twelve months, they were consequently called "the Chamber of the Parhedrin".'

This Baraita (which is likewise obscure in many respects and which we shall again examine below) seeks to explain the change of name, from 'the Chamber of the Bouleute' to the 'Chamber of the Parhedrin', as a result of the deterioration of the image of the occupants of the Chamber (apparently, the High Priests). Hence it could apparently help us to elucidate the statement in the Palestinian Talmud under discussion, which is juxtaposed to the similar Baraita cited first, which also speaks of the change of name referred to. This is precisely how Austersetzer sees it.

This scholar accepts the tradition of the Babylonian Talmud as absolute historical testimony, and is of the opinion that 'the Chamber of the Palhedrin' was indeed originally none other than the Chamber of the High Priests. In his view 'Palhedrin' signifies 'the Heads of the Courts',[6] and this designation was used by the people who coined it[7] to denote the primary value and function of the High Priests at the end of the epoch of the Second Temple in their relation to the Sanhedrin, namely, that they were the heads of the High Court; in other words, that the holiness attaching to them at first departed from them, in the estimation of the people, after they had taken to evil ways. They were subsequently regarded as secular authorities

3 This is the MS reading; see *Diqduqe Soferim*.

4 שנותנין עליה וכו' is the correct reading in accordance with the MS, see *Diqduqe Soferim* and Tosafot Yeshanim.

5 The Munich MS, and MS II read אותן, 'them' [instead of אותה, 'it'], i.e. the High Priests. But even according to our reading — אותה — the reference is certainly not to the chamber 'which every (High) Priest who entered upon his office there anew would demolish and rebuild more beautifully that it might be called after him' (Rashi), but to the High Priesthood.

6 προεδ of δικαστήρια in Egyptian papyri.

7 In truth, 'the Chamber of the Palhedrin' was not a popular byname, but a permanent title like 'the Chamber of the Bouleute', with which it is conjoined, and it was undoubtedly used (officially) in the Temple; it is only the *explanation* of the name given by tradition that has a 'popular character'. See further on in the article.

only the presidents of the Sanhedrin. Consequently, the Chamber that to begin with was called after the Bouleute and did not bear the name of the High Priests, since at that time they were considered to be ministering in holiness, their judicial office being of secondary importance, was later designated 'the Chamber of the Palhedrin' in order to underline the primary character of the High Priests from the aspect of their civil-secular function.

On this basis Austersetzer seeks to arrive at a decision in the well-known contradiction — which has exercised the minds of many scholars — between the Tannaitic tradition, which does not know of the High Priest as the head of the Sanhedrin, and the witness of Josephus and the Christian Gospels (and the *Acts of the Apostles*) that the High Priests always presided at the Great Sanhedrin. For the name *Palhedrin* (according to Austersetzer's interpretation) testifies to the fact that the High Priests were actually the heads of the High Court, and furthermore that the people regarded this function of theirs as their primary one. We thus find that the Mishna and Talmud support the tradition of external sources and refute the evidence of the Tannaim.

Austersetzer then proceeds to interpret the Palestinian Talmud. He holds that the tradition of the Yerushalmi is identical with that of the Bavli, and that the statement alluded to contains a question (juxtaposed to the preceding Baraita: 'Abba Saul. . . At first they used to call it,' etc.): 'Why was the Chamber called after the "Parhedrin"?' And the succeeding dictum — 'In the First Temple', etc. — provides an answer resembling that of the Babylonian Baraita: 'Because many High Priests who served in the Second Temple were changed every twelve months (we complete the text according to the Babylonian Talmud), hence it (the Chamber) was given a pejorative designation.' And this is how our dictum is to be construed: פראירתין is the Greek word προαιρετοί, which signifies: those elected, appointed (to anything); the word מילא is to be divided into two, מי לא. The question will then be: For [the use of] the Par'irtin, the appointees (i.e. the High Priests) — is it (the Chamber of the Bouleute) not made for (discussing) the needs of the state and of the Temple? Why then was it called 'the Chamber of the Palhedrin' (and not after the High Priests or the Bouleute, as at first)? To this the Talmud answers: At first they served, etc.

We have no need, it seems, to refute at length the forced and questionable explanation of this scholar.

(a) Austersetzer compels us to insert into the dictum an essential initial-word that it does not contain (בשביל, 'for [the use of]').[8]

(b) Why did the Palestinian Talmud see fit to choose this obscure word (found nowhere else), προα, which has no permanent or specific significance for the High Priesthood, when it enquires why this chamber was not called 'the Chamber of the High Priests' or 'the Chamber of the Bouleute'? This apart, it is difficult to suppose that the Talmud would use a strange word of this kind in a statement without *ulterior motives*.

(c) The very question is difficult. How do we know that the Chamber of the Bouleute must necessarily be for the use of the High Priests?

(d) The use of the word מי in the sense of 'is it' in an interrogative sentence is purely a Babylonian Aramaic usage, and is not found at all in the Palestinian Talmud. Austersetzer's explanation must undoubtedly be rejected.

Let us now revert to his interpretation of the word 'Palhedrin', the Babylonian Baraita, and the historical deductions derived therefrom by the savant.

It stands to reason that *Parhedrin* or *Palhedrin*, which undoubtedly represent the Greek πρόεδροι (and not πάρεδροι),[9] is to be connected with the Bouleute, who are mentioned with them in the two Baraitot cited above, that is to say, they were the heads of the Boule, who constituted the executive authority, like those that we find in many Greek cities.[10] For at the close of the period of the Second Temple

8 Austersetzer posits that the ancient version may have had פרא פראירתין, as we find in a number of passages of the Palestinian Talmud (*Rosh ha-Shana* i, 57a) פרא בסיליאום (*Shabbat* iii, 3), and the copyists omitted the word פרא, thinking that it had arisen (by dittography) from the following word. But the word פרא, which is found 'in a number of passages' of the Palestinian Talmud only means 'less' and has no bearing therefore on our subject; and as regards the dictum in *T.P. Shabbat*, it is obscure and apparently also corrupt. In *T.P. Rosh ha-Shana* 57b, the word פרא is used in the sense of *by* (παρα) in a statement that is entirely in Greek (π. βασιλέως ὁ νόμος ἄγραφος), and should not be compared with our dictum. Thus פרא is never used in the signification of 'for'.

9 Although a number of modern scholars still maintain this reading (Baneth, Strack, Fiebig, Danby, in their translations of and commentaries on the Mishna, and Lieberman, *op. cit.*) it is disproven, particularly by the analogy of the bilingual inscriptions of Palmyra (see Schürer, II, p. 60, and Austersetzer, p. 296, where פלהדרותה corresponds to ἐρὶ προέδρου).

10 Of the places close to the Land of Israel, we find them (at various periods) in *Tyre* (Dittenberger, *OGIS* II, No. 595), *Gerasa* (*ibid.*, No. 621), *Kanatha* in

the Jerusalem authorities were organized in the form of a Greek πόλις (city), with ἄρχοντες (heads), βουλή[11] (council), and even δέκα πρῶτοι[12] (the first ten) (exactly as all these were mentioned at that period in Tiberias,[13] whose government was primarily modelled on that of the Hellenistic cities). The Palhedrin are therefore none other than the heads of the Jerusalem Council and the leaders of the city in all respects (see Appendix I). This statement of fact is in no way invalidated by the serious doubt regarding the relationship between the Boule in Jerusalem and the Great Sanhedrin and the Supreme Court in the Chamber of Hewn Stone. For as is well known, the vast majority of scholars are of opinion that these three institutions are identical, while Büchler argues to the contrary that they

Transjordania (see Schürer, *op. cit.*, p. 169) and *Bozrah* in the same country; Brünnow-Domaschweski, *Provincia Arabia* III, p. 202. As regards פרוהדרוס in a city of the Land of Israel in the time of Commodus, see the inscription discussed by Clermont-Ganneau in *RAO*, VIII, pp. 173–174.

11 Claudius in his rescript of the year 45 writes in regard to the return of the garments of the High Priest to the possession of the people (to have them in their custody throughout the year), 'Ἱεροσολυμιτῶν ἄρχουσι βουλῇ δήμῳ, Ἰουδαίων παντὶ ἔθνει ('To the archons, the Boule, the citizens of Jerusalem and the Jewish people as a whole') (*Ant.* xx, 1, 2). Clearly, even δῆμος here means 'the people of Jerusalem', in accordance with the use of the word in similar formulas in documents pertaining to the Hellenistic cities, for 'the Jewish people as a whole' are specifically mentioned afterwards.

12 *Ant.* xx, 8, 11; these went with 'Ishmael, the High Priest, and Ḥilqiah, the Keeper of the Treasure (the Temple treasurer), to make religious-political representations to the emperor Nero. The βουλή, it should be noted, is also mentioned in other passages: *Wars*, ii, 16, 2; iv, 3, 13; v, 13, 1 (καὶ ὁ γραμματεὺς τῆς βουλῆς Ἀριστεύς — Aristeas the scribe of the council); v, 4, 2 (in the sense of 'the building of the Council'; *ibid.* βουλητήριον as above — vi, 6, 3). Similarly, we find Bouleutin in Jerusalem (apart from 'the Chamber of the Bouleutin') mentioned in several sources. ἄρχοντες καὶ βουλευταί (*Wars*, ii, 17, 1; here, too, there can be no doubt that this formula, which is identical with that found in the documents pertaining to Greek cities, denotes 'a municipal administrative association', and as Büchler also understood it, *Das Synedrion*, etc., p. 233). Luke xxiii 3, Ἰωσὴφ βουλευτής [being parallel to Mark xv 43 — εὐσχήμων βουλ]. In *Lamentations Rabbati* (ch. i, on 'Her adversaries are become the head'): 'There were in Jerusalem four *Bouleutin*, Ben Ṣiṣit, and Ben Gurion', etc. In the Palestinian Talmud (Ta'aniyyot, iv, p. 69a) — *Bouleutin of Jerusalem*. A reference to βουλευταί in Jerusalem, belonging to the same period as the last two sources, is found in Dio Cassius (Reinach, *Textes*, etc., p. 193; 66, 6), where they are mentioned alongside the people (δῆμος) and the priests.

13 See the passages cited by Schürer, II, p. 218, n. 529.

are separate and different.[14] Even if we accept Büchler's view, the Jerusalem Boule undoubtedly had a definite connection (of function and influence) with the Sanctuary. Hence, we need feel no surprise that the Chamber of the Bouleutin or the Chamber of the Parhedrin was situated in the holy precincts. Now the name *Parhedrin per se* certainly does not signify 'High Priests', although, in point of fact, it may be presumed that they comprised 'some of the noblest families of the priesthood'.[15] Moreover even the Babylonian Baraita itself provides no decisive proof that it refers to them. Since, however, the Baraita cannot be explained in any other way except with dif-

14 *Op. cit.*, pp. 193 ff., 227, 232. For a view approximating to that of Büchler, which distinguishes between Boule, which is only the municipal administration and the Sanhedrin (γερ., which is the same as the Boule), see Schürer, p. 247, n. 26.

15 It seems clear that *Palhedrin* is not a plural of kind [i.e., indicating a number of individuals] but denotes a group or association, like Bouleutin in the phrase 'the Chamber of the Bouleutin'. Although we sometimes find individual Parhedrin even in Hellenistic cities (in the inscriptions of Palmyra and Tyre), these cities are generally referred to in the plural; see (already at the end of the classical period) Pauly-Wissowa *Real-Enz.*, V, p. 1026, and for the Hellenistic period, Dittenberger, index to προεδ., in *OGIS* (p. 698), and the index for *Sylloge* under the aforementioned word and under 'Egypt' in Preisigke's *Lexicon*, III, ch. 8, p. 148. The Palhedrin is, therefore, a plural like ἄρχοντες. As regards the question of the connection between the High Priest and the presidency of the Sanhedrin, if we regard the Boule as a separate institution in accordance with Büchler's view, then without doubt the High Priest was not associated with the Parhedrin. Our sources do not support this separation (Appendix I), but even without it there is no difficulty. For it seems certain that when the Boule (Sanhedrin) was concerned with ordinary municipal matters, the High Priest had no need to attend the deliberations, and the Parhedrin presided, but when it dealt as a court with public and judicial affairs that had political significance (or any other general importance, like the instances cited by Josephus, the Gospels and the *Acts of the Apostles*), the High Priest could convene it and preside over it (just as in matters of religion and halakhic decisions one of 'the Jewish Sages' could be chairman in his capacity as *Nasi* [Patriarch] or *Av Bet Din* [Father of the Court], *Muphla shel Bet Din* [instructing Judge], *Gadol she-be-Dayyanim* [Chief Judge] or *Rosh Bet Din* [Head of the Court]; regarding different chairmen at the Great Sanhedrin in connection with the various matters with which it was concerned, compare the view of Jelski, Schürer, *op. cit.*, p. 255, note 54). We still need to consider the nature of the relationship between the High Priest and the Sanhedrin, and his right to convene it and preside over it, only this is not the place for this discussion (one thing, however, is certain, that despite the close connection of the High Priest with the Great Sanhedrin, his authority and power were independent, and his association with the Sanhedrin essentially constituted a *dyarchy*).

ficulty, and seeing that the Babylonian Talmud (*Yoma* 9a) cites in connection therewith a tradition approximating to that of the Palestinian Talmud to the effect that in the time of the Second Temple the years of the High Priests were shortened, we must therefore conclude that the Tannaitic tradition actually comes to inform us what the meaning of the name is.

But is the tradition sufficiently reliable to be accepted as evidence of actual fact?

The Baraita seeks to resolve a problem arising from the name 'Chamber of the Palhedrin' used in the Mishna as against 'Chamber of the Boulesate', which was employed, apparently, in another tradition. We must therefore regard our Baraita as 'harmonistic', its object being to reconcile conflicting (or different) traditions on the basis of development (the circumstances, to which the differing traditions apply, changing in the course of time) — a pseudo-historic approach. For we read in *Tosefta Yoma*, i, 1: 'R. Judah used to call it the Chamber of the פלווטין — nothing more.' And even the passage from the Palestinian Talmud quoted at the beginning, 'Abba Saul used to call it the Chamber of the Bouleutin', appears to be an isolated statement unconnected with the tradition that follows: 'At first they used to call it the Chamber of the Bouleutin', etc., which is a different Baraita, with the same 'harmonistic' purpose as that of the Babylonian Talmud.[16] We have before us, therefore, traditions that differ from our Mishna and conflict with it, and the Babylonian Baraita is only 'an expression of opinion' to reconcile the discrepancy between them.

We find a similar instance in *Sanhedrin* iii 3: 'Which are disqualified? One that gambles with dice, one that lends on interest, those who fly pigeons, those who trade in (produce of) the Sabbatical Year, and slaves. R. Simeon said: At first they called them only "Gatherers of (the produce of) the Sabbatical Year", but when the oppressors increased, they changed their name to "Traders in (the produce of) the Sabbatical Year".' Now R. Simeon's dictum is elucidated by the *Tosefta* (*ibid.* v 2), which notes with reference to our Mishna: 'R. Meir used to call them "Gatherers of (the produce of) the Sabbatical Year"; R. Judah used to call them "Traders in the produce of the

16 Actually, if we wished to draw an inference from the expression '*And now they call it* the Chamber of the Palhedrin', we should have, it appears, to conclude that this diction was not formulated in the generation following the destruction of the Temple.

Sabbatical Year".'[17] It seems clear that we have here before us two conflicting traditions, and R. Simeon seeks to reconcile in the manner stated.[18]

But it appears that we can prove positively that the Chamber of the Palhedrin did not from the outset denote the Chamber of the High Priest.

It is stated in the Mishna, *Middot* v 4: 'On the south[19] were the Wood Chamber, the Chamber of the Captivity, the Chamber of Hewn Stone. With regard to the Wood Chamber, Eliezer b. Jacob said: I have forgotten what it was used for. Abba Saul said: The Chamber of the High Priest', etc. Now a number of the Earlier Authorities [*Rishonim*],[20] and also later scholars,[21] wish to identify the Chamber of the High Priest with the Chamber of the Palhedrin and base themselves on the discussion in *T.B. Yoma* 19a. But the identification itself is difficult, for it is inconceivable that Abba Saul should for no reason call one chamber by two names — the Chamber of the High Priest in the Mishna and the Chamber of the Bouleute in *T.P. Yoma* (see Appendix II). What then was the Chamber of the Bouleute or the Chamber of the Parhedrin?

At first blush, it might be regarded as the βουλητήριον mentioned by Josephus, the seat of the 'Boule'. But it appears that the βουλητ

17 This view of R. Judah conforms with his ruling in the Mishna that all those mentioned there are disqualified 'if they have no other occupation but this', for obviously 'the Gatherers of Sabbatical produce' do not fall within this category (R. Judah's statement is incorrectly worded in the Tosefta, *ibid.*).

18 As it is stated in the Tosefta, *ibid.*, further on, in the recension of the printed editions and the Vienna MS: 'R. Simeon said I validate both views. How (are they to be reconciled)? Before the oppressors increased they were called "Gatherers of Sabbatical produce" (and were disqualified)', etc.

19 This is the reading in all the MSS of the Mishna and the one known to the Earlier Authorities [*Rishonim*]. But in the Gemara, *T.B. Yoma* 19a the text has 'And on the north', and it is evident from the end of the discussion there (see Tosafot Yeshanim) that the Talmud actually had this ruling (Maimonides, *Hilkhot Bet ha-Beḥira*, v, 16, retains the reading of the Gemara).

20 Maimonides, *Hilkhot 'Avodat Yom ha-Kippurim*, i, 3; *Hilkhot Bet ha-Beḥira*, *ibid.*; *Midrash ha-Gadol* (see Maimonides' commentary) on Leviticus, ed. Rabinowitz, p. 403; the commentary of R. Shemaiah on *Middot* and that of Me'iri on *Yoma* (in *Seder ha-'Avodah* by Jose b. Jose, Siddur of R. Saadia Gaon, p. 269: מערש יצוע שארו יבדילו מקום עצרת סגנים — an obscure passage, but at least it is not the High Priest that is referred to).

21 I. Levi, *Mishnat Abba Shaul*, Hebrew, p. 125, note 1, is in doubt; Schürer, p. 257 (he thinks πρόεδρος = High Priest, and seeks to prove, on this basis, that the High Priest always acted as the head of the Sanhedrin, as does Austersetzer, see Appendix I).

was situated outside the area of the Temple Mount, as Büchler has shown.[22] Thus it is not possible to regard it as the Chamber of the Bouleute, which was certainly located in the Temple area. It would seem that this chamber served only as a meeting-place for the Bouleute, that is the Boule, when their presence was required by their colleagues in connection with given matters relating to the Temple. As a central communal, political body, which was linked from a number of aspects with the highest sacred institution of the nation, in which and around which were concentrated and decided also communal, political issues, the Chamber of the Bouleute was given a place in the Temple precincts, where a number of its members as its representatives repaired, at times, and worked, especially it seems in connection with activities concerning the Temple itself. We find a similar situation in the time of the Second Temple in the generation of Nehemiah, when a man who enjoyed a high public status was allotted 'a chamber in the House of our God', namely, Tobiah the Ammonite; for thus we read in Scripture (Nehemiah xiii 4–5; 7–9): 'Now before this, Eliashib the (High) Priest, who resided in the chamber of the house of our God [נתון בלשכת בית אלהנו] being allied unto Tobiah,[23] had prepared for him (Eliashib for Tobiah)

22 Page 18, and before him already Herzfeld, *Geschichte*, Pt. I, p. 395.

23 This verse is explained by scholars (see Batten in *ICC*, and also Siegfried Nowack's *Handkommentar*, and Kahana) to mean that Eliashib was appointed over the chambers (the text reads: לשכת ['the chamber of']) of the Temple and was connected by family (and we are dealing here with the genealogical relationship of the Sons of Tobiah to the High Priesthood) or friendship with Tobiah. But, even though the Vulgate reads, *praepositus*, etc., the Septuagint accords with the Masoretic text: οἰκῶν ἐν γαζοφυλακίῳ οἴκου θεοῦ ἡμῶν ἐγγιῶν Τωβίᾳ. But this apart, the interpretation referred to cannot possibly be maintained. First, the expression נתון בלשכות is not to be explained in the sense of 'appointed' (as though it were equivalent to נתון על הלשכות). Secondly, Eliashib was High Priest, and in any case was in charge of the whole of the Temple. What was the point then in making him a special officer in control of the chambers? (Nor can it be suggested that he was in charge of the chambers before he was appointed High Priest, see Nehemiah iii 1–20.) The verse therefore appears, according to its form and plain meaning to signify that Eliashib resided (נתון, as in the Septuagint) in his own chamber, namely, the High Priest's chamber mentioned in our Mishna (we already find 'the chamber of Jehoḥanan the son of Eliashib', the High Priest, in Ezra x 6; so, too, in pseudepigraphical Ezra III ix, 1). The verse comes to tell us that he made a chamber for Tobiah next to his own chamber (for the next verse, 'and had prepared for him', etc., is an explanatory statement informing us how they came to have adjacent chambers in the Temple).

a great chamber where aforetime they laid the meal-offerings, the frankincense, and the vessels... and I came to Jerusalem and I understood... therefore I cast forth all the household stuff of Tobiah out of the chamber. Then I commanded, and they cleansed the chambers; and thither brought I again the vessels of the house of God, with the meal offerings and the frankincense.'[24]

This being the case, we need not regard the traditions that speak of the Chamber of the Parhedrin and the Chamber of the Bouleutin as presenting a substantive contradiction but only a difference of wording (just 'the semantic difference between them'). For these two names may represent the same thing, since the same men who acted in the name of the Boule were, generally, the Parhedrin, for they came from the Boule and were incorporated in it, in accordance with the practice obtaining in the Hellenistic cities.

However, if the testimony of the Babylonian Baraita is not acceptable to us in regard to the character of the Chamber of the Palhedrin, we are obliged to examine the facts that it attributes to the High Priests themselves and on the basis of which it explains the aforementioned name in the manner indicated.

To this end it is desirable to cite all the remaining sources that likewise speak of the deterioration of the image of the High Priests at the close of the Second Temple period and of the strange character of the High Priesthood in those days, in order to distinguish the various elements in them and to determine how far these traditions, which undoubtedly derive from Pharisaic anti-priestly sources, accord with the known reality and to what extent they contain evidence of substance concerning facts that are unknown to us.

The Baraita states three facts: (a) The High Priests did not remain in their office throughout their lifetime, nor did they beqeath the High Priesthood to their heirs in accordance with the law of the priesthood obtaining in former times; (b) they changed every twelve months, in accordance with the practice among the Greeks, and

24 In II Kings and in Jeremiah we find a number of chambers of given individuals (of standing), and it is unnecessary to assume that they all had some kind of appointment in the Temple, directly and specifically (as against the view of Yeivin, *Tarbiz*, XII, p. 261, nn. 144, 145); 'door-keeper' and 'keeper of the robes' do not prove, therefore, that these were keepers of the door and garments in the Sanctuary. Similarly it is not to be supposed that the 'princes' in 'the chamber of the princes' [שרים] in Jeremiah xxxv 4, if we avoid identifying it with the 'chambers of the singers' [שרים] in Ezekiel xl 41, are necessarily the princes of the priests.

among the Jews when they conducted public affairs in places where Hellenistic institutions existed; (c) the High Priesthood was bought for money.

Nearest to this tradition is the *Tosefta Yoma* i 7: 'When the kings multiplied, they enacted that ordinary priests should be appointed (to the High Priesthood) and displaced each year.' In this tradition we find the first two elements that we discerned in the Babylonian Baraita, but it does not mention the acquisition of the High Priesthood for money. On the other hand, you find here evidence of an 'enactment', of a kind of law ordained by 'the kings'. Likewise a new fact is stated here relative to the High Priests, namely, that they were only 'ordinary priests' and ineligible for appointment.

Different is the Baraita in the Sifre, *Balak*, §131 (Horovitz, p. 173), which is basically incorporated also in the Palestinian Talmud, in our passage, in *Lev. Rabba*, § 21, and *Pesiqta de-Rav Kahana*, Aḥăre Mot (Buber, p. 159a): 'Thus it is stated, "Behold, I give unto him (Phinehas) my covenant of peace" — this teaches us that eighteen High Priests arose from him in the First Temple <but in the Second Temple eighty (High) Priests arose from him.> And because they hired it for money, their years began to be shortened. It once happened that a man sent with his son two measures of silver filled with silver and their strikes were of silver; again it happened that a man sent with his son two measures of gold filled with gold and their strikes were of gold. It was said: "The foal has overturned the menorah [Temple lamp]".'

This tradition comes to inform us that in contradistinction to (the period of) the First Temple, the promise given to Phinehas that the High Priesthood would be 'peace', that it would be transmitted from father to son, and that its incumbents would serve therein many days was not fulfilled in the epoch of the Second Temple. But apart from the abolition of the law of inheritance ('for they hired it for money') this tradition does not include all the other matters mentioned in the aforesaid sources. For it does not refer to the displacement of the High Priests in their lifetime,[25] and certainly not to the limitation of the High Priesthood to twelve months. For it appears that 'the shortening of the years' of the High Priests signifies only, as the Sifre understood it, a punishment inflicted by Heaven upon

25 Actually, the reading שוכרין or משכירין ['hire' or 'hire out'] (see below, §3) cannot refer here to acquiring the right of office for life; but hiring for a lifetime is possible.

those who acquired the High Priesthood with money. This is most clearly seen from the addendum to this tradition in the Palestinian Talmud and in the Midrashim cited: 'But in the Second (Temple), because they obtained it for money — *and some say that they killed one another by means of sorcery* — eighty High Priests served therein.'[26] This also seems to be the meaning of the dictum in the Palestinian Talmud mentioned further on: 'R. Aḥa said, it is written "The fear of the Lord prolongeth life" — this refers to the (High) Priests who served in the First Temple. "But the years of the wicked shall be shortened" — this refers to those who served in the Second Temple.' Similar to it is the statement in Babylonian Talmud, *Yoma* 9a: 'Rabbah bar bar Ḥanah said in the name of R. Joḥanan: What is the meaning of the verse "The fear of the Lord prolongeth years", etc.?' It seems that none of these dicta refers to the limitation of the High Priesthood by restriction of tenure and the displacement of the incumbents in their lifetime, but to actual shortening of days.[27] Let us then examine the different elements in the changing traditions that we have quoted.

A. *The Abolition of the Order of Succession and the Right of the High Priest to Hold Office for Life*

On this subject most of the sources under discussion are *ad idem*, and it is even well known from Josephus. Tradition considers that the Torah law[28] was infringed thereby and that the High Priesthood was given an alien image. In truth from the point of view of both Pentateuchal[29] and rabbinic[30] legislation, the law of inheritance is firmly established, even though a number of facts appear to cast

26 The MS Munich certainly understood the dictum thus, for it reads: 'and they are changed by *Heaven* every twelve months'.

27 According to the recensions of the Sifre: 'But in the Second Temple there rose *from him* [ממנו] eighty (High) Priests.' This tradition, therefore, did not regard the High Priests in the Second Temple as [genealogically] ordinary priests, as does the Tosefta. But other recensions are differently worded.

28 So, too, Josephus, *Ant.* xix, 9, 6 (with reference to Alcimus); *ibid.* 20, 10 (with regard to Herod); *Wars* iv, 3, 7 (relative to Phannias of the village of Aphthia).

29 Exodus xxix 30; Numbers xxvi 13; Leviticus vi 15.

30 *T.B. Yoma* 72b-73a; *T.P. Horayot* iii, p. 47d (*Torat Kohanim, Ṣaw*, v; *ibid.* below: 'This teaches us that a son comes before any one else [לכל שבעולם; MS Rabed: לכל אדם]).

doubt upon it, both theoretically and practically, in various periods (see Appendix III). Such was the practice through the days of the First Temple and even in the time of the Second Temple[31] up to the reign of Herod (except for the period of Antiochus Epiphanes and Antiochus Eupator),[32] who rescinded it and even removed High Priests in their lifetime. So, too, Julius Caesar in his edict in favour of Hyrcanus decreed that the High Priesthood should be granted to him and to his sons after him (*Ant.* xiv, 10, 4); and Josephus already charged Herod with annulling the law of inheritance and the unlawful displacement of High Priests.[33] Now Herod's innovation was undoubtedly brought about by political considerations, for he wished to diminish the power of the High Priests so that they should be subordinate and subservient to him, as a number of scholars have

31 Compare also *Ecclesiasticus* xlv 30. Now I have noted that Bickermann states (*Der Gott der Makkabäer*, p. 58) that in the days of the Greeks and in the last period of the Persians, the High Priest, although chosen from among the sons and brothers of his predecessor, was appointed by the state, which also had the right to depose him. I am at a loss to understand whence he derives this. For Josephus testified that until the time of Antiochus Epiphanes no High Priest was ever displaced (see the note below), and we find no reference in the sources to such a status of the High Priest in the period in question. On the contrary, the episode concerning Onias and Joseph b. Tobias seems to show that the king (in the days of the Ptolemies) was not permitted to depose the High Priest. For Ptolemy threatened only that if he did not pay the tax, 'he would divide the land of Eretz-Israel among the soldiers', but not that he would remove him from the High Priesthood (*Ant.* xii, 4, 1; so it also appears from the continuation of the story further on). For the last period of the Persian monarchy we may infer the same from the incident of Bagoses (*Ant.* xi, 7, 1), who promised John, the brother of the High Priest Joshua 'to procure him the High Priesthood' (τὴν ἀρχιερ. παρέξειν) and the latter, relying on this promise, provoked his brother in the Temple and was slain by him. Had the satrap (to use Bickermann's expression) been legally permitted to depose the High Priest, then the course of events would have been different. It seems, therefore, that Bagoses who was Joshua's friend (*ibid.*), intended to remove John by a certain intrigue (and this was certainly in the power of the rulers) in order to make way for his brother (this is the significance of the word παρέξειν).

32 In *Ant.* xv, 3, 1 he states that Epiphanes was the first to do this (Josephus' assertion that Aristobulus was the second transgressor, in that 'he took away the High Priesthood from Hyrcanus', is valueless, for the latter resigned of his own accord in conformity with the agreement made between them, even though he did this under duress), but in *Ant.* xx 10 he speaks of Antiochus Eupator as the first offender.

33 *Ant.* xv, 3, 1; *ibid.* 5, 10.

emphasized. However, it seems that the Hellenistic example served as the legal-political basis for his conduct. For it was the prevailing practice, as we know, in the Hellenistic cities to appoint a high priest for a limited period, although we sometimes find there high priests who became dynasts by virtue of the right of inheritance (διὰ γένους) or retained their office for life (διὰ βίου). It would appear that Herod sought here, too, to establish a Hellenistic political principle just as he did in the sphere of *culture* (Greek institutions even in Jerusalem: theatre, amphitheatre, hippodrome and stadium), of *administration* (his senior officials were Greeks and the system of administration was likewise Hellenistic), of *justice* (the law he promulgated in regard to the selling of Jewish thieves into slavery in foreign lands) and of the (official) *language* (his coins bore Greek legends and not a word of Hebrew) (see Appendix IV). This principle of policy that he introduced finds expression also in his enactment to hold the garments of the High Priesthood in his custody, since no other purpose can be attributed to this enactment except the desire to emphasize thereby that the High Priesthood was subordinate to the state and subject to its supervision.[34] Now this fact is primarily stated in the Tosefta — 'When the kings multiplied, they enacted that ordinary priests should be appointed', etc. For these kings are undoubtedly Herod and his descendants (Archelaus, Agrippa I, Herod of Chalcis and Agrippa II).

B. *The Change of High Priest Every Twelve Months*

This circumstance is mentioned, as we have seen, only in some of our sources, and on the face of it the testimony of the Tosefta and the Babylonian Baraita appears puzzling. For although we do actually find a number of High Priests serving for one year only,[35] yet the majority of them ministered for a longer period, and some of them

34 I do not think that keeping the garments of the High Priest under his control gave Herod any real power (as Otto supposes, *RE*, Supplement vol. II, p. 113), for it is highly improbable that he would at any time have prevented the service of the Day of Atonement from taking place. The people's indignation did not stem from any fear on this score but was due to the fact that they regarded Herod's conduct as a blatant expression of his wish to subjugate the High Priesthood and, indirectly, to control the Temple.

35 In Herod's reign: Matthias b. Theophilus; in the days of Valerius Gratus: Ishmael b. Fiabi, Eleazar b. Ḥanan, Simeon b. Kamḥit; in the time of Agrippa I: three High Priests in the three years of his reign.

even for many years;[36] it is not possible, therefore, to speak of an 'enactment' of changes 'like those of the Parhedrin'.

But even in the tradition of the early Christians this matter is mentioned. Thus we read in the Gospel of John, in two or three passages, that the High Priest serves as a rule only one year:

1) xi 49: Caiaphas, the High Priest, said to the Sanhedrin that it was expedient that Jesus should die, provided that the whole people should be delivered from punishment by the Romans — ἀρχιερεὺς ὢν τοῦ ἐνιαυτοῦ ἐκείνου (being High Priest that year).

2) *Ibid.* xi 51: Τοῦτο δὲ ἀφ' ἑαυτοῦ οὐκ εἶπεν. ἀλλὰ ἀρχιερεὺς ὢν τοῦ ἐνιαυτοῦ ἐκείνου, ἐπροφήτευσεν. ('He did not say this of his own accord, but being High Priest that year he prophesied').

There are recensions, however, that omit here the words τοῦ ἐνιαυτ. ἐκ. (see Merx's commentary).

3) xviii 13: Jesus was led to Annas, the father-in-law of Caiaphas ὃς ἦν ἀρχιερεὺς τοῦ ἐνιαυτοῦ ἐκείνου ('who was high priest that year'). Similarly we read in Eusebius, *Ecclesiastical History*, i, 13, where Annas seeks to limit Jesus' activity to four years, since he appears between the priesthood of Annas and that of Caiaphas, a period in which according to his estimation four High Priests ministered — τῶν γάρ τοι κατὰ τὸν νόμον ἤδη πως καθαιρουμένων ἐξ ἐκείνου θεσμῶν, λέλυτο μὲν ᾧ διὰ βίου καὶ ἐκ προγόνων διαδοχῆς τὰ τῆς τοῦ θεοῦ θεραπείας προσήκοντα ἦν, ὑπὸ δὲ τῶν Ρωμαικῶν ἡγεμόνων ἄλλοτε ἄλλοι τὴν ἀρχιερωσύνην ἐπιτρεπόμενοι, οὐ πλεῖον ἔτους ἑνὸς ἐπὶ ταύτης διετέλουν ('For from that time on the laws according to the Torah were abrogated, since [the statute] was annulled whereby the heritage of the fathers and the practice throughout life belonged to the sacred service of God. And the High Priests, owing to the fact the Roman consuls used to give the High Priesthood sometimes to the one and sometimes to the other, did not remain in office for more than a year').

A similar statement is made by Chrysostom, 'In inscriptionem Altaris', Migne, *PG*, vol. 51, p. 73, on the verse in John xi 49: Καὶ γὰρ καὶ τοῦτο τῆς Ἰουδαϊκῆς ἐγένετο πονηρίας. κατῄσχυνον γὰρ τὸ τῆς ἱερωσύνης ἀξίωμα, ὠνητοὺς ποιήσαντες ἀρχιερέας. Ἔμπροσθεν δὲ οὐχ οὕτως ἦν, ἀλλὰ τῇ τελευτῇ μονῇ κατελύετο ἡ ἱερωσύνη τοῦ ἀρχιερέως. τότε δὲ καὶ ζῶντες παρελύοντο τῆς τιμῆς. ('For this

36 Like Simeon b. Boethus in the days of Herod, who remained in office many years; Ananus b. Seth in the time of Quirinius; Ananias son of Nebedius, who was appointed by Herod, king of Chalcis.

thing, too, was part of the Jewish evil [corruption]. Because [they] disgraced the honour of [the status of] the priesthood by appointing High Priests bought [for money], but originally this was not so, for only upon the death of the High Priest did his ministration come to an end. In those days, however, their high honour was taken away from them in their lifetime').

The differences between the explanation given by Eusebius and that by Chrysostom of the cause of the innovation with respect to the tenure of office of the High Priesthood is clear: according to the former the practice of changing the High Priests was introduced by the Roman procurators, whereas Chrysostom puts the blame on the Jews in that they desecrated the priesthood consciously and of their own volition. But essentially the evidence of both in regard to the cause does not amount to much, because Chrysostom stresses the fact out of excessive hatred for the Jews and Judaism, a feeling that finds expression in very many sections of his other works, while Eusebius's reason apparently refers to 'the tradition' found among the early Christians in many places to the effect that statehood and priesthood were taken from Israel with the coming of their Messiah.[37]

More important than the difference referred to is the fact mentioned by Chrysostom, which is also recorded in the Tannaitic tradition, that the High Priesthood was obtained for money. For this shows that Chrysostom drew his information from tradition and did not just adapt for himself the aforementioned statement of Eusebius. Hence it would appear, since we find the matter referred to in John's tradition, which speaks of the subject without any ulterior motive, and in the statement of Eusebius, which seeks to determine the chronology of the acts of Jesus, and in the words of Chrysostom, which contain an element absent in the others just cited, that the early Christians, from the beginning of the second century (John) to the end of the fourth (Chrysostom) also knew the Tannaitic tradition that the High Priesthood changed in the epoch of the Romans and assumed a Hellenistic form.

37 The view of Eusebius in regard to the beginning (and cause) of this practice is certainly of no account; for there is no difference between the time of Herod and that of the procurators in respect of the length of the High Priests' tenure of office. If this practice in the form of Eusebius's tradition (one year) is to be attributed to any one, it is Herod. Indeed there were Christians who thought so (so writes Agapius, *Patrologia Orientalis*, VII, p. 461; likewise Barhebraeus, *Chron. Eccles.*, ed. Lamy, Pt. I, pp. 30, 67 — 'just as... and we shall abolish their customs.' He makes a similar statement in *Chron. Syr.*).

We revert, now, to our question: What is the significance of this tradition, which, taken literally, does not fit the historic reality?

To begin with, it must be regarded, in my view, as a complete expression of the process that was started by Herod, namely, the Hellenization of the statutory position of the High Priesthood. Later generations, who understood the basic character (and aim) of this innovation, sought to give it an absolute character by making its motivating factor completely consistent and set the duration of the priesthood at one year in conformity with the practice prevailing among the Greeks.

Note should be taken, in this connection, of a tradition, similar to the one under discussion, stemming from a parallel period, from the time of Antiochus Epiphanes and Eupator, who were the first to introduce the practice of displacing the High Priests.

In *II Maccabees* xi 2–3 we read that Lysias, the guardian of Antiochus Eupator, went up against Judea — λογιζόμενος τὴν μὲν πόλιν Ἕλλησιν οἰκητήριον ποιήσειν, τὸ δὲ ἱερὸν ἀργυρολόγητον, καθὼς τὰ λοιπὰ τῶν ἐθνῶν τεμένη, πρατὴν δέ κατ' ἔτος τὴν ἀρχιερωσύνην ποιήσειν. ('He intended to make the city [Jerusalem] a home for Greeks, and to levy tribute on the Temple as he did on the sacred places of the other nations, and to put up the High Priesthood for sale every year').

Here, too, the fact of Hellenization[38] has assumed an absolute aspect, both relative to the sanctities and to the priesthood (the Temple, the City and the High Priesthood). And at the same time as it defines the monetary contribution made by High Priests in those days in the form of taxation[39] as the purchase price of the priesthood, tradition gives to the displacement of the High Priests the stamp of a fixed law, in keeping with the actual position obtaining among the Greeks.

38 The testimony of the Book of Lysias' intention to make Jerusalem 'a home for Greeks' is not to be interpreted literally, but in the sense of the conversion of Jerusalem to a Hellenistic city, as it is related in *I Maccabees* (i 15) of the days of Antiochus Epiphanes.

39 The sums specified in *II Maccabees* (iv 8, 24) are, it is self-evident (since they are so large), the total tribute of the country (this is shown by v. 8 [*ibid.*], which speaks of 'and, from another source of revenue, eighty talents'). Although Rostovtzeff (*CAH* vii, p. 20) states in all innocence that the House of Seleucus could impose on the High Priests in the Land of Israel payments in the form of the sale of the High Priesthood, as was the practice in Greek countries, there is no real evidence for this.

Nevertheless, it seems probable that the actual cause of the formulation of our tradition is in the fact that in the reign of Agrippa II six High Priests served in the course of six years (59–65). It was in those days, apparently, that this tradition also received its present form. This fact, which is to be regarded as something purely fortuitous, provided a basis, in relation to the fundamental reality — the abolition of the Jewish traditional, statutory position of the High Priest — for our tradition to evolve its current pattern.

This view appears more probable when we remember that the criticism of the High Priests and the references to their corruption found in Josephus (*Ant.* xx, 8, 8; xx, 9, 2) appertain to this period. Similarly, the famous Baraita (*Tosefta Menaḥot* xiii, 21; *T.B. Pesaḥim* 57a), which is taught in the name of Abba Saul b. Boṭnit and Abba Jose b. (Jo)ḥanan, which deals with the evil of the High Priests, concludes with those who served at this time ('woe unto me because of the House of Ishmael b. Phabi [II], who are High Priests, and their sons are (Temple) treasurers and their sons-in-law are Amarkals [Temple trustees], and their servants come and beat us with staves').

C. *The Buying of the High Priesthood for Money*

It is not, (apparently) absolutely clear whether this practice, which is mentioned in a Baraita of the Babylonian Talmud, the Sifre, the Palestinian Talmud and Midrashim, represents an established institution — legal and public — or whether the sources refer only to acts of bribery. Similarly, from the Talmudic story that Joshua b. Gamla was only appointed upon the delivery by Martha daughter of Boethus of three *qabs* of golden denars to 'king Jannai' (read: Agrippa — *T.B. Yoma* 18a; *T.B. Yevamot* 61a) we cannot determine the true nature of this payment. Nevertheless, from the simple sense of the traditional account and from the above-mentioned testimony of Chrysostom it would appear that actually an established institution is intended.

Now the practice of selling priestly and high-priestly positions, which is primarily known from inscriptions (of Asia Minor), was most prevalent in the Hellenistic period, although recently it was shown to have existed also in the classical epoch (Otto, 'Kauf und Verkauf von Priestertümern bei den Griechen', *Hermes*, XLIV, pp. 594–99). We also find it widespread even in Egypt in the era of the Ptolemies and Romans, and in other countries.

Thus our tradition likewise intends to testify that at the close of the Temple period a Hellenistic institution was revived in the sphere of the High Priesthood in the form of the sale of the position for money.

However, on examining our sources we find a version of the tradition that speaks not of selling but of hiring; thus we read in Sifre according to one formulation (*Midrash Ḥakhamim*): 'and because they used to hire it for money'. However, three other recensions give the reading 'sell'. But in the parallel in *Leviticus Rabba* we again read 'hire out' (so, too, the London MS of the Sifre reads *mazkîrîn* = *maśkîrîn*). Similarly in the *Pesiqta de-Rav Kahana* we find: 'Since they reverted to hiring it (read *'ôtāh* [f.] for *'ôtō*) out for money' (on the other hand, the Palestinian Talmud reads 'take [*nôṭĕlîn*] for money' — a neutral expression). According to this version, we are thus dealing with the institution of hiring out the priesthood, which among the Greeks took the form of selling.

But from whom was the priesthood bought or hired, and to whom was the money given? On the face of it, the matter is simple: it was acquired from the kings of the Herodian dynasty and from the Roman procurators, as the Talmudic tradition testifies concerning Joshua b. Gamla that he was appointed by giving money to the king; and the Tosefta states 'When the kings multiplied, it was instituted' etc.

However, when we examine the Babylonian Baraita carefully, we arrive at a different conclusion. For it is difficult to explain the text: ומתוך שנותנין עליו [read: עליה] ממון לכהונה ומחליפין אותה [v. l: אותן 'them', i.e. the priests] כל י״ב חודש [rendered above, 'but because they used to pay money for the office of (High) Priest [לכהונה], and they changed it every twelve months...'], in accordance with the accepted interpretation — in the manner of the Early Authorities — as referring to the payment of money to the government, and to interpret לכהונה as meaning '*for* the office of high priest'. Apart from the intrinsic difficulty of explaining the word in this way, there is the further objection that the Baraita has already said earlier שנותנין עליה [literally, 'they pay for it'], that is, for the priesthood. There would thus be an unnecessary and meaningless duplication here.

It therefore appears that the statement means that they (the candidates for appointment) used to pay money for the High Priesthood *to the priests*. The word כהונה is thus used here as a collective noun, and the intention of the tradition is to inform us that the priests (apparently the High Priests, for in the Rabbinic as in the Biblical idiom 'priest' may mean 'High Priest' and 'priesthood' may mean

'High Priesthood') used to sell or hire out their office to others for money.[40]

Now, on the face of it, this fact appears surprising and most improbable, and needless to say it is unsupported by other sources (Josephus invariably speaks of the appointment of High Priests by the kings and rulers). Nevertheless it should not be denied, at the outset, some substance.

We know already from Josephus and from the Christian Gospels and from the Mishna that in the period under discussion the ἀρχιερεῖς (or 'the sons of the High Priests' in our Mishna — *Ketubbot* xiii, 1–2; *Oholot* xvii, 5)[41] formed a kind of united and organized association (or class), which tended to blur and swallow up the personality of the serving High Priest. This fact stands out so clearly that Büchler[42] sought to infer therefrom that the serving High Priests at that time lost their governing power, which was actually transferred to the domain of the association of the ἀρχιερεῖς. Although this conclusion arrived at by Büchler is exaggerated, nevertheless the fact itself is authenticated: the families of the High Priesthood constituted a cohesive class, which possessed recognized communal-political and decisive authority, especially in respect of the Temple and its administration. We shall not, therefore, be putting forward any incredible suggestion if we posit that the office of High Priest appeared to the aforementioned families, and to many others, as the property of the class and the concern of the association. Hence it should

40 A possible interpretation is that it was the Bouleutin who paid the money to the priesthood for the appointment of the candidates, and that instead of serving throughout their lifetime (the members of the Sanhedrin, apparently, served thus) they were appointed for twelve months (in the period with which we are dealing, the Bouleutin in the Greek cities served as a rule all their life, but the Parhedrin and the Elders, and likewise the Executor, held office for one year). Actually, Büchler is inclined to this view (p. 26, note), because 'as far as we know the priests had no influence on the election of the Hight Priest'. However, from the Talmud, at any rate, it is evident that the High Priests and not the Bouleutin are intended. Attention should perhaps be drawn to the version of one MS (see *Diqduqe Soferim*) that reads לכהן ['to the priest'], for if we adopt this reading, the tradition must certainly be understood to refer to the *High Priest*, to wit, that he received money and sold his priestly office to another (there is no need to point לכהן, as does the author of *DS*). See the text further on.

41 It has already been rightly pointed out (Jeremias, *Jerusalem*, II, p. 36) that 'the sons of the High Priests' is equivalent to 'High Priests', for 'sons' serves to indicate the sex.

42 Pp. 202, 206, *et al.*

occasion no surprise that tradition attributed the arrangement of the succession of the High Priests to priestly families of noble lineage, who bestowed reciprocal favours upon each other for monetary gifts.[43] One scholar (Derenbourg, *Massa' Ereṣ Yisra'el* I p. 56) thought that the priests voluntarily rotated the office of the High Priesthood among themselves in turn, in order that all the members of the class might enjoy equal benefit. In our time Dessau has written (without proof) that we may presume that the discharge of the High Priests in the reign of Herod took the form of the voluntary resignation of the retiring High Priest and the election of his successor by his colleagues (*Geschichte der römischen Kaiserzeit* 2^2, p. 757, n. 1).

But even this practice was to be found in the Gentile world, for along with the *state*, the *priesthood* in Egypt (in the period of the Ptolemies and the Romans), both in the institutions of the Egyptian cult and in that of the Greeks, exerted a great influence in the appointment of priests to high positions (Otto, *Priester* etc., I, 242). We find that the priests in one temple appoint their high priest each year.[44] But most pertinent to our subject is the practice, found among the Greeks, of priestly offices being sold by their original buyers — ἐπίπρασις (Stengel, *Griechische Kultusaltertümer*, p. 42), for our own tradition, understood according to its simple connotation, intends to testify that the High Priests sold (or 'hired out') their priestly office to others.

Now it is clear that we have no supporting evidence for this tradition; seemingly, it is even contradicted by Josephus, who constantly speaks about the appointment of High Priests by the kings and rulers. But if we bear in mind that Josephus' historical account of this period is truncated and lacks elaboration, we shall not completely deny all value to our tradition. It may further be assumed that there was a struggle between the State (and the government) and the priesthood in regard to the right of appointing the High

43 It is true that we find Joshua b. Gamala (Gamaliel in Josephus), who was appointed by Agrippa II entered into strife and wrangling with Jesus b. Dammai (Damneus), his predecessor, whom Agrippa had removed from office (*Ant.* xx, 9, 4). But, on the other hand, we find Jonathan b. Ḥanan (Ananus), whom Agrippa I had appointed to serve a second time, withdraw in favour of his brother Matthias, whom he suggested in his stead and the king appointed him (*Ant.* xix, 6, 4). Nevertheless the exiguous tradition recorded by Josephus in this chapter of our history cannot serve as a decisive factor, especially by virtue of its silence, in refuting other sources.

44 Otto, *loc. cit.*, p. 237.

Priests and filling important offices and matters related to the administration of the Temple generally (see Appendix V), in the same way as rivalry of this kind obtained also in Egypt in the period with which we are concerned,[45] and that often in practice a way of compromise and reconciliation was found (in the form of arranging a partnership between the contending parties). It is possible, then, that Josephus in his presentation adopts one version — the official account — and overlooks the other aspect of the reality, which is equally valid.

At any rate, the tradition cannot be denied the value of historical testimony in the sense of potential truth supported by the communal background.

D. *The Appointment of Common* (Hedyoṭot) *Priests*

The Tosefta, as stated, testifies that the 'kings' ordained that 'common' (*hedyoṭot*) priests should be appointed. Although the expression itself is obscure, because 'common priest' as a rule connotes only one who does not act as High Priest and not one who is disqualified and defective for appointment, it is nevertheless clear from the context of the statement that here this designation serves to denote those who are not fit to be appointed and were disqualified to minister as High Priests after being appointed, only the nature of the defect is not clear. At first it would seem that we could elucidate the matter by reference to the preceding Halakha (6), which our Baraita adjoins and was given its present place only because of its connection with the theme of this Halakha. For we learn as follows: 'The law with regard to the High Priest requires that he should excel his brethren in beauty, strength, wealth, wisdom, and appearance', etc. The disqualification of these priests may therefore be caused by the absence of one of these attributes (wisdom — and needless to say if he lacks the quality of piety he is invalidated). We find such a complaint in the case of Jo'ezer, the brother-in-law of Matthew b. Theophilus, who was appointed by Herod. When, however, Archelaus began to reign in his father's stead, the people demanded that Jo'ezer be removed from office: νομιμώτερόν θ' ἅμα καὶ καθαρὸν ἀρχιερᾶσθαι ἄνδρ' αἱρεῖσθαι (*Ant.* xvii, 9, 1; *Wars* ii, 1, 2) [εὐσεβέστερον καὶ καθαρώτερον] ('and to choose a man more fitting according to the law, and also more pure, as High Priest'). Nevertheless, a probable interpretation of 'common priests' in the Tosefta is to understand

45 See Otto, *Priester*, Pt. I, pp. 233, 237, 238, 242.

the term as involving a genealogical defect, to wit, that they did not belong to 'the priestly families of noble descent', to whom the High Priesthood was vouchsafed as a heritage.[46] This reproach is first encountered in respect of Ḥanan'el the Babylonian who was first appointed by Herod (*Ant.* xv, 2, 4–5 — τῶν ἐπικλήτων τις 'one who came from outside', 'a common priest'. Similarly in the case of Phinehas (Phannias) of the village of Aphtha [*Wars*, iv, 3, 8], who was nominated by the Zealots and thereby — κληρωτοὺς ἐπεχείρησαν ποιεῖν τοὺς ἀρχιερεῖς, οὔσης, ὡς ἔφαμεν, κατὰ γένος αὐτῶν τῆς διαδοχῆς ['they ventured to choose the High Priests by lot although the right of succession belonged only to the families of the Hight Priests'] and they chose a man — ἀνὴρ οὐ μόνον οὐκ ἐξ ἀρχιερέων κτλ ['who was not descended from the High Priests' etc.]).

But after the High Priesthood had been taken away from the family of the Sons of Zadok, which had served up to the time of Antiochus, and from the House of the Hasmoneans (who had been appointed High Priests by the people) thereafter, there was certainly a case for denouncing all the other High Priests that followed them, and disqualifying them as commoners who had risen to high office by the (unprincipled) desire of the House of Herod and the Roman governors, and not by the right of ancestral succession.[47] Indeed, in the account of the chain of High Priests given by Josephus (*Ant.* xx, 10, 5), we read with regard to Herod: οὐκέτι τοὺς ἐκ τοῦ 'Ασαμωναίου γένους καθίστησιν ἀρχιερεῖς, ἀλλά τισιν ἀσήμοις καὶ μόνον ἐξ ἱερέων οὖσι... τὴν τιμὴν ἀπένεμε — 'Not from the House of the Hasmoneans did he appoint High Priests, but he gave the

46 The connection with the preceding Halakha is in this instance only indirect (it would be far-fetched to say that our tradition contains a denial of the legality of the choice of Phinehas, for he was the son-in-law of Rabban Gamaliel! — although it is not impossible that our tradition emanates from the School opposed to the Zealots and all their doings, like the passage in Josephus on this theme).

47 Possibly the Zealots, although they based themselves in choosing Phinehas as a High Priest by lot 'on an ancient Halakha', acted as they did because they disqualified these High Priests for the reason stated (Jeremias, *Jerusalem* etc., Pt. II, p. 54, states simply that the Zealots 'proclaimed that the families from which the High Priests were appointed', whether Hasmoneans or those who succeeded them, 'were not legal', whereas Phinehas was of the sons of Zadok, to whom the Zealots restored the High Priesthood; but it is not stated in the sources that Phinehas was of the sons of Zadok. Similarly it is not expressly stated that they disqualified those families, especially the Hasmonean dynasty; only it is possible to assume this with regard to those who were appointed by Herod and subsequently, as we have stated).

honour to undistinguished men who were descended from the priests only' (= ordinary priests).

Later on he states: 'Archelaus also, Herod's son, did like his father in the appointment of the High Priests, as did the Romans also, who took the government into their hands afterwards'.

Our Tannaitic tradition gives expression therefore to a widely held view among the Sages and the people of those generations.

Let us now revert to our opening theme.

It seems to me that underlying the word *par'irtin* is the Greek verb προϊερατεύω or προϊεράομαι, whose meaning is identical. These verbs are not found in literary Greek, but they occur in inscriptions and signify 'to serve in the priesthood in place of another, to deputize for a priest'. The first to draw attention to this was M. Frankel, *Die Inschriften von Pergamon*, I, pp. 167–168, with reference to inscription No. 248.

King Attalus II rules: Since Sosandros, the high priest of Dionysus, is ill and cannot perform the priestly functions, therefore — τὸν υἱὸν αὐτοῦ 'Αθήναιον ἐκρίν[αμε]μ προϊέρασθαι. Similarly we find in the inscription of *Chios* (fourth century B.C.E.), Dittenberger, *Sylloge*, III, No. 1013, which contains regulations regarding the priestly gifts of the temple of Heracles [Hercules] — ἐάν δ[ε ὁ] ἱερέος μὴ παρῆι, προϊερη[τεν]έτω τις ὧν αἱ λόγχαι εἰσ[ιν[48] τὰ] γινόμενα ἀποδιδό[ναι τὸν] θύοντα τῶι ἱερεῖ. ('And if the priest will not be present then there shall serve in his stead one of those who have a share [in the sacrifices of Heracles]').

Thus in the first inscription the deputy is appointed by the king and ministers in every respect like the high priest, only he is not actually (in theory) the high priest. In the second inscription the substitute who takes the priest's place is clearly distinguished from the ἱερέος. Akin to this is the ruling in the inscription from *Miletus*, which also comprises regulations like those of the *Chios* inscription (Dittenberger, *ibid.* III, No. 1037) — ἢν ξένος ἱεροποιῶι τῷ 'Απόλλονι προϊερᾶσθαι τῶ[ν] ἀστῶν ὃν ἂν θέληι ὁ ξένος, διδόναι δὲ τῷ ἱερεῖ τὰ γέρεα ('If a stranger sacrifices to Apollo, then the priest's place shall be taken by one of the men of the city that the stranger shall choose, but the [priestly] gifts shall be given to the priest').[49]

48 For the meaning of the last words see the remarks of Dittenberger: 'quorum ex numero capitur sacerdos'.

49 See the other inscriptions to which Frankel refers in his commentary, and cf. the observations of Haussoulier, *REG*, vol. XXXII, p. 259.

This expression and the cognate verbs προαρχιεράομαι, προαρχιερατεύω are also found in a number of inscriptions from *Stratonicea* (Asia Minor), apparently in the aforementioned signification.[50]

I am of opinion, therefore, that the word *Par'irtin* is the Greek word προϊρατεύοντες and denotes those who serve in place of the (High) Priests, performing priestly tasks without being officially and legally proper priests. The Palestinian Talmud seeks to explain the word *Parhedrin* as signifying *High Priests* who are not qualified as such (the 'common priests' of the Tosefta). The intent of the Talmud in offering this explanation is, apparently, to give the term a cacophemistic connotation, as though to say that these High Priests bear a Greek stamp and their appointment came about only by virtue of Hellenistic practice.

But the following suggestion appears to me even more probable. In two inscriptions we find the verb ἱεράομαι in the form of the aorist passive participle in the sense of middle voice I (צילפרי), *Philologus* LXXI, p. 41 (Dittenberger, *Sylloge* II, p. 134, No. 602): Ξένων Βούλωνος τὰν γυναῖκα Πάσιχον καὶ τοὶ υἱοὶ Βούλων, Μνάσων, Πειθαγόρας καὶ ἱεραθεῖσαν Ἐλειθυίαι.

The word ἱεραθεῖσαν signifies (see the observations of the publisher in *Philologus, ibid.*) 'she acted as priestess'. The meaning of the inscription is: 'Xenon son of Boulon and his sons Boulon, Mnason and Peithagoras [erected] the [image] of the wife [of Xenon], who served as a priestess of [the goddess] Ἐλειθυία.'[51]

Of a similar type is the second inscription (*Philologus, ibid.*) —
[ὁ δεῖνα τοῦ —
δεῖνος τὰν γυναῖκα] Ἡρα[καιναν?]
ἱεραθεῖσαν Ἐλειθυίαι ἀνέθηκε.
('So-and-so son of So-and-so erected the image of his wife Herkina, who served as a priestess to Eleithvia').

It is not difficult, therefore, to my mind to regard the word *par'irtin* as the Greek προϊεραθέντες in the sense of men who deputized in the past for [High] Priests. This suggestion comes nearer than its predecessors to the form of the word (*par'irtin* corresponds to the Greek stem) and more especially to its signification. For it is with

50 They were published in vol. xv of *Bulletin de Correspondance Hellenique*, in which we find the following expressions: 1) Ἱερύς... ὁ κα[ὶ προ]ηρχιερατευκως 2) προϊερατεύσαντες; 3) ἱερεία... καὶ προηρχιερατευκία 4)...καὶ προϊερατευκυία 5) προ[ιερα]τευκότες.

51 I discussed the meaning of the inscription with the scholars Fuks and Hack.

this in mind that the Palestinian Talmud states that the Parhedrin are actually *former* High Priests, a statement that is historically correct, since many of the Parhedrin of the Jerusalem Boule belonged to these priests. But this is not the case with regard to the first conjecture, which obliges us to attribute to the Palestinian Talmud the view that the Chamber of the Parhedrin was the Chamber of the High Priest (the view taken by the Babylonian Talmud).[52] But we must ask ourselves: What historical reality of the world of the High Priests among the Jewish people could have served as the background for our tradition?

Now first we must recall the testimony of our Mishna that every year, on the eve of the Day of Atonement, there was held in readiness for the High Priest 'another priest to take his place in case he (the High Priest) becomes disqualified', as for instance the occasion when Josephus b. Ulam [Ellemus] of Sepphoris who served temporarily

52 It remains for us to explain the words מילא עבידה. I regard them as a popular expression meaning 'a thing that is done; something that is common and without importance'. By this addition the Talmud seeks to gloss the word *Par'irtin*, in the sense that they are not actually High Priests. Possibly *T.B. Nazir* 2b is also to be explained thus (once, when I discussed the matter with my teacher, Prof. Epstein, he drew my attention to this passage): [Tosafot — הא; Venice ed. and Rosh — הדא] נזירא (Seeing that becoming) a Nazir is מילתא דעבירה ואמרינן ליה נאה... actually a sin, can we call it comely? Now the MS Munich reads מילת' עביד', and this reading is also cited by the Rosh in his commentary ('and some read'); it is likewise the text of R. Azriel in *Shiṭṭa Mequbbeṣet*, of Tosafot and of Me'iri. It is also evident from the annotations attributed to Rashi that he, too, had this reading. The Early Authorities [*Rishonim*] (Tosafot, the Rosh, *Shiṭṭa Mequbeset*, and Me'iri) understood מילתא עבידה in an obligatory sense: Is it [Naziritehood] then a thing that ought to be practised (so, too, it seems that the scribe of the Munich MS interpreted the passage, and in conformity with this he read in the continuation: ואמרינן ליה נאה ואפילו לר״א וכו' ['and we say to him, "It is comely", and even according to R. Eleazar' etc.], and he did not read אין [see Tosafot and Me'iri]. So we have not here an objection and answer but a single dictum read in the indicative mood) and it is hardly necessary to say that this interpretation is far-fetched. Hence it appears that here, too, מילתא עבידא has the aforementioned connotation, i.e. a common happening that involves no good deed or act of piety (although if we accept R. David Luria's emendation in the *T.P. Yoma, loc. cit.* — see *Tarbiz*, III, p. 339 — and read מילה עבירה, we could explain it in the sense of 'something transient', that does not endure; yet there is no need to emend the text, as I have stated). At any rate these words represent only a late gloss to 'Par'irtin', and cannot therefore fully explain the connotation of the word under discussion.

(*Tosefta Yoma* i, 4 and the parallel passages; *Antiquities* xvii, 6, 4). This apart, there were undoubtedly occurrences of another type that prevented the High Priest from performing the service and another had to take his place.

However, relative to our subject it behoves us to consider the statement in *II Maccabees* iv, 29 in regard to Menelaus, who went to Antiochia to excuse himself before Antiochus regarding the money that he had promised to give him every year for his having been appointed to serve as High Priest, but had failed to do so — ἀπέλειπεν τῆς ἀρχιερωσύνης διάδοχον Λυσίμαχον. Thus Menelaus himself appointed his deputy for the period of his absence from Jerusalem, namely, his brother (διάδοχος is undoubtedly used here in the sense of 'one who accepts a duty temporarily', and not, of course, in the connotation of inheritor).

Particularly we must take note of what is stated *ibid.* xiv, 26 concerning Alcimus — that he complained to Demetrius about his general Nicanor, who had been sent to fight against Judas Maccabeus but had made peace and concluded a treaty with him — τὸν γὰρ ἐπίβουλον τῆς βασιλείας αὐτοῦ 'Ιούδαν διάδοχον ('for he had appointed that conspirator against the kingdom, Judas, to be his successor').

Obviously this statement is not to be interpreted as if it meant that Nicanor deposed Alcimus and appointed Judas in his stead (the appointment could only be made by the king). The meaning of our passage is that Nicanor, who came to destroy Judas and his army, upon realizing the latter's strength, sought to end the war and the rebellion by peaceful negotiations. But since he was unable to depose Alcimus and appoint Judas in his place (for this he would have required the authority of Antiochus), he appointed Judas as 'acting High Priest',[53] so that he might enter officially into negotiations with him and reach a peaceful settlement. Since this fact, which implied the *de facto* recognition of Judas by the government as head of the people, deprived Alcimus, in reality, of his status (which in any case was shaky), hence he complained to the king and endeavoured, it seems, to have the appointment and the treaty annulled. We thus have before us an instance of the appointment of 'a common priest' to act instead of a High Priest, *without the latter's consent*, by the authority of a governmental order.

In solving the question we must also bear in mind that according to the Halakha 'an Ex-Substitute High Priest' (one who had once

53 Alcimus was absent from Jerusalem at the time, being then in Antiochia.

served in place of the High Priest) is subject to all the laws of the High Priesthood, and even according to the Tannaim who differ, he remains in an intermediate position between the common priest and High Priest. Thus in practice Ex-Substitute High Priests were included in the company of 'the High Priests' and were integrated with them.

This fact could have served as a basis for the tradition that invalidated all the High Priests and regarded them as *Par'irtin*, i.e. usurpers, whose Halakhic status was only that of acting High Priests, but in practice they were the *only* High Priests, a situation that as a *permanent institution* — the reference being to the complete removal of the statutory High Priests — emerged in Judaism through the influence of the Hellenistic tradition.

We have examined a number of sources in the Tannaitic and Amoraic tradition relative to the High Priests at the close of the Second Temple period, and we have seen that they all adopt a censorious attitude towards the High Priesthood, which they regard as essentially Hellenized. Although our traditions are to be considered generally as Pharisaic (popular), anti-priestly reactions — according to our conjecture they date from the early sixties — and hence we cannot in all instances treat them as historic testimony, nevertheless many of the statements are undoubtedly historically correct. And as for the others, where the sources are divergent, we must bear in mind that even they reflect socio-political conditions of substance, even though in their form and expression they cannot be substantiated.

Appendix I (to p. 51)

The existence of a municipal administration in Jerusalem organized on Hellenistic lines is not in doubt. It is true that Zucker, *Studien* etc., pp. 78–79, tries to effect a compromise; but his view is linked to his theory that ἄρχοντες mentioned in the rescript of Claudius 'are clearly none other than the High Priests'. However, this hypothesis is incorrect. The proof he advances from the testimony of Josephus, *Ant.* xx, 10, that after the deposition of Archelaus the regime in Judea became again an aristocracy, which he assumes to imply the rule of the High Priests, is groundless. Firstly, it is agreed by all that the High Priest had authority of his own, and it was not necessary for the ἄρχοντες who are mentioned here in conjunction with the βουλή, all to be 'High Priests'. Furthermore, when Josephus speaks of the 'aristocracy' of Judea, he has in mind the combination of the *High Priest* and the γερουσία, and it also appears that primarily this word is sometimes used by him specifically of the second element of this dyarchy. This is particularly evident in Josephus' account of Gabinius (*Ant.* xiv, 5; *Wars* i, 8, 5), who divided Eretz-Israel into five Sanhedrins (or, in the terminology of the *Wars*, σύνοδοι) after he had committed to Hyrcanus 'the care of the Temple', and in this way he restored the aristocratic order. Obviously not every (independent) Sanhedrin included 'archons' — 'High Priests', but in view of the fact that in each one of these administrations the reins of power were handed over to the ἄριστοι (the term used in the *Wars*), i.e. the 'Elders', hence the Jews 'were liberated from monarchic rule and attained freedom' (see *ibid.*). But Zucker's approach is to separate; he is of opinion that the βουλή is not the same as the γερουσία, which, he holds, was abolished in the days of the early Hasmoneans and thereafter became 'the High Court' (p. 68; see on this subject below).

However, two questions arise in relation to this fact: (1) When was this form of administration established? (2) What was its relationship to 'the Great Sanhedrin' (γερουσία) and 'the High Court'? Now Dessau (*Geschichte* etc. 2^2, p. 795, n. 3) simply states, without supporting evidence, that 'Agrippa bestowed upon Jerusalem a municipal council'. Seemingly his statement has a basis, for Claudius' rescript, which constitutes 'the first and entirely suitable testimony concerning the existence of a municipal council in Jerusalem', was written shortly after the death of Agrippa. However, apart from the mention of Joseph, a member of the council, in Luke and Mark as living in the days of Jesus (although it may be assumed that the writers of these books attributed a fact of their own times to the preceding generation), it is difficult to explain why Agrippa saw fit to 'bestow' a Hellenistic institution upon the men of Jerusalem. Undoubtedly the latter were not keen on this, and Agrippa, both according to the evidence of Josephus and according to the Tannaitic tradition, was a good and pious king (in the Pharisaic sense), who did not have Hellenistic tendencies such as his father Herod had evinced.

It seems to me logical to attribute this innovation to Herod. The man who introduced Hellenistic institutions into Jerusalem and into the country as a whole in all spheres of life — political, social and cultural — was also the person who foisted an alien aspect on the Jerusalem administration (and I observe that Zucker, too, *op. cit.*, takes the same view); only I consider that the matter is connected with the status of the Great Sanhedrin in Herod's days. For one cannot imagine that Herod would have introduced a new public administrative body and thus added to his worries in maintaining his rule against the people, a situation that we have to posit according to Büchler's theory, which envisages the existence of three separate bodies (the municipal council, the Great Sanhedrin, which dealt with legal and administrative matters, and the Supreme Court, sitting in the Chamber of Hewn Stone, which decided Halakhic and religious issues). We may conjecture, almost with certitude, that Herod completely abolished the Great Sanhedrin. For although scholars, who all concede that Herod severely restricted its authority, rely on *Ant.* xv, 6, 2 (Hyrcanus was brought by Herod before the Sanhedrin) to show that the Great Sanhedrin existed in those days (30 B.C.E.) in Jerusalem as at first (Hoffmann, *Der oberste Gerichtshof* etc., p. 44; Schürer, *op. cit.*, pp. 244–245; W. Otto, *Herodes*, p. 118), it must be stated that this 'Sanhedrin' is not different from the others mentioned elsewhere, before which Herod was wont to summon accused persons (συνέδριον τῶν φίλων), that is to say, it was his private council, and the judicial proceedings accorded with the practice of gentile rulers and were not conducted under Jewish law (see Wellhausen, *Die Pharisäer und Sadducäer*[2], p. 28; Büchler, *op. cit.*, p. 222; Momigliano, *CAH*, X, p. 326, and note 3; Zucker, *op. cit.*, p. 70).

But the γερουσία and συνέδριον (first, in the episode of Gabinius, who divided it into five separate bodies — see the passages indicated above — and secondly, in the incident in which Hyrcanus summoned Herod before the Sanhedrin, *Ant.* xvi, 9, 3. However, Büchler, *op. cit.*, p. 229, followed by Zucker, *op. cit.*, p. 62, seek to deny that this Sanhedrin was the Great Sanhedrin, on the ground that the Halakha ordains that capital cases should be tried by a court of twenty-three. But I have already explained in *Tarbiz*, V, pp. 244–246 — see also below, pp. 103 ff. — that all capital cases of which we know were tried at the Great Sanhedrin in Jerusalem, and that in practice, at least, such cases were adjudicated by this Sanhedrin alone) have not the character of a Jerusalem municipal institution (see Zucker, *op. cit.*, pp. 9–10, for the First Temple period, and p. 30, for the beginning of the Second Temple epoch, who points out that Jerusalem was not treated as a separate city, like the other cities of Judah, in respect of self-administration). The fact is even more clearly established by the way the γερ. is depicted in documents from the time of the early Hasmoneans γερ. τοῦ ἔθνους (the time of Jonathan, *I Maccabees* xii, 6; *ibid.* xii 35, οἱ πρεσβύτεροι τοῦ λαοῦ, see Schürer, p. 241), *II Maccabees* xi 27: τῇ γερ. τῶν 'Ιουδαίων, and by the phraseology in *Judith* (iv 8) — ἡ γερ. παντὸς δήμου 'Ισραήλ, and *ibid.* xv 8 — γερ. τῶν υἱῶν Ἰσραήλ. It is also to be inferred from the coins of the Hasmonean dynasty — from John Hyrcanus the High Priest to Antigonus — which refer to the High Priest and *ḥever ha-Yehudîm* (*ḥever* means κοινόν, the administration of the nation, in accordance with the view of many scholars, but contrary to the opinion that regards the word as a term for the whole people). For the early period, however, note should be taken of II Chronicles xix 8: 'Moreover in Jerusalem Jehoshaphat appointed certain Levites and priests and heads of families of Israel, to give judgement for the Lord and to decide disputed cases. And they returned to Jerusalem [וישבו ירושלים].' Present-day scholars (see Madsen in *ICC* and Kittel in Nowack's *Handkommentar*) follow, on account of the difficulty presented by the last two words, the Septuagint (so too the Vulgate), καὶ κρίνειν τοὺς κατοικοῦντες ἐν Ἰερουσαλήμ, and read לריב יושבי ירושלים ['to decide disputed cases of the inhabitants of Jerusalem']. Now if we adopt this version, the High Court of Jerusalem was confined to Jerusalem itself. But this reading is erroneous, for in *v.* 10 that determines the authority of this court, we read 'whenever a case comes to you from your brethren who live in their cities'. Furthermore the parallelism 'to give judgement for the Lord' — 'to decide disputed cases of the inhabitants of Jerusalem' is difficult. Therefore we should retain the traditional text, but we must point וַיֵּשְׁבוּ ['And they had their seat'], in accordance with the version of one MS. cited by Ginsburg. The sense of the verse would then be that the judges gathered together from the whole of Judea and took up residence in Jerusalem so as to serve at the High Court which was appointed over the whole country. Thus the character of the Sanhedrin, at least during the period of the author of the Book (recently scholars have expressed the view that this testimony holds good also for the time of Jehoshaphat), was the same as that which it had subsequently. On the other hand, we have already seen the communal character of the Jerusalem Council during the closing era of the Second Temple. We must therefore suppose that when Herod abolished the Sanhedrin as a body concerned with the affairs of the whole of Israel (possibly evidence of this fact — even in relation to the High Court in the Hewn Chamber, which many scholars wish to regard as a separate institution and to posit its existence even in Herod's time, latterly Zucker, p. 68 — is to be seen in the famous Baraita of R. Jose in the Tosefta, *Ḥagiga* ii, 5, and the parallel passages, see above, p. 37), he provided Jerusalem with a municipal organization, having a limited local function, and, in accordance with his custom, gave it a Hellenistic image. But it cannot be doubted that after Herod's death and Archelaus' exile, the former position was restored in *practice*, as scholars point out, and the Sanhedrin's rule embraced the whole of Israel (Schürer, p. 230, writes unequivocally that after Herod's death the Sanhedrin's authority was restricted to Judea only. But there is no proof that the division of the land into an ethnarchy and tetrarchies resulted in a division of the internal administration of the people in legal, communal and religious matters). However, the outward form given to the Council, having become established, was left unchanged. From now on, the Sanhedrin served formally as the administrative body of Jerusalem, and because of its standing as the highest court of the land, its authority spread of its own accord over all the other cities. This course of development is extremely similar to that of the Roman Senate (see Otto, *op. cit.*, p. 117, only he does not distinguish between the various periods). Now this fact, which is lacking in clarity, confronts us with certain contradictions, in theory and in practice, in regard to the designations and composition of the Sanhedrin. On the one hand it is termed a municipal council in the documents that we have noted (and elsewhere, too); and it is especially known by the designation κοινὸν τῶν Ἱεροσολυμιτῶν (the government of Jerusalem), which is found, in connection with the war against Rome, several times in Josephus' *Life* (xii, 28, etc.) and συνέδριον τ. Ἱεροσολ. (*ibid.* xii). This nomenclature certainly denotes the rule of the Sanhedrin, which operated in those days with the Assembly of the People (and there is no absence of organization here as Dessau thought, *op. cit.*, p. 809, n. 1; only this is not the place for detailed elucidation). On the other hand we find in *The Acts of the Apostles* (v 21) πᾶσαν τὴν γερουσίαν τῶν υἱῶν Ἰσραήλ. ('all the senate of the children of Israel'), and the identical expression used in *Judith* xv 8. So, too, it appears that among the 'Bouleutim' there were men from other cities. Thus Joseph who is mentioned in *Mark* and *Luke* was ὁ ἀπὸ Ἀριμαθαίας (from Arimathea), and Aristeus, the scribe of the council (*Wars* v, 13, 1) was γένος ἐξ Ἀμμαοῦς (of Emmaus stock); and also in our Mishna (*Ta'anit* iii, 6) we find: 'It once happened that the Elders went down from Jerusalem to their own cities', thus indicating that there were in the Sanhedrin Elders from other towns (in conformity with the testimony of Chronicles, *loc. cit.*, and of the Baraita of R. Jose). So, too, we may infer from the seventy elders appointed by Josephus in Galilee and associated with his government, who were local inhabitants of places throughout Galilee (*Wars* ii, 20, 5).

This vague situation could have lent support to the resistance to the authority of the Sanhedrin outside Jerusalem and aided the separatists (it is possible that Josephus also relied on that fact in establishing the Galilean Sanhedrin and in his subversive activity, under Galilean incitement, against the Jerusalem emissaries who had come to Galilee). This position served, apparently, as a factual basis for the Tannaitic dispute, relating to many matters of halakhic importance, as to whether 'Jerusalem was divided according to tribes'. This is not the place to examine the question in detail, but we must consider certain references that would seem to indicate that even in early generations (before Herod) there were those who regarded the Sanhedrin as the administrative body of the city of Jerusalem.

Thus we find in II Kings xxiii 1 the expression 'the elders of Judah and of Jerusalem' (Zucker, *op. cit.*, p. 10, holds that the phrase 'elders of Jerusalem' is not justified in a legal-political sense, but signifies that they lived in Jerusalem, and is simply a geographical term. But this apart, it is possible to combine 'Judah and Jerusalem' as a comprehensive concept, found in the Bible, and the 'elders' therefore relate to the whole country). In Josephus, in the account of the end of the Persian empire, the expression occurs οἱ τῶν Ἱεροσολυμιτῶν πρεσβύτεροι, 'the elders of Jerusalem' (*Ant.* xi, 8, 2; Zucker, *ibid.*, p. 30, n. 1, explains it as above. But possibly it should be regarded as the application of a phrase used in later times). This, too, is the reading of the Septuagint in Chronicles, *loc. cit.* If we accept this to be the case, then in this instance also Herod sought to base himself on some kind of precedent in order to undermine the Sanhedrin and to Hellenize it, in conformity with the method he adopted in all his other evil innovations. (See below App. IV).

Appendix II (to p. 55)

The Talmud certainly does not take 'Palhedrin', when used alone, to denote High Priests. For if so, why should R. Papa (or the Gemara) be in doubt whether the Chamber of the Palhedrin was in the north or the south, since it is expressly stated in the same Mishna that the Chamber of the High Priest was in the north (according to the reading of the Talmud; *Mĕle'khet Shelomo* to *Middot*, *ibid.* raises the question, and his suggested solution is that this is the very doubt expressed by the Talmud, namely: What is the correct reading in our Mishna? But this explanation is far-fetched). The Gemara, however, which does not think that 'the Chamber of the High Priest' referred to in *Middot* was used by him the whole year round (Büchler, *op. cit.*, p. 9, n. 6), assumes that it denotes the one that he used on the Day of Atonement, and hence it is in doubt where the Chamber of the Parhedrin and the House of Avtinas, both of which he used during the seven days, were situated. Only at the end, the Gemara wishes to deduce by reasoning (but the argument is far-fetched) that the Chamber of the Palhedrin lay to the south (thus, according to our Mishnaic text, it is equivalent to the Chamber of the High Priest; but in the light of the Gemara version this is the Chamber of the House of Avtinas. However, the entire section is difficult and composed, apparently, of changing elements; but we cannot enlarge upon this here). But in favour of the view that the Chamber of the High Priest is to be differentiated from the Chamber of the Palhedrin we must further point out first the difficulty of assuming that Abba Saul in *Middot* (and others with him) would designate as 'the Chamber of the High Priest' a place which the latter occupied seven days in the year (the expression 'and it was next to his chamber' in *Tosefta Yoma* i, 20, is to be interpreted as meaning that the House of Parva was next to the High Priest's chamber, and not the Water Gateway, although this is not the view that apparently emerges from the Talmudic discussion, *ibid.* 19a, and that is held also by scholars, e.g. Büchler *op. cit.*, p. 8, n. 5. The Tosefta statement seems to conflict with that of Abba Saul, who places the Chamber of the High Priest in the south, for the Chamber of the House of Parva was in the north. Indeed in the Sifra, in the passage paralleling the Baraita, this statement is wanting). Secondly, from the Mishna in *Middot* — Abba Saul says the Chamber of the High Priest was behind both of them, etc. — it is clear that this Chamber was situated west of the Hewn Chamber (the simple interpretation is that Abba Saul was looking at the plan of the Temple from east to west). It is difficult therefore to say that there was the High Priest's lodging-place (although there is found in *Midrash Psalms* i, 2, a tradition that 'the High Priest was allowed to sit in the Temple-court', in opposition to that of *T.P. Pesaḥim* v, 32d, *T.P. Soṭa* vii, 22a, and *T.B. Soṭa* 40b). Notwithstanding that one of the Early Authorities (see Büchler, *op. cit.*, p. 24) held it improbable, that the Chamber of the Palhedrin was in the Rampart and we must agree with the other Early Authorities (Tosafot, *Yoma* 8b, etc.) that it was open to ground that was not holy (Büchler's explanation of the non-holy character of the Chamber of the Parhedrin, *op. cit.*, p. 25, n. 20, is far-fetched), it is nevertheless reasonable to suppose that the High Priest was not made to spend the night in the inner precincts of the Holy, where the Chamber of the High Priest was situated according to Abba Saul. The Chamber of the Parhedrin was therefore in another place (we can, however, determine its site if we identify 'the Chamber of the Palhedrin' with the 'chamber that was opposite the north-eastern corner of the Temple-building', to which 'the priest that was to burn the heifer' — in practice he was always the High Priest — was removed 'seven days before the burning of the heifer' (*M. Para* iii, 1), an interpretation that is plausible. In this case the difference will be in name only, the one being Hebrew the other Greek (see Büchler, *Die Priester* etc., p. 113); or the change of nomenclature may be due to the fact that the Palhedrin did not always sit in that chamber).

Appendix III (to p. 59)

That the law of the succession to the High Priesthood is not absolute, like the succession to the throne, can be proven, to my mind, from the Baraita in the Sifra, *Ṣaw, Mekhilta de-Millu'im* (cf. *Tosefta Sanhedrin* iv, 11; *T.B. Horayot* 11b; *T.B. Keritot* 5b; *T.P. Sheqalim* iv, 49c; *T.P. Soṭa* viii, 22c; *T.P. Horayot* iii, 47c): 'and even a High Priest, the son of a High Priest, requires anointing, but a king, the son of a king, is not anointed'. The meaning of the Halakha is that the succession to the throne is absolute, but the inheritance of the High Priesthood implies no more than the *prior right to be appointed.* Similarly the Sages taught in the *Sifre* (in an analogy with kingship), Shofetim, § 162: 'So far the law in this respect (i.e. with regard to the king). Whence do we know that all Jewish leaders are succeeded by their sons. . .?', which undoubtedly refers only to *ḥazaqa* [i.e. prior claim to the office] (That this rule was applied to the high offices of the priesthood, is apparently to be inferred from *Wars* iv, 3, 6, which speaks of the 'High Priests' but not of the High Priest proper; for the story of Phannias of the village of Aphthia is later (par. 5) related as a separate episode. Thus the reference is to the leading priests who performed distinct functions in the Temple. But the entire section appears to be out of place and confused.) This teaching must be related to the statement found also in Hecataeus (at the beginning of Greek history; see Reinach, *Textes* etc., p. 17): τῷ δοκοῦντι τῶν ἱερέων φρονήσει καὶ ἀρετῇ προέχειν ('to the priest who is seen to transcend the others in understanding and virtue') (Schürer already, *op. cit.*, p. 240, n. 5, drew attention to Hecataeus' observation, only in his view it is not to be doubted that in the Greek period the office of the High Priest was actually passed on by inheritance). That even in practice the High Priesthood was *never* transferred *automatically* by the fixed law of inheritance is to be deduced, to my mind, from what Joseph b. Tobias said to Onias the High Priest, who refused to give king Ptolemy — Euergetes — the tax money and thereby angered the latter: δι' ἃ λαβεῖν καὶ τοῦ λαο ῦ τὴν προστασίαν αὐτὸν... καὶ τῆς ἀρχιερατικῆς τιμῆς ἐπιτυχεῖν ('through love of gain had he received the government of the nation... and obtained the office of High Priesthood') (*Ant.* xii, 4, 2) — for love of money (Onias sought) to take over the leadership of the people and to succeed to the High Priesthood. Thus he did not apparently enter upon the High Priesthood by a fixed, unchallengeable order of succession.

In abolishing inherited succession, Herod had therefore some slight basis for his action, and did not brazenly uproot a Halakha and practice that were wholly impeccable (see Wellhausen, *Israel. u. jud. Gesch.*, p. 236, who also states that in practice the High Priesthood was not always bequeathed).

Appendix IV (to p. 61)

On this subject and its Greek character see Otto, *op. cit.*, pp. 105, 106, 109; Pauly-Wissowa, Supplementum II, pp. 101–103, *et al.*

In recent times scholars have drawn attention to Herod's policy not to infringe the Jewish religion (not because of his righteousness but for political reasons), but all of them point to definite instances of infringement, which constitute absolute offences. However, it seems to me that even these, despite the fact that Josephus (i.e. the tradition in his possession) denounces them severely, are nevertheless not a breach of a fixed Halakha accepted by all Israel. For notwithstanding his non-Jewish, Hellenistic leanings and his estrangement from Judaism and his actions, which in general undoubtedly offended against religion, he still endeavoured, on account of his political astuteness, to refrain in his public acts from unquestionably grave offences. In this way he even succeeded in assuaging the resentment of many and to conceal his general intention, namely, to free himself from subjection to the Torah and Halakha and to give a Hellenistic aspect to his kingdom. Let us begin with matters mentioned in the text.

1) The theatre (we find it in his reign even in Jewish Jericho) and the amphitheatre etc. that he established in Jerusalem. Josephus (*Ant.* xv, 8, 1) denounced the breaching of the ancestral teaching implicit in these deeds. In truth from *II Maccabees* (iv 10–12) we learn that the establishment of these institutions were regarded as

tantamount to apostasy. But in the Halakha we find the Tannaim disputing whether these things were forbidden even when idolatry and bloodshed were not involved, or not. And Josephus himself subsequently relates that when the men who were angered at this and stirred up the people against the king were invited by him to the theatre and were shown that the trophies were not human images as they had imagined (human faces are halakhically forbidden according to all views) they were appeased. Others, however, did not retract from their opposition (thus Herod sought to appease the people by showing respect for the accepted Halakha, but was not deterred by those authorities whose interpretation of the Halakha was not universally regarded as unquestionable). See below, p. 144–45. With this should be compared the fact that he imprinted no face on his coins, except the form of an eagle on one of them.

2) The law with regard to the enslavement of thieves. Otto already has pointed out, *op. cit.*, p. 105, (the fact) that this ordinance conflicts with the Torah and Halakha, and was derived from Graeco-Roman legislation; and he was followed by Gulack (*Sefer Klausner*, pp. 132–135). But on further study the matter is seen not to be so simple. For we have learnt in Baraita (*T.B. Bava Meṣi'a* 73b): 'If you see a man whose behaviour is unseemly, whence do we know that you may make him a slave? Because the Torah teaches "They shall be your bondmen for ever and your brethren" [as well] (and Rava gave an actual ruling to act thus). We thus see that it is permissible to make slaves for ever of Jewish offenders (the aforementioned statute also refers to thieves that are guilty of breaking in, who commit a grave offence). It is possible, therefore, that even in earlier generations there were some Sages who ruled according to this Tannaitic Halakha. However, Herod was able, without this, to promulgate the new law referred to as a state law (see Maimonides, *Yad*, Hilkhot Melakhim, iii, 10, and compare, for the validity and nature of a state law, *Torat Kohanim*, Lev. Ḥova, §1; §4; §5; and §7, on the Scriptural phrase '"the precept of the Lord" — but not the precept of the king nor the precept of the court', for one might have thought that one should be obliged to offer a sacrifice for an infraction of a state law). Undoubtedly the Sages and the people, for the most part, did not acknowledge Herod's right to be king (and kings, even when entitled to the monarchy, had to subject themselves to the authority of the Sanhedrin, as we can see from the Haggada that praises King David in this regard). But Herod himself, and those Pharisees who sided with him, could act thus lawfully.

This argument may also be applied to —

3) The fact that Herod judged capital cases outside the Sanhedrin and not through court executions carried out according to the Halakha (the burning of the zealots who tore down the eagle from the Temple, *Ant.* xvii, 6, 3; *Wars* i, 33, 4; and the stoning of the army officers, because at that period apparently the injunction of stoning was not generally carried out in the Torah manner but according to the Halakha, by hurling down, *Ant.* xvi, 11, 6–7; *Wars* i, 27, 6. Possibly Herod in sentencing these offenders at a public assembly, ἐκκλησία, wished to base himself on the ancient custom, mentioned in the Torah, of the judgement of 'the congregation'; so, too, with regard to the stoning).

4) Momigliano (*op. cit.*, p. 333) regards Herod's marriage to Malthace, the Samaritan, a grave and brazenfaced transgression. However, although already in former times the taking of a Samaritan woman in marriage was deemed a transgression (like marrying a non-Jewess), and this caused, according to Josephus' tradition (*Ant.* xi, 8, 2), the completion of the breach between the Samaritans and the Jews, as well as the building of the temple on Mount Gerizim at the end of the Persian period, nevertheless the Tannaitic dispute as to whether a Samaritan was legally like a Gentile or an Israelite undoubtedly gives expression to a prolonged halakhic argument in the Second Temple period (just as later in the days of the Amoraim). Furthermore, who can tell whether this Samaritan woman was not converted to Judaism (Herod himself refused to let his sister Salome marry Sylleus, the Arabian, who did not consent to be circumcized), even though the question whether proselytes are to be accepted from the Samaritans is the subject of dispute in our sources (from the tradition of the early Christians we know that Samaritan converts were accepted in the days of the Tannaim). However, unless they are partly Gentile, the Samaritan women are prohibited to a Jew (even if converted to Judaism, on account of the possibility of forbidden relationship). But even if we date this prohibition as early as Temple times, it cannot be doubted that this ruling was not universally accepted (the whole subject requires detailed clarification, but this is not possible here; see 'The Origin of the Samaritans in Halakhic Tradition').

Appendix V (to p. 69)

In the method of appointing High Priests four competing factors are to be discerned: (1) inheritance, of which we have already spoken earlier; (2) the king; (3) the people; (4) the priests, by lot or not by lot.

All these factors — which were also to be found among the Greeks, with the exception of inheritance, which according to Stengel existed only in cults that were first founded in families as private forms of worship and subsequently became public — are to be found, it seems, in the sources.

The King. There is no evidence either in Josephus or in Rabbinic tradition for denying his right to appoint the High Priest, although, as far at least as the kings of the House of Herod were concerned, it is reasonable to suppose that many of the Sages and the people did not consider them entitled to this right (see for halakhic purposes especially *Tosefta Yoma* i, 4; *T.P. Horayot* iii, 47d. The king referred to was Herod). Furthermore, it appears that we may infer that the Pharisaic Halakha in Temple times give this ruling on the basis of Queen Salome's action, for according to the tradition in *Wars* she appointed Hyrcanus, by her own volition, as High Priest in her lifetime (i, 5, 1; *Ant.* iii, 16, 2). Now all that Salome did was in accordance with the teaching of the Pharisees. However, in *Ant.* xx, 4, 10, Josephus explains that Alexander Jannaeus, before his death, permitted Salome to appoint whichever of her sons she wished as High Priest. Thus it is possible to regard the episode as the carrying out of the deceased's will, and the appointment as an inheritance by virtue of the will; and we find a parallel to this in the Tannaitic tradition in regard to the story of Onias who built a temple in Egypt, *T.B. Menaḥot* 109b; *T.P. Yoma ibid.* vi, 43d. At all events we must note that there were some Sages who contested Salome's right to the throne, for in *Sifre*, *Shofeṭim*, § 157, they expounded '"king" — but not a queen').

The people. We learn in *Tosefta Sanhedrin* iii, 4: 'Neither a king nor a High Priest may be appointed except by a court of seventy-one' (Lieberman, it is true, in *Tosefet Ri'shonim* Pt. II, p. 153, refers to a responsum of R. Abraham the son of Maimonides, to the latter's *Yad*, Hilkhot Melakhim, i, 3, and to Hilkhot Sanhedrin v, 1, which do not read 'High Priest'. But Lieberman did not point out that in Hilkhot Kle ha-Miqdash iv, 15, the Halakha is quoted correctly. It is clear, therefore, that the version of the Tosefta is not to be faulted). This Halakha intends to teach the people's right in the appointment of the High Priest. But it contains no explicit testimony against the king's right, and it may be said that it purported to associate the Sanhedrin with the king in the appointment of the High Priest.

The priests. From the story of Phannias of Aphthia we learn, both from the account in Josephus and from the Tannaitic tradition, that it was the priests who appointed him (they relied on an ancient law — Josephus; this appointment, however, was by lot). This seems also to be implied in the wording of Hecataeus quoted above.

Supplementary Notes on 'Par'irtin'

1. To p. 61, l. 26. The Tosefta and the Baraita in the Babylonian Talmud state this, but on the other hand the Sifre, the Palestinian Talmud (and the Midrashim) do not have this tradition. This difference is clearly apparent in the disagreement between the Babylonian Talmud and the Palestinian in regard to the number of High Priests who served in the Second Temple; according to the latter eighty High Priests served there ('another view' is that there were from 81–85) while the Babylonian Talmud holds that there were 300, since it maintains that no High Priest was appointed in the Second Temple, from the outset, for more than a year (the Temple stood 420 years; 297 High Priests — apart from Simeon the Just and Joḥanan the High Priest and Ishmael b. Phabi whose united priesthood totals 130 years — served for 290 years, indicating that they did not respectively complete their full year of service. The Talmud does not distinguish, as do the Baraitot cited above, between the earlier years and the time 'when the kings multiplied', and postulates the restriction of the High Priesthood to one year for the entire Temple period).

2. To p. 63, l. 7. It is true that in the *Chronicle* of Jerome (ed. Helm, p. 161), which is a copy of that of Eusebius (up to the year 326 C.E.) we read that the High Priests after the reign of Herod *a Romanis imperatoribus sacerdotum emebant* ('bought the High Priesthood from the Roman rulers'); thus the tradition concerning the purchase of the High Priesthood for money is found even in Eusebius. But the author states in the same passage in regard to the service of the High Priests in those days: *et nonnulli unius anni sive modice amplius* etc. Not all the High Priests, therefore, served one year; here Eusebius contradicts his own statement in the *Ecclesiastical History*, the statement which Chrysostom denied in the passage cited. Hence it seems difficult to suppose that the latter derived his information from this source. The matter requires further investigation.

3. To p. 64, l. 3. It may be worth noting that according to Rostovtzeff, *Gott. Gel. Anzeigen*, 1909, pp. 612–639, the Romans acted similarly in Egypt. For in his view the office of ἐπιστάτης, which is sometimes also called ἀρχιερεύς (this is questioned by some scholars), and which in the days of the Ptolemies was a hereditary position and was theoretically considered by the government a kind of liturgy, was completely abolished in the times of the Romans, who in place of a single person set up an association of priests in the form πρεσβύτεροι, ἡγούμενοι, who were replaced every twelve months. See also Wilchen, *Grundzüge*, I, p. 127; Oertel, *Die Liturgie*, p. 39.

4. To p. 68, l. 17. Rostovtzeff (*op. cit.*, pp. 612–613) seeks, it is true, to restrict to a minimum the practice of electing the priests by their colleagues (contrary to Otto); but Oertel (*op. cit.*, p. 40) regards his arguments as unconvincing.

5. To note 24. Undoubtedly the keepers of the door mentioned in II Kings xxv 8 and Jeremiah lii 24 were Temple officers, as Josephus already explained

(*Ant.* x, 8, 5) Τοὺς φυλάσσοντας τὸ ἱερὸν ('The administrators who supervise the Temple'); see Büchler, *Die Priester*, p. 95. But this does not prove that the doorkeeper under discussion was also like them, for undoubtedly the monarchs also had keepers of the door and the robes.

6. To Appendix III. This question is possibly alluded to also in the Slavonic *Book of Enoch* xxi 1–3, where it is stated that 'the elders of the people' offered the (High) Priesthood to Methuselah the son of Enoch after the latter's passing, but he refused to accept it 'until the Lord the God of my father Enoch will Himself choose unto Him a priest from among his men', and he did not accept it until the Lord had revealed Himself to him in a dream of the night and enjoined him to accede to the request of the people, and he was 'written down as the High Priest' only when a heavenly wonder appeared before the eyes of the people (*v.* 24). Compare the statement there (xxii 23–24) regarding the appointment of Nir the son of Lemech who succeeded Methuselah.

7. To Appendix IV (p. 85). That the king, according to the Halakha, could pass sentence in matters of state without consultation with the Sanhedrin is evidenced, particularly for the period of the Second Temple, by the action of Herod in executing Hezekiah the Galilean and his companions, when he served as Hyrcanus' governor in Galilee. From the episode (*Wars* i, 10, 6; *Ant.* xiv, 9, 3) we learn that if Herod had not been a *hedyot* [an ignorant fellow] but had acted under orders from Hyrcanus (who had the status of king among the Jews), he would have had the right to carry out the execution without the consent of the Sanhedrin, in accordance with the law of the Torah.

8. To Appendix IV (p. 85). Even in taking possession of the vestments of the High Priest, Herod followed a precedent, for it was the practice of the Hasmonean Dynasty (*Ant.* xv, 11, 4) from the time of Joḥanan the High Priest onward (*ibid.* xviii, 4, 3) to keep them in the citadel. Only these were High Priests and it was in their capacity as High Priests (and not as rulers) that 'they took charge of the vestments, for they alone had the right to put them on' (in the words of Josephus in the last cited passage). But apparently Herod exploited the fact and continued to hold the vestments of the High Priest as ruler and king. Thus in this instance, too, Herod introduced a bad enactment on the pretext of a precedent that obtained, as it were, before his time.

ON PHILO'S HALAKHA

I

After detailing the priestly dues[1] (*De Spec. Legibus* I, 132–150), Philo states (*ibid.* 152): ὑπὲρ δὲ τοῦ μηδένα τῶν διδόντων ὀνειδίζειν τοῖς λαμβάνουσι, κελεύει τὰς ἀπαρχὰς εἰς τὸ ἱερὸν κομίζεσθαι, εἶτ' ἐνθένδε τοὺς ἱερεῖς λαμβάνειν ('And in order that none of the donors should put the recipient [priest] to shame [the Torah] enjoins that the gifts should first be brought to the Temple, from where the priests would receive them subsequently). He goes on to explain further on that the realization of the priests that they are not receiving their gifts at the hands of man but from heaven saves them from a sense of humiliation.

This statement of Philo conflicts with the Halakha,[2] which permits the owners to give the priestly dues anywhere and to whichever priest they desire. Since Philo, on the other hand, explains the

1 In §132–142 Philo enumerates four priestly dues. The first is the dough-offering, the third is the first-born of land animals and the firstling of an ass (which, according to Philo but contrary to our Halakha, implies every unclean animal) and the redemption money of a first-born son. As for the second gift it seems, as Ritter maintains (*Philon u.d. Halakha*, 122), to be the heave-offering. The fourth is the tithe (according to Albeck in his study, 'Das Buch der Jubiläen und die Halakha', published in the *Jahresbericht* of the *Lehranstalt für die Wissenschaft des Judenthums*, 1929, p. 56. Another explanation is offered by Heinemann, *Philons Griechische und Jüdische Bildung*, 36).

2 *M. Beṣa* i, 6; *Tosefta Pe'a* iv, 7. On the redemption of the first-born son and the firstlings of cattle see *Sifre*, Qoraḥ, §118, and *Mekhilta*, *Bô'*, xvi. Regarding the firstling, cf. *Sifre Deut.*, §77 (יכול אף מעשר ובכור כו' 'I might have thought also tithe and the firstling' etc.) and *Midrash Tannaim*, *loc. cit.*, p. 54. With respect to heave-offering and tithe, see *M. Giṭṭin* iii, 3, and *Midrash Tannaim* in Ch. xiv 22 (Hoffmann, p. 77: שומע אני אפילו בריחוק מקום...ת״ל מעשר דגנך וכו' 'Thus I learn even when one is at a distance...therefore Scripture says "the tithe of thy corn" etc.'. See the editor's note *ibid.* It appears that two Baraitot were combined here, one dealing with the bringing of the firstling and tithe of corn from a distant place in Eretz-Israel, and the other with bringing them from abroad.).

ordinance to bring the gifts to the Temple by the intent of the lawgiver that the priests should regard themselves as receiving gifts from the hands of heaven, Heinemann[3] thinks that Philo came to the conclusion that the individual priests do not receive gifts from the donors because of the verses Numbers xviii 8, 11, 19.[4]

But undoubtedly it was not the exegesis of the above-mentioned verses that caused Philo to write as he did, but a tradition of Halakha and custom that he had in his possession.[5]

3 In his German translation of the aforementioned work, ed. Cohn, p. 53, n. 1.

4 These verses *per se* do not prove that the gifts have to be brought to the Temple, for the expression 'heave-offering' etc. does not imply that they must necessarily be brought to the Temple itself. If there is an express verse in this respect, it is that of Deuteronomy xii 6 ('And thither ye shall bring your burnt-offerings, and your sacrifices, and your tithes' etc.; cf. v 11). Although the Halakha, in the exposition of R. Akiba (*Sifre Deut.* §63, and *Midrash Tannaim, ibid.*, p. 50), explains the verse to refer to the second tithe and the tithe of cattle, the passage, according to its simple meaning, speaks of all the tithes. So, too, Naḥmanides interprets this verse, stating: 'According to the plain interpretation the verse mentions the burnt offerings and the sacrifices that must be eaten there in the sacred area before the Lord, and it also mentions that one must bring there the tithe and the heave-offering, giving them to the priests and to the Levites, the ministers of the Temple etc., as it is said "Bring ye the whole tithe into the store-house" etc., and so it was ordained in the Second Temple in respect of the heave-offering etc., as it is said "that we should bring ... to the chambers of the house of our God" ' (so far Naḥmanides). Likewise it is stated in Amos iv 4 'Come to Beth-el, and transgress, to Gilgal, and multiply transgression; and bring your sacrifices in the morning, and your tithes after three days'. Thus an analogy is established between tithes and sacrifices: just as sacrifices must be brought to the Temple, so, too, must the tithes be brought there. Compare the remarks of Bertholet in Kautzsch's German translation of the Bible, first edition, II, p. 36, note e in the commentary to the Bible.

5 Although Philo states here that the Torah (νόμος) enjoined the bringing of gifts to the Temple, this does not prove that he inferred this rule from Scriptural interpretation. For we find that Philo employs this expression even when the matter is not specifically stated in the Torah, but is only a halakhic tradition and custom. Thus, for example, he declares in *De Septenario* 61 that the Torah admonishes the Jews to occupy themselves on Sabbaths with philosophical and ethical studies (that is to say, with the reading of the Torah in public and homilies on the pericopes). Similarly in *De Virtutibus*, 137, he states that the Torah forbids a pregnant animal to be offered up on the altar. But this is not stated in the Torah; he must without doubt have been in possession of a halakhic tradition. So, too, in other passages. Similar instances are found in Josephus; for example, *Ant.* iii, 12, 2, where it is stated that a priest may not marry a captive, and *ibid.* iv, 8, 14, in regard to 'seven men to judge in every city'. Likewise in *Against Apion* ii, 206, in respect

That the heave-offering and the tithe were brought, at the beginning of the Second Temple period, to the store-house at Jerusalem is attested by Scriptural passages Malachi iii 10; Nehemiah xii 44; xiii 5, 12; ii Chronicles xxxi 5 ff.[6]

However, the sources cited below show that subsequently, too, during the greater part of the Second Temple era, the people were accustomed to bring the heave-offering and tithes to the Temple store-house, where they were distributed to the priests (and Levites) *pro rata*. And even at the end of the Temple period, when the Halakha permitted the gifts to be given to a priest or Levite anywhere and without the supervision of the central authority at Jerusalem, it was still apparently deemed the ideal way of fulfilling the commandment to bring the gifts up (if possible) to the Temple. Philo thus transmitted here, as in many other passages, the ancient Halakha and the custom that obtained in practice in Eretz-Israel and in the Diaspora.

(1) *I Maccabees* iii 49–50: Καὶ ἤνεγκαν τὰ ἱμάτια τῆς ἱερωσύνης καὶ τὰ πρωτογενήματα καὶ τὰς δεκάτας καὶ ἤγειραν τοὺς Ναζιραίους οἳ ἐπλήρωσαν τὰς ἡμέρας καὶ ἐβόησαν φωνῇ εἰς τὸν οὐρανὸν λέγοντες Τί ποιήσωμεν τούτοις καὶ ποῦ αὐτοὺς ἀπαγάγωμεν ('And they brought the priestly garments, and the firstfruits, and the tithes; and they shaved the Nazirites who had accomplished their days. And they cried aloud toward heaven, saying: 'What shall we do with these, and whither shall we carry them away?'). The assembled people were therefore in perplexity when they were unable to bring the tithes to Jerusalem, which was occupied by the enemy, since they were obliged to bring the tithes to the Temple exactly like first-fruits. Moreover, the very fact that they collected the tithes at Mizpeh, which served them as a temporary centre, testifies that they were not accustomed to distribute the tithe at any place and to each priest (and Levite) individually.

(2) *I Maccabees* x 31 (Demetrius in his letter to 'the nation of the Jews' writes): Καὶ Ἱερουσαλὴμ ἤτω ἁγία καὶ ἀφιεμένη καὶ τὰ ὅρια αὐτῆς, αἱ δεκάται καὶ τὰ τέλη ('And let Jerusalem be holy and free, together with the outlying districts, (regarding) the tithes and the tolls'). The meaning of the words can only be that the tithes and the revenues that come into Jerusalem would be free of state taxation.

to the precept to bury the dead and erect tombstones. The prevailing custom, which dated from ancient times, was regarded as 'Scriptural'.

6 Cited by Ritter, *op. cit.*, p. 116, n. 1; Heinemann *loc. cit.*

So, too, Kautzsch[7] and Charles[8] understood the passage. Thus the tithes are accounted the assets of Jerusalem, undoubtedly because they were brought to the Temple (the aforementioned privilege was granted only to Jerusalem and its 'environs').

(3) *Judith* xi 13: καὶ τὰς ἀπαρχὰς τοῦ σίτου καὶ τὰς δεκάτας τοῦ οἴνου καὶ τοῦ ἐλαίου, ἃ διεφύλαξον ἁγιάσαντες τοῖς ἱερεῦσιν τοῖς παρεστηκόσιν ἐν Ἱερουσαλὴμ κτλ ('the firstfruits of the corn, and the tenths of the wine and the oil, which they had sanctified, and reserved for the priests that stand before the fact of our God in Jerusalem', etc.).

The statement intends to say that the men of Bethulia kept the heave-offerings and tithes in their city in order to send them (apparently for the time of the festivals; see further on) to Jerusalem so that the priests should receive them there.

(4) *Tobit* (i 6–7) relates: κἀγὼ μόνος ἐπορευόμην πλεονάκις ἐν Ἱεροσολύμοις ταῖς ἑορταῖς, καθὼς γέγραπται παντὶ τῷ Ἰσραὴλ ἐν προστάγματι αἰωνίῳ, τὰς ἀπαρχὰς καὶ τὰς δεκάτας τῶν γενημάτων καὶ τὰς προκουρίας ἔχων. καὶ ἐδίδουν αὐτὰς τοῖς ἱερεῦσιν τοῖς υἱοῖς Ἀαρὼν κτλ ('And I alone used often to journey to Jerusalem at the feasts, as it hath been ordained in all Israel by an everlasting decree. I used to go to Jerusalem with the firstfruits and the firstlings and the tenths of the cattle and the first shearings of the sheep, and gave them to the priests, the sons of Aaron' etc.).[9]

Incidentally we learn that they used to bring up the priestly and Levitical dues to Jerusalem at the three pilgrim festivals. It stands to reason that they would combine one precept with another and thus lessen the trouble of the journeys.

(5) In i Samuel i 21 the Septuagint adds: 'and all the tithes of his land' (καὶ πάσας τὰς δεκάτας τῆς γῆς αὐτοῦ); thus Elkaṇah also brought up to Shiloh the tithes together with his sacrifices. It may be assumed that this addition was inserted because the interpolators knew the custom obtaining in their day to bring the tithes to the Temple at Jerusalem. Since Shiloh served as the national sanctuary in Elkanah's time, they added (possibly on the basis of a tradition

7 In his German translation, vol. I, p. 62, note h.

8 In his English rendering, vol. I, p. 103, in the note to this verse.

9 *Codex Sinaiticus* reads: καὶ τὰς δεκάτας τῶν κτηνῶν κτλ ('and the tithe of the herd'). The verse speaks, therefore, of the tithe of the cattle. But it also reads 'the first shearings'; and in verse 7 it is stated: 'and I gave them to the priests... and the tenth of the wine and the corn... I gave to the sons of Levi, who ministered at Jerusalem'. Thus he also brought the tithe of corn to Jerusalem

of haggadic Midrash, just as there were interpolated a number of other exegetical additions on the basis of halakhic and haggadic Midrashim) the aforementioned phrase to the verse.

Similarly Josephus states (*Ant.* v, 10, 13) that Elkanah and his wife brought sacrifices and tithes to Shiloh after Samuel's birth (did he possess a haggadic tradition? or did his text have an addition at the end of the chapter like the one cited above?).

(6) *Luke* ii 22: καὶ ὅτε ἐπλήσθησαν αἱ ἡμέραι τοῦ καθαρισμοῦ αὐτῆς κατὰ τὸν νόμον Μωυσέως ἀνήγαγον αὐτὸν εἰς Ἱεροσόλυμα παραστῆσαι τῷ κυρίῳ καθὼς γέγραπται ἐν νόμῳ κυρίου ὅτι πᾶν ἄρσεν διανοῖγον μήτραν ἅγιον τῷ κυρίῳ κληθήσεται κτλ ('And when the days of her purification according to the law of Moses were accomplished, they brought him to Jerusalem, to present him to the Lord, as is written in the Law of the Lord that every male that openeth the womb shall be called holy unto the Lord').

The presentation of the first-born son in the Temple has redemption only as its purpose. We thus learn that it was the custom to redeem the first-born (by giving five *selaʿim* to a priest) in Jerusalem and at the Temple (as stated by Philo).[10]

From our Mishna, too, we learn that they used to bring up the dough-offering from outside Eretz-Israel to Jerusalem. For we thus learn in the Mishna (*M. Ḥalla* iv, 10) 'Nittai of Tekoa brought dough-offerings from Be-Jattir, but they did not accept (them) from him. The men of Alexandria brought their dough-offerings from Alexandria, but they did not accept (them) from them.'[11] Although they did not accept the dough-offering from them in these instances, yet there can be no doubt that it was the ancient custom to bring the dough-offering from outside Eretz-Israel to Jerusalem,[12] only the

10 Nehemiah x 37.

11 The dough-offering (*Ḥalla*) brought from Alexandria to Jerusalem was certainly not in the form of dough (for it would inevitably have gone bad in the course of the journey), but was baked. Ostensibly this is contrary to the established Halakha, which forbids the separation of dough-offering from the bread (*Sifre Num.* §110 and §67, p. 283) and supports Philo's view (*loc. cit.*, 132. However, if the offering was not separated from the dough, it may be separated from the bread even according to the Halakha, *Sifre*, *loc. cit.*) that the dough-offering is given from the baked bread. The matter requires further investigation.

12 Undoubtedly the bringing up of the dough-offering to Jerusalem is to be equated with that of the first-fruits and firstlings cited in the same Mishna.

later Halakha enacted not to accept the dough-offering nor the heave-offerings and tithes that came from outside Eretz-Israel.[13]

We have thus learned from the above sources that according to the ancient Halakha the priestly (and Levitical) gifts used to be brought, in the time of the Second Temple, to Jerusalem, to the Temple store.

13 Although the Halakha states in a number of places that heave-offering and tithe (and the dough-offering) do not obtain outside the Land of Israel (*M. Qiddushin* i, 9 and *Midrash Tannaim* to Deuteronomy xii 23: 'Should you suppose that just as the second tithe obtains only in the Land' etc.). With regard to the dough-offering see *M. Ḥalla* ii, 1; *M. Demai* i, 3 according to the interpretation of *T.P. ibid.* i, 1; *T.B. 'Avoda Zara* 58b; *T.B. Ḥullin* 6b; *T.B. Shabbat* 119a; *T.P. Shevi'it* vi 1; *T.P. Berakhot* iv, 1; *T.P. Sanhedrin* vii, 13. It was customary (at least in certain places) to separate heave-offerings and tithes even outside the Land. Thus we learn relative to Babylonia and Egypt from *M. Yadayim* iv, 3 (cf. Maimonides, *Code*, 'Hilkhot Terumot', i, 1, and Isaac b. Samuel the Elder (Ri) in Tosafot, *T.B. 'Avoda Zara,* 59a) and from *Tosefta Pe'a* iv, 6 (*T.B. Ketubbot* 25a). Similarly in *'Avot de-R. Nathan,* Recension I, xx (end) we learn: ' "They made me keeper of the vineyards" — this refers to Israel who were exiled to Babylon; there rose up unto them prophets from among them and said unto them: Separate heave-offerings and tithes' etc. (in *T.P. 'Eruvin* iii, 9, likewise in *Pesiqta de-Rav Kahana* 118a and *Cant. Rabba* i another version of this dictum is cited. But the Baraita in *'Avot de-R. Nathan* is not to be emended in accordance with the Palestinian Talmud, as Schechter proposed in his edition of *'Avot de-R. Nathan,* because these are two separate traditions). So, too, the statement in *T.P. Ḥalla* iv, 4, testifies with regard to Babylonia: 'Our teachers in Exile [i.e. Babylonia] used to separate heave-offerings and tithes', etc. [heave-offerings were separated even after the intervention of 'the youths' (i.e. sons of R. Ḥiyya); see *T.B. Beṣa* 12b; *T.B. Bekhorot* 27a], and they used (as far as possible) to bring up the heave-offerings and tithes and dough-offering to the Land of Israel (as we learn from our Mishna). Büchler has correctly interpreted (in his essay 'Die priesterliche Zehnten' etc., *Jubilee Volume in honour of Steinschneider*, p. 95) the edict of the proconsul of Asia Minor to the Melesians (Josephus, *Ant.* xiv, 10, 21) enjoining the people of that city to permit the Jews τοὺς καρποὺς μεταχειρίζεσθαι καθὼς ἔθος ἐστιν αὐτοῖς ('to deal with the fruits according to their laws'), which intended to permit the Jews to separate the tithe of their produce, and undoubtedly the permission referred to bringing up the tithes to Jerusalem. 'The 'fruits' were already likened there to 'the payment of the sacred dues' (τὰ ἱερὰ πάτρια τελεῖν), by which 'the sacred monies' (ἱερὰ χρήματα) are meant, namely, the money of the half-shekel — just as half-shekel has to be brought to Jerusalem so the fruits must be brought to Jerusalem. It seems to me that when Philo speaks (*loc. cit.*) of the negligence of individuals in the separation of the priestly gifts, and rebukes and admonishes them at length (*ibid.* 153–155) on this subject, his words are directed to Jewish readers in Alexandria and Egypt — that they should set aside their heave-offerings

This is a logical view. For the precept regarding the priestly gifts was intended only for the maintenance of the Sanctuary, so that the priests should be free to attend to its service.[14] If now the heave-offering and tithe had been given to individual priests without supervision by the central authority and not by systematic apportionment, an invidious situation would have arisen, for many of the priests would have lost their livelihood and would not have been able to devote themselves to the Temple service.[15] Nor should we be surprised at the trouble involved in collecting the heave-offerings and tithes in the Temple store and their distribution to the priests, for we have learned (*Tosefta Shevi'it* viii, 1) of a similar position obtaining with regard to the disbursement of the produce of the Sabbatical year to the poor by the law courts in the cities: 'At first the agents of the Bet Din used to sit at the entrances of the towns. If anyone brought produce in his hand, they took it from him...and the rest they placed in the city storehouse. When the season of the ripening of the figs arrived, the Bet Din agents hired workmen, who picked the fruit and made them into a pressed fig cake and placed it in the city storehouse...and distributed them on Sabbath eve to each one according to (the needs of) his house.' If now in the case of the

and tithes, and bring them up to Jerusalem. As regards Asia Minor (Cilicia), the ancient custom of bringing the heave-offering and tithe to Eretz-Israel is substantiated by the story of Epiphanius (*Haeres*. 30, 11) about Joseph the apostate, who, until his conversion to Christianity, served as an 'emissary' of the Patriarch and was sent to Cilicia, where he collected in each city the 'tithes' and 'heave-offerings' (τὰ ἐπιδέκατα καὶ τὰς ἀπαρχάς) from the Jews of the country. The collections of 'tithes' and 'heave-offerings' by the Patriarch was undoubtedly based on the custom of the Jews of Cilicia, prior to the Destruction, to send their heave-offerings and tithes to Jerusalem and to the Temple (instead of the Temple came the centre that replaced it, namely, the Patriarchate. The money was apparently intended for 'the associates' in Eretz-Israel — belonging to the category of 'funds collected for the scholars'; and as R. Abba said in *Pesiqta de-R. Kahana*, 'Aśser Te'aśśer: 'This contains an allusion to the travelling-merchants and sea-farers, who give a tenth to the students of the Torah').

14 Cf. Philo, *loc. cit*., 132; *ibid*. iv, 98.

15 However, when the number of the priests grew and they spread throughout the land and were divided into 24 watches, each of which served in the Temple two weeks in the year (and on festivals), and some priests acquired landed estates (cf. Josephus, *Life*, 422), for many of them the priestly gifts were no longer a necessary basis of their livelihood. Possibly this factor contributed to the fact that at the end of the Hasmonean era the system of bringing the heave-offering and tithe to the Sanctuary and distributing them on an equal basis began to languish; see below.

produce of the Sabbatical year, which it is not a religious duty to give away, the Bet Din took great trouble to have them ready and distributed to the needy, so that some should not be the gainers and others the losers, how much more so would they have been concerned to collect the priestly gifts, the giving of which is prescribed as a religious duty by the Torah, and to distribute them to the priests proportionally.

However, it appears that at the end of the Temple period heave-offering and tithe were distributed to the priests even outside Jerusalem, in accordance with our Halakha.

In his *Life*, xii, Josephus relates that his two fellow priests (Joezer, [Joazar] and Judah [Judas]), who were sent with him to Galilee at the beginning of the war, took the tithes unto themselves, although they were wealthy. He also declares in his own praise (*ibid.* xv) that he did not accept the tithes that were brought to him. It is also clear from his statement (*Ant.* xx, 8, 8, and similarly *ibid.* xx, 9, 2) that in the reign of Agrippa II the 'high priests' (i.e. the priests who were of noble lineage and power) used to send their servants to the threshing floors to take the tithes. And thus, he declares, it came about that the poor priests died of poverty. From this is to be inferred that at the end of the Temple period the system of bringing the tithe to the Temple treasury and its equal distribution among the priests was abolished, or at least languished, and the tithe was given to individuals; hence the aggressive priests secured the gifts and the modest ones were the losers.

Now we must clarify when the ancient custom ceased to be the fixed usage and the Halakha was changed permitting the priestly dues to be given in any place and to any individual himself. It appears to me that we have the means of determining the period in which this change occurred.

In *Antiquities* xiv, 10, 6 Josephus cites a decree of Julius Caesar, in which after exempting the Jews from paying tribute of the produce in the Sabbatical Year and ordaining them to bring the agricultural levy — a quarter of that which was sown — to Sidon,[16] he states:

16 The instructions of Julius Caesar with reference to giving the tithes to Hyrcanus are addressed to the Jews in Judea; so, too, are his injunctions with regard to the tribute of produce, which must be brought to Sidon (his words are not directed to the inhabitants of Sidon, as Prof. Klausner, *Historia Yisre'elit*, Pt. II, p. 205, wished to explain). He ordered the tribute to be brought to Sidon, because Sidon was the depot for the cities of Palestine and Phoenicia, where the fruits paid to the government were collected. Cf.

πρὸς τούτοις ἔτι καὶ Ὑρκανῷ καὶ τοῖς τέκνοις αὐτοῦ τὰς δεκάτας τελῶσιν, ἃς ἐτέλουν καὶ τοῖς προγόνοις αὐτῶν ('and besides this, they are to pay the same tithes to Hyrcanus and his sons, which they paid to their forefathers').

These were obviously none other than the tithes ordained in the Pentateuch to be distributed among all the priests. It would have been senseless, then, for Julius Caesar to have ordered that all tithes be brought to Hyrcanus and his sons alone. Instead, he must have ordered these gifts to be brought to Jerusalem and deposited there, as had previously been the custom (in the days of their fathers) in the custody of the High Priest, the supervisor of the Temple treasury, for distribution among the priests.

This document informs us on the one hand what was proved at the outset, namely that till the time of Hyrcanus it was the practice to take up the tithes to Jerusalem; and on the other hand we learn from here that in the days of Hyrcanus they (at least many) ceased to bring the priestly gifts to the Temple treasury. Otherwise Caesar would not have explained in his order something that was the established practice from earliest times (just as the Syrian kings, Demetrius and Alexander Balas, did not explain the matter in their injunctions in favour of Jonathan the Hasmonean; see *I Maccabees*, x: 25–45; xi: 32–37; xviii–xxi).

When we look for the reason for the change, we cannot assume that it was due to disregard for the observance of the precept for separating the tithe that occurred just at that time. Undoubtedly a politico-communal factor brought this about.

It seems that on account of their opposition to the rule of Hyrcanus and Antipater and his sons many (of those who followed Aristobulus) refrained from bringing their gifts to the Temple treasury, which was under the authority of the High Priest Hyrcanus, for they did not recognize him as High Priest and were sure that he was not making distributions from 'his treasury' to the priests who opposed him. These, therefore, gave their heave-offerings and tithes to the priests not through the agency of the High Priest and outside Jerusalem.[17] Since, however, the dependence of the priests on the

O. Roth, *Rom u. die Hasmonaer*, 67; Graetz, *Geschichte*, 4th edition, III, revised by Baron, p. 667, note 1.

17 It is, however, very possible that the division of Eretz-Israel into five separate regions and the severance of the other four districts from Jerusalem by the setting up of special Sanhedrins in their chief cities, which Gabinius had put into effect in the days of Hyrcanus (in the year 56 — Josephus, *Ant.* xiv, 5, 4; *Wars* i, 8, 5) also contributed to the fact that the gifts were no longer brought up to Jerusalem as at first.

Temple treasury could serve as a decisive means in the power of Hyrcanus with which to suppress the hostile priests, he was anxious to restore the old system of bringing the tithe to Jerusalem and requested Julius Caesar to help him issuing an imperial decree.

We are unable to determine to what extent Hyrcanus succeeded in restoring the former arrangements for bringing the priestly dues. But although it may be presumed that many (comprising those who sympathized with Hyrcanus and the 'neutrals') never stopped bringing their heave-offerings and tithes to the Temple as usual, Hyrcanus did not succeed in fully reviving for his benefit the old order (for throughout his period of office the opposition to him did not cease). It stands to reason that since that time and on the basis of the change of custom in practice, the Halakha was revised, permitting the dues to be given to the priests also outside Jerusalem, and as usual this new Halakha remained valid even after the original reason for it no longer obtained. However, since the ancient Halakha and the custom of earlier generations (which never became completely nullified, as I noted above) regarded the bringing of tithe to Jerusalem as obligatory and permanent, the zealous made every endeavour, as far as possible, to bring the heave-offering and tithe to the Temple.

Support for the document in Josephus, cited above, is to be found in the following source, which, despite the differences between it and the document referred to corroborate the main facts.

In *T.P. Maʿaser Sheni* ch. v, end (*T.P. Soṭa* ix, 11) we read: 'R. Joshua b. Levi stated some of them [the enactments of Joḥanan the High Priest, i.e. John Hyrcanus] were blameworthy and some praiseworthy. For R. Jose said in the name of R. Tanḥum and R. Ḥiyya in the name of R. Joshua b. Levi (this is the reading in *Soṭa*): At first the tithe was divided into three parts, a third was given to friends among the priests and Levites,[18] a third to the Temple treasury, and

18 The 'friends among the priests and Levites' cannot be officers 'who performed some specific public task' and who alone received the tithe from the Temple treasury, as S. Lieberman (*Tarbiz*, III, p. 211) wishes to conjecture, for we do not hear that tithe was distributed from the treasure solely to appointed priests, nor is such a practice probable. Furthermore the word *makkarim* [rendered above, 'friends'] bears no connotation of officialdom. As for the observations of Hecataeus, cited in Josephus, *Against Apion*, on which Lieberman bases himself, Büchler already explained (*Die Priester und Cultus* etc.) that the number 1,500 refers to the priests of Jerusalem, and the 'friends of the priests and the Levites' referred to in our discussion are, it appears, only groups of priests and Levites organized on the basis of family relationship and simply means all the priests, since they were all organized in watches

a third to the poor and scholars [literally, 'Associates'] who were in Jerusalem... When Eleazar b. Paḥora and Judah b. Pekhira came and took them [the priestly gifts] by force, it was within his [the High Priest's] power to put a stop to this, but he did not; he also did away with the avowal concerning the (second) tithe — and this was blameworthy.'

The tradition in its present form is difficult. If the High Priest Joḥanan did away with the avowal concerning the tithe because Eleazar b. Paḥora etc. took the gifts by force and the command to give was thus not fulfilled, he was therefore opposed to their taking the tithes in this manner, and if, as the passage states, 'it was within his power to stop them', why did he not do so? Nor does it stand to reason that Joḥanan should allow the regular system to be abolished for the benefit of individuals and to the detriment of the public and of himself (for he thereby gave up control over the priests). According to the tradition, taken literally, it was not the abolition of the avowal that deserved censure (since the precept of giving was not fulfilled), but the fact that he did not put a stop to

and fathers' houses. It is impossible to interpret otherwise *T.P. Ma'aśer Sheni* v, 5, 56b (cf. *T.P. Demai* v, 9, 24d): 'And although you say tithe is not given to priests, you must admit that we do not take it [once given] away from them. What is the reason? Scripture declares "When ye take of the children of Israel the tithe" etc. — you take (it) away from Israelites, but you may not take (it) away from the *friends among the priests and Levites.*' Here it is clear that the whole tribe is meant. So, too, Onqelos translates Deut xviii 8: 'They shall eat like portions except the *watch* that comes on the Sabbath, for thus have the fathers instituted.' Thus he interprets ממכריו [JPS, new translation, 'patrimonies'] = 'from his watch' (apparently he read the singular [*mimkaro*]). The source of Onqelos' rendering is the Baraita in *Midrash Tannaim* on that verse (p. 109: 'Another interpretation is: לבד ממכריו etc. because they were sixteen etc. I might have thought if they wished to change, they could, therefore Scripture teaches לבד ממכריו על האבות — except for what the fathers instituted.' Thus the Baraita understands מכריו in the sense of 'watches'). Similarly the Vulgate translates מכר in II Kings xii 6 and 8 by *Ordo*, and we have already found that this translation renders the word משמר ['watch'] (Neh. xii 24) by *Ordo*. However מכרי כהונה ולויה in the Babylonian Talmud (*T.B. Giṭṭin* 30a; *T.B. Bava Batra* 123b; *T.B. Ḥullin* 133a; cf. *T.B. 'Arakhin* 6a) means 'friends of the priests and Levites from among Israelites' (there it is based on the verses II Kings xii 6; xviii 9). This may also be the sense in *T.P. Giṭṭin* iii, 7, 44a. But *T.P. Bikkurim* iii, 2, 65c — 'like Jehoiarib ומכיריו etc. it is possible to explain the term here as, namely the watch of Jehoiarib and his fathers' houses (who came up with the Israelites and Levites of their district to Jerusalem).

the practice; yet the Mishna speaks of doing away with the avowal in respect of the tithe.

It seems, therefore, that essentially the tradition was as follows: Eleazar b. Paḥora is certainly none other than Eleazar b. Poʿira, who is mentioned in the Baraita in *T.B. Qiddushin* 66a.[19] Now in this Baraita Eleazar is an enemy of the Pharisees and it is he who instigates Jannai to fight against them. But according to Josephus (*Ant.* xiii, 10, 5) Eleazar was a Pharisee and he was the one who said to Joḥanan (instead of the 'Elder' Judah b. Gedidia of the aforementioned Baraita) 'Be content with the royal crown' etc. This tradition, which is basically to be found in the Palestinian Talmud, apparently adopts Josephus' version of the story. Eleazar b. Paḥora was, therefore, an opponent of Joḥanan, who at the end of his life became a Sadducee, and consequently neither he, nor his fellow priests who shared his views, received their portions from the Temple treasury and so they made their way to the farmers and took the tithes without Joḥanan's permission,[20] and these farmers, who had already distributed their tithes to Joḥanan's opponents, ceased to bring the tithe to the treasury (as we learn from the edict of Julius Caesar). Hence the High Priest Joḥanan enacted that these farmers should not be permitted to make the avowal in the Sanctuary. Without doubt he ruled, in accordance with the ancient Halakha, that tithe could only be given at Jerusalem and to the treasury. Since, however, the new — the current — Halakha allowed the tithe to be distributed even outside Jerusalem, the abolition of the avowal constituted an annulment of a Torah precept, and consequently the Sages condemned it.[21]

However, Joḥanan's ruling was for his own benefit. For primarily this enactment — the prevention of saying the avowal — had as its

19 Cf. Graetz, *op. cit.*, 3rd ed., note 9.

20 ונטלו אותן בזרוע [literally, 'and took them with the arm'; rendered in the text 'and took them by force'] simply means that they took their dues defiantly (i.e. as rebels against Joḥanan). The word בזרוע ['with the arm'] does not necessarily denote violence. Thus we read in *T.B. Berakhot* 17b: 'The whole world is sustained by charity, whereas they are sustained בזרוע', which means: by justice and by their own merit and not by grace and charity. This, too, is the connotation of ישראל בעלי זרוע [literally 'Israelites possessing an arm', i.e. having power] in *T.P. Nedarim* iii, 4–5, 38a (q.v.), namely they are upright [have moral force].

21 The stereotyped expression 'it was within his power to stop them from doing so, but he did not' derives from another source, and is not an original part of this tradition.

purpose the suppression of his opponents and served as a means to restore to himself the supervision and control over the economic sources of the maintenance of the priests.

But Joḥanan did not content himself with this means alone. He also installed 'Pairs' (*T.P. loc. cit.*), that is, he appointed officers to supervise the separation of tithes and their transportation to Jerusalem (for a state is not interested in appointing officers for the benefit of individuals, so that they should acquire, without having to give account and without advantage to the community, gifts of grain and fruit). For this reason 'in his days there was no need to enquire about *demai*' [produce about which there was a doubt as to the tithes having been properly taken] (*M. Soṭa* ix, 10), for he had forced the farmers to separate the tithes and to hand them over to him.

We thus find in the Palestinian Talmud a tradition that corroborates the main content of the imperial document cited by Josephus (irrespective of the merits of our interpretation of the passage in the Palestinian Talmud, it is at any rate evident from this tradition that in the reign of the High Priest Joḥanan the system of bringing the tithe to the treasury and distributing it proportionately was impaired),[22] but the sources are divided in regard to the date of the event. The edict of Julius Caesar implies that it took place in the days of Hyrcanus (II), but according to the tradition of the Palestinian Talmud in the time of the High Priest Joḥanan (Hyrcanus I). However, if we examine this type of interchange, which is found in Talmudic literature in historical traditions, we shall not be surprised at the possibility that Hyrcanus I was substituted for Hyrcanus II. (Such an interchange, apparently, occurs also in the tradition recorded in *T.B. Sanhedrin* 19a–b. The incident took place, according to this tradition, in the reign of King Jannai. But Josephus, *Ant.* xiv, 9, 5, states that it happened in the days of Hyrcanus. It seems, therefore, that Hyrcanus II was replaced by Hyrcanus I, that is, by the High

22 It is also possible to interpret the passage in the Palestinian Talmud as follows: Eleazar b. Paḥora, who is to be identified with Eleazar b. Po'ira of the Baraita in *T.B. Qiddushin* 66a, was a Sadducee, as is stated in this Baraita, and he and his associates used to take possession of all the tithe with the consent of Joḥanan (this is the meaning of the expression 'it was within his power to stop them from doing so, but he did not'), for they were his familiars and supporters. The farmers, however, who were opposed to Joḥanan refrained from bringing their tithes to the Temple and gave them instead to the priests who, because of their antagonism to the rule of Joḥanan and his faction, did not receive their portions from the treasury. Hence Joḥanan prevented them from making the avowal in the Temple, as explained in the text.

Priest Joḥanan, and the Talmud actually declares — *T.B. Berakhot* 29a — that Jannai and Joḥanan are identical.)

Although the internal political situation in Judea in the time of the High Priest Joḥanan makes it possible for the occurrence of such an event (note the conflict between him and the Pharisees at the end of his days), the haggadic tradition in the Palestinian Talmud is not to be preferred to the source cited in Josephus.

We thus learn that according to the ancient Halakha, which remained entirely valid until the beginning of Hyrcanus' time (the end of the sixties B.C.E.), the priestly dues used to be brought to the Temple treasury (as Philo states). From then onward the ancient custom declined and in the course of time a new Halakha arose permitting the distribution of heave-offering and tithe to individuals and outside of Jerusalem, exactly as the owners wished. Hyrcanus, however, endeavoured to restore the earlier practice. Although he was not entirely successful, there were many in his days and after him who acted according to the Halakha of the earlier generations and used to bring their tithes from within Eretz-Israel and from outside its borders to Jerusalem. Thus Philo referred in his statement to the custom followed by many in his days (Philo visited Jerusalem and the Temple and undoubtedly wrote as he did from actual observations; his book *De Spec. Legibus* was composed after he had been to Eretz-Israel), retaining, as he does in other places, the ancient Halakha, which had not yet been entirely ousted by the new Halakha.[23]

II

When Philo describes the procedure with regard to giving the *Soṭa* [the wife suspected of unfaithfulness (see Num. v: 12 ff.)] the bitter waters to drink (*De Spec. Leg.* III, 52–63) he states that the husband must write out his charge (πρόκλησις) and go up with his wife to

23 According to the ancient Halakha, which permits heave-offerings and tithes to be given only in Jerusalem, it is manifest that the precept of heave-offering and tithe was no longer in force after the Destruction. Indeed this is what we learn in the Baraita in *T.P. Sheqalim* viii, 6 (end), 51b: 'For it is taught: We may not consecrate anything, or vow a valuation [Lev. xxvii 3]... or separate heave-offerings and tithes nowadays' etc. Although the recension of the Baraita in the Babylonian Talmud (*T.B. Yoma* 66a; *T.B. Bekhorot* 53a; *T.B. 'Avoda Zara* 13a) does not read 'or separate heave-offerings and tithes', which accords with the Halakha in the Mishna (*M. Sheqalim* viii, 8), yet the Baraita in the Palestinian Talmud is in agreement with the ancient Halakha and gives expression to it.

Jerusalem and stand with her before the judges and put his case against her at the court. In stating his case, however, he must not act as a prosecutor or malicious person who seeks to win (his case) by any means, but he must desire the truth to be revealed. The woman, if she is clean, should defend herself, and if not should confess. If the statements (of the husband and the wife) are of equal weight and there is no means of deciding in favour of one, they must go to the Temple and stand before the priest, who, after the husband has disclosed to him the suspicion he entertains with regard to his wife, and after he [the priest] has brought her meal offering, gives the woman to drink the water of a *Soṭa.*

Philo's account, which is undoubtedly a tradition as well as a fixed Halakha that he knew, is fundamentally similar to the Halakha in the Mishna (*M. Soṭa* i, 4), but differs from it in two respects: a) According to our Mishna the husband must first have recourse to the court in his town (*ibid.* i, 3), while Philo holds that the case is first instituted in Jerusalem; b) according to the Mishna the High Court is only required to prevent the blotting out of the Divine Name by admonishing the woman to confess, but in Philo's view the Jerusalem court has to determine at the outset whether there is any guilt of whoredom (and apparently also to give a verdict of innocence or guilt). Only if the court is unable to decide, the woman is taken to the Temple and given the drink.[24]

These divergences in the Halakha according to Philo can be explained simply by the postulate that capital cases are everywhere brought before the High Court at Jerusalem.[25]

24 The 'discrepancies' that Heinemann enumerates in his German translation of *De Spec. Leg.*, p. 199, n. 2, and in his work *Philons Griechische u. Jüdische Bildung*, 23–24, are non-existent, since it is not Philo's practice in this treatise to enter on all occasions into the details of the Halakha. The very nature of the book, which summarizes the precepts of the Torah and arranges them as detailed laws emanating from the Decalogue, which comprises them, does not allow the author to elaborate each precept, just as it prevents him from including in his work a number of laws that are expressly mentioned in the Torah, but could not be incorporated into this framework (e.g. the regulations concerning forbidden foods).

25 The court at Jerusalem, which according to Philo is composed of priests, does not merely serve, he states, to decide the doubtful cases brought before it from the provincial courts (*De Spec. Leg.* iv, 190–91; his observations here correspond to the halakhic rulings in *M. Sanhedrin* xi, 2; *Tosefta, ibid.*, vii, 1 and the parallels, and are not far different from Josephus' statement, *Ant.* iv, 8, 14), but also deals with cases from the outset, especially, it appears, with capital cases. For he states (*op. cit.*, III, 131–139), when he comes

Now the Philonic tradition is contrary to the prevailing Halakha, which prescribes that capital cases should be tried in the Small Sanhedrins consisting of twenty-three judges.[26] However, it appears that in practice capital cases, in the period of the Second Temple, were judged at the Great Sanhedrin only.[27]

In *Wars* iv, 5, 4 Josephus relates that the Zealots appointed a court of seventy to try Zechariah son of Baruch. The Zealots would certainly not have taken the trouble to set up a high court if it had been customary to try capital cases before twenty-three judges, for they wished Zechariah to be put to death and even slew him after he had been found not guilty. This shows that capital cases were always tried by a court of seventy only.

This is also proved by the fact that Josephus established in Tiberias a court of seventy elders, which had jurisdiction over the whole of

to explain the reason for the commandment in the Torah that the homicide exiled to a city of refuge must remain there until the death of the High Priest, for the latter (who according to Philo stood at the head of the Sanhedrin in Jerusalem and to whom he undoubtedly referred when speaking *ibid.* of ὁ τῶν ἱερῶν ἔξαρχος) was in the position of a general blood-redeemer, since he tried the antagonists according to the Torah law and judged the living and the dead (his remarks resemble those of Josephus, *Against Apion* ii, 23). In *De Vita Mosis* (i, 214), when recounting the story of the man who gathered sticks on the Sabbath and was put to death, he states that they brought him to the ἄρχων (Moses) and to the priests, who sat with him in judgement, and to the congregation, who were (only) listening. In the Pentateuch (and in the Septuagint) it is said (Num. xv 33): 'unto Moses and Aaron, and unto all the congregation'. Philo, however, depicts the trial of the stick-gatherer after the manner of capital cases in the era of the Second Temple, which were tried in the High Court, whose members were priests (according to his view), headed by the High Priest. Hence Philo was careful to exclude the congregation from active participation in the trial and introduced the priests (in lieu of Aaron in the Bible) for the composition of this court, over which Moses presided (in Philo's opinion, he was High Priest; see *De Vita Mosis* ii, 21, *et al.* Cf. on this subject the passage in *T.B. Zevaḥim* 101b–102a and in *T.B. Ta'anit* 12a). When he observes in connection with the law of 'one who brings an evil name' [see Deut. xxii 13 ff.] (*op. cit.*, iii, 80) ἀθροιζέσθω μὲν ἡ γερουσία πᾶσα, he may be referring either to the court at Alexandria (so Goodenough, *The Jurisprudence* etc., 249), or — and this seems more probable — to the High Court at Jerusalem.

26 *M. Sanhedrin* i, 4 and 6; xi, 1; *Tosefta Sanhedrin* iii, 9 (*T.B. Sanhedrin* 17b; *T.P. ibid.* i, 19c); *ibid.* xi, 7; *ibid. Horayot* i, 4; *Sifra*, 'Emōr (end); *Sifre Num.* §160; *Sifre Deut.* §144 (*Midrash Tannaim*, p. 67). The Halakha stated in the name of אנשי המשוחות ['the surveyors'] (*Sifre Num.*, *loc. cit.*) that capital cases require thirty judges is unique.

27 See Juster, *Les Juifs dans l'Empire Romain*, II, 128, n. 2.

Galilee, and ordered that there should be brought before him, as head of the Sanhedrin, and before the aforementioned court, the 'greater cases' and those wherein life and death were concerned (*ibid.* ii, 20, 5). This Sanhedrin appointed by Josephus in Tiberias teaches us implicitly about the Great Sanhedrin at Jerusalem: just as this court alone (and not the courts of seven judges that he set up in the cities of Galilee) dealt with capital cases, so the High Court at Jerusalem was solely empowered to judge cases involving capital punishment.

This may also be inferred from the story that Josephus relates (*Ant.* xiv, 9, 3; but cf. *Wars* i, 10, 6) about the chief men of Jerusalem who came before Hyrcanus and complained before him that Herod had slain Hezekiah and his associates, declaring that Herod had transgressed the law of the Torah, which forbids the execution unless his sentence had been decided by the Sanhedrin; thus we learn from here, too, that capital cases were tried only by the Jerusalem Sanhedrin. For 'Sanhedrin' referred to in this narrative was undoubtedly the Great Sanhedrin, this being the meaning of the term in the paragraph in question, in the continuation of the story (paragraph 4), and *throughout* Josephus.

'An argument from silence' in support of this thesis is to be found in the fact that all the episodes known to us in which capital cases were tried in Eretz-Israel[28] (with the exception of those executed by the state under Herod) and whose location is known to us, occurred in *Jerusalem.* Herod had to stand trial before the Sanhedrin in Jerusalem (Josephus, *loc. cit.*). Zechariah b. Baruch was tried by a court of seventy. Jesus was tried in Jerusalem; and likewise his brother James and his companions (*Ant.* xx, 9, 1). Paul stood trial before the High Priest and the Sanhedrin at Jerusalem (*The Acts* xxii 30; xxiii 1). The apostles that were put in prison by the High Priest (*ibid.* v, 17) were brought before the Great Sanhedrin (*ibid.*

28 The father and son who were stoned by the Bet Din in Egypt (*T.B. Giṭṭin* 57a) may have been tried (if the incident is historical) by a court of seventy at Alexandria (cf. on the question of the authority of the Alexandrian Bet Din to adjudicate in capital cases, Fucks, *Die Juden Aegyptens*, 91 and Goodenough, *op. cit.*, p. 156, and n. 7, and Heinemann, *Philons Griechische u. Jüdische Bildung*, p. 80. Immarta the daughter of Tali who was burnt by Rav Ḥama bar Tobiah was apparently sentenced by the Exilarch of Babylonia. As regards the story of Susanna, which took place in Babylonia, the narrative seems to lack historical foundation. At all events the author set the episode in Babylonia because he wished to link it to Daniel. Cf. Juster, *op. cit.*, p. 158, n. 1.

vv. 27 ff.). Stephen, too, was tried at the High Court in Jerusalem (*ibid.* vi 12). The case of the priest's daughter who committed adultery and was encompassed with bundles of branches and burnt, to which R. Eliezer b. Zadok testified as an eyewitness who saw the incident in his childhood, undoubtedly took place in Jerusalem (*M. Sanhedrin* vii, 2; *Tosefta ibid.* ix, 11; *T.B. ibid.* 52b; *T.P. ibid.* 24b).[29] The episode in which Judah b. Tabbai (or Simeon b. Sheṭaḥ) executed a *zōmēm* witness [a false witness subject to the law of retaliation; cf. Deuteronomy xix 19] (*Tosefta Sanhedrin* vi, 6; *Midrash Tannaim*, p. 117; *T.B. Makkot* 5b; *T.P. Sanhedrin* vi, 23b; *Mekhilta*, Mishpāṭîm, xx. Cf. *Mekhilta*, ed. Horovitz, p. 327, n. 11) also occurred apparently in Jerusalem.[30] And, so too, the incident when Ben Zakkai (= R. Joḥanan b. Zakkai) cross-examined witnesses about the twigs of figs (*M. Sanhedrin* v, 2). Similarly R. Judah b. Bava testified that a cock was stoned in Jerusalem (*M. ʿEduyot* vi, 1). R. Simeon b. Pazzi reported in the name of R. Joshua b. Levi, who said in the name of Bar Qappara that once a woman came to Jerusalem with a child sitting on her shoulder, and when she had reared him, he had intercourse with her, and they were brought before the court and stoned (*T.B. Qiddushin* 80a). Also the Baraita (*T.B. Sanhedrin* 43a), which tells of the noble women of Jerusalem who brought them as a gift, speaks apparently of the drinks given to those who were executed by the High Court in Jerusalem. Furthermore the wording of the Baraita shows that the wine and frankincense were provided by the women of Jerusalem to *all* who were executed by the court. Now it is difficult to suppose that the Jerusalem women brought wine and frankincense to those who were sentenced in remote parts of the country so that they might drink when going forth to execution.[31]

On the basis of our premise that in the era of the Second Temple capital cases were tried in practice by the Great Sanhedrin, we are

29 In the Tosefta 'in Jerusalem' is expressly mentioned. However, in the Baraita in the Babylonian Talmud and in the Palestinian Talmud (so, too, in Zuckermandel) the words 'in Jerusalem' are missing. But R. Eliezer b. Zadok and his father were of the priests of Jerusalem.

30 Judah b. Tabbai (or Simeon b. Sheṭaḥ) was the Patriarch and in this capacity he ordered the execution of the *zomem* witness in contradiction of the view of the Sadducees. At all events his seat was in Jerusalem.

31 I hope, on another occasion, to elucidate the incident of the eighty women in Ashkelon who were hanged by Simeon b. Sheṭaḥ (*M. Sanhedrin* vi, 4), and the case of the stoning of Ben Saṭda at Lydda (*Tosefta Sanhedrin* x, 11).

able to elucidate a number of dicta in both Halakha and Haggada, which according to the prevailing tradition can be explained with difficulty only.

In *Mekhilta*, Massekhta di-Nĕzîqîn, iv (end) (*Mekhilta de-R. Simeon b. Yoḥai*, p. 126) we learn: ' "Thou shalt take him from Mine altar, that he may die" — from this we learn that the Sanhedrin sat beside the altar' etc. It is difficult to explain this halakhic interpretation according to the tradition that states that capital cases are tried by the Small Sanhedrins sitting in the provincial towns. But if we assume that capital cases are tried only by the High Court at Jerusalem, which sat in the Temple, the Midrash can be understood literally. Likewise the Halakha that cases involving capital punishment can be tried only when the Sanhedrin is seated in its place in the Temple (even when the Temple existed. *Mekhilta de-R. Simeon b. Yoḥai, loc. cit.*; *Sifre Zuṭa*, p. 334; *T.B. 'Avoda Zara* 8b), for the place is a vital factor (*T.B. 'Avoda Zara, ibid.*), can be explained quite simply by the premise that capital cases can be dealt with only by the Great Sanhedrin. In *T.B. Sanhedrin* 42b we learn in a Baraita: 'The place of stoning was outside the three camps'; and *ibid.* further on it is stated: 'The Rabbis have taught: "Bring forth him that hath cursed without the camp" — without the three camps' (cf., however, with reference to the second Baraita *Sifra*, 'Ĕmōr, xix, and *T.P. Ketubbot* iv, 28c). The Baraitot, in speaking of capital punishment, refer to the court at Jerusalem quite as a matter of fact (cf. Rashi and Tosafot *ad loc.*). In *Pesiqta Rabbati*, Kî Tiśśā (ed. Friedmann, 34a) it is stated: ' "Thy navel" — this means the Great Sanhedrin that used to try capital cases in Jerusalem'. That capital cases were primarily tried only at the High Court is implied also in the halakhic exposition in *Sifre*, Shōfĕṭîm, §144: ' "In all thy gates" — Scripture comes to compare the Small Sanhedrin to the Great Sanhedrin: just as the Great Sanhedrin tries (the accused) and executes so the Small Sanhedrin may try and execute'.[32]

We thus learn that in the period of the Second Temple capital cases were judged only at the High Court in Jerusalem.[33]

32 In *Midrash Tannaim* the teaching is cited in the name of R. Josiah.

33 On the basis of this premise it is possible to explain, without difficulty, the Halakhot that require the participation of the High Court in the rite of the heifer whose neck is broken (*M. Soṭa* ix, 1; *Tosefta ibid.*, ix, 1; *Sifre Deut.* §26; *Midrash Tannaim*, p. 123) and in the case of *Soṭa* (*M. Soṭa* i, 4). As far as the heifer whose neck was broken is concerned, the Halakha may also be explained in the light of the fact that they went forth to measure

It should not surprise us that a number of sections of the Torah testify to the fact that capital cases were judged in various places, for a distinction must be drawn between the Biblical era and that of the Second Temple. In the period of the First Temple the provincial cities guarded their ancient rights and Jerusalem had not yet prevailed even over the separatism obtaining in the cult, whereas in the age of the Second Temple Jerusalem served from the outset as the heart of the nation and the settlement was formed from the beginning in unity and centralization. It is also possible that the general tendency of the Halakha to be lenient in capital cases helped to remove from 'the elders of the congregation' in the provincial

between the towns and it stands to reason that the High Court of Jerusalem would be required for this, since it stood above the city courts. Büchler, *Das Grosse Synhedrium usw.*, pp. 49–52, sought to give a rather forced explanation of this Halakha by pointing to the 'cultic' element in the heifer ceremony. But it appears that the Halakha of R. Eliezer b. Jacob, which requires that the king should also accompany the High Court to perform the measurement, underscores the legal basis of this ruling. It is particularly difficult to accept Büchler's interpretation (*ibid.*) with reference to the drink given to the *Soṭa*, namely, that it was the cultic element in the ordeal that required the participation of the Great Sanhedrin. If, however, we shall explain the Mishnaic tradition to mean that the High Court was required not only to admonish (as it appears at first blush), but also to investigate and decide, and that the husband's attendance at the court of his city is only a preliminary procedure, we shall have a Halakha identical with Philo's and we can interpret it likewise as a tradition attesting the practice of trying capital cases at Jerusalem. Indeed Büchler has already noted (*op. cit.*, p. 50) that according to the *Sifre* (*Numbers* §12) the words (of admonition) that the Mishna (*M. Soṭa* i, 7) ordains to be said to the woman at the High Court, were spoken by the priest who gave the *Soṭa* the drink. Possibly this is also to be deduced from the *Tosefta* (*Soṭa* i, 4–6), which places the Halakha concerning the admonition given to the woman after the Halakha that she is to be taken up to the Gate of Nicanor (which is not the order of the Mishna, *Soṭa* i, 4–5). It should also be pointed out that in dealing with the laws of the *Soṭa* (*Ant.* iii, 11, 6), Josephus does not mention that the woman has to be taken up to the High Court, and that in *M. Sanhedrin* (i, 5) the giving of the drink to the *Soṭa* is not included in the number of things that require a court of seventy (however, the elder that rebels against the decision of the court is also not mentioned there; cf. 'Tosafot of Sens' on *T.B. Soṭa* 7a). But it is possible (if we wish to avoid the assumption that we have before us two conflicting traditions) to reconcile this contradiction by supposing that the priest also sought to persuade the woman to retract. This may also be inferred to some extent from Philo (who states that the husband again discloses his suspicion against his wife to the priest). As regards Josephus, it should be noted that in that chapter he speaks only of *sacrifices* and *puri-*

cities the authority to sentence a man to death. There is no branch of Torah legislation into which the Halakha has introduced so many innovations as to uproot, in practise, the Biblical ordinances as the laws of capital punishment.

It is also possible that the Halakha in the Mishna (*Sanhedrin* i, 4) — that capital cases must be tried by twenty-three judges — did not basically refer to Small Sanhedrins sitting in the provinces, but to the number of the judges who had to try the case and who had to be members of the High Court in Jerusalem. This perforce is the way we have to interpret the Halakha (*ibid.* Mishna 3) that requires the laying on of the hands by the elders [see Leviticus iv 15; *aliter* it refers to ordination of a Sage] and the breaking of the heifer's neck [see Deuteronomy xxi 1 ff.] to be performed by three who were members of the Great Sanhedrin. Similarly the Halakha concerning the intercalation of the month and the intercalation of the year (*ibid.* Mishna 2), which were effected by three (or seven) judges certainly refers to members of the High Court in Jerusalem, since the sanctification of the new moon and the intercalation of the year fell within the jurisdiction of the High Court (after the Destruction these functions were carried out by the Patriarch and his Bet Din).[34]

Support for the view that these twenty-three judges, who tried capital cases, were only part of the court of seventy is to be found in the law concerning the supplementation of the court of twenty-three, when opinion is (almost) equally divided or one of the judges declares 'I do not know' (*M. Sanhedrin* v, 5), which ordained that the number of judges may be increased [two at a time] till seventy (-one).[35] This Halakha can be easily understood on the supposition that the court of twenty-three was only a part of the High Court,

fications (as he phrases it *ibid.* iii, 9, 1) and he mentioned in regard to the *Soṭa* only what is relevant to the subject of the sacrifice).

34 On the basis of this assumption that the court of twenty-three consisted only of members of the High Court it is possible to understand the Halakha of 'the surveyors' (*Sifre Deuteronomy* §144) that capital cases required thirty judges. For it is difficult to suppose that 'the surveyors' come to testify that the permanent Small Sanhedrins in the provinces were comprised of thirty members. But if the Halakha refers only to the minimal number of the members of the High Court who participate in capital cases, it is not surprising that there were some who required at least thirty judges.

35 With this should be compared the Halakha in the *Tosefta* viii, 1 (*T.P. ibid.* i, 19c; *T.B. ibid.* 37a): if one of them (of the judges of the High Court) had need to leave the court, we must see if there are twenty-three left, then he may leave, otherwise he may not.

and hence was increased, in the circumstances mentioned, until its original and basic composition — to the total of seventy.[36]

If we accept the plausible conjecture of Derenbourg (*Maśśa' Ereṣ Yiśra'el*, III) that the High Court of Jerusalem was composed of three courts that sat, respectively, at the entrance to the Temple Mount, at the entrance to the Temple Court, and in the Chamber of Hewn Stone (*M. Sanhedrin* xi, 2; *Tosefta ibid.* vii, 1; *Tosefta Ḥagiga* ii, 9; *T.B. Sanhedrin* 88b; *T.P. ibid.* i, 19c),[37] that is to say, that the two courts of twenty-three judges that sat at the entrance of the Temple Mount and the entrance to the Temple Court were only sections of the Great Sanhedrin, then capital cases were dealt with by one of these permanent courts.[38]

When we wish to explain, in the light of what we have elucidated, the Halakha that places capital cases in the hands of the Small Sanhedrins of the provinces, we must regard it as a theoretical Halakha, which could not displace express Torah ordinances. Since the Jews were deprived of the right to judge capital cases some considerable time before the Destruction, the theoretical Halakha did not en-

36 Maimonides ('Hilkhot-Sanhedrin', viii, 2) rules that even in civil cases we continue to add until the number seventy-one is reached. But the Mishna (*Sanhedrin* iii, 6) merely states in monetary cases that the number of judges is increased, but it does not say to seventy-one, as it explains elaborately with regard to capital cases (*ibid.* v, 5). The RAbaD [R. Abraham b. David of Posquières] in his Haśśagot [critical notes] *ad loc.* writes (according to the amended version of *Migdal 'Oz* [Shem Ṭov ibn Gaon]): 'but the number (of judges) in civil cases does not reach seventy-one. Me'iri likewise states 'There are some who disagree and say that this (rule) applies only in capital cases, but in civil suits if any judge says "I do not know", he is removed and another put in his place'. Although the *Tosefta* (*Sanhedrin* vi, 3–4) speaks of adding two (cf. RABaD *loc. cit.*), it nevertheless does not fix a limit of seventy-one. According to my explanation of the underlying reason of the Halakha in the text it appears that in civil cases there is no law of supplementation to seventy-one. Cf. the statement of R. Osha'ia in *T.P.* iii, 21d (and the commentary of RaDBaZ [R. David b. Solomon ibn Abi Zimra] *ad loc.*).

37 In *T.B. ibid.* the reading is 'and two courts of twenty-three, one sitting at the entrance to the Temple Mount' etc. But in the *Tosefta* and *T.P.* the reading is: 'and two courts of three each' etc. But it is difficult, in the light of the Mishna (*ibid.*), to accept the text 'three each' as correct.

38 At all events the trial of Zechariah shows that they were accustomed to judge capital cases only before a full complement of judges of the High Court; and the Halakha merely speaks of the possibility of having twenty-three judges in given circumstances.

counter, in the generations after the Destruction, a conflicting actuality and was not compelled to disappear because of it.[39]

The tradition regarding the giving of the drink to the *Soṭa* reported by Philo thus reflects the practice that obtained among Jews in the era of the Second Temple as a practical Halakha.

Addendum

It seems that the assumption that capital cases were tried only in Jerusalem can also be proved from our Mishna. For we have learned in the Mishna (*Qiddushin* iv, 5): 'There is no need to trace descent beyond the altar, or beyond the platform [where the Levites sang in the Temple], or beyond the Sanhedrin (however, the words 'or beyond the Sanhedrin' are wanting in the Mishna of *T.P.*); and all whose fathers are known to have held office as public officers or almoners may marry into the priestly stock and there is no need to trace their descent,' because it seems that the Mishna referred to the Great Sanhedrin only (the sense that the term has in Josephus); for the Baraita of Levi testifies that our Mishna speaks only of Jerusalem, and so, too, does Abbaye (*T.B. Qiddushin* 76b). Even if the Baraita and Abbaye refer only to the words 'and all whose fathers are known' etc., nevertheless since the sentence preceding the clause 'or beyond the Sanhedrin' (i.e. 'There is no need to trace descent beyond the altar, or beyond the platform') and that after it ('and all whose fathers are known' etc.) speak of Jerusalem, undoubtedly this clause, too, refers only to the Great Sanhedrin (cf. the commentary of R. Obadiah of Bertinoro and the criticism of 'Tosafot Yom Ṭov' [Additional Comments of Yom Tov Lipmann Heller] *ad loc.* Note also the clause 'Israelites who may marry into priestly stock' alongside the *Great Sanhedrin* in *Tosefta Sanhedrin* iv, 7, and the parallel sources in *T.P. ibid.* ii, 20c, and *Midrash Tannaim*, p. 105).

However, the Halakha in *M. Sanhedrin* iv, 2 (cf. *M. Nidda* vi, 4) states: 'But not all are qualified to try capital cases — only priests and Levites and Israelites who may give (their daughters) in marriage to priests.' If so, whoever was a judge in a court of twenty-three should be exempt from genealogical investigation. But according to

39 The courts of twenty-three, which sat apparently in the provincial towns, also dealt — apart from its jurisdiction over all other matters such as public affairs, religion, lawsuits (except capital cases) — with scourging (according to the view of R. Ishmael in *M. Sanhedrin* i, 2). This is also evidenced by Matthew x 17 (q.v.).

our hypothesis the Mishna in *Qiddushin* can easily be understood, since capital cases were tried only by the Sanhedrin in Jerusalem.

III

After Philo has set forth the teachings of the Torah that grant proselytes the same rights as the homeborn and enjoin that they should be loved and forbid their gods to be blasphemed[40] (*De Spec. Leg.* I, 51–53), he declares (*ibid.* 54–55):

> But if any members of the [Jewish] nation betray the honour due to the One [God], they should suffer the utmost penalties. They have abandoned their most vital duty, their service in the ranks of piety and religion, have chosen darkness in preference to the brightest light and blindfolded the mind which had the power of keen vision. And it is well that all who have a zeal for virtue should be permitted to exact the penalties [from the transgressors] offhand before jury or council or any [other] kind of magistrate at all, and give full scope to the feelings which possess them, that hatred of evil and love of God which urges them to inflict punishment without mercy on the impious. They [who punish] should think that the occasion has made them councillors, jurymen, high sheriffs, members of assembly, accusers, witnesses, laws, people, everything in fact, so that without fear or hindrance they may champion religion in full security.

40 In Philo's view (here and in *De Vita Mosis* II, 26) the Torah enjoins not to blaspheme the gods of the Gentiles and he interprets accordingly the verses in Exodus xii 27 (his interpretation fits the Septuagint version) and Leviticus xxiv 15. This is also the opinion of Josephus (*Ant.* iv, 207 and *Against Apion* II, 237). It appears that this Halakha was current in the Hellenistic Diaspora and flowed from the prevailing circumstances of Jewish life among the Gentile nations. This fact is emphasized by the reason Philo gives for this precept, namely to obviate the danger of Gentiles' retaliating with blasphemies against the true God and thus the name of Heaven would be desecrated (the point is especially stressed in Philo's work *Quaestiones in Exodum* on Exodus xxii 27, in the passage where he adds another reason for the prohibition, to wit, for the sake of peace, to prevent dissensions between the peoples — *nobis autem ut pulcherrimam possessionem nunciavit lex fontem pacis* ('The Law commanded us the fountain of peace as the most precious possession'). However, in *De Vita Mosis* Philo gives the following reason for the prohibition: Lest the 'disciples of Moses' get into the habit of treating lightly the name 'god' and come to commit an offence). If we examine closely Josephus' statement in *Against Apion*, we shall find that his explanation of the Halakha is similar to that of Philo (cf. *Me'or ʿEnayim*, *'Imre Bina*, viii).

Philo adjoins to this subject the story of Phinehas (*ibid.* 56–57). The execution of the transgressor by zealots we find in Philo not only in the case of an idolater but also in that of a sorcerer.[41] For he states (*ibid.* III, 94): 'Therefore the Torah ordains that sorcerers and witches (here in the sense of poisoners who seek to kill) should not be allowed to live a single day, but should be slain as soon as they are detected, since no reason can be given for delay or for postponing their punishment.' Further on (*ibid.* 96) he observes: 'And therefore it is right that even the most reasonable and mild-tempered should seek the blood of such as these...and should hold it a religious duty to keep their punishment [i.e. of the transgressors] in their own hands and not commit it to others.' In § 102 he declares: 'All these things (enumerated earlier, § 94–101) our lawgiver had in view, I believe, when he prohibited any postponement in bringing poisoners (here he also refers to *sorcerers*) to justice and ordained that the punishment should be exacted at once.'[42]

41 Philo understands the word מכשף (Deut. xviii 10) and מכשפה (Exod. xxii 17) both as a poisoner and as a sorcerer (like the twofold meaning of the word φαρμακεύς in the Septuagint), while Josephus (*Ant.* iv, 279) comprehends it in the first sense only. Although Philo's observations about sorcerers do not specifically mention lynching, nevertheless it cannot be doubted that his remarks in this respect have to be understood in the same way as his statements about poisoners. Also the fact that he places the laws of the sorcerer in juxtaposition to those of the poisoner (although this is not their correct place, for he treats in that section of the laws of murder, in connection with the commandment 'Thou shalt not kill') supports this assumption. Apparently Philo knew a Halakhic tradition that did not require the execution of the מכשף to be carried out by the court, and he attributed the Halakha to all the senses comprised by the term מכשף. This being the case, this Halakha of Philo's is not to be limited by the influence of the Greek and Roman law (Heinemann, *Philons usw.* 387; Goodenough, Jewish Courts, 109).

42 Goodenough's statement that Philo posits lynch law for a man who commits adultery (*ibid.* 79), for one who is guilty of sodomy or of bestiality (*ibid.* 87. Goodenough quotes Philo here incorrectly; see *ibid.*), for a harlot (*ibid.* 88), for one who strikes his father, for one who causes an abortion, or murders his slave is improbable (see Heinemann, *op. cit.*, 224). His proof from the woman taken in adultery mentioned in John viii 1–11 is not relevant to our theme, (a) because in several recensions this story is entirely wanting; (b) there is no real evidence that they wished to kill the woman who had committed adultery without a court decision (that apart, this account is not reliable, for it has a fictitious air). However, in the case of one who swears falsely by the name of the Lord, Philo (*De Legibus*, II, 252–253) appears to permit zealots to assault him. But even in this instance there is no proof that this was his intent; for possibly he had only execution by the court in mind. Furthermore

These observations of Philo are contrary to the Halakha that ordains that idolaters and poisoners-sorcerers [מכשפים] must be tried by a court like other transgressors (*M. Sanhedrin* vii, 4); but since Philo bases himself on the episode of Phinehas and states elsewhere[43] that the Levites were vouchsafed the priesthood because they slew the makers of the calf, hence Heinemann is of opinion that Philo conjoined these incidents (interpreting Zimri's action as idolatry, which is contrary to the true meaning of the verse and contrary to the Halakha, according to Heinemann;[44] but see below) and formulated his own Halakha, that all idolaters are punishable by zealots.

However, Philo did not teach this Halakha of his own accord, but on the basis of an ancient Halakhic tradition that he knew and which was acted upon in Eretz-Israel and in the Diaspora in Philo's days.

Juster[45] already drew attention to the verses (*Acts* ix 23–24), according to which the Jews of Damascus wished to kill Saul of Tarsus when he lived in their city and incited them to change their religion; and Goodenough[46] pointed to *III Maccabees* vii 10–15. This may also be deduced from *Acts* xxiii 12–15 (the story of the four Jews who vowed to slay Saul). Likewise Mattathias' action in slaying the Jew who sacrificed to Zeus in Modin was an act of zealotry (*I Maccabees* ii 24).

But it is also possible to prove, on the basis of Mishnaic and Talmudic literature, that according to the ancient Halakha those who offended against the fundamental of religion (which included the sorcerer and idolater) were handed over to zealots for punishment; the new Halakha, however, abrogated this law and ordained that all these must be tried by a court like all other transgressors liable to death.

We learn in the Mishna (*Sanhedrin* ix, 6): 'If a man stole a sacred vessel [strictly: vessel for libation], or cursed by *Qôsēm* [the name of an idol or a disguised Divine Name], or had intercourse with an Aramaean woman [i.e. a non-Jewess], the zealots may fall upon him. If a priest ministered in a state of defilement, his brother priests do

one who desecrates the name of Heaven is subject to severe punishment; see below.

43 *De Legibus*, I, 79, and *ibid.* III, 126.

44 In *op. cit.*, p. 227, and in his German translation of *De Legibus* see also p. 26, note 1. Heinemann does not deal with the subject of the sorcerer who is assaulted by zealots.

45 *Les Juifs dans l'Empire Romain*, p. 158, note 2.

46 *Op. cit.*, p. 36.

not bring him to the court, but the young priests take him outside the Temple Court and split open his head with clubs.'[47]

These four acts violate the fundamental principle. For one who steals a sacred vessel desecrates the Sanctuary; the same applies to a priest who ministers in a state of defilement; and a man who curses by *Qôsēm* desecrates the name of Heaven; while one who has intercourse with an Aramaean woman is guilty of idolatry and of apostasy, and as R. Ḥiyya bar Avuya said in the Talmud (*T.B. Sanhedrin* 82a): 'Whoever is intimate with a Cuthean it is as though he married into idolatry.' Similar to this teaching is the dictum of R. Ishmael, which is cited by the Palestinian Talmud here in connection with our Mishna (ix, 27b; *Megilla* iv, 75c; *Midrash Tannaim*, p. 109; *Sifre Deut.* §171; cf. *M. Megilla* iv, 9): ' "Whosoever he be...that giveth of his seed unto Molech; he shall surely be put to death" — R. Ishamel said this refers to one who was intimate with an Aramaean woman and raises up by her a son who is an enemy of the Omnipresent.'[48]

Now in respect of all these transgressions the Halakha exempts the transgressor from capital punishment. For whoever has intercourse with the Aramaean (except of the seven nations) only transgresses a prohibition of the Scribes (*T.B. Sanhedrin* 82a),[49] and it is doubtful if the priest who ministers in a state of uncleanness is liable even to death by the hand of Heaven. And for him who steals a sacred vessel we have found no punishment prescribed by Torah law or by the Halakha, while he who curses by *Qôsēm* only 'appears to be cursing the Name'[50] (*ibid.* 82b).

Nevertheless it is difficult to suppose that the Halakha permits a person exempt from death by law to be killed, even if caught in the act. Even the Talmud struggled with the issue (*ibid.*).[51] Hence it seems

47 Cf. Juster, *loc. cit.*, note 2.

48 Cf. the Targum Yerushalmi to Lev. xviii 21, and see H. Albeck, *Das Buch der Jubiläen und die Halacha*, pp. 27–29, and note 193.

49 Cf. *T.B. 'Avoda Zara* 36b. Even according to R. Simeon he is guilty only if he is intimate with her with a view to making her his wife. At all events capital punishment does not apply here.

50 Literally 'He appears to "bless" the Name'.

51 Actually the Talmud presumes that if the offender is liable to death by the hand of Heaven no objection can be raised to the fact that it is permissible for the zealots to assault him, and it rests its case on the preceding Mishna (*Sanhedrin* ix, 5): 'He who received stripes twice (and transgressed again) is placed by the court in a cell', which refers, according to Resh Laqish, to scourging for transgressions punishable by extinction (81b). But it is difficult

that when this tradition came into existence, the (ancient) Halakha imposed death at the hands of man for all the aforementioned offences. And thus indeed we read in *The Book of Jubilees* (xxx 7) with reference to one who has intercourse with an Aramaean woman: 'And if there is any man who wishes in Israel to give his daughter or his sister to any man who is of the seed of the Gentiles he shall surely die, and they shall stone him with stones; for he hath wrought shame in Israel; and they shall burn the woman with fire, because she has dishonoured the name of the house of her father, and she shall be rooted out of Israel.'

It may well be that one who stole a sacred vessel was liable to death by the Bet Din according to the ancient Halakha, just as his penalty was death in the Hammurabic Code[52] (Müller, §6). The

to suppose that even those who are liable to death at the hand of Heaven would be left to the zealots to be dealt with. It is likewise difficult to believe that the Halakha ordained 'indirect' execution for one who had been scourged twice (and transgressed again), even in the case of flagellation for transgressions involving extinction (*kārēt*). It seems, therefore, that the Talmudic interpretation (*ibid.*) of our Mishna, namely that the transgressor was placed in a cell and was deliberately caused to die, does not accord with the ancient Halakha of the Mishna. It may be stated that *kippa* [rendered 'cell'] simply means *prison*. The Mishna's statement, 'and feed him with barley until his belly bursts', is merely rhetorical language; it only meant to say that the offender is imprisoned and fed with inferior rations (barley being the food of the poor), in the same way as the Mishna subsequently uses Biblical phraseology (Isa. xxxvi 20) 'and feed him with "the bread of adversity and the water of affliction"'. So, too, R. Judah's Halakha is to be interpreted (*M. Sanhedrin* 9, 3): 'If a murderer mixed up with others... R. Judah says: They are placed in a cell.' The reference is to the imprisonment of the suspected persons; the interpretation of the Babylonian Talmud is far-fetched. Incidentally we have to explain the Halakha thus according to R. Joḥanan in the Palestinian Talmud (*Sanhedrin* ix, 27b): 'It was taught with regard to a murderer who became mixed up with innocent people'. In this way the objection raised in the Palestinian Talmud (*ibid.*) is comprehensible: 'If it is taught with regard to an ox who got mixed up with (other) oxen, would we in such an instance rule that he has to be put in *kippā*?' What have oxen to do with prison! Similarly the *kippā* into which the one who killed without witnesses being present is none other than a prison-house.

52 This was also the case according to the ancient Greek and Roman codes. Cf. Goodenough, *op. cit.*, p. 100, n. 77. This provides an answer to the contention of Heinemann (*op. cit.*, 39) and Goodenough (*op. cit.*, 243) that there is no basis in Judaism regarding one who thieves from the Temple as a major transgressor and that Philo's view of the gravity of the sin of stealing sacred objects emanates from Egyptian, Greek and Roman thinking on the subject.

priest who served in a state of defilement (with unwashed hands and feet — *Tosefta Kelim* i, 6)[53] also desecrated the Sanctuary.[54] So, too, a non-priest who serves in the Temple is liable to death according to R. Akiba,[55] and in the reign of Herod the penalty of death was imposed on a non-Jew who entered the Sanctuary.[56] One who cursed by *Qôsēm* was sentenced, apparently, according to the ancient Halakha as a blasphemer or idolater. The Halakha of the Mishna did not come, therefore, to permit the zealots to kill a man who was exempt from death by law, but only to fall upon those who were liable to death by the court before their sentence was determined by the Sanhedrin, as is prescribed by the Halakha in Philo.

In this respect, too, the Halakha in Philo's writings conforms to that in our Mishna. Just as the Halakha in the Mishna permits the zealots to assault the transgressors only when they perpetrate the deed or soon after (*T.B. Sanhedrin* 82a),[57] so Philo, when he stresses the 'feeling' of zealotry that is aroused in the heart and when he deduces the Halakha from the action taken by Moses, Phinehas, and the sons of Levi, he refers only to immediate assault.

Now the Halakha in the Mishna certainly does not 'generalize cases that once occurred'.[58] But it nevertheless appears that *au fond* there are embedded in the Halakha events that actually took place, which were responsible for the creation and formulation of the law in the form before us. For only by this assumption is it possible to explain why the Halakha refers to *qaswā* [a vessel for libation]

53 My attention was drawn to this law in the Hammurabi Code and to the passage in *Tosefta Kelim* by my teacher Prof. J. N. Epstein.

54 It is already stated in a Baraita (*Sifre Num.* §161; *Tosefta Yoma* i, 12; *T.B. ibid.* 23a; *T.P. ibid.*, ii, 39c): 'This teaches you that the defilement of the knives (in the Temple) was of graver import for them than the shedding of blood.'

55 This was also the view of R. Ishmael and R. Johanan b. Nuri in the *Sifre* (Numbers §116. But cf. *T.B. Sanhedrin* 84a).

56 *Wars* vi, 2, 4. Cf. in this regard the inscription confirming this statement of Josephus in Schürer, *Geschichte* etc. II, 329, n. 57. Possibly there was an ancient Halakha that interpreted the verse (Num. xviii 7) 'and the stranger [zār] that draweth neigh shall be put to death' as referring to a non-Jew, a Gentile who enters the Sanctuary (even if not with a view to performing the service).

57 The Munich MS. reads: קנאים פוגעין בו בשעת מעשה ['zealots fall upon him *when he is perpetrating the deed*']. Even if this recension is only a gloss, there can be no doubt that the words of the Talmud in interpreting the aforementioned Mishna refer to the Halakha in its original connotation.

58 Heinemann, *op. cit.*, p. 237.

and not to a service vessel (for undoubtedly the law of the libation cup is not different from that of other vessels used in the Temple service).[59] It also seems probable that the Halakha that permits transgressors to be assaulted and exempts such cases from being brought to the Bet Din originated at a time when it was not possible to try the offenders legally and the transgressions enumerated in the Mishna were extremely common, and the situation necessitated the swift action of the zealots either because of the large number of transgressors or on account of the impossibility of trying them in the courts. When we proceed to estimate the time that best fits these conditions, we can find no more suitable time than the beginning of the Hasmonean era (the period of the wars waged by Mattathias, Judas Maccabeus, and his brother Jonathan). An allusion to this is found in the tradition of the Babylonian Talmud (in the name of Rav Dimi and Ravin; thus the source of the tradition is Eretz-Israel) that states that the Hasmonean Bet Din (which is mentioned here *only* in Talmudic literature) issued a decree concerning one who has intercourse with an Aramaean woman.

But it appears that we are able to prove this conjecture from the *Book of Jubilees*. For there, chapter xxx 14–15, after prescribing the penalty of stoning for one who marries his daughter to a non-Jew and burning for the woman who is married to the Gentile, it is stated: 'And Israel will not be free from this uncleanness if it has a wife of the daughters of the Gentiles, or has given any of its daughters to a man who is of any of the Gentiles. For there will be plague upon plague, and curse upon curse, and every judgement and plague and curse will come (upon him); if he do this thing, or hide his eyes from those who commit uncleanness (marriage to a non-Jew), or those who defile the sanctuary of the Lord, or those who profane His holy name' etc. In a single sentence are included one who marries a Gentile woman, one who desecrates the Temple, and one who curses the Name, in the way that they are incorporated in the Mishna (one who marries a Gentile woman — one who had

59 D. Hoffmann (in his edition of the Mishna, *Sanhedrin*, p. 187, n. 49) conjectures that this *qaswā* is one of those *qaswā'ôt* concerning which R. Judah testified (*T.B. Sukka* 48b) that they were used for the libation of wine and water, and that the Mishna speaks of Sadducees who stole the *qaswā* for the libation of water, for they were opposed to that Halakha. Hoffmann, apparently, endeavours to explain the Halakha regarding the lynching by zealots, which seemed difficult to him and not in keeping with the laws of the Mishna, by the assumption that our Mishna refers only to Sadducees. But his thesis is far-fetched; cf. the two Talmuds.

intercourse with an Aramaean woman, he that curses the Name — he that curses by *Qosem*, he that desecrates the Temple — he that steals a sacred vessel and a priest that ministered in a state of defilement) and punishments incurred (mentioned here and nowhere else in the book in respect of any other prohibitions or commandments) by all who witness the act but remain passive (i.e. it devolves upon the bystanders to fall upon the transgressors). Seeing that *The Book of Jubilees* was composed in the days of Joḥanan the High Priest, we may posit that this Halakha (of the Mishna and of *Jubilees*) was created at the beginning of the Hasmonean era under the influence of acts of the Hellenizers, who desecrated the Sanctuary and desecrated the Name and intermingled with the Gentiles.[60]

We have thus learned that the ancient Halakha permitted zealots to assault transgressors who dishonoured the sanctity of the Name and the Temple and intermingled with Gentiles.[61] Although we do not find in this tradition express references to idolatry, we may learn — by argument from minor to major — from the case of one who is intimate with an Aramaean woman that a man is assaulted by zealots only on account of the idolatry involved in his actions. And it stands to reason that the Sages did not make the penalty for idolatry less stringent than that for desecration of the Sanctuary.[62]

60 Although *The Book of Jubilees* does not specifically mention the lynching of transgressors enumerated in that chapter, nevertheless the strong resemblance between the language of *Jubilees* and our Mishna supports the interpretation of the statement in *The Book of Jubilees* in accordance with the ruling of the Halakha in the Mishna.

61 My intuition tells me that the ancient Halakha ordained execution by the court for all those who, according to our Halakha, are only liable to death by Heaven (the cases are enumerated in *Tosefta Zevaḥim* xii, 17, and *Keritot* i, 5, and the Baraita is cited in *T.B. Sanhedrin* 83a). For they are all instances of the desecration of the Temple and of holy things, the ancient Halakha being particularly severe in these matters. It will thus be seen that the later Halakha, in conformity with its general trend to be more lenient in capital cases, removed the penalty of execution by the court from these transgressors and handed over their case to Heaven.

62 Special information relative to the punishment of an idolater, which has no parallel among other offenders, is to be found in the Targum Yerushalmi to Exod. xxii 19: 'Whoever sacrifices to the idols of the Gentiles shall be slain with the sword and his possessions destroyed.' Since the verse speaks of individuals, the translator cannot be referring to the inhabitants of a condemned city, whose property perished. It would seem, therefore, that the translator knew an ancient Halakha that expounded: 'He that sacrificeth unto the gods... shall be utterly destroyed' — both he and his possessions. Apparently it was to counteract this the *Mekhilta de-R. Simeon b. Yoḥai* expounds (149):

But we possess an express Halakha that states that the instigator or inciter to idolatry [*mēsit u-maddîaḥ*] was not slain by order of the court. For we learn in the Talmud (*T.B. Sanhedrin* 8b; 80b): 'But others liable to the death penalty by order of the court (except 'an instigator') under Torah law are put to death only by *a congregation* (on the testimony of) witnesses, and (after) warning' etc. Thus the instigator does not require a congregation (i.e. a court) and he is slain without the Sanhedrin's order. In the *Tosefta* (*Sanhedrin* xi 1), however, the word 'congregation' is wanting. So, too, the Mishna ordains that the instigator should be brought before the Bet Din (*M. Sanhedrin* vii, 4). Nevertheless the tradition of the Babylonian Talmud cannot be set aside. It appears, therefore, that we have before us two divergent traditions, and that the Babylonian Talmud has transmitted here an ancient Halakha in regard to the instigator, who is subject to the same law as all those enumerated in the Mishna and he, like them, is assaulted by the zealots.[63]

As for Philo's statement concerning sorcerers, it seems to me that we possess decisive proof that the ancient Halakha did not require a court sentence for them to be put to death; it is provided by the story of Simeon b. Sheṭaḥ, who hanged women in Ashkelon. Now R. Eliezer already observed to the Sages that Simeon b. Sheṭaḥ acted illegally in hanging eighty women, for two are not tried in one day (*M. Sanhedrin* vi, 4). However, a still greater objection may be raised: How could they be tried, since a person may not be judged *in abstentia*? For it is certain that the Sanhedrin did not sit in Ashkelon and try the witches in their presence, for Ashkelon was in the hands of non-Jews in the days of Simeon. We also learn from the account of the episode in the Palestinian Talmud (*ibid.* 23c; *Ḥagiga* 11, 77d–78a) that Simeon was compelled to use various devices in order to

'He that sacrificeth unto the gods...shall be utterly destroyed' — you might think that it is forbidden to benefit from the property of one who serves idols', etc.

63 Above, p. 103 ff., I tried to show that in practice capital cases were tried in the period of the Second Temple only before the Great Sanhedrin at Jerusalem. In the light of this conclusion it is possible to explain the Baraita in the *Tosefta* (*Sanhedrin* x, 5; *T.B. Sanhedrin* 67a; *T.P. Sanhedrin ibid.* vii, 25d): 'And so they did to Ben Saṭda in Lydda, two disciples of the scholars were appointed for him and stoned him.' Even if we interpret the passage to mean that he was tried in Lydda (which is not proven), it must be borne in mind that Ben Saṭda was an instigator and inciter (and also a sorcerer — *Tosefta Shabbat* xi, 15; *T.B. ibid.* 104b; *T.P. ibid.* ii, 13d), who is not tried by 'the congregation' and is not affected by the other restrictions that apply to capital cases.

execute the witches. However, in the light of the Philonian Halakha there is no difficulty, for a sorcerer's trial has not to be completed at the Bet Din, and Simeon b. Sheṭaḥ and the eighty young men who assisted him were acting as zealots.[64]

The conclusions that we have reached enable us to confirm the tradition of the Synoptic Gospels in regard to the day of Jesus'

64 The Jerusalem Talmud (*Ḥagiga* ii, 77d) explains Simeon b. Sheṭaḥ's action in hanging eighty women in one day, which, contrary to the law, was an emergency measure called for by the circumstances of the time. Thus the Babylonian Talmud also cites the Baraita: 'R. Eliezer b. Jacob said: 'I have heard that the Bet Din beat and impose penalties on an offender though not required by the Torah, not with the intention of transgressing against the ordinances of the Torah, but in order to safeguard it', etc. But it is doubtful if there existed such a direction that gave the court permission to put a person to death, contrary to Torah law, even if 'called for by the circumstances of the time'. For the case of the one who rode on a horse on the Sabbath in the days of the Greeks and was brought before the Bet Din and was stoned may be explained by the premise that the ancient Halakha was stringent in regard to desecration of the Sabbath and imposed the penalty of death even on one who committed a transgression that was only a 'Rabbinic' prohibition according to the new Halakha [see Meir Ish Shalom (Friedmann), '*Me'ir 'Ayin*', to *Mekhilta*, Pisḥa, ix, §22]. The author of *The Book of Jubilees* likewise prescribes death for one who draws water on Shabbat (1, 8). Similarly Philo explains (*De Vita Mosis* ii, 220) the death of the stick-gatherer, that he became liable to capital punishment because he collected wood for kindling, which was intended for lighting a fire. Thus he became liable to stoning on account of *muqṣe* [something that may not be used or handled on the Sabbath or Holy Day, because its use is not counted on] (cf. *Sifre Num.*, §113; *T.B. Shabbat* 96b; *T.P. Sanhedrin* iv, 22d). It appears that the ancient Halakha did not differentiate, in regard to penalties, between Torah law and 'Rabbinic enactment', and ordained death for every kind of work forbidden on the Sabbath. As for the case of the man who had intercourse with his wife beneath a fig tree and was brought before the court and flogged, it is a daily occurrence for the Bet Din to inflict corporal punishment for disobedience on the basis of Rabbinic enactment; thus 'Rav ordered a lashing for anyone who betrothed his wife by intercourse without previous negotiations [*shiddûkhê*]' (*T.B. Qiddushin* 12b; so, too, did Samuel according to *T.P. ibid.* iii, 64b). It should be noted that in the Palestinian Talmud (*Ḥagiga* ii, 78a) the account of the second incident does not conclude (as in the Babylonian Talmud, and also in the Palestinian Talmud, earlier, in connection with one who rides on a horse) with the words 'not because he merited this punishment legally, but because the circumstances of the time called for it'; instead it reads: 'But was she not his wife? Only he behaved disgracefully.' It may therefore be assumed that this ruling of R. Eliezer b. Jacob was based on incidents that occurred in early generations who convicted and punished not in conformity with the *new* Halakha, and we simply have here an attempt to explain the earlier and contrary Halakha as 'a temporary measure'.

conviction and crucifixion. For according to this tradition, contrary to that of John, who fixes the day of his death on 14 Nisan, Jesus was convicted and his sentence executed on the first day of Passover. Now although the Talmud (*T.B. Sanhedrin* 44a) supports John's tradition, it is nevertheless possible that the tradition found in the Synoptic Gospels is correct, since in the view of R. Akiba 'the instigator and inciter' is put to death only on a festival.[65] The Sages already found it difficult to answer the question: How did the Sanhedrin try Jesus on Passover, seeing that trials do not take place on the Sabbath or on a festival (this Halakha was widely current already in the time of Philo; cf. *De Migratione Abrahami*, 16).[66] But even more difficult is the fact that we do not find in the tradition of the Gospels that the court sat in judgement on Jesus. For the discussion between the High Priest Caiaphas and Jesus has not the appearance at all of a session of the Sanhedrin. Nor do the words of Jesus, on account of which, apparently, he was sentenced to death, contain, according to the Halakha, blasphemy for which one would incur death at the hands of the court. It therefore seems that Jesus, who was tried as 'an instigator and inciter' and as a sorcerer (cf. the Baraita in *T.B. Sanhedrin* 44a),[67] did not require conviction by the court according to the ancient Halakha. The dialogue between him and the High Priest had as its purpose only to determine the truth of the reports concerning him that had reached the High Priest from witnesses,[68] or, at least, it seems, to test him and see whether he would retract and repent (as they used to say to an 'instigator': 'How shall we leave our God, who is in heaven' etc., in order that he should retract; *M. Sanhedrin* vii, 10). But since Jesus evaded any retraction[69] and made statements from which the High Priest could infer that the testimonies (which he had previously received in Jesus'

65 *Tosefta Sanhedrin* xi, 7.

66 Cf. for the elucidation of the various views on the subject, Strack-Billerbeck, *Kommentar usw.*, II, 812–853.

67 Yeḥezkel Kaufmann (*Gola we-Nekhar*, Pt. I, pp. 391–393) is of opinion that Jesus was convicted as a false prophet. But both the Talmudic tradition and that of the Gospels concerning Jesus' trial are opposed to this conjecture.

68 See Billerbeck (*op. cit.*, p. 820).

69 Noteworthy is the view of R. Abbahu that Jesus hesitated and retracted when he was being investigated (*T.P. Ta'aniyyot* ii, 65b): 'If a man says to you "I am a god" he is lying; "*I am the son of man*" (in the sense of Messiah, as in the Gospels) he will retract in the end (the reference is to the evasiveness of Jesus during his dialogue with the High Priest); "I shall ascend to heaven", he will not fulfil what he has said.'

absence) were true, he therefore sentenced him to death and handed him over to Pilate. For the Sages prohibited holding a trial on Sabbaths and Holy Days only if the matter to be considered required judicial investigation and formal conviction, but in a case where legally a court is not required, but only the ascertainment of the facts and the determination of guilt by the evidence of the accused himself, the investigation was not forbidden even on Sabbath and Festival.[70]

But the later Halakha abrogated this rule, which permitted the execution without a court trial of transgressors who offended against the basic principle of the faith and imperilled the nation, and put the law in respect of these offenders on the same footing as that relating to all offenders liable to death under Torah law;[71] only it seems that, even according to the new Halakha, where the Jewish authorities were unable to convict the transgressor (one of the aforementioned offenders; but possibly only in the case of an 'instigator and inciter') in court, they used at times to do away with him by consent of the leaders of the day after ascertaining the facts. For only such an assumption can explain the statement of Origen (*Responsio ad Africanum*) that the Nasi of his time used to sentence Jewish transgressors to death secretly. Undoubtedly it is not to be inferred from his obscure remark that the *Nasi* tried *all* transgressors; for the right to impose capital punishment had already been taken away from

70 Tosafot, *T.B. Sanhedrin* 35a, s.v. ליגמריה it is stated: 'Although we have learnt in the Mishna in *Tractate Beṣa*, v, 2: "The following are culpable by virtue of the rules concerning Sabbath rest: One may not judge", this ruling applies to civil cases, since it is a preventive measure lest he write. But capital cases are not to be prohibited on this ground, because on the previous day already the views of those who hold the defendant to be innocent and those who hold him to be guilty had been committed to writing.' In the opinion of Tosafot, therefore, capital cases could be judged even on the Sabbath if it were not for the fact that it entails delay in the execution of the sentence. This appears also to follow from the question raised in the Gemara: 'Let sentence be pronounced on the Sabbath' (this question is also asked in *T.P. Sanhedrin* iv, 22b). But undoubtedly capital cases were not tried on the Sabbath on account of the precept of Sabbath rest. Thus, too, the Romans and the ancient Babylonians were not accustomed to hold trials on their festival days. 'Nimmuqe Joseph' [R. Joseph Ḥabiba, in his commentary on Alfasi] disagrees with Tosafot and solves the Talmudic question differently (q.v.).

71 The replacement of the ancient Halakha by the later Halakha finds sharp expression in a Baraita of the Palestinian Talmud (*Sanhedrin* ix, 27b): 'It is taught: Not with the consent of the Sages'; and according to R. Judah b. Pazzi (*ibid.*) they wished to put Phinehas under the ban.

the Jews before the Destruction. But it may be supposed that Origen came to know of certain instances of the execution of apostates who instigated and incited Jews to forsake Judaism. For the instigator need not be tried by the Bet Din; and even the new Halakha required a trial by the court only when possible, but did not seek to abrogate the ancient Halakha completely.

At any rate we learn that Philo's Halakha, which prescribes that idolaters and sorcerers should be handed over to zealots was in conformity with the ancient Halakha that was in force from the beginning of the Maccabean period to the end of the Second Temple era.

IV

1) After Philo has set out, in the section dealing with the festivals, the laws of the Festival of Passover, the Festival of Unleavened Bread, and the Festival of Weeks, he states (*De Spec. Leg.* II, 188): Εξῆς ἐστιον ἱερομηνία, καθ' ἣν ἅμα ταῖς ἀναγομέναις θυσίαις ἐν τῷ ἱερῷ σαλπίζειν ἔθος. αφ' οὗ καὶ σαλπίγγων ἐτύμως ἑορτὴ προσαγορεύτεαι κτλ. (Thereafter, the Festival of the Sanctification of the month, on which it is the custom to sound the horn in the Temple when the sacrifices are offered up; therefore the festival is properly called also 'The Horn Feast').

According to Philo, therefore, the Shofar ['the horn'] was blown on Rosh ha-Shana [New Year] only in connection with the sacrifices; this is contrary to the Halakha, which ordains that the Shofar should also be sounded outside Jerusalem.

Treitel[72] and Heinemann,[73] who believed that Philo did not know the Halakha that was in force in his time in Eretz-Israel, endeavoured to explain the antithesis between Philo's ruling and the Halakha in the Mishna by supposing that there is a mix-up of laws in the statement of Philo, who confused the passage in Leviticus xxiii 24 with that in Numbers x 10 (which ordains the blowing of the trumpets over the sacrifices at all the appointed seasons and new moons, and according to the Mishna — *Sukka* v, 5; *'Arakhin* i, 4 — over every 'continual burnt offering'; compare the statement of R. Nathan in

72 *Philonische Studien*, p. 54.

73 *Philons usw.*, pp. 99, 536, and his German translation of *De Spec. Leg.*, p. 160, note 1. Heinemann is hard on Philo here (p. 99) for not knowing the nature of the Shofar, while the Gentile Plutarch was acquainted with it. However, as we shall see further on, note 97, Plutarch does not refer at all to the Shofar of Rosh ha-Shana; there is no reason therefore to make the pagan appear 'wise' and to honour him at the expense of Philo.

Sifre Numbers §77, and also *Sifre Zuṭa*, Horovitz, p. 262) and interchanged the special blowing prescribed for Rosh ha-Shana with that performed over the sacrifices.

Now before we proceed to elucidate the teaching of Philo from the aspect of the Halakha that was observed in his days in Eretz-Israel, we must first note the fact that definitely emerges from his words, namely that at that period they were not accustomed to blow the Shofar on Rosh ha-Shana in Alexandria of Egypt, for otherwise Philo would not have listed a Halakha contradicted by the actuality. And although there is no proof for it, we may nevertheless infer by analogy from Alexandria and Egypt for the entire Diaspora and state that in Philo's generation it was not the practice to blow the Shofar in the Diaspora on Rosh ha-Shana.

But there are indications that till the end of the Temple period the precept of blowing the Shofar on Rosh ha-Shana was not observed even in Eretz-Israel outside Jerusalem. For it appears that till near the time of the Destruction the Shofar was blown on Rosh ha-Shana only in the Temple, and even this blowing, which was a specific ritual of the day, was performed only over the sacrifice.

We learn in the Mishna (*Rosh ha-Shana* i, 4): 'If the festival-day of the New Year fell on a Sabbath they used to blow the Shofar in the Temple but not in the provinces.' The Talmud[74] discusses the reason of the Halakha and in the end concludes 'This is a prohibition designed to obviate one's taking it in his hand and going to an expert to learn and (thus) carrying it four cubits in a public domain.' But in *Torat Kohanim* [Sifra] (Behar, pericope 2) we learn: 'You might suppose that the blowing of the Shofar on New Year should override the Sabbath, therefore Scripture teaches "throughout all your land—Then shalt thou make proclamation...." The blowing on the tenth of the month overrides the Sabbath throughout your land, but the blowing of the Shofar on New Year does not override the Sabbath throughout your land, only at the Bet Din.'[75] It will thus be seen that the annulment in the provinces of the commandment to blow the Shofar, when New Year falls on a Sabbath, is a Pentateuchal regulation.[76]

74 *T.B. Rosh ha-Shana* 29b.

75 Cf. *T.P. Rosh ha-Shana* iv, 59b.

76 This Baraita in *Torat Kohanim* therefore takes the view that the blowing of the Shofar on New Year that falls on the Sabbath in a place that has a Bet Din is a law of the Torah and not an enactment of Rabban Joḥanan b. Zakkai. Now this approach is akin to the opinion expressed by R. Judah,

Furthermore from another Baraita we may infer that the Shofar is not blown on New Year outside the Bet Din even on a *weekday*, for we learn in the Talmud (*T.B. Rosh ha-Shana* 30a): 'The Jubilee and New Year are alike in respect of the blowing of the Shofar and the benedictions, save that on the Jubilee the Shofar is blown both at a Bet Din where the New Moon had been sanctified and at a Bet Din where the New Moon had not been sanctified, and every individual is obliged to blow, while on New Year they blew the Shofar only at a Bet Din where the New Moon had been sanctified and individuals were under no obligation to blow.' The Talmud, apparently, interprets this Baraita as dealing with New Year that falls on a Sabbath. But the plain meaning of the Baraita undoubtedly refers to any day of the week, and it is not to be wondered at that there is preserved here in the Baraita an ancient Halakha that had no cognizance of the later Halakha.

At any rate the Halakha in the Mishna that forbids the blowing of the Shofar in the provinces on New Year that falls on a Sabbath must be explained by the premise that primarily the precept of blowing the Shofar pertained only to the Temple and that at first they were accustomed to blow only in Jerusalem. Hence when a new Halakha was introduced prescribing the blowing of the Shofar even in the provinces, it had not the power to supersede the law of the Sabbath.[77]

We also learn this from the teaching of R. Simeon in the Palestinian Talmud (*Rosh ha-Shana* iv, 59b): 'R. Simeon b. Yoḥai taught "And ye shall bring an offering" — that means in the place where the sacrifices are offered up.' It is true that the commentaries connect R. Simeon b. Yoḥai's statement with those of Kahana and R. Levi cited earlier in that discussion: 'One verse states "a day of blowing the horn" and another verse says "a memorial of the blast of horns". How are the two texts to be reconciled? When it falls on a weekday it is "a day of blowing the horn", when it falls on the Sabbath it is "a memorial of the blast of horns" — we commemorate but do not

who disagrees with the tradition that attributes the prohibition (to eat the new corn) throughout the day of waving to an enactment of Rabban Joḥanan b. Zakkai, and declares (*Torat Kohanim*, 'Emor, pericope 10; *T.B. Menaḥot* 68b; *T.B. Rosh ha-Shana* 30b): 'Is it not forbidden by the law of the Torah?' (R. Judah and this Baraita, needless to say, disagree with the tradition that ascribes nine enactments to R. Joḥanan b. Zakkai; *T.B. Rosh ha-Shana* 31b) etc. We must conclude, therefore, that the author of this 'anonymous passage of the *Sifra*' is R. Judah.

77 Cf. Abraham Krochmal, *Yerushalayim ha-Benuya*, p. 43a.

blow.' In answer to the Gemara's objection 'If so let (the Sabbath) not be overridden even in the Temple', the Palestinian Talmud cites the aforementioned Baraita of R. Simeon, who derives from the Scripture 'And ye shall bring an offering' that the text 'a day of blowing the horn' refers only to the Sanctuary. But this interpretation is difficult,[78] and it seems that R. Simeon b. Yoḥai's teaching is not connected with the statements of the Amoraim mentioned earlier, but only seeks to answer the original question: 'If it is a Biblical law [that the blowing of the Shofar supersedes the Sabbath], it [the Sabbath] should be superseded in the provinces, too; if it is not a Biblical law, it [the Sabbath] should not be overridden even in the Temple.' The answer is, therefore, simple: that the blowing of the Shofar does not override the Sabbath in the provinces, because the precept primarily applies 'to the place where the sacrifices are offered up'.

That the blowing of the Shofar on New Year was linked originally to the sacrifice of the day, as is stated by Philo, can also be deduced, to my mind, from the Halakha in the Mishna (*M. Rosh ha-Shana* iv, 7): 'Of those who pass before the ark [to lead in prayer] on the festival-day of the New Year, the second [reader, who recites the *Musaf* ('Additional Prayer')] blows the Shofar; but [on festive days] when *Hallel* is recited, the first [reader, who recites *Shaḥarit* (the Morning Prayer)] reads the *Hallel*.' R. Joḥanan (*T.B. ibid.* 32b; *T.P. ibid.* iv, 59c) explains that this Halakha resulted from a given episode;[79] it was thus a Rabbinic enactment. However, if we assume, in accordance with Philo's view, that the blowing of the Shofar on New Year was related only to the sacrifice, the Halakha is intrin-

78 The unsatisfactory character of this interpretation is particularly noticeable in the light of the recension, cited above, that we find in the Palestinian Talmud ' "And ye shall bring an offering" — that means to say in the place' etc.; for if this interpretation were correct the text should have had 'And ye shall prepare', which is the reading in pericope Phinehas [Num. xxix 2], where the expression 'a day of blowing the horn' occurs. See the commentaries whose explanations are forced. However, *Lev. Rabba* xxix and *Pesiqta de-R. Kahana* (Buber, 155, §2) read 'And ye shall prepare a burnt-offering'; but possibly the text was amended in the Midrashim.

79 The Halakha in *M. Shabbat* vi, 2 ('A man may not go out with nail-studded sandals') is explained in the Talmuds as due to a given incident (*T.B. Shabbat* 60a; *T.P. ibid.* vi, 7b). However, the simple sense of the Halakha is that it is forbidden to go out with a nail-studded sandal in the same way as it is prohibited to go out with a coat of nail, a helmet, or greaves, because they are weapons of war.

sically quite comprehensible. Since in the Temple the Shofar used to be blown on New Year over the sacrifice of the day (that is, over the *Musaf* sacrifice), therefore even when the blowing of the Shofar was introduced into the *Tefilla* [Prayer, *Amida*] and in all places, it was inserted, in conformity with the original usage, during the *Musaf Tefilla.*

The statement made by R. Aḥa b. Papa to R. Zeʿira approximates this view (*T.P. ibid.*): 'It (the blowing of the Shofar) is different (from the *Hallel*), for the observance of this precept on the day is at the time of the *Musaf* sacrifice.'

Support for Philo's Halakha is to be found in the fact that in the time of the Temple the blowing of the Shofar in respect of other precepts was performed specifically by the priests. Thus the priests used to blow the Shofar at *Haqhel* [assembly of pilgrims in Jerusalem on Sukkot soon after a Sabbatical year to hear the king read from the Book of Deuteronomy; see Deuteronomy xxxi 10–13] (*Tosefta Soṭa* iii, 15–16; *T.P. Yoma* i, 38d, and the parallel passages; *Sifre* Be-haʿalotekha §75) and in the *Jubilee* year (*Sifre ibid.*). So, too, it is explained in this Halakha in the *Sifre* that also on New Year the precept of blowing the Shofar was performed by the priests (according to the recension of the Venice edition and Leiden MS. Although this reading is to be doubted on account of the other versions — see Horovitz *ibid.* — it nevertheless seems probable that these versions emended the Baraita according to the accepted Halakha). The same applied to a public *fast*, as we learn from *M. Taʿanit* ii, 5 (*Tosefta ibid.* i (end); *T.B. ibid.* 16b). R. Ḥalafta in Sepphoris and R. Ḥanina b. Teradion in Sikhnin also introduced the practice of blowing the Shofar according to this procedure in the provinces. Notwithstanding that the Sages disagreed with them and said 'We acted thus only at the Eastern Gate and on the Temple Mount',[80] we nevertheless learn from a number of sources that it was customary for the priests to blow the Shofar on a public fast even after the close of the Talmud. Thus in the Second Targum to the Book of Esther it is stated, in the account of the procedure of the fast service ordained by Esther and Mordecai, that the priests blew the Shofar. Likewise Rav Sar

80 The principle followed by R. Jose b. Ḥalafta and Ḥanina b. Teradion to observe the customs connected with the blowing of the Shofar on public fast days in the manner that obtained in Temple times also finds expression in the practice they introduced in their cities to blow on a public fast with both a Shofar [horn] and with trumpets, as they did in the Temple (*T.B. Rosh ha-Shana* 27a).

Shalom and R. Sherira and R. Hai testify in their responsa[81] that it was the custom, ordained in their Academies, to make the priests blow the Shofar on public fasts.

This practice also obtained when the Shofar was blown in the case of excommunication [*Nidduy*], as we learn from *Pirqe de-R. Eliezer* (xxxviii) and *Midrash Tanḥuma* (pericope *Wa-yēshev*). So, too, the blast that was blown on Sabbath eves to cause the people to cease from work was performed in Jerusalem only by a priest as is clear from *M. Sukka* (v, 5; cf. *M. ʿArakhin* ii, 3) and from the explanation of Josephus (*Wars* iv, 9, 12, where he also testifies that a priest used to blow a trumpet at the termination of the Sabbath to distinguish between the holy and profane).[82] It may therefore be stated that in Temple times blowing the Shofar and likewise the trumpet was regarded as a service belonging to the priests.[83]

However, with regard to blowing the Shofar on New Year we learn that near the time of the Destruction this ritual ceremony also spread beyond Jerusalem, but at first the Shofar was blown only

81 See *Oṣar ha-Ge'onim* to *Taʿanit*, pp. 23–25 and the notes *ibid.* It is noteworthy that the author of the *Ṭurim* [R. Jacob b. Asher] (*Oraḥ Ḥayyim*, Laws of Fasting, §579) and Me'iri (*T.B. Taʿanit* 15a), who quote 'the Prayer Book of the Ge'onim' on the prayers and Shofar-blowing of a public fast, omit the call 'Blow (the Shofar), O priests, blow!'; but not so Naḥmanides (in his Novellae to *T.B. Taʿanit* 15a) and the author of the *Eshkol* (ed. Albeck, pp. 133, 135, 136; cf. Naḥmanides' sermon for the New Year, *Ha-Ṣofe me-'Ereṣ Hagar*, I, p. 154).

82 With regard to the blowing at the termination of the Sabbath cf. *M. Ḥullin* i, 7 and *Tosefta ibid.* i, 26. But Maimonides rules ('Hilkhot Shabbat' v, 20) that the Shofar is also blown at the end of the Sabbath. Apparently he deduced this Halakha from *T.B. Shabbat* 114b (cf. *Maggid Mishne* [Don Vidal di Tolosa], *Hilkhot Shabbat, loc. cit.*), but the Early Authorities (Rishonim) differ from him (cf. Naḥmanides, R. Solomon b. Adret, R. Yom Ṭov b. Abraham [of Seville], and Tosafot of Riṣ on this Talmudic theme and *Maggid Mishne, loc. cit.*). With regard to Sabbath eve we have certainly learnt in a Baraita (*Tosefta Sukka* iv 11–12) that 'the superintendent of the congregation' blows the Shofar everywhere (cf. *T.B. Shabbat* 35b). But even if we understand the blower, as is implied by the general language of the aforementioned phrase, to be an Israelite, we can draw no inferences therefrom for the period preceding the Destruction. The matter requires further study.

83 This appears to refute the view of Büchler who conjectures that the Shofar was not to be found in the Temple and its use was not restricted to the priests; see *ZATW*, 1899, p. 102 and cf. p. 103, n. 1. For even if we interpret the verses as he does, we can make no deductions from them for the latter half of the Second Temple period.

within the confines of the capital and only later did they begin to do so in every city.[84]

Different from the prevailing view is also Philo's conception of the festival of the first of Tishri as ἱερομηνία (the festival with which the holy month, the month of the festivals, opens). But in order to elucidate Philo's attitude in this respect to the early tradition we must first understand his approach to the Jewish New Year.

Philo speaks in several passages, in connection with the explanation of Pentateuchal verses, of two New Years, one in Tishri and the other in Nisan (*De Spec. Leg.* II, 150; *Quaest. in Exodum*, XII, 2), and he explains this duality from the aspect of ἰσημερίαι (*aeguinoctia*), which also led, in his opinion, to the establishment of the two festivals, Passover and Tabernacles, in these months. Although he holds that the Torah appointed New Year to fall in Nisan, he nevertheless states explicitly, when he seeks to explain the fact that the Torah ordained that only one bull be offered up on the first of Tishri (and not a double oblation as in the case of the other sacrifices), that the Torah intended to emphasize unity on this day, which is the *New Year.*

Now this duality is found also in the Mishna and in Josephus (*Ant.* vi, 3, 3).[85] But whereas in our Mishna (and in Josephus' teaching) the principal New Year falls in Tishri, Philo regards Nisan as the main New Year and Tishri as subsidiary to it.[86] Hence Philo holds that the world was created in Nisan[87] (in conformity with the

84 *M. Rosh ha-Shana* iv, 2. This Halakha, which prescribes that the Shofar is to be blown on Rosh ha-Shana, if it fell on a Sabbath, in 'every town that sees (Jerusalem) and that hears (the Shofar blown in Jerusalem)' etc., is late, since the simple meaning of the earlier Mishna (*ibid.* iv, 1) is that the Shofar was blown in the Temple but not in the provinces. It thus comes to exclude Jerusalem, in accordance with Rashi's view that Jerusalem is not included in the Sanctuary, and contrary to the opinion of Maimonides (in his commentary to this Mishna). Cf. *T.B. Rosh ha-Shana* 29b, s.v. *'Avāl.*

85 In Babylon, too, there were two New Years in connection with the two *aeguinoctia* (cf. Philo's statement above); see Jeremias, *Handbuch der Altorientalischen Geisteskultur*, p. 156.

86 Josephus states that for sacred things the New Year is in Nisan, and for business matters and secular requirements the New Year falls in Tishri. However, it seems that in practice this division was not fixed and final. For we learn in the *Tosefta* (*Rosh ha-Shana* i, 1; cf. *T.B. ibid.* 7a): 'Some say, also for the renting of houses' (New Year is on the first of Nisan). On the other hand, Josephus himself, when he enumerates the laws of the festivals puts Tabernacles before Passover (*Ant.* iii, 10, 3, *et al.*).

87 The author of *The Book of Jubilees* also holds that the world was created in

view of R. Joshua, *T.B. Rosh ha-Shana* 11a–b, and contrary to that of R. Eliezer, *ibid.* 10b and 11b, and *T.P. ibid.* i 56a). Consequently when he proceeds to expound the section of the sacrifices (*op. cit.* I, 180) and the section of the festivals (*ibid.* II, 145) he begins with Passover, while Josephus puts, in the section of the sacrifices (*Ant.* iii, 10, 3 ff.), the festival of Tabernacles before Passover.

There are some scholars who are of opinion that from earliest times the Israelites used to celebrate New Year in Tishri as the day of the enthronement of Heaven, like the ancient Babylonians, and base their views on Psalms xlvii and lxxxi.[88] However, Pap has already shown (*Das israelitische Neujahrfest*, 91–92) that this theory, in regard to the period of the First Temple, is groundless. However, we have no proof even for the era of the Second Temple that New Year had the character described above. On the contrary, we have 'an argument from silence' proving the reverse in the writings of Josephus, who, in referring to the sacrifices of the first of Tishri, in no way indicates the significance of this festival (as he does in the section of the three Pilgrim Festivals and that of the Day of Atonement).

When we come to consider the aspect of New Year as a day of judgement, we must note that, apart from the fact that we find no evidence for this in the tradition for the period preceding the Destruction, the Tannaim disagree on the very concept. For according to R. Jose (*Tosefta Rosh ha-Shana* i; *T.B. ibid.* 16a) 'A man is judged every day'. And even our Mishna (i, 2), 'At four periods of the year the world is judged' etc., is but synthesis of two traditions, according to one of which the world is judged at each season, and according to the other on 'New Year all mankind pass before him like a legion of soldiers (of fixed number)'. Also the fact that the Shofar was blown, till shortly before the destruction of the Temple, only in the Sanctuary militates against ascribing to the first of Tishri the character of a day of judgement in the earlier period. This likewise applies to the view of those scholars who regard it as the festival of the enthronement of Heaven, for the Israelites did not go on pilgrimage therein, and consequently the majority of the nation did not observe the 'precept of the day'.

Nisan, as his calculation of periods everywhere shows. But Josephus follows the view of R. Eliezer (according to both of them the Flood began to come down in Marḥeshvan; see *Ant.* i, 3, 3).

88 Cf. for the elucidation of this theory Pap, *op. cit.*, pp. 13–18.

We have thus seen that Philo, who restricts the blowing on the New Year to the Temple,[89] follows the earlier Halakha that was observed in the Diaspora and in Eretz-Israel till near the time of the Destruction, and the fact that he makes no mention of the aspect of the first of Tishri as New Year[90] and the day of judgement only serves to show that in his time this tradition was not yet dominant.[91]

89 The Karaites are divided in their views. Some declare that *Tĕrûʿā* on New Year is performed only by mouth (prayer), and some prescribe blowing the Shofar. And of those who ordain blowing, some hold that it takes place only in the Temple and is performed by the priests. Cf. Revel, *The Karaite Halakha*, p. 78, note 114. See also Ginzberg, *Ginze Schechter*, II, p. 479, and *ibid.* pp. 484–485.

90 The Falashas (who also, like Philo, call New Year 'the Festival of Trumpets') likewise do not attribute the character of New Year to the first of Tishri (A. Epstein, *Eldad ha-Dani* etc., p. 162). As regards *The Book of Jubilees*, in which the reference to the 'Memorial', which is related in that book to the first of Tishri, is regarded by some scholars as an allusion to New Year and the enthronement of Heaven, it should first of all be noted that *The Book of Jubilees* does not distinguish the first of Tishri from the beginnings of other seasons [*tĕqûfā*, equinox and solstice]. Furthermore, the idea of 'Memorial' is usually attached by this work to all the precepts that it enumerates. Finally the Torah speaks of 'A memorial proclaimed with the blast of horns', and in what way is the use of this expression in *The Book of Jubilees* more significant than that in Scripture, from which, too, we are unable to infer anything with respect to our subject?

91 It seems that when we find variant traditions in regard to a halakhic or religious institution we may not always assume that one is later than the other, even if we only have late sources for the tradition in question, for it may well be that these different views existed together at an early period. We may only deal, in such instances, with the question: Which of these traditions was dominant at this or that period. Nor should we ascribe this multiplicity of opinions, even in fundamental matters, to different *sects* but to rival *schools*. Take, for example, the character of the Feast of Weeks as the festival of the giving of the Torah, a fact for which we have evidence only since the period of the Amoraim (*T.B. Pesaḥim* 68b). Nay more; according to R. Akiba and R. Jose (*'Avot de-R. Nathan* i and Recension II i; *T.B. Shabbat* 86b; *T.B. Yoma* 90b) the Torah was given on the seventh of Sivan, in which case the Feast of Weeks cannot be the anniversary of the giving of the Torah. Nevertheless it appears that in Temple times there were some who regarded this festival as the celebration of the giving of the Torah, for this is how it is seen in the tradition of the Falashas and the Samaritans (Epstein, *op. cit.*, p. 161). Also the fact that the author of *The Book of Jubilees* fixed the giving of the Torah on the 16th of Sivan (i, 1), the day on which, in his view, the Festival of Weeks fell, seems to attest this circumstance. Cf. Finkelstein, *HTR*, xxii, p. 204, note 47. I must point out that A. Epstein (*op. cit.*, p. 156), Heinemann (*op. cit.*, p. 128), and H. Albeck (*Das Buch der Jubiläen*, pp. 15–16) claim that *The Book of Jubilees* provides express

2) In the section that Philo assigns to the Festival of Tabernacles (*De Spec. Leg.*, II, 204–209) he omits the precept to take four species.

and *absolute proof* that the Festival of Weeks was regarded as the festival of the giving of the Torah. But this is not so. For the covenant referred to in that chapter of *The Book of Jubilees* [vi] is actually the covenant of the rainbow, which the Lord had made with Noah and in connection therewith had prohibited the shedding of blood and the eating of blood. Nor is it surprising that this covenant is linked with the giving of the Torah, since the verses testify that the Torah was given in Sivan, and in the same chapter, v. 21, the Book portrays the festival as having two aspects — the Feast of Weeks and the Feast of the First Ripe Fruits (sic). We thus find that the author only gives expression here to his general aim, namely, to link the festivals with events that occurred prior to the giving of the Torah and to give them an earlier origin, but on no account may we ascribe to the author, on the basis of Biblical verses cited in chapter vi (on which the aforementioned scholars base themselves), the intention to attribute to the Feast of Weeks the primary character of the festival of the giving of the Torah. Nor are we to see in this juxtaposition of the covenant of Noah and 'the renewal of the covenant' at Sinai, more than can be found in the fact that the author connects (further on in the same chapter) the beginnings of the four seasons [equinoxes and solstices] with events that happened to Noah in the year of the Flood. But the fact cited above — the fixing of the giving of the Torah on the fifteenth of Sivan — does imply such an assumption. It should also be noted that Heinemann thinks he found complete proof of the precedence given to the aspect of the Feast of Weeks as the day of the giving of the Torah in the statement in *The Acts*, chapter ii, that the Holy Ghost rested on the Christian community on Pentecost. See his aforementioned book, p. 128. But what has this episode to do with the giving of the Torah! We can, however, explain this Christian legend only by reference to the belief widespread among the people that the pilgrimage (to Jerusalem) and the Temple vouchsafed the Holy Ghost to the worshipper, as we are told in *T.P. Sukka* v, 55a, 'Jonah b. Amittai was one of the pilgrims, and on entering the Bet ha-Sho'eva [The well-head, from which water was drawn for libation on the festival of Sukkot] the Holy Spirit rested on him.' Although the Holy Spirit rested on worshippers particularly on the water-drawing festival, nevertheless the primary factor was the Sanctuary. And since this episode occurred near the time when their messiah was crucified, it was inevitably dated to the first festival that came around — to the Feast of Weeks. The matter was rightly understood already by Strack and Billerbeck (*Kommentar* etc. II, p. 604). The same applies to the Day of Atonement. For apparently the testimony of R. Simeon b. Gamaliel in the Mishna (*Ta'anit* iv, 8) comes to teach us that formerly the character of this day was completely different from that which tradition ascribed to it. But from Philo we learn that in his days all the Jews were accustomed to sit the whole day in synagogue and occupy themselves with confessions and supplications before the Almighty, and so, too, we may infer from *The Book of Jubilees* xxxiv, 19; cf. Albeck, *op. cit.*, p. 18 (only we must take into consideration, in this regard, the custom of the Falashas, who devote most of the Day of Atonement to prayer and supplications, and

Treitel[92] conjectures that Philo understood the Pentateuchal commandment 'And ye shall take you on the first day the fruit of goodly trees' etc. in the sense that the Torah enjoined the making of a booth out of the four species, which is contrary to the Halakha, and he bases his conjecture on Nehemiah viii 14–15. But this interpretation of the Torah precept, which was adopted by the Samaritans and by some of the Karaite scholars, who likewise base themselves on those verses in Nehemiah,[93] is completely refuted by a number of sources that attest that in the period of the Second Temple the Jews observed the commandment of taking the four species according to the Halakha.[94] Thus Josephus relates (*Ant.* xiii, 13, 5) that King Jannaeus was pelted by the people with citrons.[95] This is also to be seen from *II Maccabees* x 6–7. Likewise from *The Book of Jubilees* (xvi 35–36) we learn that the four species were to be carried and not used for the making of the booths. Similarly Plutarch's statement, cited below, testifies to this.

However, Philo's silence is to be explained by the fact that in his days the four species were used only in the Temple.[96]

This assumption is verified by Josephus' presentation of this precept. For he states (*Ant.* iii, 10, 4): τῇ δὲ πέμπτῃ τοῦ ἀυτοῦ μηνὸς καὶ δεκάτῃ...σκηνὰς πήγνυσθαι κελεύει κατὰ οἰκίαν ἕκαστον... παραγινομένους εἰς ἐκείνης τὴν πόλιν ἣν δία τὸν ναὸν μητρόπολιν

part of the day to dancing; cf. *Eshkol*, German Section, iv, p. 1908). See also Moore, *Judaism*, I, p. 61.

It may well be, therefore, that even before the Destruction there were some who regarded the first of Tishri as New Year and the Day of Judgement. But there was another view, akin to that of Philo, which did not attribute these features to the day. Both conceptions were rooted in Palestinian Judaism. But after the Destruction the tradition embedded in the Mishna prevailed and became the established view for the future.

92 *Philonische Studien*, 63.

93 This is also the view of Anan. See '*Misēfer ha-Miṣwot le 'Anan*' [(Fragments and Remnants) of Anan's Book of Commandments], Harkavy, p. 148, n. 7, *et al.* Cf. 'Gan Eden' on the subject of the Festival of Tabernacles.

94 Although it seems probable that there were some who, on the basis of the verses in Nehemiah, used to make the booths out of the four species, as the Halakha of R. Judah shows (*Sifra*, 'Emor, Sec. 12; *T.B. Sukka* 36b), yet this manner of fulfilling the precept did not exclude the practice of carrying the four species. Cf. D. Hoffmann, *Das Buch Leviticus*, II, pp. 288–292.

95 Cf. Hoffmann, *op. cit.*, p. 289.

96 This is the actual meaning of the text in Lev. xxiii 40: 'And ye shall take you on the first day... and ye shall rejoice *before the Lord your God*', etc. Cf. *T.P. Sukka* iii, 54a.

ἕξουσιν, ἐφ' ἡμέρας ὀκτὼ ἑορτὴν ἄγοντας... ἐν ταῖς χερσὶν εἰρεσιώνην μυρσίνης καὶ ἰτέας σὺν κράδῃ φοίνικος πεποιημένην, τοῦ μηλοῦ τοῦ τῆς περσέας προσόντος ('On the fifteenth day of this month...it is enjoined to erect booths for every family...They must come to the city that on account of the Temple will be regarded as the capital and celebrate a festival for eight days... while carrying in their hands a bunch of myrtles and willows with a bough of the palm-tree together with the citron').

Thus while he stresses that it is the duty of every Jew to erect a booth in his home wherever it may be, he links the carrying of the four species with a pilgrimage to Jerusalem and the offering of the sacrifices in the Temple. We learn therefore from this tradition in Josephus that the ceremony of the Lulav [palm-branch] was not practised in the provinces.

We learn this also from the description of the celebration of Tabernacles by Plutarch,[97] namely that the rite of the four species was in the Temple. For he states: ἔστι δὲ καὶ κραδηφορία τις ἑορτὴ καὶ θυρσοφορία παρ' αὐτοῖς, ἐν ᾗ θύρσους ἔχοντες εἰς τὸ ἱερὸν εἰσίασιν...καὶ κιθαρίζοντες ἕτεροι προσίασιν οὓς αὑτοὶ Λευίτας προσονομάζουσιν κτλ. ('They also have a festival on which they take branches of [fig trees] and branches of ivy [*thyrsus*], and holding the branches of ivy they come to the Temple, and others called Levites, playing on cithara drew near to the Temple'). Thus Plutarch also confines the carrying of the palm-branch to the Sanctuary.

Our Mishna (*Sukka* iv, 4), too, when setting out the manner of the Lulav ritual, speaks incidentally of the Temple.[98]

This postulate explains the twofold character of the precept of the willow ('one for the Temple and one for the Lulav' — *Tosefta Sukka* iii, 1; *Sifra*, 'Emor, sec. 12; *T.B. Sukka* 34a; *T.P. ibid.* iii, 53c; iv, 54b). To begin with the willow was used only in the Temple and the precept was carried out in the manner taught in the Mishna

97 *Quaestiones Conviviales* vi, 6, 2, and cf. Reinach, *Textes* etc., pp. 143–144. *Ibid.*, p. 144 n. 4, he observes in perplexity: 'On the one hand Plutarch speaks of blowing with trumpets (καὶ γὰρ σάλπιξι μικραῖς... χρῶνται) — 'For they use small trumpets'), and on the other he refers to the carrying of palm-branches etc., as though he confused New Year with Tabernacles. But it appears that Plutarch had in mind only the Festival of Tabernacles and that he simply refers to the blowing of the trumpets at the time of the water libation during the festival (*M. Sukka* v, 4).

98 Although in ch. iii, 4 the Mishna speaks of carrying the Lulav in the Synagogue (even in the provinces), yet the Talmud has already stated (*T.B. Sukka* 43a) that this Mishna was taught after the destruction of the Temple.

Sukka iv, 5; afterwards, when the precept of the four species also began to be observed in the provinces, a second willow was assigned to the Lulav and was carried with it in the bunch.

If we examine carefully the ruling of R. Joḥanan b. Baroqa, we shall see that according to the tradition in his possession the Lulav was used in the same way as the willow in conformity with the view of the Sages, who used to stand it up at the side of the altar throughout all the seven days of the festival.[99] Thus this duality existed also in the case of the Lulav. Similarly we learn from *The Book of Jubilees* (xvi 31) that they made seven circuits round the altar on each day of the festival, carrying a palm branch, a citron, and a willow.[100]

This premise makes the Halakha (*M. Sukka* iii, 12) perfectly clear: 'At first the Lulav was carried seven days in the Temple, but in the provinces one day only.' For primarily the commandment had to be performed in the Temple, while in the provinces the carrying of the Lulav was only a reminder, as it were, of the Temple ritual. Hence it was practised on the first day only.

But undoubtedly during the last days before the destruction of the Temple the rite of the four species was widely practised even in 'the provinces', as is shown by this Mishna. Similarly R. Eleazar b. R. Zadok[101] attests that they also used to carry the Lulav outside the Temple. However, we have testimony only concerning the last days of the Temple and only with regard to Jerusalem.

Now we learn that if the first day of the festival fell on a Sabbath it was not the custom in Babylon to carry the Lulav (*T.B. Sukka* 43a), and so, too, in Alexandria of Egypt they did not use the four species when the first day fell on the Sabbath, until R. Abbahu came and made them carry them (*T.P. ʿEruvin* iii, 21c). In Eretz-Israel, however, the Lulav would be carried even when the first day of Sukkot fell on the Sabbath (*T.P. Sukka* iii, 54a). This difference of practice between the Jews of Eretz-Israel and the Diaspora is to be explained by the fact that the custom of carrying the Lulav outside Jerusalem was established in Palestine before the Golah; hence

99 Ch. iv, 6, and according to Tosafot (45b, s.v. *'Aḥat*), who are of opinion that R. Joḥanan b. Baroqa holds that throughout the seven days of the festival they used to bring palm-branches.

100 According to *The Book of Jubilees* the precept called for seven circuits to be made round the altar each day (contrary to the Halakha in the Mishna iv, 5).

101 *Tosefta Sukka* ii, 10; *T.B. ibid.* 41b; cf. *T.P. ibid.* iii, 53c.

the Jews of the Exile adopted the strict ruling not to carry the Lulav on Sabbath even if it was the first day of the festival.

Thus we learn that until shortly before the Destruction the precept of the four species was observed only in the Temple. The fact that Philo overlooks this precept, which is certainly not to be explained as due to ignorance of the Halakha, since it is explicitly stated in the Torah, must emanate, therefore, from the circumstance that it was not commonly practised either before or in his days. Seeing that this precept was only one facet of the festival rejoicing and of the public celebration at the Temple, he did not mention it as he did the blowing of the Shofar on New Year, which is a precept *per se*.[102]

102 The carrying of the four species in the Temple was only an expression of public, rejoicing (cf. *T.P. Sukka* iii; cf. also *Lev. Rabba* xxx; *Midrash Tanḥuma*, 'Emor), which was practised in former times, it appears, also on other occasions of public celebration. Hence *The Book of Jubilees* (xvi) mentions in addition to the taking of palm-branches and willows the setting of wreaths upon their heads, for it was customary to wear wreaths of olive leaves at festival celebrations.

ON THE HALAKHOT OF THE EARLY SAGES

We have learned in the Mishna:[1] 'R. Judah said: Heaven forfend that ʿAqavia should have been put under the ban! For the Temple Court was never closed before[2] any man in Israel as wise and sin-fearing[3] as ʿAqavia b. Mahalal'el. Whom then did they ban?' etc.[4]

This Mishna is explained in the Talmud (*T.B. Pesaḥim* 64b) and accordingly by all the commentators, to mean that when they closed the Temple Court on Passover eve before the multitude of those that entered (*M. Pesaḥim* v, 5) there was not to be found among this vast assembly any one as great as ʿAqavia in wisdom and the fear of sin.

However, this interpretation is far-fetched. First, our Mishna is couched in general terms and does not allude to the eve of Passover at all. Secondly, R. Judah, according to this interpretation, wishes

1 *M. ʿEduyot* v, 6; *T.B. Berakhot* 19a; *T.B. Pesaḥim* 64b.

2 Hebrew בפני כל אדם, but some texts read על כל אדם ['upon any man'] etc. This is the reading in Lowe's edition of the Mishna, the Munich MS, *et al.*

3 The citation of the Mishna in *T.B. Berakhot* reads בחכמה ובטהרה וביראת חטא ['as wise and as *pure* and as sin-fearing']. But the word ובטהרה is not original in the Talmud; see *Diqduqe Soferim, ad loc.*

4 R. Judah follows his practice here of denying the tradition attesting the banning of great scholars. Thus we learn in *T.B. Rosh ha-Shana* 22a: 'R. Judah said: Heaven forfend (that we should suppose) that R. Akiba detained them! It was Shazpar, the head of Geder, who detained them' etc. The purport of his remark is that it is impossible that R. Akiba should have been involved in this incident and have been banned on account of it. This is corroborated by the wording of the Palestinian Talmud (*ibid.* i, 57b): 'Heaven forfend! R. Akiba was not banned.' In the Palestinian Talmud, however, the author of the statement is R. Judah the baker. But the basic tradition relating to our theme is already found in possession of R. Judah b. Betera — *Sifre*, Be-haʿalotekha, §105. R. Judah's view is apparently rooted in the Halakha ascribed by tradition to the Sages of Usha 'not to ban an elder' (*T.P. Moʿed Qaṭan* iii, 81b; *T.B. ibid.* 17a) and which is alluded to by R. Meir, who said to his colleagues when they wished to put him under the ban: 'I shall not listen to you until you tell me *whom you are banning*' etc.

to say that ʿAqavia was quite unique in his generation in respect of Torah learning and piety; if so, he should have used a striking metaphor more suited to this portrayal. But the capacity of the Temple Court was small[5] and the people that gathered there did not represent a vast assembly. Finally, the *wording* of our Mishna cannot bear, even with difficulty, the interpretation mentioned.

It therefore seems that the Mishna has to be explained by the assumption that in the time of the Second Temple the Halakha was that people under the ban were forbidden to enter the Temple Court. The point of the Mishna, therefore, is that the tradition concerning the banning of ʿAqavia must be rejected, for had he been banned the Court would have been closed to him, but this wise and pious man was not barred from entering the *Temple.*

Now it appears that this Halakha may be deduced from the Talmud (*T.B. Moʿed Qaṭan* 15b): 'May one who is under the ban send his sacrifices?' Thus it is to be inferred that he himself is not permitted to bring his offering, for he cannot enter the Temple Court,[6] just like a leper, in regard to whom, too, the Talmud subsequently (*ibid.*) raises the question: 'May he send his sacrifices?'

From the Mishna and the Baraita,[7] it is true, we learn that banned persons (and mourners) are permitted to enter the *Temple Mount.* But it may be argued that this Halakha comes to exclude the Temple Court, into which they are not allowed to go.

This premise, that the Halakha in Temple times prohibited those under the ban to enter the Temple Court, is supported by what we learn from the sources, namely that serious transgressors, who deviated from the ways of the community, were prevented from entering the Temple. For the ban was simply an official recognition that the banned person had departed from the ways of the majority.[8]

5 *M. Middot* ii, 6; *ibid.* v, 1. On the calculation of the capacity of the Temple Court see Chwolson, *Das letzte Passamahl Jesu.*

6 In שיטה לתלמידו של רבינו יחיאל מפריש ['Interpretation of the Disciple of R. Jeḥiel of Paris'] (כתבי מכון הערי פישל [Publications of Harry Fischel Institute], vol. I) the author notes here: מנודה a man under the ban, 'is one not permitted to come among the people, one in whose four ells it is forbidden to stand', but his explanation is not determinative. Me'iri, however, correctly stated 'but in the case of the מנודה, who is forbidden to enter the Temple, it is not clear if he postpones his sacrifices' etc.

7 *M. Middot* ii, 2; *Tractate Soferim* xix, 9; *Tractate Semaḥot* vi, 11; *Pirqe de-R. Eliezer* xvii.

8 This applies to a communal ban, not to one imposed by an individual.

This Halakha is stated anonymously in a late source of the Rabbinic tradition, which is found in the Targum to the verse (ii Samuel v 8) 'Wherefore they say: "There are the blind and the lame; he cannot come into the house".' — 'Wherefore they say: "Sinners and transgressors may not enter the House".' The sense of the passage is that the wicked are prevented from entering the Temple.[9]

But with regard to the earlier period we learn this Halakha from the tradition contained in Josephus, which is set forth below:

In *Antiquities* xix, 7, 3–4 after the author has portrayed the character of the reign of Agrippa (I), who cared for Jews and Gentiles alike, and fulfilled the Torah and precepts, and dwelt permanently in Jerusalem, and allowed not a single day to pass without offering a sacrifice, he states: Καὶ δή τις ἐν τοῖς Ἱεροσολύμοις ἀνὴρ ἐπιχώριος ἐξακριβάζειν δκῶν τὰ νόμιμα, Σίμων ἦν ὄνομα τούτῳ, πλῆθος εἰς ἐκκλησίαν ἁλίσας τηνικάδε τοῦ βασιλέως εἰς Καισάρειαν ἐκδεδημηκότος ἐτόλμησεν αὐτοῦ κατειπεῖν, ὡς οὐχ ὅσιος εἴη, δικαίως δ' ἂν εἴργοιτο τοῦ ναοῦ τῆς εἰσόδου προσηκούσης τοῖς εὐαγέσιν.[10] ('Now there was a certain man of the people of Jerusalem, called Simon, who was deemed to be well versed in the laws, drew a great multitude to an assembly, while the king was staying at Caesarea, and dared to accuse him of being wicked and that rightly he should be prevented from entering the Temple, a privilege to which only those whose deeds were righteous were entitled').

Now let us consider the nature of the wickedness on account of which Simon wished to debar Agrippa from entering the Temple court, for, needless to say, not every light, or even serious, transgression was punished by this severe penalty.

9 The Septuagint also adopts the interpretation that Scripture referred to the Temple, for it translates εἰς οἶκον Κυρίου — 'to the House of the Lord'. Now the Aramaic translation also renders *v.* 6 above, *ibid.*, as mentioned earlier — חטאיא והייביא 'sinners and transgressors' for the 'blind and lame'. But in *Pirqe de-R. Eliezer* xxxvi the explanation given is: 'These are the images' (see R. David Qimḥi *ad loc.*). Cf. Dalman, *Orte und Wege Jesu*[3], p. 406.

10 This is the reading in Niese. But in older editions we find εὐγενέσιν — who were of unblemished descent. According to this recension, the aim was to disqualify Agrippa on account of his Idumean origin. However, we do not hear of proselytes being forbidden to enter the Temple court. Moreover we learn from the continuation of the story that Simon was satisfied after he realized that nothing forbidden was done in the theatre. Thus he criticized Agrippa only on account of his deeds. Hence the reading given in our text is to be accepted.

Now we learn from the subsequent narrative, *ibid.*, that the anger aroused against the king was due to the fact that he went to Caesarea to sit in a theatre,[11] implying that this was the reason why he was adjudged a transgressor who was to be banned from the Temple. For we read that Agrippa invited Simon to the aforementioned city and seated him beside him in the theatre and asked him to tell him what things he saw there that were contrary to the Torah.

But for further assessment of the episode, and especially of the fact mentioned at the conclusion of that story, namely that Simon agreed with the king and was reconciled with him, it is necessary to clarify the basis of the Halakha that prohibits sitting in a theatre (and, needless to say, their construction, in which Agrippa engaged) according to the view of the Sages and the testimony of extraneous sources.

We have learnt in the Tosefta (*ʿAvoda Zara* ii, 5–7): 'It is forbidden to go up to the theatres of the Gentiles on account of idolatry; this is the view of R. Meir. But the Sages say that when they offer sacrifices it is forbidden on account of idolatry; if they do not offer sacrifices it is forbidden because it is "the seat of the scornful". He who goes to stadiums or camps [*castra*] and sees (the performance of) the sorcerers... this is "the seat of the scornful"... To go up to the theatres of the Gentiles, if one shouts[12] on account of the country's need, is permitted; if he conspires [with the Romans], it is forbidden. If a man sits in a theatre, he sheds blood; R. Nathan permits this for two reasons: because he shouts and thereby saves lives, and (he may go) to a camp because he helps to maintain order in the country, but if he conspires, it is forbidden.'[13]

We thus see that R. Meir and the Sages disagree. According to the latter not every theatre falls within the category of idolatry, only a place where sacrifices are offered up, whereas R. Meir, apparently, holds that even if no sacrifices are offered up theatres are forbidden

11 Needless to say, he also denounced the establishment and renovation of theatres, in which respect Agrippa followed in the footsteps of his grandfather Herod, although he did not indulge in the practice to the same extent.

12 Hebrew: אם היה ציירו מפני צורך מדינה. The printed editions and the Vienna MS read: אם צווח מפני צורך מדינה [so, too, in *T.P. ibid.*: העולה לתיאטרון צווח וכו׳ ('He who goes up to a theatre and *shouts*' etc.); likewise in the subsequent dictum of R. Nathan both in the *Tosefta* and the Palestinian Talmud and the Babylonian Talmud, ציירו is a corruption of צייח as in Arabic, meaning the same as רודף].

13 See the Baraita in *T.B. ʿAvoda Zara* 18b; *T.P. ibid.* i, 40a.

on account of idolatry. But all are agreed that they are prohibited as 'the seat of the scornful'.

Now this dispute of the Tannaim, which is to be explained by the fact that in their days sacrifices were not offered up wherever there was a theatre, and that there were different customs among the Gentiles, is to be found also among the *Christians* of that generation, some of whom took a lenient attitude for the reason stated, while others viewed the matter with stringency.[14] Even Tertullian, who strictly forbids attendance at a theatre, amphitheatres or stadium, rules that one may not sit in a theatre in the first instance because it is 'the seat of scorners' (and he also applies the verse at the beginning of the Book of Psalms 'to the gladiators')[15] and especially because, even when there are no sacrifices, nevertheless the theatre is primarily dedicated to a given idol. Even the names of the games attest this, and likewise the other customs, which demonstrate the idolatrous nature of the theatre.[16] He similarly prohibits the amphitheatre on account of the shedding of blood.[17]

We thus find that, according to R. Meir's opinion, which approximates the view of the Church Father just mentioned, it is forbidden to go up to a theatre on account of *idolatry*, even though sacrifices are not offered up, while the Sages say that this is not the reason.

Hence Simon the Pharisee, who was reconciled with Agrippa and agreed with him that there was no reason to be afraid that one would commit a sin by sitting in a theatre, followed the view of the Sages, and consequently when he saw that there was no 'infringement of the Torah' (i.e. that no sacrifices were offered up) ceased to arraign the monarchy.

But it can be shown that even in those days and in the preceding period, there were those who interpreted the Halakha more stringently and prohibited theatres and all similar institutions, not because idols were worshipped there, but for another reason, as we shall see immediately. Thus Simon's permissive view was even at that time the opinion of individuals.

We have learnt in the *Sifra* ('Ahărē Môt viii; Weiss 86a): ' "Neither shall ye walk in their statutes." Now what did Scripture omit to say?... Why then does the Torah enjoin "Neither shall ye walk in

14 Tertullian, *De Spectaculis*, 3.
15 *Ibid.*
16 *Ibid.*, 4–14.
17 *Ibid.*, 19.

their statutes"? The meaning is that you should not follow their customs in matters that are statutory for them, such as theatres, circuses, and gladiatorial shows.'

Now this Halakha, which prohibits these institutions on the ground that they represent non-Jewish culture, although they transgress no law, apparently existed at an early period and was even current among the nation as one of the established laws.

For we read in *II Maccabees* iv 10–12 that Jason asked the king's permission to set up a gymnasium and ephebeum in Jerusalem: „ἐπινεύσαντος δὲ τοῦ βασιλέως καὶ τῆς ἀρχῆς κρατήσας, εὐθέως πρὸς τὸν 'Ελληνικὸν χαρακτῆρα τοὺς ὁμοφύλους μετέστησε... καὶ τὰς μέν νομίμας καταλύων πολιτείας, παρανόμους ἐθιςμοὺς ἐκαίνιζεν. ἀσμένως γὰρ ὑπ' αὐτὴν ἀκρόπολιν γυμνάσιον καθίδρυσεν κτλ" ('And when the king had given his assent, Jason at once exercised his influence in order to bring over his fellow-countrymen to Greek ways of life... and seeking to overthrow the lawful modes of life, he introduced new customs forbidden by the law: he deliberately established a gymnasium under the citadel itself').

We thus learn that the author looked upon the establishment of the gymnasium as an infringement of Torah law and a grave sin — apostasy, as it were — because it involves 'introduction of the new ways of life' of the Greeks.

Similarly we learn from the testimony of Josephus, *Antiquities* xv, 8, 1, in the passage in which we read that Herod built a theatre and amphitheatre in Jerusalem: „τοῦ δὲ κατὰ τοὺς 'Ιουδαίους ἔθους ἀλλότρια χρῆσίς τε γὰρ αὐτῶν καὶ θεαμάτων τοιούτων ἐπίδειξις οὐ παραδίδοται" ('But [these institutions] foreign to Jewish custom, for the use of such buildings and the exhibition of such spectacles have not been traditional [with the Jews]').

Similarly we read later on, in the same paragraph, of the games of the amphitheatre organized by Herod in Jerusalem — the fights between wild beasts and men: „τοῖς δ' ἐπιχωρίοις φανερὰ κατάλυσις τῶν τιμωμένων παρ' αὐτοῖς ἐθῶν. ἀσεβὲς μὲν γὰρ ἐκ προδήλον κατεφαίνετο, θηρίοις ἀνθρώπους ὑπορρίπτειν ἐπὶ τέρψει τῆς ἀνθρώπων θέας, ἀσεβὲς δὲ ξενικοῖς ἐπιτηδεύμασιν ἐξαλλάττειν τοὺς ἐθίσμους" ('But to the natives it meant an open break with the customs held in honour by them. For it seemed glaring impiety to throw men to wild beasts for the pleasure of other men as spectators, and it served a further impiety to change their established ways for foreign practices').

We thus learn that the reason why sitting in theatres is forbidden is that it is a Gentile custom, as the Sages taught in the *Sifra*, and that this transgression of 'Neither shall ye walk in their ordinances' is equivalent to bloodshed, contrary to the view expressed by R. Nathan in the aforementioned Baraita of the Tosefta, which permits one to sit in a theatre because 'he shouts and saves lives'.

Now even in respect of this episode of Herod we encounter divergent Halakhic opinions as to the reason of the prohibition. For Josephus subsequently relates that the people were chiefly displeased because of the trophies that he had erected in the theatre, since they took them to be human faces.[18] Herod, fearing the anger of the Jews, invited the elders of the people to the theatre and showed that they were not sculptures of faces at all (*ibid.* 2). But — Josephus adds (*ibid.* 3) — although the feelings of the multitude were appeased, nevertheless: τινὲς αὐτῶν ἐπέμενον τῇ δισχερείᾳ τῶν οὐκ ἐξ ἔθους ἐπιτηδευμάτων, καὶ τὸ καταλύεσθαι τὰ πάτρια μεγάλων ἡγούμενοι ἀρχὴν κτλ ('But some of them persisted in their resentment of these practices as departures from tradition', etc.).

Since they deemed the violation of ancestral customs would be the cause of much tribulation, therefore some of them resolved to jeopardize their lives and slay Herod after the manner of the zealots,[19] so

18 Actually one should deal, in connection with this episode, with the question of sculptured faces according to the Halakha of the early Sages. But since the prohibition of images merits separate treatment, I am postponing the elucidation of the subject for the time being and will deal with it at an early opportunity.

19 From the Halakhic aspect it is not impossible that the conspirators sentenced him under the law of רודף ['pursuer', 'persecutor'] for his actions persisted in their sinfulness and in causing the public to sin. For although according to the fixed Halakha of the Mishna (*Sanhedrin* viii, 7) 'He that pursues after a beast, or that profanes the Sabbath, or that commits idolatry may not be delivered (from transgression) at the cost of their lives', yet from the Mishna of R. Simeon we learn that 'An idolater must be delivered (from Sin) at the cost of his life' (*T.B. Sanhedrin* 74a). A similar ruling is given also by R. Eleazar b. R. Zadok (*Tosefta, loc. cit.*, xi, 11) and by R. Eleazar b. R. Simeon (*T.P., loc. cit.*, viii, 26c). According to the tradition of the Babylonian Talmud (*loc. cit.*), R. Eleazar b. R. Simeon even teaches that one who profanes the Sabbath must be delivered (from sin) at the cost of his life. Nevertheless it appears that they judged him under the law of *zealots*. For as long as his deeds persisted he is to be judged as one caught in the act or close to it. In the same way Mattathias the Hasmonean and his sons judged the Jew who offered up a sacrifice at Modi'im to an idol under the same law; having seen the act, they recalled the Halakha of *Phinehas' deed* (*I Maccabees* ii 26; see above, p. 114).

long as they would prevent „ἐξαλλαττομένης αὐτοῖς τῆς πολιτείας... Ἡρώδην πρὸς βίαν ἐπεισάγοντα τὰ μὴ δι' ἔθους ὄντα κτλ" (Herod's forcible introduction of practices not in accord with custom, etc.). Indeed ten men, including a blind man, gave their lives for the precept, and rose up against Herod to kill him, and in the end they were caught and put to death with cruel tortures.

We have learnt that from earliest times there was a Halakha in Israel that considered it forbidden to sit in theatres and like places, not only because of the idolatry (and bloodshed) practised in them, but also — where there was no idol worship — on account of the ways of the Gentiles. This transgression was regarded with the utmost gravity, because they looked upon it as a departure from the ways of the mass of the people, while the acceptance of the light yoke of foreign culture seemed to them like apostasy.

On account of the gravity of the sin, they sought to ban the transgressors from the Temple and ruled that they were like Gentiles, who were likewise forbidden to enter the Temple court.[20]

Our Mishna is therefore to be explained according to its plain sense, namely that it is impossible that ʿAqavia, whose learning and fear of sin were so great, should be prevented from entering the Temple court, a penalty imposed only on the gravest sinners.

20 In *Ant.* viii, 3, 9, in the account of the building of Solomon's Temple, Josephus says concerning the Court of the Israelites: εἰς τοῦτο τοῦ λαοῦ πάντες οἱ διαφέροντες ἁγνείᾳ, καὶ παρατηρήσει τῶν νομίμων εἰσῄεσαν ('Into this precinct all the people who were distinguished by purity and their observance of the laws might enter'). Ostensibly we must infer from this statement that whoever treats the precepts contemptuously is forbidden to enter the courtyard, in accord with the tradition of the Aramaic translation of Samuel. However, it is possible that he refers only to those precepts that are connected with levitical purity, namely the sacrifices that those who still require the rite of atonement are obliged to bring, and who are prevented on account of them from entering the Temple Court (*M. Kelim* i, 12); the matter calls for further study. However, Josephus' statement that the Essenes were precluded (apparently by the Israelites) from visiting the Temple (*Ant.* xviii, 1, 5) constitutes proof, to my mind, for our thesis, since Josephus' observation implies that the Essenes were judged as seceders from the ways of the community and were consequently denied access to the Temple. However, since this passage is a subject of dispute among scholars, I intend to revert to the question and to deal with it specifically elsewhere.

THE LEVITICAL UNCLEANNESS OF GENTILES

A number of scholars, both Jewish and non-Jewish, have given attention to this subject, which forms an important chapter in the history of the relations between Judaism and the Gentile world, and have revealed various aspects of it.[1] But they, too, dealt with the matter incidentally and did not delve into it adequately by fully investigating the sources and elucidating them, until Dr. A. Büchler came and devoted a comprehensive study[2] to the question. He gathered together the vast amount of material relating to the theme, analysed it, interpreted it, and built thereon his exposition, which is explained below.

However, although great credit is due to this distinguished scholar for collecting almost all the sources dealing with Halakha and practice, nevertheless a number of his interpretations cannot be regarded, to my mind, as consonant with the simple sense of the sources, nor does his exposition as a whole approximate to the truth. I propose, therefore, to examine the subject anew and to suggest the view given below, which differs fundamentally from that of the aforementioned scholar, but it appears to me to accord more with what we know from the sources.

Now ostensibly, the correct procedure would be first to cite the sources, one by one, and finally to deduce from them the view that is grounded on them. But it seems to me that from the reader's viewpoint it is preferable to deal with the subject generally and then to go into details. Furthermore I consider it desirable to underline the distinctive features of the approach I suggest by comparing it with the essential aspects of that of Büchler. I shall therefore first present his exposition and afterwards submit my own opinion.

1 Schürer, *Geschichte*, etc.[4] III, 182–183; II, 89–92; Bertholet, *Die Stellung der Israeliten*, etc., 307, 324; Strack-Billerbeck, *Kommentar*, etc. I, 102–105; iv, 375; Zeitlin, *HUCA*, I, 359–362; Ginzburg, *MGWJ*, 1912, 434; Gavin, *The Jewish Antecendents*, etc., 29–30, 55; H. P. Chajes, *Sefer ha-Yovel le-Harkavy*, p. 109.

2 'The Levitical Impurity' etc., *JQR*, NS, XVII, 1–81.

Following are the basic elements of Büchler's view:

(a) The idea of the levitical uncleanness of non-Jews was unknown to the Jews till the close of the period of the Second Temple, when the eighteen decrees were enacted [see *M. Shabbat* i, 4]. And even when the Sages decreed that the Gentiles should be regarded as levitically unclean, they intended thereby only to keep the Jews away from the Romans, who were on the point of waging war against them, and from the neighbouring nations who assisted them. Thus this decree was only a political enactment and not a factor emanating from a fundamental concept of the faith.

(b) It is true that already earlier, about fifty years before the destruction of the Temple — in the first instance, at the beginning of the Hasmonean era — the non-Jews were deemed unclean; but this impurity was not inherent within them on account of their being Gentiles, but was due to the fact that they had relations with menstruous women. For although according to the Halakha non-Jews are not liable to defilement under Torah law, nevertheless the Sages decreed that their wives should be subject to menstruous impurity.

(c) The law of the intrinsic levitical uncleanness of non-Jews, which the Scribes revived near the time of the fall of Jerusalem had no practical consequences, since this form of impurity affects only the Temple and holy things, with the exception of the priests.

As against these postulates the following conclusions are, in my opinion, to be drawn from the sources:

(a) The impurity of non-Jews is one of the early Halakhot, current among the nation a long time before the destruction of the Temple. Although this law, which is not enjoined in the Torah, is only one of the *hilkhôt ʿimʿûm* [irregular laws passed in an emergency], it was nevertheless rooted in ancient tradition and was consolidated in the course of time and became in many respects a practical law.

(b) Basically this Halakha, which regards Gentiles as impure, is embedded in the Halakhic tradition that ascribes levitical uncleanness to the idol itself and to its attendants. The defilement of non-Jews is therefore an extension of the ambit of the uncleanness of the idol itself, incorporating its worshippers.

(c) The tradition that testifies that Gentile impurity is one of the eighteen decrees, merely seeks to state that this 'anaemic Halakha' gained new strength that day and 'was re-established'. This decree serves only to confirm the fact that it developed organically from a given basic conception which existed in the nation from early times, even though not all agreed to it, nor did the practice at all times conform to it, nor did the Sages rule according to it. Although undoubtedly the decree that made the Halakha permanent was motivated by political factors, yet intrinsically the Halakha is ancient and a product of religious thinking.

(d) In regard to the nature and intensity of the defilement three views are to be discerned in the sources, as follows:

(1) Light defilement (like that of contact with a reptile); (2) the impurity of one suffering from gonorrhea; (3) the uncleanness of a corpse.

Correspondingly we find in idolatry itself the defilement of a reptile, the impurity of a menstruous woman or of leprosy, and the uncleanness of the dead.

This fact is sufficient in itself to make us realize the connection between the defilement of idolatry and that of Gentiles and obviate the assumption that the uncleanness of Gentiles was *primarily* only a decree necessitated at the time by national political considerations.

(e) The impurity of non-Jews served as the initial reason for the ritual immersion of proselytes. For although in the course of time this nexus between a Gentile's impurity and a proselyte's immersion was as it were forgotten, and those who expounded the precept sought to explain it on another basis, nevertheless to begin with this immersion was no different from all other immersions enjoined in the Torah, whose purpose is to purify a person from his bodily defilement. The same may be said of his sacrifice, which is basically only like the precept of those who require the ritual of atonement, who bring a sacrifice for the completion of the purification.

(f) The Halakha that ordains uncleanness for non-Jews led to definite consequences in the transactions between Jews and other peoples. For although according to the fixed and generally accepted Halakha defilement applies only to the Temple and its holy things, nevertheless a number of laws, relating to the impurity of Gentiles and other kinds of uncleanness, were prescribed as obligatory and absolute like unqualified prohibitions — because an early tradition, which extended the commandment of purity beyond the Temple and its holy things, existed alongside this fixed Halakha.

Since, however, this Halakha was not essentially absolute and fixed, Jews did not refrain from having dealings with non-Jews, even in circumstances in which they might contract and impart uncleanness. But this sphere of transactions with Gentiles was liable to be restricted whenever there was no need for such dealings or there was no factor making them compulsory. Thus the application of the Halakha was dependent on circumstances of place and time; however, generally its influence was very evident in the life of the nation.

(g) The development of the Halakha, especially after the destruction of the Temple, was directed towards restricting the early tradition and the annulment and limitation of a number of laws founded on the uncleanness of Gentiles, and later generations sought to advance other reasons for those that remained. This fact, to which undoubtedly the political and economic conditions, which underwent a change after the destruction of the Temple, contributed considerably, is essentially in fundamental opposition to the entire conception of the early Sages, which attributed uncleanness to the Gentiles. Since even at the outset the Halakha was not acceptable to all Israel, it was possible to annul the tradition of this Halakha in several respects and to deprive it of the character of a Torah law and present it as a decree. Similarly, even the uncleanness of idolatry itself was weakened, for there were Sages who classified it as a Rabbinic enactment.

Now let us return and present the main sources that treat of the law of Gentile defilement in early times.

M. Ṭohorot v, 8: 'If there was in the town a woman imbecile, or a Gentile woman, or a Samaritan woman, all the spittle in the town is unclean.'

M. Makhshirin ii, 3: 'If in pots in which Israelites and Gentiles urinated the greater part (of the contents) is from unclean persons, the whole is unclean' etc.

M. Nidda x, 4: 'If a man or a woman that had a flux [of gonorrhea]... died, they defile by carriage, until the flesh has decayed. If a Gentile died, he does not defile by carriage.' The reason is that the Gentile's uncleanness in his lifetime diminishes with his death, even though the flesh is not decayed, as the matter is explained in the Baraita: 'And so R. Simeon said: If a Gentile dies, he does not defile by carriage, because his uncleanness is only a Rabbinical law.'[3]

3 *Tosefta Nidda* ix, 14; *T.B. ibid.* 69b the Halakha is taught in the name of Rabbi. Now Büchler (*op. cit.*, p. 18) explains the Baraita as though it referred to the Gentile's *corpse-uncleanness.* Thus R. Simeon rules that a Gentile's corpse defiles under Rabbinical law. Guttmann, too, gives a similar interpretation (*Mafteaḥ ha-Talmud* III, ii, p. 68). But the Halakha actually speaks of a Gentile's flux uncleanness, which only continues as long as he lives, and in point of fact the main law is stated in the Mishna in relation to a man or woman that had a flux and died etc. This is also the case in the Tosefta, and is likewise so explained in the Baraita in the Talmud. R. Simeon does not, therefore, speak at all of a Gentile's corpse-uncleanness and does not ascribe to it Rabbinical defilement, but refers to the Gentile's unclean-

M. Pesaḥim viii, 8: 'If a man became a proselyte the day before Passover, the School of Shammai say: He immerses himself and eats his Passover sacrifice in the evening; while the School of Hillel say: He that separates himself from the foreskin is as one that separates himself from a grave.' Our Talmud, it is true, explains the reason of the School of Hillel thus: 'It is a preventive measure [literally 'decree'] lest he should become defiled the following year and reason: Did I not undergo immersion last year and eat? Now, too, I shall perform immersion and eat.'[4] Thus he has no intrinsic uncleanness (due to his being a Gentile); but the expression 'He that separates himself from the foreskin is as one who separates himself from a grave' implies that on a man that becomes a proselyte there actually rests the uncleanness of seven days. No less far-fetched is the explanation of the dispute between the School of Shammai and the School of Hillel given in the Palestinian Talmud, according to which they differ as to whether a Gentile is subject to the uncleanness of a corpse or not: in the opinion of the School of Hillel a Gentile is subject to corpse-defilement, but in the view of the School of Shammai a Gentile is not subject to corpse-uncleanness. 'What is the reason of the School of Shammai? "Ye and your captives"; just as you did not become defiled until you entered into the covenant, so your captives did not become defiled until they entered into the covenant. What is the reason of the School of Hillel? "Ye and your captives"; just as you require sprinkling on the third and the seventh day, so your captives require sprinkling on the third and on the seventh day.'[5] This interpretation is not consonant with the language of the

ness in his lifetime (the impurity of one that had a flux) and declares him clean of this defilement, since to begin with (in his lifetime) this uncleanness is only a preventive prohibition of the Sages, who decreed that non-Jews should in all respects be like those who suffer from gonorrhea.

4 In the Gemara this interpretation is attributed to R. Joḥanan (*T.B. Pesaḥim* 92a). But after careful examination it may be said that primarily R. Joḥanan's statement consisted only of the words 'The dispute concerns an uncircumcized Gentile, but all agree that an Israelite immerses himself and eats his Passover sacrifice in the evening', that is to say, R. Joḥanan cited the gist of the Tosefta and the explanation, which is given in Aramaic, was interpolated into the body of R. Joḥanan's dictum by an anonymous tradition of Babylonian Sages.

5 *T.P. Pesaḥim* viii, 36b. [I have already pointed out in *Tarbiz*, III, 236, that according to the Palestinian Talmud, *loc. cit.*, the School of Shammai and the School of Hillel dispute over the same matter as R. Eliezer b. Jacob and R. Meir in *Sifra Zuṭa*, 305 (in my edition, p. 15): 'R. Liezer b. Jacob

Mishna, which ordains uncleanness for the Gentile generally and as an intrinsic impurity and not for fear of defilement that does not inhere in his person. It also appears that the expression 'He that separates himself from the foreskin' does not imply that it is the foreskin that is responsible for the Gentile's uncleanness — although there is evidence indicating that there were Sages who attributed unclean-

said the reason that Scripture declares "And it shall be unto the children of Israel" is that Israelites receive sprinkling, (but) Gentiles do not receive sprinkling. Said R. Meir to him: But has it not already been stated "Purify yourselves... and your captives"? He replied: Master, it is certainly as you have said, but you have left out one thing, which we need, namely "Ye and your captives" — just as you, children of the covenant, receive sprinkling, so the female captive, when, after entering into the covenant, becomes unclean, shall receive sprinkling. Indeed R. Eliezer b. Jacob in *Tosefta Pesaḥim* vii, 13 (according to the recension of the Vienna MS and the London MS, as well as *T.P. loc. cit.*) undoubtedly agrees with the School of Shammai and supports their views: '*R. Eliezer b. Jacob* said: There were officers and gatekeepers in Jerusalem who used to immerse themselves and eat their Passover sacrifices in the evening'; now the 'officers' [איסטרטיות] were certainly Gentile proselytes. In truth even the preceding Baraita in the Tosefta, *loc. cit.*, proves that the dispute centred on whether an uncircumcized Gentile may 'receive sprinkling' or not, for we learn: '*R. Jose* (the words 'b. Judah' are wanting in the London MS, and have been duplicated, by a copyist's error, from Halakha 12) said that the School of Shammai and the School of Hillel agree (Zuckermandel: 'the School of Shammai and the School of Hillel do not disagree') that an uncircumcized זר ['stranger'] (read: זכר 'male') receives sprinkling and eats [i.e. the Passover sacrifice]; the point of dispute is an uncircumcized Gentile, the School of Shammai holding that he immerses' etc.; this means to say that the dispute of the School of Shammai and the School of Hillel concerning a proselyte who became converted on the day before Passover (he was circumcized but did not undergo immersion) is linked to the Halakhic question whether a Gentile who is uncircumcized receives sprinkling. Now since it is *R. Jose* who also included this dispute, in *M. ʿEduyot* v, 2, among the more lenient rulings of the School of Shammai, there can be no doubt that the version of the London MS is the correct one, and it is also certain that the tradition of the Tosefta is correct as against that found in *T.B. Pesaḥim* 92a: 'The School of Shammai and the School of Hillel do not disagree about an Israelite who is uncircumcized, (but concur) that he *may immerse himself and eat his Passover sacrifice in the evening*', a recension that Tosafot already found difficult. Furthermore R. Joḥanan's statement is reported in *T.P. loc. cit.* as follows: '*Sprinkling is performed* on an uncircumcized Israelite, for we find that our ancestors in the wilderness received sprinkling when they were uncircumcized' etc., as it is reported in *T.B. Yevamot* 71b, and contrary to the form in which it is given in *T.B. Pesaḥim, loc. cit.*, in the name of R. Joḥanan. — Epstein].

ness to the foreskin[6] — and simply means that one who separates himself from the state of non-Jewishness is unclean for seven days.

M. Sheqalim viii, 1: 'Any spittle found in Jerusalem is regarded as clean except that of the Upper Market; so R. Meir.' The reason is undoubtedly that given in the Palestinian Talmud: 'The fuller of the Gentiles was there (in the Upper Market).'

M. Ṭohorot vii, 6: 'If a Gentile or a woman was with them all becomes unclean.'

T.B. Shabbat 127b: 'The Rabbis taught: Once a certain thing was needed from a noblewoman... Said the Sages: "Who will go?" R. Joshua responded: "I will go"... After he left, he descended and had a ritual bath, and taught his disciples. He then said to them... "When I descended and had a ritual bath, of what did you suspect me?" "We thought: Perhaps some spittle spurted from her mouth onto the Rabbi's garments." Said he to them: "By the Temple Service! this is precisely what happened...." '[7]

Tosefta Yom ha-Kippurim iv (iii), 20: 'It once happened that Ishmael b. Qimḥit went out to talk with the Arab king and spittle from the latter's mouth spurted onto his garments; thereupon his brother en-

6 Thus it is taught in a Baraita in *T.B. Pesaḥim* 92a: 'The School of Shammai and the School of Hillel do not disagree about an Israelite who is uncircumcized, (but concur) that he may *immerse himself* and eat his Passover sacrifice in the evening' etc. *Tosafot* does, indeed, state 'The Riva [R. Isaac b. Asher ha-Levi] is surprised at this, for we nowhere find immersion to be required by a circumcized Israelite even under Rabbinic law' (the explanation offered by *Tosefot Yom Tov* [R. Yom-Tov Lipmann Heller] that this refers only to the immersion undergone by all Israelites before the pilgrim-festival, is difficult). But we find elsewhere, too, that there were Sages who ruled that the foreskin contains uncleanness. For this Halakha is linked to the question discussed in the Talmuds (*T.B. Yevamot* 71b–72b; *T.P. Pesaḥim* viii, 36b; *T.P. Nazir* viii, 57a), namely whether an uncircumcized person can perform and receive sprinkling. In *T.B. Yevamot* (72b; also *T.B. Ḥagiga* 4b) the Talmud rules, according to the view of R. Akiba, that an uncircumcized person is like an unclean person in respect of sprinkling and appearance at the Temple [See my observations in the preceding note. The Sages did not say 'that the foreskin contains uncleanness', but only compared them, stating that R. Akiba 'includes the uncircumcized in the same prohibition as that of the unclean'. In *T.B. Yevamot* 72b they also rejected the proof based on the uncircumcized person's exemption from appearing at the Temple: 'There (i.e. the uncircumcized person is exempt from appearance at the Temple) because he is repulsive' — Ep.].

7 Cf. *Avot de-R. Nathan*, Recension II, xix (21b) and *Seder Eliyyahu Zuṭa* (ed. Ish Shalom [Friedmann] — *Pirqe Derekh Ereṣ* i, p. 7).

tered and served as High Priest in his stead. Thus their mother saw both her sons (ministering) as High Priests on the same day.'[8]

Tosefta Shabbat ix (x), 22: 'It is not permitted to suck either from a Gentile woman or from an unclean beast, but if the child is in danger, nothing stands in the way of saving life.' This prohibition to suck from a non-Jewish woman is to be explained only on the basis of Gentile defilement, and in *T.P. ʿAvoda Zara* (ii, 40c) we learn: 'It has been taught: A child may suck regularly from a Gentile woman and from an unclean beast, and milk may be brought for him from any place, and there is no need to have scruples about anything detestable or unclean.' In this Baraita, too, the milk of a Gentile woman is likened to that of an unclean beast, and only a minor is permitted to suck it.[9]

Tosefta ʿAvoda Zara viii (ix), 2 (*T.B. ibid.* 75b): 'If one buys utensils from Gentiles, then articles known to be unused should be immersed (in a ritual bath) and are clean' etc. This Halakha, which requires the vessels of non-Jews to be immersed even though they have not been used and there is no reason to fear admixture of forbidden foods, is explained by the Amoraim as though it were a special precept and its purpose was not to purify from uncleanness. According to the plain sense of the Halakha, this ritual immersion is not different from all other immersion and results from Gentile uncleanness.[10]

Josephus, *Wars*, ii, 8, 10: 'They (the Essenes) are divided according to the duration of their discipline into four grades; and so far are the junior members inferior to the seniors, that a senior if but touched by a junior, must take a bath, as after contact with an alien.'

8 The Baraita in *T.B. Yoma* 47a, after recounting the story of the *Tosefta*, adds the following narrative: 'It is further told that once R. Ishmael b. Qimḥit went out and talked to a certain general (this is the correct reading, cf. *D.S.*) in the street and spittle spurted... and Joseph his brother entered', etc. However, Büchler already rightly conjectured (*op. cit.*, p. 8, note 13) that the Babylonian Baraita simply contains two versions of a single tradition. Although the tradition in the Jerusalem Talmud and the Midrashim agrees with that of the Tosefta ('Arab king'), yet in *Avot de-R. Nathan* (Recension I, xxxiv) it corresponds to the second account in the Babylonian Talmud ('general').

9 Cf. *Tosefta Nidda* ii, 5 and *T.B. Yevamot* 114a. With regard to the theme of *M. ʿAvoda Zara* ii, 1, see below p. 182 f. and note 65 (see also Rashba (R. Solomon b. Abraham Adret) on *T.B. Yevamot, loc. cit.*).

10 Cf. *Tosefta Ṭohorot* vi, 11: 'If a person is pressed to work at a mill where there is a Gentile or menstruant, his garments contract the uncleanness of *midras* [literally 'treading'; denotes uncleanness resulting from the immediate contact of a gonorrhoeist].

Undoubtedly the defilement by a Gentile's touch, spoken of in this statement, is not restricted to the doctrines of the Essenes, but applies to Jewish teaching as a whole, and the analogy is the author's own observation.

Idem, Antiquities, xiv, 11, 5 (*Wars* i, 11, 6): Hyrcanus enjoined Herod, when he came from Galilee, not to bring his (Gentile) soldiers into the gates of Jerusalem, on account of 'the people who were purifying themselves' for the festival (of Weeks). We thus see that the Gentiles were liable to defile the Israelites and thereby prevent them from entering the Temple and offering sacrifices.

Idem, Antiquities, xviii, 4, 3: In the days of the earlier Roman governors the vestments of the High Priest were left in the capital in the custody of the ruling authorities and seven days before the Day of Atonement or the pilgrimage festivals Israelites would take them out and purify them (on account of defilement through Gentile contact).

Judith xii 5–8: During her stay with Holofernes, Judith used to go in the morning watch outside the camp to take a ritual bath and to pray, and scholars have conjectured that this immersion was on account of defilement by Gentiles, with whom she mingled.[11]

The Acts of the Apostles x 28: 'And he (Peter) said unto them, ye know how that it is an unlawful thing for a man that is a Jew to keep company, or come unto one of another nation; but God hath showed me that I should not call any man common or unclean.'[12]

Now these sources that teach the law of Gentile defilement do not explain the cause of this uncleanness. However, it certainly cannot be stated, as does a certain Christian scholar,[13] that non-Jews were deemed unclean because they failed to observe the laws of purity like Israelites. For this Halakha, that Gentiles are not subject to the Torah laws of uncleanness, is stated fully in many contexts. Thus it is stated in the Mishna with regard to menstruous impurity (*M. Nidda* vii, 3): 'All blood-stains that come from Reqem are clean. . . Those that come from Gentiles are clean', for the reason that they

11 Chajes, *loc. cit.* But the matter requires further study, for it is possible that it was not Gentile uncleanness that was the cause of this immersion. I shall deal with this in my next article.

12 John xviii 28 is apparently not relevant here, for the uncleanness mentioned there was on account of Gentile dwelling-places, which is based on the fear lest abortions were thrown down the drains etc. (*M. Oholot* xviii, 7–8). See, however, below, note 75.

13 Schürer, *op. cit.*, p. 91, II. Cf. Büchler, *op. cit.*, p. 2.

are not liable to menstruous impurity by Torah law (or Rabbinic enactment). Similarly the Sages ruled (*Torat Kohanim* [Sifra], *Tazriaʿ*, Sec. i) with regard to the uncleanness of a woman in confinement (and of a menstruant, who is included in the pericope): 'This matter concerns Israelites but not Gentiles.'

In respect of leprosy-signs it is taught (*M. Negaʿim* iii, 1): 'All can contract leprosy uncleanness except Gentiles and resident aliens [one who renounces idolatry; see *M. Dem.* ii, 3]; so, too, with regard to leprosy-signs of garments (*ibid.* xi, 1): 'All garments may contract the uncleanness of leprosy except those of Gentiles'; the same applies to leprosy of houses (*ibid.* xii, 1): 'All houses may contract the uncleanness of leprosy except those of Gentiles.' In the *Sifra* it is taught (Meṣoraʿ, Sec. v): 'R. Ishmael says: (The houses of) your possession contract leprosy uncleanness, but (the houses of) the possession of Gentiles do not contract leprosy uncleanness; and just as (the houses of) their possession are not subject to leprosy defilement so are their garments not subject to leprosy defilement' (cf. *ibid.*, Sec. x, and *Tosefta Negaʿim* vii, 10).

Similarly the Sages excluded their semen from uncleanness (*M. Miqwa'ot* viii, 4) and ruled that a Gentile is not susceptible to uncleanness if he suffered a flux (except the uncleanness due to his being a Gentile; see *M. Zavim* ii, 1 and 3).

The same applies to defilement by a corpse, concerning which the Sages taught (*Tosefta Ahilot* i, 4): 'If a Gentile etc. comes in contact with a corpse, vessels touching them are clean.' Similarly it is stated there (xiv, 6):[14] 'Grass that has been plucked up and placed in the window etc. and a Gentile or animal — all these reduce (the window space)', (for anything that is not susceptible to uncleanness forms a partition before the impurity).

The Talmud (*T.B. Nazir* 61b) expounds and deduces from Scripture that Gentiles are not susceptible to uncleanness like Israelites.[15]

14 *T.B. Bava Batra* 20a.

15 Katzenelson, *MGWJ*, XLIII, pp. 194–196 takes the opposite view and seeks to prove that according to the Torah non-Jews are susceptible to uncleanness the same as Jews; furthermore, even in the period of the Second Temple, until near the time of its destruction, this was the established halakhic ruling. This opinion is the corollary of this scholar's theory that primarily the Pentateuchal laws of defilement are based on public considerations, and therefore, needless to say, the Gentile, too, is subject to the regulations concerning cleansing and purification. But we are concerned only with the Oral Law and the period of the Second Commonwealth, and for this halakhic chapter

Thus Gentile uncleanness is not due to impurity that comes to them from elsewhere, but as the Rabbis stated (*Tosefta Zavim* ii, 1; *Torat Kohanim* [Sifra], *Zavim* Sec. 1; *T.B. Shabbat* 84a; *T.B. Nidda* 43a): 'Gentiles and a resident alien do not defile by reason of a flux, but although they do not defile because of a flux, they are unclean in all respects like those who suffer a flux, and heave-offering is burnt on their account, but an offering is not incurred on their account for defiling the Temple and its holy things.'

Now we have to consider when Gentiles began to be regarded as unclean.

Ostensibly an answer is given to this question in the Talmud, in the statement of Rav Naḥman b. R. Isaac, who said (*T.B. Shabbat* 17b; *T.B. 'Avoda Zara* 36b): 'They decreed that a Gentile child should defile by reason of flux, so that an Israelite child should not associate with him for sodomy.' This implies that this Halakha is one of the Eighteen Edicts, which were decreed a few years prior to the destruction of the Temple, as is also stated in the Palestinian Talmud (*Shabbat* i, 3c): 'It is taught: They decreed eighteen edicts. . . as follows: They decreed concerning the bread of Gentiles. . . and on their daughters and their semen and their urine.'

However, if we examine this tradition of Eighteen Edicts, we see that not all the decrees introduced innovations into the Halakha, but were intended to decide in respect to certain early laws and to validate them, because they had not at the outset been firmly established and they were disputed, and the strange practices of those who took a lenient or different view served to undermine them. For this tradition of the Baraita in the Palestinian (and likewise in the Babylonian) Talmud includes the prohibition of the oil and bread of non-Jews among the Eighteen Edicts, yet we know from a number of sources that this interdict was in force in the days of the Second Temple many generations before the Destruction.[16]

Thus Josephus (*Wars* ii, 21, 2)[17] attests that the Jews living in Syria 'refrained from using oil not prepared by their brethren'. Although this episode belongs to the time of the war of Vespasian, nevertheless we learn that the prohibition of non-Jewish oil was in force long

Katzenelson is unable to produce any convincing proof to reverse the established Halakha that Gentiles are not subject to the laws of cleanness and uncleanness.

16 See *Dorot ha-Rischonim*, Part I, vol. iii, pp. 294–297; and cf. Zeitlin, *REJ*, LXVIII, p. 36.

17 Cf. also *Life*, ch. xiii, and *Ant.* xii, 3, 1.

before then, since at that time it had spread among all Jews, including those in the Diaspora. He similarly relates (*Life*, 3) that the priests that were sent by Felix to Rome to plead their cause before Nero subsisted on a diet of figs and nuts. This incident certainly preceded the Eighteen Edicts.

We also learn from Josephus (*Ant.* xii, 3, 1) that the Jews used to refrain from using the oil of Gentiles already in the days of Seleucus Nicator, and the state was compelled to order the cities to give the Jewish citizens money in lieu of oil.

Judith, too, did not wish to partake of Holofernes' food and she lived on the oil and wine and bread that she brought with her from her house (*Judith* x 5; xii 1–4). Similarly Tobit kept himself from eating 'the food of the Gentiles' (*Tobit* i 11), like Daniel and his companions, and *The Book of Jubilees* (xxii 16) admonishes the Jews not to dine with a Gentile.

There is no need, therefore, to state that the prohibition of non-Jewish oil, wine, and bread was observed long before the promulgation of the Eighteen Edicts (and before the time of the Hasmoneans). But since it is not written in the Torah and is only a tradition of the early Sages, it required reinforcement; it also appears that not all accepted this Halakha, nor acted in conformity with it.

The same applies to the daughters of Gentiles, who were interdicted at the same time; this edict is to be understood literally as a prohibition of marriage and sexual intercourse. However, there is not the slightest doubt that even Gentiles who did not belong to the seven nations [of Canaan] were subject to the interdiction of marriage and congress in the period of the Second Temple. For so the Mishna (*Sanhedrin* ix, 6) teaches: 'If a man has intercourse with an Aramaean [i.e. non-Jewish] woman, the zealots may fall upon him.'[18] *The Book of Jubilees*[19] ordains the death penalty for a man

18 Although according to tradition one who has intercourse with an Aramaean woman is not liable to the death penalty, and the prohibition is only a Rabbinic enactment (*T.B.* *'Avoda Zara* 36b; *T.P. Shabbat* i, 3d), yet above, p. 118, I endeavoured to show that this Halakha was *au fond*, when first taught, based on the Halakha that imposes death at the hands of man on one who was intimate with the Aramaean woman (as well as on all the other transgressors enumerated in the same Mishna).

19 Ch. xxx 7, 14–17. Cf. also *The Testaments of the Twelve Patriarchs*, Levi, ch. ix. Philo (*On the Special Laws*, III, 29) likewise states that the Torah forbids intermarriage with any Gentiles whatsoever. Cf. further Ritter, *Philon u.d. Halacha*, pp. 71–76, and Heinemann's notes 281–282, *Philons u.s.w.*

who gives his son, or daughter, or sister in marriage to a Gentile. Even the House of Herod scrupulously refrained from marrying their daughters to Gentile kings before they were converted to Judaism. Josephus[20] criticizes Drusilla, the sister of Berenice, for marrying a non-Jew contrary to the law of the Torah. And undoubtedly when Ezra separated the Israelites from their Gentile wives, he did not restrict his action only to the daughters of the seven nations.

Perforce, therefore, we must conclude that this 'edict' was only promulgated in order to establish the ancient Halakha on a firm basis[21] and to give it permanence. And the same applies to the ritual defilement of Gentiles as well, namely that the decrees were not enacted for the first time then, but were reinstated and reinforced as permanent Halakhot.

This is also proved by the sources. For 'the camp of the Gentiles' in Jerusalem existed there only prior to the War of Vespasian, that is before the Eighteen Edicts were decreed.[22] It also is difficult to restrict the dispute between the School of Shammai and the School of Hillel recorded in the Mishna of *Pesaḥim* to the period after the destruction of the Temple; and the Jewish custom to purify the vestments of the High Priest seven days prior to the Day of Atonement and the three pilgrim festivals dates from thirty to sixty years before the Destruction. Certainly the *Book of Judith* was written in

20 *Ant.* xx, 7, 2.

21 Since the edicts were only intended to consolidate a weak law, it is not surprising, therefore, that Rabbi Simeon includes here the prohibition concerning the daughters of Gentiles among these decrees, although in his view it is forbidden to marry non-Jewish women, even if they do not belong to the seven nations of Canaan, by Pentateuchal law (*T.B. Avoda Zara* 36b). Similarly Gentile testimony is interdicted here, despite the fact that according to tradition this Halakha is of Torah origin; this was possible because the Sages sought only to reinforce commandments that were laxly observed.

22 According to Graetz (Fünfte Auflage, Dritter Band, Zweite Hälfte, p. 471 ff.) the episode occurred after the defeat of Cestius Gallus and the expulsion of the Romans from Jerusalem. Zeitlin thinks (*op. cit.*, p. 36) that the event occurred a few days earlier (66 C.E.). At any rate, even according to this view, the camp (קצרן) could have continued to exist after the edict for but a negligible period (the קסטרא [castra] in Jerusalem is also mentioned in *Shir ha-Shirim Zuṭa* [end], Schechter, p. 47; Buber, p. 41). Weiss (*Dor Dor we-Dorshaw*, second ed., p. 175 and note 1 to p. 176) conjectures that the Eighteen Edicts were decreed near the time of Agrippa I's death (in the forties), but his theory is unfounded.

Temple times; while the story of Ishmael b. Qimḥit preceded the Eighteen Edicts by approximately fifty years.[23]

Now the late Prof. Büchler, who seeks to establish that Gentile uncleanness stemmed from the Eighteen Edicts, also realized that the episode of Ishmael b. Qimḥit constituted an objection to his theory, and endeavoured to sustain his argument by a hypothesis that implies no little novelty. He maintains that the inherent uncleanness of non-Jews originated shortly before the Destruction, as already stated; but he suggests that in the time of Ishmael b. Qimḥit uncleanness was decreed upon Gentiles because they had intercourse with menstruants. Although under Torah law Gentiles are not susceptible to defilement, according to the established Halakha, nevertheless the uncleanness of a menstruant was decreed on non-Jewesses in that generation.[24]

This assumption led this scholar to yet another, namely, that in the last days of the Commonwealth the Halakha prevailed that made Gentiles susceptible to defilement by a corpse, and thus the Sages of that generation made non-Jews equal to Jews in respect of the laws of purity and impurity. But the proofs advanced by Prof. Büchler are unable to establish this theory, and there is evidence from other sources that refutes his assumptions.

23 Josephus (*Ant.* xvii, 6, 4) relates that Matthias son of Theophilus suffered a nocturnal pollution on the night of the Day of Atonement and refrained from performing the service in the Temple. From the manner of his narration it appears that he is reporting here a tradition concerning a unique event that occurred in the days of the Second Temple, when a High Priest was prevented from ministering on the Day of Atonement. Ostensibly this tradition contradicts the one found in Talmudic sources (cf. *Avot de-R. Nathan*, Recension I, xxxv; Schechter, liii, 1: 'Seminal pollution never occurred to the High Priest on the Day of Atonement, except in the case of R. Ishmael b. Qimḥit, who went out to speak with a certain general', etc. This combination of the experience of a pollution with the uncleanness emanating from a Gentile's spittle indicates that *au fond* the tradition is based on the uniqueness of the occurrence that a High Priest should become unclean on the Day of Atonement at all), which also has as its purpose to relate an exceptional story. At all events there is no reason to deny the truth of the Talmudic tradition regarding the story of Ishmael b. Qimḥit (but, needless to say, Josephus contradicts *M. Avot* v, 5).

24 Gavin, *op. cit.*, 29–30, 55, accepts Büchler's view, but misunderstands his meaning. For whereas Büchler said that since the uncleanness of a menstruant was decreed upon the wives of Gentiles, the Gentile husbands are unclean like those who have intercourse with menstruants, and Gavin writes that the defilement of non-Jewish wives (on account of their state of menstruation) makes *Gentile men* unclean with *secondary degree of uncleanness*!

Prof. Büchler uses an analogy to support his conjecture that the Sages issued a decree that Gentile women should defile like menstruants. He argues as follows: Just as in the story of the High Priest, who was conversing with a Sadducee when spittle from the latter's mouth spurted on him, and he turned pale, etc. (*Tosefta Nidda* v, 3; *T.B. Nidda* 33b) the uncleanness of the Sadducee stemmed from the fact that he was deemed as one who has intercourse with a menstruant, so the uncleanness of the High Priest who spoke with the Arabian king etc. was due to the same reason.

But against such an analogy it may be argued: 'Were the two matters then taught conjointly?' — 'The two cases are unrelated'. For there is no basis for combining the two incidents and drawing conclusions from the one relative to the other, in order to create a new Halakha, which is completely contradicted by a number of sources. Only Prof. Büchler wished to prove that the Sages had decreed susceptibility to menstruation uncleanness on non-Jewish women from the following statements of Rav Dimi and Rabin in *T.B. Sanhedrin* 82a (*T.B. ʿAvoda Zara* 36b): 'The Bet Din of the Hasmoneans decreed that an Israelite who cohabits with a Gentile woman should be culpable on account of (intercourse with) a menstruant, a non-Jewish maidservant, a Gentile woman, and a married woman. When Rabin came (back from Eretz-Israel) he said: On account of (cohabiting with) a menstruant, a non-Jewish maidservant, a Gentile woman, and a harlot.'[25] It cannot, however, be proved that this tradition comes to testify that it was decreed that a non-Jewess should be regarded as actually having a menstruant's uncleanness and that in every respect. For the ruling can be explained as referring only to the prohibition of congress (with which the passage in question deals), and does not refer to defilement brought about through her contact, place of lying, place of sitting, etc., nor to the uncleanness of her partner. Furthermore, it appears that this tradition merely attempts to explain the prohibition of intimacy with a non-Jewess decreed by the Sages with the help of a number of 'auxiliary factors', which are not actually halakhically valid, as Rashi explained in Sanhedrin (a variant of his gloss, in *ʿAvoda Zara*): 'Although the blood of a non-Jewess' (menstruation) is like that of a beast, nevertheless it is repulsive and constitutes religious desecration.'

25 Büchler is of opinion that this uncleanness was decreed near the time of the Hasmoneans, or at the beginning of this period, but the edict was subsequently annulled or forgotten and was renewed near the time of Ishmael b. Qimḥit (17–18 C.E.).

The same may be said of the following Haggadic statement in the *Tanḥuma* (Buber, Meṣoraʿ xxvi, 2; see note 72), which could ostensibly be cited in support of Büchler's thesis: 'Because the Gentiles do not refrain from intimacy with a menstruant they are liable to "extinction" [literally 'to be cut off'; a Talmudic term denoting Divine punishment in the form of premature or sudden death, or childlessness]', etc. It is not to be inferred from this that the uncleanness of menstruants is ascribed to Gentile women by Torah law, for the Haggada seeks only to give a reason for the verse 'When the Lord thy God shall cut off the nations', and attributes their punishment to an act that is forbidden to Israelites, but is in no way prohibited to Gentiles (for whom there is no actual uncleanness in the blood of their menstruants, nor is intercourse with them sinful).

Even if we accept the statement in Sanhedrin at its face value, this late tradition cannot be regarded as evidence for an early period. For it is unconfirmed by any other source.

Büchler seeks to adduce further proof for his theory from the Mishna (*ʿEduyot* v, 1; *Nidda* iv, 3): 'The blood of a non-Jewess and the non-defiling blood of a leprous woman that is a leper the School of Shammai declares clean, but the School of Hillel say: It is like her spittle or her urine', and he explains the passage as though the School of Shammai and the School of Hillel differed with regard to the Halakha. According to the School of Shammai a Gentile woman has no menstruation uncleanness, while the School of Hillel holds that she has, but it is not as stringent as that of a Jewish menstruant.

However, the Mishna can be interpreted in another way, namely that the School of Shammai and the School of Hillel agree that the blood of non-Jewish menstruants does not defile with menstrual uncleanness, but differ in regard to the law of a *zav*'s discharge [a *zav* is one who suffers a flux; see Lev. xv 1–15; 25–30]. In the view of the School of Shammai the blood of her menstruation does not defile even on account of a *zav*'s discharge, just as the Halakha declares the semen of a Gentile clean even in respect of the uncleanness of *zavim*, which the Sages had decreed upon them (*M. Miqwaʾot* v, 4).[26] But the School of Hillel were of opinion that although Gentile

26 According to its plain meaning the purpose of the Halakha is to declare the semen that she discharges to be ritually clean even under Rabbinic law (cf. *T.B. Nidda* 34a–b). It would appear, however, that the Baraita in the Palestinian Talmud (*loc. cit.*): 'And these are the things that they decreed... that the semen the Gentile women discharge and their urine (be unclean)' disagrees with our Mishna, even though the Talmud subsequently reconciles

women are not subject to menstrual uncleanness, their blood nevertheless defiles like a discharge, and consequently it is like it, defiling when wet but not dry. All, however, hold that a non-Jewess is not susceptible to a menstruant's uncleanness even under Rabbinic law.[27]

the Halakha in the Baraita by stating 'For a discharge of semen cannot possibly pass out without urine'.

27 My explanation follows the view of the Talmud, which explains that the School of Shammai declare the blood of a Gentile clean, because they wished to make a distinguishing rule by means of time-purification to show that her primary uncleanness (in regard to her spittle and her urine) is Rabbinical. I understand at its face value the objection raised in the Babylonian Talmud 'But do not the Shammaites accept the tradition: "Speak unto the children of Israel", etc., but a preventive measure has been enacted against them that they should be regarded as *zāvim* in all respects?'; that is to say, the Gemara considers the blood of menstruation as the discharge of a *zāvā* [a female suffering a flux] both according to the School of Shammai and the School of Hillel, and it does not seek to draw an analogy between the preventive measure concerning the uncleanness of *zavim* and the uncleanness of a menstruant, applying the Halakhic position of the former to the latter. First, how is such an analogy possible? For the uncleanness of Gentile *zavim* is not due to *their flux*, but is a general uncleanness, having no physical cause (as in the case of an Israelite); whereas here we seek to declare her blood unclean on account of actual *menstruation*. Furthermore, is it feasible to assume that according to the view of the Talmud Gentiles would be susceptible to other specific forms of uncleanness, such as leprosy, according to Rabbinic law? Again, if this uncleanness is that of menstruation, what distinguishing rule is there according to the Shammaites, when they declare a Gentile woman exempt from menstruation uncleanness, that her flux uncleanness is Rabbinical in respect of her spittle and her urine. Even the juxtaposition of a Gentile woman's menstruation blood with the non-defiling blood of a leprous woman in our Mishna shows that just as in the case of a leprous woman the defiling factor is leprosy, so in the case of a non-Jewess the factor that makes her unclean lies not in the blood of menstruation *per se*, but is due to the flux. However, our Mishna may be explained to mean that the School of Shammai and the School of Hillel differ on the basic Halakha, namely that the Shammaites do not regard the blood of menstruation as the source of a *zav*, while in the view of the Hillelites it is like the other sources, and hence defiles like them both when wet and when dry. This would also be the basis of the difference between the two schools in regard to the blood purifying of a leprous woman, as is stated in the Tosefta (v, 3) 'The blood of a Gentile woman etc. The School of Shammai say they are like the blood of her wound' (R. Obadiah of Bertinoor, in his commentary on *M. 'Eduyot*, explains 'blood of a non-Jewess' as blood of flux; but this interpretation is improbable). Cf. Maimonides' commentary to *M. Eduyot* v, 1 (and the observations of Rabad [R. Abraham b. David] *ad loc.*) and to *M. Nidda*, *loc. cit.*

Professor Büchler's hypothesis is also intrinsically difficult. For if Gentiles were declared unclean fifty years before the destruction of the Temple (and in the first instance before the Hasmonean era), because they were accounted like those who have intercourse with menstruants, why did they find it necessary to decree again subsequently (shortly before the Destruction) that they should be deemed unclean as *zavim* in order to keep them away from Israelites, seeing that they were already kept apart by a strict degree of uncleanness from the outset?

In conjunction with his theory that the Scribes had introduced an enactment ascribing a menstruant's uncleanness to a Gentile woman, Büchler further conjectures that near the time of the destruction of the Temple there were Sages who ruled that Gentiles were subject to uncleanness in every respect, and made them susceptible to cleanness and uncleanness in all respects like Israelites. He deduces this Halakha from the ruling of the School of Hillel in the Mishna in *Pesaḥim* ('If a man became a proselyte the day before Passover' etc.). For the Palestinian Talmud explains that the dispute between the School of Shammai and the School of Hillel in this Mishna centres on the fitness of Gentiles to acquire corpse uncleanness, as it is stated: 'What is the reason of the School of Shammai? "Ye and your captives"; just as you did not become defiled until you entered into the covenant' etc. (see above). Büchler also cites here in addition the dispute between R. Simeon and the Sages, as to whether Gentile graves defile or not (*T.B. Yevamot* 60b–61a and the parallel passages, and he holds, contrary to the view of the Talmud, that R. Simeon declares a Gentile corpse to be clean also in respect of contact and carrying), and since — so he argues — we learn from the testimony of Abba Yudan of Sidon in the name of R. Eliezer (*Tosefta Ahilot* xviii, 7) that a non-Jewish corpse, in the opinion of the Sages who disagree with R. Simeon, defiles, hence it is to be inferred that shortly before the Destruction Gentiles were declared liable to uncleanness, to wit, that their bodies (upon death) should defile others as with their own uncleanness. In view of the fact that R. Eliezer's testimony informs us that the Sages ruled that a Gentile corpse defiles, consequently we must conclude that this Halakha also declared Gentiles fit to receive uncleanness like an Israelite, and that this is the ruling of the Hillelites.

However, it must first be realized that the uncleanness of a Gentile corpse, which defiles an Israelite, cannot be ascribed to a living Gentile's susceptibility to uncleanness, for even according to the Halakha that exempts a Gentile from becoming defiled like an Israelite, it is still possible for a non-Jewish corpse to convey uncleanness through contact and carrying, and even in a 'tent'. As for the dispute between the School of Shammai and the School of Hillel, we have already seen that the Mishna in question must be explained according to its plain sense as centring on the primary uncleanness of the Gentile *per se*, and not on his fitness to receive uncleanness emanating from elsewhere.

It is true that we have learnt from the discussion of the Palestinian Talmud on this Mishna that there were Sages who held that Gentiles are subject to laws of uncleanness. This is also to be inferred from *Sifre Zuṭa* (edition of my teacher Prof. Epstein, *Tarbiz*, I, p. 15; cf. ed. Horovitz, 305) ' "And it shall be unto the children of Israel" — (this means) Israelites require sprinkling, (but) Gentiles do not require sprinkling. It is related that once R. Liezer b. Jacob was sitting and expounding (the laws of) the Red Heifer in Tiberias, and R. Meir and R. Leazar b. Shammuaʿ were also sitting there. Said R. Liezer b. Jacob: The reason why Scripture states "And it shall be unto the children of Israel" is that Israelites require sprinkling, (but) Gentiles do not require sprinkling. Thereupon R. Meir said to him: But has it not already been stated "purify yourselves... and your captives"? He replied: Master, it is certainly as you say; but you have omitted one thing there, which we need, namely "ye and your captives", which means that just as you who are sons of the covenant require sprinkling, so too the female captive, when she enters into the covenant and becomes unclean, requires sprinkling.'[28]

But to begin with we must consider the anonymous sources that state the Halakha in accordance with the view that denies fitness for purification to Gentiles. Thus it is taught in the Sifre (Numbers § 117) ' "Ye and your captives" — (this means) just as you are sons of the covenant, so your captives must be sons of the covenant'; a similar anonymous statement is found in *Sifre Zuṭa* itself (*loc. cit.* and in another passage, Horovitz 329). Also in the Tosefta (Para xii (xi), 11) we learn: 'If he sprinkled upon something not fit for sprinkling, on a Gentile, or on a beast' etc. It is thus seen that the Halakhic trend even in late times was to disallow Gentiles fitness for purification (or defilement).

Secondly, we nowhere find the early Tannaim expressly stating that Gentiles are fit to acquire uncleanness, and we have already seen

28 See Büchler, *op. cit.*, p. 17, note 32.

earlier a considerable number of sources, which all indicate that Gentiles are not at all susceptible to uncleanness.

Hence we must conclude that the early Sages were inclined to deny Gentiles the fitness to become defiled, although from the Torah it is possible to infer (from the story of Midian) their susceptibility to contract uncleanness, and the dispute between R. Meir and R. Eliezer b. Jacob establishes the existence of such a Halakha, which was renewed by some of the later scholars. It is not improbable that this new trend is connected with the aim of the later Halakha to restrict the prohibitions flowing from the law of non-Jewish defilement due to Gentile status, and to remove this category of uncleanness from the sphere of Biblical law and to transfer it to Rabbinic legislation (enacted on account of the prohibition of intermarriage), since fitness for defilement and permanent uncleanness because of Gentile status are mutually exclusive.

Therefore, having learnt from the story of Ishmael b. Qimḥit that Gentiles were regarded as unclean at least fifty years before the Destruction, we must perforce conclude that this defilement was intrinsic. Furthermore the tradition found in Josephus that Hyrcanus enjoined Herod to refrain from bringing his troops to Jerusalem so that they should not defile the multitudes shows that this Halakha was already observed in the middle of the first century B.C.E.

The great antiquity of this Halakha and its powerful hold on the life of the nation is evident from the tradition prohibiting non-Jews to enter the Temple beyond the Rampart [*Ḥêl*] (or Lattice Railing [*Sôreg*]), if we assume that this Halakha, which is non-Biblical, emanates from the fact that uncleanness was ascribed to Gentiles. It is logical to assume that this prohibition was due to defilement, although it is not impossible to explain it differently. This is evidenced by the fact that at times the sources compare the prohibition of Gentiles' entering to that of defiled Israelites' going into the Temple court, as we shall see later.

The Halakha itself is attested by Josephus in several passages,[29] and so, too, by Philo,[30] and there are scholars who deduce from *I Maccabees* vii 33, where it is recorded that when Nicanor went up to the Temple Mount, the priests and elders went forth to greet him etc., that Nicanor did not enter the sanctuary, where the elders of Israel were to be found. So, too, I consider, it is possible to infer

29 *Ant.* xv, 11, 5; *Wars* v, 5, 2; vi, 2, 4; *Against Apion* ii, 8.

30 *Legatio ad Caium* 31, 213; cf. *The Acts of the Apostles* xxi 28.

this from *III Maccabees* i 13–15, where it is narrated that Ptolemy Philopator wished to enter the Holy of Holies, but the priests prevented him: 'He also asked why those present had not hindered him from entering the sanctuary in the first place. And some one answered thoughtlessly that he did wrong to make this boast. But since this is so, he (the king) said, be the cause what it may, why should he not enter in any case, whether they wish it or not?'[31]

It appears that this obscure passa gecan only be explained on the basis that the author knew that Gentiles were forbidden to enter the Temple, and he was surprised at the early tradition concerning Ptolemy, who wished to go into the Holy of Holies. For how, in the first instance, was he permitted to enter the sanctuary at all? Therefore he added this question and answer to the basic tradition.

Similarly Josephus (*Antiquities* xii, 3, 4) cites an order issued by Antiochus III, from which we learn that already in those days (before the Maccabees) Gentiles were not allowed to enter the Temple. Even if we deny the authenticity of this document, it is nevertheless evident that several generations before the Destruction this Halakha was assigned to the pre-Maccabean age. If we accept the view of scholars[32] that the *Soreg*, which was torn down by 'the Gentile kings' (*M. Middot* ii, 3) or by their High Priest Alcimus (*I Maccabees* ix 54), was the partition that divided off the Temple area where Gentiles were permitted from the part where they were forbidden, it can be inferred that in Maccabean times this Halakha was ascribed to the beginning of the Second Temple period.[33] At all events this Halakha was in existence a long time before the Hasmonean era proper.

Now in the same decree of Antiochus, where he prohibits non-

31 The interpretation of the statement depends on the various versions of *v.* 13; cf. Charles, *Apocrypha* I, 163, note 13; Kautzsch, *Apokryphen* I, 122, note k. It seems to me that only the reading and interpretation given in the text are to be accepted (Kautzsch translated similarly), since any other version does not give a good sense.

32 Cf. Schürer, *op. cit.*, 225–226, note 6.

33 'The works of the prophets' in *Maccabees* are, like 'the works of the prophets' in the Mishna (*Yadayim* iv, 3), the enactments of the last prophets (akin to 'custom of the prophets' and 'institution [literally 'foundation'] of the prophets', *T.B. Sukka* 44a and *T.P. ibid.* v, 54b), who are Haggai, Zechariah, and Malachi, whose name is attached to a number of Halakhot (*T.B. Yevamot* 16a; *Nazir* 53a; *Qiddushin* 43a; *Rosh ha-Shana* 19b; Ḥullin 137b) and they act as intermediaries between the Men of the Great Synagogue and the 'Prophets' (or the 'Elders', *Avot de-R. Nathan*, Recension I and II, i, 1b).

Jews to enter the Temple, he declares: 'It shall be unlawful for any foreigner to enter the enclosure of the temple; which is forbidden also to the Jews, unless to those who, according to their custom, have purified themselves'; thus he likens the prohibition of the Gentiles to that of unclean Israelites.[34] The Mishna (*Kelim* i, 8) also links them together: 'The Rampart is still more holy, for no Gentiles or one defiled by a corpse may enter therein.' It is likewise stated in *Sifre Zuṭa* (228): 'The Rampart is holier than the Temple Mount for Aramaeans [i.e. Gentiles] and those defiled by a corpse may enter the Temple Mount but not within the Rampart.'

We may therefore conclude that the law prohibiting Gentiles from entering the sanctuary is based on the ascription of uncleanness to them.[35] But even if we do not interpret the Halakha thus, we nevertheless learn that the law of Gentile uncleanness was widely current before the time of Herod.

Therefore we should not seek the source of the Halakha in political factors of the last days of the Second Temple, or base it on similar factors in other periods, but we should regard it as the product of the religious thought of the ancients, as the outcome of the fundamental outlook of a certain spiritual trend in Judaism concerning the uncleanness of the uncircumcised and idolaters, just as the Halakha

34 However, this analogy is not decisive, for it is possible to discern here an attempt to defend the Jewish attitude towards the Gentile world by showing that Judaism is not more stringent towards Gentiles than towards Israelites who have not sanctified themselves.

35 Josephus and Philo declare that a Gentile who entered the prohibited area of the Temple was sentenced to death. This is also attested by the inscription found by Clermont-Ganneau (cf. Schürer, III, p. 329, note 57). Although Derenbourg (*Journal asiatique*, 1872, pp. 178–195) seeks to explain that the reference here is only to death at the hands of heaven, his interpretation is improbable, for the sources, according to their plain sense, show that the punishment was carried out by human agencies; cf. Bertholet p. 312. It would thus seem that the assumption that Gentiles were forbidden to enter the Temple on account of uncleanness that they had contracted (like one defiled by a corpse) is untenable, for an unclean person entering the sanctuary is only liable to *kārēt* ('extinction', i.e. premature death imposed by heaven). But there is no reason for surprise, for even a Gentile who partook of the Passover sacrifice (*T.B. Pesaḥim* 3b) was slain, and it is difficult to suppose, with Derenbourg, that this was an act of the zealots. Although it is possible that a more stringent attitude was adopted in the case of Gentiles, it may yet be assumed that some (at least) of the transgressions for which the penalty, according to the Halakha, was only *kārēt*, or death by an act of God, were punished by death at the hands of the court in conformity

is found among the Falashas[36] and the Samaritans,[37] who declare foreigners completely unclean.

However, even though essentially the uncleanness of Gentiles is one of the earliest Halakhot, nevertheless not all the authorities hold like views about its degree of defilement, some being more stringent and others less.

Most of the relevant Mishnayot and other Tannaitic statements accord with the Baraita that states that Gentiles were 'declared to be like *zavim*', and regard their uncleanness as that of gonorrhea. But from the Mishna in *Tractate Pesaḥim* we learn that in the view of the Hillelites the uncleanness of a Gentile is like that of one defiled by a corpse. The same is to be inferred from the Mishna in *Tractate Kelim*, which compares non-Jews to those defiled by a corpse and permits Gentiles to enter the Temple Mount, an area forbidden to *zavim*.[38] On the other hand, according to the Shammaites, who rule that a proselyte 'immerses himself and eats his Passover sacrifice in the evening', a Gentile's uncleanness is only like the light degree of defilement resulting from the contact of a reptile. We are similarly informed by a Baraita in *T.B. Shabbat* 83a: 'Contact by a Gentile man or woman, by an idol or its service utensils defiles but not their motion,'[39] a Halakha that is contrary to the law that ascribes the

with the earlier Halakha, and especially where the defilement of the Temple and its holy things was concerned (see above, p. 119, note 61).

36 Cf. Schechter, *Documents of Jewish Sectaries*, I, p. xxv; A. Epstein, *Eldad ha-Dani*, p. 172; Eshkoli, *Tarbiz* VII, p. 124.

37 Epiphanius, *Haeres.* IX, 3 (ed. Prussian State Academy), vol. I, p. 200; *Itinerarum Antonini*, ed. Geyer (*Itinera Hierosolymitana*), p. 164 (first version; the second version is faulty here) — 'Descendentes per campestria, civitates et vicos Samaritanorum; et per plateas, unde transivimus sive nos sive Iudaei, cum paleas vestigia nostra incendentes' etc. From the continuation of the passage we learn that the Samaritans used to declare anything touched by a Gentile (vessels, liquids, and food) unclean; cf. Büchler, p. 48, note 139. A similar account to that recorded in connection with Antoninus (where the custom is assigned to the time of Hadrian) is found in the Samaritan *Book of Joshua* (*Karme Shomeron*, 87, 88).

38 The Rash [R. Samson b. Abraham of Sens] comments on this Mishna: 'And as regards the heathens, too, although it was decreed that they should be like *zavim* in all respects, with reference to exclusion from the camps [i.e. the areas of graded sanctity in Jerusalem] it was decreed that they should be deemed like those defiled by a corpse.'

39 This is the principal reading, given by R. Ḥananel, and the Oxford MS (= *Diqduqe Soferim*) and the Early Authorities. Rashi, however, emends: 'The words "contact by a Gentile man or woman" are to be omitted, for the Sages imposed upon them the uncleanness of *zavim*.'

uncleanness of *zavim* to non-Jews.[40] Although the Talmud raises an objection to this Baraita and endeavours to reconcile the contradiction between it and the current Halakha in various ways (all of which are difficult), nevertheless the simple sense of the Baraita is that Gentiles do not defile like *zavim* but possess the uncleanness resulting from contact with a creeping thing.[41]

By distinguishing three differing views concerning the uncleanness

40 In the Baraita in *T.B. Shabbat* 21b (*Megillat Ta'anit* ix) it is stated: 'For when the Greeks [i.e. Graeco-Syrians] entered the Temple, they defiled all the oils' etc. This defilement, understood in its plain sense, refers to the uncleanness resulting from the Gentile status of the Greeks. Now the Early Authorities raise the question: Why, then, did not also the cruse of oil that bore the High Priest's seal become defiled by being moved? However, we have seen that there were Sages who ruled that the uncleanness of a Gentile is like that conveyed by a reptile's contact, and consequently a non-Jew does not defile by carrying. But even according to the other view that regards Gentiles as possessing the uncleanness resulting from corpse defilement, there is no difficulty, for one defiled by a corpse likewise does not convey uncleanness through carrying.

41 By means of this differentiation of conflicting views regarding the stringency of Gentile uncleanness, we are able to resolve the contradiction found in Josephus in respect of the High Priest's vestments (a difficulty pointed out by Büchler), namely, that in the tradition cited in our text earlier Josephus states that the garments were purified for seven days, whereas elsewhere (*Ant.* xv, 11, 4) he states that they were taken out on the eve of the festival. Thus the first tradition accords with the view that a Gentile is unclean like one defiled by a corpse, who defiles articles with seven-day uncleanness, while the second statement follows the more lenient opinion that regards Gentile uncleanness as equivalent to that produced by the contact of a reptile, and a person defiled by a reptile does not convey uncleanness to articles (Büchler, *op. cit.*, p. 29 endeavours to resolve the contradiction in a far-fetched manner; but the solution offered on p. 30 approximates to what has been stated here).

However, ostensibly the contradiction could be reconciled by the assumption that the ruling powers changed. For the Sadducees it would seem did not accept the law of Gentile uncleanness, and consequently when they were in power they did not insist on the cleanness of the vestments (compare *Tosefta Ḥagiga* iii, 35, and *T.P. ibid.*, iii, 79d, where the simple meaning of the text would appear to indicate that the Sadducees ruled that Temple furniture does not contract uncleanness). But in the first place it should be noted that although this Halakha is only 'a tradition of the elders', it is nevertheless not inconceivable that the Sadducees, like the Samaritans, also concede it. Secondly, Josephus (*Ant.* xviii, 1, 4) and the Tannaim (*Tosefta Yom ha-Kippurim* i, 8; *T.B. Yoma* 19b; *T.P. ibid.*, i, 39a) already attested that the Sadducees, willingly or unwillingly, followed the custom of the Pharisees.

of Gentiles we are able to understand the connection between it and the uncleanness inhering in the body of the idol, in regard to the stringency of which we also find three conflicting opinions, as we mentioned above.

It is stated in the Mishna (*Shabbat* ix, 1; *ʿAvoda Zara* iii, 6): 'R. Akiba said: Whence do we learn of an idol that, like a menstruant, it conveys uncleanness when carried? Because it is written "Thou shalt cast them away like a menstruous thing; thou shalt say unto it, Get thee hence". Just as a menstruant defiles when carried, so does an idol defile when carried.'[42] This menstruant's uncleanness of idols refers to the 'gonorrhea' uncleanness of Gentiles, and approximating to it is the leprosy uncleanness, which is likewise ascribed to idols, as is stated in *T.P. Pesaḥim* ix, 36c: 'The uncleanness of idols has been made equivalent to that of one unclean through gonorrhea or leprosy.' So, too, R. Alexandri began his exposition (*Lamentations Rabbati*, Petiḥta, xxi) ' "And the leper in whom the plague is" etc. — "the leper" means the Temple; "in whom is the plague" this means the idols, which defile like the plague (leprosy)' etc.[43]

As against these traditions we find another view that the uncleanness of idols is like corpse defilement. For it is stated in the Talmud (*T.B. ʿAvoda Zara* 32b; *T.B. Ḥullin* 13b): 'It is taught (in a Baraita), R. Judah b. Bathyra said: 'Whence do we learn that offerings to idols defile whatever is in the same tent? For it is stated in Scripture "They joined themselves also unto Baal of Peor and ate the sacrifices of the dead" — just as a corpse defiles all that is in the same tent, even so do offerings to idols defile whatever is in the tent.'

Now the Babylonian Talmud (*ʿAvoda Zara* 48b) understands the teaching of R. Judah b. Bathyra as referring only to the uncleanness of offerings to idols and not to the idols themselves,[44] and hence it

42 Although the Talmud rules (*T.B. Ḥagiga* 10b and parallels) that 'No inference may be drawn concerning statements of the Torah from statements of post-Pentateuchal Scripture', nevertheless a number of decided questions of law have been derived from post-Pentateuchal Scripture, which have the authority of Torah law; cf. Chajes, *Torat ha-Nevi'im*, 7–8.

43 Cf. *Tosefta Zavim* v, 5: 'He who touches... In the case of one who has intercourse with a menstruant and in the case of an idol one is defiled and one invalidated.'

44 The view of the Babylonian Talmud, which takes a more stringent attitude to idolatrous offerings than to the idol itself, is also found in the following passage (*T.B. ʿAvoda Zara* 50a): 'R. Giddal said in the name of R. Ḥiyya b. Joseph that Rav said: Whence do we know that idolatrous offerings can never be annulled? For it is stated "They joined themselves also unto Baal

explains the reason underlying the Halakha of the Mishna (*'Avoda Zara* iii, 8) 'None may sit in its shadow, but if he did so, he remains clean. Nor may anyone pass beneath it, but if he did so, he is defiled' as follows: 'It is not possible that there should be no (remains) of idolatrous offerings left there. Whose teaching does this ruling follow? That of R. Judah b. Bathyra' etc. But it is inexplicable that offerings to idols should be subject to a more stringent law of defilement than the idols themselves. Therefore it appears that R. Judah b. Bathyra seeks, by his exposition, to include idolatrous offerings and not to exclude the idols themselves, which *a fortiori*, possesses the uncleanness of corpse-defilement. We can now explain our Mishna to mean that the Asherah itself defiles in a tent and not on account of our fear that (remains of) idolatrous offerings remained underneath it. In the Palestinian Talmud the verse cited above is expounded with reference to the idol itself.[45]

Finally the view of the Sages who dispute R. Akiba's opinion is that idols defile like a reptile.

We thus see that the Sages discussed the defilement of idols, some inclining towards leniency and some to stringency, just as they were lenient and stringent in regard to the uncleanness of Gentiles. It ap-

Peor, and ate the sacrifices of the dead" ' etc. Similarly the Talmud attributes to R. Joḥanan a Halakha that an idol's uncleanness can more easily be annulled than its offering (however, in the Palestinian Talmud [*ibid.* iv, 43d] we read: 'R. Samuel (and) R. Abbahu said in the name of Rav: Stones of Mercurius that were scattered can never be annulled on account of idolatry. When R. Joḥanan heard this, he said: The master has taught us correctly, for if one prostrates himself to an idolatry of foodstuffs, [ע״ז של אוכלים] they can never be annulled.' Now *Pene Moshe* explains the meaning of the passage in the Palestinian Talmud in accordance with the view of the Babylonian Talmud; but *Yefe Enayim* understands R. Joḥanan's expression ע״ז של אוכלים to signify that the foodstuffs themselves constitute the idol, contrary to the interpretation of the Babylonian Talmud).

45 *T.P. 'Avoda Zara* iii, 43a; *T.P. Shabbat* ix, 11d: 'R. Ze'ura, R. Isaac b. Naḥman, R. Eleazar, and R. Abbahu in the name of R. Joḥanan said: "They joined themselves also unto Baal Peor, and ate the sacrifices of the dead", (this signifies that) just as a piece of a corpse the size of an olive defiles, so does a piece of an idol the size of an olive defile.' However, in the case of the Halakhot of the Tosefta (*'Avoda Zara* vi (vii), 2, 3; *Zavim* v, 7) 'If one makes his house the shrine of an idol, all of it defiles whoever enters it'; 'If one puts his head and the greater part of his body into the shrine of an idol, he becomes unclean' etc., the tent-uncleanness must be explained as based on leprosy uncleanness (for in the tent of a corpse one becomes unclean as soon as one inserts the tips of one's fingers).

pears, therefore, that the defilement of Gentiles has its roots in the uncleanness of the idol, which spread to its worshippers.

In connection with the uncleanness of Gentiles we must also consider the ritual immersion of proselytes.

It is not specifically stated in the teaching of the Tannaim that this immersion serves to purify the proselyte from his Gentile uncleanness[46] and they derived this Halakha by analogy with Israel's entry into the Divine Covenant in the Wilderness.

However, it was not the analogy that brought about this immersion,[47] but the practice and the Halakha that caused the analogy to be made and ritual immersion (and circumcision and a sacrifice) to be ascribed to the early fathers of the nation for the purpose of their entering the covenant.

Since it is unlikely that the immersion of proselytes was primarily similar to the baptism of repentance of John the Baptist[48] or that mentioned in the Sibylline Oracles,[49] a symbolic act for sanctifying the spirit or a token of the acceptance of a new religion, after the manner of baptism among Christians, we can only interpret this lustration according to its simple significance, namely that like all other Halakhic immersions its purpose is also to purify the proselyte from uncleanness, to wit, the defilement due to Gentile status. Since

46 In *T.P. Qiddushin* iii, 64d: 'For Bar Qappara taught: If a proselyte was circumcised but did not undergo immersion, he is nevertheless a valid convert, for every proselyte has at some time undergone immersion for his pollution. And the question is raised: Does the immersion that purifies him from a light degree of uncleanness avail him for a stringent degree of defilement? R. Jose be R. Bun answered: Since both lustrations are undergone for the sake of Jewish sanctity, it (the immersion for pollution) avails him.' The wording should be compared with that of R. Jeremiah in *T.P. 'Avoda Zara* v, 45b, regarding the immersion of new vessels acquired from Gentiles: 'Because they have left Gentile uncleanness and entered Jewish sanctity.' But it is not explicitly proven that this form of defilement is actual uncleanness like other forms of uncleanness, for it is possible to explain this lustration as a special symbolic precept for induction into 'Jewish sanctity'.

47 The circumcision of Israel upon entering the covenant in the wilderness and their immersion at the same time is deduced with difficulty (*Keritot* ix, 1; *T.B. Yevamot* 46b).

48 For the explanation of the nature of John's baptism cf. Brandt, Beihefte zur *ZATW*, xviii, pp. 77–85; Strack-Billerbeck, I, p. 112.

49 iv, 164 published Prussian State Academy, vol. III, p. 184. Some scholars have used this source in order to prove the antiquity of the immersion of proselytes. But this lustration is only baptism of repentance, as stated by Brandt (*op. cit.*, 70–87).

we have already learnt the antiquity of the Halakha concerning Gentile uncleanness, we are not, therefore, compelled to agree with the Jewish scholar[50] who maintains that the immersion of proselytes originated only when the Temple was destroyed and after the enactment of the Eighteen Decrees (according to tradition the uncleanness of Gentiles was decreed at that time) and that the Christians who took over the lustration from the Jews also knew nothing of it till that time, only the latter — the authors of the Gospels — anachronistically ascribed their later custom to the time of the Apostles.

We may therefore posit that in the days of Jesus — and before — it was customary to immerse proselytes in order to purify them from Gentile uncleanness. We can also infer that the lustration of converts dates from before the Destruction from the dispute of R. Eliezer and R. Joshua as to whether this immersion is indispensable or not.[51]

50 Zeitlin, *HUCA*, vol. I, pp. 357–363.

51 According to the version of the Baraita in the Babylonian Talmud (*Yevamot* 46a) R. Eliezer and R. Joshua also differ in respect to circumcision. For according to R. Eliezer circumcision suffices for a proselyte but R. Joshua holds that immersion is all that is needed. But it is difficult to suppose that circumcision would be dispensed with in the case of an intending convert, for Josephus attests in a number of places that conversion was dependent on circumcision; and although Ananias instructed Izates, king of Adiabene not to be circumcized (*Ant.* xx, 2, 4), he did so only on account of the danger, lest his Judaism become public to his subjects and they slay him, as is explained in the passage referred to. It therefore seems that preference should be given to the recension of the Palestinian Talmud (*Qiddushin* iii, 44d), according to which R. Joshua says 'Immersion is also indispensable' (the version in *Tractate Gerim* ii, 5, likewise inclines towards that of the Palestinian Talmud).

It is true that on the face of it the tradition of the Babylonian Talmud is supported by another Baraita (*ibid.* 46b) 'If (a proselyte) came and said: "I have been circumcized but I have not performed the ritual ablution", he is permitted to have the immersion, and (the validity of the circumcision) does not matter' etc., for the Talmud explains it as though in the view of R. Judah, circumcision is not indispensable. But in the Palestinian Talmud (*Qiddushin* iv, 66a) the Baraita referred to reads 'If a proselyte underwent circumcision but not immersion, and had children, and he declared I have been circumcised but have not performed the ritual ablution, he is believed and permitted to undergo immersion on the Sabbath', etc., and obviously according to this recension R. Judah permits him to undergo immersion on the Sabbath because he is believed that he circumcised himself and the ablution is not indispensable, which accords with the opinion of R. Eliezer (in a number of matters R. Judah adopts the ruling of R. Eliezer), while R. Jose holds, like R. Joshua, that the lustration is also indispensable. Hence he prohibits the immersion of the proselyte on the Sabbath (in keeping with

For they differ only in regard to the definition of the precept but concur as to the practice itself. Hence we may conclude from this debate that this precept was observed before the time of these scholars, namely before the destruction of the Temple.[52]

the recension of the tradition of the Babylonian Talmud, the Baraita there reads 'Therefore a proselyte is permitted to have his ablution on the Sabbath', indicating that the latter part of the Baraita speaks of a different case — of one who was seen to have circumcised himself — but in the Palestinian Talmud the reading is 'and he is permitted to undergo immersion on the Sabbath', implying that the entire passage deals with a single case). We thus have two conflicting traditions here, one Palestinian and the other Babylonian (nevertheless it is far-fetched to connect this dispute with the fact that Ananias, a Babylonian, permitted Izates to dispense with circumcision, while Eleazar, a Galilean, insisted on his being circumcised). Now Levi (*REJ*, LIII, 59–61) seeks to prove, from the silence of the Baraita in *Tractate Gerim* (i, 1; Higger 68–69) concerning circumcision in connection with the reception of proselytes — as it is explained in the parallel tradition in *T.B. Yevamot* (46a–b) — that according to this Halakha circumcision is not indispensable. But Levi himself already noted that the preceding Halakha (*ibid.*) makes no reference whatsoever to R. Joshua's view that circumcision is not indispensable. Secondly, is it to be supposed that according to R. Joshua circumcision is not even a precept to be observed by the intending proselyte? The difficulty, therefore, remains. Apparently this Halakha, from the words 'they take him down', sets out the order of acts to be performed by the proselyte *after* circumcision (there is no reference to circumcision, because it does not require the presence of scholars or instruction in Jewish law etc.). Since the Palestinian tradition is to be preferred, the force of Guttmann's argument is weakened (see *Das Judentum und seine Umwelt*, 95–96).

52 Nevertheless it is not to be inferred that the ablution was in those days a *conditio sine qua non* (Bertholet, 325; Schürer, III, 183–185), for possibly it was just a *miṣwa* ['precept', i.e. a desirable religious act, but not indispensable]. On the other hand, even if the ablution of the proselyte was not practised in the early days, this did not imply the abolition of Gentile uncleanness, for according to the decided Halakha uncleanness only affects the Temple and its holy things. Hence it is of no consequence that the proselyte retains his defilement, since many Israelites remain unclean without concern. But because the uncleanness of the convert is *Gentile defilement*, the lustration was made a precept and a duty. However, the fact that the proselyte's immersion is distinctive in that it is a precept and indispensable does not necessarily imply that it obtained at the beginning. Indeed, there are scholars who argue from Josephus' silence on the subject that the ablution was not observed in Temple times. But in reply it has rightly been pointed out that argument from silence does not constitute proof, for Josephus had no occasion to attest it. Only Zeitlin supposes that he had the opportunity in relating the story of Izates, where he speaks of circumcision only (*op. cit.*, 359). However, here too, there was no occasion for such a reference. Josephus

Now the prevailing tradition declares that it suffices for a proselyte to undergo immersion (and bring a sacrifice) in order to be able to enter the community of Israel (after circumcision). But we have already seen that some of the Sages took a stricter view of Gentile uncleanness and regarded it as the uncleanness of one defiled by a corpse. Logically these scholars must require the proselyte to undergo sprinkling.

Indeed according to the School of Hillel immersion is insufficient for a proselyte and he requires sprinkling, as is apparent from *Mishna Pesaḥim*. But this ruling is also to be inferred from another source; for it is stated in *Sifre Zuṭa* (251): 'The Levites were sanctified by sprinkling etc.; the Israelites were sanctified by the heifer of purification, as it is said "Speak unto the children of Israel, that they bring thee a red heifer" etc.' We thus learn that the Israelites entered the covenant only through sprinkling.[53]

However, Israel's entry into the covenant serves in all the sources, including *Sifre Zuṭa*, as a basic example of Halakhic exposition for the induction of proselytes, as it is stated (*Sifre Numbers* § 108; *M. Keritot* ix, 1; *Tractate Gerim* ii, 5): 'Just as the Israelites entered the covenant only through three things — circumcision, immersion and sacrifice — so, too, do proselytes.' Similarly it is taught in *Sifre Zuṭa* (261): ' "Ye shall have one statute, both for the stranger, and for him that is born in the land" — just as the home-born did not become fit to eat of the Passover sacrifice until the blood of the covenant was thrown upon him, so, too, the proselyte does not become fit to eat of the Passover sacrifice until the blood of the covenant is thrown upon him.' Thus we are taught by the example

dealt at length with the question of circumcision, because his mother and Ananias deterred him from performing this, on account of the Gentile inhabitants of the country, since the circumcision was likely to become known; but this did not apply to ablution. Moreover immersion is not an important and distinctive act (and Izates had already been observing the precepts prior to this), but this is not the case with circumcision, which is a difficult operation.

53 [The whole of this paragraph is to be found in *Num. Rabba*, *Naso'*, xii, 15 and in *Midrash ha-Gadol*, 'and I can find no evidence that it derives from the *Sifre Zuṭa*,' as is stated by Horowitz on p. 250, note 26. Without doubt the whole passage is a *late* Midrash, nor does it at all refer to 'sprinkling' as part of the ritual of entering the covenant, for the text does not say 'they (the Israelites) were sanctified by sprinkling' as in the case of the Levites; see the commentary of *Maharzaw* (Z. W. Einhorn). [— Epstein].

of the early fathers that a proselyte is prevented from eating of the holy sacrifices until he brings his offering.[54]

According to the tradition mentioned earlier, which is expressly opposed to the second tradition[55] and posits that the fathers of the nation entered the covenant after being sprinkled, it would appear that a proselyte required sprinkling on the third day and the seventh, in conformity with the Halakhic ruling of the School of Hillel and in keeping with the Halakhic view that Gentile uncleanness is like that which issues from defilement.

Our subject also requires that we should carefully examine the Halakhot that oblige the proselyte to bring a sacrifice.

This law, which is mentioned in a number of sources was undoubtedly observed in Temple times, as is stated in a Baraita (*T.B. Rosh ha-Shana* 31b; *T.B. Keritot* 9a; *T.P. Sheqalim* v, 51b)[56] 'A proselyte at the present time must set aside a quarter [of a shekel or a denar] for a nest of pigeons. R. Simeon said that R. Joḥanan

54 So, too, *ibid.* pp. 282–283: 'This teaches us that he (the proselyte) is not permitted to partake of sacrifices until he brings an offering made by fire.' In both these passages the anonymous statements of the Midrash conform to the view of R. Eliezer b. Jacob (cf. Horowitz in his introduction to the Sifre and *Sifre Zuṭa*, p. xviii, note 29, and the observation of my teacher Prof. Epstein, *Tarbiz*, I, p. 41; III, p. 236). Possibly we have another anonymous Halakha that accords with the view of R. Eliezer b. Jacob in *Sifre Zuṭa, loc. cit.*: ' "And if a stranger sojourn" etc. You might have thought that this refers to a proselyte who was converted among Gentiles overseas. Note, therefore, that Scripture states only "with you". So far we learn that only those who went up with you from Egypt (may be proselytized). Whence is it to be inferred that those who are with you at present (may be converted)? Observe that Scripture states "Whosoever may be among you throughout your generations".' From the phrasing of the Baraita we learn that one who was proselytised abroad is not a valid convert, a view that contradicts the parallel Baraita in *Sifra, Qedoshim*, viii and in *T.B. Yevamot* 46b–47a: 'From this is to be inferred that proselytization may take place in Eretz-Israel; how do we know that conversion may also be carried out abroad? Therefore Scripture states "with thee" — wherever you may be. If so, why does the Torah say "in your land"? It teaches us that in Eretz-Israel he must produce evidence, whereas outside Eretz-Israel there is no need to produce proof.' If this is the meaning of the Halakha in *Sifre Zuṭa*, as the plain sense of the text implies, it is apparently to be explained by the fact that the sacrifice of the proselyte is indispensable, in accordance with the opinion of R. Eliezer b. Jacob in *Tractate Gerim* (ch. ii, 4; however, the reason may possibly be that the proselyte requires sprinkling). But the subject requires further study.

55 See Horowitz, 251, note 7.

56 In the *Tosefta Sheqalim* iii, 22 it is not actually stated that it was Rabban Joḥanan b. Zakkai who abolished the practice.

b. Zakkai had already taken it to the vote and annulled it lest the money be misused.'

However, we find that the Tannaim are disagreed as to whether the sacrifice is indispensable or not. Thus it is stated in *Tractate Gerim* (ch. ii, 4; ed. Higger, p. 72): 'Just as the Israelites entered into the covenant by three precepts, so proselytes are inducted by circumcision, immersion and a sacrifice. (The first) two are indispensable, but (the third) one does not debar (him); R. Eliezer b. Jacob says that the sacrifice is likewise indispensable.' So, too, apparently, we may infer from the dispute of R. Eliezer and R. Joshua as to whether immersion and circumcision are indispensable to proselytization that they agree with the Sages who are opposed to R. Eliezer b. Jacob, since they are silent on the question of the sacrifice, thus implying that both of them are of opinion that the omission of the sacrifice does not hinder (the proselyte's conversion).[57]

Similarly we find conflicting opinions also in regard to the kind of sacrifice to be brought by the proselyte.

In the Tosefta (*Sheqalim* iii, 20–21; *Keritot* i, 11–12; *T.B. Keritot* 8b): 'A proselyte is prevented from partaking of sacrifices until he has offered up his bird sacrifices... In the case of all those who are required by Pentateuchal law to bring sacrificial birds, half of them are sin-offerings and half burnt-offerings, except the proselyte's bird offerings, which, although they are obligatory, are both burnt-offerings. If he wishes to bring his obligatory sacrifices from the cattle, he may do so... The prescription to offer up bird sacrifices was intended only to make it easier for the proselyte.' Thus according to the Sages the proselyte's sacrificial birds are not a rigid and obligatory ordinance and the convert is permitted to fulfil his sacrificial duty even by bringing an offering from the cattle.

But in the Sifre (*Numbers* § 107) it is taught: ' "And he (the proselyte) will offer an offering made by fire" — a blood sacrifice. You

57 However, this does not provide absolute proof; for their silence (on the question of the sacrifice) may be due to the fact that they are discussing the matter from the halakhic and practical viewpoint, and after the Destruction the proselyte's sacrifice was annulled (the Sages differ only as to whether the convert is obliged to set aside a quarter, and in this regard, too, it was testified that Rabban Joḥanan b. Zakkai annulled it). As regards the indispensability of the sacrifice, it appears that the Halakha in *Tractate Gerim* speaks only, like the Mishna, of holding up the proselytization and not of debarring the proselyte from partaking of holy things. See, however, *Tarbiz* III, p. 236.

say a blood sacrifice, but perhaps the reference is to a meal offering? Therefore Scripture states "as you are" — just as you bring a blood sacrifice, so must the proselytes offer up a blood sacrifice. But perhaps as the Israelites bring a sacrifice from the cattle, so, too, the proselytes must offer a sacrifice from the cattle? Therefore Scripture writes "for you" — you have I sanctified with the blood of cattle, but I have not sanctified proselytes with the blood of cattle.'

The plain sense of the Baraita appears to indicate that the proselyte's bird sacrifices are obligatory and that he may not bring his sacrifice from the cattle. This is even more evident from the subsequent statement of Rabbi, *ibid.*: 'Rabbi said... Should you think that just as the Israelites were initiated by means of the blood of burnt-offerings and peace-offerings, so too are proselytes... therefore Scripture enjoins "And he will offer an offering made by fire, of a sweet savour unto the Lord". Go now, and see which blood-sacrifice is wholly a burnt-offering made by fire and no part of it is permitted (for human use). You will find none but the burnt-offering of birds... Hence the Sages said: Of all the bird-offerings prescribed in the Torah half of them are burnt-offerings and half sin-offerings, except those of a proselyte, because they are wholly offerings made by fire.'

But the bird-sacrifice is in all cases brought by those who still require a ceremony of atonement (for complete purification before being permitted to partake of consecrated things); they are four who are defiled with a severe form of uncleanness, namely the *zav*, the *zava*, a woman after childbirth, and a leper. Consequently we must conclude that also in the case of the proselyte his sacrifice proves that he, too, requires a ceremony of atonement. Now this conclusion supports the view of R. Eliezer b. Jacob, who rules (*M. Keritot* ii, 1) 'A proselyte's atonement is incomplete until the blood (of his sacrifice) has been tossed for him.' However, the law of one who lacks atonement, who is debarred from partaking of sacrifices until he brings his offering, applies only to a person who comes to purify himself of severe uncleanness, from among the four types enumerated. Thus the proselyte, too, in the opinion of R. Eliezer b. Jacob, comes to cleanse himself of defilement similar to the kinds mentioned, namely of Gentile uncleanness, which was subject to the same law as gonorrheal uncleanness.[58]

58 In *Tosefta Pesaḥim* vii, 13 (according to the recension of the Vienna MS) and *T.P. ibid.*, viii, 36b, R. Eliezer b. Jacob states 'Roman soldiers acted as

Now we must distinguish, among the varied and conflicting Halakhot relating to proselytization, the three views that we pointed out in differentiating the Halakhot in regard to Gentile uncleanness. These are as follows:

1) The prevailing Halakha that requires immersion only (apart from circumcision; the sacrifice is not indispensable); accordingly Gentile uncleanness is no more than that of the contact of a reptile.

2) The tradition that prescribes sprinkling for the proselyte; the Gentile uncleanness to which he is subject is as grave, therefore, as that of one defiled by a corpse.

3) The Halakha that obliges the proselyte to offer up specifically a bird sacrifice, and not a burnt-offering from the cattle; this Halakha includes the proselyte among those who require a ceremony of atonement. According to this view the uncleanness is like that of *zavim*.[59]

However, one might disregard the effect in the early period of the laws of Gentile uncleanness on the dealings between Jews and non-Jews, for the Halakha ordains that the uncleanness applies only to

guards of the hinges (of the Temple gates) in Jerusalem, and they immersed themselves and partook of their Passover sacrifices in the evening'; thus R. Eliezer b. Jacob is in agreement with the School of Shammai (cf. the remarks of my teacher Prof. Epstein, *Tarbiz*, *loc. cit.*). But, it appears, that this R. Eliezer b. Jacob cited in the Tosefta is the first of that name, who lived in Temple times and whose testimonies are recorded in other parts of Rabbinic literature, and to whom the Talmud attributes the Mishna of *Middot* (*T.B. Yoma* 16a) [This is no proof; for *R. Judah*, the colleague of R. Eliezer, testified on a number of matters relating to Temple times. It would be arbitrary, therefore, to antedate R. Eliezer b. Jacob. — Epstein]. But the R. Eliezer b. Jacob referred to here is R. Eliezer b. Jacob II, a disciple of R. Akiba, with whose view a number of anonymous passages in *Sifre Zuṭa* agree; the conflicting opinions thus belong to different authorities.

59 It is indeed difficult to explain why half the sacrifices of the proselyte is not a sin-offering, like all bird-offerings. But possibly R. Eliezer b. Jacob holds that the convert's bird-offerings are like others in this respect too. Furthermore, from R. Simeon's statement in the Baraita (*T.B. Nidda* 31b and parallels; cf. *Gen. Rabba* xx) concerning a woman in confinement that 'when she kneels in bearing, she swears impetuously that she will never make herself available to her husband again; therefore the Torah ordained that she should bring a sacrifice'. It is to be inferred that the sacrifices of the others whose atonement is incomplete (without the sacrifice) were regarded as expiation for sin. Since, however, a proselyte is like 'a new-born child' (although the Tannaim differ on the subject; see *T.B. Yevamot* 48b; *Gerim* ii, 5), he has no need of a sin-offering

the Temple and its holy things, and consequently it would appear to follow that these contacts were but little affected or reduced, as Büchler contends.

But in fact, it appears, the influence of Gentile uncleanness on the life of the nation was considerable. For although the settled Halakha voided the uncleanness of any significance for whatever was extraneous to the Temple and its holy things, nevertheless concern with cleanness spread in the days of the Second Temple in a number of directions beyond the ambit of the Sanctuary. This enlarged scope finds expression first in the extension of levitical cleanness to 'sacred things' apart from the sanctity of the Temple, and secondly the people became accustomed to observe levitical cleanness even in respect to their non-consecrated food, and quite a number of fixed Halakhot were based on the fact that concern with levitical purity had spread beyond the sphere of the Temple, the offerings, and the priests, as I shall endeavour to show elsewhere. But for the present it will suffice if we deal with the things we noted, at the beginning, in regard to the immersion of new vessels derived from Gentiles, which the Sages ruled to be a precept and a fixed obligation, and so, too, in connection with the proselyte's lustrations, which some of the Rabbis interpreted to be indispensable.

Now when we examine the Halakhot relating to Gentile uncleanness in the teaching of the Tannaim and Amoraim, we observe a general tendency to set aside the early tradition concerning the levitical impurity of the Gentile status and to restrict the laws flowing therefrom. This development finds expression, to begin with, in the fact that the original cause of the prohibition and precepts was forgotten and new reasons were invented; and secondly — and because of this — the restriction of their application, or their complete annulment.

We have already dealt with the Halakhot connected with the acts of the proselyte who comes to be converted, and we have observed that the sources do not prescribe the precept of immersion on account of the Gentile levitical uncleanness attaching to him, although no other reason can be given for this ritual. This tendency is even more clearly proven by the fact that the Halakha rules that the bird-sacrifices of the proselyte are not fixed offerings. It appears that all the Sages agreed that in practice the proselyte brought a bird burnt-offering, but the latter scholars, because they denied the connection between the proselyte's sacrifice and his gonorrheal uncleanness and learnt from the fathers of the Halakha to regard it as a special precept, were unable to rule that his bird-sacrifices were fixed offerings.

Similarly the Sages ruled that the omission of the offering does not debar the proselyte from partaking of the sacrifices, so that he should not also be classified as one lacking an atonement ceremony. For if the offering is not ordained on account of uncleanness, and does not serve the purpose of cleansing, it cannot debar the proselyte from eating consecrated food.

The same applies to the immersion of new, unused Gentile utensils; according to the simple meaning of the Halakha this immersion was prescribed only on account of Gentile uncleanness. But the Babylonian Talmud (*ʿAvoda Zara* 75b) states 'The ruling applies only to purchased (utensils) and according to the circumstances of the occurrence (the Midianite utensils), but not to borrowed (utensils).' It is similarly stated in the Palestinian Talmud (*ʿAvoda Zara*, v, 45b) in the name of R. Joḥanan: 'The ruling applies only to one who purchases, but in the case of one who borrows it is permitted.' Thus in the view of the Amoraim the prohibition to use new Gentile vessels prior to their immersion is not due to uncleanness but constitutes a special precept of the Torah 'and according to the circumstances of the occurrence'. In the words of Maimonides ('Laws of Forbidden Foods', xvii, 5): 'The law that requires dining utensils purchased from Gentiles to be immersed before they are permitted to be used for eating and drinking is not based on the principles of levitical purity and impurity' etc. Because the original reason of the Halakha was removed, its application became restricted and borrowed Gentile utensils were permitted and the prohibition was even limited to metal vessels only (*T.B. ʿAvoda Zara loc. cit.*).

But intrinsically the Halakha is only to be explained on the basis of Gentile defilement, and the dictum of R. Jeremiah in the Palestinian Talmud approximates to this interpretation. He states 'They (the utensils) must be immersed because they left Gentile uncleanness and entered into Israelite sanctity', and hence (according to R. Jeremiah) purchased vessels are not to be differentiated from borrowed ones. Likewise no distinction ought to be made between metal and other vessels that are subject to defilement.

The prohibition of the oil, bread, wine, and stewed and preserved foodstuffs of Gentiles, which tradition explains in some cases as due to the admixture of forbidden foods (only) and in others as based on a prohibitive decree (intermarriage), is to be similarly understood. For it appears that all these things were originally forbidden only on account of Gentile uncleanness — even though the prohibition did not extend to all articles of food and drink capable of absorbing uncleanness and the Halakha was not completely consistent[60] — but the later Halakha removed the basis of defilement from these prohibitions and related them to the decree (cited above) and to the suspicion that they might have absorbed forbidden foodstuff from the walls of Gentile vessels.

The same applies to a Gentile wet-nurse, for it is stated in the Mishna (*'Avoda Zara* ii, 1): 'But a Gentile woman may suckle the child of a Jewess in the latter's premises.' Now there is reason to believe that the earlier Halakha prohibited suckling by a non-Jewess in all circumstances, even on Israelite premises on account of the levitical impurity of her milk, and there is a reminiscence of it in the story that Moses refused to suck at the breasts of Egyptian women.[61] Although this Haggada explains this tradition by the fact that Moses was destined to speak with the *Shekhina* and it was improper that this mouth 'should suck that which was unclean'; yet the explanation seeks to obviate any contradiction between this tradition and the Mishna in *Tractate 'Avoda Zara* (in *Exodus Rabba*, i, an objection is expressly raised by reference to this Mishna), which states that all Israelite infants may be suckled by Gentile women.[62] However, Josephus also cites this Haggadic tradition in its original

60 This conjecture rests on the fact that there is no other general basis that suffices to explain the Halakha. However, the Halakha of the Falashas (*Tarbiz* VII, p. 48) may be compared: 'If one has unwittingly partaken of Gentile foods, he must immerse himself in water', and this ordinance is certainly due to the levitical uncleanness of their foodstuffs. Reference should also be made to *M. 'Avoda Zara* ii, 7: 'The following may be eaten... and honey and grape-clusters, for even though they exude moisture, they do not come under the law of food rendered susceptible to uncleanness by a liquid'. The 'grape-clusters' are to be explained as saturated grapes, whose juice is dripping out, and the Mishna comes to teach us that the law of wine does not apply to them. But honey cannot be related to the prohibition of 'food rendered susceptible to uncleanness by a liquid', unless we assume that it was forbidden on account of the *defilement* of liquids through contact with a Gentile. On the other hand, it is not to be inferred from the Halakha in *Tractate Gerim* (iii, 2) 'His (i.e. a resident proselyte's) spittle, his seat, his couch, and his urine are unclean; his bread, his oil, and his wine are *clean*', nor from the statement in Josephus (*Life* xiii) ἐπεδὴ οὐκ ἔχουσιν ἔλαιον ᾧ χρήσονται καθαρόν κτλ. ('Since they had no oil that was pure for their use'), that the oil was forbidden on account of defilement, for there are 'unclean' things that are 'forbidden'.

61 *T.B. Soṭa* 12b.

62 In *Sefer ha-Yashar* the problem is solved differently: 'For this [the refusal to suck the Egyptian women] came to the child from the Lord, so that he might be restored to his mother's breast.'

form,[63] and from his formulation is to be inferred that in this tradition is embedded a Halakha that forbids a Jewish infant to suck a Gentile woman in any circumstances.[64] If such a Halakha is assumed, the prohibition of a Jewish child being suckled by a Gentile can only be due to the uncleanness of her milk.[65]

Nor is it surprising that children were not allowed to suck 'that which is unclean', for we learn of a similar position from 'Divergent Palestinian and Babylonian usages'[66] in respect of a menstruant, whom the Palestinians treat with particular stringency and 'refrain from touching anything, even the utensils in the house, and with difficulty did they permit her (the menstruant) to suckle her child.' But when the reason of Gentile uncleanness was set aside, the later Tannaim explained the Halakha on the ground of danger and retained it when 'the Gentile woman was not on Jewish premises.'[67]

A similar development, it seems, is also to be found — and in an even more salient form — in the laws relating to Gentile territory. The basis of the earlier Halakha was abandoned and it was differently interpreted; nevertheless the former laws continued to be observed

63 *Antiquities* ii, 9, 5.

64 Cf. Revel, *JQR*, N.S., XIV, p. 301, who refers to Josephus in connection with our Halakha and notes that the Karaites forbid a Jewish infant to be sucked by a Gentile woman.

65 With regard to our Mishna, which permits a Jewish child to suck a non-Jewess on Jewish premises, it must be stated that it is based on the view that the milk of a Gentile woman is entirely permitted (unlike the rulings of the Tosefta and the Palestinian Talmud cited in the text above); cf. [R. Solomon b. Abraham Adret (RaShBA) on *T.B. Yevamot* 114a] R. Nissim b. Reuben Gerondi (RaN) to *T.B. 'Avoda Zara* ii, and R. Yom Ṭov b. Abraham Ishbili (RIṬBA) 26a. However, it may be argued that only a child was permitted to drink the milk of a non-Jewess (cf. *T.B. Yevamot* 114a) [But how can one explain the dispute between R. Meir and the Sages in the Baraita in the Babylonian Talmud (*T.B. 'Avoda Zara* 26a): 'Nor may a Gentile woman suckle the child of a Jewess, *because of the suspicion that she may murder it*; this is the view of R. Meir. But the Sages say that a non-Jewess may suckle' etc. In the Palestinian Talmud (*loc. cit.*) it is further stated: 'For it is written "And kings shall be thy foster-fathers *and their queens thy nursing mothers*".' — Epstein].

66 *Ha-Shaḥar*, vii, 580. Cf., however, *Tosefta Miqwa'ot* vii, 7, and *T.B. Keritot* 13a.

67 From *T.P. Bava Qamma* iv, 90b, it might, apparently, be inferred that the Halakha 'But a Gentile woman may suckle the child of a Jewess in the latter's premises' already existed in the days of Rabban Gamaliel. But in the Babylonian version of this Baraita (*loc. cit.* 38a) and in the Sifre (*Deut.* §344) this Halakha is missing (it occurs, however, in *Midrash Tannaim* 212).

in detail, although at times they do not fit the interpretation of the later Sages.

This uncleanness is ascribed by tradition to the decree of Jose b. Joezer of Zeredah and Jose b. Joḥanan of Jerusalem, or to the days of Hillel and Shammai, or to the enactment of the Eighteen Decrees.[68] But it appears that there also existed another tradition according to which this Halakha preceded the era of the Second Temple. For it is stated in *Tosefta Para* iii, 10: 'R. Simeon said: Their ashes (i.e. of the red heifers) went down with them [i.e. the exiles] to Babylon and came up [on their return to Eretz-Israel]. Said the Sages to him: But did not the ashes become defiled in Gentile territory? He replied: The decree that Gentile territory be regarded as unclean came into force only after the return from exile.' Thus according to the Sages who disagree with R. Simeon the laws relative to the uncleanness of Gentile territory were observed before the return from the Babylonian exile.

Now we learn from *M. Ṭohorot* iv, 5, that the defilement of Gentile territory is due to doubt; but the nature of the doubt is not clear, and the earlier authorities are disagreed on the subject. Some explain that the doubt concerns a bone of minimum size, others that it relates to corpse-mould; while the uncleanness of 'air space' is interpreted as based on doubt as to the presence of graves. But none of these interpretations is able to explain, even with difficulty, the laws of the defilement of Gentile territory of Tannaitic teaching.

It is stated in the Tosefta (*Kelim*, Bava Meṣiʿa, vii, 1): 'A clod of clean earth and a clod of earth from a grave-area, and a clod of clean earth and a clod from Gentile territory — their minimum size is like that of a large stopper (seal) of the sack-carriers. . . R. Ṭarfon said (the minimum size of) earth from a grave-area is a quantity sufficient to cover a bone as large as a barley-corn.' Thus according to R. Ṭarfon, at least, the uncleanness of Gentile territory is not due to doubt about the presence of a bone of minimum size, since he distinguishes, in respect of the size of the clod, between earth from Gentile territory and that from a grave-area.

In another Baraita (*Tosefta Ahilot* xvii, 6) it is stated: 'R. Judah said: R. Eliezer and the Sages are agreed that earth taken from a grave-area that comes with vegetation is clean unless there is a quantity in one place the size of the seal of a packing bag; they differ about earth coming from Gentile territory with vegetation, R. Eliezer

68 *T.B. Shabbat* 14b; *T.P. ibid.* i, 3c–d.

holding that they combine' etc. If now the reason of the Halakha were the doubt regarding the presence of a bone, why does R. Eliezer apply a more stringent measure in the case of earth derived from Gentile territory than in respect of soil taken from a grave-area?

Needless to say that according to this view it is not possible to explain the Halakha that ordains air-space uncleanness for Gentile territory (*Tosefta Ahilot* xviii, 1, 5; cf. *T.B. Nazir* 55a and the parallels). According to the other explanation that the defilement was due to the doubt that corpse-mould might be present, it is difficult to understand why the Halakha did not fix the minimum quantity of dust from Gentile territory as a ladleful and more, which is the minimum quantity of grave-dust that defiles on account of corpse-mould,[69] and instead determined it as the large stopper of the sack-carriers, which is less than this.

The explanation that the space-uncleanness of Gentile territory is due to the doubt that graves might exist there is likewise inadequate, for according to this view R. Simeon, who maintains that Gentile graves do not defile because a Gentile corpse does not cause tent-uncleanness, must necessarily hold that Gentile territory does not defile whatever enters it. But we learn from the Tosefta cited above that even R. Simeon holds that utensils and liquids that enter Gentile territory are defiled.[70]

According to all the explanations it is difficult to understand how the Sages purified Gentile territory so that 'one could enter it in purity' (*Tosefta Ahilot* xviii, 1–2), which undoubtedly means complete cleanness, including even a clod taken from it.[71]

Similarly it is hard to comprehend how they purified 'Towns that formed enclaves in Israelite territory, like Susita (Hippos) and its sister towns and Ashkelon and its sister towns, although they are exempt from tithe and the observance of the Sabbatical year' (*ibid.* 4), and how they stated (*ibid.* 3) that 'It is presumed that the routes of the pilgrims from Babylon, although enclaves in Gentile territory — are clean.' It is also stated in Midrash Tannaim (112) 'That the fees

69 *M. Oholot* ii, 2.

70 For if it were due to contact with the carrier (who is subject to the doubt of corpse-defilement), he could carry their dust without its touching him, for it does not defile by carrying.

71 According to the interpretation of R. Samson b. Abraham of Sens [RaSh] (but contrary to Maimonides, '*Hilkhot Ṭum'at Met*', xi, 6). From the Tosefta it is clear that this Halakha does not refer only to Syria, as one might ostensibly infer from the Mishna, *loc. cit.*, xviii, 7), but to any Gentile territory.

(of the pilgrims) to Eretz-Israel purify Gentile territory', and needless to say cities in Eretz-Israel itself, even if inhabited by Gentiles, are not defiled as is Gentile territory.

On the other hand, the Sages ruled in regard to Gentile territory that 'its virgin soil is unclean and cannot be purified (by examination as a grave-area).' It is also stated in the Mishna (*M. Oholot* xviii, 6): 'If a man travels in Gentile territory over hills and rocks, he becomes unclean; but if (he travels) by sea or along the strand, he remains clean.' It is unreasonable to suppose that a bone or corpse-mould of minimum size, or a grave should be found in rocks.

It therefore appears that originally the uncleanness of Gentile territory was not due to the doubt about the presence there of a corpse, but stemmed from the uncleanness of the Gentile status, which was regarded as spreading and involving non-Jewish territory. Hence the Sages ruled that all land that had some link with Eretz-Israel (which was conquered by those who left Egypt;[72] towns that formed enclaves in the Land of Israel; the feet (of the pilgrims) [i.e. the routes which they travelled] to Eretz-Israel; areas where one can enter in purity) was clean, and whatever had no complete nexus to Gentile territory for habitation or walking and was not encompassed by it (the sea and the strand)[73] was also clean; but subsequently it was forgotten that the impurity of the Gentile status inhered in Gentile territory,[74] and the Halakha was based on the doubt about the presence of a corpse.[75]

72 Cf. *Kaftor wa-Ferah*, Edelmann, p. 28. However, the statements of Resh Laqish (*T.B. Ḥagiga* 25a) and R. Joshua b. Levi in the name of R. Pedayah (*T.P. ibid.*, iii, 79c) seem to imply that there were conflicting traditions on the subject. Cf. Tosafot, *T.B. Ḥagiga* 25a) *s.v. She-rĕṣû'ā*.

73 Excluding the rivers, which are within the land (*Tosefta Ahilot* xviii, 5; *T.B. Nazir* 55a).

74 Cf. Joshua xxii 19: 'Howbeit, if the land of your possession be unclean'; and Amos vii 17: 'And thou thyself shalt die in an unclean land'.

75 The uncleanness of Gentile dwelling-places is on account of the abortions, as the Mishna (*Oholot* xviii, 7–8) and the Tosefta (*loc. cit.* xviii, 7–10) explain. Nevertheless it is possible that in this case, too, the 'Gentile status' was the cause of the defilement, for only on such a premise can we avoid the conclusion that according to R. Simeon (who declares that a non-Jewish corpse does not give rise to tent-defilement) Gentile dwelling-places are not subject to the law of uncleanness. This will also enable us to account for R. Simeon b. Gamaliel's Halakha (*M. Oholot*, xviii, 9): 'A Gentile city that has been destroyed is not regarded as subject to the laws of Gentile dwelling-places.' If this was on account of the dead, then why should its having been destroyed make any difference? — Let an inspection be made.

In the course of this study it became clear to us that the concept of Gentile uncleanness was earlier at least than the reign of Herod. Furthermore, there is reason to believe, if we interpret the prohibition of non-Jews entering the Temple as due to their impurity, that this Halakha existed before the Hasmonean age, and according to the tradition current at that period, dates from the time of the last prophets, that is, from the beginning of the era of the Second Temple.

We have learnt, further, that the prohibition of non-Jewish oil, bread, and wine was likewise in force from before the time of the Hasmoneans until the destruction of the Temple. And we have seen that even this is to be explained, in the first instance, by the uncleanness of Gentiles.[76]

Similarly tradition attests that the uncleanness of Gentile territory is also of pre-Hasmonean origin, and we have learnt that there is reason to believe that this defilement was initially only 'Gentile impurity'.

We likewise noted the connection between the laws of Gentile uncleanness and the defilement of idols, a fact that inclined us to assume that both have a single root, that is, that Gentile impurity was begotten of idol uncleanness.

These facts show the groundlessness of the theory that basically these Halakhot resulted from political factors obtaining at the close of the Second Temple period.[77] Although it is possible to find similar causes (the Greek penetration into the country and the struggle against Hellenization) in pre-Hasmonean times, it is nevertheless logical to suppose that underlying these Halakhot there is an ancient national concept that finds expression in prophetic utterances[78] and is discernible even in the teaching of the Samaritans and Falashas, concerning the uncleanness of idols and their worshippers. This concep-

76 We should not be surprised at the Halakha (*Gerim* iii, 2) concerning the resident alien [who renounces idolatry for the sake of certain rights of citizenship in Eretz-Israel], which declares that 'His spittle, his seat, his couch, and his urine are unclean'. For although he is not an idolater, nevertheless, since he has not entered the covenant, no distinction is made between him and other Gentiles.

77 Strack and Billerbeck (iv, p. 353) hold that the aforementioned Halakhot were renewed in the reign of Herod as a weapon against the spread of Roman paganism.

78 There is no need to mention idolatry, which the Scripture declare unclean; and as regards the Gentiles cf. Isaiah lii 1; xxxv 5 (the reference is to Gentiles); Joel iv 17; Zechariah xiv 21 (all these verses are cited by Büchler, *op. cit.*, 21–22).

tion in the form of Halakha, is to be assigned, on the basis of the preceding explanation, to the beginning of the Second Temple period. At all events it is possible that it originated in a still earlier age; for we have an ancient tradition that evolved, in a manner paralleling the Bible, in the course of many generations, like so many other Halakhot of the Oral Law.

On the other hand we have discerned a decisive tendency on the part of the later Halakha to remove the primary reason from the prohibitions, which are rooted in the idea of Gentile uncleanness, and to explain them on different grounds. This trend finds expression (apart from the restriction of these Halakhot and the eradication of their cause) in concentrated form in the fact that the law of Gentile uncleanness was based on a Rabbinic edict and deprived of its Pentateuchal character. A second general expression of this trend is found in a Halakha that was renewed in the days of R. Akiba's disciples concerning Gentiles' fitness for uncleanness and cleanness (according to R. Me'ir's view), a fact that removes the basis of the earlier Halakha in respect of the intrinsic defilement of non-Jews.

A similar development, although in a much smaller compass, we also find in the laws regarding the uncleanness of idols, only here the process evolved later. For the Tannaim still teach that this Halakha is of Pentateuchal origin, but the Amoraim mostly take the view that the uncleanness of idols is only a Rabbinic enactment.[79]

Although we may wish to know the factors that led to this development, we are certainly unable to determine their nature clearly by means of decisive proofs. However, it may be conjectured that, in a general sense, the *historical factor* operated here in the first instance, that is to say, force of circumstances compelled the Jews to come in contact with the Gentile world (particularly after the destruction of the Temple and the fall of Bethar), a fact that could even bring about changes in the fundamental conception of Judaism in respect of the spiritual nature of Gentiles. For just as the changing reality could result in the promulgation of new prohibitions, so it was also able to lead to adaptation.

Secondly, there was the *halakhic factor*; for all the categories of uncleanness with which it deals pertain essentially to the body of the defiled, except for Gentile and idol impurity, which is due to a spiritual fact. Consequently this type of uncleanness was extruded

79 *T.B. Shabbat* 83b; *T.P. ibid.* 11d (but in the Palestinian Talmud the Amoraim are divided on the subject). Cf. also *T.P. 'Avoda Zara* iii, 43b.

from the system of defilements, since it is basically different from them.

Finally, it appears that from the outset, and throughout the period that the Halakha was in existence and operated in many forms, it was not completely recognized by all circles, even of the Pharisees, and its existence alongside the Torah law — the silence with regard to it being evidence of its desuetude — was not absolutely affirmed.

At all events, the Halakha's development, as it finds expression in the sources, was primarily only in the direction of limitation and the removal of its basis; but in certain periods there was a desire to establish it firmly, before it became unduly restricted and its Torah nexus was severed.[80]

80 When we examine the development of the process marking the removal of the Halakhot from the sphere of Pentateuchal law (and Rabbinical enactment), we first observe the lifting of Gentile uncleanness from non-Jewish territory (in the days of the Tannaim) even according to Rabbinic law, by taking away the foundation of the Halakhot that remained in essence. Thereafter the law of Gentile uncleanness was undermined, because it was deprived of its Torah status and the Tannaim declared it to be a Rabbinic enactment, only the Amoraim still further reduced its foundation of defilement due to Gentile status by interpreting the Halakha as a prohibition decreed to prevent intermarriage and transgression. Last of all came the weakening of idol-uncleanness, which the Tannaim still taught as a Pentateuchal law, and only the Amoraim regarded it as a Rabbinic regulation. This chronological order of the removal of these categories of impurity from Torah law is related to their proximity to the primary source of the defilements — idolatry, for the uncleanness of Gentile lands is less proximate to the primary source of uncleanness than Gentiles themselves, and more proximate to idol-uncleanness than to that of its worshippers. Here Maimonides' statement should be noted ('Laws of Primary Forms of Uncleanness', iv, 1; my teacher Prof. Epstein drew my attention to Naḥmanides' commentary and the *Pesiqta Zuṭarti* on Genesis xxxv 2): 'The uncleanness of idols is a Rabbinic regulation, *but there is an allusion to it in the Torah* "Put away the strange gods that are among you, and purify yourselves, and change your garments".' But according to the plain interpretation of the text the injunction was on account of the Shehemites that the sons of Jacob had slain (see Naḥmanides *ad loc.*).

THE BOUNDS OF THE LAWS OF LEVITICAL CLEANNESS[1]

It is well known that the established Halakhic tradition prescribes the Pentateuchal laws of levitical cleanness only in respect of priests, the entering of the Temple, and the eating of consecrated foods.[2] When the Halakha encounters verses that appear to imply that the law of impurity applies outside the Temple precincts and that the prohibition of defilement obtains in any circumstances, even for Israelites, it deflects them from their plain meaning and refers them to the Temple and the priests.[3]

1 This essay complements my previous study in which I endeavoured to prove the antiquity of the Halakha relating to Gentile uncleanness. Its purpose is to buttress the hypothesis that I advanced in the earlier article, namely that the laws of Gentile uncleanness, like all other forms of defilement, were likewise valid in theory and in practice for Israelites and were not confined to the Temple only.

2 A general and outstanding expression of the current Halakha is found in the following statement of Maimonides ('The Laws of Food Uncleanness', xvi, 8, 9): 'All that is prescribed in the Torah and in other parts of Scripture regarding levitical cleanness and uncleanness applies only to the Temple, its holy things, heave-offering, and second tithe... but no prohibition attaches to ordinary food at all and it is permitted to eat unclean ordinary food... Just as it is permissible to eat and drink ordinary food that is defiled, so it is permitted to defile ordinary food in Eretz-Israel... Similarly a man may touch anything that is unclean and become unclean thereby' etc.

3 The verse, Leviticus xi 8, which according to its plain sense comes to prohibit the uncleanness of a carcass and to teach us that this defilement is forbidden to all Israel, is expounded in *Torat Kohanim* as referring only to the state of uncleanness required before a festival; see below. 'Others' (*ibid.*) give a different, but forced interpretation to the verse, which is likewise inconsonant with its simple meaning.

Similarly the verse Leviticus xiv 36, whose wording clearly shows that it is obligatory to save the articles from defilement, is explained by R. Meir in the Mishna (*Nega'im* xii, 5) and in the *Sifra* ('Mĕṣôrā' §5) to imply that 'the Torah wished to spare' Israel financial loss, that is that they should not suffer loss through the fact that the articles would not be usable for levitically clean objects. R. Judah bases the law on the Scriptural injunction, and does not relate it to defilement (as RABaD [R. Abraham b. David of

But a number of laws that militate against this tradition attest that, during the Second Temple period and after, the concept of levitical cleanness was not restricted to the spheres just mentioned. This is particularly evidenced by Josephus and Philo, as we shall see later.

The 'extension'[4] of the applicability of the laws of uncleanness beyond the aforementioned confines proceeded in three directions and encompassed:

(a) *sacred objects* (not included in the sanctity of the Temple and its sacred objects);

(b) the eating of *unconsecrated food*;

(c) the intrinsic obligation of cleanness and the prohibition of uncleanness.

I. *The Precept of Cleanness in Respect of Holy Objects*

These Halakhot, which will be explained below, and which manifest an 'expansion' of the area of the laws of cleanness set for them by tradition, give expression to a basic aim at variance with that of the established Halakha, namely, *the application of the precept of cleanness to all Israel and the extension of the priestly sanctity to the entire nation.*

Now let us begin to examine the Halakhot seriatim.

1) *The laws of uncleanness appertaining to sacred objects. The uncleanness of nocturnal pollution*

From a number of Mishnayot and Baraitot[5] we learn that one who has suffered a pollution is forbidden to study Torah or to recite prayers. There seem to be conflicting traditions in regard to this

Posquières] explains in his commentary on the *Sifra* and RaSh [R. Samson b. Abraham of Sens] in his annotations to the Mishna), and R. Simeon, it seems, agrees with him (or with R. Meir, according to RaSh; cf. *Mishne le-Melekh* to Maimonides, 'Hilkhot Ṭum'at Ṣara'at', 4).

Likewise the Tannaitic interpretations that regard the Pentateuchal sections which speak of sending the unclean out of the camp as referring only to the camp of the Divine Presence and the camp of the Temple attendants [priests and Levites] are no nearer to the plain meaning of the Scriptural passages.

4 At the end of this article I deal with the question and incline to regard these Halakhot, which deviate from the established tradition, not as a development thereof, but as the expression of another view, which was opposed to it from the outset. Hence I can speak of the 'extension' of the applicability of uncleanness etc. only in inverted commas.

5 *M. Berakhot* iii, 4–6; *M. Terumot* i, 6 (cf. *Tosefta ibid.* ii, 1, and *T.P.* to this Mishna); *Tosefta Berakhot* ii, 12–14; the Baraitot in both Talmuds *Berakhot loc. cit.* and *T.P. Shabbat* i, 3d.

Halakha, as to whether it is a Biblical law or a Rabbinic regulation. According to R. Joshua b. Levi and R. Eleazar it is a Torah injunction;[6] but the Tannaitic tradition,[7] as interpreted in the Talmud,[8] considers it only an enactment of Ezra.

However, upon examination we see that these traditions do not contradict each other. For in the sources that speak of the laws of pollution we must distinguish the following three Halakhot:

(a) A Halakha that requires immersion for the study of the Torah and the recitation of prayers, on account of the prohibition against performing these duties in a (i.e. this) state of uncleanness.

(b) A Halakha that makes it incumbent upon one that has suffered a pollution to undergo ritual immersion when he goes to eat or drink.

(c) A Halakha that ordains the precept of immersion for the sake of cleansing oneself from the impurity in all events, even when one does not need to study Torah or partake of a meal.

It therefore appears that the anonymous tradition that states that Ezra 'instituted immersion for those to whom a pollution happened' does not refer to the prohibition of occupying oneself with Torah study but to the commandment of purity *per se*.[9]

Hence this Halakha does not affect the tradition of the Amoraim who teach that the prohibition that one who has suffered a pollution may not study Torah or say his prayers is a Biblical ordinance. Furthermore, it may well be that a man may be obliged to undergo immersion on account of uncleanness and yet be permitted to study Torah before his lustrations. It is not therefore necessary to conclude that R. Judah b. Bathyra, who declares that 'Words of Torah are not subject to defilement',[10] disagrees with the tradition that ascribes this enactment to Ezra.[11]

6 *T.B. Berakhot* 22b; *T.P. ibid.* iii, 6c.

7 *T.B. Bava Qamma* 82a; *T.P. Megilla* iv, 75a and *T.P. Yoma* viii, 44d.

8 *T.B. Bava Qamma, loc. cit.*; *T.B. Berakhot* 22b.

9 Zeitlin, *JQR*, N.S., LXXIII, pp. 63–66; also *HUCA*, I, pp. 369–371, advances the view that this enactment of Ezra had as its purpose only to make it easier for the defiled person, that he should not have to wait for sunset (or even to be sent outside of Jerusalem) as he must if he wishes to enter the Temple. However the expression 'he instituted ritual immersion [תיקן טבילה]' shows that the reference is to the initiation of a religious observance and not to the annulment of another precept. So, too, all the other enactments attributed to Ezra are new laws.

10 *T.B. Berakhot* 22a; *T.P. ibid.* iii, 6c.

11 The Early Authorities found this matter difficult. See Tosafot, *T.B. Bava*

The duty incumbent on those who have had a seminal issue to perform immersion though it is not their intention to study Torah may be inferred from *T.P. Berakhot* iii, 6c: 'The real reason for instituting immersion in this instance was to prevent Israelites from behaving like cocks, having sexual intercourse, going up and down and eating'. Thus the purpose of this immersion is to enable the person to eat. A similar inference is to be drawn from the story of R. Jose b. Ḥalafta who was sailing in a ship, when one of the passengers wished to perform immersion in the sea, but R. Jose forbade him on account of the danger. 'Said the passenger to him: "I wish to eat."[12] R. Jose replied: "Then eat!" (The other then said:) "I wish to drink." (R. Jose answered:) "Drink!" When, however, they reached port, the Rabbi said to him: "There I permitted you (to eat and drink) only because you would have endangered your life (by performing your lustrations in the sea). But here you may not taste a thing until you purify yourself."' Since in both these sources the tradition is silent as to the reason and does not explain the prohibition on account of the benediction, we must interpret it according to its plain sense and assume the prohibition to flow from the precept prescribing cleanness for meals.

In accordance with this Halakha is also to be explained the other story concerning R. Jose, which is cited in *T.P. ibid.* Once he was walking 'in an alley[13] at night and his ass-driver, who was following him, passed by a pool. Said the ass-driver to him: "I wish to purify myself"' etc. For it is improbable that the ass-driver wanted to immerse himself for the purpose of Torah-study.[14]

But from the general character of the tradition it seems that he did not even intend to perform his lustrations for the purpose of eating but in order to fulfil the precept of cleanness in any circumstances.

That it is obligatory for one who has suffered a pollution to bathe ritually even when he does not intend to study Torah or take a meal is also to be deduced from R. Ḥanina's statement (*T.B. Berakhot* 22a) 'They set up a great fence thereby', and from the following Baraitot, which explain the nature of this fence. 'Once a man asked a woman

Qamma 82b (s.v. '*Ātā*'), Rosh [R. Asher b. Jeḥiel] *ad loc.*; Rashba on *Tractate Berakhot*.

12 According to the correct recension of the Rome MS.

13 איסמטא; aliter איסרטא as in the Rome MS.

14 These incidents were already explained, as in this essay, also by Brandt, *Beihefte zur ZATW*, XVIII, pp. 39–41, and in the supplement of this periodical vol. XVIII, pp. 124–125.

to have illicit relations with him. Said she to him: "You good for nothing! Have you forty *se'a* to bathe in?" Forthwith he desisted.' It is thus seen that the precept of immersion applies immediately (after pollution) and is unconditional, not being linked either to the need for Torah-study or eating. A similar inference is to be drawn from the following story: 'Once a watchman wished to have intercourse with a married woman. But while they were preparing a bathing-place for themselves, people passed by and the offence was not perpetrated.'[15]

This Halakha also emerges from the following Baraita:[16] 'One who suffered a pollution may immerse himself throughout the day [of Atonement]. R. Jose said from the *Minḥa* onwards he need not bathe.' Thus in the view of the Sages he may continue to immerse himself even though it is not for the purpose of studying Torah or of eating food in purity.

Consequently the tradition regarding Ezra's enactment that requires those who had a seminal issue to immerse themselves must be understood as referring to the precept of purification *per se*, and not as a necessary preliminary of Torah-study. Furthermore, it appears that the Palestinian Talmud supports this view. For it is stated there (*T.P. Yoma* viii, 44d): 'As regards sexual intercourse, seeing that bathing is prohibited, does it not follow that coition is forbidden? You must therefore explain the Mishna as legislating for a place

15 I find it necessary to comment on the statement of Heinemann (*Philons jüdische und griechische Bildung*, p. 73), who, after quoting Philo's explanation of the reason underlying the precept concerning the uncleanness of proselytes, which, in Philo's view seeks to teach the gravity of the crime of bloodshed, writes: 'Nach einer anderen Auffassung (scil. Philons) soll die Vorschrift der Reinigung der Verbrechen verhüten. Verwandtes findet sich in der rabbinischen Literatur nicht.'

But these incidents and the dicta of R. Ḥanina and R. Joshua b. Levi show that even in the school of the Rabbinic Sages the duty of purification was regarded as 'a great fence' that keeps a man far from grave transgression (Philo uses the very same language in writing about the law of immersion after coition, stating that it serves 'to keep one far from adultery and suspicion'). Tannaim already taught in a Baraita (*Sifre Numbers* §161; *Tosefta Yoma* i, 2 and *Tosefta Shevu'ot* i, 4; *T.B. Yoma* 23a and *T.P. ibid.* ii, 39c): 'This teaches you that the uncleanness of knives was graver in their estimation than bloodshed.'

Josephus also explains the reason of the law of defilement in connection with the dead in the same way as Philo (see below).

16 *T.B. Yoma* 88a; *Tosefta ibid.* iv, 5 (in the printed editions and the Vienna MS.; it is wanting in the Erfurt MS. and was possibly omitted on account of its similarity to other passages).

where the people do not immerse themselves after sexual congress, or as having been formulated before Ezra instituted bathing for those who have a pollution.' Thus the Palestinian Talmud holds that after Ezra's enactment there is no need for a special prohibition of sexual intercourse on the Day of Atonement, since this is forbidden in any case in order that one should not be liable to immersion and so bathe on the fast day. But 'from the *Minḥa* onward' he will certainly not be studying Torah or reciting prayers, and *a fortiori* not eating. We must perforce conclude that in the view of the Talmud Ezra instituted immersion for the defilement of seminal issue even where Torah-study is not involved.[17]

We now have a *single tradition* in regard to the origin of the Halakha ordaining immersion for those who suffered a pollution before they may study Torah, a tradition that derived the rule from Scripture. But actually this Halakha was not accepted by all the Sages; there were some who objected to it and there were places where it was not complied with. R. Judah b. Bathyra criticized it, declaring 'The words of the Torah are not subject to defilement' and R. Judah b. Ileʿai adopted a similar attitude to that of R. Judah b. Bathyra.[18]

17 This assumption makes it possible to reconcile the contradiction in the Palestinian tradition in regard to the enactment of immersion for those who have suffered a pollution, namely that in *Tractates Yoma* and *Megilla* the Talmud ascribes the regulation to Ezra, whereas in *Tractate Shabbat* (i, 3d) it is counted among the Eighteen Edicts. The explanation is that the passage in *Tractate Shabbat* speaks of the immersion, for the purpose of studying Torah, of one who has had a seminal issue, but this is not the case in the other two passages, which refer to the precept of immersion *per se*.

18 *M. Berakhot* iii, 5, 6; *Tosefta ibid.* ii, 14; *T.B. ibid.* 22a and *T.P. ibid.* iii, 6c.

It seems difficult, however, to understand why R. Judah is not consistent with regard to these Halakhot. For in this instance he is lenient and the Sages are strict, but elsewhere (*Tosefta Berakhot* ii, 12; *T.B. ibid.* 22b; *T.P. ibid.* iii, 6c) it is stated: 'If a sick person who had a pollution (in the Babylonian Talmud, too, this recension should be adopted, in accordance with the text of the Munich MS. and other versions, and also the reading of *T.P. ibid.* and *M. Miqwa'ot* iii, 4) poured nine kabs of water over himself, he may read the *Shĕmaʿ*, but he may not act on behalf of others until he immerses himself in forty *se'ā*. R. Judah says forty *se'a* are required in either case.' Thus we see that R. Judah is stricter than the Sages.

It may perhaps be conjectured, if we eschew the answer that 'Two disciples (holding different views) taught this', that R. Judah's ruling 'forty *se'a* are required in either case' was not enunciated originally in connection with the Halakha discussed here, but is only an excerpt from the Baraita in *Tosefta Miqwa'ot* vi, 1, where he states 'Because one who had a seminal issue may

It appears that, in the earlier generations, many Sages agreed with R. Judah b. Bathyra's view, although in the later Mishna his opinion, it would seem, is that of one individual only. For we see that our Halakha underlies the custom of the former 'morning bathers' who used to immerse themselves every day before saying their prayers lest they had suffered a pollution. It is actually stated in the Tosefta [*Yadayim* i, 20, according to the complete reading given by the RaSh in his commentary on the last Mishna of that tractate]: 'The "morning bathers" say "We bring a charge against you, O Pharisees, for pronouncing the Divine Name in the morning without prior immersion." The Pharisees answer: "We charge you, O 'morning bathers', with uttering the Name from a body containing impurity."' These Pharisees who by their reply wish to prove to their opponents that it is impossible to achieve absolute cleanness when pronouncing God's name, use this argument only for the sake of refutation, adopting the 'premises' of their adversaries; but actually their remarks are oriented towards the Halakha that rules that no heed need be

perform immersion in any place [בכל מקום]', expressing a more lenient view (in opposition to R. Meir who holds a stricter opinion) and teaching us that there are places forbidden to people who have been defiled by other forms of uncleanness but are permitted to one who has had a pollution. Now the 'Tanna' of our Baraita took over this tradition holus-bolus and attached it to a subject with which it had nothing to do in the first instance. This combination resulted in the introduction of an antithetic usage, בכל מקום 'in any place' being changed to מכל מקום 'in either case'.

It should be noted that the Halakha that originated in the school of Naḥum of Gimzo, R. Akiba and Ben 'Azzai, which permits pouring water over the person who had a seminal issue (*T.B. Berakhot* 22a) finds a parallel in another source of that period, namely *The Teaching of the Twelve Apostles* [Didache], a work that is rooted in Jewish Halakhot and customs. It is stated there (vii, 1–3), after the injunction concerning the baptism (of Christians) in spring water: 'If there is no spring water, bathe in other water. If you cannot do so in cold water, bathe in warm water. And if you have neither, throw water three times over your head' etc.

From this we learn that it is permissible to perform the lustrations (in an emergency) by pouring water over the head, and that one may bathe in warm water (cf. *Berakhot, loc. cit.*); we are also given here the limits of leniency and stringency, which are found in this connection in the Palestinian Talmud: 'R. Jannai said: I have heard that some are lenient and that some are strict in this regard. Those who are lenient permit bathing in drawn water and those who are strict insist on immersion in spring water.'

Josephus, however (*Ant.* iii, 11, 3), understands the Halakha as it was prior to the introduction of leniencies and states that one who suffered a pollution must immerse himself in cold water.

given to uncleanness, when mentioning the Divine Name, since 'The words of the Torah are not subject to defilement.' Thus the 'morning bathers' follow the view of the Sages, while the early 'Pharisees' adopt the opinion of R. Judah b. Bathyra. The subject, however, requires further study.[19]

2) *The relationship of other forms of uncleanness to the words of the Torah*

The settled Halakha teaches us that only those who had a pollution are forbidden to occupy themselves with Scripture. For it is stated in a Baraita:[20] 'Men and women who suffered a flux, menstruants, and woman after childbirth are permitted to read the Torah... but those who had a seminal issue are forbidden to do any of these things.' This Halakha is explained by the Early Authorities to be due to the fact that all other defiled persons 'may be in a state of awe and trembling, but a pollution can only result from frivolity and arrogance'.[21] This interpretation serves to undermine the foundation of the Halakha concerning the relationship of uncleanness to Torah and to base the prohibition debarring those who have suffered a pollution from occupying themselves with words of the Torah on the principle that they should have nothing to do with sacred matters while in a state of frivolity.

However, since it has been established that the tradition knows of no view conflicting with that of the Amoraim in the Talmuds that this Halakha was derived from the Torah, given at Mount Sinai, the Baraita must be assumed to mean that the Sages did not wish to equate all other forms of uncleanness to that referred to here and based the Halakha on what is expressly stated in Scripture.

But from the sources to be cited later we learn that other kinds of defilement should logically entail the prohibition of Torah-study. Hence the following Geonic interpretation seems probable:[22] 'Why is one who had a seminal issue, unlike other defiled persons, prohibited (from studying Torah)? Because the others (those who have gonorrhea, etc.) have no remedy on the day that the uncleanness occurs, whereas he has a remedy on the very same day; hence he was forbidden.' Thus, according to this view, other defiled persons

19 For it may well be that they used to bathe in order to sanctify themselves before praying, even if there was no fear of defilement; see further on in this article.

20 *Tosefta Berakhot* ii, 3; *T.B. Berakhot* 22a.

21 Rashi *ad loc.*; *Ṭur*, Oraḥ Ḥayyim, §88.

22 *Eshkol*, Pt. I; Urbach p. 3; Albeck p. 5.

ought also to be forbidden to occupy themselves with words of the Torah, only it was not feasible to debar a man from Torah-study and prayer, when he has no means of purifying himself on the same day.[23]

So, too, it is stated in regard to the impurity of Gentiles (*T.B. Shabbat* 127b): 'The Rabbis taught: The Sages were once in need of something from a certain matrona... said they: "Who will go?" R. Joshua answered: "I will go"... On coming out, he went down, immersed himself, and taught his disciples... "When I went down and immersed myself, of what did you suspect me?" They replied "Perchance some spittle spurted from her mouth onto the Rabbi's garments." "By the Temple Service!"[24] he exclaimed "It was even so...."' Now Gentiles' uncleanness, according to that tradition, is the *defilement of those who suffer a flux*. It follows that this form of impurity also prohibits occupying oneself with words of the Torah.

It was similarly taught that a menstruant may not recite prayers, nor pronounce a benediction, nor enter a synagogue. Nay more, the Sages declared that even one who is defiled by a menstruant's touch or sitting accommodation is required to bathe for Torah-study.[25]

23 This refutes the view of Prof. Ginzberg, who stated *MGWJ*, 1912, p. 448, n. 1, that the Halakha prohibits only one who had a pollution from prayer and not any one defiled by any other form of uncleanness, for only the Karaites forbid also those who suffer from any other kind of impurity.

24 This episode occurred *after the destruction of the Temple*, for prior to it R. Joshua certainly had no disciples; nevertheless it is not surprising that he uses the expression העבודה 'By the Temple Service!' For not only did the generation that witnessed the destruction of the Temple use this oath (we find R. Joshua employing this expression after the Destruction also in *T.B. Giṭṭin* 58a. My attention was drawn to this passage by my colleague H. Finkel), but even Sages who lived long after the destruction of the Temple used to swear in this fashion. For the linguistic usage did not cease among the Jews, even though the Service had ceased. Thus we find the phrase used by R. Jose b. Durmasqit (*Pesiqta de-R. Kahana*, ed. Buber, 128a), by R. Nehorai (*Mekhilta*, Be-shallaḥ; *Mekhilta de-R. Simeon b. Yoḥai*, *ibid.* p. 38), by R. Ḥiyya and Bar Qappara (*T.B. Yevamot* 32b), by R. Ḥiyya's disciple (or R. Meir, *Sifre*, Shelaḥ, §115; *T.B. Menaḥot* 44a) and by R. Joḥanan (*T.P. Yevamot* v, 9c; *T.P. Qiddushin* iv, 65c. In *T.B. ibid.* 71a — היכלא in the same sense as העבודה). Lieberman was wrong, therefore, in stating (*Hayerushalmi Kiphshuto*, p. 51) that this oath formula is appropriate only to Sages who lived in Temple times. Likewise Hyman did not note these passages (*Toledot Tanna'im wa-'Amora'im* s.v. Benjamin the Righteous).

25 The *Baraita of Tractate Nidda*, pp. 3, 33, 17. Although this is a late work, it nevertheless appears that its basically underlying tradition goes back to early times. There were even some Geonim, although most of them ruled that

With regard to defilement by the dead, although the unclean were not obliged to immerse themselves, they were nevertheless forbidden to study Torah in a place of impurity. For the following is stated in *T.P. Berakhot* (ii, 4c *init.*): 'If a man was occupied with a corpse in a grave and the time for reading the *Shema'* arrived, he must go to a place of purity and put on phylacteries and recite the *Shema'* and say the *Tefilla* [Eighteen Benedictions].' So, too, we learn in *Tractate Semaḥot* (iii, 7, ed. Higger, p. 202): 'If a man was making a chamber in a burial place and the time arrived for reciting the *Shema'*, he may not read (the *Shema'*) nor say the *Tefilla* (there), but must go to a place of purity and recite the *Shema'* and say the *Tefilla*, and thereafter enter.'[26]

The nexus between all other categories of defilement and occupation with Torah, as well as the obligation to purify oneself wherever possible, may be deduced from the tradition that ordains that the benediction for the precept of immersion should be pronounced after it has been performed, unlike the procedure in the case of other commandments (*T.B. Pesaḥim* 7b; *T.P. Berachot* ix 13a). The Geonim are divided in regard to this Halakha;[27] some of them hold that it refers only to a proselyte, in order to harmonize this law with the Baraita that permits other unclean persons to occupy themselves with Torah; while others interpret it according to its plain and true meaning, namely that it applies to all who require immersion. For once a person proceeds to purify himself, no further concession may be made in infraction of the essential rule, which requires cleansing from all forms of defilement for words of the Torah, since the law was waived only when its observance was not possible. Consequently the benediction is not to be uttered while 'the individual is not yet fit'[28] but after purifications.

Thus the Halakha basically ordains that *every form of impurity* prohibits Torah-study and prayer.[29]

it was permitted, who prohibited a menstruant from entering a Synagogue or occupying herself with hallowed matters (cf. *Otzar ha-Geonim* to *Berakhot*, Responsa, p. 49).

26 [*T.B. Berakhot* 14b].

27 See *Otzar ha-Geonim* to *Berakhot*, Responsa, p. 48; to *Pesaḥim*, p. 8 (see the notes *ibid.*); to *Rosh ha-Shana*, p. 27.

28 This is the expression of the Gemara, *T.B. Berakhot* 51a, and R. Yehudai Gaon likewise holds that the benediction is to be pronounced after the performance of the lustrations also in the case of other forms of defilement (*Toratan shel Ri'shonim*, Halakhot Qeṣuvot, p. 25).

29 In the Baraita of *Tractate Nidda*, p. 26, it is stated: ' "That they die not in

3) *The uncleanness of one who suffered a pollution in respect of phylacteries*

Although the established Halakha prohibits an unclean person only from engaging in Torah and prayer, but not from occupying himself with other holy observances, nevertheless we find that some of the Sages forbade even the putting on of phylacteries in a state of defilement.

Thus it is stated in the Talmud (*T.B. Sukka* 26b): 'The Rabbis taught: He who goes to sleep during the day may, if he so wishes, take off (his phylacteries), or, if he desires, put them on; but at night he must remove (his phylacteries) and not put them on. This is the view of R. Nathan. R. Jose says: Youths must always take off (their phylacteries) and not put them on, because defilement is frequent with them.' In the same passage the Talmud raises the question: 'Is it to be presumed that R. Jose takes the view that one who had an issue is forbidden to wear phylacteries?' Abbaye replies: 'We are dealing here with youths accompanied by their wives, for fear that they will become habituated to sinful conduct.' But the plain meaning of the words teaches us that in R. Jose's view it is forbidden to put on phylacteries in a state of impurity due to a seminal emission.

Furthermore it appears probable that this Halakha is also accepted by Rava, the opponent of Abbaye, who permits one who has suffered a pollution to wear phylacteries. For it is stated in *T.B. Shabbat* (49a; 130a): 'R. Jannai said: Phylacteries require a pure body like that of Elisha, the man of wings. What does this imply? Abbaye said that one should not pass wind while wearing them. Rava said that one should not sleep with them on.' According to the simple meaning of Rava's statement, 'a pure body' means *undefiled*, that one who has had a seminal emission is not permitted to put on phylacteries. And although the *Rishonim* [Early Authorities] raised objections by referring to the same theme in *T.B. Sukka*, nevertheless it may be said that Amoraim differ on the subject. For the anonymous

their uncleanness": This teaches that a Jew may not enter a house of prayer when he is unclean, because he defiles the sanctuary of the Holy One, blessed be He' etc. The implication is that every unclean person is prohibited. But later it is added: 'Now what is the impurity of a man? "And this shall be his uncleanness in his issue" ' etc. It is thus seen that the reference is to one who has had a pollution.

discussion of the theme follows the view of Abbaye,[30] who also explains in *T.B. Shabbat* that R. Jose's Halakha is not due to the fear of seminal pollution, but is based on the principle of cleanliness, while Rava construes this Halakha in conformity with the opinion of R. Jose, stated in the Baraita *ibid.*, according to its plain meaning.[31]

4) *Washing the hands for prayer*

This Halakha is taught in the Talmud only by Amoraim.[32] But in essence the Halakha is of great antiquity, and was practised by many long before the Amoraic period. Thus the author of *The Letter of Aristeas* testifies concerning the seventy-two elders, who translated the Torah into Greek,[33] as follows: 'And as is the custom of all the Jews, they washed their hands in the sea and prayed to God' etc. The following verse expressly states that this washing of the hands was on account of prayer.

30 In a number of places the Rishonim note that there are Talmudic discourses where the anonymous questions cited there were actually asked by those who answer them (cf. Tosafot, *Bava Meṣi'a* 21a, and Ramban *ibid.*, who writes 'and this is the case in many passages of the Talmud', *et al.*).

31 A Gaon was already asked 'Whether a man may put on phylacteries after sexual intercourse or not' (*Otzar ha-Geonim* to *Berakhot*, Responsa, p. 56), and he permitted it on the basis of the discussion in *T.B. Sukkot*. Possibly the fundamental reason of our Mishna (*Terumot* i, 6), in ordaining that one who has suffered a pollution may not, at the outset, set aside heave-offering, is not the fact that he has to *utter a benediction* (*Tosefta, ibid.* i, 1; *T.P. ibid.* i, 40d), but the sacred character of the act of *separating heave-offering* (the same applies to a naked person, while a dumb person is debarred from separating heave-offering because of his inability to enunciate the designation), and this is also the case in regard to the dough-offering (*M. Ḥalla* ii, 3).

32 *T.B. Berakhot* 14b; 15a; *T.B. Pesaḥim* 46a; *T.B. Ḥullin* 122b. The Halakha 'For prayer and for washing the hands — up to four *mils*' apparently refers to washing the hands for prayer (cf. *Otzar ha-Geonim*, to *Berakhot*, Responsa, p. 42, and Tosafot, *Ḥullin, loc. cit.*, s.v. *û-lĕ-gabbal* ['And for a kneader']), although R. Sherira Gaon explains the reference to be to one who had a seminal issue. Nor should it be deduced from the statement in *T.B. Berakhot* 51a: 'R. Ishmael b. Elisha said: Suriel, Prince of the Presence, told me three things... and do not let one who has not washed his hands wash your hands' etc. that washing of the hands for this reason is meant. Furthermore, the tradition in question explains the prohibition as due to evil spirits.

33 [Charles, *Pseudepigrapha*, p. 120, ll. 305–306]. Cf. Schürer, *Geschichte*⁴ etc., II, p. 519, n. 63. Although the author of the Letter explains the lustrations symbolically, the reason he gives is only intended to adapt the observance to the taste of the Greek readers and to make it acceptable to the Jewish allegorists.

Similarly we read in the *Sibylline Oracles*:[34] 'But they instead raise heavenwards holy arms, rising early from their bed and ever cleansing their flesh with water, and they honour Him alone who reigns for ever, the Eternal, and after him their parents.'

Now having seen above that in strict law all other categories of uncleanness disqualify a person from praying, we must explain that this washing of the hands serves to purify one from light forms of defilement that were to be found among all people. Hence it is also possible to interpret Judith's practice, during the period of her stay with Holofernes, to go out in the morning watch outside the camp to bathe and pray, as due not to the uncleanness of the Gentiles, with whom she came in contact in those days,[35] but as a custom that she always observed, even when she was among Jews. For this immersion, like the washing of the hands, preceded her prayer everywhere, in order to purify herself from other forms of defilement.

If now we assume this, we find that in the time of the Second Temple two customs obtained among Jews — one to purify themselves for prayer by washing the hands, and the other, which is more stringent, to purify themselves by immersing the whole body.[36] But it may well be that these Halakhot, which ordain immersion or washing of the hands for prayer, are not based on the suspicion of actual defilement, but on the fact that the service of the heart is likened to the Temple service, which requires washing of the hands and immersion even by those who are clean.[37] A similar Halakha,

34 [Charles, *op. cit.*, *The Sibylline Oracles*, Book iii, p. 389, ll. 591–594]. II, 591–594, ed. of the Prussian Academy, p. 78: ἀλλὰ γὰρ ἀείρουσι πρὸς οὔρανον ὠλένας ἁγνὰς ὄρθριοι ἐξ εὐνῆς αἰεὶ χρόα ἁγνίζοντες ὕδατι καὶ τιμῶσι τὸν ἀεὶ μεδεόντα ἀθάνατον καὶ ἔπειτα γονεῖς. The text I have copied here is not in agreement with my translation, because I did not wish the Greek to differ from the version of the aforementioned edition. But I have decided to render it in accordance with the two recensions (see the notes *ibid.*) that read χέρας instead of χρόα χειρες. But the reading of the other (single) version, which implies the washing of the whole body, is not ruled out, for as stated in the article it is probable that there were some Jews who were accustomed to bathe regularly before prayer.

35 See above, p. 154.

36 We have the testimony of the Church Fathers regarding the custom of the Jews to bathe every day (before prayer). Likewise the practice of the Judeo-Christian sects to immerse themselves, which earned them their name [Baptists], undoubtedly stemmed from the Jewish custom, see Brandt, the Supplement to *ZATW*, XVIII, p. 49, and the following chapters on sectarian baptism.

37 *M. Yoma* iii, 3,

likewise based on this analogy, is found in *T.B. Berakhot* 53b: 'Just as a dirty person is disqualified from performing the Temple service, so dirty hands disqualify one from reciting grace.'[38]

But in any case these Halakhot mark an expansion of the sphere of purity beyond the Temple precincts.

5) *The precept of purity on festival and Sabbath*

It is stated in the *Sifra* (Shemini, iv, ed. Weiss 49a; *T.B. Rosh ha-Shana* 16b): ' "And their carcasses ye shall not touch" — I might have thought that the Israelites were enjoined not to touch carcasses... How then am I to explain "And their carcasses ye shall not touch?" This refers to festivals.' A similar exposition is given in *Sifre Zuṭa* (Horovitz, p. 229): ' "Every leper, and every one that hath an issue, and whosoever is unclean by the dead"; "and whosoever is unclean" comes to include all other defiled persons — that they must become fit before the festival.' This may also be inferred from what is subsequently stated there for we learn with regard to the Nazirite (p. 242): 'I might argue that he should defile himself for a *mēt miṣwā* [literally 'a corpse of religious duty', i.e. an unattended corpse, whose burial is obligatory on everyone] on a festival; indeed Scripture teaches "He shall not make himself unclean... for his mother" — but he must defile himself for a *mēt miṣwā* on a festival.' It thus comes to teach us that although two Pentateuchal injunctions are incumbent upon him prior to the festival to avoid defilement — one on account of his naziriteship and one on account of the festival — nevertheless he is obliged to defile himself for a *mēt miṣwā*.

Now the Rishonim and Geonim[39] explained that the reason of

38 R. Abraham, the son of Maimonides writes (his *Kifāyat al-'Ābidīn*, published by S. Eppenstein in *Israel Levy Jubilee Volume*, pp. 33–59, together with his translation, on which the following English rendering is based): 'It is still necessary to add his explanation of the duty to purify the hands (for prayer) — but it is preferable by far to wash the hands and feet together — namely that the prayers were instituted to correspond to the daily burnt-offerings, and since the services take the place of the sacrifices and the Torah enjoined "Thou shalt also make a laver of bronze... And Aaron and his sons shall wash their hands and their feet thereat", it is incumbent upon us to endeavour to wash our hands at every service and not refrain from doing so. For there is an analogy here to the Temple service; one of the things observed punctiliously, the Sages declare, was this: "It was the rule in the Sanctuary that whoever eases himself requires immersion and whoever passes water must purify his hands and feet." '

39 RABaD (R. Abraham b. David of Posquières) to *Torat Kohanim*, *loc. cit.*, Maimonides, 'Hilkhot Tum'at Okholin [Laws concerning the uncleanness of foods]' xvi, 9 (so, too, Alfasi, who does not cite this Halakha); Asheri at

the Halakha was the need to offer the (festal) sacrifice and to visit the Temple (pilgrimage); hence only the pilgrims were enjoined to observe this precept. Ostensibly this view is supported by the last Baraita of *Sifre Zuṭa*, where 'festival' [*regel*] refers to 'the slaughtering of the Passover sacrifice' found in the parallel Baraitot.[40] Nevertheless it appears that the Halakha was not confined to pilgrims, as is to be seen from the responsum of the Gaon cited in *Geone Mizraḥ u-Maʿarav* (§78; *Otzar ha-Geonim* to *Rosh ha-Shana*, p. 26), who considers our Halakha to apply to all Israel. For the unqualified character of R. Isaac's statement (*T.B. Rosh ha-Shana, loc. cit.*) that 'It is incumbent upon a man to purify himself for the festival' and the fact that the Talmud juxtaposed this dictum to the preceding saying of R. Isaac 'It is a man's duty to pay his respects to his teacher on festivals', which perforce does not refer just to Temple times, implies that the precept of purification is not due only to the need to offer up the sacrifice and to enter the Sanctuary, but also to the sanctity of the day.

The custom of purification on account of the sanctity of the day we find at an early period also in connection with the *Sabbath*. Thus we read in *II Maccabees* (xii 38): 'And Judas took his army to the town of Adullam, where, as the seventh day was coming on, they purified themselves according to custom and kept the Sabbath there.'[41]

Possibly this may also be inferred from the Mishna (*Shabbat* ii, 7) with regard to the Tannaitic era, for most of the acts enumerated there were performed for the sake of the Sabbath, and it may be presumed that the immersion of vessels (which was carried out for unconsecrated food, as is explained in the Palestinian Talmud) was practised by many Jews on account of the holiness of the day, and actually the Rishonim[42] explain the reason underlying the Mishna

the end of *Tractate Yoma*; and Naḥmanides in his commentary to Lev. xi 8. This is also the view of the Geonim (Eshkol, Urbach 3; Albeck, p. 5; *Shaʿare Teshuva* No. 175).

40 *Sifre Numbers* §26; *T.B. Nazir* 48b. Thus we can see that at least according to *Sifre Zuṭa* this is a proper Pentateuchal precept, and not a Rabbinical enactment based on a Biblical intimation, as Naḥmanides maintains in his commentary on the Pentateuch, *loc. cit.* (see *Mishne le-Melekh*).

41 Attention was drawn to this passage by Ginzberg, *MGNJ*, XLIII, p. 435.

42 Rashi on *T.B. Beṣa* 17b; Ha-Me'iri and RaN *ad loc.* Although Rabban Simeon b. Gamaliel formulates that Halakha in the Tosefta with reference to a priest and heave-offering, this can nevertheless not serve as a criterion for the interpretation of our Mishna, for possibly there were two traditions.

in *Tractate Beṣa* (ii, 2): 'If a festival-day fell on the day after the Sabbath, the School of Shammai rule: All [requiring purification] must be immersed before the Sabbath. But the School of Hillel say: Vessels are to be immersed before the Sabbath and men on the Sabbath' (see also the next Mishna), to be the precept to purify oneself for the festival.

Indeed we find that in the time of Rav Yehudai Gaon there were communities who were accustomed to bathe on the eve of every Sabbath and festival and they regarded this lustration as a permanent religious duty, so that they even wished to say a benediction in connection with it.[43] It is possible, therefore, that the sequence of acts to be performed on the eve of the Sabbath, which is prescribed in the Mishna, refers to the custom of others to purify themselves before every Sabbath and festival.

II. *The Eating of Unconsecrated Food in Purity*

When we proceed to discuss this subject, we cannot overlook the particular difficulty involved in the examination of the sources relating to the Halakha under discussion. For many Tannaitic Halakhot that deal with levitically clean foods and doubts arising in connection with them are couched in general terms, and in most instances we have no means of deciding with certainty whether the reference is to unconsecrated food prepared in purity or to pure food which is heave-offering, dough-offering, or tithes. Now we are inclined to interpret these laws in the latter sense, since the established Halakha generally applies the laws of purity specifically to holy things and

43 *Sha'are Teshuva*, *loc. cit.* (*Otzar ha-Geonim* to *Rosh ha-Shana*, p. 26, n. 9). It is true that the Gaon replies: 'Thus the Sages taught: Since the destruction of the Temple there is no purity or impurity and there is no obligation for ritual immersion neither on the eve of the Sabbath nor on the eve of a festival, for the Pentateuchal duty of immersion applies only to entering the Sanctuary' etc. Nevertheless this was not the universal opinion, especially in Eretz-Israel. This refutes the view of Prof. Ginzberg, who states (*loc. cit.*, n. 3) that it is apparently to be inferred from the Damascus Document that the members of this sect were accustomed to purify themselves for the Sabbath, a practice of which there is no trace in tradition (except in *Maccabees*, *loc. cit.*). He only points to the Karaites (*Eshkol ha-Kofer*), who ordain immersion on the Sabbath eve. With reference to the main thesis of the aforementioned Gaon that immersion on Sabbath eve and on the eve of a festival is not obligatory, it should be noted that Rav Saadia Gaon (R. Isaac ibn Ghayyat, *Mē'ā Shĕ'ārîm*, Laws of the Day of Atonement) rules that one who immerses himself on the eve of the Day of Atonement must say a benediction on arising from the ritual bath. Thus this immersion is obligatory.

to priestly gifts. This is the line of interpretation followed by the distinguished scholar, Prof. Büchler (in his work *Der galiläische 'Am ha-'Areṣ* from which I quote many passages), who sought to harmonize the sources — often with great difficulty — with the trend to restrict the application of levitical purity prescribed in the established Halakha.

But it appears to me that since we know of a number of Tannaitic Halakhot that undoubtedly prescribe levitical purity for ordinary food as an act of piety or duty, we should study the sources with the following two premises in mind: (a) every Halakha that is formulated in general terms (or its terms of reference are defined, but its date is not stated) and can be referred to the purity required for heave-offering with difficulty, is to be interpreted according to its plain meaning and applied to unconsecrated food (and its observance dated to the generation to which tradition assigns it); (b) any Halakha whose terms are not specific is to be explained on the assumption that it refers to the purity of ordinary food, unless the reverse can be proven.

This being so, it is unnecessary to say that a number of the conclusions, which are stated later, in my interpretation of the sources are only probable conjectures; nevertheless they combine, to my mind, with the complete proofs to provide a basis for the overall view advanced in this chapter.

Let us now go back and examine the actual Halakhot.

In many passages the sources testify that both early and late Sages ate their ordinary food[44] under conditions of levitical purity. Similarly the Haggadah ascribes to the early ancestors of the Jewish people the practice of eating unconsecrated food in purity.[45]

Now ostensibly it may be inferred from some of the sources cited

44 See Büchler, *Der galiläische 'Am ha-'Areṣ*, 119–124. However, his evidence regarding R. Joshua from the Baraita in *T.B. Shabbat* 127b is not valid. For the expression 'He went down and immersed himself and taught' shows that the lustration was on account of the teaching. But to the list of those who ate their ordinary food in purity there are to be added, apparently, Rabban Joḥanan b. Zakkai and R. Eliezer, who declared at the time of their death 'Clear the house on account of uncleanness' (*T.P. Soṭa* ix, 24c; *T.P. 'Avoda Zara* iii, 42c). However, it is not impossible that both of them were priests.

45 Abraham (*T.B. Bava Meṣi'a* 87a; Gen. Rabba xliv), Saul (*Midrash Tehillim*, Ps. vii; ed. Buber 32a; *Pesiqta de-R. Kahana*, ed. Buber, 78; *Pesiqta Rabbati* xv, ed. Ish Shalom, 68a).

above and from their formulation[46] that this observance was limited to a few individuals and that the eating of unconsecrated food in levitical purity was not actually a religious duty (*miṣwā*) but only an act of piety.[47]

But the fact that tradition depicts the practice of these Sages as an extreme, self-imposed stringency does not prove anything. It may be explained (1) as reflecting the view of later generations when not many (even among the Sages) were meticulous in observing this precept; (2) as due to the great difficulty of maintaining the practice *all the time* and of observing all the necessary minutiae;[48] (3) by the circumstance that since the time of the Sages there were certain scholars who did not refrain from expounding and ruling that halakhically only holy things and heave-offerings required levitical cleanness, and consequently the law was in suspense. In truth we learn from a number of passages that in the days of the Tannaim the eating of unconsecrated food in purity was a widespread custom and was not restricted to a few pious souls. We further learn that in a number of respects this religious practice was regarded as obligatory and was taught as one of the established Halakhot, although the eating of defiled ordinary food could not be declared absolutely forbidden, for such a ruling was impossible.

It is stated in a Baraita:[49] 'He who gives the following four undertakings is accepted as an Associate: That he will not give heave-offerings and tithes to an *ʿAm ha-ʾAreṣ*, that he will not prepare levitically pure food next to an *ʿAm ha-ʾAreṣ*, and that he will eat secular food in purity.'

In a Mishna it is taught:[50] 'He that undertakes to be an Associate may not sell to an *ʿAm ha-ʾAreṣ* wet or dry (foodstuff) or buy from him wet (food)' etc. It is not to be supposed that the restriction was made on account of heave-offerings and tithes, for the Halakha unequivocally forbids the sale of foodstuff to an *ʿAm ha-ʾAreṣ*, even

46 The rest prove nothing. For example, Joḥanan b. Gudgada is distinguished by the fact that he ate his ordinary meals 'in accordance with levitical regulations applying to sacred food'. Likewise R. Joḥanan the son of the freedwoman may possibly have been unusual in eschewing doubt.

47 Büchler, *op. cit.*, p. 119, pp. 124–126.

48 Note should be taken of the expression 'all the time' [literally 'all his days'] used with reference to R. Joḥanan b. Gudgada, Rabban Gamaliel and ʿAqilas.

49 *Tosefta Demai* ii, 2; *ʾAvot de-R. Nathan*, Version I, xli (ed. Schechter, p. 66b).

50 *M. Demai* ii, 3.

if the vendor had first set aside the heave-offering and tithe.[51] Furthermore one is not permitted to sell (to an *'Am ha-'Areṣ*) produce from which the sacred gifts have not been separated.[52]

It is similarly taught in a Mishna:[53] 'If an Associate and an *'Am ha-'Areṣ* inherited jointly the estate of their father who was an *'Am ha-'Areṣ*... he may not say to his coheir "you take the wheat and I will take the barley", or "you take the wet produce and I will take the dry".' Here, too, the Mishna prohibits selling to an *'Am ha-'Areṣ* foodstuff that is fit to contract uncleanness (exchange being equivalent to selling), like the preceding Mishna, and like that Mishna it also speaks, apparently, of secular food prepared under conditions of levitical purity.

In the Tosefta[54] it is taught: 'An Associate may not say to an *'Am ha-'Areṣ*: "Take this loaf and give it to Associate So-and-so", because levitically clean food may not be sent by an *'Am ha-'Areṣ*. If an *'Am ha-'Areṣ* said to an Associate: "Take this loaf and hand it to So-and-so, an *'Am ha-'Areṣ*", he may not do so, for levitically clean food may not be delivered to an *'Am ha-'Areṣ*. If an *'Am ha-'Areṣ* said to an Associate: "Give me this loaf to eat", or "this wine to drink", he may not do so, because levitically prepared food may not be given to an *'Am ha-'Areṣ* to eat.' Now here the prohibition is not due to the fact that the articles were prepared according to

51 The RaSh [R. Samson b. Abraham of Sens] and Maimonides also interpret the Mishna as referring to ordinary food levitically prepared.

52 *M. Demai* v, 8; *T.P. ibid.*, 24d. Now Büchler (p. 163) is at first inclined to explain the Mishna as applying to priests and heave-offering, because the *midras* [couch, seat, etc.] of one that has a flux does not defile secular foodstuff. But the commentators have already pointed out that if his wife, during her period, sat on his garments, they become unclean even in respect of unconsecrated food (see RaSh here and on *M. Ṭohorot* vi, 5); and it is this that we are afraid of.

53 *M. Demai* vi, 9.

54 ii, 20–22. Büchler (154–155) maintains that we must understand these Halakhot as referring to heave-offering (actually, if we concede that the Baraitot may be dealing with unconsecrated food, in any respect, what compels us then to explain them as applying specifically to priests?). He infers this by analogy from the *Tosefta Demai* vi, 8, that speaks of levitically prepared food of an *'Am ha-'Areṣ*, which must be burnt; and in his opinion this Halakha can only be explained with regard to heave-offering. But, in the first instance, the laws relating to levitically clean food are not to be compared, nor can the unstated be inferred from that which is explicitly stated. Secondly, Büchler himself concedes that it is possible, at least according to the Sages of Usha, that the Halakha refers to the burning of secular food that was levitically prepared (p. 151).

the rules governing sacred food, but to the levitical purity of the ordinary food itself.

It is further taught:[55] 'Who is an *'Am ha-'Areṣ*? Whoever does not eat ordinary food levitically prepared. This is the view of R. Me'ir.'

Thus we learn that the preparation of secular food under conditions of levitical purity was not the practice of the few, but was a religious custom observed by all the Associates. However, we have still to consider, first, whether this ritual purity comes within the framework of the Halakha, or is no more than a purificatory embellishment. Secondly, we must determine whether, if it is a Halakha, it is confined to the community of Associates, who 'undertook' to observe this practice, or is basically a specific custom of all Israelites, only the Associates took it upon themselves to keep the observance scrupulously.

Now as regards the first question, the wording of the Halakhot cited above apparently indicates that this is a permanent religious duty, for they are formulated as fixed laws. Indeed this is a primary inference to be drawn from the Mishnayot and Baraitot that deal with purity relative to ordinary food in juxtaposition to that of heave-offering — that this levitical cleanness is a permanent regulation like that of its companion and is a fundamental Torah teaching.

Thus it is stated in *M. Zavim* (iii, 2): 'If they (the clean with the one that suffered a flux) were unloading an ass or leading it and the load was heavy, they (the clean) become unclean, but if it was light, they remain clean. In either case[56] they are clean for members of the congregation and unclean for heave-offering.'

It is further taught (*M. Para* xi, 5): 'Whoever requires immersion according to the ruling of the Scribes defiles hallowed things and invalidates heave-offering; but he is permitted common food. This is the view of R. Me'ir', etc.

In the Tosefta (*Miqwa'ot* vi, 7) it is stated: 'All those who were declared (above to be unclean) are clean for ordinary food and unclean for heave-offering, except a woman who discharges semen, who is unclean for common food, too.'

With respect to the second question, we must consider the sources cited below, which show that in a number of cases the Sages prescribed levitical purity for secular food as an actual obligation, and

55 *Tosefta 'Avoda Zara* iii (iv), 10; *T.B. Giṭṭin* 61b.

56 With regard to the textual reading compare RaSh *ad loc.*; Tosafot, *T.N. Nidda* 7a, s.v. וכולן; and *Mĕle'khet Shĕlomo, ad loc.*

absolutely forbade *all Israel* to eat it in a state of uncleanness. For they formulate their ruling in general terms and teach this Halakha, like all other Halakhot, without differentiating between Associates and others.

Thus it is stated in *M. Ḥullin* (ii, 5): 'If a man slaughtered cattle or a wild animal or a bird, and blood did not issue, they are valid, and they may be eaten with unclean hands, because they (the animals) have not been rendered susceptible to uncleanness through the blood. R. Simeon said: They have been made susceptible to defilement through slaughtering.' Thus R. Simeon and the Sages agree that they are not to be eaten in uncleanness, and we are certainly dealing here with unconsecrated food, for a wild animal and bird are mentioned.[57]

Similarly, the Tosefta (*Berakhot* vi(v), 2–3)[58] makes it clear that in the dispute between the School of Shammai and the School of Hillel in *M. Berakhot* (viii, 2–3) on the question whether the washing of the hands or the mixing of the cup comes first, and with regard to where the napkin is to be placed, both schools are agreed that it is forbidden to defile the food during the meal and that they differ only on the best way of avoiding the contingency of its defilement.

This general prohibition of the eating of common food in a state of uncleanness is to be inferred from the Halakha that forbids 'causing the defilement of secular food in Eretz-Israel', even if it is not subject to sacred gifts, for primarily the reason of this second Halakha is that it should be eaten in purity.

We learn this from *M. ʿAvoda Zara* (iv, 9): 'One may tread a winepress together with a Gentile, but not gather grapes with him', because he would help thereby to make the grapes susceptible to defilement by the Gentile. Now the fruit of the non-Jew are not subject to sacred gifts,[59] nevertheless the Sages forbade defiling them.

In the Tosefta (*Makhshirin* iii, 7) it is taught: 'Although the Sages ruled that a man is not permitted to defile his produce, they permitted the owner to defile a small quantity and put it in a *kefisha* [an inverted basket of twigs].'

We have already seen[60] that R. Jose forbade a man who had

57 Cf. *T.B. Ḥullin* 33a; *T.P. Ḥagiga* iii, 78a (indeed the Talmuds refer this to secular food prepared according to the levitical requirements of hallowed food).

58 *T.B. ibid.*, 52a–b; *T.P. ibid.*, viii, 12a.

59 Even under Rabbinic law, when the produce is in the Gentile's possession. See Maimonides, 'Hilkhot Maʿasér', xi, 15, and RABaD *ad loc.*; *ibid.*, 'Hilkhot Terumot', i, and Kesef Mishne *ad loc.*

60 Above, p. 193.

travelled with him in a ship to eat or drink until he had immersed himself on account of uncleanness due to a seminal discharge. And the man in question was even prepared to risk his life rather than fail to observe this religious duty.

Therefore we must conclude that this precept was regarded by the Sages as basically incumbent upon every Israelite, but owing to the difficulties involved many did not keep it, or did not observe it constantly. Hence the Sages (and other people who undertook to do so) had to form an association and dedicate themselves by a specific undertaking to observe the rite of purity scrupulously and to eschew all doubts.[61]

Consequently it is not surprising that the Mishna calls those who eat unconsecrated food in purity 'members of the congregation' (*M. Zavim*, *loc. cit.*), a term that implies all who are Israelites — the usage is also found in other passages[62] — because the eating of secular food in purity is a precept devolving upon all Jews.

However, the question of the institution of the Halakha — when it was taught and where it was introduced — must be discussed

61 Most of the precepts that the Associate undertook to observe, and which tradition testifies the *'Amme ha-'Areṣ* did not observe scrupulously, are entirely obligatory, like tithes, the recitation of the *Shĕma'*, phylacteries, fringes, *mĕzûzā*, the prohibition of raising small cattle, and even recklessness in vowing, which can lead to transgression (*M. Demai* ii, 3; *Tosefta 'Avoda Zara, loc. cit.*, *T.B. Giṭṭin, loc. cit.*, *T.B. Soṭa* 22a; *T.B. Berakhot* 47b). Although there were some who spoke of Torah-study and attendance on Sages (R. Judah in M., *loc. cit.*, and 'others' in *Soṭa* and *Berakhot*), this was certainly not the primary concern of the early Associates. Furthermore, we find in connection with the Associations only the following two precepts mentioned: levitically prepared food and tithes (except for the Mishna cited above). Hence it appears probable that the main purpose of the Associations was to facilitate their observance of the precepts relating to food — that they should have no dealings with those who were untrustworthy and prone to fall into sin. We must not, therefore, attribute to the Associates the aim to acquire greater sanctity by observances that were not generally obligatory, but we must conclude that they sought to help one another to keep those commandments that, for some reason, were treated with disrespect.

62 *M. Bekhorot* v, 5; *Tosefta Sanhedrin* i, 2; *ibid. Bekhorot* iii, 25. The fact that 'members of the congregation' (בני הכנסת) are paralleled here by 'an expert' (מומחה) testifies that they are any members of the community. Büchler regards them, by a forced interpretation (p. 74, n. 2), as Sages. But the expression בני כנסת in *Tosefta Megilla* iii, 1, and iv, 12, is not relevant here, for there it means the members of a given Synagogue; cf. Tosafot, *Nidda* 7a, s.v. וכולן, and Tosefot ha-Rosh *ad loc.* and also to *M. Zavim, loc. cit.*, as well as to RaSh *ibid.*

first. For Prof. Büchler adopts a particular view on this subject, in that he is inclined to regard the tradition that restricts the application of levitical purity to the sphere of the Temple and the priests as valid and without challenge, for all places and times up to the age of the last Tannaim. In his opinion, the stringent laws of defilement, which prohibit doubtful cases in relation to the *'Am ha-'Areṣ*, came into being only after the Destruction, some in Jabneh but the vast majority in Usha after the fall of Bethar; and even these refer primarily only to the priests and to heave-offering,[63] save that at

63 Büchler wishes to posit that wherever the Halakha teaches the laws of levitical purity in general terms the reference is to heave-offering (pp. 83-85). But this premise (which he himself assumes only as 'a very sure conjecture') is merely based on the principle 'of inferring from the stated for that which is not stated', which is not particularly applicable to the laws of purity, because there were conflicting Halakhot, and it is generally agreed that the levitical regulations are more concerned with heave-offering than with secular produce, whose need for cleanness is obscure (and this assumption is not weakened by the fact that in a number of passages the 'levitically pure foodstuff' spoken of is heave-offering). Thus no deductions may be made from the *Tosefta Yom Ṭov* ii, 7 (which is in accordance with Rabban Simeon b. Gamaliel) for the anonymous Mishna in *M. Beṣa* ii, 2 (Büchler, p. 84). Even weaker is his proof from *M. Ṭohorot* viii, 2 — (If 'the *'Am ha-'Areṣ*) knew him to be one that ate of heave-offering, they [i.e. the vessels] do not become unclean with corpse-uncleanness, but they are unclean with *midras* uncleanness' — for all the other Halakhot in chs. vii and viii *ibid.*, which treat of vessels and foodstuffs that are deposited with an *'Am ha-'Areṣ*, are concerned with priests and their heave-offering (p. 49). For the meaning of this Midrash, according to its plain sense, may be the equivalent of stating: 'If the depositor was a priest and the depository knew him as such' etc., that is to say that the Halakhot speak of an Israelite (Büchler was forced by his interpretation, referred to above, to explain the expression 'one that ate of heave-offering' in this Mishna as implying that there are priests who do not eat heave-offering. But 'one that ate of heave-offering' is only a general epithet for a priest, when levitically clean foodstuffs are dealt with, as is shown by its parallelism to 'members of the congregation' in *M. Zavim, loc. cit.*).

Similarly, no inference is to be drawn from *M. Ṭohorot* vii, 5, which R. Mani in *T.P.* (*Ḥagiga* ii, 78c) explains as referring to heave-offering (Büchler, p. 48), for R. Judah b. Pazzi disagrees with him and interprets the Mishna as relating to secular foodstuff, and his view appears to be supported by the statement in the *Tosefta* (*Ḥagiga* iii, 21): 'If any doubt existed as to whether an object was in the domain of an *'Am ha-'Areṣ*, any form of uncleanness that, in the case of one suffering from flux, would have defiled it — such as *midras* [leaning or sitting on it], *ḥaṣiṣ* [shaking it indirectly, when there is a partition between the person and the object], and *hesseṭ* [shaking it indirectly], does not render it unclean in respect of foodstuffs, but does so for heave-offering', for the Mishna cited here likewise declares his doubtful

times the priests also observed levitical purity with respect to their unconsecrated food 'to preserve uniformity with heave-offering'.[64] Hence, except for a few Halakhot ordained by the Sages of Usha,[65]

hesseṭ clean. With regard to Büchler's statement that the RaSh (on this Mishna) also explains *M. Ṭohorot* viii, 6 and vii, 1 as referring to heave-offering, the latter only writes: 'And *perhaps*, just as the Palestinian Talmud relates the Mishna here to heave-offering, the same applies to all the subsequent Mishnayot' etc., for it can be argued that we are concerned, even in respect of ordinary food, lest his wife, during her period, indirectly shook it (*hesseṭ*), and therefore the vessels that are tightly closed are nevertheless unclean (viii, 1), if the owner dwells in the same courtyard as an *'Am ha-'Areṣ*. But with regard to the interpretation of these Mishnayot in relationship to other Mishnayot that appear to contradict them (see RaSh *ad loc.* and on *M. Demai* ii, 3; Tosafot, *T.B. Giṭṭin* 61b; Ramban on *T.B. Giṭṭin ibid.* and on *T.B. Nidda* 33b), we must conclude that there were *divergent views* among the Tannaim in respect of the principle of the uncleanness of those who suffer from flux applied to an *'Am ha-'Areṣ*, just as we find similar differences of opinion among the early Tannaim concerning the uncleanness of Cutheans [= Samaritans], for some regarded them as unclean from flux *per se*, while others declared them unclean because they had sexual relations with menstruants (a subject that I intend to clarify elsewhere).

64 P. 86, *et al.* Büchler (p. 161) carefully analyses the expression ושיהא אוכל חוליו בטהרה ['and that he will eat *his* secular food in purity'] and endeavours to deduce from it that this Halakha referred at the outset to priests, for it implies that he has other food apart from secular foodstuff, namely heave-offering. He finds support in the *Tosefta Ḥagiga* iii, 2, which states: 'Rabban Gamaliel used to eat secular food (חולין) in purity'. This teaches us that wherever חולין occurs, without further qualification, the reference is to an Israelite (and we have to understand 'חולין של כהנים' 'secular food of priests' i.e. in accordance with the rules of levitical purity), whereas whenever חוליו [his secular food] is used, priests are spoken of. But in the first instance it should be noted that the Baraita in *Tosefta Demai, loc. cit.*, has vv. ll., and that the Vienna MS. and printed edition read חולין. This is also the reading in *'Avot de-R. Nathan*. Elsewhere, too, we find such textual changes; for example, *Tosefta Sukka* ii, 3, where the printed edition and the Erfurt MS. read חולין, whereas the Vienna MS. has חוליו. Secondly, no inferences can be drawn from the expression referred to, for it simply means אוכליו של חולין 'his secular food', i.e. that he will undertake to eat all his food in levitical purity.

65 On p. 124, note 1, Büchler concedes that the Baraitot in *Tosefta Makhshirin* iii, 7, 9, 10, 5, 6, and Tosefta *'Avoda Zara* iv, 11, speak of an Israelite's ordinary food and not specifically of that of priests, only in his opinion these were not taught before the time of the Sages of Usha. He supports his contention by adducing evidence from *M. Makhshirin* vi, 2, which proves that 'the fathers of these Halakhot were R. Me'ir and R. Judah'. But not only does this Mishna not affirm his view, but actually shows that these Halakhot predate the period of these Tannaim. For this Mishna states: 'All the bundles

wherever the Halakha speaks of levitical cleanness with regard to secular foodstuff the reference is to priests. However, even Prof. Büchler admits that we also find levitical purity observed for ordinary food before the Bar Kokhba war and even in Temple times, but he holds that only a few individuals acted thus, and even they did not prescribe the practice as a Halakha, but represented it as an act of religious piety.

Now this view is intrinsically difficult. For one cannot explain what impelled the Sages to adopt a stringent attitude and to introduce new prohibitions in respect of levitical cleanness long after the Destruction, when these regulations were no longer related to the Temple and the sacred offerings. It is also far-fetched to suggest that the Sages of Usha promulgated many essential new Halakhot, that affected every Israelite and were a severe burden upon those who wished to observe them, without relying on earlier tradition. Should one argue, as does Büchler, that this was done because the people of Galilee were estranged from Torah-learning and were contemptuous of the precepts and were the very *'Amme ha-'Areṣ* referred to in Rabbinic teaching (in relation to the observance of the details of commandments), it is most difficult to comprehend how all at once the Rabbis imposed stringent enactments on a community that could not keep them.[66]

of vegetables in the market places are unclean. R. Judah declares them clean if they are fresh. R. Me'ir said: *Then why have they been declared unclean*? Only because of liquid from the mouth.' It is thus seen that they differ concerning the condition prescribed by earlier Sages with regard to the first Halakha. See on this subject below, in the text.

66 See pp. 65, 212. Büchler holds that the *'Am ha-'Areṣ* with respect to the observance of the precepts was to be found only in Galilee and after the destruction of Bethar, for in Judah only the *'Am ha-'Areṣ* in regard to Torah-knowledge was known. But Büchler himself already realized (p. 26) the difficulty encountered by his theory in Josephus' testimony that the Galileans gave tithe according to law (Life §12). The same is to be inferred with regard to matters of purity from Josephus' account in *Antiquities* (see below) about the Galileans who refused to settle in Tiberias on account of levitical uncleanness. Thus Büchler was forced into suggesting (p. 32) that perhaps the cause (of the neglect of tithing) was the Destruction. But if so, why the difference between Galilee and Judah? The abolition of the Temple service should have affected the Judeans no less than the Galileans. Furthermore, that the Galileans scrupulously observed the laws of levitical cleanness *after the destruction of the Temple and before the Bar Kokhba War*. For it is stated in the *Tosefta* (*Makhshirin* iii, 5): 'R. Jose said: *At first* the bundles of cucumbers and gourds in Sepphoris were declared unclean because they were wiped with a sponge when plucked from the ground. (Subsequently) the

Thus we cannot but conclude that all these Halakhot did not primarily originate in the academy of the Sages of Usha and were not intended, in the first instance, specifically for the Galileans, but they incorporate some of the teachings of earlier Sages, who also kept aloof from the *ʿAm ha-ʾAreṣ* inasmuch as he was not scrupulous in eschewing uncleanness in respect of secular food nor even in regard to holy things.[67] This assumption is not to be rejected on the ground that we find many of the regulations relating to these matters formulated by Sages of the first generation after the fall of Bethar, because this applies also to other Halakhot. The reason for this phenomenon is that the disciples of R. Akiba continued to inculcate the teaching of their master and of other scholars, and the Halakhot of the Sages throughout the generations became absorbed in their own learning and in the interpretations they gave to the instruction of their predecessors. But in regard to the subject under discussion here — the eating of ordinary food in levitical purity — we can learn from the following sources that even in earlier generations many practised it and taught it as Halakha.

people of Sepphoris undertook not to do so.' And we have already noted two men from Galilee (one of whom was an ass-driver) were prepared to risk their lives for the observance of purity.

67 Büchler adopted very forced explanations in order to remove the obstacles to his theory, which confines the Associates and *ʿAmme ha-ʾAreṣ* with respect to tithes and levitically clean foodstuff to Galilee and the generation after Bethar (see *op. cit.*, p. 18, n. 1, and p. 22). This view is particularly unacceptable in the light of the tradition concerning the enactment made in the days of Joḥanan the High Priest [John Hyrcanus] in regard to *Demai* [produce about which there is doubt as to whether the tithes have been duly removed from it] (Büchler went to great lengths to nullify this proof by invalidating the tradition). Now if we find that the Sages of Usha praised those who gave tithes and rebuked those who did not, this undoubtedly indicates that not all were scrupulous in observing the precept of their own accord. But it stands to reason that a difficult commandment like that of separating the priestly gifts required urging in all generations. Thus, for example, we find considerable propaganda in Philo (*De Specialibus Legibus*, i, 153–154), particularly in relation to the priestly dues, and without doubt this was prompted by the fact that the people neglected to bring the gifts on account of the financial loss involved. The same applies to levitically clean foodstuff, which it is most difficult to guard adequately against defilement. Regarding the 'Associations' of the Sages and other people established for the observance of the precepts mentioned above, it appears that the fact that tradition only reports Halakhot and not actual *happenings* suffices to attest that in their fundamental form they are earlier at least than the generation of R. Akiba's disciples, for otherwise substantial information would have

It is stated in a Baraita:[68] 'How long is the period of probation (for an Associate)? The School of Shammai say: With regard to liquids, thirty days, and with respect to clothing, twelve months. But the School of Hillel hold that it is thirty days in either case.' The Halakha refers to eating common food in purity and to all Israelite Associates. Thus this religious observance was firmly practised before the time of these disputants, since they differ with respect to only one condition relating to it.

Although Prof. Büchler suggests that this tradition was not originally taught in its present form and that it contains the 'interpretation' of the Sages of Usha, yet there is no reason to doubt the validity of the tradition or to reject it for logical reasons.[69]

Similarly it is taught in the *Tosefta*:[70] 'The Shammaites say that a Pharisee who suffers from flux may not eat with an *ʿAm ha-'Areṣ* who has the same malady; but the Hillelites permit it.' It follows that both schools agree that a Pharisee who is levitically clean may not eat with one suffering from gonorrhea, on account of food defilement, and that they differ only with regard to one who has flux and is consequently unclean *per se*, as R. Simeon b. Eleazar stated *ibid.*: 'Come and see how far the observance of levitical purity has spread in Israel! For the earlier Sages did not ordain that a man who is levitically clean should not eat with a menstruant, for the earlier generations did not eat with menstruous women, but they said that a man with flux may not eat with a woman who suffers from flux, so that it should not provide an occasion for transgression.'

reached us about the acceptance of Associates and the precepts that they undertook to keep, matters on which the contemporary Sages differ.

68 *Tosefta Demai* ii, 11; *T.B. Bekhorot* 30b.

69 Page 170, n. 2. Büchler deduces from the expression 'How long is the period of probation?' etc. that 'it is entirely unrelated' to the other Halakhot of that chapter, and from the fact that the other Halakhot emanate from the Sages of Usha that we have here a tradition which was formulated by scholars of that generation. But this is no proof, for not infrequently we find Halakhot in Tannaitic teaching that are connected with others that have not come down to us, but nevertheless their authenticity is not in question. Furthermore, in this section, too, it is possible to see that the preceding Halakha (10) is of ancient origin. That apart, R. Meir, R. Judah, R. Simeon, Rabban Simeon b. Gamaliel, and R. Joshua b. Qorḥa speak in this chapter only of *details* about which they disagree, and it is by no means impossible that their disputes stem from different ways of interpreting the tradition of the earlier scholars.

70 *Tosefta Shabbat* i, 15; *T.P. ibid.* i, 3c.

Now in this case, too, Prof. Büchler sought to explain[71] that the first Baraita, the dispute between the School of Shammai and the School of Hillel, contains an explicatory addition by R. Simeon b. Eleazar and that originally the tradition was worded thus: 'A man who suffers a flux may not eat with a woman that suffers a flux.' R. Simeon b. Eleazar, however, proceeded to augment it and to formulate it on the basis of the later Halakha adopted by him and his school.

But this conjecture, too, is not grounded in the Baraita itself, nor is it supported by any other evidence. Hence we have no right to deprive the Baraita of its trustworthiness without due cause.

The antiquity of the Halakha is also proved by the following Baraita:[72] 'At first all vessels that had been used by women who died during menstruation were subjected to ritual ablution; subsequently this was done in all cases out of respect for the women. To begin with (all vessels) used by those who died while suffering from flux were immersed ritually, and the living who had flux were put to shame; (later) it was instituted that this procedure should apply to all out of deference to the living suffering from flux.'

There is no need to state that the tradition refers to any Israelite and not to priests only, and it is also reasonable to suppose that 'At first' means before the generation of R. Akiba's disciples.[73]

The same inference is to be drawn from another Baraita:[74] 'At first (the Sages) said B.D.D.[75] — that (Israelites) may not harvest grapes together with a Gentile (and bring them) into the winepress, because it is forbidden to cause defilement to secular foodstuff in Eretz-Israel; but subsequently they ruled ... but they may harvest them together with a Gentile (and bring them) into the winepress, because it is permitted to cause defilement to secular foodstuff in Eretz-Israel.' In this case, too, it seems that 'At first' (when the Sages forbade defilement to be caused to the ordinary foodstuff of

71 P. 167. He is led to reject the tradition by his view that 'the *'Amme ha-'Areṣ* and Associates' did not exist till the time of R. Akiba's disciples. But I could not understand his deduction from the wording of the Baraita in *T.B.* and *T.P.*

72 *Tosefta Nidda* ix, 16; *T.B. Mo'ed Qaṭan* 27b.

73 The Halakha appears to be old, because we find no mention of this custom in the tradition of the later Sages. Furthermore, in the next Halakha (*Tosefta, loc. cit.*, 17), which belongs to the same group as that cited above, the expression 'At first' precedes the words 'Rabban Gamaliel introduced'.

74 *T.B. 'Avoda Zara* 55b–56a; *Tosefta ibid.* vii (viii), 1; *T.P. ibid.*, iv, 44b.

75 B.D.D. = בד״ד is a mnemonic of the three Halakhot of the Baraita.

a Gentile, although it is not subject to sacred gifts) signifies before the time of the Sages of Usha.[76]

Similarly it appears possible to prove the antiquity of the Halakha from *M. Demai* (vi, 6): 'The School of Shammai say that a man may only sell his olives to an Associate. The School of Hillel say that he may also sell them to one who only gives tithes.' For although it is possible to explain the reason of the tradition to be the avoidance of the defilement of the heave-offering and tithes contained in the olives, nevertheless the Shammaites and Hillelites probably differ only in regard to the levitical purity of unconsecrated food, the view of the former being very stringent and that of the latter lenient.[77]

The early origin of the Halakha is likewise attested by the dispute between the Shammaites and the Hillelites in *M. Berakhot* (viii, 2, 3) which it is most difficult to explain except in accordance with the interpretation of the Tosefta. Hence we have no reason to regard Mark as mistaken and to understand otherwise than at their face value his observations about 'The Pharisees and all the Jews...and

76 This is evidenced by the statement in the *Tosefta, loc. cit.*: 'At first (the Sages) ruled that (Israelites) may not harvest grapes together with a Gentile... However, they may convey new but not old casks with him. This is the view of R. Meir, but the Sages said: Both new and old.' Now it appears that R. Meir and the Sages differ about the meaning of 'casks' in the earlier tradition; thus it follows that this Halakha antedated them (even if we assume that the last part of the Baraita, which is preserved in the Babylonian, was omitted from the Tosefta — see *T.P. loc. cit.* — the Halakha concerning the conveying of the casks is linked to it as in our Mishna). Hence the improbability of the thesis advanced by Büchler (p. 41, note 1), who deduces from the above Tosefta that the *Mishna 'Avoda Zara* iv 9 was formulated in the generation of R. Meir and the Sages, who were 'the fathers of these Halakhic questions', and that in their time they made the Halakha stricter, prohibiting Jews from both trading and harvesting the grapes (together with non-Jews). But, as stated, this Halakha antedates them (and in the Mishna 'casks' are mentioned without further qualifications, their nature still being unexplained).

77 Thus Maimonides explains that the reason of the Shammaite ruling is that it is forbidden to cause unconsecrated food in Eretz-Israel to become defiled. It appears that the dispute between the School of Shammai and the School of Hillel as to whether the buyer must be an Associate, who is trustworthy in matters of levitical purity, or it suffices that he 'gives tithes', is simply based on that between R. Meir and the Sages in *Tosefta 'Avoda Zara,* where R. Meir states: 'Who is an *'Am ha-'Areṣ*? Whoever does not eat his ordinary food in purity', while the Sages declare: 'Whoever does not give tithes'. Büchler, however, who posits that 'the Associate, *'Am ha-'Areṣ*, and one who gives tithes are terms of a later period', rejects the tradition also in this case and regards it as representing the views of later generations, which have been attributed to an earlier period.

when they come from the market place, they do not eat unless they purify themselves; and there are many other traditions which they observe, the washing of cups and pots and vessels of bronze'; Because there is nothing to prevent the assumption that in the days of the writer (and also of Jesus) the Associates and many of the people were accustomed to eating their ordinary food in levitical purity, as he expressly testifies.

The applicability of uncleanness to the eating of secular food in the early days, as a settled Halakha, is best shown by the precept concerning the washing of the hands for unconsecrated meals. Indeed Prof. Büchler[78] treats of this subject at length in order to explain away the contradiction it poses to his theory, which denies the antiquity of this Halakha; only he is compelled to date the origin of the washing of the hands a little earlier. Thus he states that the washing of the hands for unconsecrated food was only initiated in the school of Rabban Gamaliel of Jabneh, *circa* 100 B.C.E., for Hillel and Shammai only ordained levitical purity for the hands in connection with holy things. Although there were individuals even prior to this who practised washing of the hands for secular food, this was not an established Halakha, and even those who were accustomed to observe this were none other than the disciples of the School of Shammai, who were actually the originators of the Halakha that was accepted at Jabneh also by the other Sages. Should it be argued that the Gospel writers refer to this religious practice as a 'tradition of the elders', kept by 'the Pharisees and all Israel', his reply is that the evangelists were merely transferring a usage of their own day to that of their messiah and generalized the ruling given by individual Sages (of the School of Shammai) as a fixed and widely recognized Halakha.

However, this approach is difficult, because the hypothesis makes it very hard to explain the sources. For the Shammaites and Hillelites differ regarding the order of the washing of the hands at mealtimes, and it is obvious that this precept was observed before their time, since they disagree about details. It is difficult to suppose, as Prof. Büchler suggests, that this dispute is not concerned with a Halakhic question but with the dining routine followed by the rich not as a matter of religious requirement but on account of etiquette. For although we find Tannaitic traditions relating to 'dining procedures', without any Halakhic implications, nevertheless it seems that the

78 Pp. 130–138.

sources contain no Rabbinic dispute on a matter that is wholly without relevance to the Halakha.[79]

It is further taught in a Baraita:[80] 'Over wine unmixed with water we say the benediction "Who createst the fruit of the tree" and we may use it for washing the hands. If water has been added to it, we say over it the blessing "Who createst the fruit of the vine" and we may not use it for washing the hands. This is the view of R. Eliezer. But the Sages say: Whether it be unmixed or mixed with water, we say over it the benediction "Who createst the fruit of the vine" and we do not use it for washing the hands.' Now R. Eliezer and the Sages differ as to whether wine unmixed with water is fit for washing the hands or not; it follows that the actual Halakha antedates the time of these Sages.[81]

However, Prof. Büchler seeks to find support for his thesis that the Halakha originated in the generation of Rabban Gamaliel of Jabneh, and that in those days it was not yet accepted by all the Sages, in the Baraita of *T.B. Eruvin* (21b). There R. Akiba is reported

79 For even their dispute concerning the washing of the hands after the meal and sweeping the house, which Büchler cited as proof that they differ only with regard to dining customs, is explained in the Tosefta (and so, too, in *T.B.* and *T.P.*) as 'based on the principle of avoiding waste of food', which tradition forbids (cf. 'eatables may not be passed by').

Büchler deduces from the statement in *Tosefta Berakhot* iv, 11 ([*T.B. Yoma* 30a] *T.B. Berakhot* 43a) in respect of meal procedure — 'This is the Halakha relating to meals: If one goes out to pass water, he must wash his one hand' — that just as this washing of one hand is not a religious duty, for 'the washing of one hand is unknown in the washing of the hands for the purpose of levitical purity', so, too, the washing of both hands for meals is not a precept (p. 138). But it stated in the Mishna (*Ḥagiga* iii, 2): 'In the case of heave-offering if one of his hands became defiled, the other remains clean; but with respect to hallowed things, he must immerse them both.' Compare *Tosefta ibid.* iii, 8–10, and also *M. Yadayim* (ii, 1): 'If one poured water over one hand with a single rinsing, his hand is clean.' It follows *a fortiori* that one hand would be clean for unconsecrated foodstuff, too. What should prevent us, then, from regarding this washing of one hand as a precept, for we assume that he used only one hand. Indeed this is how Tosafot, *T.B. Pesaḥim* 115a, s.v. כל, explain the Halakha discussed there, 'When wine is brought to them, each one washes one hand', namely that it takes account of the uncleanness of one hand.

80 *Tosefta Berakhot* iv, 3; *T.B. ibid.* 50b; *T.P. ibid.* vi, 10a.

81 Büchler writes (p. 133): 'Es sind Kollegen des R. Akiba, die hier den Beschluss des Lehrhauses in Jamnia über das Händewaschen bereits voraussetzen könnten.' But R. Eliezer and the Sages were not 'colleagues of R. Akiba', and if they base their views on an earlier Halakha, it follows that his Halakha originated before the time of Rabban Gamaliel of Jabneh.

as saying to his disciple R. Joshua ha-Garsi ['dealer' or grits-dealer', or an inhabitant of Geres], who brought him water to drink, but it did not suffice for washing the hands as well as drinking, and consequently R. Akiba refrained from drinking: 'But what can I do, since one is deserving of death for disobeying the ruling of the Sages? It is better that I myself die rather than that I should transgress against the view of my colleagues.' From this Prof. Büchler infers: (a) that the Halakha was new at the time and was enacted by R. Akiba's colleagues; (b) that R. Akiba himself did not agree with it.

But it would seem that this Baraita provides no evidence for our subject, for the language is stereotyped and the expression 'rather than that I should transgress against the view of my colleagues' need not be understood here precisely according to its plain meaning. It merely states that R. Akiba preferred to die rather than transgress any Rabbinic regulation. 'Colleagues' simply means Sages who teach this Halakha in any case, and were not necessarily contemporaries of his. We find this expression elsewhere, where, too, it is to be understood in this way, namely the Baraita that narrates that R. Judah b. Bava took a goat 'and tied it to the legs of his bed and used to suck hot milk from it whenever he suffered an attack of angina... and when he was dying he said: I am guilty of only this sin, that I transgressed against the words of my colleagues.'[82] Now the prohibition concerning the breeding of small cattle was not enacted by the colleagues of R. Judah b. Bava, for Rabban Gamaliel and R. Eliezer were already questioned about this Halakha.[83] Thus we must conclude that 'words of colleagues' simply means Rabbinic regulations and that R. Judah b. Bava, like R. Akiba in the story in *Tractate 'Eruvin*, comes to teach us that whoever transgresses against the words of the Sages is deserving of death, and hence a man must give his life for them.

However, it is reasonable to suppose that till the time of the Destruction of the Temple, and possibly even later, washing of the hands for ordinary food was not accepted by *all the Sages*, nor practised by *all Israel*. This is evidenced by the doubt expressed by Eleazar b. Enoch. Hence the statements in the Gospels to the effect that 'all Israel' observed this practice in the days of Jesus[84] are to be regarded as an exaggerated generalization. Nevertheless it is not

82 *Tosefta Bava Qamma* viii, 13; *T.B. Bava Qamma* 80a; *T.B. Temura* 15b; *T.P. Soṭa* ix, 24a.

83 See Büchler's own statements, p. 193.

84 Matthew xv 1; Mark xvii 1–5; Luke xi 18.

possible to reject the premise that essentially this precept was in force already prior to the Destruction, even though it was uncertain and subject to dispute.[85]

Now it is certain that it cannot be inferred from the washing of the hands that all other laws of levitical purity pertaining to unconsecrated foodstuff were firmly established and kept in practice. For the purification of the hands is easy, whereas the observance of other acts of purification is difficult. Hence it may not be deduced from this usage that the other laws of purity relating to ordinary food, too, were as settled and commonly practised as this precept. But as regards the *basis of the Halakha*, it may be argued syllogistically that since the Sages paid attention to the washing of the hands, which serves only to purify from the doubt of a light degree of uncleanness, they were even more concerned with the need to avoid definite uncleanness of a severe form.[86]

85 If we date the regulation to wash the hands for ordinary foodstuff as late as the post-Destruction period, the tradition relating to the enactment of Hillel and Shammai concerning the purification must refer to holy things. Büchler thinks so, too, but in Judith xi 13 it is stated: 'The heave-offerings (or, first fruits) of the corn, and the tithes of the wine and oil, which they had sanctified, and reserved for the priests that stand before the face of our God in Jerusalem; the which things it is not fitting for any of the people so much as *to touch with their hands.*' Thus in the case of heave-offerings and tithes the hands defile even by touching (which is contrary to the solution offered by both Talmuds to the contradiction between *M. Bikkurim* 1, 5 and *M. Ḥagiga* ii, 5, on the question whether tithe requires washing of the hands for touching; see *T.B. ibid.* 18b and *T.P. Bikkurim* ii, 64d. More probable, therefore, is the first answer given by *T.P.* and *T.B. ibid.*, that the matter is the subject of a Tannaitic dispute). It follows that the washing of the hands for holy things was practised before the time of Hillel and Shammai. Only Büchler (p. 68, note 1) casts doubt on this tradition, because it is not clear to him what is meant by 'the first fruits of corn and tithes of wine' etc., which ostensibly — so he declares — refer to *holy things*. The basis of his doubt lies in the fact that according to the Halakha the heave-offerings and tithes were given to the priest anywhere; but I have already endeavoured to show (above, pp. 83 ff.) that it was customary, in the days of the Second Temple, to bring heave-offerings and the tithes to Jerusalem. The verse is therefore to be construed at its face value and is not to be rejected.

86 Ostensibly the observance of levitical purity in respect of common foodstuff in the earliest period of Israel's history may be deduced from the Bible, i Samuel xx 26 (possibly this verse was the basis of the Haggadah that states that Saul used to eat unconsecrated food in purity. For the verse, i Samuel ix 24, from which the author of *Midrash Shoḥer Ṭov* vii derives this tradition does not prove it). And Josephus (*Antiquities* vi, 11, 9) writes: „ἁγνεύσας ὡς ἔθος εἶχεν ὁ βασιλεὺς ἧκεν ἐπὶ τὸ δεῖπνον" ('The king, after purifying himself as

But the Halakha as such, which calls for levitical purity when eating unconsecrated food, was left undecided from the outset, for others ruled that uncleanness applies only to the Sanctuary and to holy things (it is possible that this fact caused the purification of the hands to be questioned).[87] Hence the Halakha could not be firmly established and applied to all things, but remained for many 'a precept of piety [literally, 'abstinence']' and succeeded in being firmly applied in given cases only.

III. *The Precept of Purity and the Prohibition of Uncleanness*

We have already established from the Talmuds above[88] that there were Sages who ruled that immersion was obligatory for one who suffered a pollution, even if he had not the intention to study Torah or eat a meal; in other words that a man must purify himself from this uncleanness on account of the religious duty of purification *per se*.

This teaching may also be derived from *Tanna de-be Eliyyahu* (xv, ed. Ish Shalom, xvi, p. 78): 'If a man suffered a pollution he must perform immersion by Torah law.' The unqualified character of the statement appears to imply that it speaks of immersion as a regular duty unrelated to Torah-study or eating.[89]

the custom was, came to the feast'). But no proof may be adduced from this tradition, for 'sacrifices' in those days were regarded as holy things. Furthermore, the verse speaks of the New Moon, which was considered in those days as a festival in all respects, and it may well be that purity was required on account of the sanctity of the festival.

87 Cf. *M. Ṭohorot* iv, 11.

88 Pp. 191 ff.

89 I should like to observe that these Halakhot in *Tanna de-be Eliyyahu* would appear to indicate that the work was composed in Eretz-Israel, because in Babylonia the attitude to immersion after an emission of semen and to menstrual uncleanness was lenient. For we learn from *T.B. Berakhot* 22a — from the statement of Rav Naḥman bar Isaac — and so, too, from the testimony of *T.P. ibid.*, iii, 6c, that in Babylonia they were accustomed to be lenient in the matter. For the Geonic period we have the evidence of חילופי מנהגים בין בני ארץ־ישראל ובני בבל [Differences of Custom between the Palestinian and the Babylonian Jews] (579, השחר ז), where it is stated: 'The Jews of the East do not bathe (ritually) either after an accidental seminal emission or after intercourse, but in Eretz-Israel they immerse themselves as usual even on the Day of Atonement' etc.

But undoubtedly even in Babylon not all followed the same practice or held the same opinions. For the contemporaries of Rav Naḥman bar Isaac (R. Papa, R. Huna the son of R. Joshua and R. Ḥama) ruled in favour of immersion (*T.B. Berakhot* 22b). In the Geonic period we find that they were

This is also shown by an earlier passage *ibid.* (p. 40): 'Why did the plague of blood [come upon them]? Because when they saw that the Israelites performed immersion after congress and that the Israelite women immersed themselves after menstruation and congress, they denied them access to water so that they might not immerse themselves, have intercourse and multiply. The defilement of the emission of semen is thus put in the same category as that of menstruation, indicating that just as immersion in the latter case was obligatory, so was it also in the former.[90] However, this applies not only to this form of uncleanness, but all other kinds of defilement necessitated immersion as an established religious precept, an observance referred to by the Talmud as 'immersion at the right time is a religious duty', and as we learn from a Baraita 'A man or woman that suffer a flux, a male or female leper, and one who has intercourse with a menstruant, and one defiled by a corpse may immerse themselves in the usual way on the Day of Atonement.'[91]

accustomed to follow the strict view and there were some Geonim who ruled that immersion was obligatory for prayer.

This is also true of the menstruant, for although in *Differences of Custom*, etc. we read (*ibid.* p. 580) that in Eretz-Israel the Sages adopted a strict rule forbidding her to touch any vessel and in Babylon they permitted in all respects, yet we learn from Geonic responsa even in this regard that some authorities in Babylon followed the stricter view. Thus there was no difference between Babylon and Eretz-Israel, except that the majority in the latter adopted the stringent practice, while in the former the lenient view predominated. Hence this difference provides no proof that the book was composed in Eretz-Israel.

90 From *T.P. Nidda* ii, 50a, we learn that the purification of a menstruant is a permanent duty as a precept on its own account. For it is stated thus: 'R. Ḥanina said: This implies that it is forbidden for a woman to abide in her uncleanness'. In *'Avot de-R. Nathan* (Version I, ii, Schechter v, 1; the printed editions do not contain the statement concerning one who suffers a pollution; possibly the omission was due to homoeoteleuton): 'Another explanation is: "Thy belly is like a heap of wheat" — this refers to the Congregation of Israel...How is this to be understood? If his wife during her menstruation period is with him in the house, he can, if he so wishes, have intercourse with her...thus he is afraid only of Him who enjoined him not to have relations with a menstruant. If he suffered a seminal emission, he can, if he so wishes, take a ritual bath or not. Thus he is afraid only of Him who enjoined him to perform immersion'.

91 *Tosefta Yom ha-Kippurim* v (iv), 5; *T.B. Yoma* 88a. Because the Halakha appeared difficult to the Early Authorities, therefore they wished to emend the text. Me'iri writes: 'Consequently our leading ancient authorities are surprised that the others who are obliged to undergo immersion may perform their ablutions on the Day of Atonement, for they are able to recite their

In another Baraita[92] it is taught: 'Then there was another story concerning a certain maiden who was taken captive and two pious men went after her to redeem her...In the morning he said to them: Immerse me...He asked them: With regard to the immersion of this maiden, of what did you suspect her? They replied: Throughout the period that she stayed among Gentiles she ate their food and drank their drink, now you told me to immerse her in order that she should be purified. He rejoined: By the Temple Service! it was even so' etc. Now this uncleanness is that (arising from the eating) of *nĕvēlôt* [beasts not slaughtered according to ritual law], and although the maiden was not going to study Torah, she was nevertheless obliged to purify herself. Similarly we learn in a comparable Baraita:[93] 'Once R. Joshua...and when he returned he went down to take a ritual bath...They replied: We thought that when you were among the unclean Gentiles, you were like one who eats swine's flesh, and so when you returned to Jewish people you decided: I shall go down and immerse myself and become clean like them. He rejoined: It was exactly so; you did not err in the slightest.' Tradition did not specify whether this purification was for the purpose of Torah-study (or for a meal), in order to teach that a man must be clean in any case.

The duty of levitical purity as a permanent precept is also taught by Philo. Thus he states: 'So careful was the lawgiver to guard against anyone helping to bring about the death of another that he considers that even those who have touched the corpse of one who has met a natural death must remain unclean until they have been purified by aspersions and ablutions. Indeed he did not permit even the fully

prayers, only those who have suffered a pollution being forbidden to do so', etc. But there is no need to emend the Baraita, because, as we have already seen (above, p. 200), *fundamentally* the Halakha forbids even the others who have to immerse themselves to say their prayers, if a remedy is available to them on the same day. Only the simple meaning of the Baraita is that in the view of the Sages the duty of purification is a permanent precept, while R. Jose differs and holds that it is to be observed on account of prayer (or that the latter precept itself does not override the prohibition of washing on the Day of Atonement).

92 *'Avot de-R. Nathan*, Version I, viii (Schechter, p. 19a).

93 *Ibid.*, Version II, xix, p. 21a. Now R. Joshua did not contaminate himself by eating forbidden foods; only he ineluctably ate Gentile bread (compare the expression used by R. Eliezer, his colleague, in *M. Shevi'it* viii, 10: 'He that eats the bread of the Samaritans is like one who eats swine's flesh'). We thus learn that the eating of Gentile foods defile like *nĕvēlā* (cf. above, p. 181).

cleansed to enter the Temple within seven days and ordered them to purge themselves on the third and seventh.[94]

Now the last Halakha is to be explained by the fact that they were obliged to purify themselves on account of the doubt of possible corpse-defilement. At all events we expressly learn that one who has been defiled by a corpse is bound by law to purify himself, even if he does not intend to visit the Temple.

Josephus writes in similar vein concerning defilement by the dead, which he explains, like Philo, as designed to serve as a fence against the shedding of blood (*Against Apion* ii, 26): 'After the funeral, the house and its inmates must be purified [in order that anyone guilty of murder may be very far from thinking himself pure].'[95] He further declares (*ibid.* 23): 'Apart from the Sacrifices, the Law has prescribed purifications for various occasions: after a funeral, after child-birth, after conjugal union, and many others which it would be tedious to mention.'[96]

This fundamental conception, which regards the precept of purity as a duty *per se*, without any connection with the Temple or holy things, also finds expression in the Halakha that forbids the defilement of common food, as the Talmud states in a number of places, explaining thereby Tannaitic teachings, and as we learn in *Tosefta Makhshirin*, cited above. For even if the object of the Halakha was

94 DSL., III, 205: Τοσαύτην δὲ πρόνοιαν ἐποιήσατο τοῦ μηδένα παραίτιόν τινι γενέσθαι θανάτου, ὡς καὶ τοὺς προσαψαμένους νεκροῦ σώματος, ὅ τελευτὴν ἐνδέδεκται τὴν κατὰ φύσιν, οἴεται δεῖν μὴ εὐθὺς εἶναι καθαρούς, μέχρις ἂν περιρρανάμενοι καὶ ἀπολουσάμενοι καθαρῶσιν. εἰς μέντοι τὸ ἱερὸν οὐδὲ τοῖς σφόδρα καθαροῖς ἐφῆκεν εἰσιέναι ἐντὸς ἡμερῶν ἑπτά, τρίτῃ καὶ ἑβδόμῃ κελεύσας ἀφαγνίζεσθαι.

95 καθαίρειν δὲ καὶ τὸν οἶκον καὶ τοὺς ἐνοικοῦντας ἀπὸ κήδους, ἵνα πλεῖστον ἀπέχῃ τοῦ δοκεῖν, καθαρὸς εἶναί τις φόνον ἐργασάμενος.

96 ἁγνείας ἐπὶ ταῖς θυσίαις διείρηκεν ὁ νόμος ἀπὸ κήδους, ἀπὸ λέχους, ἀπὸ κοινωνίας τῆς πρὸς γυναίκα, καὶ πολλῶν ἄλλων, ἃ μακρὸν ἄν ἔιη νῦν γράφειν. Cf. also *ibid.* II, 24. This refutes R. Joshua b. Levi's statement (*T.P. Berakhot* iii, 6c) 'קרי [seminal emission] results only from conjugal union'. It is far-fetched to interpret the sentence in the sense of 'purifications for the sake of the sacrifices', for apart from the fact that the language can bear such an interpretation only with difficulty (and this applies also to the order of the statements in the section), we have seen that Josephus arranges the precept of the sacrifices and that of levitical purification separately and in complete parallelism, placing between them the section of forbidden foods; see *Ant.* iii, 9, 1 to iii, 12, 1. It should be noted that in *Ant. ibid.* (and following) the order of the sections is identical with that in *Against Apion*, namely *sacrifices*, purifications, and *forbidden relations*. I am grateful to Dr. Schwabe who corroborated my explanation of the passage.

to prevent the eating of unconsecrated food that is unclean, nevertheless its formulation shows that it is a prohibition on its own, namely not to cause needless defilement of foodstuff.

This Halakha, too, which, according to the Amoraic tradition, is the subject of Tannaitic dispute, forms part of Philo's teaching, for he states in the aforementioned section (*loc. cit.* 206): 'Further too, those who enter a house in which anyone has died are ordered not to touch anything until they have bathed themselves and also washed the clothes which they were wearing.'[97]

Similarly he declares (*ibid.*, III, 63): 'So careful is the law to provide against the introduction of violent changes in the institution of marriage that a husband and wife, who have intercourse in accordance with the legitimate usages of married life, are not allowed, when they leave their bed, to touch anything until they have made their ablutions and purged themselves with water. This ordinance extends by implication to a prohibition [literally 'forbidding from afar'] of adultery, or anything which entails an accusation of adultery.'[98]

We likewise read in Josephus (*Ant.*, iii, 11, 3): 'He banished from the city alike those whose bodies were afflicted with leprosy and those with contagious disease [gonorrhea]. Women, too, when beset by their natural secretions, he secluded until the seventh day, after which they were permitted, as now pure, to return to society. A like rule applies to those who have paid the last rites to the dead: after the same number of days they may rejoin their families.'[99]

The removal of the menstruant from pure things and her separation from the public on account of uncleanness, to which Josephus testifies, is also taught by tradition. For we read in *Tanna de-be Eliyyahu* (Ish Shalom, xvi, 75–76): 'Thus whoever says to his wife and to his household: Touch the vessels and do whatever you please, since the

97 ἔτι μέντοι καὶ τοῖς εἰσιοῦσιν εἰς οἰκίαν, ἐν ᾗ τετελεύτηκέ τις, προστάττει μεδενὸς ἅπτεσθαι, μέχρις ἂν ἀπολούσωνται καὶ τὰς ἐσθῆτας αἷς ἀμπίσχοντο προσαποπλύσαντες.

98 τοσαύτην δ' ἔχει πρόνοιαν ὁ νόμος τοῦ μηδὲν ἐπὶ γάμοις νεωτερίζεσθαι, ὥστε καὶ τοὺς συνιόντας εἰς ὁμιλίαν ἄνδρας καὶ γυναῖκας κατὰ τοὺς ἐπὶ γάμοις θεσμούς, ὅταν εὐνῆς ἀπαλλάττωνται, οὐ πρότερον ἐᾷ τινος ψαύειν ἢ λουτροῖς καὶ περιρραντηρίοις χρῆσθαι. πόρρωθεν μοιχείας ἀνείργων καὶ τῶν ἐπὶ μοιχείαις ἐγκλημάτων.

99 ἀπήλασε δὲ τῆς πόλεως καὶ τοὺς λέπρᾳ τὰ σώματα κακωθέντας καὶ τοὺς περὶ τὴν γονὴν ῥεομένους. καὶ τὰς γυναῖκας δὲ αἷς ἡ τῶν κατὰ φύσιν ἔκκρισις ἐπίοι, μετέστησε πρὸς ἡμέραν ἑβδόμην, μεθ' ἣν ὡς ἤδη καθαραῖς ἐνδημεῖν ἐφίησιν, ὁμοίως δὲ καὶ τοῖς κηδεύσασι νεκρὸν μετὰ τοσαύτας ἡμέρας νόμιμον τὸ ἐνδημεῖν.

Torah does not enjoin immersion for a menstruant, never knows peace of mind.' From *Mishna Nidda* (vii, 4), which refers incidentally to menstruants' 'chambers of uncleanness', it is evident that it was the practice in the days of the Tannaim to place women during the period of their menstruation in special chambers,[100] so that they should not defile people, vessels, or foodstuff as is the custom of the Samaritans and the Falashas.[101]

Now these Halakhot, which obligate the unclean to avoid contact with levitically clean people and food, so as not to defile them,[102] teach by syllogistic reasoning that the clean are forbidden, from the outset, to have aught to do with uncleanness, as far as possible. We thus reach the limits to which the laws of purity extend, the prohibition of defilement resting on all Israel, just as the priests were subject thereto by Biblical law (in respect of corpse-defilement).

However, the priests' injunction not to defile themselves can be observed completely and permanently, but this is not the case with other Jews, who must perforce attend to the dead. Nor is it possible to avoid having dealings with the unclean except partially, depending on circumstances.

We also learn from R. Judah's teaching (*M. Demai* ii, 3) that one who accepts the duties of an Associate must undertake 'not to contract corpse-defilement'.[103] Josephus, too, supports the view of

100 Cf. *Tarbiz*, vi, p. 124, the note of my teacher, Prof. Epstein. See also Ramban on Genesis xxxi 35.

101 A. Epstein, *Eldad ha-Dani*, p. 177; Eshkoli, *Tarbiz*, *loc. cit.*, pp. 123–124.

102 Rav Hai Gaon also enjoins that one who suffers from flux should be separated from the general public so as not to defile them, and he ordains that he should occupy a special place in the Synagogue. See *Geonica* II, p. 38; cf. Maimonides' commentary to *M. Zavim* iii, 2.

103 Büchler (pp. 204–207) was compelled to interpret R. Judah's ruling as referring to a priest. But he himself realized the great difficulty involved in this assumption, for in that case why should the Sages disagree with him? Moreover, all the other restrictions enumerated do not necessarily concern priests. But R. Judah's view that it is forbidden to contract corpse-uncleanness (when it is not incumbent as a religious duty; this solves Büchler's difficulty in understanding why R. Judah teaches that Torah-study is to be interrupted in order to attend a funeral) also underlies his ruling that even an Israelite is prohibited from going outside Eretz-Israel without approval, for it is thus taught in the Tosefta (*Mo'ed Qaṭan* ii (i) 2): 'R. Judah further said: Those who come from the coast and from abroad are forbidden to cut their hair and to wash their clothes; but the Sages permit this. Rabbi said: R. Judah's view seems apposite where the person had set out without approval, while the Sages' opinion appears apposite where he had set out with approval.' Cf. *T.B. ibid.* 14a, *T.P. ibid.* iii, 81c, and *T.P. Pesaḥim* iv, 30d, whence it

R. Judah (which is disputed by the Sages). This is evident from his account of the building of Tiberias by Herod Antipas, which cost him much trouble. He was compelled to bring inhabitants from all kinds of distant places, including the lowest strata of the people — even slaves — to whom he allocated lands and houses, so long as they agreed to dwell in the new city: 'For he knew that this settlement was contrary to the law and tradition of the Jews because Tiberias was built on the site of tombs that had been obliterated, of which there were many there. And our law declares that such settlers are unclean for seven days.'[104]

This passage teaches us two things: one refers to the Halakha — that corpse-defilement must be avoided, and the other relates to the current practice — that Jews (except for the riff-raff types and slaves) in the generation before the Destruction were accustomed to eschew this type of uncleanness as sinful.[105]

seems that R. Judah's reason is that Gentile territory is unclean, the defilement being halakhically based on the suspicion that it has contracted corpse-uncleanness. Hence the Palestinian Talmud (*Mo'ed Qaṭan, loc. cit.*), immediately after citing R. Judah's view raises the point: 'In that case a priest (who, the Sages admit, is forbidden to go abroad, on account of defilement) who went abroad, seeing that he did so without the approval of the Sages, should not be allowed to shave.'

104 *Antiquities* xviii, 2, 3: εἰδὼς παράνομον τὸν οἰκισμὸν ὄντα καὶ ἀπὸ τοῦ Ἰουδαίοις πατρίου διὰ τὸ ἐπὶ μνήμασιν, ἃ πολλὰ τῇδε ἦν, ἀνῃρημένοις τὴν ἵδρυσιν Τιβεριάδι γενέσθαι, μιαροὺς δὲ ἐπὶ ἑπτὰ ἡμέρας εἶναι τοὺς οἰκήτορας, ὡς ἀγορεύει ἡμῖν τὸ νόμιμον.

105 Büchler (96), who criticizes Schürer for taking Josephus' statement literally, asks how it is possible to infer from this passage that an observant Jew was forbidden to live in Tiberias, when Rabban Joḥanan b. Zakkai and others dwelt there before R. Simeon had purified it. Hence he explains, with Graetz, that Josephus did not mean that it was actually prohibited to dwell in the city, but that he was referring to the sprinkling with the waters of purification that the inhabitants would be obliged to undergo when they went on pilgrimage to the Temple, or — the view accepted by Büchler finally — that Josephus, in conformity with the tradition of the Sages, was alluding to the priests.

However, the first explanation is improbable, for it was surely of no consequence that the inhabitants would have to cleanse themselves, since ever so many Jews (if not all of them, on account of doubt) sanctified themselves in Jerusalem before the festivals; such an obligation could not possibly deter them from taking advantage of the numerous benefits that Herod offered them. As for the interpretation preferred by Büchler, it is obvious that he distorts the plain sense of the words. For even if there was a large number of priests in Galilee at that time, it must certainly be presumed that, if Herod was compelled to liberate slaves in order to populate the city and to transport

Thus the Halakha and custom removed the application of the laws of purity from the narrow sphere to which the established Halakha had confined them — Temple, consecrated objects, and priests — and expanded it in many ways and aspects.[106]

Now we must consider the fundamental nature of these Halakhot from the viewpoint of their relationship to the general, fixed Halakha. In other words, we must examine the basic aim underlying all these laws — whether it is in any way antagonistic to this Halakha, or whether it originally emanates from a peculiar, primary conception of the Pentateuchal regulations pertaining to levitical uncleanness.

First, however, we must distinguish between the Halakhot that enlarge the operative area of the laws of purity with respect to holy things and the others. For the former do not differ, in their basic conception, from the levitical laws of the fixed Halakha, which

'worthless and reckless fellows' there, the Israelites, too, had eschewed settling there. But actually, upon closer scrutiny, Büchler's primary question falls away, since we learn from the Talmud (*T.B. Shabbat* 34a) that Ben ʿAzzai (this, it appears, is the correct reading instead of Ben Zakkai of the printed editions; in accordance with the recension of the *ʿArukh* and the Munich MS. For we find Ben ʿAzzai permanently settled in Tiberias, as is attested by the oft-repeated dictum of Abbaye and Rava in the Babylonian Talmud 'I am like Ben ʿAzzai in the market-places of Tiberias' [*T.B. Eruvin* 29a and parallels] and Rav's pronouncement in *T.P. Pe'a* vi, 19d and *T.P. Soṭa* ix, 23c — 'I am the Ben ʿAzzai of this place [Tiberias]') regarded Tiberias as levitically clean. In *Genesis Rabba* (lxxix, 6) R. Simeon exclaims: 'I swear that I know as many Halakhot as the hairs of my head to prove that Tiberias is clean!'. This shows that R. Simeon did not purify the city by his acts, but relied on the ruling of earlier authorities. On the other hand, we learn from the Talmudic and Midrashic tradition that even after this pronouncement that the city was clean, there were Sages who disagreed with R. Simeon and declared it unclean. Consequently the fact that Sages dwelt therein constitutes no difficulty, for the majority considered it clean from the beginning. Possibly the difference of opinion about the cleanness of Tiberias goes back to the Tannaitic dispute as to whether Gentile graves defile or not. It may well be that the tombs on which Tiberias was built belonged to the 'Canaanites', the ancient inhabitants of the land, and that R. Simeon, in declaring them clean, follows his principle that Gentile graves do not defile.

106 I should like to draw attention to the tradition that prescribes the observance of purity by all Israel as obligatory even in the Amoraic period. In *T.P. Berakhot* vi, 10a, it is stated: 'R. Ḥaggai and R. Jeremiah went up for waters of purification (according to the correct reading of the Rome MS and that of Sirillo). R. Ḥaggai made haste to pronounce the benediction over them. Thereupon R. Jeremiah said to him: You acted well, for all religious observances require a blessing.' This shows that purification by sprinkling was considered a religious duty, in the full sense of the term, even for Israelites.

teaches that uncleanness relates only to sacred objects. Although these new laws contributed considerably to the observance of levitical purity among the Israelites, nevertheless there are no grounds for ascribing to them the motivation of endowing the Israelites with priestly sanctity. They may rather be regarded only as evincing a tendency to enlarge the sphere of 'holiness', just as we find in the case of other Halakhot of the Second Temple period, which aim at assigning to the Synagogue some of the religious practices that were originally limited to the Temple.

However, the Halakhot that prescribe laws of purity for unconsecrated food and those that make levitical cleanness obligatory and prohibit uncleanness are all directed towards one objective, which is in fact twofold: the extension of the priestly sanctity to all Israel and of the purity of holy things to common foodstuffs.

This underlying motive of the Halakhot under discussion is well expressed by the author of *Tanna de-be Eliyyahu* (Ish Shalom, xvi, p. 72), who makes the following statement concerning the washing of the hands for ordinary food: 'Now we learn that the obligation to wash the hands is Pentateuchal... But what does Scripture say with regard to the Israelites? "Sanctify yourselves therefore, and be ye holy." On the basis of this verse Rabban Gamaliel used to eat common food under conditions of levitical purity. The Sages declared: Holiness was not bestowed upon the priests only, but to the priests, the Levites, and to the Israelites. Hence the Rabbis said: If one treats the washing of the hands lightly, it is a bad augury for him.'

We still have to consider whether these Halakhot and practices did not begin merely as an *extension of purity*; that at the outset they were observed only by the pious and scrupulous, but in the course of time they grew into a general observance and established Halakhot. In other words, it could be presumed that these Halakhot gradually crystallized at a later period on the basis of the general Halakha by a process of expansion and the augmentation of precepts, but that originally the laws of purity applied — both in theory and in practice — only to priests and to the Temple and holy objects.

This conjecture is ostensibly attractive for two reasons. First, because traditionally these Halakhot are regarded as Rabbinic regulations, that is to say, as later enactments that were promulgated on the basis of the definite Halakha, which was of Pentateuchal origin. Secondly, because the fixed Halakha is not explicitly disputed in the teaching of the Sages of the Oral Law.

But, in the first place, it should be noted that the fact that tradition considers a certain Halakha as a Rabbinic law does not necessarily imply that it originated in later generations. For we possess many ancient Halakhot that are as old as the Torah, and some that are even older.[107] Nor does the absence, according to tradition, of any difference of opinion concerning a given Halakha indicate that it was never challenged, because many early laws were completely forgotten and replaced by the later Halakha. It may be postulated, *a fortiori*, that an earlier conflicting Halakha existed, when tradition contains a number of Halakhic and practical pointers in that direction.

However, in our case it appears that we must rely largely on the definitive and express statements of Philo and Josephus, which not only show that in their days the popular usage and official ruling were not in accord with the established Halakha, but that they (and the schools that received their teaching) interpreted the Torah in this way.

It would therefore seem that we must posit that in the period of the Second Temple two conflicting trends established themselves: one insisted on restriction, and limited the laws of purity to the sphere of the Temple and priests, while the other aimed at enlargement and taught that laws of uncleanness applied to all Israel.

These two traditions are to be regarded, in the first place, as two contrary methods of exegesis, that differ on the interpretation of Scriptures. But, in truth, this dispute has its origin in a certain duality that is already found in the Torah itself, and is only a sequel to the variant approaches that find expression in conflicting verses. For there are Biblical passages that speak of uncleanness only in connection with priests, the Temple, and holy things,[108] whereas others are unqualified and are addressed to all Israel and to the prohibition of uncleanness in all circumstances, and not necessarily to sacred objects.[109] This duality is also found in respect to other Halakhot, which in one place are prescribed for priests and in other passages for all Israelites.[110] As is well known, this is the case with regard

107 Compare *Dorot ha-Rishonim*, Pt. I, xxx–xxxv.

108 Leviticus vii 19–21; xii 4; xxi 4; xxii 4–8; Numbers xix 20.

109 Leviticus xi speaks entirely of the defilement of Israelites, declaring (v. 8) 'and their carcasses ye shall not touch', and ordains the breaking of unclean vessels (v. 33) and the washing of garments, but does not mention the Temple or hallowed things. It concludes with 'Sanctify yourselves therefore, and be ye holy' as an injunction to Israelites to eschew uncleanness from the outset. Similarly the verses concerned with the person suffering with gonorrhea (xv) speak of the precept of purity *per se*.

110 With respect to making tonsures, cuttings of the flesh, and shaving the edges

to *nĕvēlā* ['that which dies of itself'] and *ṭĕrēfā* ['that which is torn of beasts'] in Ezekiel, when combined with the teaching of the Torah itself.[111]

Now these two antithetic traditions prevailed — quite independently and without ulterior motive — among the various sects. The expansionist tendency entrenched itself among the Essenes, whereas the inclination towards restriction was most powerful among the Sadducees.[112] But in the Pharisaic teaching neither was able to oust the other entirely, although the tendency towards limitation was the stronger.[113]

When we seek the reason for this Halakhic struggle among the Pharisees, we must regard it as the result of the clash between two general fundaments on which Rabbinic doctrine rested: one was the adaptation of the Halakha to the needs of life; the other was the extension of sanctity to all Jews (even those who were not priests) and to all places (apart from the Temple) and at all times.

This second principle compelled the Sages to instruct all Israel in levitical purity and to enjoin complete abstention (from uncleanness).

of the beard, compare Leviticus xxi 5 with xix 27, and with Deuteronomy xiv 1.

111 The Karaites are divided on the subject: some have ruled that the laws of uncleanness are absolute prohibitions, which apply equally to Israelites and to priests, while others agree with the established Halakha, see Ginzberg, *Ginze Schechter*, Pt. II, pp. 192–193.

112 That the Sadducees should have limited the laws of uncleanness to the priests and the Temple is self-understood, for they were essentially the priesthood. But the point is also evidenced by the dispute recorded in the Gospels between Jesus and the Pharisees with regard to the observance of levitical purity with respect to unconsecrated food (requiring washing of the hands and the immersion of vessels). Jesus rejected the purity regulations on the ground that they were merely a 'received tradition' and a 'tradition of the elders', which are not written in the Torah. On Jesus' adoption of the Sadducean viewpoint, see Leszynsky, *Die Sadduzäer*, pp. 280 ff.

113 On the basic idea see Geiger, *Urschrift*, 223, and *Zeitschrift*, II, 31–33. But he (and after him, Leszynsky, *op. cit.*) adduces proof for this concept from *II Maccabees* (whose author was a Pharisee) ii 17: ὁ δὲ θεὸς ὁ σώσας τὸν πάντα λαὸν αὐτοῦ, καὶ ἀποδοὺς τὴν κληρονομίαν αὐτοῦ πᾶσιν καὶ τὸ βασίλειν καὶ τὸ ἱεράτευμα καὶ τὸν ἁγιασμόν, κτλ. ('Now God, who saved all his people, and restored to all the heritage, and the kingdom, and the priesthood, and the hallowing', etc.). From this passage Geiger infers that the author wishes to stress that the priesthood and the hallowing do not appertain to the priests only, but are the heritage of the whole people, contrary to the teaching of the Sadducees. But the verse has no bearing on our subject, for it does not speak of the relationship between 'the people'

But life demands the limitation of levitical purity, since it is not always possible to comply with it, and where it is feasible, it involves much effort. Consequently (and for the reason that for Israelites the Halakha could certainly not apply *in all circumstances*) the Halakha that exempts Israelites from the rules of uncleanness, where the Temple was not concerned, prevailed and became norm. The second tradition, on the other hand, found expression in a number of particular regulations, which were not difficult to observe[114] or appertained to special cases,[115] and in practices of abstention from uncleanness.

and the priests, but comes to tell the Jews of Egypt, to whom the letter is addressed with the object of persuading them to accept and observe the festival of *Hanukkah* [Dedication], that the national possessions, in their entirety, belong to the whole Jewish people, and do not appertain to the Jews of Eretz-Israel alone, that the kingship (the dominion to which the Hasmoneans attained) and the priesthood and the Temple (which had been desecrated by the Greeks and Hellenists) and the land belong to the entire nation. Hence the Egyptian Jews, too, were involved in that miracle and have a duty to observe the precept of the festival. Thus the writer proceeds to add in the next verse that 'In God have we hope, that he will speedily have mercy upon us, and gather us together from under the (wide) heaven', implying that they are also destined to be settled in Eretz-Israel, and that consequently there is no difference between them and the Jews in the homeland in respect of the observance of the festival.

114 E.g. washing the hands for a meal.

115 Like the menstruant and the person suffering from gonorrhea, and even Gentile uncleanness.

BY THE (EXPRESSED) NAME

In the order of the High Priest's confessions in the Temple on the Day of Atonement there is a difference, according to the Mishna version of the Mishnayot, in the recitations of the (Expressed) Name [i.e. the Tetragrammaton] between the first two confessions and the last. In the confession pronounced over his own bullock and that of the priests, the High Priest used to say, both in the confession proper and at the end in the supplication for atonement: אנא השם *'Annā' ha-Shēm* ['Pray Thee, O Lord', literally 'O Name'] (*M. Yoma* iii, 8; iv, 2: 'I pray Thee, O Lord, I have sinned... O Lord, atone, pray...'), whereas in the confession for all Israel, uttered in connection with the scapegoat (*ibid.* vi, 2), he used to say: אנא בשם *'Annā' ba-Shēm* ['I pray Thee, by the Name...'].

Needless to say the Mishna recension cited above is not authoritative, for what significance is there in the textual divergence between the last confession and the first two? Undoubtedly our version preserves a reminiscence of two variant traditions of the Mishna, one of which read, in the entreaty for forgiveness *in all three confessions* *'Annā' ha-Shēm*, and the other, *'Annā' ba-Shēm*.

In truth the manuscripts of the Mishna display this difference. The Parma MS, the Kaufmann MS, and the Munich MS read throughout: *'Annā' ha-Shēm.*[1] On the other hand, in Lowe's edition (*Matnitā' di-Bênê Ma'ărāvā*) the reading in all three petitions for atonement is *'Annā' ba-Shēm*, in conformity with the testimony of R. Ḥaggai in *T.P. Yoma* iii, 40d: 'In the first part (of the confession) he said *'Annā' ha-Shēm* and in the second *'Annā' ba-Shēm.*' The same varia-

1 The Naples and Pesaro editions read: *ha-Shem*. *Kesef Mishne* (D.S. to *T.B. Yoma* 66a) and R. Ḥananel (*T.B. Yoma* 36b) state: 'Our Mishna in both parts (of the confession) has *'Anna' ha-Shem*... and we disregard the version of R. Ḥaggai' etc. See *'Ahăvat Ṣiyyôn wi-Yĕrushālāyim* to *Tractate Yoma*, 43–44.

tion is also found among the Tosefta MSS. (*ibid.* ii, 1)[2] and the recensions quoted by the Rishonim from the *Sifra* ('Aḥărê Mŏt, Sec. ii, chs. 1 and 2; Sec. iv, ch. 4; ed. Weiss, 80d, 81a, and 82a).[3] The same applies to the variant versions in the Order of the (Temple) Service on the Day of Atonement described in the *piyyuṭim*.[4]

It is reasonable to suppose that the reading in the Mishna *ba-Shem* (thrice) is original. It was subsequently ousted from many works because the Divine Name is not commonly mentioned in our sources in this form, and because the meaning of the word is not quite clear.

It is imperative now to deal with the signification of the expression and the reason for its use.

Derenbourg[5] and Baneth (in his Mishna commentary) regard *ba-Shem* as a form of oath in the sense 'I adjure Thee by Thy Name to atone' etc. (or 'I entreat Thee by Thy Name to atone'),[6] an interpretation that is extremely difficult to accord with the prayer of the High Priest.[7]

Lieberman explains the sense to be: 'Atone, I pray Thee, with Thy great Name', the phrasing being styled in the manner of Psalms liv 3 ('O God, save me by Thy name') *et al.*

2 The Erfurt MS. and the London MS. have *ba-Shem* in the second part. The Vienna MS. (printed) reads: *ha-Shem.* On the vv. ll. in the quotations of the Rishonim from the Tosefta see Lieberman, *Tosefet ha-Ri'shonim*, Pt. I, p. 188.

See *Tosefet ha-Ri'shonim, ibid.*, cf. *Leqaḥ Ṭov*, ed. Buber, pp. 93–94 (Wa-Yiqra') and *Midrash ha-Gadol* (Wa-yiqra', Rabinowitz), pp. 410, 411, 427, who invariably read *ha-Shem.*

4 Compare J. Derenbourg, *Essai de restitution de l'ancienne rédaction de Masséchet Kippourim*, p. 35 (on the MSS. of the Order of the Temple Service). In *Siddur Rav Saadia Gaon* in the *'Avoda* of Jose b. Jose (272, 273, 274) we find *ha-Shem* three times in the last part. Further on (*'Attā Kônantā*, 277, 278, 279): *ha-Shem.* In the Appendices *ibid.*, 412: *ha-Shem.* So, too, in Elbogen, *Studien zur Geschichte des jüdischen Gottesdienstes*, p. 166: "*Anna ha-Shem*, atone, pray'; but on p. 167: "*Anna ha-Shem*', etc. (This variant reading also occurs in other passages of the Genizah fragments *ibid.*).

5 *Loc. cit.*, p. 36 ('une adjuration addressé au Dieu').

6 'Bei deinem heiligen Namen beschwöre ich dich, flehe dich an'.

7 Such expressions were to be expected in the prayers of the mystics and in adjurations. Goldzieher in his study 'Zauberelemente im islamischen Gebet' (*Orientalische Studien, Th. Nöldeke gewidmet*, I, p. 303–329) informs us that worshippers (pietists and holy men) in the ancient Islamic age were accustomed to adjure the diety and thus compel it to do their will. Only he finds this practice also among Israelites in the prayer of Ḥoni ha-Me'aggel, who drew a circle and stood therein etc., saying 'Nun beschwöre ich dich bei

This suggestion, too, appears improbable, for if the High Priest had prayed thus, he would not have said just *ba-Shem* ['by the Name'], but more explicitly *bĕ-Shimĕkhā* ['by Thy Name']. Another point is that this explanation is feasible only if we assume that the Mishna cites the word *ba-Shem* as it was actually pronounced by the High Priest, whereas according to the Tannaitic tradition the six Names under discussion (*ha-Shem, ba-Shem*) were included in 'the ten times that the High Priest mentioned the Expressed Name on the Day of Atonement'. This necessarily implies that the Mishna uses a surrogate designation, whereas the High Priest himself used to utter: *ba-YHWH* (the Tetragrammaton).[8]

We shall, however, revert to this subject later and deal with it specifically.

To me it seems that *ba-Shem* is simply a secondary form of *ha-Shem*, which was crystallized during the Second Temple period and remained popular with many generations after the Destruction; it was used in precisely the same sense as the prevailing designation *ha-Shem*.

This fact emerges, to my mind, from a number of Greek invocation papyri, which, although non-Jewish in content and form, contain inherent Israelite elements, including the word under consideration.

In the great papyrus published by Preisendanz, *Papyri Graecae Magicae*, Pt. II, pp. 87–138, 'which was originally derived from the liturgical work ('Book of Creation') of a Gnostic community and was not initially written for magical purposes',[9] we read in Version I (pp. 93–94) and similarly in Version II (p. 109) Ἐπικαλοῦμαί σε τὸν πάντα περιέχοντα, πασῇ φωνῇ καὶ διαλέκτῳ, ὡς πρ«ῶ»τος ὕμνεσέ σε

deinem Grossen Namen usw.' But all the formulas in the Mishna and the parallel Baraitot in *Tractate Ta'anit* read 'I swear by the Great Name' etc.

8 There is also another fact that militates against this suggestion. The expression 'by the Name' or 'by Thy Name' (or 'Name') never occurs in the Bible in the sense of by the 'means' or 'aid' of the Lord's actions on behalf of people, but has the connotation 'by might and by salvation' (see Psalms xliv 6: 'Through Thy name do we tread them under that rise up against us'; *ibid.* cxxiv 8: 'Our help is in the name of the Lord, who made heaven and earth'; *ibid.* xx 2: 'The name of the God of Jacob set thee on high'; Proverbs xviii 10: 'The name of the Lord is a strong tower'). The reason is quite clear: the word *ha-Shem* expresses the quintessence of Divine power (hence the use of *ha-Shem* in the Haggada and in magic formulas). But we do not find that it is employed in other acts, such as the atonement of iniquities ('By Thy Name atone, we pray Thee').

9 See the introduction *ibid.* to Papyrus XIII, pp. 86–87.

ὁ ἀπὸ σοῦ ταχθεὶς καὶ πάντα πιστευθεὶς τὰ αὐθεντικὰ Ἥλιος... οὗ ἡ δόξα... ὅτι διά σε ἐνεδοξάσθη «ἀέρας», εἶθ' ὡσαύτως ἀγλαομορουφμένους τοὺς ἀστέρας ἱστὰς καὶ τῷ φωτὶ ἐνθέῳ κτίζων τὸν κόσμον... ἐν ῷ διέστησας τὰ πάντα Σαβαωθ 'Αρβαθιάω Ζαγουρῆ. οὗτοί εἰσιν οἱ πρῶτοι φανέντες ἄγγελοι 'Αρᾶθ, 'Αδωναῖε, Βασημμ, 'Ιάω ('I invoke thee, thou who dost encompass all, with every voice and every tongue, as he that was appointed by thee for every dominion and authority first praised thee, Helios. . . whose praise. . . for he was by thee as one who established the atmospheres and the shining stars, and created the world with the divine light, whereby thou didst distinguish everything. These are the angels who appear: Arath, Adonai, Ba-Shem, Ja [יהו]').

In my opinion the word *Ba-Shem* is not to be linked to Iao as a *nomen regens* to a *nomen rectum*.[10] *Ba-Shem*, it seems, stands here by itself as one of the angels who were first created, for there is no adjuration or supplication here, only a presentation of 'the work of creation'.

Needless to say these angels (with the exception of Arath) are of Israelite origin: and Gnostic doctrine actually states: the God of Israel is one of the two divine powers. Only our author himself attests, so to speak, his nexus with the Jewish tradition, for in his introductory remarks, second version, he states (p. 105): Βίβλος ἱερὰ ἐπικαλουμένη Μονὰς ἢ 'Ογδοὴ Μουσέως... περὶ τοῦ ὀνόματος τοῦ ἁγίου. The 'Eighth Book of Moses[11] on the Holy Name' alludes to the use of a Jewish magical source. Similarly in the continuation of the papyrus (pp. 98–99) he states: Πλήρης ἡ τελετὴς τῆς Μονάδος προσεφωνήθή σοι, τέκνον. ὑποτάξω δέ σοι, τέκνον, καὶ τὰς χρείας τῆς ἱερᾶς βίβλου, ἅς πάντες οἱ σοφισταὶ ἐτέλησαν ἀπὸ ταύτης τῆς ἱεράς καὶ μακάριδος βίβλου, ὡς ἐξεώρκισᾶ σε, τέκνον, ἐν τῷ ἱερῷ τῷ ἐν 'Ιεροσολύμῳ· κτλ. ('As I have adjured thee, my son, by the Temple at Jerusalem').

The oath 'by the Temple of Jerusalem' likewise testifies to a connection with Jewish tradition.[12]

10 Preisendanz translates thus: 'Adonai im Namen Jahwe'.

11 In Papyrus XIII, p. 88, 'Moses' Key (κλῆΐς)' is cited; in Papyrus vii, Pt. II, p. 28, we find 'The Diadem of Moses' — ἐκ τοῦ διαδήματος Μοῦσέως, which is an ancient source of Moses' 'Crown of Glory' (both are, undoubtedly, magical works); similarly, mention is made (Papyrus vii, 28, II) of Moses' βίβλος' Αρχαγγελική.

12 On 'the Jewish Hebrew-Aramaean basis' of the magical papyri see Th. Hopfner, *Archiv Orientalni*, III, 2, pp. 336 ff. Note especially Papyrus XXII

Similarly we read in 'version II' of this papyrus: Ἐπικαλοῦμαί σε, κύριε, ὡς οἱ ὑπό σου φανέντες θεοί, ἵνα δύναμιν ἔχωσιν, Αχεβυκμω οὗ ἡ δόξᾰ... Σαβαωθ, Ἀρβαθιάω, Ζαγουρῆ, ὁ θεὸς Ἀραθ, Ἀδωναί, Βασυμμ, Ἰάω ('I invoke thee, O Lord... *Adonai, Ba-Shem, Iao*').

The word βασυμμ may simply be another form of *Ba-Shem*, but, conceivably, it represents בשום *be-Shûm*, which would be quite appropriate.

So far *ba-Shem* has occurred immediately preceding Iao, and the expression could still, with some difficulty, be equated with the formula בשם ה׳, *be-Shem Y* ['in the name of the Lord'], which was taken over from a Jewish source (magically or even liturgical),[13] without the non-Jews (when uttering their prayers and magical formulas) realizing its meaning.

But in the following papyrus the word occurs detached from Iao. Thus we read in the adjuration *ibid.*, Pt. I, pp. 184–186, which is replete with many Jewish elements (headed: 'Inscription of Iao' [יהו]):[14] Σὲ καλῶ τὸν ἀκέφαλον τὸν κτίσαντα γῆν καὶ οὐρανὸν... οὐ εἶ Ὀσορροννώφρις σὺ εἶ Ἰαβας, σὺ εἶ Ἰαπως, σὺ διέκρινα τὸ δίκαιον καὶ τὸ ἄδικον. Ἐγώ εἰμι Μωσῆς ὁ προφήτης σοῦ, ᾧ παρἒδοκας τὰ μυστήρια σοῦ τὰ συντελοῦμενα Ἰστραηλ, οὐ ἔδειξας ὑγρὸν καὶ ξηρὸν καὶ πάσαν τροφὴν, ἐπακούσόν με, ἐλὼ εἰμὶ ἄγγελος τοῦ Φαπρω Ὀσοροννόφρις τοῦτο ἐστιν σοῦ τὸ ὄνομα τὸ ἀληθινὸν τὸ παραδιδόμενον τοῖς προφήταις Ἰστραηλ, εἰσακούσόν με καὶ ἀποστρέψο[ν] τὸ δαιμόνιον τοῦτο,... ἀπόλλαξον τὸν δεῖνα Αωθ, Ἀβαωθ βασυμ, Ἰσακ, Σαβαωθ, Ἰάω κτλ ('I invoke thee, O Headless One,[15] who hast created earth and heaven. Thou art Osoronnophris (good Osiris), thou art Iabas... thou hast distinguished righteousness from unrighteousness. I am Moses, thy prophet, to whom thou didst deliver thy mysteries, which are completed [or celebrated?] by Israel. Thou hast made known the wet and the dry and all manner of food. Hear me, who am the messenger of Phapro Osoronnophris — the true name, which was transmitted to the prophets of Israel; hear me and

(Pt. I, pp. 149 ff.), which is an adjuration that was originally an actual prayer (it even bears the name 'Prayer of Jacob', προσευχὴ Ἰακῶβ) and is essentially a Jewish formulation. So, too, Papyrus VI (the Parisian), 170, I, which is full of distinctly Jewish phrases.

13 See Reitzenstein, *Poimandres*, pp. 184–189 (Jewish theology and magic exerted a joint influence, for they are interrelated).

14 Cf. Hopfner, *loc. cit.*, p. 332.

15 The 'headless' god is identical here with *Y.* (Tetragrammaton); Hopfner, *ibid.*, pp. 342–343.

banish this demon. . . deliver N----O, Aoth, Abaoth, *Be-Shum*, Isaac, Sabaoth, Iao' etc.).

Clearly *Be-Shem* stands by itself and has a specific identity.[16]

The same occurs in Pt. II, p. 110 (Papyrus XIII): Βεσεν, Βουρειθεν, Βεριο. It appears that here the epithet *Besen* = *Be-Shem* with the usual transformation of *Mêm* at the end of a word to *Nûn*.[17] Thus in this instance, too, the term *Be-Shem* stands by itself in the sense of god (or supreme power).

We likewise read *ibid.*, Pt. I, p. 126 in the adjuration (love charm) called 'the sword of Dardanos' (ξίφος Δαρδάνου) — and similarly further on, p. 128 — [Κρύφιε καὶ πρεσβύτατε], αχαπα 'Αδωναιε, Βασμα, Χαρακω, 'Ιακωβ, 'Ιαω, Χαρουήρ... ('Lord and Elder, [an obscure magical word], Adonai, Basma. . .').

Apparently we have here the word בשמא *bi-Shema'*, the Aramaic form of the Hebrew *be-Shem*, and in this instance, too, it is followed by a non-Jewish magical term, which cannot be related to it.[18]

Thus these papyri, which date from the time of the Tannaim and Amoraim,[19] use *be-Shem* (*be-Shum*; *bi-Shema'*) in the sense of a Divine Name, similar to *ha-Shem*.

Undoubtedly the Jewish sources, to which the Gentile Gnostics and sorcerers were indebted, need not necessarily have employed this usage, for it is not completely ruled out that these sources (if we assume that they were of a magical character, for in prayers and benedictions recited outside the Temple there was no question of pronouncing the Expressed Name, *YHW*) always employed the combination *be-Shem YHW*, but the non-Jews, in the course of time, separated the words and this *be-Shem* became an independent divine power.

Nevertheless, I consider it more probable that the usage in the papyri is to be explained on the assumption that it was also found

16 Isaac is a separate divine name, just as the other Patriarchs represent divine powers in these papyri. I disagree with Preisendanz's translation: 'Im Namen Isak'.

17 See *Mavo' le-Nosaḥ ha-Mishna* by my teacher J. N. Epstein, Pt. II, p. 1232.

18 Contrary to the view of Hopfner, who renders, *op. cit.*, p. 338: 'Adonai im Namen des Charako' (apart from arguments based on the content of the prayer, the words cannot be construed thus, for *bi-Shema'* βασμα should, in that case, have been followed by 'די *di* [of] Charako', but the word *di* is missing from the adjuration.

19 The papyri under discussion belong mostly to the beginning of the fourth century C.E., but some date from the time of Hadrian.

among the Jews, both in prayers (blessings) and in adjurations. This conjecture is supported by the Tannaitic sources that I adduce below. Let us revert to the Mishna in *Yoma*.

Be-Shem in the High Priest's confession, when he supplicates for atonement, simply means the same as *ha-Shem*, which occurs at the beginning of the prayer in the recitation of the sins. This is actually self-evident, for apparently the High Priest is citing the Hallel formula of *'Annā'* *Y*, even when he uses the expression *'Annā' ba-Shem*; consequently the *Bêt* is not to be construed as a preposition. The introduction of the form *be-Shem* in the latter part of the High Priest's confession was prompted, it seems, by the desire to conjoin the two forms of the enunciation of *ha-Shem*, so that each is given its due.

Possibly R. Haggai in the Palestinian Talmud sought to decide, in the same harmonizing and compromising spirit, between conflicting traditions regarding all the six utterances of the Divine Name. For there were some who cited the High Priest as always saying *ha-Shem*, while others invariably preferred the word *ba-Shem*, until R. Haggai came and 'arbitrated' between them, ruling that equal use be made of both forms.

Now we must discuss again a question that we touched upon at the outset: Does the Mishna give the Divine Name exactly as the High Priest pronounced it in his prayer, or is the word a surrogate for the Expressed Name, which he uttered according to its true enunciation?

Ostensibly the High Priest pronounced the Divine Name as it is written, for it is stated in *M. Yoma* vi, 2: 'And when the priests and the people who stood in the Temple Court heard the Expressed Name come forth from the mouth of the High Priest' etc. It is furthermore stated in *T.B. Yoma* 39b, *T.P. ibid.* iii, 40d, and *Tosefta ibid.* ii, 2: 'Ten times did the High Priest pronounce the Name on the Day of Atonement, six times in connection with the bull, and thrice in connection with the he-goat, and once in connection with the lots.'

However, the principal recensions do not read in our Mishna: 'And when the priests and the people', etc.;[20] it seems that this paragraph was added to the Mishna from the Order of the 'Avoda as it is portrayed in the piyyuṭim. Must the Mishna tradition necessarily

20 See *D.S.* to *T.B. Yoma* 66a, and especially J. N. Epstein, *Mavo' le-Nosaḥ ha-Mishna*, Pt. II, pp. 971–972.

accord with that of the Baraita, so that the former, too, is construed as using a surrogate for the Expressed Name, which the High Priest used to pronounce?

Now Geiger[21] already pointed out certain Tannaitic sources which ostensibly indicate that even in the Temple the Expressed Name was not used. For in *Tosefta Soṭa* xiii, 8 (*T.B. Yoma* 39b) it is stated: 'When Simeon the Just died, his brethren refrained from pronouncing the (Expressed) Name in the (priestly) benediction.'[22] A similar tradition is found in *T.P. Yoma* 40d end (*T.B. Qiddushin* 71a; *Sifre Zuṭa*, ed. Horovitz, p. 250): 'At first he [the High Priest] used to pronounce it [the Expressed Name] aloud, but when the number of impious men increased, he began to utter it softly.'[23] R. Ṭarfon said: I was standing among my brother priests in the line and I inclined my ear to the High Priest and I heard him swallow [i.e. muffle] it in the chanting of the priests. At first it [the pronunciation of the Name] was transmitted to every man, but when the impious multiplied it was transmitted only to those who were worthy.'

Undoubtedly we cannot accept Geiger's view that these traditions reflect the early Halakha, whereas the Halakhot that attest the enunciation of the Expressed Name in the Temple are later and represent a reaction against the sect of Minim, which adopted the earlier Halakha and completely forbade the pronouncing of the Name in any place.[24] Essentially the cited traditions clearly bear testimony to the later development.[25] Nor is it difficult to understand the nature of this development: the same pietism that stopped the pronunciation of the Expressed Name in the Prayer [Eighteen Benedictions] in synagogue necessarily influenced, in turn, Temple worship conducted in the presence of a large congregation (such as the Priestly Benediction).

21 *Qevuṣat Ma'amarim*, pp. 98–103; *Urschrift*, etc., pp. 263–5.

22 Another reading is: 'They *ceased* [פסקו instead of נמנעו] to pronounce the Name in the priestly benediction.'

23 The other traditions speak of the priestly benediction in the Temple. But this passage apparently refers to the High Priest on the Day of Atonement.

24 *Urschrift*, *loc. cit.*; *Qevuṣat Ma'amarim*, pp. 123 ff. (these Minim are the Dosithean-Samaritans). See Ginzberg's reply, *op. cit.*, p. 409.

25 'Simeon the Just' mentioned here is undoubtedly the same as the one of whom the Baraita (*Tosefta Soṭa* xiii, 6, and parallels) attests that he 'heard' of the assassination of גסקלגס (Caius Caligula), that is to say, he was one of the High Priests who lived at the end of the Temple period (see Graetz, *Divrê Yĕmê Yisrā'ēl*, II, pp. 16–17, note), since several other traditions (on the 'evil signs' that appeared upon the death of 'Simeon the Just') definitely refer to him (or else the Haggada 'skips' periods in the chronology).

For the barriers that divided the Temple service from 'the service [*'avôdā*]' in the synagogues gradually disappeared in the course of time. It is not surprising, therefore, that a trend developed among the 'pietists' of the priests and the people to 'conceal' or 'swallow' the Expressed Name in the Temple as well.

But is this to be regarded as a settled Halakha that crystallized among the Sages of a given school in complete contrast to the many later Halakhot[26] that prescribe the pronunciation of the Name in the Temple 'as it is written'? It seems that no such inference may be drawn from the sources in our possession; the traditions cited merely attest a trend that was still inchoate and had not yet established a firmly decided Halakha.[27] Thus the Mishnayot in *Yoma* must be interpreted as only employing a substitute for the Expressed Name, which was pronounced by the High Priest in accordance with its spelling; in other words, at the beginning of the confession he said אנא ה׳ *'Anna' YHWH* and at the end אנא בה׳ *'Anna' b-YHWH.*

It seems to me that these two forms of pronunciation of the Divine Name in the Temple are again at issue among the Tannaim in the dispute between R. Judah and the Sages in *M. Sukka* iv, 5: 'Each day they circuited the altar once, saying "Save now, we pray Thee, O Lord [אנא ה׳]..." R. Judah said "*'Anî WHW* [אני והו], save us pray".' For the interpretation of R. Judah's ruling given in the *T.P.* (54c), which reads אני והוא *'Anî wa-Hû* ['I and He'], explaining it in the manner of Haggadic tradition as referring to the Holy One, blessed be He, who also shares Israel's trouble and is, as it were, saved together with them, is only a homiletical exposition.[28] Rightly the Sages already sought to interpret this expression as a given form of the Divine Name, as it was pronounced in the Temple, only their suggested explanations are not satisfactory.[29]

26 *M. Sota* vii, 6; *M. Tamid* vii, 2; Mekhilta, Jethro, *Massekhta de-ba-Ḥodesh*, xi; *Sifre Numbers* §39, Horovitz, p. 43; *Sifre Deuteronomy* §62; *T.B. Sota* 38a; *T.B. Sanhedrin* 101b, *et al.*

27 See Appendix.

28 Although L. Ginzberg wishes to substantiate it (*Qevuṣat Ma'amarim*, p. 395), with the added comment: הוא is one of the Divine Names.

29 L. Blau, *Das altjüdische Zauberwesen*, p. 134, No. 2, regards אני as an abbreviation of אדני, and הוא = YHWH. A similar view is expressed by M. Gaster, *Ḥarba' de-Moshe*, Introduction, p. 12. Geiger, *Qevuṣat Ma'amarim*, p. 101, note, reads the two words as one, אניוהו, because they combined אנא ה׳ (Tetragrammaton) with a view to blurring the Divine Name, for the same reason as they coalesced — and blurred — the word יה with the pre-

Apparently *'Ani WHW* in R. Judah's tradition corresponds to *'Anna' YHWH* of the Sages,[30] that is to say, the two versions are really the same, except for a slight textual variation.

Hence I construe the word **והו** *WHW* in the sense of **ביהו** *b-YHW*, for at first the people pronounced **אנא ביהו** like **אנא בה׳** in the High Priest's prayer on the Day of Atonement. Now the name *YHW* is found, as is well known, not only in Biblical theophoric names, but also in the Elephantine papyri and *Sefer ha-Yeṣira* [Book of Creation], as well as many incantation texts.[31] It is not difficult, therefore, to suppose that the tradition continued in the Temple of pronouncing the Divine Name in this form. And since the *Bêt* in the word **ביהו** was necessarily aspirated on account of the open syllable at the end of the preceding **אנא**, it was changed to *Wāw*, as we often find in the Mishnaic idiom.[32] Likewise the pronunciation of **אני** for **אנא** was induced by the *Ḥireq* in the word *bi-YHW*.

If this conjecture is accepted, it follows that there was a struggle between the two traditions concerning the pronunciation — *YHWH* or *b-YHWH*. This strengthens our assumption that R. Haggai, who testifies that the High Priest said *'Anna' ha-Shem* in the first part of his prayer and *'Anna' ba-Shem* in the second part, is only deciding between conflicting traditions, according to one of which the High Priest always said *ha-Shem*, and according to the other, *ba-Shem*.

The latter pronunciation is apparently to be explained only as the continuation of the similar Biblical usage. Thus **ביה ה׳ צור עולמים**, in Isaiah xxvi 4, simply means **יה וגו׳** ['For the Lord God is an everlasting Rock']. The same applies to Psalms lxviii 5: **ביה שמו** is equivalent to **יה** etc. (so the Septuagint actually renders in both passages). Scholars explained this *Bêt* as *Bêt essentiae*; see H. P. Chajes on Psalms *ad loc.*

The word **בשם** is parallel therefore to **בה׳**, which was pronounced according to its spelling in the Temple and was current, in its proper form, as a Divine epithet — alongside **השם** in certain circles — in

ceding word. See Baneth's commentary to Sukka, and so, too, Bornhaüser, pp. 115–120.

30 This was noted by some of the scholars mentioned.

31 Montgomery, *Aramaic Incantations Texts from Nippur*, p. 150.

32 *Mavo le-Nosaḥ ha-Mishna*, Pt. II, pp. 1225–1226 (in regard to prefixed *Wāw* and *Bêt*).

33 Apparently the Divine Name we have suggested occurs in Invocation No. 7 *apud* Montgomery, *op. cit.*, 146: **בשום גמליאל ... בשום יהו ביהו** (he translates: *Yehu* in *Yahu*, 'a theosophic concept: God in God') and so, too, in Invocation No. 13, *ibid.*, p. 179: **בשום יהוה ביה אלאל רבה**. Thus **ביה** = **יה**,

prayers and in benedictions. This it seems, is how we must interpret the Baraita cited in the Tosefta and the Palestinian Talmud, which scholars have struggled to interpret in various ways.

The Palestinian Talmud states as follows (*Berakhot* viii, 12c; *Sukka* iii, 54a; *Megilla* i, 72a): 'It has been taught (in a Baraita): If a Gentile blessed **השם** we respond "Amen"; (but if he blessed) **בשם**, we do not answer "Amen".'[34] A similar ruling is found in *Tosefta Berakhot* v, 11, according to the correct reading: 'If a Gentile blesses **השם**, we respond "Amen", (but if he blesses) **בשם**, we do not answer "Amen", unless the entire benediction is heard.'

Geiger, Derenbourg, I. Lewy, and L. Ginzberg[35] have advanced interpretations based on recensions (or their own emendations) that are not authoritative, and certainly cannot be accepted. But S. Lieberman,[36] who establishes the correct text of the Yerushalmi passage, has recently proposed an explanation that is intended to make the Tosefta text conform to that of the Baraita, suggesting that the concluding words of the Tosefta — 'unless the entire benediction is heard' — are to be regarded as a scribal duplication in error of the

as above. Likewise the expression (*ibid.*, pp. 150–151) בשמיה יהביה is to be construed, it seems, as יה–ביה, i.e. the combination of these two forms. Similarly the Aramaic inscription published by Gordon, *Archiv Orientalni* V, 2, p. 296, which reads לבריכיהביה apparently contains the twofold Name we have discussed: בריך יה־ביה ['blessed be YH-be-YH']. I also think that בהו (i.e. ביהו = ויהו) is also enshrined in the פרוסאי papyrus (Preisendanz, I, 106) — Ο Κύριος, Βουηλ. Compare לבהו–אל. Possibly it is also implied in the name Βαυβώ = בהו־בו (or בהו–בהו?), Papyrus 13, *ibid.*, 127, II. I am also inclined to regard the expanded name (*ibid.* 121, II) ιαραββαο (ιεου) as representing יה־ריב־בהו.

34 This is the amended text also in *Berakhot*.

35 Geiger, *Qevuṣat Ma'amarim*, p. 104, reads in a note: כותי המברך השם ... כותי המברך בשם ['A Samaritan who blesses the Name. . . a Samaritan who blesses with the Name'] (with reference to the Samaritan practice of pronouncing the Expressed Name). The same text is adopted by Derenberg, *op. cit.*, p. 37: כותי וכו׳. I. Lewy, *Über einige Fragmente aus der Mishna des Abba Saul*, p. 38, reads: גוי המברך את השם... כותי המברך את השם ('Amen' is not said in response, because they were accustomed to use the Expressed Name; this resembles Geiger's conjecture). Ginzberg, *Qevuṣat Ma'amarim*, pp. 395–396, reads: ...גוי המברך בשם עונין אחריו אמן, כותי המברך את השם עונין אחריו בשם אין עונין... and explains: A Gentile may pronounce the Expressed Name, hence 'Amen' may be said in response; but this is not so in the case of a Samaritan, who, like an Israelite, is forbidden to do this, and therefore, when he pronounces a benediction with the Divine Name [בשם] (in accordance with its spelling), the response may not be said.

36 *Tosefet Ri'shonim* to *Berakhot*, p. 25.

Baraita *ibid.* iii, 26 (' "Amen" is said after the benediction of an Israelite but not after that of the Samaritan [literally: 'Cuthean'], unless the entire benediction is heard').[37] He explains as follows: If (the Gentile) blessed the Expressed Name with a surrogate designation, we may answer 'Amen' after him, but if he used the Expressed Name, we may not respond 'Amen'.

We thus have to split the Halakha, so that the last part refers to a normative benediction in which the Expressed Name was uttered instead of the usual substitute ('Adônay), while the first part deals with a benediction pronounced on the Expressed Name, which is quite unlike the benedictory formulas in use. This is a difficult interpretation to accept.

But this apart, this scholar's explanation is obscure, for how are we to understand 'If (the Gentile) blessed the Expressed Name?'

I believe that the Baraita under discussion can be explained, on the basis of the conclusions that we stated at the beginning, as follows: If a Gentile blesses the Name, i.e. if he says in the benediction, in accordance with the formula established by the Sages, 'Blessed art Thou השם' etc., the blessing is valid and we may answer after him 'Amen'. But if he says 'Blessed art Thou בשם' etc.,[38] we may not respond 'Amen', because although בשם is also found in the sense of השם, yet in view of the rarity of the usage and its obscurity in the mouth of a Gentile pronouncing a benediction, we may not answer 'Amen'.

What now is the difference between a Jew pronouncing a benediction and a Gentile doing so? It would appear that the liturgical-magical papyri, from which we have quoted, provide the explanation, for they contain בשם linked and integrated with the names of pagan deities and magical powers in invocations and prayers. Hence we are afraid that the Gentile may be using בשם in the benediction he is uttering, in the syncretistic-polytheistic sense that was current in the non-Jewish world.

However, it is quite clear to me that the version of the Baraita in the Tosefta is fundamental, and the final clause 'unless the entire benediction has been heard' is an essential part of the Halakha (and

37 This is also Ginzberg's view in conformity with his approach.

38 Although 'a benediction in which the Divine Name is not mentioned is not valid', one's obligation is certainly discharged, if a substitute designation (not *'Adônay*) is employed; for even the epithet רחמנא, 'the All-Merciful' suffices (*T.B. Berakhot* 40b). However, השם may also refer to the use of *'Adônay*, in accordance with the usual formula.

not an erroneous duplication). The underlying reason of the Halakha is self-evident — lest there be attached to the word בשם in *the very text of the benediction* any of the pagan-magical names to which the non-Jew is accustomed, and any of the themes that find expression in their prayers and invocations. Hence, if the Israelite heard the entire benediction, uttered according to its proper formulation and devoid of these interpolations, he may respond 'Amen'.

Furthermore, even the Yerushalmi version appears, in its *essential content*, to be the same as that of the Tosefta, and it likewise did not intend to disqualify a Gentile's benediction in which בשם was used, but only if the Israelite had not heard the blessing to the end. For the Baraita in the Talmud is related to the preceding discussion, which speaks of an 'orphaned Amen' in the sense of an 'Amen' that was uttered in connection with a benediction that the responder had not heard properly. Thus we read 'It is taught: We may not say an 'orphaned Amen', nor a 'cut-off Amen'. Ben ʿAzzai said: If one utters an 'orphaned Amen', his children shall be orphans, a 'cut-off Amen', his soul shall be cut-off; a long (Amen), he shall enjoy length of days in wellbeing. What is meant by an 'orphaned Amen'? Rav Huna said: If a man has to say a benediction[39] and he responds without knowing what he is responding to. It has been taught: If a Gentile blessed השם. . . .' It seems obvious, therefore, that the Baraita treats of a kind of 'orphaned Amen'. Now this conforms to the tradition of the Tosefta, which forbids 'Amen' to be said (in the case of a Gentile who blesses בשם) 'unless the entire benediction has been heard.'[40]

The Tannaitic Halakha under discussion, if interpreted as we have suggested, serves to corroborate the fact emerging from the Greek

39 This is the authoritative recension.

40 Undoubtedly the subsequent Talmudic passage, 'R. Tanḥum said: If a Gentile blessed you, answer "Amen"...', has no connection with an 'orphaned Amen', and was introduced incidentally on account of the general theme, which is concerned with a Gentile's blessings.

However, the explanation given in the text is not decisive. For the Yerushalmi passage, 'It has been taught: If a Gentile blessed השם...', may relate to the concluding Halakha of *T.P. Berakhot* viii, 9, ' "Amen" may be said after an Israelite who pronounces a benediction, but not after a Samaritan who pronounces a benediction, unless the entire blessing has been heard'; and in that case the Baraita does not constitute the continuation of the preceding theme, which treats of an 'orphaned Amen'. At any rate the recension of the Baraita in the Palestinian Talmud is not decisive evidence for that of the Tosefta.

papyri (and similar sources), namely that the spiritual, syncretistic world of the pagans was saturated, in the period of the Tannaim, with elements of the Jewish faith and liturgy, not only in the Diaspora but also in Eretz-Israel.

We further learn that, although the Sages, who were aware of the spread of this religious jumble (especially in the mystic circles of the Gnostics and Magi?), considered 'proper benedictions' of 'God-fearing' Gentiles as valid as those of Israelites, they nevertheless reserved their definite approval of these blessings, in view of the diffusion and danger of syncretism, until all doubt as to their form was removed, and ruled that Israelites should abstain from joining non-Jews in responding 'Amen' to any blessing of the Divine Name that was in doubt.

Appendix

It may be desirable to examine the tradition in *M. Berakhot* ix, 5: 'And it was ordained that a man should greet his fellow with the Divine Name' etc. For Geiger deduces from it that the later Halakhists, reacting against the Minim who were meticulous in observing the ancient Halakha, decided to permit the use of the Expressed Name (even in salutations). Now the theory itself we cannot accept, as already stated. But the tradition itself still requires clarification. For recently scholars have sought to interpret also this institution, no less than its companion, the first enactment ('It was ordained that they should say "From everlasting to everlasting" '), as a reaction against the real Minim, namely the Sadducees, like the 'Minim' mentioned earlier in the Mishna (others say: 'against the Christians', thus following the view of Rav Hai Gaon in his commentary to tractate *Berakhot* — J. Mann, *Text and Studies*, I, p. 605). This view was also adopted by Mann (*ibid.*, pp. 580–583), to wit, that the enactment was introduced against the Sadducees' denial of personal providence (for which reason they did not greet individuals with God's name).

However, this hypothesis and the like appear not only to be intrinsically difficult (we have no real basis as yet for differentiating, in the teaching of the Sadducees, between general providence, in which they believed and personal providence, which they denied; nor, as a matter of fact, have we evidence that the Sadducees deliberately refrained from saluting an individual with the Divine Name) but they do not exhaust the sources dealing with the subject. For it is thus stated in the Tosefta (*Berakhot* vii, 23) in parallelism with the

Mishna: 'At first when the Torah was being forgotten in Israel, the elders used to swallow it [אותה] among themselves', etc. We thus learn that the elders (Sages) in former times also used to refrain from uttering the Name in greeting individuals (when the Tosefta adds: 'As Scripture declares "And, behold, Boaz"', etc., it undoubtedly comes to teach, like the Mishna, that biblically it is enjoined, or permitted, to greet one's fellow with the Name, unlike the custom of these elders). It follows that the abstention from using the Name in greetings is not to be attributed to the Sadducees and the like.

As far as the subject itself is concerned, it should be stated that although the Mishna adjoins the second enactment to the first, which is directed against the Minim (the Sadducees), this fact does not compel us to interpret also the second ordinance as directed against Minut (Sadduceeism), although it certainly implies a reaction against a prevailing practice (or ideology) that was considered undesirable (at the time when the regulation was introduced).

Furthermore, we sometimes find 'Minim' who are not guilty of denying the Torah (of the Pharisees), but whose exceptional stringency and meticulousness have assumed the aspect of dogmas among certain definite groups, a phenomenon with which we shall deal below.

It appears to me that the object of the enactment was to demonstrate against the schools of the 'Hasidim' (Pietists) who made it standard practice, on account of the sanctity of the Name, and because of the duty to be in a state of purity when mentioning it (even by its substitute, *'Adonay*), to refrain from 'secularizing' the use of the Name for the purpose of greetings in their contacts with individuals. These circles, it seems, had affinity with the 'morning bathers', who were similarly meticulous in regard to the mention of the Name. Indeed, we find friction and disputes between them and the Pharisees recorded in the Tosefta (*Yadayim* ii, 20, according to the complete reading of the RaSh [Samson b. Abraham of Sens] in his commentary on the Mishna *ibid.* iv, 8): 'The morning bathers say: We cry out against you, O Pharisees, that you utter the Name without first undergoing immersion. The Pharisees answered: We cry out against you, O morning bathers, that you utter the Name out of a body that contains uncleanness.' However, many of the Pharisees themselves also scrupulously follow 'the Hasidic practice' of avoiding the frequent utterance of the Name, their sentiment being with the strict pietists. The Baraita already (*T.B. Rosh ha-Shana* 18b; *Megillat Ta'anit* vii) attests: 'On the third of Tishri the practice of mentioning the Divine Name in bonds was abolished... but when the Hasmoneans prevailed and defeated the enemy, they ordained that the Name of God should (again) be mentioned in bonds, and they wrote as follows: "In the year so-and-so of Joḥanan the High Priest of God Most High". But when the Sages heard of this, they said: Tomorrow this man will pay his debt and the bond will be found lying on the dustheap; consequently they annulled the practice. That day was made a festive day.' However, later Sages wished to combat 'an erroneous usage', that the people should not diminish the use of the Name of God and cause it to be forgotten by removing it from the greetings of friends and acquaintances as they were accustomed to do. Hence they decided to abolish the practice of the Hasidim in their midst and ordained it a religious duty to use the Name in greetings (unquestionably a contributing factor was also the emergence of sectarian dogmatics among the organized circles who made their abstention from mentioning the Name in saluting their fellow-creatures, one of their distinguishing characteristics; there is thus also a polemical reaction here against sectarians).

Therefore the Tosefta seeks to find an excuse by interpreting the custom of the elders, who 'at first' refrained from uttering the Name in greeting individuals, as due to 'the neglect of the Torah' in former generations, which impelled the Sages to adopt a practice 'contrary to Torah teaching'. In the same way it cites below (*loc. cit.*, 24; see also both Talmuds) in the name of Hillel: 'When you see that the Torah is beloved of Israel and all rejoice therein, scatter it abroad. . . but when you see that the Torah is forgotten of Israel and is generally unheeded gather it in (for yourself)'. Even the Mishna, which supports the Halakha under discussion by reference to the verse 'Despise not thy mother when she is old' apparently implies a similar kind of apology for the Halakha, which fell into desuetude in later generations (who prescribed using the Name in greetings, as the Tosefta attests), but which is nevertheless still valid. The same applies to the citation of the verse 'It is time to work for the Lord; they have made void Thy Law'. For at all events according to R. Nathan's tradition ('They have made void the Law — it is time to work for the Lord.' This is a Baraita interpolated into the Mishna; see J. N. Epstein, *Mavo' le-Nosaḥ ha-Mishna*, Pt. II, p. 975; in *Tosefta, loc. cit.*, 24, it is attributed to R. Meir) it purports to explain the enactment concerning the use of the Name in greetings as due to prevailing circumstances ('on account of the insinuations of the Minim'), although it involved 'voiding the Law'.

Now we have only to consider if the Sages ever use *Minut* not in the sense of denial of Pharisaic teaching, but to signify an accretion to it, and as such is exceptional, forming organizationally and ideologically a special entity *vis-à-vis* the Pharisees.

Apparently this is to be found in *M. Yadayim* iv, 8: 'A Galilean Min said: I cry out against you, O Pharisees, that you write the name of the (Roman) governor together with Moses in a bill of divorce. The Pharisees answered: We cry out against you, O Galilean Min, that you write the name of the governor together with the Divine Name on the (same) page', etc.

This Galilean Min was, it seems, one of the Galilean Zealots, who protested against the mention (i.e. the recognition) of Roman rule in bills of divorce, for, as is well known, they held that it was religiously forbidden to accept the authority of Caesar's government. But according to Josephus' testimony (which is authoritative) the Zealots accepted Pharisaic teaching as a whole, only they formed 'a fourth philosophy' in addition to the Sadducees, Pharisees, and Essenes, on account of the additional precepts of their stringent religious-political ideology (*Ant.* xviii, 1, 6). Thus they also qualify for the designation 'Minim' from the standpoint of the Sages.

THE BURNING OF THE TEMPLE

Josephus' testimony concerning the council of Roman commanders, which met before the burning of the Temple and at which the fate of the Sanctuary was discussed, is well known. He states that opinions were divided when the vote was taken: some demanded the burning of the Temple in any case, since it served as a centre for the Jews (both in Eretz-Israel and throughout the world) and a base foi rebellion. Others argued: if the Jewish fighters would leave it, it should be saved; but if not, it should be burnt. And others, again, agreed with Titus and decided to save the Temple from destruction, even if the Jews fought from it. But its destiny was already decreed, and through one of the soldiers, who hurled a torch at the Temple, 'as though impelled by a supernal power', the Sanctuary went up in flames. When this happened, Titus gave orders forthwith for his troops to extinguish the fire, but they paid no heed to his commands and threats, and urged one another to complete the acts of incendiarism in the presence of Caesar.[1]

As against this statement of Josephus, there is the well-known testimony of the Christian monk Sulpicius Severus (apparently he derived the account from Tacitus' *Historiae*, part of which has been lost[2]) that at the assembly of the principal commanders Titus insisted that the Temple be burned, in order to destroy the root of Judaism,[3] so that the Jewish people should have no strongpoint in the future for rebellion against the state (that is to say, Titus held the view of those who advised the first course in Josephus' tradition). Now the opinions of scholars — Jewish as well as Gentile — are divided:

1 *Wars* vi, 4; iii, 5, 6–7. In many other passages, too, Josephus makes a point of informing us that the Temple was burned down against the wish of Titus. See the Preface to *Wars* vi, 11, and *ibid.* v, 10, 5.

2 See in detail Bernays, *Gesammelte Abhandlungen*, II, pp. 159–167, 171–181.

3 'Christianity', mentioned here, was interpolated only by the last redactor.

while some prefer Flavius' version, others reject it on the basis of Severus' tradition; and the question still remains undecided.[4]

However, it appears that after thorough study of all aspects of the episode, we cannot avoid the almost certain conclusion that *the Temple was put to the torch at Titus' behest.*

This may be determined in three ways: (a) by having recourse to other sources, apart from those already mentioned; (b) by examining the events that immediately preceded and followed the destruction of the Temple; (c) by reference to records preserved by Josephus in his two major works (passages in which he writes without ulterior motives) elsewhere than in the chapter of the *Wars* alluded to. In addition we shall have to ascertain, through certain impressions relating to the period of the tragedy, the *general background* of the events and the spirit and views prevailing at the time in the camp of the Roman rulers towards Jews and Judaism, who were at war with them. It is noteworthy that the evidence contained in the second and third lines of investigation, mentioned above, refute Josephus by his own testimony, and hence are particularly effective in demonstrating the distortion of the truth in his evidence concerning the burning of the Temple, and in revealing the author's adjustment of his historical presentation to the demands of his benefactors.

(a) Apart from the testimony of Severus we have the tradition of the Sages — Tannaim and Amoraim — *the same in all the sources*, which declare that the Temple was burnt down by 'the wicked Titus'.[5]

4 Cf. the literature referred to in Schürer, *Geschichte*, I, pp. 631–632, note 115 (I was unable to obtain some of these works). To these should be added: Schlatter, *Geschichte Israels*, p. 334; Bertholet, *Das Ende d. jüdischen Staatwesens*, 630–631; Schürer, *op. cit.*, p. 158; Dubnow, דברי ימי עם עולם II, p. 274; Simḥoni מבוא למלחמות, הערות ובאורים p. 491; Jawitz, *op. cit.*, Pt. V, p. 183; Weynand in *Wissowa*, XII, 2703–2704 (accept Josephus' testimony). Bludau, *Die Juden in Alexandria*, p. 88, Willrich, *Das Haus des Herodes*, pp. 163–164; Weber, *Josephus und Vespasian*, pp. 68–73; R. Eisler, Ιησοῦς βασιλεὺς II, p. 600; Wolf-Boeckh, *Kaiser Titus und der jüdische Krieg*, pp. 27–28; Momigliano, *The Cambridge Ancient History*, II, p. 862 (accept the tradition found in Severus). Klausner, היסטוריה ישראלית, Pt. iv; S. Kraus, *The Jewish Encyclopedia*, XII, p. 163; Wellhausen, *Israelitische u. jüdische Geschichte*, p. 353, note 1 (doubtful attitude). Note should also be taken of Braun's view, in the 5th edition of Graetz, III, Pt. II, p. 540, who rejects Josephus' witness (end of note 1); similarly Thackeray, *Josephus* etc., p. 48.

5 *Sifre Deuteronomy* x, §328; *Midrash Tannaim*, p. 202; *T.B. Giṭṭin* 56b; *Genesis Rabba* x (Theodor's edition, pp. 82–83; see the other Midrashim in the notes *ibid.*); *Avot de-R. Nathan*, Version II, vii (ed. Schechter, pp. 20–21). It should be noted that the Haggada, which seeks to justify Nebuchadnezzar, would

Nay more, the Sages even attributed to him the blasphemous intention of waging war against the Almighty and of conquering Israel's God by setting his sanctuary on fire.[6] This tradition, especially the last-mentioned factor, which regards Titus as the foe of the nation's God, serves to show that the people's memory, in the period shortly after the Destruction, preserved the fact that the burning of the Temple did not occur accidentally or unintentionally, but with the knowledge and at the injunction of the emperor, to whom the destruction of the Temple appeared as a providential event in his war against Judaism. Several scholars have already noted, on the basis of other sources, that Titus (and his father) regarded this war as a struggle between the deity of Rome and the God of Israel — a fact that was clearly established by Weber and subsequently by R. Eisler.[7]

Similarly Josephus' testimony is contradicted by D. Cassius, who relates that after the Temple chambers had been burnt down and the Romans began to storm the sanctuary, the soldiers refused to enter the Temple 'for superstitious reasons', until Titus came and compelled them to go in against their will.[8] Although this tradition is not explicitly in conflict with the actual statement under discussion, it nevertheless refutes Josephus' witness by its *general portrayal* of the event. For whereas Josephus endeavours to depict the acts associated with the destruction of the Temple as an outrage perpetrated by the troops

have been particularly interested, had there been any basis for it, to regard the Destruction as an act of Providence, and not as the result of Titus' decree, the view expressed in the *Syriac Apocalypse of Baruch* iv, 1, and in *Pesiqta Rabbati* xxvi.

6 Some scholars interpret the tradition that, when Titus entered the Temple, he took hold of a harlot etc. as a reminiscence of Titus' relations with Berenice, Agrippa's sister (Krauss, *op. cit.*, p. 164). However, it appears that the tradition alluded to another event, affecting the community as a whole. For we read in *Wars* vii, 8, 7, that Eleazar, the last of the Zealots, declared at Massada: 'Where is this city that was believed to have God Himself inhabiting therein?... some unfortunate old men also die upon the ashes of the Temple, and a few women are there preserved alive by the enemy, for our bitter shame and reproach.' Thus we learn that the Romans put the captive women in brothels, which they set up near the Temple (perhaps on the Temple Mount itself), and later generations gave prominence to the act by the terrible scene depicted in the Haggada. On the dishonour done to 'the noble women in Jerusalem' see the other Rabbinic Haggadot.

7 Weber, *op. cit.*, p. 73; Eisler, *loc. cit.* Similar views are also expressed by Willrich, *op. cit.*, p. 164.

8 6, 65, Krauss, *op. cit.*, has already noted the contradiction between Cassius' statement and Josephus' testimony.

against the emperor's wishes, Cassius, on the contrary, informs us that the former were forced by Titus to act as they did despite their reluctance.[9]

We shall now proceed to examine the facts, which are related by Josephus himself and refute his testimony.[10]

(b) First let us consider the edict of the emperor (Vespasian) ordering the destruction of the Temple of Onias, after some of the Zealots, who had escaped from Judea attempted to instigate a revolt against the Romans in that country. Although the edict was suspended about three years later, it nevertheless sheds light on the policy of Vespasian

9 In several passages of Josephus we are told that the Romans assaulted the Jews, or massacred them on their own initiative, against the will of the emperor. For example in *Wars* v, 3, 3, where it is related that the men of Jerusalem pretended to surrender, and the Romans took up their arms in order to break through to the city, but were repulsed with heavy losses, Flavius attests that the soldiers acted against the express orders of Titus. Similarly he blames Antiochus, king of Commagene, for assaulting the walls of Jerusalem with his army without the consent of the emperor, who was pleased at the king's defeat (*ibid.* v, 11, 3). So, too, the splitting open of the bellies of the Jewish deserters — a brutality that was repeatedly committed for a long time — is portrayed as having been perpetrated despite the threats of Titus (*ibid.* v, 13, 4–5). He further states that after the capture of Jerusalem 'Caesar gave orders that they should kill none but those that were in arms, and offered resistance, but should take the rest captive. But, together with those whom they had orders to slay, they slew the aged and feeble' (*ibid.* vi, 9, 2). He likewise testifies (*ibid.*) that eleven thousand of the captives were starved to death, because the guards (contrary to their orders) 'withheld their food out of their great hatred towards them'. On the other hand, there has been preserved, as we know, corroborative evidence for Cassius' portrayal in the verses of the poet Valerius Flaccus, a contemporary, under the patronage of the Flavians. He tells Domitinus to depict his brother thus: 'Solymo ac nigrantem pulvere fratren spargentemque faces et in omni turre furentem' (The brother who, blackened by the dust of Jerusalem, scatters torches, rages from every tower). See Bernays, *op. cit.*, p. 165.

10 It is also known that Orosius confirms Severus. He states (*Adversum Paganos* vii, 9, 5–6): 'Quod tamen postquam in potestatem redactum... din deliberaverit utrum tamquam incitamentum hostium incenderet an in testimonium victoriae reservaret... itaque Titus, imperator ab exercitu pronuntiatus, templum in Hierosolymis incendit ac diruit.' The unqualified language of the writer indicates that the tradition he had received knew nothing of Titus' desire, and the steps he took, to save the Sanctuary, before he ordered — *after the event* — the remains of the Temple to be destroyed (as Josephus informs us), and attributes all the acts connected with the Temple's destruction, to the emperor.

and his son even in regard to our question.[11] For, according to Josephus' testimony, the Temple of Onias was closed down for the very reason advanced by the army commanders, when they advocated, at the council meeting preceding the burning of the Temple of Jerusalem, that the Sanctuary should be destroyed: 'Because the Jews would never leave off rebelling', while that House was standing.

This is confirmed by the witness of Josephus (and others) that the Roman emperors decreed, immediately after the Destruction, that Jews throughout the world must pay to the Temple of Jupiter Capitolinus in Rome the 'half shekel' that they used formerly to contribute to the Sanctuary.[12] For if Josephus' statement that Titus was opposed to the destruction of the Temple and grieved over the fate of 'the Sanctuary revered by Romans and by all the peoples'[13] was true, it is incomprehensible how immediately after the outrage to what was dear to him he could mock (the Jews) so brutally and provocatively.[14]

However, evidence is not lacking even from the time of the catastrophe itself, which points to the same conclusion.

In *Wars* vii, 1, 1, we read that upon the capture of Jerusalem, Titus gave orders 'that they should now demolish the entire city and Temple.'[15] So, too, *ibid.* vi, 5, 2, Flavius testifies that the Romans set fire (this time he himself states that it was done at Titus' command), after the burning of the Sanctuary, to all the other buildings left standing on the day of the Destruction: the halls, the chambers, and the gates. Now one wonders why, if initially the fire was started only accidentally against the express command of the emperor, the latter decided to add still further to the ruin.

It is true that Josephus stresses parenthetically in the course of his account of the incident that the Romans considered 'that it was in vain to spare the buildings round about, after the Sanctuary had been burnt down'. But this 'explanation' is hardly satisfactory; on

11 *Wars* vii, 10, 2(4), from which Willrich, *op. cit.*, and afterwards Weber, *op. cit.*, drew the necessary conclusions in regard to our subject.

12 *Wars* vii, 6, 6. As is well known, even Gentile writers attest this decree (Dio Cassius 66, §7; Suetonius, *Domitianus*). Compare, with reference to the document from that period, Schürer, *op. cit.*, III, 117, note 62.

13 *Wars* vii, 2, 4; *ibid.*, v, 10, 5; v, 8, 1.

14 This point has already been noted by Willrich, Weber, and Eisler in connection with our topic. We may likewise cite here the fact that Titus destroyed synagogues at Daphne in Antiochia and in Caesarea, and built in their stead institutions for Gentiles. See above, p. 293, note 55.

15 Compare also *Wars* vi, 6, 3; vi, 9, 1.

the contrary, one would have supposed that if Titus really thought 'it was improper to avenge oneself on this House, which is inanimate, for human sins',[16] he would undoubtedly have shown his generosity (and the reverence he felt, according to Josephus, for the Temple of the Lord) by endeavouring to spare all that he could, and not to enjoin total destruction. Thus we cannot but conclude that Titus intended from the outset 'to eradicate the evil root' of Judaism by utterly demolishing the House of its life.

Flavius similarly attests that when some of the surviving priests came to Titus, on the fifth day after the burning of the Temple and asked for mercy, he answered that 'Since the Temple, on whose account he might have been merciful in judgement, was destroyed, and it was moreover fitting that the priests should perish with their fane', he could not agree to spare their lives, and ordered them to be executed.[17] It seems that if Titus had been chagrined by the burning of the Temple, and had mourned and grieved over its destruction, as Josephus alleges,[18] it would have been inconceivable that he should have spoken in this vein.

However, there are also all but express statements of Titus and of his emissary Flavius, made during the actual events, which have to be taken at their face value, as indicated above.

Thus we read[19] that on the seventeenth of Tammuz, after the cessation of the daily offering, Titus instructed Josephus to say to John of Giscala as follows: 'If you have any malicious inclination to wage war, you can come out with as many men as wish to fight, without bringing destruction on the city and the Temple together with yourself' etc. It is evident, therefore, that Titus intended to destroy Jeru-

16 *Ibid.* vi, 4, 3; Josephus tells us that Titus wished to spare the Temple (and the city) out of *Philantropia*; only the Zealots imagined that this 'humanity' was but a sign of weakness (v, 8, 1). However, events showed that the Zealots were not very much mistaken in their distrust of Roman liberality.

17 *Ibid.* vi, 6, 1.

18 *Ibid.* vii, 5, 2.

19 *Ibid.* vi, 2, 1. See there Josephus' appeal to the men of Jerusalem to have pity on their ancestral city and to put an end to the fire that was *already licking at the Temple*. Compare also v, 10, 5, regarding the period between the capture of the second wall and the last wall: 'These men (the Zealots) destroyed the city with their own hands... and it may almost be said that they (deliberately) drew the fire, which spread slowly, upon the Temple.' This sentence indicates that the Romans were considering, long before the destruction of the Sanctuary, whether to burn it or not, and that only as time passed did they finally decide to destroy it.

salem and to burn the Temple, if the Zealots continued to fight against the Romans, in accordance with the second proposal of his army commanders at his council-meeting.

Similarly we read further[20] that at the beginning of the siege of Jerusalem, Titus sent some of the captives, whose hands had been cut off, to Simeon bar Giora and John of Giscala and ordered them to demand, in his name, that they should surrender to him 'and not force him to destroy the city; and if (he added) they would repent their deeds, they would thereby save their lives and no stranger's foot would tread in the Temple'. Now it is not explicitly stated here that Caesar threatened the Zealots with the burning of the Temple, but this is undoubtedly evident from the passage cited below. Josephus relates that the men of Jerusalem who stood on the wall replied to Titus' proposal with reproaches: 'We utterly contemn death. . . why should we be concerned for our holy city, which you declare will surely be destroyed, since God has a more exalted Sanctuary above this Temple?' Titus' message, therefore, must have contained an express threat to burn down the Temple.

So, too, Flavius says to the Zealots at Titus' injunction:[21] 'However, the Romans. . . provided they receive the tribute, will not destroy the city, nor touch its sacred places.' Thus the implied converse is obvious: If the Jews will not surrender to Titus, the Romans will destroy the city and the Temple with it.

He speaks to them in similar vein at the close of his address: 'Lay down your arms, have mercy on the city of your ancestors. . . Look back and behold the beautiful jewel, which you cast away with your own hands — the splendour of the city, *the glory of the Sanctuary*, the precious gifts of many peoples. And who would have the heart to set fire to all these?' etc. He states, in effect, that if they come to terms, the Romans will spare the Temple, but if not, it will be burnt! Also at the beginning of his speech, addressed to all the men of Jerusalem, he cries: 'Take pity on your lives and the lives of your brethren, take pity on your ancestral city and your Sanctuary', the implication being that if they will not deliver themselves into the

20 v, 11, 2.

21 v, 9, 4. Similar language was used by Rabban Joḥanan b. Zakkai, who said to the men of Jerusalem: 'My sons, why are you destroying this city and seeking to burn the Temple; for what after all does he demand of you? He only asks of you one bow, or one arrow, and he will leave you alone' (*Avot de-R. Nathan*, Version I, iv; cf. Version II, vi).

hands of the Romans, they, the city and the Temple are destined to be destroyed.

From the following story, too, it may be inferred, to my mind, that Titus had decided to burn the Temple before ever the military council had met. Josephus[22] testifies that when the story reached the Roman camp that Miriam, the daughter of Eleazar of Transjordan, had eaten her own child, Titus declared: 'Behold I have offered the Jews peace... but they have chosen war... *and their own hands have started to set fire to their Temple*, whose honour we have preserved. Therefore such food befit them. However, I shall now cover the full abomination of the murder of this child with the ruins of the city and I shall not let the sun that encircles the whole world look down upon a city whose mothers consume the flesh of their children. In truth, his food is more suited to the fathers, who refuse to lay down their arms after so many miseries.'

It is not our concern to point out the patent hypocrisy of Titus' 'holy anger' and 'sense of righteousness' with which his words reek. But it should be noted that the words in italics contain an anticipatory excuse for the burning of the Temple, which is announced here in advance, and that the Zealots are blamed for the destruction of the Sanctuary. But quite apart from this we find numerous passages[23] in the account of the disaster in which the fate of the Shrine is bound up with that of the city, implying that in the Roman view they were both subject to the same sentence. Nor is it reasonable to suppose that they only intended to destroy the city and to leave the Temple, for without Jerusalem the Sanctuary would have been without practical value and could not have survived by itself as the centre of the nation's spiritual life, whether in Eretz-Israel or in the Diaspora. It therefore appears that Josephus was afraid to explain Titus' real intention in regard to the Temple — even when he was able 'to excuse' its destruction — and restricted his testimony solely to Jerusalem. Only by revealing a little he disclosed a great deal.

We read a similar statement[24] by the fugitives of Jerusalem — whom Titus had temporarily settled in Gophnah, but now recalled for a while to show that they had not been slain by the Romans — to

22 vi, 3, 5. Weber already relates this incident to our subject, *op. cit.*, p. 72, n. 1.

23 v, 8, 1; v, 10, 5; v, 11, 2; vi, 2, 1, *et al.*; *Ant.* xx, 10; so, too, in both versions of *Avot de-R. Nathan*, and in the passages mentioned above.

24 vi, 2, 3. See also *ibid.* 1: 'Behold God... is bringing upon you, together with the Romans, *the fire to purge the Sanctuary*', etc.

the effect that they said to the men of Jerusalem (doubtless at the command of Titus), as they stood between the Roman lines and the wall: 'Pray, open the gates of Jerusalem to the Romans and save the city of our ancestors. Should you refuse to do this, depart all of you from the Temple Mount and let the Temple escape destruction, for the Romans will not venture to set fire to the Sanctuary, *except under the most pressing circumstances.*' Even Titus himself, when the Jewish fighters had replied to the deserters' appeal with reproaches and arrows, declared to the men of John of Giscala, after denouncing 'the unclean wretches' with harsh words, 'that they defile the Temple with Jewish and Gentile blood', unlike the Romans who have preserved the purity of the Temple all the time by forbidding Gentiles to enter them, 'and if you will set your battle lines at a distance from this place, no Roman will draw nigh to your Temple nor desecrate it'.[25] Again we clearly discern the (covert) threat of Titus to burn the Temple, if the Jews will continue to fight.

Furthermore, we read that Titus spoke in similar vein in his last address to the Zealots, after the destruction of the Sanctuary and before the conquest of the city:[26] 'And when I approached the Shrine, I was again willing to abandon the rules of war and I appealed to you *to have pity on your own sanctities and to save the Temple* for your own sake. . . .' 'But you rejected all my appeals, and with your own hands you set fire to the Sanctuary.'

It also appears to me that we have clear evidence in Josephus' statement[27] that, three days prior to the burning of the Temple, Titus ordered its gates to be set on fire, when he saw 'that his compassion

25 *Ibid.* 2, 4.

26 *Ibid.* 6, 2.

27 *Ibid.* 4, 1. Schürer and Weber already (p. 72, note 1) have remarked on the Talmudic tradition (*T.B. Ta'anit* 29a), which asserts that the destruction of the Temple began a day or two before the main destruction took place (on the ninth of Ab), and have explained the statement by the fact, referred to here, that the Romans then (on the seventh or eighth of Ab) set fire to the gates of the Temple court. But it seems that this Rabbinic tradition is substantiated by Josephus' testimony concerning the act referred to: 'And when the Jews saw the fire. . . the rebels did not take the lesson to heart, so as to save the rest of their Sanctuary, but their fury against the Romans was still further enflamed, as though the Temple itself was already ablaze.' Thus contemporaries, who took part in the events, regarded the act as the commencement of the destruction (needless to say, Josephus' vexation with the Zealots who actually witnessed the Romans setting fire to the Temple, was prompted by his desire to exculpate the latter from responsibility.

on a foreign temple resulted in injury and death to his soldiers'. Thus Caesar preferred already then to burn 'foreign temples', provided this would make it easier for him to capture the Temple Mount. In other words, his view (even before that council meeting) was in accord with those of his officers who proposed that the Temple should be destroyed, if the Jews fought for it and to save it only if they surrendered.

(c) A number of matters recorded by Josephus, though not actually connected with the event, also prove that the author *knew*, when writing the *Wars* and the *Antiquities*, that the Temple was not burnt down by Titus accidentally but (almost) as an inevitable result of the war.

Thus we read[28] in a speech attributed by Flavius to Agrippa upon the outbreak of the revolt: 'Is there one so simple among you as to believe that the Romans will wage war against you according to an agreement, and that when they gain the upper hand they will deal mercifully with you *and not burn the holy city*. . . Have pity, I beseech you, on this city of your fathers *and on the holy vestibules*, spare our sanctuary and take care of the Temple and its sacred things, for the Romans will show no restraint when they gain the ascendancy over you, and they will no longer spare our sanctities after you have shown your ingratitude to them.' Needless to say, Agrippa did not utter these words verbatim, but the writer, as usual, ascribes them as 'a retrospective prophecy' to earlier times. However, if Josephus 'had remembered' at the time that the Temple was set on fire only accidentally, and not as a necessary consequence of the revolt, he could not have written as he did.

Similarly the author[29] testifies later on that, when Agrippa sent his troops to Jerusalem to restrain the rebels, he did so 'because he was solicitous for both the Jews and the Romans. . . and wished to save for the Romans the peace with the Jews and for the Jews *their sanctuary and the city of their glory*'.

So, too, we read in *Wars*[30] that, when the 'procurator' Cumanus punished many Jews for seeking to avenge themselves on the Samaritans for being responsible for the death of their brethren, and the enraged people were ready to revolt in anger against the vicious conduct of the Roman governor, the leading priests and Sanhedrin

28 *Wars* ii, 16, 4.
29 *Ibid.* ii, 17, 4.
30 *Ibid.* ii, 13, 5.

persuaded the multitude 'not to provoke the wrath of the Romans... but to take pity *on the city and the Temple* and on their children and wives who would be imperilled', etc. Also here, it should be noted that the formulation of the speech by the author could hardly have been in its present form, had he not 'forgotten', when writing his testimony on the burning of the Sanctuary, that it came about against the will of the Romans. A similar statement occurs on the subject in *Antiquities*:[31] 'And when the eminent men of Jerusalem perceived the terrible straits in which the people found themselves... they besought the rebels to desist from their acts on account of the danger that their ancestral city might be destroyed and *the Temple burnt'*, etc.

We likewise read in the list of High Priests given in *Ant.* xx, 10, in unmistakable language: 'From the time of Herod until the day when Titus destroyed the Sanctuary and the city', etc.

Now let us re-examine the views and sentiments current among contemporaneous Romans, in the period under discussion, towards the Jews and Judaism, in case they shed light on our subject. We have already seen that those who proposed at the assembly of the commanders of the Roman forces that the Temple should be burnt argued that the Jews would always seek to rebel against the Romans as long as the Sanctuary remained standing. This view, which we find current in certain ruling circles in Rome (and in Judea) many years before the Destruction (a view that provided the evil governors with an excuse for maltreating the Jews, sometimes in the form of terrible provocation),[32] was given drastic expression by Titus, who had authorized the acts. Thus he declares to the men of Jerusalem, who wished to surrender to him upon the destruction of the Temple:[33] 'Rightly I should exterminate you from off the face of the earth, for

31 *Ibid.* xx, 6, 5. Here reference should be made to the incident of Sabinus — about seventy years before the Destruction — who burnt the vestibules of the Sanctuary during the rebellion and plundered the Temple treasure (*Wars* ii, 4, 3; *Ant.* xvii, 10, 2). Thus the Romans even then had no compunction in destroying the Temple.

32 For the time of Agrippa I compare Philo, *Legatio ad Gaium*, and Tacitus, *Historiae* v, 9. The latter, too, attests that at this period the Jews were ready for armed revolt, and in general he portrays the Jews, in his account of the war against Vespasian and Titus, as *almost ceaseless rebels* against the government, from the days of Pompey onwards (cf. especially *ibid.* 12, where he asserts that in Claudius' reign the Jews fortified the walls of Jerusalem and the Temple in preparing themselves for war). For the period following Herod's death cf. *Wars* ii, 6, 2 and *Ant.* vii, 11, 2.

33 vi, 6, 2.

since earliest times, when Pompey subdued you by force, you have not ceased to rebel', etc. Does not this prove that Titus did not hold views very different from those of his aforementioned advisers, namely that 'the evil root' of 'the everlasting rebels' must be uprooted?

Another factor contributing to the malicious designs of the leading Romans at that time against the Jewish people is to be found in the wrath of Vespasian and his son — who were thus engaged in laying the foundations of the Flavian dynasty, after the long struggles within the Roman empire, although in the past their family had no stake in the tradition of rulership — against the Jews, who would not recognize their authority and greatly endangered the establishment of their rule. This aspect is more fully explained in the continuation of Titus' speech cited above: 'And when I went with my father to the land of Egypt, you took the opportunity to intensify your preparations for war and you were not ashamed to raise disturbances against men about to ascend the throne, whom you knew to have been benevolent as generals. Afterwards every dominion found shelter under us, and all the countries were tranquil and at peace, and even the foreign peoples sent embassies to bring us greetings, and only the Jews remained hostile to us... Thereafter I went up against this city, and my father gave me a fearful injunction in his great anger.'[34] It would seem that this 'fearful injunction' meant the destruction of the city and the Sanctuary. In other words, Vespasian gave his son a *mandatum* to burn the Temple, in order to annihilate 'the stiff-necked' Jews, who prevented him from establishing his rule in Rome, by 'the gift of peace', which he wished to offer to the empire, after the many wars, both internal and external, which started with the assassination of Nero (and somewhat earlier).

A third factor that apparently contributed to the crystallization, among the Romans, of the idea of the destruction of Jerusalem and the Sanctuary, was their negative attitude towards the Jews in general. For they held that the Jews were 'haters of humanity' and eschewed peaceful relations with any men or nation; hence they were not to be subject to the same laws of war as other peoples. This is to be seen from Vespasian's action at Tiberias, where he ordered the many thousands of fugitives from Tarichaeae to be massacred, although they had surrendered to him after he had promised them

34 In Tacitus, too, the fact is stressed that Vespasian was angry with the Jews, because 'they alone did not submit to him' after the termination of the civil war (*ibid.*, 10: 'augebat iras quod soli Iudaei non cessissent').

their lives in 'a covenant of peace'. Josephus expressly states[35] that Vespasian perpetrated this act after accepting the view of his commander-counsellors (it was they, apparently, who advised at Titus' council-meeting to destroy the Temple in any case) 'for there was no impiety (in any evil done) to the Jews'. Thus the Jews did not deserve to have the same measure of justice meted out to them as was customary in war against enemies, and judiciary principles were not to be applied to them. In other words, *they were outside the law.*

It follows, *a fortiori*, that they were not to be granted any concessions,[36] and that their Temple was not to be spared, once they were actually fighting from within it.

An echo of this thought in Vespasian's mind is to be heard, it seems to me, in the statement reported by Philostratus in the name of Apollonius of Tyana and his companions,[37] who said to Vespasian (when he was staying in Alexandria, after being proclaimed emperor by the Roman forces in Syria and Egypt) that the Jews had always risen in revolt against the Romans, and not only against them but against all peoples. For they do not eat with foreigners and are misanthropes, and hence, from the outset, they should not be incorporated into a civilized kingdom.[38] Have we not here a tradition that portrays

35 *Wars* iii, 10, 10.

36 According to Josephus' testimony the Romans considered the burning of the city and the Temple to be based on the laws of war (*Wars* vi, 4, 3). Similarly Tacitus (*loc. cit.* 9) held that when Pompey entered the Holy of Holies (and thereby desecrated the Sanctuary), he acted *iure victoriae.*

37 Cf. Th. Reinach, *Textes*, etc., p. 116.

38 Reference should be made here to the interesting parallel to our subject in Diodorus' story (taken from the work of Poseidonius), Book xxxiv, about Antiochus Sidetes, who besieged Jerusalem in the time of Joḥanan the High Priest, and the latter, being hard pressed, decided to surrender to the Greek king. Most of the king's friends counselled him to take Jerusalem by force (and not by negotiation, as Joḥanan requested) and to destroy the city and the whole Jewish people, for they alone do not become integrated with the other nations and hate mankind. Antiochus Epiphanes acted in this way; because of Jewish hostility to all nations, he sought to suppress the Jewish religion.

This attitude, which was then prevalent among the Romans, is also reflected in Tacitus' statement that numerous portents were seen in heaven and on earth, which foretold Vespasian's ascension to the throne, but the Jews interpreted them to signify that their own dominion would spread in the east 'gens superstitioni obnoxia, religionibus adversa'. Compare Bernays' statement that the Romans at that time regarded the Jews fighting against them as 'a barbarian people', who were not to be treated in war as other civilized peoples.

for us the atmosphere of contempt in which Vespasian gave Titus, in that same Alexandria and at that particular time, 'the fearful injunction'?

Upon reviewing the facts detailed above, we cannot but conclude that the burning of the Temple (and the city) had been considered by the Romans long before the meeting of the army commanders, and especially from the day that Titus came to Judea on his father's commission. However, Josephus' statement about the various opinions expressed at the council assembly indicates that there were three conflicting views among the leading Romans all the time that the question was under discussion. As the sources quoted above show, it appears that many advocated the destruction of the city and the Sanctuary, even if the Jewish fighters were to evacuate them, so that they would have no strongpoint for future rebellion. Others argued in favour of saving both, in accordance with the practice of civilized peoples to spare their enemies' sanctities. While others again adopted a middle course, namely, if the Temple were captured after fighting, it should be burnt; but if the Jews surrendered it peacefully, it should be saved.

Which of the views that were being canvassed among the Romans[39] was ultimately to prevail depended, needless to say, on a number of factors. On the one hand, the Romans never ceased to regard the vast Jewish diaspora in their empire and the Jews dwelling in the realm of the Parthians as a considerable power that should not be antagonized towards Rome;[40] nor should it be supposed that Vespasian and his son did not endeavour to avoid being stigmatized by the

39 It seems to me that all these conflicting views among the Romans are corroborated by Josephus himself. The first view is voiced by Agrippa in his speech, cited above, in which he warns the Jews that if they took up arms, 'the Romans would not wage war against them according to an agreement', and that they would bring about the destruction of the city and the Temple. The second view is aired by the author in the prolix speech of Titus about sparing the Temple (and the city). The intermediate course, which prevailed, found its expression — in action.

40 I believe that this is the true reason why Titus did not agree to the demand of the Antiochians of Syria to deprive the Jews of their time-honoured rights, and not — as Titus avers in Josephus' work — because the Jews of the Diaspora could no longer go to their homeland, which was in ruins. It is also possible that the emperors wished to maintain the rivalry between the Jewish communities and the Greek cities, in order to secure themselves against powerful enemies, who would in future be without opposition (see *Wars* vi, 5, 2).

many nations living in the empire, as well as by certain Roman circles themselves, as tyrants who treated with brutality a conquered people of heroic fighters, contrary to the 'glorious' tradition of 'generous' Rome. Perhaps there was the added reason that Titus did not wish to close the door completely to submission by peace-loving Jews and to their acquiescence to end the war, by destroying the Temple and the city that was the nation's pride. On the other hand, the harsh treatment accorded to the Jews and their sanctities was fostered by the covert and open hatred for the Jews evinced by the Syrians and Egyptians, not to mention the Arabs and other peoples living adjacent to Judea during this period of fighting. Another contributory factor was the desire of the Roman Caesars 'to finish' the war 'expeditiously', since it was jeopardizing the consolidation of their rule, and thereby to free the Romans from 'the everlasting' fear of the Jewish rebels, who could serve as an example to other peoples.[41] It may also be assumed that even the changing fortunes of war during the five months of the siege of the Temple and city were bound to affect Titus in various ways.

Hence it may be said that the young Caesar's attitude underwent certain fluctuations in the course of the war, and that the many passages of Josephus designed to exculpate him from blame for the destruction of the Temple possibly reflect a certain measure of truth, namely that Titus was not disinclined at certain periods to show clemency. But the *actual fact* that he gave orders to set fire to the Sanctuary appears to be beyond doubt. Assuming we reject Severus' statement as it stands, to wit, that Titus had all along intended to burn down the Temple, even if the besieged were to surrender,[42] it

41 See *Wars* iii, 1, 2.

42 It should be noted that even the tradition in *Midrash Ekha* (i, 31), concerning the consultation held by Vespasian (= Titus) on the destruction of Jerusalem (and the Temple?) after its conquest, apparently indicates that Caesar's attitude was not harsh, as depicted by Severus. Although this Midrashic tradition is truncated and contains only the advice of Pangar the Arab ('The serpent is killed and the chest is burnt') and of Rabban Joḥanan b. Zakkai ('A snake-charmer is procured and the serpent is charmed and the chest is spared'), nevertheless the fact that the Haggada attributes this malicious advice to evil neighbours — i.e. Arabs — seems to show that the national memory retained no recollection of the fact that the emperor had resolved to destroy the city and the Temple in any circumstances. (Incidentally it is noteworthy that the Midrash relates that Pangar did not destroy the portion allocated to him [saying that he refrained from doing so] 'for the glory of the empire... for had I destroyed it [the Western Wall] no

must at least be conceded that the position that he adopted in the course of time was to destroy the Sanctuary and the city if the fighters failed to evacuate them.

If we are surprised at Flavius' false testimony, we must realize, with Bernays,[43] that when he wrote his book (75–79) the atmosphere in Rome had changed and many of the factors that operated during the wartime 'frenzy' no longer existed. Consequently it was appropriate that the emperors should be portrayed among the Roman and other intelligentsia in a kindly light as generous and 'god-fearing' men.[44] To put it more simply, after the tremendous carnage perpetrated by the Romans in Judea, and the destruction of the city and Temple, the Romans and their emperors no longer regarded the Jews as a danger to Roman rule and therefore could afford to appear benevolent even retrospectively, and actually demanded that the writer who enjoyed their protection and bounty should relate to future generations the heroism, glory and benevolence of his masters and benefactors.[45] Despite his efforts, however, he did not succeed

one would have known what you laid in ruins, but now when people see it, they will say "see what Vespasian's troops have demolished!"' Now these are the very arguments used by Josephus — as well as by Severus, who ascribed them to others — to emphasize Titus' desire to preserve the Temple).

43 *Ibid.*

44 Perhaps one should add here that a change in general took place in Titus' mood, for to begin with he was hard (much more so than his father) and cruel to people, but in the end he wished to give the impression by his acts that he was *amor et deliciae generis humani*; see Wolf-Boeckh, *op. cit.*

45 Josephus' efforts to exculpate Titus and to speak in his praise are obvious in many passages, but special attention should be paid to his practice of finding 'excuses' for the destruction of the Temple in devious ways, as long as the emperor should appear innocent. He is particularly inclined to portray the Zealots as wicked desecrators of the Temple and its sanctities, so as to leave the reader with the impression that the sanctuary was no longer deserving of its name, and consequently it was no great crime to put it to the torch (although this last point is *nowhere* expressly stated, yet in ever so many places it is quite clearly implied). Thus he declares unctuously and with hypocritical cunning in *Wars* iv, 3, 13, where he describes how the Zealots fought against the rule of the Sanhedrin, 'And rightly it may be said that this blood (shed by the Zealots) defiled the sanctities.' Later he observes *ibid.* iv, 5, 2, after the murder of Ḥanan, 'I believe that God who had decreed the destruction of the defiled city and wished to purify its Temple (by means of the Romans, who destroyed both!) cut off these men' etc. In v, 1, 3 he breaks into a feigned lamentation: 'Is it indeed through the Romans that these terrible calamities came upon thee, when they entered the gates to purify thee *with fire* of the abominations of thy sons, for thou wast no longer the

in whitewashing all their deeds, and unwittingly (or possibly even wittingly?),[46] he himself, through many slips of the pen, tells us the truth.

dwelling-place of God, after thou hadst become a cemetery for thy sons and thy Temple had been transformed into a burial ground?' Is there not here an implicit justification of both God and the Romans? The same applies to his remarks (vi, 2, 1) addressed to the Zealots: 'Behold, it is God, and no other, who, together with the Romans, brings this conflagration upon you to cleanse the Temple and to wipe from off the face of the earth the city that is filled with such great abominations.' Needless to say, even the Sages ascribed the destruction of the Second Temple to 'causeless hatred'. But like the prophets in their day, they too, even though they regarded the disasters as a punishment inflicted by Heaven, did not seek to *exculpate the enemy*, as Flavius endeavoured to do (this refutes the surprising remarks of Weber, p. 73; nevertheless the view has still been expressed that this slave of the Romans was 'a prophet weeping to himself' like Jeremiah — see Simḥoni in his Introduction to the Wars). Furthermore, Josephus blames the destruction on the Zealots, who ate the holy food and used the Temple vessels for war purposes (*Wars* v, 1, 2; v, 1, 6; v, 13, 6; vii, 8, 1), as though he had forgotten the law that when life is at stake all these prohibitions are set aside (one is reminded of Titus' wrath against the hapless mother who devoured her child, when he declared that on account of this sin he had resolved to be the true champion of righteousness and utterly destroy the 'sinful city' from the face of the earth). Special note should be taken of *Wars* v, 13, 6, where Josephus upbraids John of Giscala for melting down the Temple utensils, asserting: 'I believe that if the Romans had delayed avenging themselves on the villains, the ground would have opened up and swallowed *the city*, or an overwhelming flood would have come and submerged it' etc. It is not difficult to perceive in these hypocritical words a covert defence of the Romans, as though to say 'They burnt a city that was already consumed'. Nay more, he censures the people of Jerusalem for not giving heed to 'the clear portents' that foretold doom (*Wars* vi, 5, 3). He also rebukes them for disregarding the fact that after making the Temple four-square by demolishing the tower, the Temple was destined to be destroyed, 'although it was written in their books that both the city and the Temple would be laid in ruins, when the Temple would become four-square'. He likewise complains that they did not interpret 'the End', predicted in those days, as referring to the kingdom of Vespasian and not to that of the Messiah. 'Eventually the fall of their city and their own calamitous end demonstrated their folly' (*ibid.* vi, 6, 4).

46 It may well be that where it was possible to evade the dread censorship of the Caesars, Josephus did not hesitate to give clandestine expression to his residual national and moral feelings, which as a rule were submerged in his servile and abject spirit; compare, for instance, the speech of Eleazar at Massada (Dinaburg [Dinur] also inclines to this view; cf. *Megillot*).

RABBAN JOḤANAN B. ZAKKAI'S REMOVAL TO JABNEH

It is the accepted view among scholars regarding the negotiations between Vespasian (or Titus) and Rabban Joḥanan b. Zakkai that the latter, when he foresaw the destruction of Jerusalem and the burning of the Temple, sought to take preventive measures to avert the collapse of the nation and its Torah by establishing 'a spiritual centre', which would assure the continued existence of the Jewish people, even when its residual political independence was gone and its homeland destroyed.[1] Therefore he decided to go to Vespasian and ask him for Jabneh, where shattered Judaism might be resuscitated by the formation of a new centre that would replace the Temple and Sanhedrin, and thus heal the wounded nation, restore its strength and unite it through Torah and precepts. Since the Roman commander, who respected only palpable physical strength, was unable to appraise the manifold consequence resulting from the seemingly inconsequential action that Rabban Joḥanan intended to take, he acceded to his 'humble' request, without sensing that he was at that moment destroying with his own hands the fruit of his victory by permitting a wretched and outcast fugitive to create a new spiritual Judaism, which was destined to outlive the victorious Roman Empire.[2]

This view, which finds support in the Haggada of the Talmudic

1 Nachman Krochmal, *Môre Nevûkhê ha-Zĕman*, Lemberg, p. 75; Weiss, *Dôr Dôr wĕ-Dôrĕshāw*[2], Pt. II, p. 35; Graetz, *Geschichte*[5], IV, p. 13; Dubnow (Hebrew), Pt. II, p. 203; Jawitz, VI, p. 5; Halevy, *Dorot Harischonim*, Pt. 1, Vol. V, p. 44; Klausner, *Historya Yisrĕʿēlīt*, Pt. IV, pp. 181, 213; Menahem Stein, *Zion*, III, p. 118; Bacher, *Die Agada der Tannaïten*, Pt. I, p. 213; Derenbourg, *Maśśāʿ 'Ereṣ Yisrā'ēl*, pp. 154, 161; Christie, *The Journal of Theological Studies*, XXVI, pp. 342–343; Bertholet, *Das Ende des jüdischen Staatswesen*, 1910, pp. 163–164; H. Loewe in Hastings *Encyclopedia of Religion and Ethics*, VII, p. 593.

2 See especially Graetz, *loc. cit.*, Jawitz and Dubnow; Wasser, *Die Stellung des Juden*, etc., p. 55.

tradition,[3] relies primarily on the events that ensued in the days after the Destruction, when the Nasi's college and Bet Din were established in Jabneh, and Judaism in Eretz-Israel was restored and had even largely recovered its influence over the entire Diaspora, both in the West and in the East.

But are we able to maintain this theory on the basis of the actual events of those days? Is it possible to confirm it by the known facts of what transpired in the country during the entire course of the great war?

To answer this question we must first deal with an obscure point. Its elucidation will, it appears, militate against the current view, but we shall thereby be able, I believe, to arrive at a truer understanding of the episode under discussion.

The question is: What prompted Rabban Joḥanan to go particularly to Jabneh? In what way did this city differ from other Judean cities and justify its role as a refuge for the Torah and a stronghold for the Jewish people? Is it because it was occupied only at the end of the Hasmonean period, and that when Pompey came to the country he proceeded to detach it from Judea, and that even when it was reintegrated into Palestine in the days of Herod it was not possible to remove from it the many non-Jews who had lived there until then?[4] Was it these facts that gave it precedence?

Scholars have already recognized this problem and sought to solve it on the assumption that Jabneh was a city of Sages and scribes long before the event referred to.[5] Furthermore, according to several authorities[6] a High Court [בית דין גדול *Bêt Dîn Gādôl*] existed there from early times. Hence it is understandable that Rabban Joḥanan b. Zakkai asked Vespasian to grant him the remaining centre, in

3 See particularly the Aggada in *Tractate Giṭṭin* and *Avot de-R. Nathan*. But on the tradition itself see the Appendix below.

4 See Schürer, *Geschichte*, etc., Pt. II, pp. 126–128; Stein, p. 119.

5 Nachman Krochmal, *loc. cit.*, is of opinion that there was a college at Jabneh in the time of Rabban Gamaliel the Elder. Jawitz takes a similar view. Halevy, *loc. cit.*, infers from the *Tosefta Sanhedrin* xiii 'On another occasion the Sages assembled at Jabneh' etc., that already in the days of Hillel, the Patriarch and Elders were accustomed to convene their council meeting there (just as in other well-known cities). But this passage does not occur in Zuckermandel's edition, or in the parallel Baraita in *Sanhedrin* 11a and in *T.P. Sota* i, 24b. It is undoubtedly erroneous and does not form an original part of the *Tosefta*.

6 See Hyman, *Toledot Tanna'im wa-'Amora'im*, Pt. II, 677; Stein, *loc. cit.*, Derenbourg, *op. cit.*, p. 154, note 1, and *ibid.*, p. 109.

Jabneh, so that it might sustain the nation after the fall of Jerusalem.

But this conjecture (which we shall also discuss presently) that there were Sages in Jabneh before the Destruction does not help very much to solve the difficulty. For we are unaware that Halakhic scholars, capable of rendering decisions, were not to be found in the Temple period also in other Judean cities. If, however, a High Court did exist in Jabneh before the Destruction, the problem is fully solved.

However, this theory is not only groundless, as we shall see further on, but the reverse can be proved, namely, that it is impossible to assume that a High Court existed at Jabneh (or at any other place) before the destruction of the Temple.

The scholars who maintain this hypothesis attempt to substantiate their view with the help of the Mishna (*Sanhedrin* xi, 4): 'He (the rebellious elder) was not executed either by the court of his city, or by the court at Jabneh, but he was brought up to the High Court at Jerusalem' etc. Thus the Halakha ostensibly speaks of the court at Jabneh, whose powers exceeded that of other city courts, that is, of the small Sanhedrins (its authority, therefore, was equivalent to that which it possessed after the Destruction), when the Great Sanhedrin of the Chamber of Hewn Stone was still standing.

If now this tradition is interpreted as suggested above, it must necessarily be concluded that the High Court at Jabneh was in existence at least forty years prior to the Destruction, for according to Rabbinic tradition the Jews were deprived of the right to try capital cases from then on, and the Halakha became meaningless. Indeed the scholars referred to actually hold this view and date the establishment of the court at Jabneh several generations before the destruction of the Temple. In answer to the question why this particular place was chosen for setting up a High Court, M. Stein has surmised[7] that it was due to the exceptional administrative status of this city, for Jabneh had been presented by Salome, Herod's sister, to the Emperor's wife as a personal gift. Since according to Mommsen it may be assumed that the superintendent of the private estates of the Emperors had the same power of judicial initiative as the 'supervisors' of the provinces, it follows that the superintendents of Jabneh also favoured the institution of an independent High Court in their territory.

However, although scholars sought to regard the Mishna in Trac-

7 *Ibid.*, pp. 119–121.

tate *Sanhedrin* as an ancient Halakha that was formulated in its present form before the fall of the State, it is nevertheless obvious that in its current recension it is of later date. If an earlier date is to be given to the origin of this tradition, the Mishna must be assumed to have read, in the first instance, as follows: 'He is not executed by his local court, but is brought up to the High Court in Jerusalem.' Subsequently Tannaim that lived after the Destruction interpolated into the passage the words 'nor at the court of Jabneh'. This is ordained by the Tosefta (*ibid.* xi, 7), which reads: 'A stubborn and rebellious son... and a rebellious elder are not executed on the spot, but are taken up to the High Court at Jerusalem' etc. Thus the court at Jabneh is not mentioned at all.

The expanded Halakha comes to teach us, therefore, that a rebellious elder is not put to death in the city courts, and *a fortiori* not in the Lower Courts [literally 'Small Sanhedrins']. But even if a High Court existed before the Destruction like that in Jabneh after the destruction of the Temple, which occupied an intermediate position (in respect of its judicial powers) between the Lower Courts and the Sanhedrin in Jerusalem, he would not be executed even there, because only Israel's highest and most perfect judicial institution, which is none other than the High Court convening in the Chamber of Hewn Stone, had jurisdiction in such a matter.

The hypothesis concerning the existence of a High Court at Jabneh in Temple times is refuted, in the first place, by the fact that all the sources alluding to the court at Jabneh refer only to the post-Destruction period, but even more so by the silence on this point of the well-known tradition transmitted by R. Jose.[8] 'Originally the disputes in Israel were few; the Court of Seventy-One (judges) used to sit in the Chamber of Hewn Stone, and there were also two Courts of Twenty-Three,[9] one of which sat at the entrance of the Temple Mount... If there was need to enquire, the local court was consulted;[10] if they said to them... and if not, they went to the one

8 *Tosefta Sanhedrin* vii, 1; *Tosefta Ḥagiga* ii, 9; *T.B.* Sanhedrin 88b; *T.P. ibid.* i, 19c.

9 In the Tosefta and the Palestinian Talmud the text has: 'And two courts of three judges each'.

10 The Tosefta and the Palestinian Talmud lack the passage found in the Babylonian Talmud: 'If they had a tradition [literally: 'heard'] (in the local court), they told them, but if not they proceeded to the nearest court.' Clearly this passage is not an original part of the tradition and is not to be found even in the Gemara in the Munich MS or the Karlsruhe MS (see *D.S.*),

at the entrance of the Temple Court... If not, then all proceeded to the Chamber of Hewn Stone.' Thus, if there had been a High Court in Temple times — from which, too, 'Instruction went forth unto all Israel' — that occupied an intermediate position between the Courts of Twenty-Three and the Great Sanhedrin at Jerusalem, they should have enquired of this court before proceeding to Jerusalem, just as they enquired from the court on the Temple Mount and at the entrance of the Temple Court,[11] prior to going to the Sanhedrin sitting in the Chamber of Hewn Stone.[12]

But this is not all; it is out of the question that a High Court existed in Temple times anywhere in Eretz-Israel jointly with the Sanhedrin at Jerusalem. For the Halakha assigns to the jurisdiction of this court (of seventy-one) only such tasks — and it is they that determine its character and name — as transcend local interests and pertain to the whole Jewish people,[13] that is to say, the High Court

for there is no reason to consult the court of another town, which was not higher than the local one.

11 On enquiring the Halakha from these two courts first see also *Mishna*, *ibid.*, xl, 2.

12 That the High Court at Jabneh was established only after the Destruction is to be inferred from *T.B. Sanhedrin* 17b: 'R. Judah said in the name of Rav: A Sanhedrin is not established in a city where there are not (at least) two who can speak (the seventy languages) and one who can understand (them). In Bethar there were three (who could speak these languages) and in Jabneh four, namely, R. Eliezer and R. Joshua etc. Thus the Talmud speaks of setting up a Sanhedrin in Jabneh for the first time, and mentions R. Eliezer, R. Joshua *et al.*, who were disciples of Rabban Joḥanan b. Zakkai and came with him to Jabneh. However, for the primary tradition, cf. *Tosefta, ibid.*, viii, 1, and *T.P. Sheqalim* v, 48d.

13 The matters appertaining to the jurisdiction of the Court of Seventy-One, as enumerated in the *Mishna* (*Sanhedrin* i, 5) are: Proclaiming an optional war (cf. also *M.*, *ibid.*, ii, 4), adding on to the City [Jerusalem] and the Temple Courts — a matter that affects the whole Jewish people — instituting Sanhedrins for the tribes (i.e. the Courts of Twenty-Three sitting in the provincial towns), declaring (a city to be) an apostate city, judging a tribe (on a charge of idolatry) or a High Priest — an issue that likewise concerns the whole nation — intercalating a year and sanctifying the New Moon (cf. R. Josiah's statement in *Mekhilta*, Bo', pericope ii, Horovitz, p. 9), and the going forth of the elders to carry out the measurements in connection with the heifer that had its neck broken (in order to determine which of two cities is nearer to the slain person). Needless to say this court decided moot questions referred to it from the city courts; see *Midrash Tanna'im*, p. 107. To be sure there was a Court of Seventy-One in Alexandria, but it served that entire country. Even when Josephus set up a Court of Seventy-One in Galilee, he

is concerned only with matters affecting the entire nation, whether in Eretz-Israel or in the Diaspora.[14] It is accordingly inconceivable that there could have been a High Court at Jabneh when the Great Sanhedrin was sitting at the Temple, 'whence instruction went forth unto all Israel'.

Consequently Stein's conjecture, outlined above, must be rejected. Even if it could be shown (and this is unlikely) that the special administrative status of Jabneh could have induced the Jews of this city to separate themselves from their countrymen in Eretz-Israel and sever their connection with the Jerusalem Sanhedrin, the fact remains that the function of a High Court, as we have seen, was only to serve the largest area within its jurisdiction, whereas Jabneh was but a single city.[15]

Likewise the assertion of scholars that men of learning were to be found in Jabneh prior to the destruction of the Temple is unfounded. They infer this from Rabban Joḥanan b. Zakkai's request to Vespasian, according to the current Talmudic recension, 'Give me Jabneh and its Sages'.[16] But in *Avot de-R. Nathan*, Version I (iv; Schechter, p. 12) the reading is: 'Said he [Rabban Joḥanan b. Zakkai] to him [Titus]: I ask of you only Jabneh, that I may go and teach *my disciples* there', etc. Thus he does not mention Jabneh's Sages, on whose account he supposedly wished to go there, but speaks of his own disciples, whom he intends bringing with him. Similarly we read in *Avot de-R. Nathan*, Version II (vi, p. 10): 'He said to him: I ask of you Jabneh, that I may teach Torah there', etc.[17]

intended thereby to remove this region from the control of the Jerusalem Sanhedrin, which, as we know, he opposed.

14 Such as the fixing of New Year and the beginning of each month.

15 Undoubtedly there were villages pertaining to Jabneh, in which, apparently, Jews also dwelt; see Schürer, *op. cit.*, p. 127. But the fact that a number of villages were attached to Jabneh has no bearing on our subject.

16 Klausner, *loc. cit.*, Stein, *loc. cit.*, Jawitz, *op. cit.*, p. 6, note 4; Horovitz in his note to Graetz, *op. cit.*, p. 13, note 3.

17 But in *Avot de-R. Nathan*, Version II (xxix, 30a), it is stated: 'But when they went forth from Jerusalem, he said: "Whither shall I go?"... but they said: "Let us go to Jabneh, a place where Torah is beloved, a place where there are many scholars"', etc. This tradition evidently refers to the scholars' exodus at the time of the event under discussion; but another tradition shows that the incident occurred when Rabban Joḥanan b. Zakkai died (see below, p. 324). Possibly, therefore, the transmitters of this tradition confused the chronology (in *Avot de-R. Nathan*, Version I, iv, the episode took place at

Hence it seems that in the tradition of the Babylonian Talmud the expression 'and its Sages' was a well-established phrase, as we find in the following Babylonian Baraita (*Qiddushin* 59b): ' "On condition that I am a Sage", we do not say, *like the Sages of Jabneh*, or like R. Akiba and his colleagues', etc. The words 'and its Sages' are thus an anachronistic insertion.

Since it is now clear that Rabban Joḥanan b. Zakkai's removal to Jabneh is not to be explained by the previous existence of a High Court, or the large number of Sages and erudite scholars in that city, we must now look for another reason. But first it will be necessary to deal with the very thorny question raised by scholars:[18] With whom did Rabban Joḥanan b. Zakkai negotiate — Vespasian or Titus?

Although the elucidation of this problem, as we shall see, has no great bearing on our main theme, according to the view suggested below, yet, being related to our theme, it can assist us to some extent in clarifying the subject.

The principal argument of the scholars who completely reject the traditional account, which everywhere speaks of Vespasian, is the fact that the Haggada depicts Rabban Joḥanan b. Zakkai's departure from Jerusalem as from a beleaguered city whereas it was Titus' forces that surrounded Jerusalem.[19] But the difficulty is removed in the light of *Wars* iv, 9, 1,[20] which states that 'Vespasian encompassed Jerusalem on all sides'. Although this was certainly no real blockade, compared with that subsequently set up by Titus, we nevertheless learn from *Wars* iv, 6, 3 and *ibid.* 7, 3, that already then the Zealots closed the gates of Jerusalem and would not permit any of its inhabitants to leave the city, so that any one who attempted to escape to the Roman camp did so at the risk of his life.[21]

The main feature of the event portrayed in the tradition could, therefore, fit the springtime of 68 C.E., when Vespasian conquered

the death of Rabban Joḥanan b. Zakkai's son, but it is not stated when this occurred). At all events there is an anachronism here, too.

18 Graetz, *op. cit.*, p. 13, note 1; Dubnow, *op. cit.*, p. 283, note 1; I. Halevy, *Dorot Harischonim*, Pt. I, vol. v, pp. 1 ff.; Klausner, *op. cit.*, pp. 212–213; Stein, *op. cit.*, p. 118, note 3. See also *Encyclopaedia Judaica* (*Eschkol* — German), IX, p. 225.

19 See Klausner, *op. cit.*, p. 212; Graetz, *loc. cit.*, Stein, *loc. cit.*

20 Cf. Halevy, *op. cit.*, p. 1.

21 Notwithstanding, many fled from the city to the Roman camp; see the two passages cited above from *Wars.*

the whole of Judea and isolated Jerusalem from the rest of the country. But other elements of the Haggada are perforce suited only to the time of Titus.

Thus the fact, recorded in *Avot de-R. Nathan*, that they signalled with arrows that Rabban Joḥanan was 'a friend of Caesar', testifies that the Romans were at this juncture close to the gates. Similarly the tradition in *Midrash Ekha* (Lamentations) attests that Rabban Joḥanan stood in the presence of Vespasian and his captains when they were discussing the conquest of the city. Likewise the description of the ravages wrought by famine in Jerusalem accord best with the period of Titus' siege. So, too, the incident of the burning of the stores, which according to two sources was the cause of Rabban Joḥanan b. Zakkai's exodus from the city, followed immediately upon Titus' blockade, as is evident from *Wars* v, 1, 4.[22]

But even the fact that tradition designates the person in question 'Vespasian' proves nothing. For according to most of the sources, except the Talmud, Vespasian was still in Judea till the end of the war and the conquest of Jerusalem (although the burning of the Temple is everywhere ascribed to Titus). Obviously the tradition suffers from chronological and factual confusion.

However, the strongest evidence, ostensibly, in support of the view that Rabban Joḥanan b. Zakkai surrendered to Vespasian is the fact that he predicted his becoming Emperor.[23] But when we recall that the same story is narrated by Josephus about himself and that Gentile writers mention an oracle uttered by a pagan priest on Mount Carmel and that various 'portents' appeared to Vespasian,[24] which foretold his succession to the throne, we must ineluctably doubt the authenticity of the tradition.

Thus the matter remains a moot question. Nevertheless, it seems that these considerations do not suffice to negate the essential validity of the account. For it may be argued that although in later times the entire episode was transferred to a time shortly before the destruction of the Temple, the central incident of the story — Rabban Joḥanan's exit — occurred earlier. The most persuasive reason in

22 Tacitus, too, *Hist*. V, 12, states that the stores were burnt at that time.

23 This is regarded as the primary reason by Halevy (*op. cit*., p. 2, n. 3), who accepts the tradition and dates the incident to the period when Vespasian was approaching Jerusalem (but his deductions, pp. 1–2, from the wording of the Haggada are not well founded).

24 See, on this subject, Weber, *Josephus und Vespasian*, pp. 45–52; Klausner, *op. cit*., p. 156.

favour of the tradition is Josephus' statement that the Jews who gave themselves up to the Romans were settled by Vespasian in the summer of that year in Jabneh, as we shall see immediately.

Let us now return to our starting-point. I believe that the scholars who adopted the aforementioned view concerning the acts and intentions of Rabban Joḥanan, did so because they confined themselves to considering the single act (and the one individual) of which the Talmudic tradition speaks. But if we are to evaluate the nature of the event correctly, we must first examine the incidents, related to our theme, about which we read in various passages of Josephus.

In *Wars* iv, 8, 1, it is stated that upon receiving news of the rebellion that had broken out in Galatia [Gaul] against Nero, Vespasian foresaw the wars that were destined to take place in the Roman empire and decided to establish order in Judea. For this purpose he set his forces in motion in the spring of 68 C.E. After conquering the toparchy of Thamna, 'he went up against Lydda and Jabneh, and when both of them had been delivered into his hands, he settled there the worthy citizens from the cities that had surrendered to him earlier.'[25] Now the nature of this action is not clear; we do not know if this was done with the consent of the settlers or not.

But it seems reasonable to assume that the Romans forced this settlement upon those Jews who had surrendered. First, their cities had already been captured by the Romans; but having made peace, why did they leave their homes and go to dwell elsewhere? Secondly, it is not to be supposed that Josephus would have passed over in silence Vespasian's great 'act of generosity' to the Jews, had he intended it for their benefit. We must, therefore, conclude that this was a compulsory resettlement decreed by Vespasian. Similarly, we read *ibid.* 7, 6, that Placidus, who at that time had conquered Abel, Beth Ramah, and Beth ha-Jeshimoth in Transjordan and the other towns and villages as far as the Dead Sea, 'settled in each city those among the [Jewish] fugitives who were useful.'

Here, too, it cannot possibly be said that this man[26] allotted the

25 Wherever I cite Josephus in the text, I render the quotations from the source in Niese's edition and do not use Simḥoni's translation, which is not an exact rendition; sometimes the expansions are unnecessary and detract from the meaning of the Greek.

26 The savagery of this general, which is evident in the battles he waged against the Jews at the command of Cestius Gallus, and later of Vespasian, finds particular expression in his treatment of the people of Mount Tabor, which is described later in the text.

cities to the Jews that surrendered as a reward for their treason, for in that case Josephus would certainly not have failed to tell us.

The nature of this transportation by the Romans of the Jews who had given themselves up to them by fleeing their birthplace, is best explained by reference to another passage (*Wars* iv, 3, 2) in which Josephus relates that Vespasian left Caesarea, after the conquest of Galilee, 'and went to Jabneh and Ashdod, and set up there a garrison and took with him a great multitude of the people who had surrendered themselves to him under a covenant.' This makes it clear that the Romans exiled their Jewish 'confederates' by force and settled them in alien parts.[27]

But what was the purpose of this practice?

To begin it appears from Josephus' testimony that these 'worthy' and 'useful' settlers (who were transported in groups) were intended by Vespasian to act as a rampart in their new abodes (if they chanced to be settled in *Judea*, for others were transported to places outside the country) against any future conspiracy by the inhabitants to revolt. This would be achieved, firstly, by their very presence and, secondly, it seems, by informing to the government.[28]

However, it appears that it was also the intention of the Romans to assemble the elite and the activists of the fugitives in particular places where they could be under surveillance by the soldiery. In other words, the Romans used to exile the fugitives and those who surrendered (i.e. the influential and wealthy among them) from their cities and shut them up in special remote habitations, depriving them of freedom of movement outside their camps.

This is clearly evidenced by the following episode, which testifies that Titus, too, acted like his father during the siege of Jerusalem.

Thus we read (*Wars* vi, 2, 2–3) that High Priests and the sons of High Priests and many others of the nobility escaped from Jerusalem and went over to the Roman camp, influenced, as it were, by the words of Josephus:

> Caesar received them kindly, and knowing that it would not be pleasant for them to dwell among the Gentiles, whose customs

27 It is not ruled out in the least that Vespasian transported them into slavery. But perhaps, in the absence of any specific statement to that effect, we should make the minimal assumption, namely that he exiled them first to Caesarea and then settled them among the Gentiles 'until the war would be over'.

28 That the Romans had (Jewish) spies, who lived among the Jewish fighters and informed them of what transpired in the camps of the rebels, we learn from *Avot de-R. Nathan*, Versions I and II. See the Appendix below.

> were different [from those of the Jews], he sent them to Gophna and persuaded them to reside there for the present [and even assured them] that he would return their possessions to them once he was free of the war. These then went willingly and with complete confidence to that small township that was given to them. But since the men were not seen again, the rebels spread the report that the fugitives had been slaughtered by the Romans, their obvious intention being to deter others from escaping by spreading terror. For a while, indeed, their conspiracy succeeded as in the first instance,[29] for [the men of Jerusalem] refrained from deserting out of fear. But after Titus had ordered the men from Gophna to be brought back, so that they might go round the wall with Josephus and be seen by the people, many [again] fled to the Romans.

Josephus' presentation of the incident ostensibly gives the impression that Titus treated these distinguished refugees with magnanimity and compassion, and that all that he did was for their good and with their consent. In truth it is certain that this is what the author intended in accordance with his practice everywhere to whitewash the ruthlessness of Vespasian and Titus towards the Jews (especially the men of peace) and he endeavoured in his polished language (which was apparently in several passages a mere transcript of the 'diplomatic' version in which the events were portrayed in the *Commentarii* of these emperors) to justify the guilty.[30]

But there is no need to delve deeply into the matter in order to understand it in its true light. The clear fact that emerges from the episode is that Titus prevented the fugitives from going where they wished and even banished them from their estates (situated in Judea, which was in the hands of the Romans) and confined them against their will in Gophna. When Josephus declares that Titus, to his credit, intended merely to save them from the unpleasantness of dwelling amongst non-Jews, he implies that a major harassment was avoided. But, following our line of interpretation, we learn from his statement

29 The first occasion, when 'the Zealots' strategy' succeeded in preventing fugitives from leaving Jerusalem and going over to the camp of the enemy is that described in *Wars* v, 11, 2 — the story of the crucifixion of the fugitives, which is cited below, in the text.

30 On Josephus' use of the *Commentarii* of Vespasian and Titus in general (a fact that he attests twice in *Life*, 65) see Weber, *op. cit.*, pp. 105–109, and elsewhere.

that the refugees might have been dealt with in one of two ways: (a) they could have been incarcerated in the Roman camp as absolute prisoners; (b) they could have been sent to non-Jewish cities. But Titus acted with 'compassion' and confined them in a Jewish city. At all events it is evident that in persuading all to reside in Gophna, he deprived the fugitives of their freedom and held them under arrest. It also shows that the restraint, which prevented the captives from 'being seen' implied complete severance from the Jewish population and the prohibition of leaving their place of detention. For only on this assumption is it possible to understand the fact that the Jews (who were not Zealots and hoped to escape to the Romans) believed that these earlier fugitives were murdered by Titus.

This practice of the Romans, followed by Vespasian and afterwards by Titus, to confine those who surrendered or deserted and to concentrate them in special places is to be explained, in the first instance, by their concern that these defectors should not change front when the opportunity offered and go over to the fighters. For it appears that as the war proceeded many of the moderates among the people and those who desired peace joined the rebels, either on account of the cruelty of the Romans towards the Jews (as a whole), as we shall see further on, or because the Roman power temporarily weakened. Thus after Cestius Gallus' defeat, the majority of the opponents of the revolt completely aligned themselves with Zealots.[31] So, too, it seems that when the Roman generals began to fight among themselves upon the death of Nero, and Vespasian halted the war against Judea, the Jewish fighters grew stronger by being reinforced by many who had at first deserted the community.[32] This trepidation even finds expression in the fact that the Romans demanded (and received) hostages from the people of Sepphoris, who made peace with the Romans at the outset and kept faith with them throughout the entire war (even helping them actively). These hostages were sent to a non-Jewish city — Dor.[33] The Roman fears are easily comprehensible when it is realized that despite the mass of information that reached

31 Compare *Wars* ii, 20, 3 ff.

32 See *Wars* vi, 6, 2, where Titus charges the men of Jerusalem with the fact that after the death of Nero, when he left with his father for Egypt, they still dared to act against the Romans and even sent emissaries to Babylon to incite them to revolt against Rome. Josephus testifies *ibid.* iv, 9, 4, that at the time, Simon the son of Giora succeeded in gathering to his camp 'many of the nobility of the people'.

33 *Wars* iii, 2, 4; *Life* §§8, 25, 67, 71.

the Roman commanders from the deserters and spies among the fighters, they could never be sure of the character of the defectors. Hence they treated (handled) them with extreme caution and severity. Moreover, certain incidents wherein Jews pretended to desert to the Romans, but, when the latter wished to receive them, they rose up and slew them — as in the episode of Castor and his ten companions (*Wars* v, 7, 4) and the story of the Jewish Youth narrated *ibid.*, vii, 6, 4, and the cunning of the Zealots portrayed *ibid.*, v, 3, 3 — contributed to this attitude. In particular this can be understood in the light of Dio Cassius' statement[34] that Jewish deserters used at times to attack individual Romans and slay them (behind the lines). It also happened that they damaged the wells and thus denied the Roman army water; hence Titus decided not to accept deserters from Jerusalem any more. However, it is by no means certain that these statements are entirely true, for it may well be that they emanated originally from among the Roman commanders, with a view to justifying thereby their brutal treatment of the Jews. Nevertheless, we have no right to reject this witness, since what we know of the bravery and the stratagems of the men of Jerusalem and the inhabitants of other cities does not permit such rejection.

But this policy of the Romans is not to be explained altogether on the basis of caution only. The confinement (and imprisonment) of the deserters is largely (and primarily) to be understood in the light of the general attitude of the Romans towards the deserters and those who sought peace during the Great War.

In a number of passages Josephus tries to tell us that Vespasian and Titus dealt strictly only with the fighters, but were compassionate and well disposed towards those who did not take part in the war, or surrendered to them under 'covenant', or deserted to them.[35]

In truth, not only did the Romans (and their Syrian and Greek allies) throughout — from the commencement of the war to the conquest of Jerusalem — act towards the Jewish fighters with inconceivable cruelty, but they often ordered the massacre of hundreds of thousands of the men of peace, who never made war against them,

34 lxvi, 5.

35 Compare, for example, *Wars* vi, 6, 2, where Titus in his speech (or in the words Josephus attributes to him) boasts: 'For a long time I took pity on the enemies who fought against me and I gave my pledge to those who came over to me, and I kept faith with the deserters', etc. However, the truth of his witness (or that of his henchman, Josephus) concerning himself may be judged from the acts mentioned further on, in the text and in the notes.

and they executed the fighters who surrendered to them and to whom they had pledged their covenant. They treated the deserters similarly, whom they slew in groups — and needless to say individuals — or sold them as slaves.[36] The ruthlessness of these acts, which despite Josephus' efforts to gloss over them as far as possible, is not diminished by the fact that occasionally the Romans used to spare the lives of the fugitives, or even to set them free.[37] For it appears that they acted thus only when they might hope for some benefit to accrue to themselves by such 'benevolence'.[38]

The episode at the fall of Tarichaeae is particularly significant in this respect. This city, according to Josephus, did not desire war and wished to surrender to the Romans. But the fugitives from among the Galilean fighters (and from 'the ten cities'), who gathered there compelled it to wage war. The struggle between the citizens and the newcomers contributed to the ease with which the city was captured. When the troops entered there, 'there was great slaughter in the city, for the refugees, who had not managed to escape, were slain in battle, and the inhabitants — without fighting. For in the hope of being granted a covenant and conscious that they had never wished to fight, the latter had refrained from taking part in the battle' (iii, 10, 5).

Now the citizens' wish for peace was well known to the Romans, as we learn from the preceding paragraph, *ibid.* Furthermore, it appears that they had earlier started negotiations with the Romans,

36 On the murder of the deserters see below. As regards their being sold as slaves see *Wars*, iii, 7, 32, where he states that the Samaritans, through thirst, deserted to the Romans, who surrounded them on Mount Gerizim: 'And many of them fled to the Romans, for they preferred a life of bondage to such a death.' Thus desertion generally resulted in slavery.

37 Wherever one meets with Roman "benevolence' one also uncovers their brutality. In *Wars* v, 10, 1, Josephus states that the wealthy men of Jerusalem deserted to Titus, 'and Titus let many go free and permitted each one to choose whatever dwelling-place he wished.' It follows that others were enslaved and imprisoned. Similarly Josephus declares *ibid* vi, 4, 2, that Titus received Ananus [Ḥanan] of Emmaus and Archelaus son of Magadatus 'and let them go free'. But this testimony is suspect, since the author immediately adds, 'although he did not treat them (as well) as he did the other defectors', for what other kindness could he have extended to them, seeing that he had let them go free?

38 They performed these acts of grace primarily where they hoped to influence thereby those who were left in the camp and induce them to go over to them. Cf. *ibid.* v, 10, 1, and similar passages elsewhere (cf. *ibid.* vi, 8, 2, in regard to the Idumaeans, who planned to surrender to the Romans).

just as the men of Tiberias had done round about this time;[39] otherwise their confidence that the conquerors would not harm them is inexplicable. But the Romans refused to differentiate between fighters and peace-makers and broke their word, just as they did in other instances, too.

A shocking deception, far worse than that of Migdal Nunaiya [Magdala] was perpetrated on the Jews who surrendered to the Romans at Mount Tabor.

Thus we read (*Wars* iv, 1, 8) of Placidus, who was sent there with his horsemen by Vespasian: 'But he found it impossible to ascend (the mount), [hence] he enticed the multitude by holding out the hope of a covenant and by calling for peace. However, they too descended with a counter design. For Placidus negotiated with them courteously, whilst trying to draw them to the plain. The latter came down as though persuaded by him, but with the intention of attacking him unawares. But Placidus' strategem prevailed; for when the Jews joined battle, he pretended to flee and drew them far into the plain; then he turned his cavalry against them and slew most of them.'

The narrative taken at its face value is, it is clear, inherently false. It is far fetched to suppose that at the moment when Placidus conspired to massacre the Jews through trickery by promising peace, they also intended to deceive their deceivers. It is also hard to believe that at this time, when the whole of Galilee was already in Roman hands, except for Tabor and Giscala, which likewise made peace with the Romans after a short while, the besieged (who were not, it seems, very strong and prepared for battle) would dare to engage the enemy in the plain, where it was almost impossible to stand against the horsemen who had all the topographical advantages for charging and attacking.[40]

39 *Ibid.* iii, 9, 8.

40 As a rule the Jews refrained from fighting against the Romans outside the fortified cities, both in Galilee (cf. *Wars* iii, 6, 3; ii, 19, 1; iii, 4, 1) and in Judea (cf. *ibid.* ii, 19, 2). But the Jewish forces were particularly at a disadvantage in the plains on account of the horsemen (see *Life*, §24, how Josephus understood the advantages of cavalry in a plain; and *ibid.* §71, how the Jews feared the horsemen. In this respect the Jewish people retained 'their ancestral tradition', dating from the period of the First Temple, Judges i, 19; 1 Kings xx, 23). However, at Taricheae the Zealots attempted to fight for a while in the plain before the city. At Bet Nimrin the Jews sallied forth against the horsemen of Placidus, in a vineyard, but these were exceptional instances and ended in utter defeat. Even at the beginning of the war, when

It therefore appears that Josephus is deliberately untruthful here (i.e. he consciously records a falsehood, for primarily, it seems, the account was contained in Vespasians' *Commentarii* and was written on the basis of the report that the person concerned, Placidus, presented to him).

In truth it may be stated that the Jews descended from their stronghold unsuspectingly in order to accept the peace offer of the Romans. The latter, however, broke their oath and deliberately drew them away from their place of refuge, so that they would not be able to escape, when the calvary overtook them. Thus the Jews were slaughtered without engaging in battle at all.[41]

In the following episode we find a similar falsification aimed at excusing dastardly acts[42] perpetrated by the Romans upon the Jews, who, in all integrity, gave themselves up to them.

in their great zeal the Jews attacked Ashkelon, where the Romans were few, they were badly beaten, because 'footmen fought against cavalry' (*Wars* iii, 2, 2).

41 If the Jews wished the Romans to believe that they came down to surrender, they would certainly not have taken weapons with them. How then could they have fallen upon the Romans and attacked them?

Regarding the weakness of the men of Tabor's defence, see Simḥoni, '*He'ārôt ŭ-Bē'ûrîm*', *Toledot Milḥemet ha-Yehudim*, p. 459.

42 A not very successful fabrication designed to justify the breaking of a promise to a Jewish city that surrendered to the Romans is to be found in the story of the conquest of Tiberias. Thus we read in *Wars* iii, 9, 8, that the elders of Tiberias came to the Romans (on behalf of the city Council; cf. *Life* §68) to make a covenant with them. Vespasian accepted their proposal and sent his troops to the city, which opened its gates to them. 'And when the soldiers who came into the city found themselves pressed together, for its entrances were very narrow, Vespasian ordered the southern wall to be broken down and the entrance widened for the soldiers... and for Agrippas' sake he spared the (rest of the) wall of Tiberias and did not destroy it completely, after the king had given his pledge for the city's inhabitants.' Now this statement is inconsistent. At first the author states that it was on account of the crowding of the multitude of those who entered that Vespasian demolished the wall, and subsequently he declares that Vespasian wished to pull down the entire wall, only he 'spared' it because of Agrippa (who entreated him to do so). But it is obvious that the writer wishes to justify the fact that Vespasian breached the wall, unlawfully, since Tiberias had surrendered under covenant, and a city wall is demolished only if conquered in battle. We learn this from *Wars* iv, 2, 5, where we read that the men of Giscala appealed to Vespasian to make peace with them, but he rejected them. When he arrived at the gates of the city, he commanded his soldiers to break down a part of the wall in accordance with the conqueror's right (and *ibid.*, iv, 7, 3, we are informed that the men of Gedud in Transjordan

In *Wars* v, 11, 1–2, we read that Titus 'sent a company of horsemen and ordered them to lay ambushes in the valley [near Jerusalem] for those who went out to gather food; some [of them] were also fighters, who were not content with what they obtained by rapine [from the people of the city]. But the majority of them [were] poor people, who out of fear for their families refrained from going over to the Romans. For they did not believe [that they could] evade the rebels, if they escaped with their wives and children, nor could they [consent] to leave them behind, lest they be slain by the robbers. . . and when they were caught [by the Romans], they could not help defending themselves, and once they fought, it was obvious to them that it was too late to sue for mercy. They were flogged and subjected to all kinds of fatal tortures, and finally they were crucified in front of the wall. Indeed Titus felt compassion for them on seeing their suffering, for five hundred and sometimes even more were captured each day. But he considered it unsafe to let [men] that were taken by force to go free, and he even considered that surveillance of so many [men] would really mean that they were keeping watch over their guards. But his main reason for not preventing [their execution] was the hope that the spectacle would induce [the men of Jerusalem] to yield, since [he thereby showed them] that they too would suffer like them [the crucified captives], if they would not surrender.'

Now the author offers three explanations of the massacres perpetrated by the Romans. First, that the Jews defended themselves, and hence were rightly to be treated as fighters. Secondly, it was impossible to incarcerate such a vast multitude. Finally, Titus wished to give the men of Jerusalem 'decisive proof' of what was in store for them from his mailed fist.

But it is obvious that the first reason was a deliberate libel (just as the second was fatuous). For Josephus himself testifies that those who went outside the city wall wanted nothing better than to desert to the Romans. Why therefore did they see fit to slay these deserters who were ready to be captured by them?[43] Furthermore, the greater

surrendered their city to Vespasian and demolished their city wall with their own hands 'before ever the Romans demanded it' etc., thus indicating that they enhanced their surrender by doing something not required of them). It appears, therefore, that Vespasian broke his covenant with the people of Tiberias (and Agrippa) and sought to justify his actions by the pretext of *force majeure*.

43 Although Josephus states that they were afraid to desert to the Romans out of fear that their families would be punished, their real concern was that

part of them (indeed, all of them, it seems[44]) did not belong to the fighters, but were utterly destitute. How, then, could they fight against their embattled foes, seeing that they had no weapons?

Even if we assume that the victims acted thus in confusion (and so, too, the Romans who slew them), it is inconceivable that such incidents should recur again and again, as a daily occurrence, involving hundreds and thousands.

We must therefore conclude that these hapless people, who had never taken part in the war, left the city to save their lives and they were not at all concerned if they were captured by the Romans. It also appears that primarily they left the city only with a view to surrendering.[45] Since they were poverty-stricken (and 'valueless' as such), Titus treated them 'in accordance with the strict letter of the law', and put them to death with every conceivable atrocity.

This is proved, if further proof be necessary, by Josephus' subsequent statement that the Zealots 'fetched the relatives of the *deserters* and the other citizens who wished to make peace with the Romans in order to show them the sufferings of the fugitives, and they told them that those who were crucified were not captives of war, but had sought refuge', and thus many who contemplated going over to the Romans were deterred from doing what they had at first intended.

Clearly the facts were as the Zealots stated. For the relatives of those executed certainly knew what was in the mind of those that left the city, and if they accepted the version of the fighters and refrained from escaping out of fear that they faced death by leaving the city, they had no doubt that those who went before them were not 'war captives'.[46]

they should not be killed for leaving with the intention of deserting. But now after being taken by force they would not be suspected of this. Why then did they jeopardize themselves in vain?

44 It appears that Josephus' observation that there were also fighting men among them was intended only to justify from another angle, the murder of the fugitives, for if such were the case, it would be difficult, in 'the furore of battle' to distinguish between combatants and non-combatants.

45 This is evidenced by the fact that subsequently — at the beginning of paragraph 2 — he 'forgets' his main contention and relates that the Zealots dragged the relatives of the *deserters* (αὐτόμολοι) etc. He thus testifies, unwittingly, that they had left with the intention of surrendering to the Romans.

46 To this episode must be added Josephus' story (*Wars* v, 13, 4–5) about the fugitives who were murdered by the Syrian, Arabian, and even Roman troops, after it was discovered that some of them had swallowed golden denars when leaving the city ('in a single night the bellies of thousands of

Now the treatment accorded by the Romans to the fugitives and those who surrendered, as depicted above, suffices to lead us to the truth concerning the subject we are discussing, namely what was the criterion of the Romans in their dealings with Rabban Joḥanan and his company, who were also fugitive. However, for the better assessment of the event we must understand that the Romans' treatment of the deserters was but one of the ways that gave expression to their general policy and also to their ultimate aim throughout the war.

For their practice of massacring the people of the towns and villages who had no wish whatsoever to fight against the Romans, and of slaying entire populations that had contained some rebels, although they had left without a struggle,[47] was of the same type. Needless

men were ripped open'). Now the author avers that Titus was angered by the incident and threatened to put to death anyone who would do this again. But this testimony is refuted by the fact that subsequently, too, the soldiers continued to split open the bellies of these hapless captives; nor is there much point in the author's philosophising about 'the overpowering avarice implanted in the human heart', which is the worst of all the lusts, since it is not even deterred by the fear of death, or in his theological speculation that 'the finger of God was to be seen in the matter, for God had condemned the whole people to destruction'. The reason was very simple. The soldiers knew full well that Titus would not prevent them from murdering thousands of Jews, who had come to seek refuge and protection with 'the delight of the human race', and that even if he was 'wroth' with them, so to speak, he would never punish them in the slightest.

47 Cestius Gallus found fifty people in Lydda, after the rest of the inhabitants had gone on pilgrimage to Jerusalem, and slew them (*ibid.*, ii, 19, 1); he suddenly raided Jaffa (Joppa) and massacred eight thousand and four hundred people (including women and children), without the Jews even attempting to give battle. He likewise destroyed the inhabitants of the district of Narbatene and burnt their villages, although they had not made war against him (*ibid.*, ii, 18, 10). Placidus burnt the fields of the men of Galilee and murdered the men who ventured outside the settlements, although they 'dwelt in peace' — that is to say, they did not lift their hand against the Romans — slew and destroyed the youths and sold the old and weak into slavery (*ibid.*, iii, 4, 1), filling Galilee with blood and fire. He also slaughtered a great many of the captives (who had not taken part in the fighting, since Josephus had never led forth the men of Galilee to fight with Placidus, except once when he went out against him near the village of Cabul, but did not join battle with him — *Life* §43), men who were old and feeble, dispirited and weary of fleeing (iii, 6, 1). Vespasian killed all the young men in the city of Arabah, which was captured without a fight, including even the aged and the children (although Josephus asserts that while Vespasian ordered only the young men to be slain, the Romans, in their hatred of the Jews, did not differentiate between the various age-groups and murdered everyone; yet here, too, his

to say, they killed mercilessly all who were found in places conquered by them during the war — men, women, and children.[48] This was the course adopted by Cestius Gallus, Vespasian, and Titus (and their henchmen) without distinction.

These facts prove that the Romans did not consider their war against Judea to be directed against a given movement of rebels *within* the nation (to which the majority were opposed) in order 'to extirpate the evil from its midst' and restore the original position, as Josephus would have us infer from his account in the *Wars*.

It appears that from the outset of the revolt the Romans waged war against the Jewish people in Eretz-Israel,[49] with the purpose of

testimony is suspect, since their deeds prove just the contrary). He likewise burnt all the villages and towns in the neighbourhood and sold their inhabitants as slaves (and in each instance the Jews had not attacked him at all, for Josephus withdrew immediately, upon Vespasian's arrival, to Tiberias, see *ibid.* iii, 6, 3). When Jaffa was conquered the second time, Vespasian sent his horsemen to cut down the *villagers* and to lay the whole land waste (needless to say these Jews never thought of fighting against the Romans; *ibid.* iii, 9, 4). When he captured Geresh (or Gezer) without fighting, he slew a thousand youths and enslaved their families, burning the villages in the vicinity and killing their enfeebled inhabitants (*ibid.*, iv, 9, 1). He did the same in Idumea and in the district of Timnah and in Antipatris (*ibid.*, i, 8, 1).

48 At Jotapata the Romans carried out a total massacre, except for the women and children who were sold into slavery (*ibid.*, iii, 7, 31; iii, 7, 36). At Tiberias Vespasian ordered all the men of Taricheae (assembled there at his injunction) that 'were useless for work', being old or weak, to be slaughtered; five thousand he sent to Nero to do hard labour, and thirty thousand and four hundred men he sold as slaves. Needless to say only a minority of them had taken part in the fighting, the majority being local residents or fugitives who had fled for fear of the war and had got 'mixed up', with the rebels. Upon capturing Gamala the Romans slew all the inhabitants of the place, without distinguishing between fighters and men of peace, and murdered the infants, dashing them against the ground (*Wars*, iii, 10; iv, 2, 10). In Yafa (Japhia) in Galilee the Romans killed the old and young men, and sold the women and children into slavery. At Jerusalem Titus gave orders, as it were, to slay 'only the armed men who engaged in combat and to take the rest of the people captive', but 'the soldiers, in carrying out his instructions, added thereto also the slaughter of the old and the feeble'. They did, however, spare the young and strong, 'who found favour with them' (being useful for service or the arena), and 'out of sheer animosity' they left eleven thousand of the survivors to starve to death (*ibid.* vi, 9, 2). When the Temple was put to the torch, they murdered the aged and infants, showing no compassion (*ibid.* v, 1).

49 This fact is to be inferred not only from the atrocities mentioned in the preceding notes, but also from Caesar's proclamations at the end of the war that the *whole* of Judea was his private domain. The same emerges from

depriving them of their political autonomy, of ending the rule of the Sanhedrin,[50] and, above all, of undermining the nation physically and spiritually, so that the Palestinian Jews should no longer be able

Titus' address to the fighters of Jerusalem after the burning of the Temple and before the capture of the city: 'Ah, miserable creatures! Wherein do you put your trust now? *Your people is dead*', etc. For the beginning of the war, it appears, we have reliable testimony in the act of Agrippa's governor, who executed seventy of the nobility of the city, and also the Jews of Caesarea Philippi entirely because the Syrians in Caesarea assured him 'that the Romans would condemn Agrippa to death for the crimes of the Jews' (*Life* §11; cf. also *Wars* ii, 18, 6). It seems that these non-Jews correctly appraised the Romans' intentions in respect of the Jews *as a whole*, although their forecast was not fulfilled in regard to Agrippa, who was the faithful and humble servant of the Romans, no less than the other gentile kings, who came with Vespasian to destroy the Jews out of extreme hatred (and not merely to fulfil their duty as *socii*). However, Agrippa exonerated Varus and merely deprived him of his office, but did not punish him otherwise. According to Josephus (*Wars, ibid.*) he did so out of deference to King Sohemus, who was Varus' relative, but in actual fact, it seems, on account of the Romans, who by no means disapproved of Varus' actions.

In this context it should also be noted that the gentile writers Tacitus, Suetonius, and Dio Cassius make no mention of the Zealots (or rebels, in contradistinction to the rest of the people, who wanted peace), and speak only of Jews and the Jewish people who are at war with Rome. Apparently their approach expresses the viewpoint of the Caesars, the authors of the acts, who did not wish to differentiate 'a rebellious group' from the rest of the nation and directed their efforts against the people as a whole.

50 These, as is known, were the results of the war (see Mommsen, *Römische Geschichte*, V). There is no reason for us not to assume that the Romans had these intentions in mind from the very outbreak of the war onwards. Indeed once the news had reached the Roman camp that Mary of Transjordan had murdered her infant child and eaten it, Titus claimed, in justifying himself to God: 'I offered the Jews peace, independence and an amnesty for all the past offences.' We, however, do not place any reliance on his protestations. In all the 'good tidings' and the 'gifts' conferred by Vespasian and his son, we hear nothing of the kind. These were only designed to encourage the Jews to surrender totally, and even to foment quarrels among them (see below, note 63). If we do wish to learn anything from that wicked man's words, then it would be preferable to rely on what he said to the inhabitants of Jerusalem between the burning of the Temple and the conquest of the city: 'Throw down your arms, surrender your persons and I grant you your lives like a lenient master of the household, punishing the incorrigible and preserving the rest for myself.' Even though this statement was made in the final days of the war, it can well serve to disclose the Romans' original intentions. All they had in mind was to subdue and enslave the Jewish people and to rule the land like the δεσπόται who held the life and death of their subjects in their hands.

to rise up against them and threaten their dominion.[51] Hence they did not differentiate as a rule between extremists and moderates, between fighters and men of peace, between war captives and deserters (for even if they sometimes spared the lives of the fugitives and peacemakers, they nevertheless banished them from their estates, exiled them, and enslaved them). For this reason, too, they often deliberately failed to respond to the appeal of the men of peace to hasten to their help in the places where they were in conflict with the Zealots.[52]

51 Indeed they succeeded in carrying out their design. For according to Josephus' testimony (*Wars*, vi, 9, 3) 97,000 were captured in the course of the war, in which 1,100,000 were slain. Even if we concede that the figures are exaggerated, it must nevertheless be reckoned that about a third of the Jewish population in the country were annihilated (and the picture is but little affected if we assume that many among the fallen were from Babylonia and other countries, as Dio Cassius seems to imply, lxvi, 4).

52 After civil war had broken out in Judea, and those who desired peace asked for the help of the Romans, 'but the garrison troops in the cities did nothing to succour the oppressed, or helped them very little, because they feared the hazards to which they would be subjected, *and also on account of their hatred* for the [Jewish] people' (*Wars* iv, 3, 3). At this juncture, when the Roman army commanders desired to exploit the opportunity and go up against Jerusalem, Vespasian restrained them not only by pointing out that at that stage it was still dangerous to assault the city, but also by arguing that if the Romans refrained from attacking the Jews now, the latter would do themselves far more harm than would the Romans by their victory, and hence the Jews should be allowed 'to slay one another till they annihilate themselves'. When Vespasian finally 'took pity' on the deserters from Jerusalem and acceded to their entreaties to invest the city 'in order to redeem it' (recalling the tribulations that they had suffered at the hands of the Zealots 'because of their love for the Romans'), he ostensibly led his forces against Jerusalem as though to fulfil their request, when in fact he made them cross the Jordan. Thus he paid no heed to the supplications of 'his friends' and postponed the 'redemption' of the city, in consonance with the intention that he had originally expressed to his commanders (iv, 7, 3).

This is also to be inferred from Cestius Gallus' action, for he, too, had no respect for Rome's friends and made no distinction between the 'people' and the 'bandits'. Thus we read (*Wars* ii, 19, 5) that when he first besieged Jerusalem, 'many of the important citizens at that time went over to Ḥanan [Ananus] the son of Jonathan and invited Cestius [to the city] with a view to opening the gates to him. But the latter in his anger [against the Jews] and because of his lack of complete trust in them, ignored them and dallied until the rebels became aware of the contemplated treachery and hurled Ḥanan's men from the wall', etc. A similar incident occurred in the case of Titus, at the beginning of his siege of Jerusalem, when one of Simeon bar Giora's officers wanted to surrender the towers in his charge so that the entire city could be conquered by the Romans. 'But some of the Romans

For their primary purpose in the war was the suppression and annihilation of the people, and not the defeat of the rebels.

This objective of the Romans in the war finds vivid and clear expression in the statement — which served as a kind of maxim — made to Vespasian by his commander-advisors (and accepted by him), when they took counsel together and decided 'to make a covenant' with the multitude of Jews remaining in Tarichaeae after the capture of the city. Their aim was to entice the survivors away from there in order to slaughter them unexpectedly in the stadium of Tiberias, and they justified their action by declaring: 'Nothing is impious (when perpetrated) against the Jews'.[53] It was this policy also that encouraged the neighbours of the Jews — the Syrians and Greeks — to participate in every stage of the catastrophe, their intention, needless to say, being to exterminate every single Jew wherever they could, so that their share in the war should be maximal.[54]

despised him out of arrogance, and others did not trust him', whilst the majority delayed [in the hope] that after a little while they would [in any case] capture the city without hazard (*Wars* v, 13, 2. Note the striking similarity to the account of the Cestius episode!).

53 *Wars* iii, 10, 10.

54 The revolt, as we know, was triggered by the malice of the non-Jewish Caesareans towards the local Jews and by the brutality of Florus, who aided the enemies of the Jews (and apparently incited them to commit the criminal acts). It was they, too, that massacred more than twenty thousand of the Jews who dwelt in the city (and Florus enslaved the survivors and sent them away to do hard labour — *Wars* ii, 18, 1). The same treatment was meted out to the Jews by the Syrians (and the Greeks) in the other cities in Eretz-Israel and in Transjordan and in Syria, and when Cestius went up against Galilee, he took with him many of the non-Jews from the cities adjoining Eretz-Israel, whose 'lust for battle as well as their fierce hatred for the Jews made up for their lack of training' (in war tactics), and 'when he returned to Acre, he left the conquered part of Galilee in the hands of the Syrians, who were devastating the land (*ibid.*, ii, 19, 9). We have already noted the view of the Gentiles, the inhabitants of Caesarea Philippi (the capital of Agrippa's kingdom!), who considered themselves free to shed Jewish blood, since the Romans wished it. It was these Gentiles who welcomed Titus after the destruction of Jerusalem and crowned him with garlands and praised him for destroying the nation (Philistratus, *apud* Reinach, *Textes* etc. 177–178). I would point out here the importance of this factor — the sending of the non-Jewish neighbours by the Romans to murder and annihilate the Jews — in the history of the two men who were renowned for their deeds during the war, namely, John of Giscala and Justus of Tiberias.

The former — powerful and loyal Zealot that he was at first — according to Josephus (*Life*, §10), opposed the war against the Romans and even

Another expression — *sui generis* — of this aim is to be seen in the religious persecutory decrees (which Josephus fails to mention in his account of the war, but reveals elsewhere) that were heaped on the Jews in those days of tribulation, followed by similar prohibitions

restrained his fellow townsmen from rebelling. But the neighbours from round about... 'assembling a large army, fell upon the people of Giscala, captured the city by force, set it on fire, and reduced it to a heap of ruins'. It was then that he (John) armed his men, attacked the neighbours referred to and severely defeated them' (this episode, apparently, must be related to the narrative in *Wars* ii, 11, 9, q.v.). Thus John subsequently became a fighter against the Romans, because they sent the malevolent neighbours of the Jews to destroy them utterly; that is to say, John perceived the Romans' intent, to wit, that they wanted to annihilate the Jewish people, and consequently he was stirred to defend his people both against the emissaries and those who sent them.

The same, *mutatis mutandis*, happened to Justus. We know that he testified (in his lost work) that he was one of those who desired peace. But Josephus falsified his image by stating that he attacked 'the ten cities' in Syria and burnt their villages (*Life* §65). Now if Justus had initiated the hostilities by attacking these cities, he could certainly be considered a rebel against Rome, since undoubtedly the Romans themselves regarded him as such. Only this testimony of Josephus is open to doubt; it may be argued that the man who gave himself up to Agrippa as soon as Vespasian came to Eretz-Israel, only protected the Jews in the Greek cities who were being slaughtered by their neighbours (that Justus wished to fight only against the neighbouring peoples is also the view of M. Stein in the introduction to the translation of *Life*, p. 12). Now ostensibly Josephus, *Wars* ii, 18, 1, implies that it was the Jews who attacked the men of those cities first. But this account is refuted by his subsequent statement (*ibid.*, ii, 18, 5) that the inhabitants of Hippos and Gadara massacred the Jews in their midst and put the survivors in custody, but the Gerasons took pity on their Jewish neighbours and spared their lives. But these were the very cities that had at the outset been 'burnt and destroyed' by the Jews who attacked them, as related earlier! Simḥoni ('*He'arot u-Be'urim*', pp. 437–438) already noted the difficulty. Furthermore, from the presentation of the events in *Life* §6 it is evident that the Gentile inhabitants of the 'cities on the Syrian border' had initiated the war. This also emerges from Eleazar's speech at Masada before his death (see *Wars*, vii, 8, 7).

Hence it must be concluded that Justus wished only to protect his fellow Jews who were attacked by their neighbours (that these Jews did not belong to the fighters is clear from Eleazar's statement, *ibid.*, that they were more hostile to the Zealots than to the Romans themselves). But John correctly inferred that the Syrians were simply Rome's shock troops and hence he felt compelled to fight against them, too, while Justus kept to his original principle and made peace with Vespasian.

imposed by the Romans even after the Destruction, immediately following the conclusion of the war.[55]

It appears that these policies of the Romans and the goal that they had in mind were responsible for the fact that the ranks of the rebels attracted many of the dignitaries and the nobility, of both the

55 In *Wars* ii, 8, 10, Josephus speaks of the Essene sect (after mentioning the Sadducees and Pharisees) and praised them as follows: 'The war with the Romans revealed their greatness of soul, which did not flinch before anything. When their bodies were racked by the wheel and their limbs distended, when they were burned alive or their bones were crushed and every instrument of torment was used on them, and their torturers demanded of them to curse the name of their lawgiver or to defile their bodies with that which was forbidden to them, they stood the ordeal and did none of these things. Nor did they plead with their torturers nor shed tears before them, but bore their sufferings with shining eyes and laughed to scorn the men who applied the instruments of torment to them, joyfully surrendering their souls to God, in the knowledge that they would be restored to them.' Needless to say it was not to the Essenes alone that this cup of bitterness was passed. For they were in no way different from others (moreover, the Essenes were probably, in most instances at least, not members of the Zealots, although we find John the Essene among the commanders who fought against the Romans at the beginning of the war; we simply encounter here the brutalities that characterized the Romans' treatment of wholly innocent Jews in many places), only these were *outstanding* in their power of endurance and the fortitude with which they suffered, and for this reason were specially mentioned by the author. It seems to me that this brief description suffices to enable us to understand the shocking atrocities perpetrated by the Romans on faithful Jews.

The same mistreatment by Vespasian (this should apparently be corrected to Titus, see Weber, *op. cit.*, p. 278) of the nation's sanctities is attested by Malalas, who states that he demolished the Synagogue at Daphne of Antioch and in its stead he built a theatre in which he erected a marble statue, inscribing on the theatre 'From the spoil of the Jews'.

Similarly the author relates that at that time the Romans set up in place of the synagogue at Caesarea, which they destroyed, an ᾠδεῖον (which, like other institutions of this kind, was also undoubtedly dedicated to an idol); see Weber, *ibid.*, pp. 277–278.

Likewise the two drachmas, which Vespasian imposed on every Jew after the Destruction as a gift to the Temple of Jupiter in Rome in lieu of the half-shekel that they originally contributed to the temple, were intended to force Jews to commit *sacrilege* by donating to idolatry (at all events the *form* of this tax was directed to this end, although Caesar kept the money for himself). The Tannaitic Halakha, which makes gifts to idols tantamount to idolatry, is an ancient law and was in force since early times, as we learn from *II Maccabees* iv: 18–20, where it is stated that when 'the vile Jason' sent men from Jerusalem with three hundred drachmas for a sacrifice to

priests and the people, and even members of the House of Herod,[56] who essentially had no wish forcibly to oppose the rule of Rome as such and were content with the limited independence that they enjoyed before the outbreak of the war. For when they saw that the Romans sought to uproot what freedom still remained to the nation and to destroy the people itself physically, especially through the malevolent neighbours that they sent against them, they decided to join the rebels and resolved to defend the soul and body of the people.[57]

In the light of the facts elucidated above, (1) that it was the Roman practice to exile the fugitives and settle them in internment camps, either in Eretz-Israel or in 'foreign parts', and (2) that the Romans intended to suppress the nation in every possible way, we must conclude that Rabban Joḥanan b. Zakkai and his company went to Jabneh not because they particularly desired this place, but because they were sent there against their will, like many other illustrious fugitives, since Jabneh served as one of the places of exile, where the peacemakers among the people were held in custody.[58] Rabban

Hercules which was offered up at the time of the games and celebrations at Tyre, but 'the very bearers judged that the money ought not to be spent on a sacrifice, because that was not fitting, but devoted to some other purpose.' Thus we see that even the servants of that wicked man were deterred from contributing money to idolatrous purposes.

I intend to revert to the main theme, the acts of sacrilege committed by the Romans until the end of the war, in an essay that I mention in note 57.

56 Antipas, who was of royal lineage (*Wars* ii, 17, 4; iv, 3, 4) remained in Jerusalem at the outbreak of the war and collaborated with the fighters, even acting as finance minister of the state. But when the Zealots overthrew the government of the Sanhedrin and established their terrorist rule, they murdered him in prison.

57 I intend to discuss further the attitude of the 'moderates' towards the Romans, on the one hand, and to the Zealots on the other, and to explain in particular the factors that led to the civil war and the abolition of the regime of the Sanhedrin in 68 C.E., in a special essay in which I shall deal more fully with the methods and aims of the Romans in this war.

58 We have already noted several cities that served as places of internment for those who surrendered; these include — apart from Jabneh — Gophnah, Lydda, Ashdod, and other cities in Transjordan. And just as Jabneh became, at first under compulsion and ultimately with the approval of the Sages, a Jewish centre through the initial settlers who were transported there against their will, so it came about that at a later period many priestly families remained at Gophnah (descendants of the priests interred by Titus), as we learn from the Talmud (Berakhot 44a). The fact that Lydda, too, served

Joḥanan's main request to Vespasian that he should be allowed 'to study Torah [at Jabneh] and make fringes and perform there all the other precepts' simply means that their captors should not make the conditions of their confinement unduly stringent, as they were, apparently, wont to do with others, and that they should grant them a certain measure of freedom of action, and not treat them as absolute prisoners. For Rabban Joḥanan could not hope to receive at that time any benefit for the general public; the only concession he could obtain from the Romans was to save some lives — his own life and the lives of his disciples and friends and relatives, the very same measure of grace that Titus showed Josephus when Jerusalem was destroyed.[59] Indeed the tradition in *Midrash Lamentations* knows nothing of Vespasian's 'gift' of Jabneh to Rabban Joḥanan nor of the permission he granted him to study Torah, etc. On the other hand it attests that the emperor allowed him to save his relatives and friends from death.

However, after the Destruction, when the war came to an end and the attitude of father and son grew more lenient towards the Jewish people, and the wounds of the nation began to heal with time and the vigour of its life was restored and renewed, Jabneh, which had served as a focus of the Sages' activities — initially against their will by Roman decree and ultimately by their own desire through the scholars who continued to flock to the academy of Rabban Joḥanan b. Zakkai — became a national centre. Under Rabban Joḥanan it was still on a small scale, but under Rabban Gamaliel it assumed large dimensions and later generations proceeded to attribute the origin of the events to the pre-Destruction period. Thus

as a centre of Torah learning in the period following the Destruction (it is doubtful whether this took place immediately after the fall of the State) is possibly to be explained in the same way.

59 Cf. *Life* §75. It appears to me that although Josephus belonged to the category of 'modern' political writers (in his day), whose entire Torah-knowledge and scholarship was used by them merely as 'a spade to dig with and a crown with which to magnify themselves', and he was prepared to forgo that which was sacred and precious to him because of his love of life, of wealth and of power and glory, nevertheless he would certainly not have refrained from asking the Caesars for some favour for the Jewish people — be it only for the sake of his honour, that he might magnify himself in the eyes of his compatriots and save himself from the disgrace of treason that clung to him — if there had existed the slightest hope that his request would be fulfilled. This is symptomatic of the attitude adopted by the Romans towards the Jews at that time!

'the end-result' of the process, which originally unfolded against the will of its authors, was deemed to have its roots in 'the original design'.

Appendix
The Sources of the Story of Rabban Joḥanan b. Zakkai

The Talmudic tradition concerning the episode of Rabban Joḥanan b. Zakkai and Vespasian is found (in its entirety) in five books, namely: (1) *Avot de-R. Nathan*, Version I, iv (Schechter, pp. 22–24); (2) *Avot de-R. Nathan*, Version II (Schechter, vi, p. 19); (3) *Midrash Lamentations* (pericope i, 31); (4) Babylonian Talmud (*Giṭṭin* 56a–b); (5) *Midrash Proverbs*, xv (Buber 79–80). But it appears that the Haggada in *Midrash Proverbs* was taken verbatim from *Avot de-R. Nathan*, Version II.[60] Hence, when we consider the differences between the divergent traditions regarding this episode, we have to speak of only four sources.

Although the primary theme of these sources is the episode of Rabban Joḥanan b. Zakkai, yet they sometimes include certain elements that were not, it seems, originally mentioned in the Academy in relation to this incident. For example, the conquest of Jerusalem is combined in the Midrash with this story as a single narrative, but from the silence on the subject of the parallel accounts it must apparently be inferred that this subject formed a separate narrative. Similarly the burning of the stores in *Avot de-R. Nathan* constitutes a chapter on its own, without any connection with the tradition regarding Rabban Joḥanan, which in the other accounts is completely integrated with his departure from Jerusalem.[61]

Nevertheless, it is desirable to collate all these references, for we learn from the views of the Sages concerning the factors that induced the early scholars to offer their surrender and caused Rabban Joḥanan b. Zakkai and his company to leave the city, as well as the role that he played in the Roman camp.

For examining the sources we not only acquaint ourselves with

60 This accords with the view of S. Buber in his edition of *Midrash Proverbs* xv, note 9.

61 The passage concerning the Jerusalem senators and the burning of the stores, as well as the story of Rabban Joḥanan b. Zakkai and Ben Baṭiaḥ found in *Midrash Lamentations*, likewise occurs in *Midrash Ecclesiastes* on the verse 'Wisdom is good with an inheritance' (Eccl., vii, 11).

the many deviations in the variant traditions, but also with the historical background of the incidents that these traditions portrayed in different shades, whilst preserving, amid all the divergences, the basic truth and spirit of the events.[62]

(1) *Avot de-R. Nathan, Version I*

When Vespasian came to destroy Jerusalem he said to them [the people of Jerusalem]: 'O fools, why do you wish to destroy this city and to burn your Temple? For what did I ask of you? Merely that you send me one bow or one arrow and I shall depart from you.'[63] They replied: 'Just as we went forth (to battle) against the

62 I do not deal with the emendation or elucidation of the texts, except when necessary to the main subject under discussion.

63 Dio Cassius also relates (66, 4) that, when Titus was sent by his father to besiege Jerusalem, he first attempted to use suasion, and only after they had rejected his overtures did he commence hostilities. On the other hand, Josephus tells us that when Vespasian came to Galilee, he delayed the start of the war in order to frighten the Galileans by the spectacle of his vast army, so that they might have second thoughts (μετάνοια) before the commencement of the fighting (Titus, himself, in the speech attributed to him by Josephus, declares that Vespasian deliberately went up first against Galilee and not against Judea and Jerusalem, in order to give the Zealots time to mend their ways, and that he acted thus only out of his 'love for humanity' — *Wars* vi, 6, 2). Similarly Josephus attests (*ibid.*, v, 9, 16) that Titus halted his siege of Jerusalem for a short time, so as to give the rebels time to reconsider the position in case they would agree to surrender (but he immediately adds that the rebels did not submit, because they realized 'that they would die a vile death, if they surrendered to the Romans, and considered it far better to die in battle'. That their fears were justified is proved by the tradition referred to by S. Severus and cited by Reinach, *op. cit.*, p. 324: *Iudaei obsidione clausi qiua nulla neque pacis neque deditionis copia dabatur* etc. This shows the extent of Roman φιλαναθρωπία (love of humanity), even when they wished, as it were, to persuade the Jews 'to mend their ways' and thus save their lives!). Weber is of the opinion (*op. cit.*, p. 130, note 1) that Vespasian's waiting tactic implies that he issued a proclamation to the Galileans to change their conduct. But his arguments in support of this conjecture — 'ohne ein solches Manifest is das rücksichtlose Verfahren nicht ganz verständlich' — are not convincing, since the cruelty of the Romans in this war requires no 'explanations'.

But, at all events, even if the Romans made proposals and issued manifestoes to the people, these must have contained only a demand for surrender and dire threats in the case of refusal, which is essentially Weber's view, *ibid.* So, too, we must understand the messages sent by Vespasian and Titus to the Jews, according to our own tradition and according to Dio Cassius.

first two (generals), who preceded you, and slew them,[64] even so we shall go forth against you and slay you.' When Rabban Joḥanan b. Zakkai heard this, he sent for the leaders of Jerusalem and said to them: 'My sons, why do you destroy this city and why do you wish to burn the Temple? What, after all, does he demand of you? He only asks you for one bow or one arrow and he will depart from you.' They answered him: 'Just as we went forth (to battle) against the two (generals), who preceded him, and slew them, so we shall go forth against him and slay him. Now Vespasian had men stationed beside the walls (inside) Jerusalem and whatever they heard they would write down on an arrow and shoot over the wall, and thus reported that Rabban Joḥanan b. Zakkai was a friend of Caesar. After Rabban Joḥanan b. Zakkai had spoken to the leaders of Jerusalem one day and two and three, and they would not accede to his request, he sent for his disciples R. Eliezer and R. Joshua, saying to them: 'My sons, arise and bring me forth from here; make me a coffin and I shall sleep in it'. R. Eliezer held his head and R. Joshua held his feet and they carried him till sunset, until they reached the gates of Jerusalem. When the gatekeepers asked: 'Who is this?' They replied: 'This is a corpse. Do you not know that a corpse may not be left overnight in Jerusalem?' Thereupon they [the gatekeepers] said: 'If this is a corpse, then carry it out.' So they brought him forth and carried him (till sunset), until they came to Vespasian. They then opened the coffin and he [Rabban Joḥanan] stood before him [Vespasian]. The latter asked: 'Are you Rabban Joḥanan b. Zakkai? Tell me what I should give you.' He replied: 'I ask of you only Jabneh, so that I may go and teach my disciples there and institute prayers there and perform there all the precepts.' He [Vespasian] answered: 'Go and do all that you desire!' He (Rabban Joḥanan) then said to him: 'Would you allow me to say something to you?' Vespasian replied: 'Speak!' He [Rabban Joḥanan] then said: 'You are about to become emperor. [Said Vespasian] to him: 'How do you know?' He answered: 'We have a tradition that the Temple will not be delivered into the hands of a commoner but only to a king, for Scripture declares: "He will cut down the thickets of the forest

64 'The first two' were apparently Cestius Gallus, preceded by Metilius with his troops (*Wars*, ii, 17, 10), in agreement with Graetz as against the view of Ewald, *Geschichte des Volkes Israel*, who explains the reference to be to Gallus and Vespasian, who also retreated from Jerusalem, for the men of Jerusalem made no attempt to go forth to fight against him; see also the view of Derenbourg, *op. cit.*, 152.

with an axe and Lebanon shall fall by a majestic one".' It is related that within a day or two or three a despatch [*aliter*: two envoys] arrived from his city to inform him that Caesar had died and that he had been elected emperor. They brought him a battering ram [קשת זירים, literally 'a bow of branches'] which he directed [ותיפ"א][65] against the wall of Jerusalem. They then brought him logs of cedar, which he inserted into the battering ram and smote the wall therewith until he breached it. (Thereafter) they brought him a pig's head, which he put into the battering ram and hurled it towards the sacrificial limbs on the altar. At that moment Jerusalem was taken.

Ibid. Chapter VI [*pp. 32–33*]

Why was he called Kalba Savuʿa? Because whoever entered his house hungry as a dog (*kelev*) used to leave sated (*saveʿa*). When Vespasian Caesar came to destroy Jerusalem, the Zealots wished to burn all this wealth. Said Kalba Savuʿa to them: 'Why do you destroy this city and why do you wish to burn all this wealth? Wait till I enter and see what I have in the house.' He went in and found that he had sufficient food to provide a meal for every one in Jerusalem for twenty-two years. He immediately gave orders and they heaped up stacks, selected, sifted, kneaded and baked and prepared [food] for twenty-two years. But they paid no heed to him. What did the leaders of Jerusalem do? They brought the loaves [reading *ha-ʿiggulim* for *ha-ʿagalim* as proposed by Jastrow *s.v.*] and sawed them through and plastered them with mud. Furthermore, the leaders of Jerusalem seethed the straw and ate it. Now every Israelite resident near the wall would say: 'If I were given five dates, I should go down and remove five heads.' He was given five dates and he went down and removed five heads of Vespasian's men. Vespasian inspected their excrement and saw that it contained no kind of cereal. Thereupon he observed to his soldiers: 'If these who subsist on straw only can slay so many of them, how many more of you would they slay if they ate and drank like you!'

(2) *Avot de-R. Nathan, Version II*

When Vespasian came and invested Jerusalem, he encamped near the wall of Jerusalem and said to the leaders of Jerusalem: 'Deliver to me [according to Schechter's emendation; the extant text means

65 The meaning of this word is not clear to me; see Schechter, *op. cit.*, p. 23, note 71.

literally 'break from me'] one bow and one arrow and I shall depart from you in peace.' He spoke to them thus once and twice, but they did not accede to his request. Thereupon Rabban Joḥanan b. Zakkai said to them: 'You will cause this city to be destroyed and this Temple to be burnt.' They answered him: 'Just as we went forth (to battle) against the first-commanders and slew them, so we shall go forth against (these and slay them [this one and slay him]. Whatever Rabban Joḥanan b. Zakkai said to them) they recorded in documents, which they tied to arrows and shot over the wall, (saying) Rabban Joḥanan b. Zakkai is the emperor's friend. When Rabban Joḥanan b. Zakkai saw that they did not wish to hearken to him, he said to his disciples: 'Colleagues, arise and bring me forth from here.' So they placed him in a wooden coffin and R. Eliezer took his head and R. Joshua [and R. Judah] his feet. They bore him thus until they reached the entrance of the city. When they came to the entrance of the city, they said to them (the gatekeepers): 'Arise and open up for us that we may go out and bury him.' They (the gatekeepers) answered (them): 'We shall not open (the gates) before we have run him through first with the sword.' They replied: 'You will bring evil repute upon your city. Tomorrow it will be said that they even stabbed Rabban Joḥanan b. Zakkai.' In the end they (the gatekeepers) arose and opened for them. When Rabban Joḥanan b. Zakkai left the entrance of Jerusalem, he went to greet Vespasian as one hails a sovereign, (addressing him: '*Vive domine imperator*!' Thereupon he asked him: 'Are you Ben Zakkai?' He answered 'I am'). Said he (Vespasian) to him: 'You have grieved me.' He replied: 'Fear not; we have a written tradition that this Temple will be destroyed only by a king as it is said: "And Lebanon shall fall by a mighty one."' He then handed him over to two officers. Three days later despatches reached from Rome, announcing that 'Emperor (Nero) is dead and the Romans have proclaimed you emperor'. Thereupon he sent for Rabban Joḥanan and said to him 'Make a request'. He replied: 'I ask of you Jabneh that I may study Torah there and make fringes there and observe there all the other commandments.' He answered: 'You may have it as a gift.'

Ibid. Chapter VII

When Vespasian came and invested Jerusalem, he encamped over against the eastern part of Jerusalem. Thereupon all the terrorists arose and burnt all the stores of victuals that were in Jerusalem, their intention being to leave no provisions. And the men of Jerusalem boiled straw and drank its water and went forth to do battle with them (the Romans), slaying [numbers] of them. When Vespasian observed that the excrement of the men of Jerusalem was void of any kind of cereals, he called all his soldiers and said to them: 'Come and see, famished and parched men go forth to battle you and kill [numbers] of you. If they ate and drank, how many more would they slay!' They brought him logs of wood and he made a kind of catapult. He made two big missiles, which they hurled at the wall until it was breached. He (also) made a bow of branches in which he placed a pig's head. They split it like dog-stitching and (the pieces) came down upon the sacrificial limbs lying on the altars and defiled it. They destroyed the whole of Jerusalem until they reached the Temple. When they reached the Sanctuary they said to one another 'Who shall enter first?'[66] Now there was present there a wicked man Titus, the son of Vespasian's wife, who had the impudence to enter first, thus fulfilling the verse 'A wicked man puts on a bold face' (Proverbs xxi 29). Furthermore, he took his sword and slashed the Veil, etc.[67]

(3) *Lamentations Rabbati*

Vespasian invested Jerusalem three and a half years. He had with him four *duces*: The *dux* of Arabia, the *dux* of Africa,[68] the *dux* of Alexandria, and the *dux* of Palestine. With regard to the *dux* of Arabia, two Amoraim express divergent views: one says his name was Qillus ('Praise') and the other said it was Pangar ('Encomiast').

66 This episode, which indicates that the Romans were afraid to enter the Temple in order to burn it, on account of its sanctity, also occurs, with variations of form, in Dio Cassius, who relates that the soldiers were unwilling to go into the Temple because of δεισιδαιμονία (superstition), and refrained from doing so until Titus forced them.

67 Here should be added the following passage found in this work (Schechter, p. 31): 'It was said of Ben Kalba Savu'a that he had three years' food for every citizen of Jerusalem, and when the *Sicarii* burnt the stores of provisions in Jerusalem, they measured all that he possessed and found three years' food for every person in Jerusalem.

68 The current editions read אפריקה '*Afriqa*', but the correct version is apparently that of S. Buber's text of *Lamentations Rabbati*. דוכס דאפניקא *Duks de-'Afniqa*', which refers to Phoenicia, according to the editor's conjecture, *ibid.*, p. 65, note 246. I would observe here that all the passages found in this pericope in that edition, but not in the ordinary recension, are taken (sometimes with variants) from the Talmud, and do not belong to the text proper of the Midrash.

There were at the time four senators in Jerusalem — Ben Ṣiṣit, Ben Gurion, Ben Naqdimon and Ben Kalba Savuʿa — and each one was able to supply the city's food provisions for ten years. Ben Baṭiaḥ, the son of Rabban Joḥanan b. Zakkai's sister, who was in charge of the stores, was there, and he burnt all the stores. When Rabban Joḥanan b. Zakkai heard of this, he cried 'Woe!' Informers went and told Ben Baṭiaḥ 'Your uncle said 'Woe!' He thereupon sent for him, and said to him 'Why did you say "Woe!"?' He replied, 'I did not say "Woe!" [וי *way*], but "Ah!" [װה *wa*, an expression of joy]'. He then said to him 'you said "Wa!"; why did you say "Wa!"?' He answered 'Because you burnt all the stores, and I said to myself that as long as the stores last they will refrain from risking their person in battle. Between *way* and *wa*, Joḥanan b. Zakkai succeeded in escaping, and he applied to himself the verse 'And the advantage of knowledge is, that wisdom preserves the life of him who has it.' Three days later Rabban Joḥanan b. Zakkai went for a stroll in the street and saw people boiling straw and drinking its water. Said he 'Can people who boil straw and drink its water stand against the troops of Vespasian?' He said 'The main thing is that I should get out of here.' Accordingly he sent word to Ben Baṭiaḥ 'Take me out of here!' He replied 'We have decided among ourselves that none but a corpse may leave this place.' Said he: 'Take me out as a corpse!' So R. Eliezer carried his head and R. Joshua his feet and Ben Baṭiaḥ walked in front. When they reached [the gateway], they [the guards] wished to stab him. Said Ben Baṭiaḥ to them 'So you wish it to be said that their teacher died and they stabbed him!' When he spoke to them thus, they left him alone. Upon leaving the gates, they carried him and put him in a cemetery and returned to the city. Rabban Joḥanan b. Zakkai then went forth and walked among Vespasian's soldiers. He asked them 'Where is the emperor?' So they went and told Vespasian 'A certain Jew wishes to salute you.' He answered 'Let him come! When he (Rabban Joḥanan) arrived he said to him 'Vive, domine imperator!' He replied 'You hail me as an emperor, but I am not an emperor, and when the emperor hears of this he will slay me.' (Rabban Joḥanan) replied 'If you are not emperor (now), you will be so eventually. For this Temple will be destroyed only by a king, for it is said 'And Lebanon shall fall by a mighty one'. They then took him and put him inside seven cells and asked what the time was by night and he told them, and what the time was by day and he told them. How did Rabban Joḥanan b. Zakkai know? From his study. Three days later Vespasian went to bathe in

Gafnah [= Gophnah].[69] When he had bathed and put on one of his shoes, a message came announcing that Nero was dead and that he had been proclaimed emperor by the Romans. He wished to put on his other shoe, but it would not go on. So he sent for Rabban Joḥanan b. Zakkai and said to him: 'Can you tell me why all the time I have put on both shoes and they went on, but now one goes on and one does not?' He answered him 'You have received good tidings, for it is written "A good report maketh the bones fat".' Said Vespasian to him 'What am I to do that it should go on?' He replied 'Let them cause a man that you dislike or has sinned against you to pass before you and your flesh will shrink, for it is written "But a broken spirit drieth the bones".' They then began to speak in parables before him: 'If a serpent nested inside a jar, what is to be done with it?' He replied 'A snake-charmer should be brought and the serpent should be charmed and the jar left intact.' Pangar said 'The serpent should be killed and the jar broken.' 'If a snake nested in a chest, what should be done?' Rabban Joḥanan answered 'A snake charmer should be brought and the serpent charmed and the chest left intact. Pangar said 'The serpent should be killed and the chest burnt.' Said Rabban Joḥanan b. Zakkai to Pangar 'All neighbours [it seems] that are bent on evil do it to their neighbours. Not only do you not speak in our favour, but you argue to our detriment.' He replied 'It is your benefit that I seek. For as long as this Temple stands, the kingdoms will attack you. If, however, the Temple be destroyed, the kingdom will cease to attack you.' Rabbi Joḥanan b. Zakkai replied 'The heart knows whether it is done for עקל *ʿēqel* [a legitimate purpose] or for עקלקלות *ʿaqalqallot* ['perverseness'].'

Vespasian said to Rabban Joḥanan b. Zakkai 'Make a request and I shall grant it.' He said 'I request that you raise the siege of the city and depart.' He replied 'Did the Romans make me emperor so that I should raise the siege of the city? Make (another) request and I shall grant it.' He then said 'I ask you to relax your watch on the western gate, which leads to Lydda, so that whoever leaves

69 This proves that Rabban Joḥanan b. Zakkai was a captive at Gophnah. When we bear in mind that, according to the tradition of this Midrash, Rabban Joḥanan made no mention of Jabneh whatsoever in his conversation with Vespasian, we must conclude that, according to this tradition, Rabban Joḥanan b. Zakkai was held in detention at Gophnah, where the High Priests and the notables of the people were also imprisoned by Titus after their submission to him. Thus we obtain an essentially different picture from that depicted by the Talmudic Haggadah.

before the fourth hour[70] may be saved.' When he had conquered it (Jerusalem), Vespasian said to him 'If you have a friend or relative send for him before the troops enter (the city). So he despatched R. Eliezer and R. Joshua to fetch R. Zadok. They went and found him at the gate of the city. When he arrived, Rabban Joḥanan stood up before him. Said Vespasian to him 'You rise before this shrivelled old man!' He answered 'By your life, if there were (one other) like him and you had twice the number of soldiers, you would not have been able to conquer (the city).' Vespasian asked him 'Wherein lies his greatness?' He replied 'He eats one fig (or, carob) and teaches on the strength of it a hundred sessions.' He then asked him 'Why is he so emaciated?' He replied 'As a result of the many fasts he kept.' He sent for physicians and they fed him a little at a time...

When Vespasian captured Jerusalem he assigned (the demolition of) the four ramparts to the four *duces* and the western gate fell to Pangar. But it was decreed by Heaven that it should never be destroyed. Why? Because the Divine Presence dwells in the west. The others destroyed theirs; he did not destroy his. Vespasian sent for him and asked him 'Why did you not destroy your sector?' He replied 'By your life, I acted for the glory of the empire. For had I demolished (my rampart), no one would have known what you destroyed. Now, however, people will see and say "Behold the power of Vespasian; see what he destroyed"!' He replied 'By your life, you have spoken well. But since you have disobeyed my orders, go up to the top of the roof and throw yourself down. If you live, you live; if you die, you die.' He ascended and threw himself down and died. Thus the curse of Rabban Joḥanan b. Zakkai overtook him.

(4) *Giṭṭin 56a–b*

He then sent Vespasian Caesar against them, and he came and besieged it (Jerusalem) for three years. There were three rich men in it — Naqdimon b. Gurion, Ben Kalba Savuʿa, and Ben Ṣiṣit Ha-Keset... One said to them (the people of Jerusalem) 'I shall provide them with wheat and barley'; and another said '(I shall provide them) with wine and salt and oil'; and the third said '(I shall provide them) with wood'... They had enough to keep (the population) for twenty-one years.[71]

70 In Buber's edition — 'before the *third* hour'.

71 Tradition has preserved four divergent numbers in regard to the period that 'the great men of Jerusalem' were prepared to provide the besieged city with food, to wit, twenty-two years (*ARN* Version I), twenty-one years (Talmud),

There were also in it (the city) the *Biryonim* ['terrorists'; originally, perhaps, 'palace-guards']. The Rabbis said to them 'Let us go forth and make peace with them (the Romans).' But they would not let them; (instead) they demanded 'Let us go forth and engage them in battle.' The Rabbis answered 'Your plan will not succeed.' They (the *Biryonim*) then arose and burnt the stores of wheat and barley and famine reigned. Martha, the daughter of Boethius...

Abba Siqra, the head of the *Biryonim* of Jerusalem, was the son of R. Joḥanan b. Zakkai's sister. (Rabban Joḥanan) sent him a message 'Come to me secretly.' When he arrived, he said to him 'How long will you go on acting thus and starve the people to death?' He replied 'What can I do? If I say a word to them (the *Biryonim*), they will slay me.' Said (Rabban Joḥanan) to him 'Find a way for me to leave (the city); perhaps I may save a little.' He replied 'Feign illness and let all the people come and enquire about you. Fetch also some putrid matter and put it by you, so that it will be said that you are dead. Then let your disciples come in to attend to you, but no one else, so that they do not notice that you are light, for it is known that a living person is lighter than a corpse.' He did so... R. Eliezer came in to hold him at one end and R. Joshua at the other. When they reached the gateway, they (the guards) wished to stab him. He (R. Eliezer) said to them 'It will be said that they stabbed their teacher.' So they wished to give him a push. He said to them 'It will be said that they pushed their teacher.' So they opened the gate for him and he (Rabban Joḥanan) went out. When he reached his destination, he said 'Peace unto you, O Emperor, peace unto you, O emperor!' He (Vespasian) replied 'You deserve death on two counts. For one thing, I am not an emperor, yet you call me emperor. Secondly, if I am emperor, why did you not come to me before now?' He replied 'As for your saying "I am not an emperor", in truth you are an emperor, otherwise Jerusalem would not be delivered into your hand, for it is written "And Lebanon shall fall by a mighty one", and "mighty one" means none other than a king, for it is written "And their mighty one shall be of themselves" etc.; and Lebanon refers to the Temple, for it is written "This goodly mountain and Lebanon". As for your query "If I am

ten years (*Midrash Lamentations*), three years (*ARN* Version II). They are all standard numbers: twenty-one years consists of three septennia; twenty-two corresponds to the twenty-two letters of the Hebrew alphabet (cf. for example, *The Book of Jubilees*, ch. ii, 15: two and twenty kinds were created in the six days of creation).

an emperor, why did you not come to me before now?", the *Biryonim* among us did not permit me.' Said (Vespasian) to him 'If a serpent was wound round a jar of honey, would they not break the jar on account of the serpent?'[72] Rabban Joḥanan remained silent. Rav Joseph, and some say R. Akiba, applied to him the verse '(God) turneth wise men backward and maketh their knowledge foolish.' He should have answered 'We take a pair of tongs and remove the serpent and kill it, but we leave the jar intact.' In the meantime a courier arrived for him (Vespasian) from Rome and said to him 'Arise! for Caesar is dead and the notables of Rome have decided to appoint you head (of the State).' (Vespasian) had put on one shoe and wished to put on the other, but it would not go on. He then wished to pull off the first, but it would not come off. So he said 'What is the meaning of this?' Said (Rabban Joḥanan) to him 'Don't worry, "A good report maketh the bones fat".' — 'What is the remedy?' — 'Let a man who displeases you pass before you, as it is written "But a broken spirit drieth the bones". Said (Vespasian) to him 'Since you are so wise, why did you not come to me before now?' (Rabban Joḥanan) replied 'Have I not told you?' Said (Vespasian) to him 'I shall depart, but I shall send someone else. However, ask me to grant you something. Said (Rabban Joḥanan) 'Grant me Jabneh and its Sages and the dynasty of Rabban Gamaliel, and physicians to heal R. Zadok.' Rav Joseph, and some say R. Akiba, applied to him the verse '(God) turneth the wise men backward and maketh their knowledge 'foolish'. He should have asked him to let them off this once. But Rabban Joḥanan considered that he might not concede so much and there would not even be a small measure of relief.[73] How did the physicians heal R. Zadok? The first day

72 In the Talmud the parable of the jar round which the serpent was wound is presented as though Vespasian was reproaching Rabban Joḥanan for the fact that the peace-loving men of Jerusalem did not rise up against the Zealots, even though the war doomed the city to annihilation. But it seems that originally it had the same meaning as in *Midrash Lamentations*, namely that they (Vespasian and Rabban Joḥanan) were debating the destruction of the city by the Romans. But in the Gemara the connection between this element of the tradition and its original source was severed, and hence it was displaced and its sense distorted.

73 According to the Talmudic tradition Rabban Joḥanan left the city in the hope that 'perhaps I may save a little'. But in all the other sources there is no trace of the fact that Rabban Joḥanan intended, by his departure, to save the population.

they gave him to drink bran water; the next day (they gave him) coarse flour water; the third day, flour water, until little by little his bowels expanded.

(Vespasian) departed and sent Titus, who said 'Where is their God, the Rock in whom they trusted?' This is the Titus that blasphemed and abused Heaven.

On relating these sources one is struck, first of all, by the discrepancies between them in respect of their compass and the structure of their component parts. Whilst the tradition in *Avot de-R. Nathan*, Version I, concludes with Rabban Joḥanan b. Zakkai's request for Jabneh etc., that of the Midrash does not add to the main acts of Rabban Joḥanan b. Zakkai even his participation in the deliberations of the *duces* that preceded the conquest of the city. On the other hand, we find in the Talmud and *Avot de-R. Nathan*, Version II, the narrative concerning Titus' burning of the Temple and his punishment. But both in the Babylonian Talmud and in *Avot de-R. Nathan* these matters do not constitute a basic element of the tradition about Rabban Joḥanan b. Zakkai. Only in the Gemara these incidents follow upon and are related to the episode of Rabban Joḥanan b. Zakkai, since the Talmud has preserved for us a complete tradition concerning the destruction of the Temple, beginning with its initial causes and ending with the final fate of the destroyer of the Sanctuary. In *Avot de-R. Nathan*, on the other hand, these events form part of a parallel tradition to that of Rabban Joḥanan. Similarly a distinction must be made between *Midrash Lamentations* and the Talmud, on the one hand, and *Avot de-R. Nathan*, according to both versions, on the other, in regard to the burning of the stores of Jerusalem. For the former connect this account with Rabban Joḥanan b. Zakkai's departure from the city, whereas the latter records it without reference to this occurrence. It will thus be seen that in *Midrash Lamentations* the essence of the episode under consideration is preserved in a complete unit of tradition, transcending that of all the other sources.

Now let us proceed to examine the actual tradition, with its manifold differences, as given in the various sources mentioned above.

The Haggadic tradition has to be considered from three aspects: (a) the cause that led to the departure of Joḥanan b. Zakkai from Jerusalem; (b) his exit from the city and his audience with Vespasian; (c) his negotiations with the latter. We shall now investigate these themes seriatim.

I

These sources advance in this regard two conflicting views and one intermediate and unifying view. These variant traditions are symptomatic of divergent traditions among the Sages respecting the attitude of the Pharisees towards the Zealots on the question of war and peace with the Romans. According to the tradition found in both versions of *Avot de-R. Nathan*, Rabban Joḥanan b. Zakkai decided to leave the city and to give himself up to the Romans after the Zealots had refused to accept his suggestion to accept Vespasian's demand that 'the men of Jerusalem' should surrender to him completely. Thus Rabban Joḥanan was opposed to the war with Rome in any form, hoping at the same time that by submitting, the Jews would save the Temple and the city from destruction. But according to the presentation of the episode in the Midrash, Rabban Joḥanan resolved to surrender to the Romans only after the Zealots had burnt the stores of food, which could have lasted many years. Rabban Joḥanan b. Zakkai's opposition to the Zealots, in that case, was not directed towards immediate submission to the Romans, but against the methods employed by the Zealots in the war. For the latter wished to fight an offensive war against Vespasian (or Titus), beyond the wall, whereas Rabban Joḥanan, together with the 'Senators', who apparently held the same view,[74] favoured entrenching themselves in Jerusalem, and hence had accumulated much food in order to maintain a long defensive war.

Accordingly, the differences of opinion between Rabban Joḥanan b. Zakkai and the Zealots were only tactical. These two variant traditions we find in juxtaposition in the Babylonian Talmud. Thus after the Talmud has described the negotiations between 'the Rabbis' and 'the *Biryone*',[75] the former proposing 'let us go forth and make peace

74 Halevy (*Dorot Harischonim*, Pt. I, Vol. V) correctly deduces from *Avot de-R. Nathan*, Version II, ch. xiii — 'He [R. Eliezer b. Hyrcanus' father] went up to Jerusalem in order to ban (his son) from his possessions and he found Rabban Joḥanan b. Zakkai celebrating a festival there, which was attended by all the great men of the city, namely Ben Ṣiṣit ha-Keset and Naqdimon b. Gurion and Ben Kalba Savu'a' — that these men were intimate friends and admirers of Rabban Joḥanan b. Zakkai (cf. also Version I, ch. vi, as well as *Gen. Rabba*, xlii). Hence it may be inferred that they were all in agreement with Rabban Joḥanan's policy.

75 It should be noted that the name '*Biryone*' is found in the Talmud only (in *Lam. Rabbati*, ed. Buber, this epithet is taken over from the Gemara). But in *Avot de-R. Nathan*, both versions, they are called 'Zealots' in a meliorative sense (and even in *Lam. Rabbati* no prejorative term is applied to them),

with them', and the latter, 'let us go forth and engage them in battle', it tells us the accumulation of provisions by 'the rich men' of Jerusalem and of the burning of their stores by Abba Siqra and of Rabban Joḥanan b. Zakkai's protest to his sister's son for this act of sabotage, which was primarily responsible for his leaving the city. The Gemara, it will be seen, combined the two traditions, which actually stem from different sources, and covered up the discrepancy between them by harmonizing them, implying that both incidents contributed to Rabban Joḥanan b. Zakkai's visit to Vespasian.

II

Regarding the story of Rabban Joḥanan's departure from Jerusalem, we must first note the obvious and most important difference between the two sources. In *Avot de-R. Nathan*, both versions, we read that Vespasian's men (from among the Jews), who were in Jerusalem, informed him before Rabban Joḥanan left the city, that he was one of 'Caesar's friends'.[76] Hence Rabban Joḥanan b. Zakkai's audience with the Roman general was absolutely simple. He was brought directly to Vespasian, who welcomed him as one of whom

and Rabban Joḥanan addresses them as 'my sons', which the tradition itself takes pride in them and in the deeds of the 'men of Jerusalem'. Likewise the tradition of *Pesiqta Rabbati* (ed. Ish Shalom, 140a) is also aware of 'the men of Jerusalem', who fought against the Romans, and glorifies their heroes. Generally, the attitude of tradition (except the Talmud) to the Zealots is that they are men who err in their policy and acts, but are not wicked or depraved, as Josephus portrays them.

76 Note should be taken of the story contained in the Talmud, in the Midrash, and in *Avot de-R. Nathan*, Version II (but not in Version I), that the Zealots wanted to stab the 'corpse' of Rabban Joḥanan, in order to determine whether he was alive or not, but refrained from doing so lest they 'besmirch the name of their state'. Tradition thus gives expression to its estimation of the Zealots as men who had the honour of their nation at heart, although they were concerned that their opponents should not exploit this fact to their detriment, showing that they observed in wartime the standards of civilized conduct. (This, too, confutes Josephus, according to whom the Zealots' behaviour was the diametrical opposite of this). Dio Cassius, in similar vein, relates (66, 5) that after Titus had decided not to spare the lives of any more deserters from Jerusalem, there were Romans who despaired of victory and gave themselves up to the Israelites, 'and the Jews, even though they were themselves short of food, treated them with love' (that Romans went over to the Jewish side may be inferred even from Josephus, who mentions the fact incidentally — *Wars*, v, 6, 3). Thus this non-Jewish writer also condemns Josephus for concealing facts favourable to the Zealots, and not hesitating 'to besmirch his state'.

he had already heard and said to him 'Are you Rabban Joḥanan b. Zakkai?' But in *Midrash Lamentations* and in the Talmud there is no reference to the fact that the Romans knew the Rabbi and his attitude towards them. Consequently his audience was also not achieved directly, but his disciples, who brought him forth, left him in a cemetery and went away, and he 'went forth and walked among Vespasian's soldiers' and asked them to inform Vespasian that 'a certain Jew wishes to salute him'. Then when he came before him, Vespasian did not receive him like one of whom he had known before. According to this tradition, Rabban Joḥanan b. Zakkai left the city like a deserter, whose fate was unclear, and who had to find a way to the leading officers in order to win favour for himself.

Another important difference. According to the tradition in the Midrash and Talmud, Ben Baṭiaḥ (or Abba Siqra) was in collusion with Rabban Joḥanan b. Zakkai and his disciples, and it was he who helped them to take him out of the city. But in *Avot de-R. Nathan*, both versions, there is no allusion to this incident.

Another detail. In the Midrash it is related that Vespasian ordered Rabban Joḥanan b. Zakkai to be put 'inside seven cells' — one room within another — in darkness, so that he should not be able to tell day from night.[77] Although this episode is not mentioned in the Talmud, we nevertheless read there twice that Vespasian asked Rabban Joḥanan b. Zakkai 'Why did you not come to me before now?' From both narratives we learn that Vespasian did not receive Rabban Joḥanan b. Zakkai trustfully and gracefully, but queried his courage and actions, and treated him with severity.

These differences in the sources are not accidental but interrelated, and are to be explained by the divergency in the various traditions that lies at the root of these accounts. Thus according to the tradition in both versions of *Avot de-R. Nathan*, Rabban Joḥanan b.

77 Also in *Avot de-R. Nathan*, Version II, we read that Rabban Joḥanan b. Zakkai was handed over to 'two officers', but according to this tradition it is possible (with difficulty) to explain that he was put in ward until his prophecy would be confirmed or not (cf. the story of Josephus, who, too, was released from his chains only after Vespasian was informed of Nero's death, and the former's prophecy was fulfilled). But it is not possible to explain thereby the fact that Rabban Joḥanan b. Zakkai was put in a dark dungeon. Undoubtedly tradition has preserved here the essential fact that when Rabban Joḥanan b. Zakkai came to the Romans, he was put in prison (just as the notables of Jerusalem, who surrendered to Titus together with the royal family of Izates, were kept in custody — *Wars* vi, 6, 4), an act that was unrelated to the initial greeting of the emperor.

Zakkai was opposed to the war from the outset and wished the Jews to submit to the Romans without reservation. Hence it follows that before he ever decided to leave the city, his intention was already revealed to the Romans, and consequently it was quite impossible for him to receive the assistance of one of the leaders of the Zealots. For the same reason we can also understand the 'gentle' treatment accorded him by Vespasian when he came before him.

However, the tradition found in the Midrash and Talmud held that Rabban Joḥanan b. Zakkai was also an opponent of complete surrender, but he disagreed with the Zealots regarding the tactics of the war, and he eventually acted as he did only when he reached the point of despair after the people had been deprived of the means of defending themselves. Hence it was not inconceivable that one of the Zealots should secretly agree with Rabban Joḥanan, when he saw the cruel consequences of their tactics, and should even help him clandestinely to save his life. In the light of this tradition it is quite comprehensible that Vespasian received Rabban Joḥanan ungraciously and questioned him and put him in prison.

III

With regard to Rabban Joḥanan b. Zakkai's negotiations with Vespasian, the following aspects have to be noted: (a) the prophecy that Vespasian would become emperor; (b) Rabban Joḥanan's requests; (c) his participation in the deliberations of the commanders. In order to ascertain the nature of the tradition it is most important to determine the sequence of the first two acts, i.e. which preceded, the royal salutation or the request. Here, too, there is a difference between *Avot de-R. Nathan*, Version I, on the one hand, and the Midrash and Talmud (and even *Avot de-R. Nathan*, Version II), on the other. According to the former tradition, the request was made prior to the prophecy; nay more, Vespasian took the initiative and said to Rabban Joḥanan b. Zakkai, before the latter began to speak, once he knew that it was Rabban Joḥanan b. Zakkai who stood before him: 'Are you Rabban Joḥanan b. Zakkai? Tell me what I should give you.' But according to the other sources, the greeting as emperor preceded the request. This difference is also but one link in a chain of numerous variations in the sources, all of which are to be explained by their primary divergence, as pointed out above. Thus according to the first tradition Rabban Joḥanan had already gained the esteem of the Romans by the fact that he had sought to persuade the people to surrender to them and he had no need to acquire their favour by any further act. Hence as soon as he appeared before Vespasian, the latter said to him 'Tell me what I should give you.' But this was not the case according to the second tradition, which does not portray Rabban Joḥanan b. Zakkai as 'one of Caesar's friends' to begin with; nor did he possess 'deeds' to his credit in the eyes of the Romans. Consequently he was required to perform a great feat in order to convert Vespasian into a friend. And it was the royal salutation that won him approval.[78]

As for the request, the divergences in the sources are particularly numerous in this respect, and we can distinguish three traditions in regard to this episode. The tradition preserved in *Avot de-R. Nathan*, both versions, states that Rabban Joḥanan asked Vespasian for 'Jabneh, that I may go and teach my disciples there and institute prayers there and perform there all the precepts.' The Talmudic tradition avers that he also requested him, apart from 'Jabneh and its sages', for 'the dynasty of Rabban Gamaliel' (in plain language that he should spare the lives of Rabban Gamaliel and his family)[79] and for 'physicians to heal Rabbi Zadok'. But according to the tradition in the Midrash, Rabban Joḥanan b. Zakkai did not ask for Jabneh at all. Instead he appealed to Vespasian to raise the siege of Jerusalem, but he refused. He also asked him for a concession in respect of 'the western gate, which leads to Lydda, so that whoever leaves before the fourth [or third] hour may be saved.'[80] This request, too, it appears, from the tradition's silence on the subject, he did not grant. In the end he allowed him (apparently on the basis of the previous

78 In *Avot de-R. Nathan*, version II, apparently the basic tradition about the salutation was inserted in the wrong place.

79 The reference to 'the dynasty of Rabban Gamaliel' is undoubtedly an anachronism; see below, p. 336.

80 Rabban Joḥanan's request to Vespasian to leave 'the western gate leading to Lydda' unguarded, so that whoever left by it would be saved, is to be explained in the light of the story recounted by Josephus (*Wars*, vi, 6, 7) that after the Destruction, but before the conquest of the city, Titus appealed to the Zealots to surrender to him, but they replied that they could not do so, because of their oath, but they were prepared to leave the city with their wives and children 'in order to go to the wilderness and abandon the city to him'. 'The western gate leading to Lydda' indicates therefore, that Rabban Joḥanan b. Zakkai was entreating on behalf of those who fled to the Romans (Lydda, as we have seen, was a depot for the deserters), in contradistinction to the Zealot fighters, who wished to go east, to the desert, without submitting to the Romans, for Rabban Joḥanan could hope that the peace-loving people might be spared, but on no account would this concession be granted to the rebels (only this request was also turned down).

request) to bring forth his friends and relatives from Jerusalem and so deliver them from death. He also took out R. Zadok and he was healed.[81]

Now according to this tradition of the Midrash, Rabban Joḥanan did not succeed in obtaining from Vespasian any benefit for the general population; only the lives of his relatives were spared. It seems that this tradition is nearest to the historical truth. Likewise according to the other sources, the narrative must be understood, as stated earlier, to mean that Rabban Joḥanan b. Zakkai only had in mind a certain freedom of action where he was going; but these sources transferred events that occurred at a later stage to the beginning of Rabban Joḥanan's labours with his disciples at Jabneh. Since his actual translation there was not due to his initiative or for his benefit, the Midrash tradition did not include it among the requests made by Rabban Joḥanan to Vespasian.

81 The saving of R. Zadok by Rabban Joḥanan is recorded in the Talmud and Midrash. But there is no mention of it in either version of *Avot de-R. Nathan*. Furthermore, from *Avot de-R. Nathan*, Version I, xvi (Schechter, p. 63) it is evident that R. Zadok was captured and brought to Rome. This is also to be inferred from the story of the Matrona who wished to make him commit a sin against his will, of which we read in the Talmud (*Qiddushin* 40a). Also in *Midrash Lamentations* i 46, we learn that the two sons of Zadok the priest were captured and brought to Rome. Therefore, if we wish to avoid the premise that we have divergent traditions before us (see below, p. 319), we must reluctantly conclude that Rabban Joḥanan only succeeded in saving R. Zadok's life, but not in delivering him from captivity or servitude.

THE PATRIARCHATE OF RABBAN JOḤANAN BEN ZAKKAI

The period immediately after the destruction of the Second Temple is one of the obscurest chapters in Jewish history. From this crucial era, which determined the fate of Judaism and moulded its image for many generations, after the annihilation of its cardinal, existential foundations of former days, there have been preserved only a few fragmentary sources, insufficient to furnish data for a chapter of history. Hence we sometimes struggle with basic questions and cannot solve them.

Out of the mystery enveloping these days emerges the outstanding figure of Rabban Joḥanan b. Zakkai, the leader of his generation, whom tradition regards as the central personage of the epoch and the man who created and consolidated the Jewish renascence. But even in this respect the position is perplexing and we possess only scraps of information, which cannot provide us with explicit answers to fundamental questions: What was the communal and official position of Rabban Joḥanan b. Zakkai during the period of his work at Jabneh, at the close of the Temple era and after the Destruction, and what was the attitude of Palestinian Jewry to the man and his work?

These questions can be formulated in another, more concrete form: Did Rabban Joḥanan b. Zakkai function as Patriarch, and if so, to what extent was he recognized as such by the nation?

Now to the first question, regarding which latter-day scholars differ[1] (the Rishonim regard Rabban Joḥanan b. Zakkai as Patriarch in all respects[2]), despite the fact that we lack firm and express evi-

1 Nachman Krochmal (*More Nevukhe ha-Zeman*, ed. Rawidowicz, p. 105), Weiss (*Dor Dor we-Dorshaw*², Part II, p. 34), Graetz (*Geschichte*⁴, p. 14), and Jawitz (vol. vi, p. 8) consider Rabban Joḥanan b. Zakkai to have been Patriarch. Zacharias Frankel (*Darkhe ha-Mishna*², p. 67), Jakob Bruell (*Mevo' ha-Mishna*, vol. I, p. 50), N. Bruell (*Jahrbuch*, vol. vii, p. 10) and Halevy (*Dorot Harischonim*, Part I, vol. v, p. 52) deny this.

2 Rav Sherira Gaon (in the responsa cited below, note 3); R. Samson of Chinon (*Keritut*, Yemot 'Olam, Sha'ar I); R. Simeon b. Zemach Duran (*Magen Avot*, on *Avot*, i, 16).

dence in our sources, the answer, it seems, can be absolutely positive. Rabban Joḥanan undoubtedly officiated as Patriarch; this is substantiated by two facts:

(a) The title 'Rabban', which is accorded him by tradition everywhere,[3] is restricted to the Patriarchs only;[4] this is attested by Rav

3 R. Zacharias Frankel (*Darkhe ha-Mishna, ibid.*) writes: 'In all the recensions of the Mishna and Baraita we find Rabbi Joḥanan b. Zakkai and not Rabban'. This statement is incomprehensible to me, since in the extant versions, both in manuscript and in the works of the Rishonim and in the printed editions, the reading is Rabban. We may rely on the testimony of Rav Sherira Gaon (in the responsa published in the 'Appendices' to Rav Sherira Gaon's Epistle, ed. Lewin, pp. 125, 128), and of Maimonides (in the Introduction to the *Perush ha-Mishnayot*); cf. Hyman, *Toledot Tanna'im wa-Amora'im, s.v.* Rabban Joḥanan b. Zakkai.

4 The title 'Rabban' as the permanent title of the Patriarch is found from the time of Rabban Gamaliel the Elder onwards (Rav Sherira Gaon, *op. cit.*). This fact lends support to the view that this period, beginning with the establishment of Hillel's dynasty, marks a new chapter in the history of national leadership. When we add thereto the hereditary succession, which was instituted by this dynasty, and the unified rule, which was not enjoyed by the 'Pairs', we are led to the conclusion that the institution of the Patriarchate, which concentrated the powers of administration in the hands of a single individual (expressed in the title 'Rabban') originated with Hillel and his sons. Although according to the Mishna (*Ḥagiga* ii, 2), the 'Pairs' consisted in each case of the Patriarch and the Head of the Court [Av Bet Din], this is to be regarded as an anachronistic note. Since Hillel lived at the close of an age that was passing — the period of the Pairs — when authority was vested in the hands of a duumvirate (cf. 'two judges of civil law', in *M. Ketubbot* xiii, 1, and the Baraitot in the Babylonian and Palestinian Talmuds, which are not to be considered inconsistent with the Mishna, because the third member was not a contemporary of Admon and Ḥanan), he was still counted with the 'Pairs' and was not given the title 'Rabban', which came into force when the new type of Patriarchate was established under his son.

Some scholars have already referred to this Mishna, which projects a later situation to an earlier period; but they regard the 'Pairs' as two leading Soferim and the like (Nahman Krochmal, *More Nevukhe ha-Zeman*, ed. Rawidowicz, 217–218; Bacher, *Tradition* etc., 49), suggestions that appear improbable. Now R. Jose (*Tosefta Sanhedrin* vii, 1; *Ḥagiga* ii, 9, and the parallels) praises the earlier generations, up to the time of Hillel, for the absence of disputes among them, because the High Court [*Bet Din ha-Gadol*] decided all issues. There was no difference, therefore, between the earlier period — the era of the 'Pairs' — and that of Hillel and his sons, except that at first the administrative powers were vested with two persons, but subsequently with one, and that from Hillel onward the leadership belonged to a single dynasty. It was these innovations that determined the character of the Patriarchate in contradistinction to the era of the 'Pairs', and we have the explicit evidence of the Geonim for this (*Seder Tanna'im wa-Amora'im*,

Sherira Gaon in a responsum and the testimony is fully confirmed by the use of this appellation in the sources. Although this evidence of Rav Sherira Gaon is ostensibly contradicted by the well-known Baraita in the Tosefta at the end of *'Eduyot*,[5] and Rav Sherira Gaon himself has mentioned it as an objection to his former statement, nevertheless it appears that this obscure Baraita refers only to the use of the epithet as an honorary designation, which the disciples of a Sage were accustomed to apply to the master, even in his absence, without mentioning his name (because as a rule they refrained from calling their teachers by their names); its use was restricted to the school of the elder in question. Similarly we find that a number of Amoraim in the Talmud, when teaching in public and citing a dictum in their master's name, call him *Rabbenu* ['our teacher'], without qualification.[6] But the permanent title *Rabban* ['our teacher'], which was attached to the scholar's name and was used by *all* the Sages (though not necessarily his disciples), and which served to denote an authority whose ruling received general acceptance, was limited

Neubauer, Part I, p. 671; *Kerem Ḥemed* iv, 184; *Maḥzor Vitry*, 481) — 'and from the time of Hillel they were called Patriarchs'. Cf. Abraham Krochmal (*Perushim we-He'arot le-Talmud Bavli*, pp. 15 ff.), and Jawitz, vol. v, p. 34, note 2.

Possibly the establishment of the Patriarchate and the transfer of the spiritual and religious authority to one person and one family was responsible for the fact that 'Disputes multiply in Israel and the Torah has become like two', as R. Jose stated, for Shammai and his school did not recognize these innovations and would not accept the rulings of the Patriarch's court, and thus the former unity of the nation was disrupted (Isaak Halevy, *Dorot Harischonim*, Part I, vol. iii, ch. xii, seeks to interpret the state of affairs of which R. Jose speaks as a reference to the fact that Gabinius abolished the Great Sanhedrin, with the consent, as it were, of Antipater and Hyrcanus, and transferred to them the administrative powers. But this conjecture is very far-fetched and was already refuted by Hoffmann in the *Frankfurter Jahrbuch*, V, 225–238).

5 Ch. iii, 4 (according to the reading of Rav Sherira Gaon *ibid.*): 'If one has disciples and his disciples have disciples, he is called "Rabbi" ['my teacher']; if his disciples are forgotten, he is called "Rabban" ['our teacher']' etc.

6 On rare occasions his name is also mentioned; cf. *T.B. Bekhorot* 49b; *T.B. Bava Batra* 154b; *T.B. Rosh ha-Shana* 18b; *T.B. Ketubbot* 107b (in the Munich MS there is an omission here; see *ibid.*); *T.B. Giṭṭin* 19a; *T.B. Berakhot* 38b; *T.B. Shabbat* 144b; *T.B. 'Eruvin* 11a, 16b; *T.B. Sukka* 33a; *T.B. Bava Batra* 135b; *T.B. Beṣa* 22b. The disciples of Rav Ashi called him (when signing a document) 'Rabbana' ['our teacher'] Ashi, *T.B. Ketubbot* 22a. See the observations of Rabbi Ehrentreu, *Frankfurter Jahrbuch* X, pp. 197 ff.

to the Patriarch only (just as in Babylon the Head of the Golah was called *Rabbana*, which means the same thing).

(b) Tradition attributes nine enactments to Joḥanan b. Zakkai.[7] Ordinances of the kind promulgated by Joḥanan b. Zakkai could have been instituted in the Second Temple period only by a Patriarch and his Court [*Bet Din*] (apart from those enumerated below). Wherever we find in this period that 'So-and-so enacted', in the sense that he established a general enactment, he was either a Patriarch, or one of the 'Pairs', or a High Priest (indeed Ezra and the Men of the Great Assembly were also included among them).[8]

But if it has been shown that Rabban Joḥanan b. Zakkai officiated as Patriarch, we still have to enquire whether he was recognized by all Israel and whether the whole, or the majority, of the community accepted his authority.

We are unable to give a clear-cut answer to this question on account of the paucity and obscurity of our sources. However, after a careful examination of the material that has a bearing on our subject, and drawing the necessary inference from its express or implicit statements, we may conclude that Rabban Joḥanan b. Zakkai was acknowledged as Patriarch only by a minority and that he had many opponents, who challenged his Patriarchate for various reasons. Some of them did not follow him to Jabneh from the outset, while others who were in his circle disputed his authority, until he was

7 Baraita, *T.B. Rosh ha-Shana*, 31b, but Rabbi Judah disagrees with this tradition in respect of one enactment (in connection with 'the day of the waving' — *M. Menaḥot* x, 5). From *Torat Kohanim*, be-Har, ch. i (so, too, from the Baraita in *T.B. Rosh ha-Shana* 30a) it is evident that some sages disputed the 'enactment' regarding the blowing of the Shofar in Jabneh on Rosh ha-Shana that fell on a Sabbath (this was deduced from the Torah). But none of his other enactments are challenged. Halevy's remarks (*Dorot Harischonim*, Part I, vol. v, ch. xxxii) do not invalidate the significance of this fact in regard to Rabban Joḥanan b. Zakkai's authority.

8 Hillel (*M. Shevu'ot* x, 3; *M. Giṭṭin* iv, 3; *M. 'Arakhin* ix, 5); Rabban Gamaliel the Elder (*M. Rosh ha-Shanb* ii, 8; *M. Giṭṭin* iv, 2, 3); Simeon b. Sheṭaḥ (*T.B. Ketubbot* ch. ii; *T.P. ibid.* viii, 11); Joshua b. Gamala (*T.B. Bava Batra* 22a). Cf. the enactments of Joḥanan the High Priest (*M. Ma'aser Sheni* v, 15; *M. Soṭa* ix, 1). The same applies to the expression 'So-and-so decreed'. On the other hand we find the statement 'R. So-and-so enacted in his city' in the sense of a local enactment (*T.B. Sanhedrin* 9a; *T.P. Berakhot* iii, 6a; *T.P. Sanhedrin* ii, 2. Cf. also *T.B. Nidda* 67b; but the expression 'Rav Judah has ordained (the following formula) in a deed of *ḥaliṣa* in *T.B. Yevamot* 39b, and the like, have no bearing on our subject, for it concerns the formulation of a deed of *ḥaliṣa*).

compelled to vacate his position to Rabban Gamaliel and to transfer his school from Jabneh to Beror Ḥayil, where he set up his court and resided until his death.

Let us now enumerate in detail the groups that were antagonistic to the Patriarchate of Rabban Joḥanan b. Zakkai.

I. *The Priests*

Büchler already pointed to the fact that the priests, who, we find, had information on the Temple and its service, are not found in Rabban Joḥanan b. Zakkai's society and are not dependent on him or his school.[9] This fact, which is certainly not merely coincidental, grows in significance in the light of what the Mishna states regarding the conflicts between Rabban Joḥanan b. Zakkai and the priests, and Rabban Joḥanan's inability to assert his authority over them.[10] To these incidents should be added, to my mind, the statements in the Talmud (*T.B. Bekhorot* 30b) concerning R. Ḥanina b. Antigonus (the Priest), who 'insulted the scholars'. Although the nature of R. Ḥanina b. Antigonus' insult to the scholars is not expressly stated in the Talmud,[11] it is nevertheless clear that a dispute between R. Ḥanina

9 *Priester und Cultus u.s.w.*, p. 17. Büchler enumerates: R. Ḥanina the Deputy High Priest, Zechariah b. Qevutal, R. Ẓadok, R. Zechariah b. ha-Qaṣṣav, Jose b. Jo'ezer (?), and R. Ṭarfon. With regard to the last-mentioned Sage it may ostensibly be objected that he once stated that he possessed a Halakha from Rabban Joḥanan b. Zakkai (*Tosefta Ḥagiga*, ch. iii, end). But in ed. Zuckermandel, *ibid.* iii, 6, this reading is 'from Rabban Gamaliel Joḥanan b. Zakkai'. We thus have a conflated reading of two recensions, one of which had 'Rabban Gamaliel'. No deduction is therefore to be made therefrom (Büchler, *ibid.* 26, explains the matter in a different way). We also find a variant tradition as between Rabban Gamaliel and Rabban Joḥanan b. Zakkai in *Mishnat R. Eliezer* (p. 333) in comparison with *M. Soṭa* ii, 1.

To these should be added the following contemporary priests, even though they did not testify concerning the Temple and its service: R. Judah the Priest (*M. Eduyot* viii, 4), R. Eliezer b. Ẓadok, and possibly also R. Simeon b. ha-Segan [Deputy High Priest], as well as Azariah, the father of R. Eleazar b. Azariah (*T.B. Yevamot* 16a), and, perhaps, R. Simeon the brother of Azariah (*Sifre Zuta*, ed. Horovitz, 313). Büchler (*ibid.* p. 23) notes the two priests who were with Rabban Joḥanan b. Zakkai: R. Jose the Priest and R. Simeon b. Nathaniel. But, in the light of my subsequent explanation, in the text, it appears that they, too, were not in their teacher's circle after the Destruction.

10 *M. Sheqalim* i, 4; *M. Eduyot* viii, 3 (Büchler, *op. cit.*, p. 9 and p. 20, note 1).

11 Tosafot explains: 'In connection with levitically prepared food, as did his son.' Rashi comments: 'He said so in anger, but it was not factual'; Rashi, therefore, understood the words literally, only he denied their veracity, in

b. Antigonus and the Sages is alluded to here. Seeing, however, that the Halakhic question discussed in the context (see *ibid.*) related to laws concerning levitically prepared food, which was primarily a matter pertaining to the priests, and that Rabban Joḥanan b. Zakkai has already been found in dispute with the priests in the same field of Halakhot, it may be assumed that in this case, too, we have another example of their struggle and that the Sages whom R. Ḥanina b. Antigonus 'insulted' were none other than his contemporary, Rabban Joḥanan b. Zakkai, and his disciples.

Of the priests who were not found in Rabban Joḥanan b. Zakkai's society, but were afterwards members of Rabban Gamaliel's household and school, R. Ẓadok is particularly prominent. We hear of no connection between Rabban Joḥanan b. Zakkai and this priest-sage, who served as Head of the Court[12] under Rabban Gamaliel until R. Joshua took his place, although he occupied, it seems, even in Temple times, an important position in the Sanctuary and in the state.[13] Hence it must be assumed that, like his colleagues, he, too, was alienated from Rabban Joḥanan.

Ostensibly this thesis is contradicted by the tradition in the Babylonian Talmud and in *Midrash Lamentations*, which related that Rabban Joḥanan b. Zakkai entreated Vespasian on behalf of R. Ẓadok.[14] However, the fact that Rabban Joḥanan b. Zakkai saved his life does not necessarily imply that R. Ẓadok acknowledged R. Joḥanan's authority, or agreed with his views and actions. But this apart it must be noted that in the oldest of the sources that narrate the story of Rabban Joḥanan b. Zakkai and Vespasian, namely *Avot de-R. Nathan* (Version I, ch. iv, and Version II, ch. vi), there is no trace of this episode. Furthermore, from the same source we learn that R. Ẓadok was captured and brought to Rome;[15] it is thus apparent

order, no doubt, to save the honour of this elder. Cf. Halevy, *op. cit.*, Part I, vol. v, ch. xlix.

12 *Tosefta Sanhedrin* viii, 1, and *T.P. ibid.* i, 19c. But it is not ruled out that the correct reading in *T.P.* (and so, too, in Tosefta, ed. Zuckermandel, *ibid.* q.v.) is: אבא אחיו ['Abba his brother'], i.e. the brother of Rabban Gamaliel (*T.B. Yevamot* 15a). Cf. *Eshkol* (Hebrew), vol. I, p. 17.

13 *Tosefta Yom ha-Kippurim* i, 2, and the parallels. In *M. Sukka* ii, 5, the reference is not to a single occasion (at which Rabban Joḥanan b. Zakkai, Rabban Gamaliel and R. Ẓadok dined together). Cf. Halevy, *op. cit.*, Part I, vol. V, p. 59, note 26).

14 *T.B. Gittin* 57b; *Lamentations Rabbati* ch. i.

15 *Avot de-R. Nathan* Version I, ch. xvi (the story in *T.B. Qiddushin* 40a, may be cited as a parallel). From *Lamentations Rabbati* i, 46, we learn that two

that he did not find favour with Vespasian. The tradition cited above is therefore open to doubt, and at all events cannot invalidate our premise.

Why was it that priests refused to recognize the authority of Rabban Joḥanan b. Zakkai and refrained from attending his school? It is difficult to explain the fact on the basis of nationalist zealotry,[16] because the majority of the priests were moderates. R. Ḥanina, the Deputy High Priest, explicitly enjoins in the Mishna: 'Pray for the peace of the ruling power, since but for the fear of it men would have swallowed one another up alive', and undoubtedly his words refer to the beginning of the war against Rome and to the fratricidal strife that prevailed at the time. Was the cause paucity of Rabban Joḥanan b. Zakkai's wisdom and Torah-learning? But Rabban Joḥanan b. Zakkai was the head of a school in Jerusalem and one of the leaders of the generation, and apparently even functioned as Head of the Court under Rabban Simeon b. Gamaliel I.[17]

The answer to this question, it seems, is to be sought in the special status enjoyed by the priests of that period: not only did they constitute the majority of the Sanhedrin and most of the commanders and governors were appointed from among them when the great war[18] broke out (this latter fact does not add much to the former, since these appointments were made by the Sanhedrin itself), but they had a special Court of their own and claimed extraordinary privileges for themselves in certain juridical spheres.[19] At times they even invaded the domain that belonged solely to the Patriarch, to wit, the

sons of 'Ẓadok the Priest' were taken captive and brought to Rome; apparently the reference is to the same incident.

16 Cf. Büchler, *op. cit.*, p. 18.

17 *Midrash Tanna'im*, ed. Hoffmann, 176 (Rabban Simeon b. Gamaliel and Rabban Joḥanan b. Zakkai jointly sign this letter). But some doubt attaches to this testimony, since in the parallel sources (*Tosefta Sanhedrin* ii, 6; *T.B. ibid.* 11a–b; and *T.P. ibid.* i, 18d) the name of Rabban Joḥanan b. Zakkai is not mentioned in the letter; for it would appear that despite the thematic and linguistic differences we discern between the source, cited above, and the parallels, we have here but one event and the names of Rabban Gamaliel and Rabban Simeon b. Gamaliel have been interchanged (this interchange occurs very frequently in Talmudic literature). My teacher, Prof. Epstein, gave me the following reason for this view: the Patriarch's scribe in this source is Joḥanan, whereas that of Rabban Gamaliel (the Elder) was Naḥum the Scribe (*M. Pe'a* ii, 6; *T.B. Nazir* 56b).

18 *Wars* ii, 2, 3–4.

19 *M. Ketubbot* i, 5.

fixing of the calendar.[20] The people also regarded them as having special administrative rights, as we learn from Josephus' account of the envoys that were sent by order of the Sanhedrin in Jerusalem to remove him from his high office.[21]

It seems, therefore, that as long as the Patriarchate was vested in the House of David (the family of Hillel) the priests were, generally speaking, subordinate to the Patriarchs and accepted their authority. But after the Destruction, when the Patriarch Rabban Simeon b. Gamaliel was killed by the Romans and his son Rabban Gamaliel was at first unable to expect the favour of the government (see below), and the Davidic line was temporarily interrupted, the priests sought to restore to themselves the leadership of the people and refrained from recognizing the rule of Rabban Joḥanan b. Zakkai, who was neither a priest nor a scion of the Davidic family.[22]

This special claim of the priests to the Patriarchate finds expression again in the generation following the time with which we are dealing, when Rabban Gamaliel was deposed from the Patriarchate, for on that occasion R. Joshua b. Ḥananiah, who was the Head of the Court (and therefore most entitled to fill this vacancy), was not appointed, but R. Eleazar b. Azariah, one of the younger scholars, was chosen. Undoubtedly his priesthood stood him in good stead.[23]

Furthermore, it appears that R. Ṭarfon the Priest was also privileged to officiate as Patriarch (in effect). It seems that in the intervening period, between the death of Rabban Gamaliel of Jabneh and of R. Eleazar b. Azariah (who apparently was the sole Patriarch after the former's demise) and the destruction of Bethar, R. Ṭarfon[24]

20 *M. Rosh ha-Shana* i, 7.

21 *Life*, xxxix.

22 Cf. Büchler, *op. cit.*, p. 18, note 2; lack of space prevents me from elaborating this point.

23 The Haggada attributes his appointment as Patriarch to the fact that 'he was the tenth in the line of descent from Ezra' (*T.B. Berakhot* 28a; *T.P. ibid.* iv, 7d); but the context wishes it clear that the Talmud only intends to state that he was a priest of noble lineage.

24 Halevy rightly posits, as against Graetz, that R. Eleazar b. Azariah officiated as Patriarch after Rabban Gamaliel's death, and not R. Joshua (*op. cit.*, Part I, Vol. iii, p. 334). My statement that R. Ṭarfon outlived R. Eleazar b. Azariah is substantiated by the sources in several of which we find R. Eleazar b. Azariah, R. Ṭarfon, R. Akiba, and R. Jose ha-Gelili together, while in others we have only R. Ṭarfon and R. Jose ha-Gelili with R. Akiba, or with R. Akiba alone. Furthermore, R. Judah was a prominent disciple of R. Ṭarfon, and when he cites any dicta in the name of R. Eleazar b.

reigned as Patriarch, and although there is no absolute proof of this, it is implied: (a) In several sources we find 'Once R. Ṭarfon and the Elders'[25]; this expression which equates an individual with the scholars as a whole, is found only in relation to the Patriarch.[26] (b) In the Palestinian Talmud R. Ṭarfon is given the title 'The teacher of all Israel', or 'the father of all Israel',[27] an epithet that can only be applied, when taken at its face value, to the Patriarch, the supreme leader of his generation. An echo of the tradition relating to this fact is to be heard in *T.P. Yevamot* i, 38d, which narrates that R. Dosa b. Harkinas said that R. Eleazar b. Azariah was the tenth generation in the line of descent from Ezra and adds in the name of R. Ḥanina of Sepphoris 'R. Ṭarfon was also with them and he stated the same of him as he had of R. Eleazar b. Azariah'. It is by no means far-fetched to perceive here an attempt to equate R. Ṭarfon's and R. Eleazar b. Azariah's standing in the community (for R. Eleazar b. Azariah's descent from Ezra conduced, according to the Haggada in the Talmuds, to his appointment as Patriarch). When we come to the Geonic period we find (in the tenth and eleventh centuries) two families of Palestinian Patriarchs contending with each other. One claimed descent from the House of Hillel and the other

Azariah he merely says 'in the name of R. Eleazar b. Azariah'. Apparently he did not study under him.

Although according to both Talmuds R. Eleazar b. Azariah was appointed to the Patriarchate when he was very young (at the age of 18 according to the Babylonian Talmud, and 16 according to the Palestinian Talmud), it is evident that this is an exaggeration (cf. Tosafot, *T.B. Shabbat* 54b); it seems that he was of a mature age when the Temple was still standing. As regards the exposition in the Babylonian Talmud (it is not found in *T.P. Berakhot* i, 3d) הרי אני כבן שבעים שנה ['Behold, I am as one that is (= nearly) seventy years old'], see *Mekhilta*, Bo', where R. Joshua uses the same expression ('I am nearly [כבן] seventy years old, but I have not been privileged to hear this teaching'); here undoubtedly the words have to be understood literally.

25 *Mekhilta*, Beshallaḥ, v; *T.B. Qiddushin* 40b; *T.B. Yoma* 76a (cf. *Sifre* Numbers §118 and the parallel *T.B. Zevaḥim* 57a).

26 In *T.B. Mo'ed Qaṭan* 20a, it is true, we find 'Elisha b. Avuya and the Elders who were with him', but in the parallel passage in *T.B. Nazir* 44a the reading is 'four Elders who were with him'. Furthermore, in *T.B. Mo'ed Qaṭan*, too, R. Ḥananel and the Munich MS have 'four (or, five) Elders who were with him'.

27 *Yoma* i, 38d; *Yevamot* iv, 6b; *Horayot* iii, 47d; the title 'Abba' ['father'] was originally equivalent (or similar) to 'Rav' ['Master']. The same applies to the term found in inscriptions πατὴρ συναγωγῆς, but eventually it became an honorary title only; cf. *Eshkol* (Hebrew), s.v. אב הכנסת.

was a priestly family (claiming descent from Eleazar b. Azariah). This shows how powerful was the priesthood's prerogative in respect of the Patriarchate, even in later times.[28]

Where did the priests concentrate themselves after the Destruction and what did they do to create a centre of administrative authority in Eretz-Israel? The question cannot be answered. Büchler,[29] however, maintains that they assembled at Lydda and established a school there, but his arguments are not convincing, since the sources on which he relies belong to a later date[30] and cannot be applied retrospectively to our period. Josephus (and this is confirmed by the Talmud)[31] informs us that Vespasian set aside Gophnah for fugitive priests. But this, too, does not tell us much. The question is where it was located at the time. But it seems certain that the priests (generally) were opposed to Rabban Joḥanan b. Zakkai and did not attend his school nor recognize his patriarchate (claiming the leadership of the people for themselves) until Rabban Gamaliel restored the prestige of the Davidic dynasty. It was then that the priests subordinated themselves to the authority of the Patriarchate, as they did (willingly or unwillingly) before the destruction of the Temple.

II. *Sages of the Torah* (*Political Opponents*)

Apart from the priests that seceded from Rabban Joḥanan b. Zakkai, as was shown above, we find an array of Sages — among them Elders of the generation — who were active when the Temple was still standing as well as after the Destruction, who likewise withdrew from Rabban Joḥanan and his school. Some of them subse-

28 Cf. *JQR*, 1902, p. 459.
Even at the beginning of the sixth century we find that the Palestinian priests stood at the head of the community, as is evident from the expression of Bishop Simon (Graetz, [Hebrew], vol. III, note 5) 'the Chief Priests of Tiberias'. This is confirmed by the parallel source, relating to the same time and event — Moberg, *The Book of the Himyarites*, 1924 — where it is stated (p. 7) 'Judah the Priest of Tiberias sent to them'. Can we avoid the conclusion that after the abolition of the Patriarchate of the House of David (about a hundred years earlier) the priests sought to take the reins of power into their hands, even as we see they did subsequently?

29 *Ibid.* 23–35.

30 Cf. *ibid.*, p. 27, note 1; these sources relate to the time when R. Jose ha-Gelili, R. Ṭarfon, and R. Akiba were dining together, but none of the older scholars (R. Eliezer, Rabban Gamaliel, R. Joshua, and R. Eleazar b. Azariah) were there, for they had died.

31 *Wars* vi, 2, 2; *T.B. Berakhot* 44a; *T.P. Ta'anit* iv, 68a.

quently joined Rabban Gamaliel at Jabneh,[32] and some are not found in the latter's entourage either.[33] Of the former, R. Dosa b. Harkinas stands out as one who supported Rabban Gamaliel when R. Joshua wished to challenge him openly, on the ground that he recognized the decisive authority of Rabban Gamaliel as Patriarch,[34] although R. Dosa himself disagreed with him in regard to the particular Halakha in question. Of the latter, especially prominent are R. Neḥunya b. Haqana, the teacher of R. Ishmael, and Nahum of Gimzo, the teacher of R. Akiba,[35] who laid the foundation, through these disciples of two great schools of Halakhic exposition. The absence of the leaders of the generation from Jabneh in R. Joḥanan b. Zakkai's time, although he risked his life for the sake of Israel's Torah and the salvation

32 Hezekiah, the father of 'Iqqesh (*T.B. Bekhorot* 38a), Menaḥem b. Signai, Yaqim of Hadar, R. Judah b. Bava, R. Neḥunya b. Elinathan of Kefar ha-Bavli, R. Eleazar of Modi'in (contemporary and disputant of R. Joshua), R. Papias (apparently identical with Popias of Onan-Ono, near Lydda — *Sifre Zuta*, ed. Horovitz, p. 281), *Judah b. Pappus* (*T.P. Berakhot* ii, 5d), R. Ḥalafta, the father of R. Jose, R. Joḥanan b. Nuri, R. Neḥunya (Joḥanan) b. Gudgeda, R. Dosa b. Harkinas (it is doubtful if some of those listed were adults at the time of the Destruction).

33 Naḥum the Mede, R. Neḥunya b. ha-Qana, Naḥum of Gimzo, R. Ḥanina b. Teradyon, Abba Eleazar (*T.B. Hagiga* 16b), Joḥanan b. Bagbag, Abba Saul b. Botnit, R. Eliezer b. Dalgai, R. Eliezer b. Jacob.

34 *M. Rosh ha-Shana* ii, 9.

35 *T.B. Shevu'ot* 26a. Although in *T.B. Bava Batra* 10b R. Neḥunya b. ha-Qana is reckoned among Rabban Joḥanan b. Zakkai's disciples and engages him in discussion (this source was temporarily overlooked by Büchler, *op. cit.*, 18 and by J. M. Guttmann, *Festschrift zum 75 Jährigen Bestehen des jüdisch-theologischen Seminars*, vol. I, p. 108), yet it must first be noted that in the parallel passage in *Pesiqta de-R. Kahana* (§2; ed. Buber 12b) it is not mentioned at all, although it does occur in the corresponding passage of the *Tanḥuma* (Ki Tissa', §5); but this apart, the sources differ considerably (cf. also *Midrash Proverbs* xiv). Again we observe that five of Rabban Joḥanan b. Zakkai's disciples are mentioned here, whose discussion with their master is couched in language reminiscent of *M. Avot* ii, 8. We thus have before us a tradition that is opposed to that of the Mishna concerning the five disciples of Rabban Joḥanan b. Zakkai, those mentioned here being different from those enumerated there.

As regards the reference to 'five disciples' (cf. the five disciples of R. Akiba), it would seem that they constituted a kind of association with special and permanent authority alongside the head of the school; similarly we find חמשה זקנים and חמישה סבי [both expressions mean 'five Elders'] (*T.P. Beṣa* iii, 62a; *Sifre Zuta* 314; *T.B. Giṭṭin* 33b; *M. 'Eruvin* iii, 4; cf. *T.B. Nazir* 44a and the parallel passage in *T.B. Mo'ed Qaṭan* 20a, according to the reading of R. Ḥananel and the Munich MSS.).

of the nation from annihilation (as we view Rabban Joḥanan's actions today) cannot be explained on the basis of personal factors (or any similar incidental causes). In seeking the reason, we can only conjecture that the Sages, together with many other representatives of the people, did not concur at the time with Rabban Joḥanan b. Zakkai's departure from Jerusalem, regarding the act as one of secession from the community and as lending a hand to 'Caesar's friends', many of whom actively helped the Romans to crush the Jewish fighters.[36] Although later generations (including ourselves) judged Rabban Joḥanan's actions favourably and even attributed to him the salvation of the Torah and the deliverance of the nation, nevertheless many of his contemporaries, who did not have the benefit of hindsight as did subsequent ages, did not find sufficient justification for Rabban Joḥanan b. Zakkai's leaving Jerusalem and making peace with the Roman government. For at that juncture the nation was still in the middle of the war, when the scales of victory were in the balance, and Rabban Simeon b. Gamaliel the Patriarch was living in the embattled capital and most Jews were in the battle line and trusting to Heaven's mercy. Is it difficult then to imagine that many of the people regarded Rabban Joḥanan b. Zakkai at the time as a seceder from the community in the hour of its distress?

When Jerusalem fell and the Temple was in ashes, Rabban Joḥanan was not yet cleared in the eyes of these Sages, who remained antagonistic and refused to follow his leadership and collaborate with him.

Furthermore, it appears that at this time Rabban Joḥanan b. Zakkai lost his leading disciples, who left their teacher forever.

Tradition relates in several sources[37] that R. Eliezer b. 'Arakh declined to go with his colleagues to Jabneh and departed elsewhere, forgetting thereby his learning. The Haggada, in accordance with its usage in a number of sources, adorns the narrative with an ethical-didactic motif (the good waters attracted him; and in Midrash *Ecclesiastes Rabba* there is added that his wife urged him to it). We, however, when seeking to evaluate the event historically and to find its actual cause, must first determine when the episode occurred and in what circumstances R. Eleazar's departure occurred.

In this regard we find two conflicting traditions. In *Ecclesiastes Rabba* it is evident that the incident took place after Rabban Joḥanan

36 Cf. Büchler, *op. cit.*, p. 18, whose remarks are cited with emphasis by J. M. Guttmann (*op. cit.*).

37 *Avot de-R. Nathan*, Version I, xiv, and Version II, xxix; *T.B. Shabbat* 147b; *Ecclesiastes Rabba* vii.

b. Zakkai's death. But in *Avot de-R. Nathan*, Version I, xiv, it is implied that it occurred in his lifetime. Although this source is not explicit and does not inform us whether the Sages went to Jabneh before or after the Destruction, we learn this from the parallel passage in Version II, xxix, where we read: 'Why did his fame in wisdom not grow? When they left Jerusalem, Rabban Joḥanan b. Zakkai said: "Where shall I go?" He (R. Eleazar b. 'Arakh) said: "To Emmaus [מעום][38] which is a beautiful city..." But they said "Let us go to Jabneh" ' etc. We thus learn that R. Eleazar b. 'Arakh left his master when they departed from Jerusalem to go to Jabneh with Vespasian's permission.[39]

This fact, which is expressly stated in this first source, is also corroborated by the sources that narrate the story of Rabban Joḥanan b. Zakkai and Vespasian,[40] all of which mention only R. Eliezer b. Hyrcanus and R. Joshua as the disciples of Rabban Joḥanan who were with him at the time. It is impossible to attribute this silence to R. Eleazar b. 'Arakh's insignificance *vis-à-vis* these disciples, for according to Abba Saul in the Mishna[41] R. Eleazar b. Arakh outweighed, in Rabban Joḥanan's estimation, all his other distinguished disciples, including Eliezer. Although this Mishna, in its own name, applies this encomium to R. Eliezer, nevertheless the tradition of Abba Saul is confirmed by other Tannaitic sources.[42] The silence,

38 I.e. אמאום in Judea; there is no need to locate it near Tiberias (Horovitz, p. 52, note 4). On the name, cf. Prof. Klein, *Leshonénu*, Vol. iv, p. 46, note 3 (his observations should be completed with the help of our source here). Emmaus was the seat of R. Naḥunya b. ha-Qana (*Midrash Tanna'im*, ed. Hoffmann, p. 175).

39 Halevy (*op. cit.*, Part I, vol. v, p. 67) wishes to emend the reading וכשיצאו מלפניו in *Avot de-R. Nathan*, Version I, to וכשנפטר in *Ecclesiastes Rabba*, but he forgot Version II, which is not to be 'emended' at all.

40 *Avot de-R. Nathan*, Version I, iv, and Version II, vi; *T.B. Giṭṭin* 56a–b; *Lamentations Rabbati* i; *Midrash Proverbs* xxviii.

41 Ch. ii, 8; *Avot de-R. Nathan*, Version II, xxix.

42 In *Avot de-R. Nathan*, Version I, xiv, Rabban Joḥanan b. Zakkai accepts consolation only from R. Eleazar b. 'Arakh and declares that 'he is a great man and I cannot withstand him'. Cf. *Tosefta Ḥagiga* ii, 1; *T.B. ibid.* 14b; *T.P.* ii, 1 (R. Eleazar b. 'Arakh discourses on the Chariot before Rabban Joḥanan b. Zakkai). This Baraita (*Tosefta ibid.* and in the two Talmuds), which relates that R. Joshua discoursed before Rabban Joḥanan b. Zakkai on the Work of the Chariot is undoubtedly in conflict with the first tradition. The Babylonian Talmud already noted this inconsistency. The contradiction between the sources is to be explained by the two divergent views that we find in the Mishna *Avot* concerning R. Eleazar b. 'Arakh and his greatness in the estimation of Rabban Joḥanan b. Zakkai.

therefore, can only be explained by the fact that R. Eleazar b. ʿArakh did not join Rabban Joḥanan b. Zakkai when he left Jerusalem for Jabneh.

But we still have to clarify, in the light of this assumption, the passage in *Avot de-R. Nathan*, which ostensibly attests the fact that R. Eleazar b. ʿArakh was also with his teacher when he departed from the city, thus implying that he shared Rabban Joḥanan b. Zakkai's views. But, in order to assess this 'testimony' correctly, we must realize that at any rate not all the statements in the source are to be accepted at their face value. For this Haggada stresses R. Eleazar b. ʿArakh's dispute with Rabban Joḥanan b. Zakkai and his disciples regarding his preference for 'a place of good water'. Undoubtedly this is not to be considered, having regard to the time of the event, a matter of consequence, for this is not a reason suited to the situation in which the nation as a whole and the group of Sages found themselves at that troubled juncture. Perforce, therefore, we are inclined to the view that this is a later explanation dating from a time when the nexus between the events and their causes had become somewhat blurred. Hence we may assume that the tradition before us combined two events separated from each other by some interval of time. The transmitters of the tradition knew that R. Eleazar b. ʿArakh went to Emmaus and established his seat there. This departure, which did not precede the Destruction, was connected in the course of time with the departure of Rabban Joḥanan b. Zakkai and his other disciples for Jabneh and integrated into a single event, emphasizing at the same time, by this unification, the ethical motif referred to above.

The silence of the sources that describe Rabban Joḥanan b. Zakkai's exit from Jerusalem and his meeting with Vespasian indicates that R. Jose ha-Kohen and R. Simeon b. Nathaniel (also a priest and the son-in-law of Rabban Gamaliel the Elder)[43] were not at that time with Rabban Joḥanan. It seems, therefore, that also these two, of the five leading disciples of Rabban Joḥanan b. Zakkai mentioned in the Mishna, left their master.

When we seek a reason for the secession of these Sages from Rabban Joḥanan, when he went to lay a foundation for the Torah in

43 This refutes Büchler (*op. cit.* 23), who posits that R. Joseph ha-Kohen and Rabban Simeon b. Gamaliel were with Rabban Joḥanan b. Zakkai at Jabneh (on the basis of the Mishna in *Avot*, which apparently only refers to the period before the Destruction).

the refuge of Jabneh, we must inevitably say that they, no less than other Sages of the Torah named above, did not concur with their teacher's action and because in their opposition to him they withdrew from his school permanently, 'they forgot their learning'.

III. *The Sons of Bathyra*

In a Baraita it is stated (*T.B. Rosh ha-Shana* 29b): 'Our Rabbis taught: 'Once, when Rosh ha-Shana fell on a Sabbath, Rabban Joḥanan b. Zakkai said to the Sons of Bathyra 'Let us blow the Shofar'. They replied 'Let us discuss the matter (first)'. Said Rabban Joḥanan 'Let us blow the Shofar and then discuss it'. When, after the Shofar had been blown, they said to him 'Let us (now) discuss (the question)', he answered 'The horn has already been heard in Jabneh and no objection can be raised after the act'." '

Even a cursory examination of the Baraita shows that at the time when Rabban Joḥanan b. Zakkai was debating with the Sons of Bathyra the enactment he wished to introduce, namely that the Shofar be blown in Jabneh on Rosh ha-Shana even when it fell on a Sabbath, just as they did in Jerusalem, his authority as Patriarch was not accepted by the Sons of Bathyra, who appear here as having equal standing with Rabban Joḥanan and not as subordinate to him. Hence Rabban Joḥanan b. Zakkai was compelled to resort to a subterfuge against them in order to establish his enactment. One of the Rishonim[44] already noted the position and explained the attitude of the Sons of Bathyra by the fact that the Patriarchate was vested in them before Hillel was appointed.

This source informs us, therefore, that during the initial period of Rabban Joḥanan b. Zakkai's residence at Jabneh his Patriarchal authority was impaired in the presence of the Sons of Bathyra, who had also come there with him. It is logical to suppose that they were not prepared to forgo this 'vested right' to the Patriarchate in favour of Rabban Joḥanan b. Zakkai, after it had become vacant upon the interruption of the line of Hillel, who had taken over the leadership from them.

But in order to be able to evaluate the event correctly we must first endeavour to elucidate the moot question of the origin and history of the Sons of Bathyra.

44 The author of *Yiḥuse Tanna'im wa-Amora'im* (ed. Rabbinovicz, Lyck, 10a): 'It appears to me that the Sons of Bathyra continued to maintain their father's authority and learning.'

Graetz[45] identifies the Sons of Bathyra mentioned in the Talmudic sources with the great and powerful Babylonian family that Herod brought over to Eretz-Israel and settled in northern Transjordan. Isaak Halevy,[46] followed by Prof. Klausner,[47] disagrees with this identification and holds that 'the Sons of Bathyra' in the Talmud are unrelated to the Babylonians settled by Herod in Bathyra on the border of Syria. The objections raised by Halevy and Prof. Klausner are, ostensibly, very powerful. But after closer scrutiny, the force of these refutations is considerably diminished and Graetz's view, although only a probable conjecture, remains unimpaired.

Let us first, therefore, examine the evidence on which Graetz's theory is based, and then the counterarguments. Graetz advances four reasons: (a) the joint name; the word 'Bathyra' in the designation of the family mentioned in the Talmud is certainly only a general appellation denoting a place (or genealogical origin);[48] (b) both families first appear approximately at the same time (in Herod's reign); (c) both flourished during all the subsequent generations until the Destruction (and after);[49] (d) both came from Babylon.[50]

The counterarguments are: (a) the Babylonians referred to by Josephus were great warriors, whereas the Sons of Bathyra in Talmudic literature were great scholars; (b) in the tradition of the Palestinian Talmud,[51] in its account of the abdication of the Sons of Bathyra from the Patriarchate, they say of Hillel at first: 'What can one expect from a Babylonian?'; but no one ever disqualifies another with his own infirmity; (c) according to the tradition of the Babylonian Talmud[52] 'Hillel and Simeon Gamaliel and Simeon functioned as Patriarchs one hundred years before the destruction of the Temple'; how then could the Sons of Bathyra serve in the Patriarchate before Hillel, if they were the 'Babylonians' mentioned by Josephus, seeing that they came to Eretz-Israel some 80–90 years before the Destruction?

45 *MGWJ*, Vol. I, pp. 115–120. Nachman Krochmal also inclines to this view (*More Nevukhe ha-Zeman*, ed. Rawidowicz, 118).

46 *Dorot Harischonim*, Pt. I, Vol. III, chs. vii–xii.

47 *Historya Yisre'elit*, Pt. III, 42–43.

48 Cf. *Yiḥuse Tanna'im wa-'Amora'im*, *ibid.*

49 *Life*, xi (see Dr. Stein's notes in the Hebrew translation, p. 29). See also *Wars* ii, 17, 4; also *Sifre Numbers* §115 and the parallels in *T.B. Menaḥot* 41b and *T.B. Pesaḥim* 3b.

50 Several generations later we find 'R. Judah b. Bathyra at Nisibis'.

51 *T.P. Pesaḥim* vi, 33a.

52 *T.B. Sabbath* 15b.

But these objections do not necessarily refute the hypothesis entirely. The family of the Sons of Bathyra was a large one and some of its members made soldiering their career, while others devoted themselves wholly to Torah study. Nor is there any reason to believe that in antiquity the Book everywhere ousted the Sword from Jewish life. Regarding the second objection it should be noted that in the parallel tradition in the Babylonian Talmud the expression in question is completely missing. It must therefore be presumed that the tradition in the Palestinian Talmud contains a literary embellishment derived from the prevailing popular opinion, for in Tannaitic and Amoraic times the Palestinian Jews looked upon the Babylonians as unintelligent people ('Babylonian fools', and even Hillel himself was dubbed as such — *Avot de-R. Nathan*, Version I, xii). Nothing, therefore, can be inferred from this passage concerning the origin of the Sons of Bathyra, which apparently was partly forgotten in the course of time.

More serious than these obscurities is the chronological difficulty that arises from the tradition in the Babylonian Talmud regarding the duration of the Patriarchate of Hillel and his descendants.[53] But in this respect, too, it may be stated objectively that this late tradition (which was not even accurate in listing the generations, for it included Simeon I in the line of Patriarchs that ruled after Hillel, but this does not apparently accord with the facts)[54] used a global figure and a stereotyped chronology and did not seek to date precisely.

If, however, we examine carefully the Talmudic traditions[55] concerning the commencement of Hillel's Patriarchate, we arrive at a different understanding of the source in question from the initial impression for apparently these traditions come to tell us that Hillel was appointed Patriarch immediately upon immigrating to Eretz-Israel. But, apart from the fact that Hillel was known to have sat for many years at the feet of Shemaʿya and Avṭalyon in Jerusalem it is inconceivable that an unknown foreigner would be appointed Patriarch over all Israel. Without doubt Hillel must have lived in Jerusalem for a long time before his election to the Patriarchate, and he must have been regarded by the people even before then as a great man, and he must have first officiated at the school and in the

53 This objection was raised by the first critic of Graetz's theory, namely Fürst (*MGWJ*, Vol. I, 559–561).

54 Cf. *Historya Yisre'elit*, Vol. III, p. 102.

55 But in the Tosefta (*Pesaḥim* iv, 1–2) the form of the tradition is different and approximates to the account in the text, which pictures Hillel as well-known at the time.

Sanhedrin in an important capacity. This made it possible for the Sons of Bathyra to be ousted at a given juncture and for him to reign in their stead.

Hence it must be concluded that the Babylonian tradition which dates the commencement of Hillel's Patriarchate a century before the Destruction has added the period that Hillel actually functioned as Patriarch to the earlier period when he served his generation as a Torah teacher and as an administrator on a lower level.[56] We are therefore able to confirm Graetz's theory and to regard these sons of Bathyra, who acted as Patriarchs before Hillel and challenged the authority of Rabban Joḥanan b. Zakkai after the Destruction, as members of that great family which rose to pre-eminence under Herod. In the light of this view the strong stand taken by them against Rabban Joḥanan b. Zakkai is quite understandable. For this family had served Herod throughout his reign and also his descendants Agrippas I and II, and like them had been supporters of the Romans; some of them had lived in Jerusalem at the beginning of the Great War and occupied there an important place in the community and within the influential and governmental circles.[57] If now Rabban Joḥanan b. Zakkai succeeded in gaining permission to go to Jabneh, to establish a school there and to renew the Patriarchate (although he wisely took care not to mention the question of the Patriarchate to Vespasian), because he was 'one of Caesar's friends',[58] then from this aspect, having regard to their attitude to Rome, they, too, no less than Rabban Joḥanan, were entitled to expect honours, and hence when they came to Jabneh, they revived their former claim to the Patriarchate.

But at this point we must re-examine the Patriarchate of the Sons of Bathyra *ab ovo*, since Isaak Halevy[59] has advanced a new theory, which denies that they were ever Patriarchs.

Halevy puts forward two arguments against the accepted view based on Talmudic sources as follows: if the Sons of Bathyra were

56 Just as the *Sifre* (Deut. §357) states that Rabban Joḥanan b. Zakkai served Israel (as Patriarch) for forty years, obtaining this figure by adding the few years that he acted as Patriarch after the Destruction to the period prior to that, when he officiated as Head of the Court (or in some other capacity).

57 *Life*, §xxix.

58 *Avot de-R. Nathan*, Version I, iv (similar to it is Version II, vi): 'they would write down on an arrow and shoot over the wall, and thus reported that Rabban Joḥanan b. Zakkai was a friend of Caesar'.

59 *Op. cit.*, Pt. I, vol. III, ch. xi. Essentially, however, Zacharias Frankel already posited this (*Darkhe ha-Mishna*[2], p. 43).

Patriarchs why are they not mentioned in the list of Patriarchs, found in *M. Avot*, who received the Torah tradition, and why have they been omitted from the Pairs who differed about the laying-on of hands [on the sacrificial beast on a Festival day] (*M. Ḥagiga* ii, 2)?

Halevy, therefore, maintains that the Sons of Bathyra stood at the head of the community only temporarily — during a period of transition — without actually being Patriarchs.

But Halevy's objections are without substance. The tradition of Mishna *Avot* does not purport to enumerate all the leaders of the generations that functioned in the two centuries between the first Pair, Jose b. Joʿezer of Ẓeredah and Jose b. Joḥanan of Jerusalem, and the last Pair, Hillel and Shammai; obviously more than five Pairs reigned during this long period. The Mishna mentions only the terminal and important links in the chain of the recipients of the Torah and passes over those in between. How could the Mishna state that Hillel and Shammai received the Torah-tradition from the Sons of Bathyra, seeing that they acquired their Torah-learning directly from Shemaʿya and Avṭalyon and did not study under the Sons of Bathyra at all?

Likewise in *Ḥagiga* the Mishna does not enumerate the Patriarchs and Heads of the Court for the purpose of listing the generations, but only to indicate those who disputed the practice of laying on the hands. Is it surprising then that the tradition does not recall this dispute in the time of the Sons of Bathyra? However, I think it probable that Menaḥem, who is mentioned in this Mishna ('Hillel and Menaḥem did not differ') was one of the Sons of Bathyra.

A number of scholars agree with R. Azariah dei Rossi and R. Abraham Zacuto, the author of *Sefer ha-Yuḥasin* ['The Book of Genealogies'], in regarding Menaḥem as the Essene, who, according to Josephus,[60] was honoured by Herod for prophesying as a child that he would become king of Judea. This conjecture is not, to my mind, consonant with the sources. For we read in a Baraita (*T.B. Ḥagiga* 16b; *T.P. ibid.* ii, 77d) 'He and eighty pairs of scholars went forth' etc. (in the parallel passage at the end of *Canticles Zuṭa*: 'eight hundred disciples'). Menaḥem was accordingly a great Torah-scholar and the teacher of many students. On the other hand, we learn from the version of the Palestinian Baraita 'They wore golden corselets[61] (תירקי = θώρκες; the reading תיריקי in the Palestinian Talmud is to be pre-

60 *Ant.* xv, 10, 5.

61 So, too, Geiger correctly explains it in *Zeitschrift* iv.

ferred to סירייקון in the Babylonian Talmud[62]), and from the wording of the Babylonian Baraita 'He went forth to the king's service', that Menaḥem was at the head of a big contingent that served in Herod's army. These facts — that on the one hand the tradition recalls Menaḥem's eminence as a Torah-scholar and, on the other, is aware that he fulfilled, together with a large group of intimates, the function of an army commander of the king — fit the qualities of the Sons of Bathyra, as they are known to us from the Talmudic sources and from Josephus.[63]

I wish, therefore, to suggest that this tradition preserved the memory of a large family that served in Herod's army, but, at the same time, was aware that it comprised Sages and that one of them, Menaḥem, had been Patriarch in Herod's time, and thus proceeded to link these two facts in the form of successive events, basing itself on the words of the Mishna 'Menaḥem went forth and Shammai entered.'

But, ostensibly, this conjecture is refuted by the statement in the Mishna 'Hillel and Menaḥem did not differ; Menaḥem went forth and Shammai entered', which implies, as it were, that Menaḥem formerly occupied the position subsequently held by Shammai, but Shammai was never a Patriarch![64]

62 Also in *Cant. Zuta* (end) we find 'סיריקונין of gold'. But in the Parma MS., *ibid.* (Schechter, p. 96), the reading is 'בסתרקי of gold'. Apparently the recension in the Babylonian Talmud was corrupted from 'בתרקי of gold'.

63 It should not, however, be objected that in *Cant. Zuta* it is stated 'In the days of Menaḥem and Hillel, when a dispute broke out between them', whereas the Sons of Bathyra, according to the Talmudic tradition (*T.B. Bava Meṣi'a* 85a; *T.P. Kil'ayim* ix, 32a; and the parallel passage in *T.P. Ketubbot* xii, 35a) abdicated voluntarily in favour of Hillel, because these are divergent sources.

I would comment here on the word ארחמו (or אורחמו — 'The men of ארחומו sent and set up a camp against Jerusalem' etc.), which Schechter (p. 96) and Buber (p. 41, n. 15) found difficult to explain (the observations of Jawitz, Vol. v, note 5, are far-fetched and strange). It means Rome, which in Syriac is written רהומי, *Rehumi* (the *Alef* is prosthetic and *Hē'* is to be read for *Ḥêt*). Earlier on, when the Midrash declares: '"Make haste, my beloved" — this refers to the day when I made a covenant with Aruḥuma and they offered up two lambs, one on the north of the altar' etc., it alludes to the sacrifices that were offered up every day in honour of the emperors of Rome, and gives expression to the view of the ('nationalist') Sages, who were opposed to this act (attested also by Josephus and Philo). The subject deserves to be investigated Halachically and historically, but this is not the place for it.

64 In *Avot de-R. Nathan*, Version II, xxii (end) the reading is: 'Menaḥem went forth and *Hillel* entered.' But evidently the text is corrupt for immediately afterwards (ch. xxiii) Shammai is quoted.

However, it appears that although both Talmuds (and also the Baraita mentioned above) explain the wording [יצא] of this Mishna literally in the sense of 'going forth', the plain meaning of our Mishna is simply that Menaḥem was not [literally 'was excluded from'] among those who differed on the subject of laying on the hands, because the tradition had no knowledge of Menaḥem's disputing the issue, and Shammai entered as one of the disputants. For, as stated earlier, our Mishna does not intend to relate the history of the Patriarchs, but to enumerate those who differed regarding this Halakha, and there was no need to cite the incident in question out of context. We also find this idiomatic usage in other passages where a given number occurs (in our case — five Pairs) and someone comes to exclude one or more of those enumerated from the total and to introduce others in their place, in order to complete the number fixed by tradition. This, for instance, is the phrasing of the *Tosefta Menaḥot* xii (which is based on the Mishna *ibid.* ix, 2, 'There were seven liquid-measures in the Temple'): 'R. Simeon said: The *hin* was not one of the seven measures in the Temple... What did he put in its place? A *log* and a half [לוג ומחצה]' (in the parallel Baraita in *T.B. ibid.* 87b–88a: 'What should I put in its stead?'). This, too, is the sense of this expression (in Aramaic) in the Talmud and the Midrash and the like.[65]

The Sons of Bathyra, therefore, were intimates of the king and were regarded as peace-lovers and friends of the Romans. It was they who functioned as Patriarchs before the appointment of Hillel, and consequently when the Patriarchate became vacant, upon the temporary interruption of the Hillelite dynasty, they again claimed for themselves the right to stand at the head of the nation and proceeded to challenge the authority of Rabban Joḥanan b. Zakkai. Only, in the end Rabban Joḥanan prevailed against them and his Patriarchate was firmly established at Jabneh.

IV. *Rabban Gamaliel* (*of Jabneh*)

In order to elucidate the relationship between Rabban Gamaliel and Rabban Joḥanan b. Zakkai from the time when the latter began to officiate as Patriarch until his death, we must first understand what

65 Cf. for example, *Midrash Lamentations Rabbati,* ch. ii (on verse 2: 'The Lord hath swallowed up') on the list of the Ten Martyrs executed by the Romans: 'Some exclude [דמפקין] R. Ṭarfon and include [ומעילין] R. Eleazar Ḥarsana.

it was that prevented Rabban Gamaliel from succeeding to the throne of his fathers immediately after the Destruction.

The Rishonim, and likewise a number of modern scholars,[66] are of opinion that Rabban Gamaliel was unable to act as Patriarch at the time, because he was still a minor. But this theory was already disproved by R. Ḥayyim Joseph David Azulai,[67] who proved from *M. Yevamot* xvi, 7, that Rabban Gamaliel was an adult long before the Destruction. Subsequently, Isaak Halevy adduced further proof from another source.[68]

Perforce, therefore, we must seek the explanation in the political situation prevailing in the country and in the attitude of the Romans to the first Patriarchal family after the destruction of the Temple.

This policy was naturally prompted by the acts of his father Rabban Simeon in the course of the war. For Rabban Simeon was for a long time one of the aggressive and reliable leaders who headed the people in revolt (his zealotic stance — even if not extremist — may be deduced from his attitude and actions towards Josephus, who had defected and betrayed his charge and from the friendship he showed to John of Giscala).

However, in order to understand the position adopted by Rabban Simeon b. Gamaliel towards the Romans in the last phase of the war, from the clash between the Zealots and the Sanhedrin over who should rule in Jerusalem up to the Destruction, we must clarify the question of Rabban Simeon's death.

Several modern scholars are inclined to presume that he was put to death by the Zealots.[69] This view, which derives mainly from the tendency of the scholars to equate Rabban Simeon b. Gamaliel with Rabban Joḥanan b. Zakkai in their stance towards Rome and to regard Rabban Joḥanan as the sole representative of the Pharisees as a whole in their attitude to the events of the time, is completely

66 Tosafot, *T.B. Beṣa* 23a, s.v. תליסר; R. Simeon b. Ṣemah Duran, *Magen Avot* on *M. Avot* i, 16; Graetz, *Geschichte*, iv, p. 14; Bruell, *Mevo' ha-Mishna*, p. 62; Landau, *MGWJ*, I, 285; Derenbourg, *ibid.*, I, 28^5.

67 *Petaḥ 'Enayim* on *T.B. Berakhot* 23a and on *T.B. Giṭṭin* 56b.

68 *Op. cit.*, Pt. I, vol. v, ch. xv. Although he cites this Mishna, too, in support of his argument, he does not mention Azulai. Cf. Landau, *op. cit.*, note 5. Derenbourg already inferred that Rabban Gamaliel was an adult before the Destruction from *M. 'Eruvin* vi, 2 (*Maśśa' Ereṣ Yisrael*, Pt. II, 165, note 1). See also Bruell, *op. cit.*; Frankel, *Darkhe ha-Mishna*^{2}, p. 72. R. Simeon b. Ṣemaḥ Duran, *op. cit.*, deduced from *M. Pesaḥim* iii, 2, that 'Rabban Gamaliel saw the Temple still standing'.

69 Graetz, *MGWJ*, Vol. I, 315–321; Weiss, *Dor Dor we-Dorshaw*^{2}, Pt. I, p. 180.

unfounded. Furthermore, all the sources that relate Rabban Simeon b. Gamaliel's death are unanimous that he was killed by the Roman authorities,[70] and though these traditions contain a number of difficulties that cannot ostensibly, be removed, nevertheless we have no reason to doubt the truth of the fact attested by them all. Hence we are not in a position to state, as does Simḥoni[71] (with whom other scholars agree) that 'Rabban Simeon b. Gamaliel returned to the Pharisees proper, who belonged to Rabban Joḥanan b. Zakkai's faction', for were there such he would not in the end have been put to death by the Romans.

Even if he took a leading part, as Simḥoni asserts, in the bitter struggle against the Zealots, which Josephus describes in *Wars* iv, 3, 9 ff., this only proves that Rabban Simeon wished to defend the statutory rule of the Sanhedrin and the security of the public against the fanatical Zealots who went to extreme lengths and wrought havoc in the country. It cannot possibly be inferred from this that he desired at that time to submit to the Romans, for good or ill, as did Rabban Joḥanan b. Zakkai.

Furthermore, there are two reasons for doubting Rabban Simeon b. Gamaliel's participation in that episode: (a) Josephus, who subsequently relates that three of Rabban Simeon b. Gamaliel's collaborators at the time — Gorion b. Joseph, Joshua [Jesus] b. Gamala, and Ḥanan [Ananus] b. Ḥanan — were murdered by the Zealots, makes no mention of Rabban Simeon b. Gamaliel's fate. When we recall that the Talmudic sources tell us that R. Simeon was executed by the Roman authorities, it is difficult to understand why the Zealots made an exception of him *vis-à-vis* his colleagues. (b) The final act that led to civil strife was, according to Josephus, the selection of Phinehas of Kefar Ḥavta [Aphtha] as High Priest. But this Phinehas

70 *Mekhilta, Mishpatim*, xviii; *Avot de-R. Nathan* (Version I, xxxviii; Version II, xli). *Tractate Sémahot* viii, 8; *T.B. Sanhedrin* 11a; *Lamentations Rabbati*, ch. i; *Midrash Psalms* ix; *Tanna debe Eliahu* (Friedmann) xxviii; *Megillot Taʿanit* (end); cf. *Bet ha-Midrash* (Jellinek), Ḥeder II, p. 66 and *ibid.*, Ḥeder VI, p. 20; and the piyyut '*Elle Ezkera*'. This is also the view of the *Rishonim*. Graetz's conjecture (*MGWJ*, *ibid.*, p. 320) that the name ר' שמעון בן גמליאל [Rabban Simeon b. Gamaliel] was incorrectly derived from the abbreviation רשב״נ = ר' שמעון בן ננס (R. Simeon b. Nannas) is improbable.

71 Notes and Explanations to *Wars*, p. 463. Even Zechariah b. Eucolus, who was a Pharisee (*Tosefta Shabbat* xvii, 9) and a 'humble [i.e. scrupulous] man' (*ibid.* and *T.B. Giṭṭin* 56a), collaborated with the Zealots and stood at their head after the incident referred to (*Wars* iv, 4, 1).

was the son-in-law of Rabban Simeon b. Gamaliel (or of Rabban Gamaliel his father)![72]

When we abandon misleading comparisons, we must come to the conclusion that the Pharisees were divided at that time over the question of the war; some followed in the path of Rabban Joḥanan b. Zakkai, while there were others who refused to make peace with Caesar and remained in Jerusalem until its destruction (a similar difference of opinion we find among the Sages in Bar Kokhba's time!).

Rabban Simeon b. Gamaliel's stance in the war and his execution by the Romans, when Jerusalem was conquered, support the assumption that Rabban Gamaliel was prevented from functioning as Patriarch by governmental decree. Subsequently, too, the Roman authorities persecuted, according to the testimony of the Christian tradition, the descendants of the Davidic dynasty.[73]

When we come to consider the relations between Rabban Gamaliel and Rabban Joḥanan b. Zakkai at that period, we must first stress the point of political polarity in the light of the fact, which has been elucidated previously, that Rabban Joḥanan b. Zakkai made peace with Vespasian,[74] whereas Rabban Simeon b. Gamaliel, his superior

72 *Torat Kohanim*, Emor, Sec. 2; *Tosefta Yoma* i, 5.

73 Cf. Schürer, *Geschichte*, I, p. 661, and n. 43. Halevy (*op. cit.*, Pt. I, vol. 5, xix–xx) gives an elaborate explanation of the Baraita in *T.B. Ta'anit* 29a, stating that it refers to Rabban Gamaliel of Jabneh and that the Turnusrufus mentioned there is Terentius Rufus, who was appointed commander of the Roman army in Judea after the Destruction (*Wars* vii, 2, 2). This interpretation was already suggested earlier by Z. H. Chajes, who wrote on the same lines to Jakob Bruell, 'in the name of a certain scholar' (*Mevo' ha-Mishna*, vol. I, p. 56). On the basic interpretation of the Baraita, cf. *Yuḥasin s.v.* Rabban Gamaliel of Jabneh.

74 Rabban Joḥanan b. Zakkai's moderate attitude and his desire for peace from the commencement of the war finds expression, to my mind, in the dictum that apparently dates from the initial period of the Revolt, after the defeat of C. Gallus, when the Jews dominated the neighbouring nations and the people were enthusiastic and confident of victory. He declared (in the Mekhilta fragment to Deuteronomy, which Schechter published from a MS in *JQR*, xvi, p. 447; *Midrash Tanna'im*, ed. Hoffmann, p. 56; so also *Avot de-R. Nathan*, Version II, xxxi, cf. *ibid.*): 'Be not hasty to destroy the high places of the Gentiles, lest you have to rebuild them with your own hand; lest you destroy those made of brick and they bid you make them again of stone, or make them of wood.'

Frankel already realized the relationship between Rabban Simeon b. Gamaliel and Rabban Joḥanan b. Zakkai, as explained above, and wrote (*Darkhe ha-Mishna*[2], p. 72, addendum): 'Possibly there was no real harmony between Rabban Simeon, the father of Rabban Gamaliel, who was opposed

(in rank) and Patriarch, continued to carry the burden of the war and remained in Jerusalem until it was conquered and he himself was decapitated. When we add thereto the denial of the Patriarchate to the legitimate successor and his persecution by the Roman authorities, who allowed Rabban Joḥanan b. Zakkai to conduct his Patriarchal office at Jabneh, and finally the fact that we do not find in the sources any connection between Rabban Gamaliel and Rabban Joḥanan b. Zakkai,[75] we cannot believe, as do many scholars, that Rabban Gamaliel was to be found in Rabban Joḥanan's company throughout the period of the latter's Patriarchate. This view rests on the well-known tradition in the Babylonian Talmud that Rabban Joḥanan b. Zakkai asked Vespasian for 'the dynasty of Rabban Gamaliel'. However, the meagre value of this obscure tradition[76] is negated by the fact that there is no trace of it in any of the other parallel Palestinian traditions. This omission is undoubtedly to be explained only by the fact that they had no knowledge of this request, for had they known of it they would certainly not have refrained from mentioning it on account of its importance.

If we eschew apologetics and endeavour to see and evaluate the events against the background of their time, we must presume that Rabban Gamaliel could not have agreed to Rabban Joḥanan b. Zakkai's Patriarchate, or accept his authority. Although prevented, on account of political circumstances, from inheriting his ancestral office, he certainly did not despair, but awaited an opportune moment, when the severity of Roman persecution would ease, and he could attempt to regain, with the help of the community (the great majority

to the Romans... and Rabban Joḥanan b. Zakkai, who urged the acceptance anew of the Roman yoke and personally went over to Vespasian, as we know from the story in *T.B. Giṭṭin.*'

75 Although in *T.B. Bava Batra* 10b, Rabban Gamaliel is stated to have been a disciple of Rabban Joḥanan b. Zakkai, yet we have already seen earlier (note 35) that this tradition contradicts that of *M. Avot*. Furthermore in the parallel passage in *Tanḥuma*, Ki Tiśśa', Rabban Gamaliel is not mentioned at all. In *Pesiqta de-R. Kahana*, too, one must read, with the Carmoly MS. (Buber, p. 12b, note 39), רבנן 'The Rabbis' (instead of ר״ג = Rabban Gamaliel), for the passage there commences: 'R. Eliezer and R. Joshua, and the Rabbis' (it appears that two different traditions have been conflated in the *Pesiqta*; see *ibid.*). Bacher has expressed doubt (*Die Agada der Tannaïten*, vol. I, p. 34, note 4, and *ibid.*, p. 73, note 1) about this tradition, which makes Rabban Gamaliel a disciple of Rabban Joḥanan b. Zakkai. As for *Pirqe de-R. Eliezer* ch. vii (see *ibid.*), no objections can be raised on the basis of a pseudepigraphical work.

76 *T.B. Giṭṭin* 56b.

of whom were unquestionably well disposed towards him in recognition of his ancestors' noble works and of the right of the House of David) the authority and leadership of which he was temporarily deprived.

This moment, it seems, was not long in coming. For we find Rabban Joḥanan b. Zakkai, at the end of his days, residing, together with his pupils, at Beror Ḥayil,[77] while Rabban Gamaliel's seat was consolidated in Jabneh. Rabban Gamaliel, therefore, was raised to his high office in Jabneh in the lifetime of Rabban Joḥanan b. Zakkai, who apparently could not withstand the desire of the nation to enthrone a descendant of the House of David, which had been deprived of its honours by the Gentiles,[78] to rule over them.

At this period, when Rabban Gamaliel reigned in Jabneh and Rabban Joḥanan b. Zakkai taught in Beror Ḥayil, the latter's leading pupils attended his school and his Bet Din. But even they did not wish, after their master's death, to refuse allegiance to Rabban Gamaliel's Patriarchate, and came to Jabneh and served him.[79] At that juncture Rabban Gamaliel succeeded in uniting the nation, which

77 *T.B. Sanhedrin* 32b (*Sifre Deuteronomy*, Sec. 144); *Tosefta Ma'aśerot* ii, 1. On the form of the name of this place cf. the Geonic responsum in *Teshuvot ha-Ge'onim*, ed. Harkavy, No. 361 Appendices (= Lewin, *Otzar ha-Geonim*, Appendix 16), which reads in *T.P. Ketubbot* i, 25c, בלור חיל.

78 Geiger, too, is of opinion that there was friction between Rabban Joḥanan b. Zakkai and Rabban Gamaliel and that 'Rabban Gamaliel ousted Rabban Joḥanan b. Zakkai' (*Zeitschrift* vi, 132), but he does not elaborate. His other observations, however (on *M. Avot*, q.v.), are improbable.

Halevy, who holds that Rabban Joḥanan b. Zakkai went voluntarily from Jabneh to Beror Ḥayil for the sake of Rabban Gamaliel (a view already advanced earlier by Derenbourg), endeavours to prove this thesis from *M. Rosh ha-Shana* iv, 4, 'R. Joshua b. Qorḥa said: Rabban Joḥanan b. Zakkai ordained this also that wheresoever the Chief of the Court might be, witnesses should go only to the place of assembly'. This he interprets to mean that Rabban Joḥanan b. Zakkai enacted that witnesses of the New Moon should not come to him at Beror Ḥayil (for he was 'the Chief of the Court') but to the Patriarch Rabban Gamaliel (at Jabneh), 'so as to strengthen the position of the new Patriarch, who was sitting with them (with the assembly) there'. But this Mishna is not relevant to our discussion, because its meaning is thus explained in *T.P. Rosh ha-Shana* iv, 59c: 'The Mishna means to the place of the assembly of the New Moon'. For although the fixing of the months, the years, and the festivals was in the hands of the Patriarch, he could delegate this task to others, and thus we find that Rabbi sent R. Ḥiyya to receive the witnesses of the New Moon at 'En Ṭav. So, too, R. Osha'ya received the witnesses at that place. The place of 'the assembly of the New Moon' was not necessarily the seat of the Patriarch and his Court.

79 *Ecclesiastes Rabba*, vii.

was apparently split and divided by political, social and family differences, which had their origin in the war period and its aftermath, and in establishing a strong central authority acceptable to all.

However, it appears that although Rabban Gamaliel was able to bring back those who had been alienated and to bridge the differences that had existed between him and the school of Rabban Joḥanan b. Zakkai, he was nevertheless unable to obliterate completely the effect of the earlier days. It thus came about that after friction had repeatedly broken out between him and R. Joshua b. Ḥananiah, the distinguished disciple of Rabban Joḥanan b. Zakkai, in Torah learning and political outlook, he was temporarily deposed from the Patriarchate, and the Hillelite dynasty was again in danger of coming to an end.[80] Even when his son, Rabban Simeon, succeeded him, Patriarchal authority was liable to be weakened by the disciples of R. Akiba,[81] because the influence of earlier factors had not yet ceased; they were concealed in times of peace, but manifested themselves when the opportunity presented itself. This was the position until Rabbi came and succeeded in 'casting bile among the students' [i.e. in asserting strict discipline over them] and 'in conducting his Patriarchate with men of high standing',[82] thus establishing the Patriarchal authority on a firm basis, to which all submitted. Hence it was said 'From the time of Moses unto Rabbi we do not find (pre-eminence of) Torah-learning and high office united in one person (as in their case).'[83]

80 In the sources we encounter friction between Rabban Gamaliel and R. Akiba regarding the authority of the Patriarch to decide against the view of the majority (*Tosefta Berakhot* iv, 12, and in the parallel passage in *T.B. ibid.* 37a; *Tosefta Beṣa* ii, 12).

This enables us to solve the difficulty raised in *T.P. Berakhot* i, 3a: 'Rabban Gamaliel disagreed with the Rabbis and nevertheless acted according to his own view (but how can this be justified?). For behold R. Meir, when he disagreed with the Rabbis, did not act according to his own opinion, and R. Akiba, when he differed from the Rabbis, did not act in accordance with his personal opinion... and we find that R. Simeon disagreed with the Rabbis, but did not act according to his ruling!' The answer is that Rabban Gamaliel was not like other people; he was the Patriarch.

81 *T.B. Horayot* 13b (but R. Nathan also joined R. Meir), from the fragment of a responsum by Rav Sherira Gaon, published in *JQR*, xiv, 488–491 (= Lewin, *op. cit.*, Appendix 5), it appears that R. Jose was also involved in the incident (only the statement, which undoubtedly emanates from an early tradition, is obscure).

82 *T.B. Ketubbot* 103b.

83 *T.B. Giṭṭin* 59a and the parallel in *T.B. Sanhedrin* 36a.

We find constant contention between the Patriarchs — from the time of Rabban Gamaliel to Rabbi Judah the Patriarch ('our holy master') — and the Sages who were the disciples and the disciples of the disciples of Rabban Joḥanan b. Zakkai on the question of authority to appoint Elders (ordination). Thus R. Ba' states in *T.P. Sanhedrin* i, 19a: 'At first every Sage used to ordain his own disciples; for example, Rabban Joḥanan b. Zakkai ordained R. Eliezer and R. Joshua, and R. Joshua gave ordination to R. Akiba and R. Akiba to R. Meir and R. Simeon. . . Subsequently they paid honour to this House [i.e. the Patriarchal Dynasty] declaring that the ordination of a Bet Din that ordained without the consent of the Patriarch was invalid, whereas a Patriarch's ordination without the consent of the Bet Din was valid. Later it was enacted that the Bet Din should ordain only with the approval of the Patriarch and that the Patriarch should ordain only with the assent of the Bet Din.' From the generations enumerated in this Talmudic statement it can easily be inferred that the authority to ordain became the privilege solely of the Patriarch in the days of Rabbi; and the restriction of this absolute right of the Patriarch to appoint Elders, so that it was subject to the consent of the Sages, took place in the time of Judah Nesi'a.[84] Indeed we find Rabbi appointing Elders on his own accord, whereas in his grandson's day Sages were ordained by R. Joḥanan and R. Joshua b. Levi (in consonance with this tradition, the Patriarch consenting).[85] We further learn from this passage that the Sages attributed their right in this respect to the authority of Rabban Joḥanan b. Zakkai and his disciples. Thus the relations between the scholars and the Patriarchate were long influenced by the memory of Rabban Joḥanan's

84 Abraham Krochmal (*Yerushalayim ha-Benuya*, 105) holds that it was to Rabban Simeon b. Gamaliel that the power of ordination by the Patriarch alone was granted. But J. H. Schorr already in *He-Ḥalutz*, 1853, p. 41, took the same view as that adumbrated in the text; so, too, Weiss, *Dor Dor we-Dorshaw*[6], vol. III, 56. Bornstein (*Ha-Tekufa*, vol. iv, p. 317) also inclines to this opinion. In connection with our subject it should also be noted that the enactment barring a disciple (i.e. one who was not ordained) from giving a decision was likewise promulgated by Rabbi (*T.B. Sanhedrin* 56b; *T.P. Shevi'it* vi, 35c).

85 Weiss regards R. Joshua b. Levi's act of ordination as indicative of a dispute between the scholars of the South and the House of the Patriarch. But R. Joḥanan, too, gave ordination and he was one of the intimates and supporters of the Patriarch ('R. Joḥanan of the Patriarch's House', *T.B. Soṭa*, 11b). It seems, therefore, as stated in the text, that these ordinations were carried out with the Patriarch's consent. J. H. Schorr also wrote (*op. cit.*): 'Perhaps this was done with the Patriarch's consent.'

attitude towards the family of Hillel. For the Tannaim whose learning is enshrined in the Mishna and whose wisdom was a source of strength to the Patriarchs, in governance and in formulating decisions, came from the school of Rabban Joḥanan b. Zakkai's disciple.

It also seems that *M. Avot* gives expression to this struggle between the Patriarchs and the Sages who followed the teaching of the great master, Rabban Joḥanan b. Zakkai, in its reference to two lines of Torah-recipients, the one including the Patriarchs from Hillel to Rabban Gamaliel, the son of R. Judah the Patriarch (i, 12–ii, 4), and the other assigning the receipt of the Torah tradition to Rabban Joḥanan b. Zakkai and his disciples (ii, 8–14). It would appear that this duality stems from two divergent viewpoints found among the Sages concerning the right of spiritual rulership over the nation. In this case, too, the tower of strength of those who challenged the Patriarchal Family was Rabban Joḥanan b. Zakkai.[86]

The reason why only faint echoes remain of the differences that existed after the Destruction between Rabban Joḥanan b. Zakkai and the circles mentioned above is the fact that Rabban Joḥanan b. Zakkai's disciples gave allegiance after their master's death to Rabban Gamaliel, that time served to temper the judgement of succeeding generations on Rabban Joḥanan b. Zakkai, and finally the most important factor — that the great majority of our sources emanate from the teaching of Rabban Joḥanan b. Zakkai's disciples and their

86 It seems to me not unlikely that the Mishna (*Sanhedrin* v, 2) that calls Rabban Joḥanan b. Zakkai just 'Ben Zakkai' emanates from the circles that did not regard him as having Patriarchal status. To the question why he was not called Rabban Joḥanan b. Zakkai the Talmud replies that at the time he was only a disciple sitting before his master (*T.B. Sanhedrin* 41a–b); a similar solution is also offered in *T.B. Ta'anit* 3a with reference to R. Judah b. Bathyra). This explanation, however, is difficult, for it cannot be supposed that a disciple, even though as worthy of giving a decision as Ben 'Azzai, would be allowed to examine the witnesses in capital cases (the examination would certainly have been conducted by the heads of the Sanhedrin). The fact that he is not called 'Rabbi' is rather to be explained by the fact that the use of this title came into force only in the generation after the Destruction, in accordance with the testimony of Rav Sherira Gaon in the responsum cited in Lewin, *op. cit.*, 125. (We also find Ben Bag Bag, and at times Joḥanan b. Bag Bag. Similarly there occur Ben Nannas, Ben 'Azzai, and Ben Zoma, who are also sometimes designated by their father's name. In *T.B. Shabbat* 34a Ben 'Azzai should be read for Ben Zakkai in the current text, in accordance with the recension of the 'Arukh and the Munich MS. We further find Ben 'Azzai giving instruction 'in the streets of Tiberias', *T.B. Qiddushin* 20a and the parallels).

disciples. These facts conduced to the sinking of differences and to earlier acts being forgotten, so that today Rabban Joḥanan b. Zakkai is seen as a Patriarch and Father in Israel, who saved the nation and brought about a renascence of Torah-learning.

GA'ON, GE'IM*

(On the Social History of Eretz-Israel in the Period of the Tannaim)

We learn in *Avot de-R. Nathan*, Version II, xxxi (ed. Schechter 34a): 'He (R. Joḥanan b. Zakkai) would say: Keep the children[1] away from *ga'on* and keep them apart from the *ba'ale batim*, since the ba'ale batim distract [man][2] from the words of Torah.'

It may reasonably be assumed that the word *ga'on* which, at first sight seems obscure, appears here as the regular, established name of some particular social entity,[3] and was, in the opinion of R. Joḥanan b. Zakkai, pejorative. Its nature becomes clear from the conclusion of the dictum, which, it appears, continues with the theme of the beginning: 'And separate them from the *ba'ale batim* . . .' And so *ga'on*, then, designates the world of the *ba'ale batim*.

As for these *ba'ale batim*, their nature will become evident from the passages quoted below. 'He would say: *Ba'ale batim* are handed over to the ruling power because of three sins: They lend (money) at interest, retain paid bills, and pledge to charity in public[4] but never redeem (their pledges) [and they divest themselves of the yoke and put the burden and the tax on the unfortunate poor and needy].[5]

* Prof. Allon died before he completed the notes on this study. I completed them from n. 16 onwards from what he had delivered orally, and have enclosed these in square brackets — S. Safrai.

1 In the Ms.: התלמידים, 'the students'. Ours, however, is the correct version. See below: 'Force the sons, for from them Sages emerge.'

2 Added from the Ms. by Schechter, but is unnecessary.

3 Büchler, *Der galiläischer 'Am Ha-aretz*, p. 248, explains *ga'on* to mean 'pride'. There can be no doubt, however, that the word is not to be taken in this sense in the passage in question, for here we are not dealing with any psychological-ethical characteristic, but with a factual, social situation, as the dicta that follow will indicate.

4 Sic. Even here there is no compelling reason to prefer this version to the reading in Ms. Rome, וכובשים פוסקים, 'to extract by force'.

5 So Ms. The Rome Ms. reads, however: 'And cast off the yoke from themselves and put burdens on the poor.' Ms. Parma (Suppl. 3 to Version II, lxxxvi, 1): 'And cast off from themselves and put burdens on the poor.'

It is said of them: "Cursed be he that does not fulfil the words of this Torah" (Deut. 27: 26) — these are the *ba'ale batim.*'

Accordingly, *ba'ale batim* are the wealthy property owners (especially landed property owners), who lend money at interest, oppress their debtors and refrain from making charity contributions — and even shift the burden of royal taxation levied on all from the rich to those lacking in financial resources.[6] Consequently, what we are dealing with here, is a power-wielding, monied class who, on account of their wealth, have the influence in civic affairs and with the Government to arrange the allocation and the collection of taxation to the advantage of their own class and the disadvantage of the poor.[7]

The name *ga'on* then designates this class.

The study of this essay will most likely show that the name essentially refers to the economic property aspect of the world of the *ba'ale batim*, but not to any corrupt, or socio-moral or public-administrative aspects; for the reason, that they distract one from Torah, only implies neglect and lack of application to Torah characteristic of those circles and not to any wickedness that is inherently injurious. Hence we are obliged to interpret *ga'on* as signifying that wealth which acquires for its owners powerful, public social standing, without necessarily entailing any moral depravity.

Nevertheless, the entire substance of the last element does not, it stands to reason, belong to the main, early tradition. First, because it is not to be found in the parallel passage in *Tosefta Sukka* ii, 5, where the first three items are enumerated. Instead it has: 'And who has the ability to protest, but does not protest.' The same applies to the parallel in *T.B. Sukka* 29a/b and *Derekh Ereṣ Rabba*, ii. It is included, however, in the other Baraita quoted in *Derekh Ereṣ Rabba* and *T.B. Sukka* 29b (It is a Baraita in T.B. as well, since 'Rabba said' is not essential, cf. *Diqduqe Soferim, ad loc.*): 'On account of four things is the property of the *ba'ale batim* confiscated by the hands of the treasury: On account of those who hold back the hired man's wages, on account of those who remove the yoke from their necks and place it on their fellows, and for coarseness of spirit.' Secondly, our passage begins with 'On account of three things' and proceeds to enumerate four, which shows that the fourth item is a later addition.

6 See Rostowzew, *CAH*, Vol. XII, p. 260 on the shifting of the burden of taxation by 'the urban bourgeoisie on to the lower classes' in the period of the Antonine Emperors.

7 The rich were able to accomplish this shifting of the burden of debt due the Government on to the poor indirectly, by persuading and bribing Government officials. See, for instance, the papyrus of 157 C.E.; Johnson, "Roman Egypt", p. 234, *apud* T. Frank, *An Economic Survey of Ancient Rome*, II, where it is related that bribed officials exempted the property of the 'great' from taxation and levied it on others. Cf. Rostowzew, *CAH*, Vol. XII on

R. Joḥanan b. Zakkai's warning to keep sons away from *ga'on* is directed against preoccupation with accumulating property, which supplants Torah study, as other similar observations show.[8] Consequently, he requires Torah scholars at the outset to withdraw from the wealth and the dignity of the opulent.[9]

It may reasonably be assumed that this name, in the connotation ascribed to it, also derives from the tradition below, but here the social standing entailed in it is regarded as positive.

We have been taught in Sifra, *Beḥuqotai*, v, 2 (ed. Weiss 111d): '"And I will break the *ge'on* of your power" — this refers to the Temple. And so it states: "Behold I will profane [My] sanctuary, the *ge'on* of your power." R. Akiva says: "And I will break the *ge'on* of your power" — these are the mighty warriors of Israel, like Joab b. Zeruiah and his comrades;[10] Others say: "And I will break the *ge'on* of your power" — this refers to the *ge'im* who are the pride of Israel, like Pappos b. Judah[11] and Lulianus of Alexandria and his companions.'

'the urban bourgeoisie which shifted burden of money debts due the government on to the lower classes' in the Roman Empire (second century).

8 Büchler, *The Economic Condition of Judaea* etc., p. 31, n. 1. He regards the *ba'ale batim* as the *'ammê ha-'areṣ*, like the 'traders' (lit. 'those who sit at the street corners'), and as in 'the assemblies of the *'ammê ha-'areṣ*', mentioned in that generation. But our saying does not bring out this characteristic of theirs, but their financial-social and ethical nature.

9 In his will (Baraita, *T.B. Berakhot* 28b), R. Eliezer instructed his disciples: 'Keep your children away from *higgayon* and set them between the knees of the scholars.' The word *higgayon* presents some difficulty, and scholars have wrestled with its meaning from the days of the Ge'onim until the present. It might conceivably have evolved from *ga'on* (or *haga'on*) in the passage ascribed to R. Joḥanan b. Zakkai, R. Eliezer's teacher, in *Avot de-R. Nathan*.

Then the continuation of the remarks would also be similar in content: 'And keep them away from the *ba'ale batim* — the negative figure — and place them between the knees of the scholars — the positive figure. Our hypothesis is reinforced by the statement found in *Pirqe Rabbenu Ha-Kadosh* ascribed to R. Judah b. Bathyra, and which is identical with that of R. Eliezer in the Babylonian Talmud, as it appears in Ms. Oxford, 'Things which the Sages enumerated by number' appended to *Maḥzor Vitri*, published by Enelow in R. Israel al Nakawa, *Menorat Ha-Ma'or* (IV, p. 591): 'And keep [your sons] away from *haga'on*.' (In his note Enelow remarks: 'Ms. defective.' And he gives the reading found in the editions of *Pirqe de-Rabbenu Ha-Kadosh* and in the Talmud: מן ההגיון).

10 In Ms. Rome: שהין בישראל.

11 The words 'ben Judah' do not appear in the other sources which speak of Pappos and Lulianus and have certainly been added because of the habitual mention of Pappos b. Judah of R. Gamaliel's days.

The word *ge'im* certainly is some specific term, designating a social reality, like the word *ga'on* that is connected with it in our dictum. Although there is no explicit clarification of its actual nature, we may nevertheless have the means to discover this by studying the substance of the tradition itself to some extent. It contains three different approaches to the interpretation of '*ge'on uzekhem* (of your power)'. One ascribes a spiritual connotation to the phrase, viewing the text as referring to the destruction of the Temple; the second, as denoting 'might', and takes Scripture to refer to the defeat of the warriors of Israel. It would be reasonable, then, to regard the last as a third approach to the prophecy of the Destruction predicted here. To me, it seems that here the affluent among the Jews are indicated, those who assist and lead the people, and whose defeat and the destruction of whose wealth and station will bring about the collapse of the entire community.[12] So here, too, *ga'on* and *ge'im* designate wealth and the wealthy.

This hypothesis is supported, in my opinion, by the concluding portion of the Baraita which cites Pappos and Lulianus as examples of *ge'im*.

Now, it is well known that the incident involving Pappos and Lulianus is one of the most difficult in Jewish history. Many scholars have wrestled with it, trying to shed light on the subject from the sources which seem obscure and contradictory. We cannot deal with the entire problem, but only insofar as is necessary for our topic, and so we shall content ourselves with the few remarks that follow.

Now, in the sources that speak of Lulianus and Pappos, you find three facts ascribed to them: (i) their execution by Trajan[13] — this event is certainly related to the 'War of Quietus', although it is by no means definite that this war actually took place in Eretz-Israel;[14]

12 It is certainly possible to regard *ge'im* here as signifying communal leaders. And the same applies to *ga'on* (גאונם של ישראל), in the sense of 'local rule'. The noun, *gedolim*, *gedula* bears the same two connotations: 'men of wealth' and 'men of power', and this derives from the inherent connection between the two. The tradition transcribed further on in the body of the article and culled from *Gen. Rabba* makes it apparent that the money aspect is the primary factor insofar as Pappos and Lulianus are concerned.

13 Sifra, *'Emor*, 5; *Semaḥot* viii, 15, ed. Higger, p. 164; *T.B. Ta'anit* 18b (*Megillat Ta'anit*, Chap. xii); *Midrash R. Simeon b. Joḥai*, 125; *Qohelet Rabba* iii, 17; *T.P. Ta'aniyot* ii, 66a; *Megilla* i, 70c.

14 The view most commonly held by scholars identifies the 'slain of Lod' with Pappos and Lulianus (and along with them, his brother, Shemaya). See, most recently, Malter on *Ta'anit*, p. 69; S. Klein, *Ereṣ Judah*, p. 160. There

(ii) that 'they were given water in a painted glass vessel but would not accept it from them',[15] that is to say they were pressed to convert. Now, although these traditions certainly testify to the unique character and worthiness of the persons involved, they nevertheless reveal nothing of their social standing and their activities within the nation. The last fact that emerges from the traditions, however, clearly describes their character; (iii) As we read in *Genesis Rabba*, xliv (ed. Theodor, p. 710): 'In the days of R. Joshua b. R. Ḥanania the Government decreed that the Temple be rebuilt. Pappos and Lulianus set up tables from Acre to Antioch and supplied the pilgrims from the diaspora [var. lect.: with silver and gold and all their perquisites], etc. Pappos and Lulianus must therefore have been extremely wealthy, providing public needs from their own resources, and assisting in delivering the nation.[16]

Obviously this third tradition cannot be reconciled with the first two, and especially with the first, since according to those, Pappos and Lulianus were either executed towards the end of Trajan's reign for participating in the 'War of Quietus' against Rome, or they were sentenced to death during the decree compelling conversion during and after the war, for not submitting to conversion, while according to our tradition they lived and were active at the beginning of Hadrian's reign, at the time when the Government had ordered that the Temple be rebuilt. Certainly the traditions conflict with one another and this detracts from the reliability of the one under discussion as a source of fact.

is no basis for the view which substitutes Laodicea for Lod (as the location of the execution of Pappos and Lulianus), nor can it be logically sustained either. The whole subject of the martyrdom of Pappos and Lulianus in relation to the 'War of Quietus' requires a separate study, which would be out of place here.

15 *T.P. Shevi'it* iv, 35a; *Sanhedrin iii,* 21b. The dream vision vouchsafed to R. Aḥa: 'Blessed be He Who removed the shame of Pappos and Lulianus' (*Qohelet Rabba* ix; ed. Buber, p. 122), however, apparently gives evidence of a tradition contrary to that of the T.P., and, according to it, they succumbed and failed the test.

16 [Graetz (Hebrew ed., II, p. 229, n. 2) holds the opinion that their function was to change the pilgrims' money into Roman currency. Yet even if we not accept the readings which add 'gold and silver and all building accessories', it is difficult to accept this interpretation, since טרפיזין generally signifies the lender, the one who provides the building materials. See *History of the Jews in Eretz Israel in the Period of the Mishna and Gemara* — Hebrew — I, pp. 273 and 260.]

Nevertheless even if we reject the substance of the story, the image of these personalities preserved in the memory of the nation is abundantly clear: They are depicted as men of wealth, who loved their people, and by their financial support, helped the community and provided for its needs. Such were the *ge'im* and *ga'on* of Israel.

The same signification emerges from the Tannaitic Midrash-Aggada in a Baraita in the Talmud on the verse in question. We have been taught (*T.B. Giṭṭin* 37a): ' "And I will break the *ge'on* of your power" — R. Joseph taught: These are the *Bula'ot* in Judah.' This Baraita has been the subject of intense study by the scholars, who have deliberated at length on the nature of its historical and chronological content. Recently, S. Klein[17] devoted close attention to it, and he has adopted a new approach in explicating the name, *Bula'ot*. As opposed to the majority of scholars, he holds the opinion that the two were not executed during the War of Bar Kokhba, but of Vespasian, and that *Bula'ot* is not the plural of βουλη, which occurs frequently in Tannaitic parlance, but is derived from the Latin, *vallum*, which denotes 'fortress' or 'citadel'. Accordingly the Baraita would be dealing with the conquest and razing of fortresses in Judea during the War of the Destruction. And since the traditions speak of 'twenty-four *Bula'ot* in Judea (or in the South) that were destroyed',[18] Klein proceeds to seek out twenty-four settlements which could have served as fortresses in Judea in those times.

It is difficult to uphold this view, and better to reject it.

The hypothesis that the destruction of the *Bula'ot* be ascribed to the time of the War of Vespasian, in which other scholars preceded Klein, is based on the traditions in *Avot de-R. Nathan*, Version I, xx (ed. Schechter 36b) which is ascribed to R. Ḥanina, the Deputy High Priest: ' "Look not upon me that I am swarthy, that the sun has tanned me" — these are the *Bula'ot* in Judah, who cast off the yoke of the Holy One, blessed be He, from themselves and crowned a king of flesh and blood over themselves.' Since R. Ḥanina could not possibly have lived beyond the Bar Kokhba rebellion, the incident can only be attributed to the Destruction of the Temple.

There is another Tannaitic tradition, however, which explicitly gives evidence that this disaster could only have taken place after the fall of Betar. For so we learn in *Semaḥot* viii, 9 (ed. Higger p. 154): 'When the news that R. Akiva had been executed in Caesaria reached

17 [*The Chayes Memorial Volume* (Hebrew), pp. 279–284.]

18 [*T.P. Nedarim* iii, top of 38a; *Shevu'ot* iii, 34d.]

R. Judah b. Bava and R. Ḥanina b. Teradion, they rose, girded their loins with sackcloth and said: O Israel, our brethren, hear us! R. Akiva has been executed . . . only as a sign . . . In a short time from now no place in the land of Israel will be found where the bodies of the slain have not been cast . . . Not long thereafter, it is said, war came and put the whole world into chaos. Within twelve months from now the *Bula'ot* in Judah will come to an end . . . They said: Twelve months did not pass before all they had said was fulfilled for them.'

Even though the tradition appears to be garbled to some extent, it is abundantly clear from there that the 'cessation of the *bula'ot*' occurred after the War of Bar Kokhba. And since traditions only repeated by later Sages are 'predated' in *Avot de-R. Nathan*, preference should be given to the tradition in *Semaḥot.*

Another consideration, however, has a decisive bearing. It has already been clarified by Büchler[19] that wherever traditions speak of פולמוס שביהודה and משחרבה יהודה or uses similar expressions, the reference is to the War of Bar Kokhba alone, because this war was confined to Judea, which was not the case in the war leading to the destruction of the Temple, which extended into all 'three provinces' of Eretz-Israel. Although we have some reservations in regard to Büchler's view, especially in the light of documents discovered subsequent to that scholar's publication of his study, which apparently testify to battles fought beyond the boundaries of Judea, nevertheless it is certain that the main war and the greatest battles were concentrated in that province.[20] And so the destruction of the *Bula'ot* in Judah could only have occurred in the War of Bar Kokhba or its aftermath.

As for the name *Bula'ot*, first of all the word *vallum* is nowhere to be found in Tannaitic literature. Moreover, all Latin words which have been absorbed in Hebrew or Palestinian Aramaic (and the same applies to all Oriental languages) were only adopted into the language

19 [*JQR*, 1904, pp. 143–205.]

20 [The grave of a soldier of the XIV Legion was excavated in Gadara (*RE*, XII, s.v. *Legio*, p. 1741). In Bet Shean (Beisan) the grave of a soldier of the XI Legion was found (Avi-Yonah, *QDAP*, Vol. VIII, 1938. Similarly, that the fighting spread into the districts of the Samaritans is substantiated by the grave of a soldier of the V, Macedonian Legion (*RB*, Vol. XXV, p. 421), while a second inscription tells of a holy place set aside by in upper (*RB*, 1909, p. 44). These legions were to be found in Eretz-Israel only during the time of the Bar Kokhba Rebellion.]

by way of Greek. And in that language, *vallum* is nowhere to be found. Even in Latin itself, *vallum* only denotes the earthen wall or rampart, i.e. one particular item of a fortified camp, or else the camp as such, but never the entire, fortified settlement.

Obviously, then, בולאות can only be βουλαί, 'city councils', which is the currently accepted view of the meaning of *bule*. Yet this does not exhaust the normal frame of reference of the passage under discussion. For it is far-fetched to assume that the traditions refer to the destruction of these institutions as such; undoubtedly the Aggada must be lamenting a disaster that befell the entire community. And the abolition of the autonomous administration of the Jewish settlements in the land which resulted from the war, could possibly (and certainly would) be regarded as such a disaster. The expression בולאות שחרבו apparently testifies to the social strata which conducted the autonomous administration of the settlement, supported it and constituted its essence and foundation. It was their standing that was destroyed, and their power that was abolished during the war and its aftermath, and along with them, the settlements themselves collapsed.

These circles consisted of the affluent, who generously supported public needs, both in the Greek city of the East during the Roman epoch and also, as has been explained, in the Jewish city in Judea as well. The name *Bula* which, in our study, has been taken to signify the specific social element we have been dealing with, is certainly bound up, from the outset, with the process which spread through the Roman Empire during the second century: the transformation of the Bule into a council of the affluent alone. From here onwards, the Bouleutes (βουλευταί, curiales, decuriones) are the propertied classes alone, no longer elected by the citizenry as a whole, as heretofore, but appointed to, and coopted on, the Bule by Government edict on account of their wealth. Often, these Bouleute were forced to assume the honour to their disadvantage, not only because the burden of defraying the cost of public needs in the settlements was thrust upon them, but because they had to assume the responsibility for the collection and remittance of the sums of money due the Government. Certainly the culmination of this process and the conferring of judicial status upon it, occurred in the latter half of the second century. So we would be permitted, at first sight, to regard this tradition in the light of a relatively late situation that had been transferred to the period immediately preceding the Bar Kokhba rebellion. Undoubtedly, however, city leadership, which had attained an autonomy recognised by the Government, was based to a large extent upon the property owners and their support of public needs even in those days. And so the disaster that befell the nation with the destruction of the *Bula'ot* refers to the ruin of the wealthy among the nation. This led to the disintegration of the efficient administration of the large settlements and the collapse of the communities that came in its wake, and entailed the direct and complete subservience of the urban inhabitants to the Roman administration in the hyparchy, which did great harm.

'*Ge'on uzekhem*', expounded in our tradition as referring to the *Bula'ot*, also leads to the interpretation of *ga'on* in the same sense: wealth that endows its owner with an elevated status in society (and enables him to promote the good and welfare of the public).

This explanation of ours is verified by the Talmud, which elucidates the Baraita under discussion in the manner we have suggested. For so we read in *T.B. Giṭṭin* (*ibid*): 'The Bule are the rich, as it is written: "And I will break the *ge'on* of your power." R. Joseph explained these are the *Bula'ot* in Judea.' It is clear then that a factual tradition had been incorporated in the Babylonian Talmud, although, apparently, only a popular, homiletical interpretation of a word is given here.

Yet we have not yet completed our investigation. The *Bula'ot* were apparently only to be found in the settlements organised along the lines of the Greek πόλις (city), and it is a known fact such cities did not exist in Jewish Eretz-Israel until the War of Bar Kokhba, the exceptions being the two cities of Galilee, Tiberias and Sepphoris, while in Judea there were none at all. Are we then obliged to date the tradition back to the beginning of the third century, the time when three large settled areas in Jewish Judea were organised in the form of πόλεις (cities), in spite of the fact that gentiles in the main served in *Bula'ot*, and to deny it historical reality in the days of, and preceding, the War of Bar Kokhba?

It is reasonable to conclude that although formally and completely, *Bula'ot* only belonged to the 'Greek' cities, yet in practice the other large settlements, which legally were adjudged 'villages', were nevertheless allowed the organisational elements which belonged to the polis, and so acquired some type of Government recognition of their autonomy.

In the Greek inscriptions of many large rural settlements in Bashan, Hauron and Tracheae, Bouleute are mentioned. It is far-fetched to consider these individuals as members of the Bule of other 'cities';

they certainly belonged to the local Bule, as is the view of Harper in his *Village Administration in Syria* (Yale Classical Studies, Vol. I, pp. 142–146). Although these writings belong to the end of the Augustan and the beginning of the Byzantine periods, there is nevertheless nothing to prevent us from assuming the existence of such a situation in Judea (and in other areas of the East) at the beginning of the second century. So the tradition under discussion may very well be true and accurate.

It would seem that the *ge'im* dealt with in the Baraita in the Sifra in the economic and social sense under discussion are also to be found in the famous Aggada (*T.B. Berakhot* 57b; *'Avoda Zara* 11a): ' "And the Lord said unto her: Two nations are in your womb" — Do not read "two *goyim*" ("nations") but "two *ge'im*" ("lords") instead. And R. Judah said in the name of Rav: These are Antoninus and Rabbi, whose table never lacked either radish, or lettuce or cucumbers in summer or winter.'

The reference to Antoninus and Rabbi is certainly in respect of their enormous wealth, which allowed them to have fresh vegetables and spices on their tables all year round, even out of season. The *ge'im*, then, are men of great wealth.

Moreover, it seems to me that the word *ga'on* in this sense is also to be found in the Scriptures (Ezek. 16: 49): 'Behold this was the iniquity of your sister Sodom; *ga'on,* fulness of bread and careless ease was in her hand and in her daughters'; neither did she strengthen the hand of the poor and needy.' Although the Septuagint and Vulgate translate *ga'on* after their manner as 'pride and arrogance', nevertheless it follows logically from the context that the meaning is none other than 'wealth', like 'fulness of bread', just as the word *shalva* in this passage should most likely be interpreted in the sense of economic abundance. And so it is used by the Sages in many instances which speak of the settlements and countries. The entire content of the verse leads to its conclusion: Although Sodom was blessed with great and abundant wealth, it did not deal kindly with its poor. Consequently *ga'on* in our text, as well, has the same connotation.

THE ORIGIN OF THE SAMARITANS IN THE HALAKHIC TRADITION

Rabbinic tradition in its entirety negates the Israelite origin of the Samaritans.[1] The very dispute found in Tannaitic teaching as to whether Cutheans were 'proselytes (through fear) of lions', or 'true proselytes'[2] (or 'righteous [i.e. genuine] proselytes'[3]), or whether 'a Cuthean has the status of an Israelite' or 'the status of a Gentile',[4] only concerns their Jewishness from the religious aspect, but not their historical beginnings and descent, which are not Israelite.

Nevertheless, even if the consensus [of opinion] was that essentially the Samaritans were Gentiles, it seems that upon examining our sources we can differentiate three divergent traditions that were current among the Jewish people during the Second Temple period and after the Destruction in respect of their national pedigree.

The prevailing view regarded the Samaritans as the descendants of those people who were settled in Eretz-Israel by the Assyrian kings, in accordance with the Biblical tradition. This is evidenced by the entrenched use of the designation 'Cutheans' and the discussion on the nature of their conversion to Judaism, which is also based on the Biblical tradition.[5]

1 See, for example, the argument between R. Meir and the Cuthean in *Gen. Rabba* xciv (Theodor–Albeck, pp. 1178–1179).

2 *T.B. Qiddushin* 75b, and the parallels cited there.

3 *T.P. Giṭṭin* i, 43c; *Tractate Kuthim* ii, 7 (Higger, p. 66).

4 *Tosefta Terumot* iv, 14; in the Palestinian Talmud *passim*.

5 Sometimes we also find in Palestinian sources the (Aramaic) name שמראי (exceptions are *Pirqe de-R. Eliezer* xxxviii and the parallel in the *Tanḥuma*, pericope Wa-yeshev, 13, where the tradition deals with the derivation of the name Samaritans; only it appears that its purpose is to explain the name as it is given in the Bible, II Kings xvii, 29). But one passage in the Palestinian Talmud deserves special attention (*Ta'aniyot* iii, 66d): R. Aḥa observed thirteen fasts, but rain did not fall. When he entered, a Cuthean met him and said to him 'Master, wring the rain from your cloak [*aliter*: save your cloak from the rain].' He answered him: 'By your [literally: his] life, the heavens will perform miracles and the year shall prosper, but you [literally:

Josephus, too, as we know, often calls them by that name and attests that they were aliens, who were brought to the country by the king of Assyria. He also testifies that they are thus called 'in the tongue of the Hebrews' and denies their relationship to the House of Joseph. They themselves, he asserts, sometimes admit this by terming themselves alien settlers in the land.[6] This tradition, it seems, is reflected also in II Maccabees vi, 2, where we read that Antiochus Epiphanes' envoy came to Eretz-Israel to compel the Jews to give up their religion: μολῦναι δὲ καὶ τὸν ἐν Ἱεροσολύμοις νεὼν καὶ προσονομάσαι Διὸς Ὀλυμπίου, καὶ τὸν ἐν Γαριζεί, καθῶς ἐτύγχανον οἱ τὸν τόπον οἰκοῦντες Διὸς ξενίου. ['Further, the sanctuary in Jerusalem was to be polluted and called after Zeus Olympius, while the sanctuary at Gerizim was also to be called after Zeus Xenius, as did the people who dwelt in that place']. If we refrain from emending the text needlessly,[7] the sense of the concluding words is that the king

that man] will not live.' And the heavens wrought miracles and the year prospered, but the Cuthean died. Thereupon the people said 'Come and see the bier of the sun [פורין דשמש].' Undoubtedly the correct reading is פורין דשמרי — 'the bier' (φορεῖον) of the Samaritan (who was punished in fulfilment of the curse of R. Aḥa. When I once lectured on this passage before my teacher Prof. Epstein, the Talmudic statement was elucidated between us). The use of two names — Cuthean in the national tradition, and Samaritan (שמראי) in popular speech — may perhaps indicate that the designation 'Cuthean' was more commonly used by the Sages.

6 *Antiquities* ix, 14, 3 (§§288–291); xi, 7, 2 (§302); xi, 8, 6 (§§241–242); xii 5, 5 (§257). As regards the relationship of the Samaritans to Joseph see, apart from the Haggada mentioned above in *Gen. Rabba*, also Origen's commentary on John iv, 25 (ed. Preuschen, p. 250).

7 The suggestion of certain scholars to read καθὼς ἐνετύγχανον (as the Samaritans requested of the king) in order to harmonize the tradition in II Maccabees with that of Josephus (*Antiquities* xii, 5, 5; see below in the text) καθάπερ ἠξιώκασι (see Willrich, *Urkundenfälschung* etc., pp. 14–16) is improbable. First, because it involves an emendation. Secondly, if the tradition in Maccabees referred to a petition by the Samaritans to change their religion, it would not have reported the episode with such brevity, but would have elaborated it (in order to harmonize these traditions, Willrich is compelled to mutilate the text, emending Ξενίου in II Maccabees to Ἑλληνίου as in Josephus; this is quite arbitrary. There is no connection between the two traditions).

As regards the other current interpretation that the author intended to praise the Samaritans for their hospitality, it is difficult to understand the reason or basis for such an encomium. Where do we find a Jewish tradition dating from Temple times that eulogizes the qualities of the Samaritans? Scholars have, indeed, asked this question with surprise. Hence our interpretation is to be preferred. We have here a brief and parenthetic statement

decreed that the temple on Mount Gerizim should be named after Zeus Xenius, thus hinting to the local inhabitants, the Samaritans, that they, too, were alien guests, who came from abroad (apparently, as stated in the Bible, through the agency of the kings of Assyria).

Another tradition likewise regards the Samaritans as primarily of 'Cuthean' origin, except that Jews had intermingled with them. This view is not expressed in our sources as an independent historical tradition, but is implied in the reason given for the prohibition of their marriage to Jews (even after their conversion to Judaism) and for their being debarred from intermarrying among themselves, according to R. Eliezer in the Mishna (*Qiddushin* iv, 3), namely that they were of 'doubtful' stock. Among other reasons advanced for this interdiction, the Sages also mention the opinion that the Samaritans were disqualified 'because when a Gentile or a slave has intercourse with a Jewess, the offspring is a bastard' (*T.P. Giṭṭin* i, 43c (end); *T.P. Yevamot* vii, 8b). It seems that the addition of the slave here was a *lapsus calami* due to the customary coupling of slave and Gentile[8] in the Halakha, whenever it refers to their having relations with a Jewess and the question arises whether the offspring are legitimate or not, for the Talmudic discussion links our Halakha with the problem whether the Cutheans are 'proselytes (out of fear) of lions' or 'righteous proselytes'[9] and elsewhere we learn from the Palestinian Talmud (*Ketubbot* iii, 27a) that the Sages permitted the intermarriage of Jews with the daughters of Cutheans.

Another version of this tradition concerning the intermingling of Israelites with Samaritans, which aims to explain the prohibition of their intermarrying with Jews, is to be found in those Rabbinic dicta that speak of 'the priests of high places' who intermarried with Samaritans.[10] The Babylonian Talmud, it is true, explains their interdiction as due to the fact that they came 'from the thorns of the

the purport of which is that the name given by Gentiles to the temple at Gerizim befits the status of the Cutheans, because they are alien guests in the country. Büchler already understood it thus — *Die Tobiaden und Oniaden*, p. 155, n. 148.

8 *Tosefta Qiddushin* iv, 16, and in the Talmuds *passim*.

9 It is true that Rava declares in *T.B. Qiddushin* 76a: 'A (heathen) bondman and a bondwoman had intermingled with them.' But this is an independent tradition, just as there were two traditions regarding the Palmyreans — whether their disqualification stemmed from Solomon's slaves or from the daughters of Jerusalem (*T.B. Yevamot* 15b).

10 *T.B. Qiddushin* 75b; *T.P. Giṭṭin* i, 43d; *Tractate Kuthim* ii, 7.

people' [i.e. unfit priests],[11] an exposition that apparently is based on R. Ishmael's teaching that 'the Cutheans were proselytes (from fear) of lions and the priests who intermixed with them were unfit', and also on the statement juxtaposed by the Palestinian Talmud (*Giṭṭin* i, 43d) to R. Joḥanan's dictum ('because the priests of the high places had intermingled with them'): ' "And he made (priests) from among קצות *qĕṣôt* [literally 'the ends'] of the people";[12] R. Ela said: From the thorns [קוצים *qôṣîm*] and refuse of the people.' Nevertheless, it seems that the original tradition referred only to the actual intermingling of Israelite priests — they and their daughters — with Cutheans ('proselytes [from fear] of lions'), whose disqualification stemmed from the fact that if a Gentile has intercourse with a daughter of an Israelite, the offspring is a bastard, in accordance with the view mentioned earlier that this rule applies irrespective of whether the priests are fit or unfit.[13] This juxtaposition of statements — Cutheans are proselytes (from fear) of lions and the priests who mingled with them were unfit — is primarily based on the tradition that refers to the impaired status of the Samaritans in general and is not specifically concerned with elucidating the reason for the prohibition of their marrying Jews; in the same way the other view attributed to R. Akiba — 'Cutheans are true proselytes and the priests who mingled with them were fit priests' — does not deal primarily with the disqualification to marry.

The expository character of these traditions deprives them to a

11 'Rabba bar Ḥanah said in the name of R. Joḥanan: Of the thorns of the people and for this reason they were disqualified.'

12 There is no need to emend the text and read 'And they made unto them *mi-qĕṣôtām* [E.V. 'from among themselves'] priests of the high places' (II Kings xvii, 32, as in the Babylonian Talmud, because this verse refers to the Cutheans, whereas the verse in our text is concerned with Jeroboam; see *Sha'are Torat 'Ereṣ Yisrā'el*, p. 412), for the dictum of R. Ela is juxtaposed to the story of Jeroboam and the Palestinian Talmud cited this verse verbatim in order to give a similar exposition of the Scripture referring to the Samaritans.

13 The tradition relating to the priests of the high places does not explain the nature of their disqualification and its connection with forbidden sexual relations. It is certainly possible that they were bastards; nevertheless it is not improbable that primarily R. Joḥanan's dictum in the Palestinian Talmud — which only states 'because the priests of the high places intermingled with them' (this is also the recension in *Tractate Kuthim*), without the Midrashic exposition that speaks of their unfitness — comes to disqualify them because of mixed marriages between Cutheans and daughters of Israelites (see also Hershkovitz, *Yavneh*, II, pp. 81–82, who dealt with this question).

great extent of their ancient character. But the Halakhot that forbid the acceptance of proselytes from among the Palmyreans and the like[14] lend support to the assumption that these traditions have a basis in the early Halakhot. For the reasons given in our sources for the interdiction of the proselytization of these peoples gives considerable credibility to the tradition that bases it on their intermarriage (while still Gentiles) with Jews, in conformity with the principle 'If a Gentile and a slave have intercourse with a daughter of Israel, the offspring is a bastard.'[15] Indeed we have some evidence of the 'mixed' character of these nations.[16] We are permitted, therefore, to make the necessary inference by analogy regarding the prohibition in Tannaitic teaching of Cuthean intermarriage with Jews.

The tradition under discussion could have found support in the conditions prevailing in the time of the Sages. For it is logical to suppose that Jews and Cutheans intermarried both because they lived in many cities in close proximity and because of their religious affinity. R. Abbahu already testified that 'The inhabitants of thirteen towns were merged in the Cutheans during the period of religious persecution.'[17] He also explains R. Meir's reason for his stringent ruling to regard Cutheans as Gentiles with regard to the law of the goring ox: 'It is a financial disability imposed upon them to prevent Israelites from intermingling with them.'[18] Undoubtedly this measure was due to the widespread intermarriage of Israelites with Cutheans for the reasons mentioned.

However, even in Temple times there were factors contributing to the intermarriage and merging of Israelites and Cutheans. This fact, which is a natural assumption, is actually stated in Josephus. Thus he testifies, in connection with the origin of the temple at Gerizim and the inauguration of the Samaritan community, that quite apart from Manasseh, the brother of Jaddua the High Priest, who wedded Sanballat's daughter, many others — both priests and Israelites — intermarried with the Samaritans.[19] He likewise attests that in the period after Alexander 'all the transgressors from among the Jerusalemites who had contaminated themselves with forbidden foods and

14 *T.B. Yevamot* 16a–b; *T.P. ibid.* i, 3b; *T.P. Qiddushin* iv, 85c.

15 *T.B. Yevamot* 16b–17a. See Appendix I.

16 We know, for example, how the Palmyreans were influenced by the Israelites, as is evidenced from their inscriptions.

17 *T.P. Yevamot* viii, 9d; *T.P. Qiddushin* iv, 65c.

18 *T.B. Bava Qamma* 38b.

19 *Ant.* xi, 8, 2 (§312).

had desecrated the Sabbath and had broken all the other precepts fled to the Shechemites'.[20] Possibly it was this testimony that prompted Josephus to write in one passage[21] about the Samaritans who dwelt in Shechem: κατῳκημένην ὑπὸ τῶν ἀποστατῶν τοῦ Ἰουδαίων ἔθνους ('which is inhabited by apostates of the Jewish nation'). At all events, both in the tradition preserved in Josephus and in the teaching of the Sages the view is found, expressed in diverse ways, that the Samaritans had intermarried with Israelites from earliest times.

I believe that study of the Halakhic sources of the Sages and extraneous sources — both Jewish and Christian — reveals yet a third tradition concerning the origin of the Samaritans, a tradition that was likewise current among the nation both in Temple times and in the Talmudic era, to the effect that the Samaritans, or a part of them, are none other than the descendants of the ancient Canaanites, the indigenous inhabitants of the land.

First, we must refer to the epistle sent by the Cutheans, according to Josephus (Antiquities xii, 5, 5), to Antiochus Epiphanes, in which they call themselves *Sidonians living in Shechem.* In this document they petition the king to exonerate them from the charges levelled against the Jews, for their ancestors were never Israelites, but only accepted the Sabbath as 'an ancient superstition' with a view to delivering the country from the tribulations that had befallen it.[22] They had also established a temple on Mount Gerizim to an anonymous god and offered upon it the appropriate sacrifices. Again they deny all kinship with the Jews or any affinity to Judaism and claim

20 *Ibid.*, xi, 8, 7 (§346).

21 *Ibid.*, xi, 8, 6 (§340). This passage in Josephus has no parallel, for as a rule he regards the Samaritans as Gentiles. His expression is similar to the term 'Minim' used by the Sages.

22 Most recensions read διά τινας αὐχμοὺς τῆς χώρας ('on account of a number of droughts from which the land suffered'). But in three MSS the wording is συχνοὺς τῆς χώρας λοιμούς ('frequent pestilences of the land'); and so, too, the Latin version (*crebras provinciae pestilentias*). λοιμοί, apparently this last reading underlies *Ant.* ix, 14, 3, where he speaks of λοιμός that were sent upon the early Cutheans (but makes no reference to the lions). On the other hand, however, we find a tradition among the Samaritans that approximates the former version; it mentions the blight and drought that befell the 'Persians' settled in the land and compelled them to return to their own country (see *Karme Shomeron*, pp. 81–82). Consideration of the originality of the one or other reading can help to some extent to decide the question (see below) of the authenticity of the document in general. But it is not really possible to decide one way or the other.

descent from the Sidonians, so that the king should agree to exempt them from the disabilities imposed upon the Jews, 'as they deserved', and ask his permission to name their 'anonymous sanctuary' from now on after Zeus. Antiochus likewise directs his answer to 'the Sidonians living in Shechem' and accedes to their request, since they chose to live according to 'the customs of the Hellenes' and are in no way implicated in 'the charges against the Jews'.

It seems to me that the document under discussion cannot in any circumstances be regarded as genuine — a view shared by many scholars — although there were and are other scholars who endeavour to authenticate it. It is entirely a Jewish polemical creation (apparently dating from the Hasmonean period), which seeks to attribute to the Samaritans a confession of their non-Jewish origin, their tainted Judaism, and their apostasy in the days of the religious persecution by the Graeco-Syrians.[23] Even the designation 'the Sidonians living in Shechem' (which Josephus also repeats in: *Ant.* xi, 8, 6, as a statement made by the Samaritans in their negotiations with Alexander) is only to be regarded as an epithet applied to them by Jewish tradition for accusatory and polemical purposes. It appears that the expression simply means that the Samaritans are descendants of the ancient Canaanites (Sidonians), thus demonstrating that their pedigree is very blemished.[24]

An allusion to this tradition also occurs in another source belonging to the close of the Hasmonean period. In *The Testaments of the Twelve Patriarchs*, Levi, ch. vii (ed. Charles, pp. 41–42) we read: καὶ εἶπον ἐγὼ τῷ πατρί μου, Ἰακώβ, ὅτι ἐν σοὶ ἐξουδενώσει Κύριος τοὺς Χαναναίους καὶ δώσει τὴν γῆν αὐτῶν σοι καὶ τῷ σπέρματί σου

23 Some scholars have already pointed out that the Sidonians here really stand for Phoenicians = Canaanites; see Büchler, *Tobiaden u. Oniaden*, p. 159, n. 189; E. Meyer, *Ursprung und Anfänge des Christentums*, II, p. 154, n. 3. But it was Bickerman who perceived more deeply and correctly the connection with the ancient Canaanites. Only in his view the Samaritans actually traced their descent, in that epistle, to these Canaanites, a claim that he holds cannot be substantiated, as we have stated (we know, of course, that they called themselves thus even in their negotiations with Alexander, as Josephus writes in *Ant.* xi, 8, 6 [§344]. However, the entire tradition is a (Jewish) legend, and it is self-refuting. This is not the place to deal with the subject; it will suffice to observe that this designation was not used by the Samaritans themselves. As for the Sidonians–Phoenicians–Canaanites, cf. the evidence adduced by Bickerman (add also Matthew ix, 22 in comparison with Mark vii, 26).

24 See Appendix II.

μετά σε. Ἔσται γὰρ ἀπὸ τῆς σήμερον ἡ Σύκημα λεγομένη πόλις ἀσυνέτων, ὅτι ὡσεί τις χλευάσει μωρὸν οὕτως ἐχλευάσαμεν αὐτούς, ὅτι καίγε ἀφροσύνην ἔπραξαν ἐν Ἰσραὴλ μιάναντες τὴν ἀδελφήν μου.[25] Obviously in calling Shechem 'a city of imbeciles', the author employs the defamatory and contemptuous term current among the people for Samaritans, as is evidenced by the words of Sirach (50, 26) καὶ ὁ λαὸς μωρὸς ὁ κατοικῶν ἐν Σικίμοις.[26] But the explanation given by the author of *The Twelve Testaments* of the origin of the Samaritans, which he connects with the incident of Shechem the son of Hamor and the conspiracy of Jacob's sons, which had proved successful, attests his wish to trace the genealogy of the Samaritans to the ancient Canaanites.

A similar view is found in Christian literature of the fourth century and later.

Epiphanius writing (*Haer.* 9, 1, ed. Hohl, I, 197–198) on the meaning of the name 'Samaritan' [Hebrew: שומרונים *Shômĕrônîm*) enumerates four explanations: ἑρμηνεύονται δὲ Σαμαρεῖται φύλακες διὰ τὸ ἐν τάξει φυλάκων τετάχθαι ἐν τῇ γῇ, ἢ ἀπὸ τοῦ φύλακας αὐτοὺς εἶναι τῆς κατὰ τὸν νόμον Μωυσέως διατάξεως. ἐκαλεῖτο δὲ καὶ τὸ ὄρος ἔνθα ἐκαθέσθησαν Σωμόρων, ἅμα δὲ καὶ Σωμήρ, ἀπὸ ἀρχαίου τινὸς Σομόρων, υἱοῦ Σωμήρ, οὕτω τοῦ ἀνδρὸς καλουμένου. ἦν δὲ οὗτος ὁ Σωμόρων υἱὸς ἑνὸς ἀνδρὸς τῶν ἀπὸ γένους τῶν Φερεζαίων καὶ Γεργεσαίων, οἳ κατῴκουν τὸ τηνικαῦτα τὴν γῆν, ἐκ διαδοχῆς ὄντες παῖδες τοῦ Χαναάν κτλ.[27]

25 Translation: 'And I said to my father Jacob: By the will the Lord despoil the Canaanites, and will give their land to thee and to thy seed after thee. For from this day forward shall Shechem be called a city of imbeciles; for as a man mocketh a fool, so do we mock them. Because also they had wrought folly in Israel by defiling my sister.'

26 Translation: 'And that foolish nation that dwelleth in Sichem' (*nāvāl* in the sense of 'fool'). This epithet applied to the Cutheans accords with the fact that the Minim are derived in the Tannaitic tradition from the biblical word *naval* (*Sifre Deuteronomy* §320 ' "I will provoke them with a *naval* nation" — this refers to the Minim' etc.; *T.B. Yevamot* 63b). We also find the Samaritans called fools even in the patristic literature.

27 Translation: 'The name Samaritans [*Shômĕrônîm*] signifies *Shômĕrîm* ('keepers, watchmen'); they were called thus because they were appointed keepers in the land or because they kept the ways of life ordained by the Law of Moses. Also the mountain, on which they had settled, was called Shomeron, or Shemer, after Shemer the son of the ancient Shomeron. This Shomeron was the son of one of the descendants of the Perizzites and Girgashites, who dwelt in the land, for according to their pedigree they were descended from Canaan.'

He states similarly in *On the Stones of the Breast-piece* (the ancient Latin translation):[28] *Erant itaque, qui permanserunt ex gentibus, in terra Israel, pro diversis rebus Samaritani vocati: primum a Somer, uno ex filiis Chananaeorum et Pherezaeorum, priusquam Abraham patriarcha ad eamdem terram divinitatis adveniret, et appellabatur Somer, et Somoron, tam mons, quam omnia quae montis vicina esse videbantur. Rursus praefatae gentes, ab Assyriorum rege transmissae, vocatae sunt Samaritani, qui custodes interpretantur. Habet autem et aliam contemplationem nominis huius intentio: propter custodiam, videlicet legis, quoniam qui missi fuerunt, legis putabantur custodire mandata*, etc.[29]

Epiphanius' language is obscure and confused as always; but it is clear that the Church Father has preserved variant traditions concerning the meaning of the name Samaritans. They were given the name, he states, (1) because they were the people who were brought to the land as keepers to preserve it from desolation; (2) because they kept the Torah; (3) on account of Mount Shomeron; (4) they were so named after Shemer, from whom Omri bought the mountain and built Samaria [*Shômĕrôn*] thereon, only the tradition adds the explanation that this man was descendant from the Canaanites who dwelt in the land before the arrival of Abraham.

It seems to me that it is not difficult to indicate the aim and source of these traditions. The second tradition — because they kept the Torah — is undoubtedly of Samaritan origin, and we know that the Samaritans called themselves *Shomerim* ['keepers'] in this sense.[30] The

28 *PG* 43, col. 359–360.

29 Translation: 'The people, therefore, who were left in the Land of Israel were called Samaritans for a variety of reasons: first, after Shemer, one of the sons of the Canaanites and the Perizzites, before our father Abraham came to the land of the Lord', etc. The Georgian version of our excerpt as given in Blake, *Studies and Documents*, 1934, p. 189: 'Now I shall expatiate and dwell upon the account of all this and shall investigate whence are the Samaritans or from what tribes, since they are named of the mountain and the son of Someras, who was of the tribe of the Canaanites and the Pheresites.'

30 Apparently this derivation is alluded to in *T.B. Ḥullin* 6a: 'R. Isaac b. Joseph was sent by R. Abbahu to bring wine from among the Cutheans. A certain old man met him and said to him "There are no keepers of the Torah here".' The old man referred, it seems, to the name current among the Samaritans, as if to say, there are no true observers of the Law — Jews — here, and the Cutheans in the town are breakers of the Law, not keepers thereof, as they style themselves (Montgomery, *op. cit.*, 318). Similarly we find in a Baraita in *T.B. Yoma* (4a): 'And two scholars of the *disciples of Moses* transmitting the tradition to him throughout the seven days in order to train him in the

third explanation is found in Josephus and in late Midrashim; it appears to have been Jewish originally.[31] The fourth aims to connect the Samaritans with the Canaanites, informing us that the former are called after one of the descendants of the latter, because they are his offspring; this tradition is also Jewish. The fourth tradition, in another version, also occurs in Philastrius (*CSEL* 1898, p. 4): *alii autem aiunt a filio Canan, qui hoc nomine Samareus vocabatur, a quo Samaritani sunt appellati.*'[32] The tradition known to this Christian writer, a contemporary of Epiphanius, seeks to explain the genealogical relationship of the Samaritans to the Canaanites by equating the name the Zemarite the son of Canaan (Genesis x, 18), called in the Septuagint Σαμαρεῖος, *Shomeronim*, with the Σαμαρεῖται, thus establishing that they are descended from the son of Canaan.[33]

In similar vein Procopius of Gaza writes in his commentary on Genesis (*PG*, 87, 1, col. 309): "καὶ τὸν Σαμαρεῖον" ἐκ τούτου φανερὸν ὅτι Σαμαρεῖον τοῦ Χαναὰν υἱός... ἀφ' οὗ Σαμάρεια ἡ νῦν ἐν Παλαιστίνῃ, χώρᾳ τῶν Σαμαρείων προσηγόρευται.[34]

The derivation of the name Samaria from Zemarite [*Ṣĕmārî*] certainly alludes to the relationship of the Samaritans to him in accordance with Philastrius' tradition.

service'; in this way the Halakha seeks to exclude the Sadducees, as the Talmud explains. It follows that they called themselves 'disciples of Moses' in contradiction to the Pharisees who augmented the words of the Torah with the 'tradition of the Elders'; thus the Baraita comes to tell us that the true disciples of Moses were Pharisees (the designation found in Philo: γνώριμοι τοῦ Μωυσέως, is directed against the Gentiles, who are the disciples of others, is not relevant here).

As regards the first tradition, Origen, like Epiphanius and Eusebius (in his *Chronicon*) and others, explains that the Cutheans etc. were sent by the king to the Land of Israel to preserve (keep) it from desolation. It could not, therefore, be regarded, as it stands, as a Samaritan tradition (but perhaps it evolved from another version in their possession).

31 *Ant.* x, 9, 7 (§189); *Tanḥuma*, pericope Wa-yeshev; *Pirqe de-R. Eliezer* xxxviii (see also the references to *Halakhot Gedolot* at the end of Appendix I). This explanation, however, is also found among the Samaritans (Adler, *Chronicon*, in *REJ* 44, p. 210).

32 Translation: 'Others say (that they are called Samaritans) after the son of Canaan, who was so named... and after whom they are called Samaritans.'

33 This tradition certainly could not have originated with the Palestinian Jews, but possibly it emanated from Diaspora Jews (or perhaps Christians added the exposition on the basis of the first version?).

34 Translation ' "And the Zemarite" — this clearly indicates that the Zemarite was the son of Canaan... and from him (is derived the name) Samaria, which is now situated in Palestine, (the city) of the Samaritans.'

We now come to Halakhic sources, which I consider to be based, in all likelihood, on the tradition mentioned above.

It is stated in the Talmud (*T.B. Ḥagiga* 25a) in elucidation of the Mishna (*ibid.* ch. iii): 'Greater stringency applies to the heave-offering (than to hallowed things), for in Judea they are trusted regarding the cleanness of hallowed wine and oil throughout the year (for libations)', etc. This excludes Galilee, where they are not trusted in regard to the cleanness of these commodities. The Talmud continues: 'Resh Laqish said: Because a strip of (land inhabited by) Cutheans divides them.' According to its plain meaning the dictum certainly purports to teach us that the land of the Cutheans defiles on account of the uncleanness of non-Jewish territory, as Rashi and other Rishonim explain and as the subsequent discussion in the Gemara shows.[35] The same applies to the parallel tradition in the Palestinian Talmud (*ibid.* iii, 79b–c): 'R. Simon said that R. Joshua b. Levi said in the name of R. Pedya: Because an area (occupied) by the Cutheans divides them.'[36] Now the Rishonim already objected on the basis of *Tosefta Miqwa'ot* (vi, 1): 'The land of the Cutheans is clean' etc.; obviously they represent conflicting traditions. But ostensibly the aforementioned Amoraic Halakha is inherently difficult. For even if the Cutheans are deemed Gentiles, Eretz-Israel is still regarded as clean even where Gentiles reside (except for their dwellings). It would appear, there-

35 For the question of a box, chest, turret, and a tent in motion applies only to Gentile land, as is shown by the Talmud's citation of the Baraita that deals with such territory. Revel (*Ḥoreb*, I, 2, p. 124, note 6) states that R. Ḥananel explains the dictum to be based on the principle that Gentile dwellings defile. But he explicitly mentions the uncleanness of Gentile territory, although at the end he uses the expression 'the Cuthean dwellings'.

Cf., however, Maimonides' commentary and *Kaftor wa-Feraḥ* (ed. Lunz), I, p. 230; but their observations do not accord with the sources. See the allusion to non-Jewish territory and Gentile dwellings in *Tosefta Oholot* xviii, 17, and compare it with *T.P. Shevi'it* vi, 36c; *T.P. Yevamot* vii, 8a. It should be noted, however, in this connection that according to the correct reading and interpretation there is no discrepancy between them.

36 R. Joshua b. Levi's view that the Cutheans are like Gentiles, with respect to the obligation of giving tithes, is to be inferred from his ruling in *T.P. Demai* v, 25a: 'There are three who set aside tithes without the consent (of the Sages): one whose *ṭevel* [Jastrow: 'eatables forbidden pending the separation of sacred gifts'] became mixed up with ordinary food, and one who buys produce from the Cuthean area (the first case certainly refers to one who buys plucked produce from a Gentile, as mentioned earlier in the passage), for this Halakha is undoubtedly based on the same reason as that concerning one who purchases produce from a non-Jew.

fore, that the Halakha is based on the tradition that the Cutheans are non-Jews living in their own land, or in part of it,[37] from earliest times, for they were never subjugated and their land is, as it were, Gentile territory, since it was never sanctified by the conquest of those who left Egypt.[38]

In the same way we must interpret the following passage, which scholars have found difficult to understand. In *T.P. Shevi'it* (vi, 36c) it is stated: 'R. Abbahu said: There are Cuthean towns, where it has been allowed since the days of Joshua the son of Nun and they are permitted. R. Jose asked: If so the priests should not be concerned about their dough-offering, yet we see that the Rabbis are concerned. R. Yuda [= Judah] b. Pazzi replied: Not for the reason that you suppose [דאת אמרת],[39] but that the state should not take it over permanently.[40]

The passage deals, apparently, with the permissibility of working the land[41] during the Sabbatical year. According to the testimony of R. Abbahu as taught in R. Jose's school and as the current text implies, these are areas in the Cuthean territory, where (resident) Israelites were permitted to work (the land) during the Sabbatical year since Joshua's time, the reason for this being undoubtedly that these towns were never settled by Israelites; it may thus be inferred that the Cutheans there were Canaanites who had not been 'subdued'

37 The Talmudic expression 'They let them remain, and when Elijah comes he will purify them' is to be explained, apparently, by the fact that the Talmudic Sages understood the reference to be to an unclean strip within the Cuthean territory and not to their entire country (similar to the 'path of cleanness', as explained by the Rishonim). The language of R. Abbahu's dictum, cited below in the text — 'there are Cuthean towns' — also indicates a given area in their land.

38 Undoubtedly these 'Canaanites' were, in any case, considered 'tribute-payers'. But the Sages differ as to whether 'those who were made tributary (under Joshua) are regarded as conquered' and their territories as sanctified with the sanctity of the Land, or not (*T.P. Demai* ii, 22d; *T.P. Shevi'it* vi, 36c; *Gen. Rabba* xcviii, Theodor–Albeck, p. 1263).

39 The Rome MS. reads דאמרת.

40 The Rome MS. reads בידה; current editions בידא.

41 Although the immediately preceding and following dicta speak of Gentile territory relative to uncleanness and the prohibition to go there from Eretz-Israel, as a whole the passage also deals with the laws of the Sabbatical year (in regard to Eretz-Israel and outside of it) and with tithes (at any rate it appears to me that the text under discussion is not altogether in its correct place).

(either by those who left Egypt or by those who returned from Babylon).

R. Jose queries the tradition, for if these towns are deemed Gentile territory, the priests have no need to be meticulous about the sanctity of the dough offering separated there and to eat it in a state of cleanness, for it actually has no sanctity. Why then are the Sages so punctilious and careful about the way they eat it?[42] In reply to this question R. Judah b. Pazzi adduces another reason for permitting work on the land in these areas during the Sabbatical year: strictly speaking they belong by law to Eretz-Israel and are subject to the commandment concerning the Sabbatical year, but the Israelites dwelling there were permitted by a Rabbinical enactment to cultivate the land during *Shemiṭṭa* [Sabbatical year], lest the State should take over the lands permanently[43] (the same applies to the Cutheans who observe the laws of the seventh year). This explanation is connected with the demand for land-taxes and *annonae* by the government even in the *Shemiṭṭa* year, a demand which appears to have been made of Israelites only in times of persecution.[44] But Cuthean territory was not exempted from the obligation of paying these taxes in the Sabbatical year even in normal times, at least in the course of the third century. The exemption from land taxation in the Sabbatical years, granted to the Jews by the Romans, was based, as we know, on the famous order issued by Julius Caesar in the time of the last Hyrcanus.[45] It appears that this privilege was not rescinded even after the Destruction and throughout the Talmudic period, except for isolated instances. But from Origen we learn that the Samaritans did not enjoy the dispensation, accorded the Jews, from obeying the State laws where these conflicted with their religion. Thus he attests that the Samaritans were put to death for practising circumcision, undoubtedly because Hadrian's decree prohibiting this rite (under *Lex Cornelia de Sicariis*) within the framework of the general law was

42 The question corresponds, therefore, to the parallel passage in *T.P. ʿAvoda Zara* v, 44d (where, too, it is R. Jose who raises the question with regard to the dough-offering of the Cutheans).

43 תחלטון=חלטתון.

44 See *T.B. Sanhedrin* 26a (in the parallels in *T.P. ibid.* iii, 21b and *T.P. Sheviʿit* iv, 35a, the substance of the tradition is different). See also *Lev. Rabba* i, 1: 'R. Isaac said the text refers to those who observe the Sabbatical year... and this man sees his field lying fallow and his vineyard uncultivated, yet he pays the *annona* and is silent', etc. (but in the parallels in the *Tanḥuma*, in both editions, the words 'and pays the *annona* and is silent' are missing).

45 *Ant.* xiv, 10, 6 (§202).

not set aside for them, as Antoninus Pius had done for the Jews.[46] It follows, *a fortiori*, that the Cutheans were not released from land taxation on account of the precept of *Shemiṭṭa*.[47]

It may well be assumed that the Jews, too, who formed a minority in the Cuthean area were not, in practice, differentiated from the Samaritans for privileged treatment — not at least in many cases. The authorities, who, in the course of the third century which was plagued by internal and external wars, sometimes ignored, as we have seen, even the rights of the Jews in their own settlements and levied *annonae* in Sabbatical years, would certainly not be meticulous in distinguishing between all the inhabitants, who, despite their observance of the Torah, had not been freed from taxation in the *Shemiṭṭa* year, and the Jewish minority living in their midst. Hence, according to R. Judah b. Pazzi, it was enacted that cultivation should always be permitted in these areas.[48]

It seems that the sources under discussion support, as a whole, the view that there was an ancient Jewish tradition that regarded the Samaritans as partly descended from the early Canaanites.[49] Only the Biblical tradition suppressed the others, 'since they found no support' in Scripture.

46 Contra Celsum, ii, 13 (ed. Koetschau, I, p. 14, 2): ἀλλὰ φήσει τις ὅτι καὶ Σαμαρεῖς διὰ τὴν ἑαυτῶν θεοσέβειαν διώκονται κτλ. ['If anyone should say that the Samaritans, too, are persecuted on account of their religion' etc.].
Similarly he states elsewhere that 'the scholars' among the Samaritans give their life for the Law and the precepts.

47 From Josephus' testimony (*Ant.* xi, 8, 6, §343–344) we may infer that even in Temple times the Samaritans were not exempted from land taxation in the year of *Shemiṭṭa*.

48 See Appendix III. 'The Sequestration of property' emanates from the famous statute in Roman law on the confiscation of lands whose taxes have not been paid.

49 Possibly the prohibition of intermarriage with the Cutheans should also be explained on the basis of this tradition. As we know, the interdiction of marriage with Nethinim, who are regarded as descendants of the 'seven nations', is to be explained, according to the Babylonian Talmud, by the fact that they were subject to the decree of bondage, but the Palestinian Talmud rejects this view (*Ketubbot* iii, 27a). It appears that the real reason is that underlying Rava's view cited in *T.B. Yevamot* 76a, which (in the conclusion) prohibits their marriage to Jews (on account of their 'Canaanite' origin) even if they become proselytes. Thus the Cutheans could likewise be forbidden to enter into matrimony with Jews on the basis of the last-mentioned tradition. Possibly this explanation is supported by the fact that in Tannaitic literature the Nethinim and Cutheans are juxtaposed (*M. Ketubbot* iii, 1; *Tosefta Nidda* vi, 1, and the parallels in the Talmuds).

Appendix I (to note 15)

The reason why proselytes from these nations were not admitted, namely that they intermarried with Jews while still Gentiles, emerges most clearly from the discussion in *T.P. Yevamot, loc. cit.*, and *T.P. Qiddushin, loc. cit.*: 'R. Abbahu in the name of R. Joḥanan said: The Mishna also holds that proselytes from Palmyra [Tadmor] are fit. For we have learnt elsewhere: All bloodstains (on garments) coming from Reqem are clean (*M. Nidda* vii, 3) — this implies that the Palmyrean proselytes are fit.' The passage is obscure and the commentators explain it in accordance with the discussion in *T.B. Yevamot, loc. cit.*, and in *T.B. Nidda* 56b, where R. Joḥanan deduces from the latter part of the Mishna: 'Those (bloodstains) that come from Gentiles are clean' — 'Since the statement is categorical, it applies to those from Tarmod [= Tadmor]! R. Joḥanan replied: This proves that proselytes may be accepted from Tarmod' (for they are adjudged completely non-Jewish, the Sages not being concerned that in the past Israelites might have intermarried with the Palmyreans and that in consequence their present offspring were bastards). But the deduction made in the Gemara is extremely difficult, nor is it easy to derive the proof in the Palestinian Talmud from the second part of the Mishna, which is unlikely although possible. It seems, therefore, that R. Joḥanan draws the inference from R. Judah's statement in the first part of the Mishna, namely that the bloodstains are unclean 'because the people who live there (in Reqem) are proselytes though misguided (they relapsed through forgetfulness [?], breaking the commandments and living as Gentiles)'; it thus follows that the people of Reqem are deemed proselytes. R. Joḥanan's deduction from this with regard to the Palmyreans is based on the fact that the people of Reqem (whatever its identity; see *Tarbiz*, III, pp. 328–336) were Nabateans, and we likewise know that the Palmyreans had an admixture of Arabian-Nabatean blood. Thus the statement of R. Judah (and Patristic literature corroborates this) testifies to the intermingling of Jews with non-Jews to the point where the lines of demarcation among the Nabatean inhabitants of Reqem were erased, and the same, it is known, applied to the Palmyreans. Hence R. Joḥanan was able to infer that proselytes could be accepted from them, too (on the prohibition of the acceptance of Cuthean proselytes — though permitted in the case of the Palmyreans — on account of the interdiction of intermarriage, see *Hilkhot Re'u*, p. 37; *Halakhot Gedolot*, Warsaw, p. 108b, and *ibid.*, Berlin, p. 443; *Otzar ha-Geonim* to *Qiddushin*, pp. 186–189, and to *Yevamot*, p. 173).

Appendix II (to note 24)

Bickerman devoted an essay to the document under discussion ('Un document relatif à la persecution d'Antiochos IV Epiphane', *RHR*, 1937, pp. 188–223). The author endeavours to authenticate the document, like many scholars before him, by detailed examination of its content and language. First, he argues that its phraseology accords with the literary style of the Hellenistic period and its authorship is not, therefore, to be regarded as a spurious Jewish work of the Roman age. But, even if we rule out the possibility of imitation by an expert (a possibility that is by no means precluded; at all events it is no improbable conjecture to suppose that a Jewish author utilized an original document and altered its substance, while retaining its framework), this reason does not apply to the Hasmonean period. It seems that just at this time, when Antiochus' decrees and the wars fought by the Jews in consequence of them were still fresh in the national memory, and the Samaritans living in the state government by the Hasmoneans were suppressed by them, a Jewish polemical literature could very well have arisen, whose aim was to prove the Gentile character of the Samaritans by their own admission and their desertion of Israel's faith in time of trouble, thus showing that they deserved to be adjudged non-Jews and subjugated like them.

Furthermore, Bickerman seeks to explain the content of the epistle in a way that would make its authenticity appear plausible. The Samaritans sought to deny any relationship between themselves and the Israelites, either ethnically or religiously. Hence they wrote with exactitude: 'Our forefathers... had a custom of observing the day which by the Jews is called the Sabbath'. Thus they indicated that there was no question here of borrowing from the Jews but that this was a parallel ancient practice introduced by the 'Shechemites', the ancestors of the Samaritans (see note 25). This argument of the Cutheans could have been based on the view current among the Jews (*The Book of Jubilees*), that the Patriarchs already observed the Torah before ever it was given at Sinai. Their (the Cutheans') assertion concerning the temple that they had built at Gerizim purports to attest the antiquity of their worship, that it was pre-Mosaic. This was a widespread belief among the Samaritans at this period, as we learn from Eupolemos, who tells us that Abraham was received by Melchizedek at the temple of Gerizim. The fact that they call their god the anonymous deity is to be explained by the Jewish practice not to pronounce the Ineffable Name but only its substitute (cf. Κύριος in the Septuagint). This usage was also current among the Samaritans.

When they requested the king's permission to call this god in future Zeus, they were not introducing thereby alien worship or changing their religion; they were merely giving him a Greek name — a translation, so to speak (cf. the Phoenician Baal-Shamain called Zeus; [the Arabic] Dushra = Zeus)[1]. Furthermore, their request is not evidence of their abrogating the Torah; they actually continued to observe the Sabbath as before and to sacrifice on Mount Gerizim according to the Law of Moses.

Despite the great erudition and acuity that characterizes this article, the arguments appear to me unfounded and improbable. That a Haggada was taught in a certain Rabbinic school, to the effect that the Patriarchs observed the Torah before it was revealed, does not prove that the same Haggada was current among all the Samaritans before the Hasmonean period. But even if this was so, it cannot reasonably be considered a basis for the document in question. Actually the inference from the wording of the epistle that it purported to antedate the origin of the Sabbath and to represent it as a custom that had not been borrowed from the Jews is without foundation. The main contention of the Samaritans that their ancestors had instituted it on account of the visitations from which they suffered is, according to its plain meaning, an apologia for having adopted a precept from others (the Jews). The same applies to the temple at Gerizim; there is no reference here to its antiquity dating back to the time of Abraham. The explanation that the anonymity of their god was based on the desire to avoid the enunciation of the Ineffable Name is far-fetched. It seems to me inconceivable that the Jews would designate the Lord thus for this reason. Moreover, what evidence is there that the Samaritans also refrained from pronouncing the Divine Name during the period of the Second Temple (as they did at a later stage)? We know that Theodoritus copied two different pronunciations of the Ineffable Name in use among the Samaritans in his days (fifth century; see Montgomery, *The Samaritans*, p. 213). From the Palestinian Talmud (fourth century), too, we learn that the Cutheans were accustomed to swear by the Name. In *T.P. Sanhedrin* x, 28b, with reference to the ruling in the Mishna 'Also he that pronounces the Name with its proper letters', we read 'R. Mana said: Like those Cutheans, when they take an oath.' According to its simple meaning, the dictum cites an example of the pronunciation of the Name ac-

1 This interpretation has already been suggested by others; see Thomson, *The Samaritans*, etc., p. 34.

cording to its letters. Undoubtedly *T.P. ibid.*, vii, 25b implies that Cuthean 'blasphemers' expressed the Divine Name by means of a surrogate, but when necessary and in fulfilling a *miṣwa* [precept], such as taking an oath, it appears that they pronounced the Name explicitly (see Greenbaum, *ZDMG*, 18, 137; see *ibid.*, earlier, this scholar's discussion of Bickerman's conjecture that the anonymity of the Samaritan god, mentioned in the document under discussion, was due to the prohibition of pronouncing the Name. See further I. Lewy, *Mishnat Abba' Sha'ul* [Hebrew], pp. 28–29).

Furthermore, according to one document, apparently, the Samaritans knew of a way of pronouncing the Ineffable Name as late as the nineteenth century (Montgomery, *JBL*, 1906, pp. 49–51). As regards the continued observance by the Samaritans of the Torah and its precepts, it is somewhat difficult to attribute this to their similarity to Israel, for they were compelled to abolish circumcision, to desecrate the Sabbath, and to partake of forbidden foods and to destroy Torah scrolls (we know that the author of II Maccabees likens in two passages [v, 23; vi, 12] the decree against the Samaritans to that against the Jews). Moreover, Antiochus expressly states in his reply: ἀλλὰ τοῖς Ἑλληνικοῖς ἔθεσιν αἱροῦνται χρώμενοι ζῆν ('but they choose to live by walking in the ways of the Greeks'). This implies an entire change of religious life, complete apostasy as it were (cf. the passage in the epistle of Antiochus Eupator, II Maccabees xi, 24, where he restores religious freedom to the Jews and rescinds his father's decrees: ἀκηκοότες τοὺς Ἰουδαίους μὴ συνευδοκοῦντας τῇ τοῦ πατρός εἰς τὰ Ἑλληνικὰ μεταθέσει, ἀλλὰ τὴν ἑαυτῶν ἀγωγὴν αἱρετίζοντας κτλ ('We have heard that the Jews refuse to accede to my father's intent that they should go over to Greek customs, but cleave to their own way of life'). It therefore seems that the document in *its present form* is the work of a Jew, who wished to accuse the Samaritans of abandoning the Torah and renouncing the God of Israel, as many scholars actually suppose (this is not the place to enter into a detailed elucidation of the subject). From all that we know about the Samaritans they cannot be charged, wholly or in part, with apostasy. Some, it is true, deduce from the statement in I Maccabees vi, that Apollonius brought with him a great army from Samaria — ἀπὸ Σαμαρείας — to up against Judea that the Samaritans defected from their faith and aligned themselves with the government; see, for example, Рынский Самаряне, pp. 251–252. But it appears that the reference is only to the city of Samaria, which, as is known, was inhabited, since Alexander's time, after the rebellion of the Samaritans, by Macedonians and

Greeks. And another point. Bickerman claims that the authenticity of the document is proven by the fact that it is written in Greek, which appears to be original; he argues that it would certainly not have been composed, if the writer was a Jewish forger, for the benefit of the Palestinian inhabitants — Jews or Samaritans — who spoke Aramaic at that period, but for the use of Greeks or Jews living in the Diaspora. But in that case, how could the author, whose purpose was to denigrate the Samaritans, represent the affinity of the Samaritans with Hellenic culture as a shameful thing? But the answer to this objection is contained in Bickerman's own argument. The epistle was certainly directed to Greek-reading Jews, whether living in the Diaspora (Josephus already testifies to the strife between the Jews and Samaritans in Alexandria in the days of Philometer) or in Eretz-Israel. Both the former and the latter rejected 'affinity with Greek culture' in its real connotation of apostasy from Judaism. Compare II Maccabees, the Jewish Sibylline Oracles, and other works of Judeo-Greek literature.

Appendix III (to note 48)

Some aspects of our interpretation are already to be found in *Sefer ha-Ner*. S. Lieberman, however, discusses the meaning of the passage anew in *Tarbiz*, II, p. 107. He follows the line of exegesis adopted by R. Elijah, the Gaon of Vilna, who explains the term 'permitted' as referring to entering these areas in a state of cleanness, because the cities in question belonged to Eretz-Israel, and he holds that R. Abbahu alluded to Caesarea in which there was a Cuthean population. R. Jose's query: 'If so the priests should not be concerned about their dough-offering' is explained to mean that Israelites should not be afraid to knead their levitically clean dough in Caesarea, since it is part of Eretz-Israel proper (the text, therefore, requires emendation מעתה לא נחוש על חלתן 'If so let us not be concerned about their dough!' — as the scholar explains in his article), yet, we see that the Sages are concerned and go so far as to knead it in Eretz-Israel on account of the Gentile uncleanness of the city! To this R. Pazzi replies that Caesarea is unclean because it is Gentile territory, not for the reason that it is really outside Eretz-Israel, but because the Government decided against the inclusion of Caesarea in the Jewish domain and gave it to the Greeks. R. Pazzi was thus alluding to the struggle between the Jews and Greeks over the control of Caesarea recounted by Josephus. In other words, the city originally belonged to Israel, but after the Emperor's ruling (which made the Greek settlement in the city official) and the destruction of the Jewish settlement there, the Rabbis decreed that it should come under the law of Gentile territory. The far-fetched character of this interpretation as a whole is obvious; nevertheless I should like to make the following observations:

First, it is highly improbable that R. Abbahu would designate his own city by the indefinite term 'cities of the Cutheans'. Secondly, how was it possible to call Caesarea a city of Cutheans, for what reason have we for supposing that the Samaritan population exceeded that of the Gentiles and Jews (even if each ethnic group is considered by itself)? Caesarea was known to have been, even in the third and fourth centuries, a 'metropolis' of Hellenism in Eretz-Israel and also beyond it. Furthermore, I do not believe it to be stated anywhere in the Halakha that a governmental decree to expropriate a given territory of Eretz-Israel involves its being declared Gentile territory. Indeed, Nero's entire ruling is of no real relevance to Eretz-Israel or to regions outside, seeing that even subsequently Caesarea remained, as we know, within the boundaries of Eretz-Israel. The decision in question was only concerned with the communal character of the city; it determined which national entity had the right to control its independent rule and what was to be the character of the citizenship, but did not deal with the relationship to Eretz-Israel. It is surely unwarranted to suggest that the Sages decreed the city to become Gentile territory, because it was removed from the Jewish domain and because of the destruction of its Jewish settlement, seeing that an enactment of this nature is to the detriment of the Jewish people (in Jaffa, too, the Jewish population was destroyed, but the Rabbis did not declare it a Gentile area; the same is true of Beth-Shean, which was likewise a city whose citizenship was known to be Greek)!

THOSE APPOINTED FOR MONEY

On the History of the Various Juridical Authorities in Eretz-Israel in the Talmudic Period*

Several sources in both Talmuds attest that certain Patriarchs used to appoint ignorant judges for pecuniary considerations. Some of these judges would wrap themselves in a Sage's cloak (*Tallit*) and wished to sit and teach with a *Meturgeman* ['Expounder'] at their side, after the manner of Torah scholars, but the Sages objected to them, disqualified them from judging, and demanded that the due honour and status be withheld from them.[1] These testimonies date from after the middle of the third century to the middle of the fourth century. Because this period is generally treated as one of spiritual and ethical decline in the world of the Patriarchate, since it had ceased giving Halakhic decisions and teaching Torah in the Great Bet ha-Midrash [Academy][2] and became wholly immersed in wield-

* This article follows on a lecture delivered at the First World Congress of Jewish Studies, which was held at Jerusalem during Tammuz, 5707 (1947).

1 *T.B. Sanhedrin* 7b; *T.P. Bikkurim* iii, 65d; *Midrash Samuel*, ed. Buber, p. 68. Possibly Resh Laqish's dictum in *Sanhedrin, loc. cit.*, 'Whoever appoints an unworthy judge is as one who planted an Ashera in Israel', may be linked to this question. For it was his Meturgeman who publicly denounced the judge appointed by the Patriarch on account of his ignorance.

2 Halevy, *Dorot Harischonim* (II, i, pp. 766–774; see also Dinaburg in the *Memorial Volume to Gulak and Klein*, p. 88, note 1) seeks to prove that the separation of the office of Head of the College from the Patriarchate obtained already in Rabban Simeon b. Gamaliel's day. He finds support for the conjecture in the title 'Head of the Speakers' applied to R. Judah b. Ille'ai (*T.B. Shabbat* 33b, and parallels cited *ibid.*), which according to the Talmudic explanation was given him by the Government because he had praised it, thus showing that R. Judah served as Head of the College, while Rabban Simeon b. Gamaliel as Patriarch conducted public affairs. However, the Talmudic explanation is merely a Haggada, and 'Head of the Speakers' does not mean the Head of the College, but the term is related to the procedures adopted at the College among the Sages as a whole. These procedures are referred to in the *Tosefta* (*Sanhedrin* viii, 1; *T.B. ibid.*, 17b; *T.P. Sheqalim* v, 48d): 'Every Sanhedrin that contains two members who know how "to speak" [i.e. to discuss a Halakhic matter] and all are able "to hear" [i.e. to comprehend the discussion]', etc. (cf. *Tosefta, loc. cit.*, vii, 9; *T.B. Horayot*

ing the sceptre of authority and the evil that this entailed, historians are mostly inclined to regard this facet, too, as one of the symptoms of degeneration and corruption that had spread among the Patriarchs. Some explain this practice of the Jewish Patriarchs[3] by reference to the difficult conditions prevailing in the time of crisis, economic collapse, and governmental oppression, which marked the third century.

However, we must first qualify the current view that the Patriarchate was sundered from the world of the Torah and Halakhic decision during this period. Undoubtedly, already in the days of Rabban Gamaliel 'Berabbi' we see the standing of the Patriarch in the sphere of Halakha impaired in relation to the Sages,[4] and needless to say,

13b: 'Sons of Sages and disciples of Sages, when they have the knowledge to understand', etc., since these are certainly unable 'to speak'). For only certain of the Sages would take part in public discussions to elucidate the Halakhic questions raised at the College, and some of them were 'Heads of the Speakers', as we are informed in the Palestinian Talmud (*Rosh ha-Shana* ii, 58b; *Sanhedrin* i, 18c): 'Provided each one spoke in his due place, for instance, R. Ḥanina opened the discussion, and R. Joḥanan and R. Simeon b. Laqish closed it; R. Ba bar Zavda opened it, and R. Ḥiyya, R. Yassa, and R. Ammi closed it; R. Ḥaggai opened it, and R. Jonah and R. Jose closed it.'

Furthermore, L. Ginzberg (*Perushim we-Ḥiddushim bi-Yerushalmi*, Pt. III, pp. 195–196) is of opinion that when Rabban Gamaliel of Jabneh was deposed and R. Eleazar b. Azariah was appointed in his place, the two offices were separated. For in his view (and Kämpf thinks so, too, *MGWJ*, v, 155, note 2) the Sages were able to depose Rabban Gamaliel only from the headship of the College but not from the Patriarchate, which was subject to Roman authorization. However, the argument is not decisive, and the traditions, understood according to their simple meaning, attest his removal from the Patriarchate, as well. This was actually what happened (but this is not the place to discuss the subject).

3 Among recent scholars: Jawitz, *Toledot*, viii, 107–130; Marmorstein, *REJ*, vol. 64, pp. 59–66; Zucker, *Studien*, p. 167; Strack-Billerbeck, *Kommentar*, etc., II, 150; Dinaburg, *op. cit.*, p. 91; and others.

4 *T.P. Shabbat* vi, 8a: 'Rabban Gamaliel once went down to stroll in his courtyard on the Sabbath, holding a golden key in his hand, and his colleagues rebuked him on the ground that it was an adornment'. *Ibid.*, *Ḥalla* iv, 60a: 'Rabban Gamaliel "Berabbi" wished to apply the law of *Demai* [produce concerning which there is a doubt as to whether the sacred gifts and the laws of levitical cleanness have been observed] to Syria, but R. Hoshaʿya did not permit him.' (Although Halevy, *Dorot Harischonim*, II, i, p. 332, holds that this Rabban Gamaliel was the son of R. Judah Nesi'a, his opinion is predicated on his theory that the Patriarchs' knowledge of the Torah did not decline till after the time of R. Judah Nesi'a. But we cannot but regard Rabban Gamaliel here, too, as the son of Rabbi.)

in the period under discussion the Patriarchs appear to be subject to the contemporary Sages' ruling on religious matters, to depend on them in respect of Halakhic questions, and to act under their direction.[5] Nevertheless, this does not yet prove that the Patriarchs were devoid of Torah-learning or that their connection with the Great Bet ha-Midrash had been severed. Not only were Rabban Gamaliel 'Berabbi' and R. Judah Nesi'a I leading Torah scholars having a decisive voice in Halakhic matters,[6] but their descendants living at the end of the third century and the beginning of the fourth were also at times asked Halakhic questions[7] and some Sages were even guided by their ritual practice.[8] At times a Halakhic dispute between the Patriarch and the Av Bet Din (Head of the Court) caused per-

5 Thus Resh Laqish gave the Patriarch a Halakhic direction (*T.B. ʿAvoda Zara* 6b; *T.P. ibid.* i, 39b); so, too, did R. Ammi (*T.B. Taʿanit* 14a–b; *ibid.* 25b; *T.B. ʿAvoda Zara* 33b), R. Manni (*T.P. Pesaḥim* x, 37b), and R. Abbahu (*T.P. Avoda Zara, loc. cit.*). R. Ammi was vexed at a Halakhic practice of R. Judah Nesi'a, which was contrary to his own opinion (*T.B. Moʿed Qaṭan* 12b). The Patriarchs likewise enquired of the Sages the interpretation of certain Haggadas. However, we find a similar situation in the case of Rabban Simeon b. Gamaliel, who declared (*Tosefta Sukka* ii, 2, and the parallels in the Talmuds): 'Rabbi Jose permitted me', etc. On Rabban Simeon b. Gamaliel and his status *vis-à-vis* the Sages see below.

6 See Halevy, *op. cit.*, II, i, pp. 19–49.

7 *T.B. Ḥullin* 51a: 'Rav Safra said to Abbaye: Has the Master seen the scholar who came from the West and said: My name is R. ʿAwira... once there came before Rabbi the case of a needle... He (R. ʿAwira) replied: I am the janitor [*mafṭîr kĕnêsiyyôt*; see Jastrow *s.v.*] at the meetings of scholars to His Excellency the Great Rabbi (i.e. the Patriarch; *ibid.* 54a R. Judah the Patriarch is called thus by R. Joḥanan)... and there came before Rabbi the case of a needle found in the thick wall of the reticulum... and he declared it *ṭerefa* [an animal possessing an organic defect rendering it forbidden as food].' The case came before one of the Patriarchs at the beginning of the fourth century. Incidentally, the term *mafṭîr kĕnêsiyyôt* has not yet been satisfactorily explained (Lauterbach's explanation in the *Hebrew Union College Annual, Jubilee Volume* [Cincinnati, 1925], p. 217, is not clear). However, this is, at all events, connected with the Patriarch's practice to lecture in public. As regards the teaching of Torah by the (later) Patriarchs, the requisite inference may be drawn from the expression 'The School of Rabbi teaches', which frequently occurs in the Palestinian Talmud and simply refers to Baraitot taught in the college of the Patriarchs (cf. *T.B. Berakhot* 34b: 'R. Safra said in the name of a scholar of the School of Rabbi' — this is the correct reading, although there are variant versions).

8 *T.P. Yom Tov* i, 60d: 'R. Zeʿira asked Qalla Daroma, R. Judah Nesi'a's slave: Does your Master grind spices on a Holy Day?'

plexity and transgression.[9] We also know the testimony of Epiphanius concerning the 'apostles' who used 'to sit with the Patriarch day and night in order to advise him and to cite before him responsa regarding the laws of the Torah'.[10]

Now as to his position as ruler. The status of the Patriarch in the conduct of communal and political affairs did not oust nor blur his spiritual and religious image.[11] The Sages still assigned to the Patriarch sovereign authority in the religious life of the people.[12]

9 *Deuteronomy Rabba* ii, 19: 'R. Samuel bar Naḥmani said: All that the leaders do the generation does. How is this (to be understood)? If the Patriarch permits and the Av Bet Din says: The Patriarch permits, but I forbid; and the judges say: The Av Bet Din permits, but we forbid, and the rest of the people [lit.: 'generation'] declare: The judges permit, but we forbid; who then caused the entire generation to sin? The Patriarch, who was the first to transgress' (Av Bet Din here, apparently, means the Head of the College at Tiberias).

10 *Haer.* 30, 4. Epiphanius who wishes to glorify the 'apostles' (in connection with the story of the apostate Joseph) emphasizes their outstanding knowledge of the Torah and the authority they enjoyed among the Patriarchs. But it is clear that it was the Patriarch who gave the final decision in Halakhic practice. Some scholars prove the Patriarch's paucity of Halakhic erudition from *T.P.* *'Avoda Zara* i, 39b: 'R. Abbahu said: (ואני לא is wanting in the citation of the passage in *Or Zarua'*, Pisqe 'Avoda Zara, §96) Rabban Gamaliel 'Berabbi' asked me: Is it permitted to go to a (Gentile) fair? and I forbade him... But it has been taught: It is permitted to go to a fair and to buy male and female slaves there! Resh Laqish said: Not only may not Israelite slaves (be purchased), but not even Gentile slaves... How is Resh Laqish's ruling to be explained then? *Rabban Gamaliel was a small man and R. Abbahu wished to restrain him*, but R. Judan Nesi'a was a great man! Even so Resh Laqish (who likewise forbade Rabban Gamaliel to go to a fair) wished to curb the practice.' From this, it is argued, one can see how vast was the difference between R. Judah Nesi'a and Rabban Gamaliel who succeeded him! But the correct reading, given in *Or Zarua'*, is: 'Rabban Gamaliel was a great man... R. Judan Nesi'a was also a great man...' (see *Sha'are Torat Ereṣ Yisra'el*, p. 557). The meaning is: Although the general public is permitted to visit a fair, the rule for 'an eminent person' is made stricter so that he may serve as a deterrent and prevent the multitude from breaching the law completely — a principle that is applied in other Halakhot as well (the recension of current editions does not make sense).

11 See Ginzberg, *Perushim we-Ḥiddushim bi-Yerushalmi*, Pt. II, p. 195.

12 As, for instance, the proclamation of a fast, which was not decided solely by the Sages, 'but only if the Patriarch agreed'. See *T.P. Ta'anit* ii, 65a (in Harkavy, *Teshuvot ha-Ge'onim*, §259, p. 133, the reading is: אילין תענייתא דאינון [instead of דאנן] עבדין, 'The fasts that they [not 'we'] observed', i.e. that the Babylonians keep. This accords with Samuel's dictum: 'The

The Patriarchs themselves are known to have continued to care for communal needs by sending Sages to various cities of Eretz-Israel to see to the socio-religious institutions of the community in the Jewish settlements,[13] and the last Rabban Gamaliel jeopardized his position for the sake of building synagogues in the country (thus circumventing the imperial decree forbidding this) and on account of the judicial rights of which the Government had deprived the Jews.[14]

We undoubtedly hear, at this period, of acts of oppression committed by the Patriarchal House towards the Sages[15] and of the excessive exaction of money from the Jews.[16] But over and beyond the evidence of greed and callousness of individual Patriarchs, these traditions testify to the conflict between the Sages — or some of them — and the Patriarchs on public issues.[17] In other words, these

only public fasts in Babylonia are the Ninth of Av and the Day of Atonement' — *T.B. Ta'anit* 12b and the parallels listed *ibid.* The reason is that suggested by some of the Rishonim: Since the Babylonian fasts are not appointed by the Patriarchs, they are not treated Halakhically as proper fasts. There is no need to emend the reading, as does Harkavy.) Similarly in the case of a person placed under the ban; the Patriarch can always grant absolution, whether the one who imposed it dies, or it is not known who he is (see the episodes of Resh Laqish and Rav Judah in *T.B. Mo'ed Qaṭan* 17a, and the statement of R. Joshua b. Levi in *T.P. Mo'ed Qaṭan* iii, 81d).

13 *T.P. Ḥagiga* i, 86c and the parallels in the Midrashim: 'R. Judan Nesi'a (II) sent a message to R. Ḥiyya (bar Abba), to R. Assi, and R. Ammi that they should visit the cities of Eretz-Israel and arrange for them Bible and Mishna teachers', etc.

14 The reference is to the right to judge disputes between Christians and Jews; *C. Th.* 16, 8, 22 (*C. J.* 1, 9, 15).

15 For instance, R. Judah Nesi'a's attitude towards Jose of Ma'on, *T.P. Sanhedrin* ii, 20c–d (*Genesis Rabba* lxxx, Theodor-Albeck, p. 950) and towards Resh Laqish (*T.P. loc. cit.*, 19d. But these scholars attacked the Patriarch in public). Likewise the case of R. Mani of whom we are told 'that the members of the Patriarch's House vexed him' (*T.B. Ta'anit* 23b) and the story of how 'the servants of the Patriarchate' tortured Osha'ya Ze'ira of Ḥaverya [*aliter*: 'the youngest of the members'] (*T.B. Ta'anit* 24a; he, too, lectured publicly and blamed the Patriarchs for the tribulations suffered by the people).

16 The exposition of Jose of Ma'on was directed against the Patriarch's taking money from the people. The story of the woman that brought R. Judah Nesi'a a gift is well known and is one of the incidents against which Resh Laqish protested — *Genesis Rabba* lxxviii.

17 When Resh Laqish advised the Patriarch 'that he should not accept a gift from anyone' and even the Roman officers would not oppress him, he certainly gave him good counsel, which was in keeping with the plebeian character of this Sage. However, even if at times the collection of the contributions

traditions primarily reflect the clashes between the Patriarchs and the Sages, particularly in the sphere of their interrelationship and views.[18] Hence it is not surprising that our sources, which emanate from the

of the Palestinian Jews to the Patriarchate was accompanied by unworthy actions, it must be remembered that it was difficult for the Patriarch to forgo the financial means that enabled the central administrative institutions of the nation and its activities to survive. Incidentally, it appears that the landed estates that provided the material mainstay of the Patriarchate in the time of Rabbi (land that he leased from the Imperial House) were wholly, or partly, taken away from the Patriarch in the course of the changes that took place after the Severan Dynasty. Thereafter the Patriarchs were particularly in need of the support of the Jews in Eretz-Israel and the Diaspora.

This problem arose again in the reign of Julian, who wished to deliver the Jews from the burden of the ἀποστολή, against which many of them protested (see the famous letter of this Emperor). Similarly when Honorius Caesar charged that by exacting the *aurum coronarium* the Patriarch was acting as *depopulator Judaeorum*, he undoubtedly based his case on popular criticism, only the abolition of the 'coronation tax', needless to say, did not help to solve the problem of the maintenance of the administration, whose activities in Eretz-Israel and in the Diaspora were manifold at that time.

18 Jose of Maʿon's charge that 'the king takes all' and that 'the priests', in consequence, do not receive 'their gifts' from the people actually raises the question in whose custody the contributions to the Patriarchs and the Sages should be placed. For the 'Sages' Fund' was, apparently, none other than the Patriarch's 'coronation tax'. Without doubt the cause of the contention was the question under whose control these monies should be. This is one of the aspects of the struggle between the two elements in the supreme leadership — the *Bet Din ha-Gadol* [High Court] and the Patriarch — over the issue of sovereign authority. It likewise applied to R. Judah Nesi'a's demand that the Sages should contribute to the cost of building the wall of Tiberias, an impost that Resh Laqish and R. Joḥanan foiled (*T.B. Bava Batra* 7b-8a). The Sages claimed complete exemption from all obligations towards the city, an attitude that contributed, especially in places where there were large numbers of Sages and disciples, like Tiberias, to the aggravation of the burden borne by the townspeople (these were difficult times for the empire as a whole, including Eretz-Israel). Is it to be wondered at that the Patriarchs, on whom rested the responsibility and supervision of communal life in general, wished to avoid granting excessive privileges to the Sages as a body to the detriment of others?

It is true that some scholars hold the view that the exemption of the Sages from public taxation and service is based on an ancient Jewish usage dating from the period of the Second Temple and that the Antonine Emperors released them from governmental taxes. If that were the case the action of R. Judah Nesi'a would have to be regarded as an assault on the established rights of the Sages and an act of 'despotism'. But although Rabbi already freed the Sages from paying the 'coronation tax' (*T.B. Bava Batra* 8a), there is, to my mind, no basis for the view that in practice this tradition gradually crystallized from the days of Rabbi onwards. This subject requires elucidation,

world of the Sages, present the incidents tendentiously and with some suppression of the truth.

Far greater is the need to qualify the testimony of the Church Fathers, who completely deny any spiritual virtue to the Patriarchs and compare them to 'actors in the theatre', to 'pampered women', or to 'mere youths', 'immersed in lewdness'.[19] For even if 'secular' dominion did not leave the Patriarchs unaffected and some of them indulged in luxuries,[20] basically this testimony is polemical and seeks to repudiate the Jewish claim that the sovereignty and priesthood[21] still remained in their possession — and would continue to be theirs until the advent of the Messiah — in the form of the Patriarchate.[22]

In their polemic they even accused the Sages of ignorance of the Torah and of wallowing in the pleasures of this world, a charge that

but this is not the place for it (I propose to revert to this theme in an essay entitled 'Aspects of the Political and Social History of Jewish Palestine in the Period of the Severan Dynasty' [Hebrew]).

Furthermore, the repair of the wall of Tiberias presumably occurred at a time of turmoil, when there was danger of attack (i.e. by 'robber bands') upon the city. We also find that the Sages, on occasion, acted as did R. Judah Nesi'a and imposed a monetary contribution on their colleagues at a time of trouble, and there were protests against them as well (*T.P. Mo'ed Qaṭan* iii, 81d: 'In the days of R. Jeremiah trouble came upon Tiberias, so he sent a request for a silver (*aliter*: golden) lamp to R. Jacob b. Bun. He replied: "Jeremiah has not yet changed his evil ways", and he wished to put him under the ban. . . so they banned each other.').

19 Origen, *MG*, 24, 110; Jerome, in his commentary on Isaiah iii 3, Pl. 24, 59, his introduction to Hosea, Vallarsi, vol. 6, p. XXIII (ML, 25, 820). Chrysostom, *Adversus Judaeos* vi, *PG*, 48, 911–913; Epiphanius, *op. cit.*, 30, 7.

20 Rabbi's wealthy home and 'his (lavish) table' are well known (although he himself 'did not enjoy even with his little finger' anything of this world's pleasures). See the story of 'one of the members of the Patriarch's family' who became impoverished — *T.P. Pe'a* viii, 21a. In this connection mention should be made of the Patriarchs' practice, from the time of Rabbi onward, to visit Ḥammat Gader [which had hot springs], and although Sages also went with them and sometimes they went by themselves (see the sources cited in *Sefer ha-Yishuv*, א, א, pp. 45–46, and Epiphanius, *op. cit.*, p. 69), it seems that at times these visits were connected with Rabbinic conventions concerned with public matters (*T.P. 'Eruvin* vi, 23c; Ẓuri, *Shilton ha-Nesi'ut we-ha-Va'ad*, pp. 113–114, only he overstates the case).

21 Chrysostom implies that some Jews regarded the Patriarch as taking the place of the High Priest.

22 Origen initiates this polemic (*De Principiis* 4, 1, 3, Kötschau, pp. 297–298) and Theodoritus concludes it, shortly after the abolition of the Patriarchate (*PG*, 83, 61–64).

is at any rate highly exaggerated.[23] We must therefore conclude that it is improbable that the ordination of ignorant judges for pecuniary considerations was due primarily to the cupidity of the Patriarchs. Without doubt these appointments, which continued for several generations, had a general social and historical significance. The same applies to the protests of the Sages against them.

This conclusion, it appears, is borne out by a Christian tradition of the beginning of the fifth century, which also refers to a practice similar to those previously mentioned. Palladius writes in his *History of John Chrysostom*[24] that it is the custom of the Patriarchs to change each year, or every two years, the heads of the congregations in order to enrich themselves (by receiving the appointment fee). This writer also charges the Patriarchs with cupidity, which undermines the religious administration of the Jews through the frequent changes of its leaders. But we are inclined to regard this practice — the question of the acceptance of money we shall discuss later — not as an evil innovation of the Patriarchs but as the continuation (or intensification) of the democratic tradition in the Jewish community — the appointment of the administrative authorities for one year. This usage, however, began to be impaired by occasional life-appointments, and even more so by the tendency to establish a lineal aristocracy in the form of hereditary offices among the communal leaders.[25]

These acts of the Patriarchs and the opposition thereto of the Sages were related, it seems, to the problem of the existence of communal judicatures alongside the judiciary of the expert, ordained Rabbis. However, since we still lack a methodical presentation of the judicial

23 Origen, *PG*, 24, 110, and Jerome *passim*. Even if we assume that there was a decline in Torah-learning among the Palestinian Sages at the close of the fourth century and the beginning of the fifth (and this is by no means certain) it was undoubtedly not wholly forgotten, nor did Halakhic authorities cease in Eretz-Israel. Jerome himself testifies frequently to the numerous 'teachers' and 'illustrious teachers', who were to be found in Eretz-Israel.

24 *PG*, 47, p. 51.

25 In the third and fourth centuries there are common in the Diaspora communal leaders who served (διὰ βίου) 'throughout their lifetime' and, similarly, μελλάρχοντες, μελλογραμματεῖς, and children archons, a fact which indicates that there was a kind of law of heredity in public administration (see Frey, *Corpus*, Introduction, p. 78; Baron, *The Jewish Community*, I, pp. 104–105). But Theodotus already in his inscription (first century) boasts that he is the head of a congregation, the son of the head of a congregation, and the grandson of the head of a congregation (*REJ*, 1920, vol. 71, p. 46; this inscription has been translated into Hebrew by M. Schwabe in *Sefer Yerushalayim*, vol. I, p. 362 ff).

institutions of Eretz-Israel in the Talmudic period, describing their different types, their interrelationship, and the structure of their organization,[26] we are therefore compelled to deal here with the main problems inherent in this theme. Needless to say, we have no intention of stating explicit conclusions, something that cannot be done definitely even after deep study, because of the nature of our sources. What follows is no more than an attempt to outline in general terms the framework of the problem — a few headings, as it were, for suggested investigation.

The abstract, theoretical formulation adopted by the sources on the subject of the courts, the multiplicity of conflicting opinions and the contradictions in the Halakhic and practical traditions regarding their authority and composition, including many actual facts that ostensibly attest the temporary character of the Palestinian judicial institutions at that period, have collectively induced one scholar[27] to deny completely the existence of organized courts of a permanent and regular nature. According to Chajes we only find in the sources evidence of separate, individual judges,[28] who tried cases by special authorization and on a temporary basis, but judicial bodies were entirely non-existent.

There is undoubtedly much evidence to support this assessment, only it does not embrace the entire sphere of judicial tribunals but only a part of them. For against this testimony we learn of courts that tried the accused perforce,[29] of courts that enforced certain acts upon the demand of one of the parties to the suit,[30] of courts 'that

26 Although Weinberg's article ('Organisation' etc., *MGWJ*, 1897, pp. 249–262) and the presentation of Juster and Gulak, *Yesode ha-Mishpaṭ ha-ʿIvri* (Book IV, pp. 23–40), and similar works, teach us a great deal, they do not provide us with a full picture.

27 Chajes in *REJ*, 1899, vol. 39, pp. 39–52.

28 Juster (II, p. 96, n. 2) answers that all the Sages who are represented as judging by themselves actually had others with them, and thus constituted permanent courts. But although in many instances this was undoubtedly the case, individuals also gave judgement, without holding a permanent position. See below.

29 *Sifre Deuteronomy* §144 (ed. Finkelstein, p. 198): ' "And they shall judge the people" — perforce'; *ibid.* §286 (ed. Finkelstein, p. 302): ' "And they shall judge" — perforce'. See also *T.P. Sanhedrin* i, 18a: 'If an authorized judge forced (the litigants to come before him) and judged by himself (despite the law requiring three judges), his judgement is valid'.

30 Although in regard to the Halakhot that treat of compelling one of the parties to a suit to carry out the court's decision, the nature of the enforcement is not clearly stated in the sources and sometimes the Rishonim discuss

flagellated and imprisoned',[31] of 'court messengers who administered beatings',[32] of the seizure of the lands of debtors in their absence

the question whether physical compulsion is implied, it is apparent that generally the actual use of force is meant; and this is inconceivable without a permanent court of justice, for example 'And these are they that are compelled to put away their wives' (*M. Ketubbot* vii, 9, 10). So, too, 'a bill of divorce given under compulsion' (*M. Giṭṭin* ix, 8; *Mekhilta*, Mishpatim, ed. Horovitz, p. 246), and *Ḥaliṣa* [ceremony of removing the *yavam*'s shoe; Deut. xxv 5–11] carried out under compulsion (*Tosefta Yevamot* xii, 13), and the like.

31 See the Baraita in *T.B. Sanhedrin* 17b: 'Any city where the following ten things are absent... and a court that flagellates and *imprisons* (*ḥôvĕshîn*)' — this is the correct recension and not 'imposes penalties (*'ônĕshîn*)', as in current editions. See *Diqduqe Soferim* and 'Pirqe Rabbenu ha-Qadosh' (Higger, *Ḥorev*, vol. vi, p. 143) and several works published subsequently. This is also the reading in the parallel dictum of Rav in *T.P. Qiddushin* iv, 66b. Indeed, the expression is quite old and so, too, is the institution itself, for we read in Josephus (*Ant.* xiii, 10, 6) that when Joḥanan the High Priest [John Hyrcanus] requested the Pharisees to pronounce sentence on one of their number who had slandered him (alleging that he was the son of a captive woman), they declared that he deserved 'stripes and fetters' — πληγῶν καὶ δεσμῶν. This is not the place to discuss the problem, dealt with by various scholars, whether this imprisonment was a punishment based on criminal law, or *poena extraordinaria*, and whether it was imposed before sentence was passed, or was 'a police measure' (see Katz, *Die Strafe im Talmud*, pp. 52–55; Gulak, *Ha-Ḥiyyuv we-Shi'budaw*, pp. 24 ff. On the specific question of *kippa* see Kantor, *Beiträge zur Lehre von der Strafrechtlichen Schuld im Talmud*; see also below, pp. 289 ff).

The existence of prisons in the Jewish cities of Eretz-Israel is not surprising, since these existed in Hellenistic cities of the East and were under the control of the municipal authorities; see Mommsen, *Das römische Strafrecht*, p. 309 (Sifre §309, *Midrash Tanna'im*, p. 188: 'It is like the case of a man who was standing and insulting a senator in the street. Said the bystanders to him: Fool that you are, do you stand and insult a senator? Could he not, if he wished, beat you, tear your garments, and cast you into prison...?'). However, it should be noted, on the other hand, that we do not find explicit reference in civil cases to *actual instances* in which beatings were administered and force was employed except by the order of the Patriarchs, or by the Sages who enforced their sentence by means of 'the servants' of the Patriarch (*Ecclesiastes Rabba* x; *T.P. Ketubbot* ix, 33a; *T.B. Nidda* 52a).

This apart, there is evidence to support the assumption that sometimes the Bet Din was unable in practice to enforce payment by debtors. This situation is to be attributed to the parallel Roman Judiciary (under the auspices of the Governor) and to the practice of the authorities to intervene in the autonomous judicature, both of the Jews and the Greek cities, despite the tradition and law that assured them independence and the right of jurisdiction.

32 *Tosefta Bava Qamma* ix, 1; *ibid. Makkot* ii, 5, and similar sources.

and against their will,[33] of courts that appointed administrators for orphans, for deaf-mutes, and for imbeciles, or themselves acted as administrators,[34] of 'the judges of Sepphoris',[35] and of Sages who

33 Cf. especially R. Mana's remarks to Alaxa (a Gentile) in *T.P. Ketubbot* ix, 33b and *T.P. Shevu'ot* vii, 38a on the practice of Jewish courts in the fourth century to collect by force property of the debtor for the benefit of the creditor.

34 *Tosefta Terumot* i, 1; *ibid.* Yevamot ix, 2 ('A deaf-mute, an imbecile, and a minor. . . but if the Bet Din bought for them or the administrators bought for them', etc.).

35 *M. Bava Batra* vi, 7. Büchler suggests that these may have served as judges by governmental appointment (*Der Galiläische 'Am-Ha'areṣ*, p. 139; *The Political and Social Leaders of the Jewish Community of Sepphoris in the 2nd and 3rd Centuries*, p. 25, note 1). This conjecture is intrinsically different from the tradition in *Tractate Semaḥot* xiv, ed. Higger, p. 208, where this Halakha is attributed to 'the elders of Bet Av', an obscure expression (which cannot be discussed here), but which, at any rate, signifies a Bet Din of Sages. But Büchler's entire theory concerning Jewish judges that were appointed by the Government, including Tannaim, who tried cases, in his view, according to Roman law and not in accordance with the Halakha, is doubtful. Büchler relies on the Haggadah in *T.B. Bava Batra* 58a–b concerning R. Banna'a, who was appointed a judge by the Roman authorities. But it is not stated that he acted as judge to Jews, or where he judged. Now there is a kind of parallel to this story in another Haggada relating to R. Shila in *T.B. Berakhot* 58a (according to the correct recensions it is clear that the incident occurred in Eretz-Israel and not in Babylon, and the objection raised in *Diqduqe Soferim* is without basis, because there was a Sage of that name also in Eretz-Israel). We read at the end of that narrative in the original manuscript versions: 'They put a rod in his hand and seated him at the gateway of Rome and he served as judge.' We cannot therefore make any deductions from the sources in regard to our subject. But the whole question as to whether Jews served in the Roman judiciary in Eretz-Israel is bound up, to my mind, with the problem discussed by modern authorities on Roman law with reference to the structure of the Roman judiciary in the provinces during the period of the *principatus*. As is well known, from the time of Diocletian onwards the early Roman civil law was abolished throughout the empire (apparently in the middle of the third century). The formulary proceedings, with their inherent division between judgement *in jure* by the ruler and *in judaico* by the civil magistrate, were replaced by bureaucratic *extraordinary proceedings* of the government. Only it cannot be ascertained when the latter procedure was introduced in the provinces. There is evidence to support the premise, especially in respect of the imperial states (in contrast to those of the Senate), that the *extraordinary proceedings* were in force since the time of the early emperors. If this may be assumed — and apparently it seems correct — the possibility of Jewish citizens being appointed by the Government to serve as judges in Eretz-Israel appears to be precluded (on the existence of *judices pedanei* in the Byzantine period see Wlassak, *Zum*

were specifically designated 'judges'.[36] Perhaps the strongest evidence of permanent and composite courts is furnished by the existence of Avot Bet Din ['Fathers of the courts'] in populated localities; their chief function was undoubtedly judicial.[37]

The investigation of our sources points to the existence (or the

römischen Provinzialprozess, *passim*; cf. also 'the judges of Caesarea', *T.B. Sukka* 8a and the parallel passages listed *ibid.*).

36 R. Nathan, *T.B. Bava Qamma* 53a; *T.B. Bava Mesi'a* 117b; R. Jose b. Ḥanina, *T.B. Bava Qamma* 39a. Cf. 'the judges' grotto' *T.B. Mo'ed Qaṭan* 17a.

37 *T.B. Mo'ed Qaṭan* 17a: 'In Usha they enacted that if an Av Bet Din committed an offence he was not to be put under the ban'. In the parallel passage in the Palestinian Talmud (*ibid.* iii, 81d) we read: 'They decided by vote in Usha not to put an Elder under the ban'. Similarly in *T.B. Ḥagiga* 13a 'R. Zera said: The headings of chapters may be transmitted only to an Av Bet Din and to one whose heart is anxious within him' etc., the pre-eminent Av Bet Din, the Vice-President [of the Sanhedrin of which the Patriarch was the President]. The same applies to the Baraita in *T.B. Mo'ed Qaṭan* (*Tractate Semaḥot* x, 3, ed. Higger, p. 185): 'when an Av Bet Din dies all the colleges *in his city* are closed'; this ruling refers explicitly to the Av Bet Din of a city. Likewise in *T.B. Sukka* 29a (*Massekhtot Derekh 'Ereṣ*, ed. Higger, p. 290): 'On account of four things the sun is eclipsed: because of an Av Bet Din who died and no appropriate mourning oration was delivered over him.' This statement is related to the many Talmudic admonitions concerning the observance of the *hespēd* ['mourning oration'] and *'ēvel* ['mourning'] for a Sage who died, every Sage being implied. The matter is elucidated by R. Samuel bar Naḥmani in *Ruth Rabba* ii: ' "The father of Lecah" — the Av Bet Din of Lecah; "the father of Mareshah" — the Av Bet Din of Mareshah.' So, too, the dictum in the *Yalquṭ*, Deuteronomy, §416, taken from *Sifre Zuṭa*: 'It is like the case of an Av Bet Din who had many sons all of whom were ignoramuses [*ammê ha-'areṣ*] and only his eldest son was learned in the Torah. In his will he assigned to each one his share... (To the eldest) he said: Let it suffice you that you take my place.' Unquestionably the passage speaks of the Sage of a city (although Büchler, *Der Galiläische 'Am-Ha'areṣ*, p. 174, n. 136, seeks to prove that this dictum refers specifically to the Av Bet Din who was Vice-President. As proof he adduces the fact that the Av Bet Din gives his office as a heritage to his son, for only administrative offices were hereditary, not posts concerned with Halakhic decisions. But this distinction is incorrect; see below, the article 'The Sons of the Sages', p. 436). A similar position of Av Bet Din was filled by R. Osha'ya, under whom were 'judges' who transgressed (*Ecclesiastes Rabba* ii, 16), and it is certainly possible that the 'Av Bet Din' R. Joshua b. Ḥanania (*T.B. Bava Qamma* 74b) must have held this position on a municipal level. This also applies to 'Aqavya whom the Sages proposed to appoint an Av Bet Din in Israel (*M. 'Eduyot* v, 6). See M. Guttmann, *Mafteaḥ ha-Talmud*, I, p. 82, who points to the tradition in *Ruth Rabba*, and Albeck, *Zion*, 1943, p. 91, who posited the possibility of the position of local Av Bet Din applying to R. Joshua b. Ḥanania and 'Aqavya.

possible existence) of the following three principal judicial systems: (1) the communal judiciary, which was independent of the central authority — the Patriarchate and the Sanhedrin; (2) the judicature of the Sages, who were experts or ordained judges; their authority derived, directly or indirectly, from the authorization of the central administration mentioned above; (3) private jurisdiction, which was provisional, in the form of arbitration.

The communal judiciary. It will appear, from our subsequent analysis, to have comprised three different forms of jurisdiction: that of the municipal administration, that of the citizens' tribunal, and that of the permanent 'judges'. The factor common to them all is that in each sector the judges were 'inexpert', and hence whenever the Talmudic sources speak of 'a Bet Din of lay judges' they may refer to one of these types of tribunals.

The judicature of the municipal administration. There is the well-known tradition of Josephus in *Antiquities* to the effect that Moses enjoined that a Bet Din of seven judges[38] be established in every city of Eretz-Israel. He further testifies that he himself appointed seven judges in every Galilean settlement, when he was made the governor of that province by the Jerusalem authorities.[39] From Josephus' own observation we learn that these judges were merely the members of the local administrative organization, and the Sages already equated them with the seven town representatives [שבעה טובי העיר *shivʿā ṭôvê hā-ʿîr,* literally: 'the seven good men of the town'] mentioned in the Talmuds, who were the leaders of the urban settlement.[40] Thus we see that the town administration, in the period prior to the destruction of the Second Temple, possessed judicial powers, just as 'the city Elders' also served as judges in the Biblical era.[41]

38 iv, 8, 14; *ibid.* 38.

39 *Wars* ii, 20, 5; Life §14.

40 Weyl, *Die jüdischen Strafgesetze bei Flavius Josephus*, p. 15. Although the term שבעת טובי העיר is found only in the Babylonian Talmud (*Megilla* 26a), the Palestinian Talmud also mentions שבעת מבני העיר, 'seven burghers of the town', who stand at the head of the community (*Megilla* iii, 74a). Also the epithet טב קרתא, 'town representative' is found in the Palestinian Talmud (*Taʿanit* iv, 68d; so, too, *Lamentations Rabba* v, 12, and *Midrash Samuel* xxxii, ed. Buber, p. 141).

41 Menes, *Die vorexilischen Gesetze Israels*, pp. 91–92; Ring, *Israel's Rechtsleben*, pp. 78–79; Sulzberger, *JQR*, N.S., Vol. III, pp. 48–49, 61 ff; Nicolsky, *ZAW*, 1930, pp. 156–158. Josephus' testimony concerning the municipal judicature is supported by the tradition in *The History of Susanna* (i, 5): καὶ ἀπεδείχθησαν δύο πρεσβύτεροι ἐκ τοῦ λαοῦ κριταὶ ἐν τῷ ἐνιαυτῷ ἐκείνῳ

Of the period after the Destruction we have no explicit evidence, it seems, of the existence of this type of district judicature; only it is not an improbable assumption that it continued to function also at this period. The local settlement and its administration were, to a large extent, a stable factor amid the upheavals that accompanied the war against Rome and followed it, although at times, to be sure, they also suffered in the time of crisis. Generally speaking the Roman authorities were tolerant towards the autonomous rule of the urban settlements in Jewish Palestine, primarily because an established local management could help to furnish their requirements in the administrative and financial sphere. There is no reason, therefore, to negate the hypothesis that the judicial powers of the local administration were not abolished, at least for given areas of Eretz-Israel, even in the Talmudic period.

The citizens' tribunals. Most of the sources that speak of lay persons connected with judicial proceedings, or with matters of a legal nature, generally refer to any citizens who have no public standing in their locality. These are the 'members of the congregation' [בני כנסת *bĕnê kĕneset*], i.e. the ordinary members of the community, who are contrasted with the 'experts'.[42] But our sources do not explain how these judges were appointed and what authority they and their rulings had in the local administration.

Our survey does not, of course, include actions of a judicial or religio-judicial character that do not involve the settlement of a dispute between parties, or the passing of a sentence of conviction that is enforceable, as for example the selection of arbiters entirely by those concerned, which requires no communal organization or supervision

('And the same year there were appointed two of the elders of the people to be judges'). Although this verse does not state expressly that these 'elders' were members of the urban administration, this can be seen from v. 29: καὶ ἀναστάντες οἱ δὺο πρεσβύτεροι καὶ κριταί ('Then the two elders and judges arose'). Cf. *vv.* 34, 41 (see especially the version of Theodotion in *v.* 41, πρεσβύτεροι τοῦ λαοῦ κ. κριταί 'elders of the people and judges'). But it is still uncertain where and when the book was written and what its original language was.

42 *M. Bekhorot* iv, 2; *Tosefta Sanhedrin* i, 2; *ibid. Bekhorot* iii, 25. Although Lauterbach, like Büchler, takes these *bĕnê kĕneset* to be associates of Rabbinic scholars (*Hebrew Union College Annual, Jubilee Volume*, 1925, pp. 216–218), the real meaning of the expression is that given in the text; see above, p. 211, n. 62 (= *Meḥqarim*, vol. I, p. 162, n. 62).

Undoubtedly the Rishonim are correct in stating that three lay judges can enforce their decision (see below, the views of scholars who wish to identify them invariably with arbitrators).

to speak of. But a judicial institution dealing with cases between plaintiffs and defendants is apparently inconceivable — if we exclude arbitration, with which we are not concerned here — unless we assume control and supervision by the public authority to ensure submission by the defendant to litigation and its verdict.[43]

We can posit such control vested in the hands of the entire community represented by 'the assembly of the townspeople [מעמד אנשי העיר *ma'ămad 'anshé ha-'îr*]', which took unto itself — at least in certain places — supreme authority in the administration of public affairs, both in theory and in practice.[44] The citizens, or some of them, were required and authorized to act as judges in private matters, when they were called upon to try a case by the parties to the dispute or by the plaintiffs.[45] But it is possible that it was the local

43 The Rishonim are undoubtedly correct. Three non-ordained judges can force the parties to accept their jurisdiction (but see below, the views of scholars who always seek to identity these judges as arbitrators).

44 *Ma'amad 'anshê ha-'îr* is referred to in this precise form only in a Baraita in the Babylonian Talmud (*Bava Meṣi'a* 78b; 106b) and in the Gemara (*T.B. Megilla* 26a). Furthermore, in the parallel passage to this Baraita in the Tosefta (*Megilla* i, 5) this assembly is not mentioned at all. The Tosefta likewise makes no mention of the Halakha cited in the Gemara (*ibid.* iii, 1), but makes the sale of the sacred objects of the town depend specifically on the stipulations of the town administrators. Nevertheless, the substance of the Halakha concerning the primacy of 'the citizens' over the administrators is also found in the Palestinian Talmud (iii, 74a): 'With what case are we dealing? If they accepted (an administrative authority) over them, even one (may act). If they did not do so, even many (cannot act). . .' Most of the Rishonim explain that the reference is to the assent of the townspeople to the action of the administration in selling sacred articles (in consonance with the discussion in the Babylonian Talmud). But Me'iri interprets the passage in relation to the election of administrators, which was in the hands of the townspeople as a whole. Be this as it may, the power of the latter *vis-à-vis* the administration is clearly stated here. But it is well known that in the course of the second century the ἐκκλησία progressively disappears in the Hellenistic cities of the East as a factor in administration and legislation. The fact that municipal government was placed in the hands of the affluent classes under imperial law (in the period of the Severans) also conduced to the weakening of 'the assembly of the townspeople' even in the Jewish settlements of Eretz-Israel, which were not organized in the form of πόλεις ['cities'].

45 It seems that the courts of the Essenes acted similarly; it is thus implied by Josephus (*Wars* ii, 8, 9), who attests that they did not pass sentence with fewer than a hundred judges (only these judges did not deal with civil suits). Apparently he does not refer to permanent judges but to any 'members of the congregation'. This citizens' tribunal is probably to be regarded as a development of communal judgement, for we still find traces of 'a community

administration that supervised the citizens' judicial role mentioned above. In that case the municipal authority saw to it that the law was carried out and compelled those judged liable to obey the verdict. Since those judges were not permanent nor belonged to a closed group of administrators, it appears that the composition of these tribunals of changing judges was left undecided, even in respect of fixing the lower limit.[46] It would consequently seem that it is this judicial authority to which the Halakha — ostensibly so surprising — refers in two or three passages, when it rules that each of the parties has the right to demand the appointment of additional judges even during the course of the legal proceedings right to the end.[47]

judging' even in the post-Biblical period. Thus we read in Sirach (xxiii 24) that an adulteress αὕτη εἰς ἐκκλησίαν ἐξαχθήσεται — 'she shall be led into the assembly' (i.e. for punishment. But can inferences be drawn from a book of proverbs? Perhaps the author is merely using an ancient formula). Also in the story of Susanna the people assemble for judgement, only we do not find them actively participating in the trial. Herod likewise 'handed over' to the community the trial of capital cases and the latter actually carried them out (*Wars* i, 27, 6; *Ant.* xvi, 11, 6–7, and elsewhere). It seems that Herod wished to abide by ancient tradition and to show that he observed it (or renewed it?). See above, 'Par'irtin', p. 84 (= *Meḥqarim*, I, 6, 73).

46 That civil cases require three judges was already taught by R. Akiba (*Tosefta Shevu'ot* iii, 8), but Rabbi calls for five (*ibid.*; *Tosefta Sanhedrin* i, 1; *T.B. ibid.* 3b). The Amoraim of Eretz-Israel differed, as we know, from those of Babylon in regard to judgement given by two, the former disqualifying the decision and the latter validating it (*T.P. Sanhedrin* i, 18a; *T.B. ibid.* 2b; *T.B. Ketubbot* 22a. See the similar dispute with reference to the benediction of the common grace [zimmûn] in *T.B. Berakhot* 45a and *T.P. ibid.* vii, 11a).

47 *Sifre Deuteronomy* §12 (ed. Finkelstein, pp. 19–20): 'If one of them saw that his opponent was winning the case, he would say: I am able to bring (more) witnesses, I have (more) evidence; when I argue my case tomorrow I shall add more judges.' In *Tosefta Sanhedrin* i, 4 we read: 'More judges can always be appointed until the conclusion of the case.' So, too, *T.P. Sanhedrin* iii, 22d (see ed. Finkelstein, *ibid.*, note 1).

Apparently the Baraita in *T.B. Sanhedrin* 23a, 'The perspicacious in Jerusalem [נקיי הדעת בירושלים, 'the clear-minded of Jerusalem'] acted thus... and they would not sit in judgement unless they knew who would sit with them', refers to the type of Bet Din under discussion; for citizens had the right to refuse to act as judges, when they were not sure that their would-be colleagues were worthy (נקיי הדעת בירושלים are not to be identified with יקירי ירושלים ['the noble ones of Jerusalem'] and to be regarded as aristocrats and dignitaries, as does Klein, *Madda'e ha-Yahadut*, vol. I, pp. 75–77). The expression 'clarity of mind' simply means 'understanding', 'knowledge of life' (see *T.P. Ma'aśerot* ii, 49d 'R. Ze'ira said: R. Joshua has a clear mind. R. Mani retorted: Are all other people then fools?' So, too, *T.P. Terumot* viii, 45d, with reference to the serpent, who drops venom into

A third type of communal judicature consisted of permanent 'judges', who were apparently appointed from among the city's nobility and wealthy citizens. This fact is not to be explained on a Halakhic basis,[48] for 'all are eligible to adjudicate in civil cases' and the demand for 'such as can marry (their daughters) to priests' applies only to capital cases.[49] But just as many of the town leaders were men of standing and noble lineage,[50] so it is not surprising that these judges were chosen from among them, because judgeship of this kind symbolized (and vouchsafed) high status in the community.

The image of such a judge emerges from the tradition in the *Sifre*, Numbers, *Be-ha'alotekha*, § 79 (ed. Horovitz), p. 76: ' "And he (Jethro) said to him (Moses): I will not go" — He said to him: If I did not return on account of (my) chattels, or on account of (my) land — for

liquids: 'This wicked creature has a clear mind and does not drink hot water that has been cooled.' But undoubtedly no inferences are to be drawn from this Baraita in regard to the practice in Temple times for the added reason that the relevant sentence is wanting in the *Mekhilta*, Mishpaṭim, pericope 2, ed. Horovitz-Rabin, p. 322).

48 Dinaburg, *op. cit.*; the question of the judiciary is not to be identified with the appointment of administrators.

49 However, we possess evidence that at first care was taken to appoint as judges only 'such as can marry their daughters to priests'. Thus we are told in the Mishna (*Qiddushin* iv, 5): 'Also any whose name was signed as a witness in the old archives at Sepphoris' (חתום בערכי... — this is the reading in most recensions and appears to be correct; another version is: חתום עד). Some of the Rishonim explained it to mean 'signed as a judge'. This explanation is possible, although ערכי is probably to be understood in the sense of ἀρχεῖον (Gulak, *Dinê Qarqa'ot*, pp. 46–47). It is similarly taught in the Tosefta (Sanhedrin vii, 1): 'Rabban Simeon b. Gamaliel said: Formerly a woman's *ketubba* ['marriage contract'] was signed only by priests, Levites, or Israelites who can marry their daughters to priests.' But even the expression '[those who can] marry their daughters to priests' does not imply the status of real nobility, but refers to Israelites who were born of absolutely lawful wedlock (of which marriage to priests constitutes Halakhic proof); this is, therefore, a religio-national criterion that goes beyond a social test. At any rate, the Halakha in the course of its development validated 'disqualified' citizens as judges (even proselytes, the Palestinian Talmud states — *Yevamot* xii, 12c top, and likewise *T.B. Sanhedrin* 36b — were permitted by some authorities to adjudicate in civil cases; see below, pp. 436 ff.).

50 There are undoubtedly intimations of this also in the Halakha (see Dinaburg, *op. cit.*), just as even the presumption of inheritance is expounded in the Halakha. But this represents only the view of a certain school; other traditions depreciated these things (I intend dealing with the question in the article 'The Sons of the Sages').

sometimes a man has land but no chattels, or he has chattels but no family — but I have land and chattels and family, *and I was a judge in my town*, if I did not go (home) on account of my land, I would go on account of my chattels, and if I did not go on account of my chattels, I would go on account of my kindred.'

However, another important factor contributed strongly to the appointment of rich men as judges: they were able to find the time for public service without taking payment. The fact that a judge was prohibited from taking fees for his judgement,[51] and that there was no fixed salary for public administrators in general,[52] as well as for important communal functionaries in the cities, conduced to judicial work being placed in the hands of men of means, 'the *baṭlanin*' ['men of leisure'].[53]

51 *M. Bekhorot* iv, 6. But in *Tosefta ibid.*, iii, 8 (cf. *T.B. Ketubbot* 105a; *T.P. Sanhedrin* i, 18b): 'He who is suspected of taking a fee and giving judgement... all the judgements given by him... are void. But one gives the judge a fee for his judgement [i.e. the professional fee to compensate him for loss of work]... although they said: Contemptible is the judge who takes his fee.' Is it far-fetched to suggest that just as this Halakha, which permits the taking of payment for judgement, contains evidence of the country's deteriorated economic position, so it also attests the aim to validate the judicature of people (and Sages) who do not belong to the affluent class?

52 *Tanna de-vê Eliyyahu* (ed. Friedmann, p. 54): 'There was a small town in Eretz-Israel... and they hired unto themselves the Sage [*Ḥākhām*]' etc. However, even if we ascribe this work to Eretz-Israel (I am personally inclined to this view; it was possibly written at the end of the Byzantine period), the subject-matter of the dictum apparently indicates that the reading of the *Yalkut*: 'And they hired a *ḥazzan* (attendant, official, supervisor) for themselves' is the correct version. The same applies to the parallel instance of the appointment of the Babylonian by Resh Laqish as a *ḥazzan* in Basrah (*T.P. Shevi'it* vi, 36d) mentioned in *Deuteronomy Rabba*, ed. Liberman, pp. 60–61, from which it follows he was appointed and allocated a fixed salary, and in this tradition he is not mentioned as having exercised any judicial function (as in T.P.). Indeed, the other functionaries enumerated there (teacher, scribe, etc.), as is known, did receive emoluments from the community.

53 Scholars have been extensively preoccupied in attempting to clarify the nature of the 'ten men of leisure' mentioned in *M. Megilla* (i, 3; see most recently, *JQR* 1943/4, pp. 93 ff). It would seem first of all, however, that these individuals did not constitute some kind of *council* of public leaders. Furthermore, the Halakha — 'Which is considered a large town? — One that has ten men of leisure. One that has fewer is considered a village' — only refers to a locality where at least ten rich men reside, who are able to free themselves from their businesses. This is a socio-economic indication of the multitude of inhabitants of a city. Yet others rightly wanted to regard them as men needed for the performance of public duties (such as Torah and prayer),

It seems that already in the first generation after the Destruction the Sages discussed the problem, in the manner in which it is apparently reflected in the dispute between R. Joshua and R. Eleazar of Modiʿim in the *Mekhilta* (Massekhta da-Amalek, Jethro, section ii, Horovitz, p. 198): ' "Moreover, thou shalt provide... able men", that is, wealthy people, people of means; "such as fear God", that means those who fear the Omnipresent when sitting in judgement; "men of truth", these are people of trust; "hating unjust gain", these are men that are averse to accepting fees for given judgement — this is the view of R. Joshua. R. Eleazar of Modiʿim said: "Moreover, thou shalt provide... able men", that is people of trust; "such as fear of God", those who arbitrate litigations, "men of truth", like R. Ḥanina b. Dosa and his associates; "hating unjust gain", those who are disdainful of their own money — if now they are contemptuous of their own money, how much more so of that of others.' The same applies to the subsequent dispute: ' "And let them judge the people at all seasons" — R. Joshua said: Men who are free from work shall judge the people at all times. R. Eleazar of Modiʿim said: Men who are free from work *and occupy themselves with the Torah* shall judge the people at all times.'

It is not unwarranted to perceive in these differences of opinion the disputes of the Sages concerning the kind of judges required for their own days. R. Joshua emphasizes, as a decisive factor in the choice of judges, their economic position, which enables them to find time for public service and makes no mention whatsoever of their preoccupation with Torah study.

At the time of his death, Rabbi Prof. Abrahams had translated the article and notes till here. The rest has been completed by another hand.

R. Eleazar of Modiʿim, in contradistinction, attaches less importance to this factor and emphasizes Torah study and saintly conduct as the essential precondition for judgeship. Here, then, we have before us two contradictory Tannaitic evaluations of the qualifications of the 'secular' aristocracy for judicial authority.

This negative attitude towards prevailing conditions is apparently given caustic expression by another contemporary Sage.[54] In *Deuteron-*

since from them emanated the individuals who were engaged in public affairs (*T.B. Megilla* 5a; *Sanhedrin* 17b; *T.P. Megilla*, i, 70b).

54 We certainly cannot be positive that Ben Azzai uttered these words exactly as transcribed.

omy Rabba, MS Munich (Buber, *Bet Talmud*, IV, p. 278) and MS Oxford (Lieberman, pp. 13–14), we read: 'What does *hirba etkhem* (lit. 'has made you great') [mean]? You find that Ben Azzai said: A Jew's dog is better than a Jewish judge. How? One man came and said to another: Exchange with me. Will you take this kid and give me that dog? He said to him: Yes. As they were standing, someone else came and said to him: Take two for yourself. Another came and said: Take three. Still another came and said: Take four for yourself. They would not agree. They came to trial to a judge and related the case to him. The judges began saying: Let them divide the dog among the four of them, and let each take a quarter of the dog (while the Sages say: The verdict should be in favour of the first only). But they divided it among the four men. So it happens that justice is perverted, and one receives an ear more than the next. What happens to the judges? They destroy their lives and the lives of their children and everything they have. What caused this (to happen) to them? That he gave more to one than to the other. Alas, a dog's ear is worth more than their judges.[55] Hence, "the Lord your God has made you greater than your judges".' The caustic language this tradition uses against these 'Judges of Israel' makes it clear to us that the Sages had the upper and powerful classes in mind and not the simple citizens who undertook to conduct lawsuits only occasionally. The Sages objected to these judges because they were ignorant (that is to say, they did not judge in accordance with the Halakhic norms), and just as in other Tannaitic Halakhic traditions, the insistence is repeated that only judges 'expert in law' be appointed.[56]

A similar accusation, presumably, appears in a Baraita quoted in *Sifre* Deuteronomy, § 17 (ed. Finkelstein, pp. 19–20): ' "You shall

55 It stands to reason that what we have here is a popular maxim. The Haggada, however, wished to interweave it with circumstances providing an excuse for the usage (the legally unjustified award of a dog's ear is the excuse for the exaction of retribution from the judge). This approach is adopted by the Haggada in other instances as well, as in the incident, for instance, involving R. Eliezer recorded in *Genesis Rabba*, xlii: 'And his cow fell and broke (its leg). He said: It was for my good that my cow broke its leg'; similarly in *T.P. Horayot* iii, 48a, where the remark, too, is a popular maxim. The same applies to *T.B. Shabbat* 116b: 'She brought him a golden lamp . . . R. Gamaliel said to him: An ass came and knocked down the lamp.' The lamp was introduced into the narrative in order to furnish a pretext for the emergence of the proverb (*T.P. Yoma* i, 38c, 'The donkey kicked over the Menorah.').

56 *Midrash Tannaim*, pp. 97, 161.

not respect persons in judgement" — (this is directed at) the person appointed for the placement of judges. Lest you say: This person is pleasing, I shall assign him a judgeship; this person is mighty, I shall assign him a judgeship; this person is my relative (*qerovi*),[57] I shall assign him a judgeship; this person knows Greek, I shall assign him a judgeship; this person knows all languages, I shall assign him a judgeship. It is found that he acquits the guilty, and convicts the innocent, not because he is wicked, but because he is ignorant. Scripture regards him as if he had respected persons in judgement.' Several scholars in recent times have explicated this tradition as being directed against the Patriarch (or his authorized agent), who would appoint the judges to their seats in the communities.[58] Nevertheless the expression 'appointed for the placement of judges' and the entire passage itself, which sets down the above-mentioned qualifications of the candidates, makes their conjecture far-fetched in my mind. What is dealt with here is, presumably, the making of local appointments (by the municipal administrations, which assigned the selection of city judges to one of its members), the appointments being determined solely by personal and social criteria, without knowledge of the Torah, i.e. the teachings of the Sages, being a prerequisite.[59]

The aforementioned traditions censure these judges for their lack of attachment to, and preparation for 'lawsuits conducted according to the Halakha'. Nevertheless many Baraitot make the grave accusation of moral corruption against the 'Judges of Israel' and testify against them that they pervert justice, favour persons and take bribes — and hold them responsible for the troubles that beset Israel

57 Lieberman (*Sinai* IV, p. 233) wishes to regard *qerova* as 'precentor', for the holder of this office is sometimes associated with a '*poetan*' in the Haggada, that is to say, he received his appointment in recognition of his public service and fitness. First of all, however, the recension *qerovi* should be retained, and moreover we find no *qerova* among the Tannaim (even though R. Eliezer b. R. Simeon is accorded this title in Midrashim). Nor do we learn of any permanently serving precentor until Amoraic times (the Haggada concerning R. Eliezer b. R. Simeon being unreliable in its present form). See §144 — ' "You (the judge) shall not pervert judgement" — You shall not say: Such a man is pleasant; such a man is *qerovi* [my relative].' Consequently *qerovi* is to be taken in its plain sense.

58 Guttmann, *MGWJ*, 1936, p. 353; Dinaburg, *ibid.*, et al. So Rambam in his Code and in the *Sefer Hamiṣvot* (See Finkelstein, *op. cit.*, p. 28, n. 15).

59 Cf. Büchler, *Manhige Ṣippori*, p. 30.

and for delaying the advent of the Messiah.[60] Even though similar condemnations are found in the tradition of the Sages, of the 'Elders' who do not practice what they preach, take bribes and show favouritism in lawsuits,[61] it is nevertheless clear that the above-mentioned statements refer only to the 'wicked judges' who were not learned Sages, the strong-armed, power-wielding and upper-class individuals in the settlements.[62] The truth of these testimonies is certainly not to be denied. It is only natural for the pedigreed class to give rise to social corruption, as the Sages averred (especially in the particular, political circumstances following the Bar Kokhba rebellion, in that and subsequent generations). Nevertheless we may safely ascribe a certain measure of polemical exaggeration to these statements, since they constitute a protest against the existence of powerful judges of the aristocracy of wealth and parentage, who did not, generally, belong to the realm of the learned in Torah.

How did these unqualified judges (*hedyoṭot* [lit. 'commoners']) try their lawsuits? After all, only very few laws are explicitly stated in the Torah, and these are insufficient to constitute a legal system of any kind.

Firstly, some of them must certainly have possessed some familiarity with the teachings of the Sages pertaining to monetary cases, which they must have tried to learn or else they must have relied for assistance on the legal opinions of the Sages and their disciples, whom

60 *T.B. Shabbat* 139a; *Sanhedrin* 98a; *Tosefta Soṭa* xiv, 3–4; *T.B. ibid.* 47b. Dinaburg's conjecture, *ibid.*, p. 99, that 'those who forced their goods upon the householders' were the Sages, who were judges, is far-fetched; although the expression, which is also found in *T.B. Shabbat* and was voiced by R. Judah in reference to the sons of Eli, is not altogether clear, it may reasonably be held to apply to power-wielding individuals who were not Sages. See Büchler, *Manhige Ṣippori*, p. 27.

61 *Ruth Rabba*, lxxxi, 2; *Deuteronomy Rabba* lxxxii, 9, etc. Most of these evidences date from the Amoraic period. About the same time (that of the first Amoraim), Origen complained at the Bishops, 'Elders' and ministers being ignorant boors, who love pecuniary gain, are corrupt, devour the flesh of orphans, sell the church for money, and rush after glory (Commentary on Matthew); Lommatzsh, *op. cit.*, Vol. IV, p. 202. See also, Harnack, *Die kirchengeschichtliche Ertrag* usw., Texte und Untersuchungen, 1916, I, p. 114.

62 See in detail, Büchler, *The Political and Social Leaders* etc. This scholar by far exaggerates the depravity of the city judges. He also denies the existence of judges who were Sages in Galilee prior to the Bar Kokhba rebellion, which is unsubstantiated. He also fails to mention the rivalry existing in the world of the Sages themselves in respect of the exercise of judicial functions by the urban upper classes, which we have pealt with.

they consulted. This much may be inferred from R. Eleazar b. R. Simeon's attack upon the 'disciples of the Sages who were relatives of the judges', obviously for their having assisted their relatives, affording them guidance in trying cases — and also from the Baraita which forbids 'the teaching of monetary laws to the ignorant'.[63] Yet certainly many of these 'ignorant judges' would have no truck with the Halakha and its exponents. It stands to reason, then, that they must first of all have rendered their decisions in conformity with precedents, with 'local custom', some sort of 'common law'. Secondly, their verdicts must in the main have been based on 'equity' and on their appraisal of the facts, but not according to any defined legal procedures.[64] Consequently, in all likelihood, a whole system of popular civil law became crystallized in the course of time, side by side with the official Halakha of the Sages.

The fact that these courts generally lacked all connection with the laws of the Sages emerges, it seems, from the sources. In *T.P. Sanhedrin* iii, 21a, it is stated of an Halakha in our Mishna: ' "Each party may reject the judge of the other..." (which the Palestinian Talmud takes to refer to the selection of the court to try the case by the litigants, see below) — Resh Laqish said: They said this of the courts in Syria, but not of cases tried by Torah law; R. Joḥanan said: Even in Torah lawsuits.' Resh Laqish sought to restrict the right of the parties to disqualify a judge or judicial tribunal proposed by the other party (see below) to courts of unqualified judges only, of which the 'Syrian courts' furnish an obvious example. Now these courts existed parallel to the 'lawsuits' conducted by the Sages according to the Halakha, and this parallel functioning can only be explained by the fact that the former did not base their judgements on the laws of the Sages.

It appears that the substance of this distinction is also evident in the tradition we cite here. In *T.P. Sanhedrin* i, 18a, we read: 'Two men came to R. Jose b. Ḥalafta. They said to him: (Try our case) on condition that you judge according to Torah law. He said to them: I don't know Torah law, but may He Who knows (human) thoughts exact retribution from those men. Will you accept what I

63 *T.B. Shabbat* 139a. Mar Zutra's observation, *ibid.*; 'These are the disciples of the Sages who teach communal laws to ignorant judges'; *Mekhilta de R. Simeon b. Joḥai*, p. 97.

64 Büchler, *Manhige Ṣippori*, p. 21. He regards it possible, however, that the 'heads of the settlements' exercising judicial functions were judges appointed by the Roman government.

shall say to you?' The commentators have found this seemingly obscure passage difficult to explain. It appears, however, that here the Sage had two alternatives, either to try the case as a 'qualified expert' (*Mumḥe*) or else as an unqualified judge (*hedyoṭ*) who would not be liable to suffer the penalties that misjudging a case in Torah law would entail.[65] The litigants had demanded that R. Jose try the case as an 'expert'. He, however, evaded the issue by claiming that he 'did not know' how to judge otherwise than by his personal evaluation, after the manner of the unqualified judge (since he had been approached by them to act as judge, he was acceptable to them as [having the authority of] three [judges] — *Tosefta, Sanhedrin* iv, 1). His evasion and sharp retort stemmed from his realization of their hidden intention, to reserve the right to themselves to appeal his verdict, and have it annulled as erroneous, if either of them was dissatisfied. Hence he would only consent to officiate as an unqualified judge, whose decision is irrevocable, even when he is mistaken.[66]

65 Büchler, *ibid.*, p. 21, holds that these litigants refused to be tried by Torah law, since they rejected the teachings of the Sages, somewhat after the manner of the Sadducees. This elucidation fits in with his general view (which is groundless) of the Galilean *Ammê Ha'areṣ* who were especially hard natured. Nevertheless, the tradition cited below does not lend any credence to this explanation of his.

66 The tradition concerning R. Jose's behaviour is appended to the opening of the discussion in this way: 'And it follows R. Jose.' That passage, however, is truncated and its content obscure. See Ginzberg's suggested reconstruction of the text (*Jubilee Volume in honour of Israel Levi* [Hebrew], pp. 407–409): '. . . "Before them" — to the best of them, which teaches that one does not teach monetary laws to the ignorant'. The *No'am Yerushalmi* suggests a similar reading: <' "Before them" — and not before the unqualified'>. Yet the passage still remains unclear. At all events no arguments can be adduced from R. Jose's tradition to refute our explanation. Certainly the very dread of passing judgement, and often the complexity of 'Torah' jurisprudence could well have impelled the Sage-judge to recoil from becoming involved in the gravity, and often the complexity of Torah jurisprudence.

The large measure of freedom accorded the unqualified judge, not bound by Torah law, to pronounce judgement in accordance with what is 'right and good', could also have induced the Sage to try cases not as a *Mumḥe*. It is not far-fetched, in my opinion, to assert that R. Joḥanan's dictum (*T.B. Bava Meṣi'a*, 30b): 'Jerusalem was only destroyed because they based their judgements on the law of the Torah' is relevant here. Certainly the Babylonian Talmud poses the question: 'Should they then have judged with unqualified judges?' ('by force' — Rashi). The Talmud amends the statement to 'They based their judgements on Torah law and did not go beyond the requirements of the law'. Yet the entire observation needs no emendation, and the Talmud fits in perfectly with the tradition *ab initio*. R. Joḥanan protested against

Their stipulation was based on the Halakha that the erroneous verdict of a qualified judge can be reversed, while that of an unqualified judge cannot,[67] the view of R. Joseph in the Talmud (*T.B. Sanhedrin* 33a): 'In the case of a *Mumḥe* we reverse (the verdict); in the case of a non-*Mumḥe* we do not.'[68]

The juridical authority of the ordained Sages. A relatively large

them — both litigants and judges — needing to depend on the strict particulars of the Torah of the Sages, and refusing to conduct their trials within the freer judicial framework that approximated more closely to the 'good' of the unqualified judges.

67 Our explanation agrees partially with the view of R. Jacob, the author of the *Ṭurim* (*Ṭur, Ḥoshen Mishpat*, Hilkhot Dayyanim, xii, 6). The latter, however, holds the view that R. Jose wanted them to submit to arbitration. It stands to reason, however, that the enforcement depended upon the consent of the parties, as the wording shows: 'Go out and settle' (*Tosefta, Sanhedrin* i, 6; *T.B. ibid.*, 6b; *T.P. ibid.*, i, 6b. Cf. *Mekhilta, Massekhta da'Amalek*, Jethro ii, Horowitz p. 190; ' "And his friend" — this is the law which has a compromise (*peshara*), that the two of them become tempered [*nifsharin*] to each other like friends'). Now R. Jose rebukes them: 'Will you accept upon yourselves what I say?' even where the verdict would not be to their advantage. If so, then why did he curse them? Because they did not come before him for arbitration, but for him to judge them, did they deserve to be cursed?

68 The reversal of a verdict in monetary cases, which is mentioned in the teachings of the Tannaim, is also referred to by Josephus in regard to the seven judges of the city (*Ant.* iv, 7, 14): ἢ ἄλλην τινα αἰτίαν προφέροι καθ' ἣν οὐ καλῶς ἐλέγχει αὐτοὺς ἀποφηναμένους ('Let judges have power to pronounce what sentence they think fit, always provided that no one denounces them for having receivedb a ribe or of not having pronounced aright.') Contrastingly, he testifies of the Essenes (*Wars* ii, 8, 9) that they never reverse any court verdict. Possibly the obscure tradition appearing further on in the Palestinian Talmud has some bearing here: 'We were taught there: If one had judged a case and pronounced the guilty guiltless and the guiltless guilty... What he has done is irrevocable... and he must pay from his pocket... R. Ba in the name of R. Abbahu: When they said to him: You are as acceptable to us as three [judges] on condition that you judge us in accordance with Torah law, and he erred and delivered his verdict in accordance with his own appraisal, he must pay from his pocket because he acted presumptuously in trying the case on his own assessment, for we have been taught: Do not judge alone, for no one may judge alone, except the One.' I regard 'Torah law' here as having the same connotation as in the case of R. Jose. R. Abbahu's remark purports to protest against the judge who consents to conduct a trial on his own properly and in accordance with the Torah of the Sages and does not humble himself to judge like the 'unqualified' (once they had accepted him as equivalent to three judges). For R. Abbahu always warned against judging on one's own, even a *Mumḥe* (although it is stated of him further that he himself had conducted a lawsuit singly, once the parties to

amount of source material pertaining to this field is available. Moreover, we have in our possession definitions of sorts for ordination, texts of certificates of appointment, as well as evidence of the development of ordination through its various stages. Contemporary scholars, too, have produced research studies on the subject.[69] Nevertheless, we still possess no comprehensive presentation of the history of the *Semikha* and the structure of the courts headed by *Mumḥim.* We also lack sufficient documentation in the sources to compile them.

Ordination possesses one basic significance: the co-option of the Sage to the Sanhedrin (and the Great Bet Midrash).[70] The expression *Yashav Biyeshiva* (took his seat in the Academy) used synonymously for *Ḥakham*, Sage or Rabbi (or 'was given his seat in the Academy') proves as much.[71] The same connotation applies to the term *Yashav*

the trial 'had accepted him over them', as the Baraita transcribed there in his name has it, *ibid.* Do we have conflicting traditions before us?).

In the parallel in the Babylonian Talmud, *Sanhedrin* 6a, however, we find: '...since they said to him: Judge us according to the Torah', the significance of the stipulation being that he should not err. Yet it is easy to discern that the content represents a change from the main substance of the original Palestinian tradition.

Another version of this discussion is found in the *Sefer Hama'asim Shel Bĕnê Ereṣ Israel* (*Tarbiz* I, 3, p. 10): 'What is it that we have been taught? Having judged the case... what he has done is irrevocable and he must pay from his pocket? You say that he judged in accordance with his own appraisal and they had accepted this, but in such matters as he traduces the Torah...' — the language is obscure.

69 See, most recently, Albeck, *Zion* (1943), pp. 85–93.

70 A certain scholar has, however, recently written that the 'appointment of Elders' is not to be regarded as entailing membership in the Sanhedrin (A. Weiss, *Proceedings of the American Academy for Jewish Research*, 1944, p. 273). Yet, except for the sole passage that he deals with, and which is not decisive for our discussion, as he admits, such membership is certainly included in the signification of ordination.

71 *Tosefta, Demai*, ii, 8, and the parallels in the Talmudim: *T.B. Nedarim* 62a; *Yoma* 78a, etc. Even the expression: 'On the day that they appointed R. Eleazar to the Academy' (*M. Zevaḥim* i, 3; *Yadayim* iii, 5) does not essentially convey anything else than ordination. Although this testimony of our Mishna apparently contradicts that referring to the appointment of R. Eleazar B. Azaria 'on that very day' as Patriarch, our explanation still stands, although here is not the place to deal with the topic. Similarly, too, the expression 'And they appointed him to the Academy' in reference to Menaḥem b. Sugnai in *Tosefta Eduyot* iii, 2, also signifies ordination. (His ordination was conferred on the occasion of his evidence on a question of Halakha, and is similar to R. Joḥanan's conferring ordination on R. Jose b. Ḥanina, *T.B. Sanhedrin* 30b).

berosh (or *Hushav berosh*), which never meant anything else than ordination (the last expression stems from the practice of the 'sages' to sit on higher seats than their 'disciples').[72] The actual conferring of membership in the Great Bet Din entailed, *ipso facto*, the authorization to try lawsuits, as well as other 'rights and privileges' conferred on the Sage. Insofar as the law is concerned, two elements are involved here: (a) the certification of professional competence (in the language of the Babylonian Talmud, 'learned and able to reason logically');[73] (b) the granting of authority 'to give rulings' (taking authority — *neṭilat reshut*).

These sources, however, also make mention of appointment not involving 'taking one's seat in the Academy' but as being the direct granting of authority to perform certain specific public functions alone. This aspect of ordination as appointment to public office is especially evident from what we find to have existed from Rabbi's days and onwards, the separation of functions previously included in ordination in general, and the granting of certification for single specific duties.[74] (The same would apply to appointments granted for limited periods of time, which confront us first in the third century.)[75] This last manifestation is a wide deviation from the earlier frame of reference of *Semikha*, which was essentially: the concentration of the communal authority of the Sages within the Sanhedrin. Such a development, however, proves how great was the real worth of ordination in actual practice; it constituted direct certification for public office in the settled areas of the country. And this fact of itself is tied up with the growth of the element of 'rulership' in ordination,

72 The episode involving R. Eleazar Ḥisma and R. Joḥanan b. Gudgada (in the Babylonian tradition, *Horayot* 10a; the parallel, *Sifre Deuteronomy* xvi has 'R. Joḥanan b. Nuri') whom 'R. Gamaliel appointed at the head' (the Talmudic version) does not signify that they were appointed 'supervisors in the House of Study' (as Bacher holds, *Aggada der Tannaiten*, I, p. 360, n. 1; *Studien* usw., pp. 13–30; Finkelstein in his notes to *Sifre*, p. 26) but that they received ordination by the Sages instead (like the wording of the *Sifre*: 'And R. Gamaliel appointed them to the Academy'). That they thereby obtained their livelihood (according to the Babylonian tradition, but not mentioned in the *Sifre*) was part of the general practice of supporting ordained Sages (especially); see below.

73 That the deciding factor in the performance of judicial functions is the qualification of knowledge emerges from Ben Sira's remarks, xxxviii, 33–34; xxxix, 1 ('On the seat of the judges they shall not sit', etc., and the same occurs in the Greek version).

74 See especially *T.P. Ḥagiga* i, 76c–d, and its parallel in *Nedarim* x, 42b.

75 *T.P. ibid.*; *T.B. Sanhedrin* 5b.

which corresponded to the increase in the power and quality of the *ordaining authority.*

From here we are led to the investigation of the nature of the ordaining authority. Apparently this is clearly established by that famous tradition (end of the third century) in *T.P. Sanhedrin* (i, 19a), which scholars have used as the basis for their concurring conception of the metamorphosis in ordination during the course of generations. Here is the text: 'Said R. Ba:[76] At first each would ordain his own disciples — such as R. Joḥanan b. Zakkai who ordained R. Eliezer; R. Eliezer, R. Joshua; R. Joshua, R. Akiba; R. Akiba, R. Meir and R. Simeon... They reverted and accorded honour to this House (the Patriarchal family). They declared ordination conferred by a Bet Din[77] without the ratification of the Patriarch to be void; while ordination by the Patriarch without the approval of the Bet Din to be valid. They reverted and instituted that no Bet Din should ordain without the approval of the Bet Din.'

Of the three stages in the history of ordination as viewed by this tradition, we shall briefly survey the middle one, the concentration of ordination in the hands of the Patriarch, first. As is known, scholars differ on when this state of affairs first came into being. Some assign the event to the days of Rabban Simeon b. Gamaliel, others to the time of Rabbi.

As I see it, the first view has no ground to stand on. First, we find Rabbi granting ordination in many instances, while nowhere is there any mention of the Sanhedrin of his time doing likewise. As for Rabban Simeon b. Gamaliel, we never find him granting ordination at all, even though in his days, *Mumḥim* were appointed by the Bet Din.[78] Secondly, although Rabbi controlled the Sages (as well as the nation as a whole) with a firm hand, nevertheless it is reasonable to assume that Rabban Simeon b. Gamaliel needed the Sages and was even subordinate to them, even though he was successful in the course of time in providing himself with a position of supremacy in the Sanhedrin. This fact, which is variously manifested, is not to be accounted for in terms of the personality of the Patriarch

76 In R. Judah of Barcelona's *Sefer Hashetarot* (ed. Halberstadt), p. 133, the reading is 'R. Abba b. Bîna'.

77 As is known, Maimonides (Laws of Sanhedrin iv, 5) has: *Av Bet Din.* This is the reading of the *Midrash Hagadol*, MS, *Numbers* Pineḥas. Guttmann (*Mafteaḥ* I, p. 89) accepts Maimonides' version. There are no grounds for doing so, however (our reading is also accepted by Rishonim).

78 *M. Sanhedrin* iii, 1; *Tosefta ibid.*, v, 1; *T.B. ibid.*, 23a.

only. In those days the Patriarchate became weakened *vis à vis* the nation and even the realm of the Sages.[79] Finally, the opinion is current among scholars that Rabban Simeon b. Gamaliel secured recognition for his Patriarchate from the Roman government, and furthermore that it was he who was the true founder of the Patriarchate, wielding unlimited and recognized power.[80] This view, it appears, is totally unsupported by the sources. We never find R. Simeon b. Gamaliel being accepted by the government or dependent upon the ruling power (as in the case of his successor, Rabbi, and his predecessor, R. Gamaliel). This is presumably more than a coincidence. Its cause lies in the political position of Eretz-Israel, which suffered discrimination in the days of the Antonines. At that time the government could *tolerate* the existence of the Patriarchate but could not recognize it officially.

We revert to the first period. It can be inferred that until the time of Rabbi, ordination was entrusted neither to the Patriarchate nor to the Sanhedrin, but was conferred by individual Sages, who ordained their disciples as Rabbis but not as members and delegates of the Great Bet Din. For at that time no direct relationship obtained between ordination and the central authority. Essentially ordination signified testimony to the professional competence of the candidate. This conception is to be found, as is known, in the Babylonian Talmud which regards the *Mumḥe Larabbim* (qualified to try cases as a sole judge) as one who had acquired expertise in Torah knowledge without having 'obtained authority' (*T.B. Sanhedrin* 5a).

Yet many finer points compel us to cast considerable doubt on the veracity of this evidence. Certainly, the tradition is apparently reinforced by what is related of R. Akiba in the Talmud — that he ordained his own disciples[81] — and the same applies to R. Judah b. Bava who also conferred ordination.[82] The episode involving R. Judah b. Bava, however, occurred at the time when neither Patriarchate nor Sanhedrin existed, 'in the generation of forcible conversion' (immediately subsequent to the Bar Kokhba rebellion). It is not to be wondered at, then, that this Sage arose and rescued Jewish jurisprudence from extinction. Furthermore, the very substance of this tradition concerning R. Judah b. Bava's ordination of Sages is sub-

79 I intend to deal with this point in the future, in my above-mentioned article, *Qavvim*, etc.

80 Dinaburg, *ibid.*, p. 88; Zucker, *op. cit.*, pp. 151–153.

81 *T.P. Sanhedrin* i, 19a; *T.B. Sanhedrin* 14a.

82 *T.B. ibid.*

ject to doubt.[83] It is not even known when R. Akiba ordained his disciples. Possibly, he did so immediately after the defeat of Bar Kokhba. But this apart, R. Akiba was, after all, one of the most prominent members of the Sanhedrin, and ordination by him could well have been considered as ordination by the Sanhedrin itself, which had vested the authority in him to do so (either explicitly or tacitly). The general assumption that the Head of the Great Bet Din would

83 First of all, the Talmud itself has noted the contradiction between the traditions ascribing the ordination of R. Meir and R. Simeon to R. Akiba and to R. Judah b. Bava (the explanation advanced by the Talmud is merely an attempt at harmonization, and so unacceptable). All the evidence concerning the death of R. Judah b. Bava at the hands of Roman legions, however (at the time when he was engaged in conferring ordination), is doubtful. We have been taught in a Baraita quoted in the Babylonian Talmud (*Soṭa* 48b; *Sanhedrin* 11a; *Canticles Rabba* lxxxviii, 10): 'And they sought to say the same of R. Judah b. Bava, but the hour was too turbulent, since no funeral orations were delivered over those slain by the government.' (In MS Munich, *Soṭa*, 'since funeral orations are not delivered...' alone appears. In Sanhedrin, however, the text is the same as we have given it.) Hence the text in its original form does confirm that he was slain by the Romans. So, too, is his name listed in *Midrash Pss.* ix (Buber ed., 45a) and in *Lamentations Rabba*, in the comment on the verse: 'The Lord has swallowed up unsparingly...', among those suffering martyrdom at the hands of the Romans. Yet we are disposed, first, to assume that two earlier traditions have been combined here; the one having, 'the time hour was turbulent' and the other explaining that 'no funeral orations were delivered'. 'The hour was turbulent' conveys that prevailing abnormal political conditions prevented the Sages in general from performing certain specific acts, but does not denote any Halakhic obstacle directly affecting the person in question, such as 'No funeral orations are delivered over those martyred by the Roman government', which referred to his case specifically. We may therefore infer that the first reason accounts for the other. In the parallel in *Tosefta Soṭa*, xiii, 5 and in *T.P. ibid.* ix, 24b, we only have the reading: 'But the hour was turbulent.' Is it then far-fetched to assume that tradition did not know of R. Judah b. Bava meeting his death in the manner reported in the Babylonian Talmud? This assumption is supported by the tradition in the Palestinian Talmud, *ibid.* a, and *Tosefta Bava Qamma* viii, 13, which explicitly testifies that he died a natural death in his home because he violated the prohibition against raising a sheep in his house. Certainly it is possible to argue that this last tradition is derived from the rule of the Babylonian Talmud (*Temura* 15b; *Bava Qamma* 80a) that wherever it is reported that 'It happened that a certain pious man...' the reference is to R. Judah b. Bava or R. Judah b. Il'ai, and that its first version is the same as in *T.B. Temura*, *ibid.*, and *Bava Qamma* 80a: 'It happened that a certain pious man...' At all events there were Sages who did not ascribe R. Judah b. Bava's death to the Romans, and even more so is the tradition of his having conferred ordination on that occasion questionable.

confer ordination on behalf of the Sanhedrin, and not personally as the teacher of the ordained, should rightfully be accepted as applying to the third period, as we shall see later on.

At all events, we find Rabban Gamaliel conferring ordination in the Jabneh period (and the indication is that it was he who made the decisions)[84] and also R. Akiba calling R. Ṭarfon 'qualified for the Bet Din', which would signify that he had certainly been ordained in the name of the Great Bet Din. The same expression, however, is reiterated by R. Meir and his colleagues,[85] which indicates that even in the generation of Usha, the main object of ordination was for membership in the Sanhedrin.

Furthermore the very tradition itself relating to R. Abba also reinforces our doubts. What this tradition conveys principally is the evolution of the relationship between the Patriarchate and Sanhedrin in respect of ordination. In the second period, the Patriarchate attained exclusive authority (this is substantiated by the facts), while in the third, a compromise of some sort was effected, a balance between the two contending elements for supreme control. It is reasonable to assume then, that even the first period represents a particular stage in this process; that is to say, at first ordination was completely entrusted to the Sages in the form of the Sanhedrin. During the next epoch, it rested exclusively with the Patriarchate, while finally the two authorities combined. This pattern is reasonable (although the main substance of the evidence fits the situation subsequent to the Bar Kokhba rebellion and continuing till the time of Rabbi, rather than the time of Rabban Gamaliel of Jabneh). This cannot be said of the tradition in its original form, since at first glance it would be incapable of explaining how the right of ordination, which originally had no connection at all with the central authority, should later become the exclusive province of the Patriarchate, and why, after it had reverted to the Sages, it did not accrue to them in their individual capacities but as the Bet Din.

Hence the tradition under discussion is highly suspect in respect of the first period. Nevertheless, its wording undoubtedly reflects certain concrete facts. First of all, it may reasonably be assumed that in the period immediately following Bar Kokhba's rebellion (and this lasted for a long time) and until the Patriarchate became reestablished

84 This is the incident of the appointment of R. Eleazar Ḥisma and R. Joḥanan b. Nuri. See above, n. 72.

85 *M. Sanhedrin*, iii, 1; *Tosefta* v, 1; *T.B. ibid.* 23a.

and the standing of the Sanhedrin, too, had become stabilized once more, it was possible for individual ordination to become current practice, and then not to disappear entirely even after the positions of the Great Bet Din and Patriarchate had become normalized. Yet even the discriminating investigation of the situation and opinions prevailing in the time of R. Abba can provide us with an explanation of the form the tradition has taken, as we shall see presently.

The evidence furnished by that tradition of the third period, that ordination was entrusted in general to two authorities, the Patriarchate and the Sanhedrin, is substantiated by the sources in our possession. Most of the ordinations that are mentioned were granted by the Patriarch.[86] On several occasions, however, it was the Sages, as we learn, who did the conferring.[87] Yet the Patriarch undoubtedly

86 *T.P. Ḥagiga* i, 76d; *Nedarim* x, 42b; *T.P. Terumot* xi, 48b, and the parallel, *Shabbat* ii, 4d; *Ketubbot*, i, 25a and the parallel, *Ruth Rabba*, vii 8: 'R. Pineḥas said: . . ."From this we learn that this House appoints Elders at their banquet halls".' And in *Sifre Zuṭa* ed. Horowitz, p. 271: 'It teaches that every Elder to whom the head of the generation dealt honour. . .' (in speaking of the ordination of Sages).

87 *Soṭa* 40a: 'The Rabbis decided to appoint him (*sic*, MS Munich), R. Abbahu, at the head.' In *T.P. Eruvin* viii, 28b, in the name of R. Ḥiyya (b. Abba): 'When we ordain Sages, we shall appoint you with them' (and it makes no difference to our discussion whether the remark was made 'in jest' or 'seriously').

It is in place here to deal with the passage in *T.B. Yoma* 88a–b which poses the question to us: 'Rabba b.b. Ḥana said: They asked R. Eleazar: Must an Elder who is a member of the Academy obtain permission to declare a firstborn animal permitted, or must he not?. . . R. Isaac b. Ḥaqola (the correct reading) rose to his feet and said: I saw R. Jose b. Zimra, who was both an Elder and a member of the Academy, and was superior to the grandfather of this one, yet obtained permission to declare a firstborn permissible. . .' This tradition confirms that the Patriarchs possessed the exclusive right to grant permission to rule on firstborn animals (a matter to which Patriarchs paid the most meticulous attention in granting ordination, *T.B. Sanhedrin* 5a and *T.P. Ḥagiga* i, 76c, and the parallel in *Nedarim*). This would seem at first sight to remove the right of ordination entirely from the Sages' province, for it stands to reason that the status of the 'Elder who was appointed to the Academy' was not at all dependent upon any 'securing of permission' from the Patriarch (as was the right to declare a firstborn permissible). The conclusion follows explicitly from the dictum of R. Idi b. Avin, *ibid.*: 'This matter was left for the House of the Patriarch in which to distinguish itself', which implies that all other areas of authority did not require the Patriarch's assent. From here it follows that the consent which, according to the tradition of R. Abba, had to be given by the Patriarchs for appointment to the Bet Din was not accepted by all (or not always).

held the upper hand.[88] This is most convincingly established by the tradition in *T.P. Horayot* iii, 48c:[89] 'They sought to appoint Elders. From where do they make the appointments? From Tiberias — from the South? R. Simeon said: "Judah shall go up." R. Mana said to him: This (Scriptural verse) speaks of war, but for ordination (it is) "those who see the face of the king" who sit first in the kingdom — this teaches that ordination is vested in the Patriarch' (who had his seat in Galilee).[90]

Yet many facts indicate, apparently, that even in the last period ordination was still at times held to lie within the province of the individual Sage. First, we read in many instances in the Babylonian

However, R. Abba himself denies the entire tradition transmitted by R. Isaac b. Ḥaqola (further in the same section). It is also necessary to examine the passage in order to determine the date when this took place. For it is known that R. Jose b. Zimra's teacher married off his son to the former's daughter (*Ketubbot* 62b). Hence it follows that the event in question occurred during the time of Rabbi and this implies that the Sages were not dependent upon him for their ordination. The fact, however, that there is much evidence testifying to the right of ordination being concentrated in the hands of the Patriarch, taken together with what we know of R. Isaac b. Ḥaqola — that he was a disciple of R. Judah Nesi'a (the first) — supports the identification of 'his grandfather' as R. Judah Nesi'a II's paternal grandfather, and so indicates that the episode took place in the days of R. Judah Nesi'a I. (In that event, R. Jose b. Zimra must have been extremely old at the time, or else was it, possibly, his grandson who is mentioned here?)

88 The fact of the matter under discussion: The opposition of the Sages to the nomination of judges by the Patriarchs can testify to this. (There is no doubt, however, that our sources only bring the opinions of some of the group opposed to the Patriarchate, such as Resh Laqish, to light.) Nevertheless a view currently held by scholars (see most recently, Dinaburg, *op. cit.*, p. 97) seeks to ascribe the entire regulation restricting the Patriarch's power to the cases where they received remuneration for conferring ordination. This explanation is without any basis in the sources nor is it a reasonable assumption. The denial of the Patriarchs' exclusive right in granting ordination and its being made dependent on the Bet Din stems from the earlier protracted rivalry between the Patriarchate and the Sanhedrin for control, and was facilitated in the third century by the growing power of the Sages and by the distinction drawn in practice (not in principle) between headship of the Academy and the Patriarchate.

89 *Ruth Rabba*, iv.

90 Insofar as the rivalry between the Sages and the Patriarch in the appointment of judges is concerned, it would be worthwhile to take account of Diocletian's *Rescript*, the subject of Dinaburg's research-study. Now since that document requires somewhat detailed clarification, I shall deal with it in an appendix to this article.

Talmud of R. Joḥanan conferring ordination on his disciples,[91] and the Palestinian Talmud gives evidence of R. Joshua b. Levi doing likewise to his disciples.[92] To these testimonies we must add the evidence of the Babylonian Talmud (*Sanhedrin* 5a) concerning Rabba b. R. Huna, who 'received his authority from his father, and R. Huna had received his from Rab, and Rab from R. Ḥiyya, which shows that the Rabbi could ordain his disciples without any direct connection with the Bet Din or Patriarch.

Still insofar as R. Joḥanan and R. Joshua are concerned, these testimonies apparently directly contradict the essential evidence of R. Abba, that a Bet Din might only confer ordination with the consent of the Patriarch (certainly no individual Sages could do so), for his consent to these appointments is not mentioned. Now since R. Abba was a younger contemporary of these Sages (it is reasonable to assume him to be the first R. Abba), we must perforce admit that he could not be completely mistaken in recounting the deeds of his Rabbis. Hence we must explain R. Joḥanan to have made his appointments in his capacity as head of the Great Bet Din (in Tiberias), with its approval and that of the Patriarch as well. We must assume this because of the close relationship that obtained between R. Joḥanan and the Patriarchal dynasty. This consent need not have been given in each individual instance; the Patriarch could have issued a general authorization to him.[93]

91 It follows from *T.B. Sanhedrin*, 14a, apparently, that it was R. Joḥanan who was granting ordination. The wording, 'that he was not among them' (and similarly further on), and also 'that they ordained him', or 'they did not ordain him' — would tend to convey that ordination was performed by more than one person at a time (the Sages in general, the Bet Din). So, too, *ibid.* 30b. In the parallel, *T.P. Sanhedrin* iii, 21d, however, 'the elevation of R. Simeon b. Yakim to a higher level' is spoken of. This expression is not altogether clear. It may perhaps refer to ordination (Albeck, *op. cit.*, p. 87). The same applies to *ibid.* 5b (R. Joḥanan's observation to R. Shemen = R. Simeon b. Abba. In the parallel, *T.P. Ḥagiga* i, *Nedarim* x, the individual doing the conferring is not R. Joḥanan but R. Judah Nesi'a). Resh Laqish's appointment of a 'lecturer, judge' etc. in Basra with R. Joḥanan's assent (*T.P. Shevi'it* vi, 36d) should be added to what is said here. On the other hand, this conclusion can neither be deduced, nor drawn from R. Zeira's remark in *T.P. Megilla* iv, 75b: 'He appointed him Sage'.

92 *T.P. loc. cit.*

93 Meiri puts it so: (*Sanhedrin*, p. 73): 'The Exilarch or Patriarch has the right to authorize one of the Sages to grant permission to others on their own.' And this is what R. Joḥanan said to R. Shemen: 'Behold you have our authorization. . .' (the *makhtir* [one who crowns, confers] with whom Rabbi consulted).

The same applies to Rabbi Joshua b. Levi. His ordination of 'all his pupils' has some connection, apparently, with his position as head of the 'Great Academy' of Lod and with the standing of the Academy itself and the 'Sages of the South' in the third (and fourth) centuries. The significant role played by that city in the lives of the Jewish Eretz-Israel and in the world of the Sages (and Patriarchs) from the end of the Tannaitic period onwards is common knowledge.[94] So, too, was the rivalry between the Sages and their Academy in Lod on the one hand and the Sages of Galilee on the other — a rivalry which extended even into the domain of ordination — well known.[95] In fact the Great Academy seems, as it were, to have split (and with it, of course, the Sanhedrin) into two: Tiberias and Lod.[96] The 'subordination' of the South to the overall authority of the central administration was maintained essentially through the former's dependence on the Patriarchs.[97] Yet it was only right that the Patriarchs in turn should grant the same recognition and authority to the South as they had given to the Galileans. R. Joshua b. Levi's ordination of his students might likely be attributed to the strong stand taken by the Academy in Lod. Yet this authority, too, was derived principally from the (overall) Bet Din (established in Tiberias) and the consent of the Patriarch. This should be taken for granted since Rabbi Joshua b. Levi's family relationship with the Patriarchal House precludes us from regarding him as instigating any provocative action against the Patriarch in ordaining Sages.[98]

As for the Babylonian tradition, it first of all conflicts with the Halakha set down in the Palestinian Talmud (*Bikkurim* iii, 65d)

94 It similarly played an important role even in the period prior to the Bar Kokhba rebellion.

95 The history of the relations between the southerners and the Galileans in the second and third centuries is known in particular from the writings of scholars. It is not in place here to clarify this in detail.

96 The duplication and separation of the '*Sanhedra'ot*' took place in the days subsequent to the abolition of the Patriarchate by the well-known order of the last of the Theodosians, C. Th. 16, 8, 29. There *Judaeorum primates, qui in utriusque Palaestinae Synedriis nominantur* is spoken of, where the first Palestine (the 'South', with its seat in Caesarea) is referred to, as well as the second (with its seat in Beisan, Galilee).

97 Cf. the practice of the Patriarchs of the third and fourth centuries to contract marital unions with the heads of the Sages in Lod, for instance R. Joshua b. Levi (*T.B. Qiddushin* 33b) and Ben Pazzi's house (*T.P. Shabbat* xiv, 13c; *Horayot* iii, 48c; and see also *T.P. 'Avoda Zara* iii, 42c).

98 *Qiddushin ibid.*: 'It is not fitting that I should stand up before my son... but the honor of the Patriarch's House [requires it].'

that 'Elders' were appointed outside Eretz-Israel, even by Eretz-Israel authorities, only on condition that they return, yet R. Huna (as well as his son) lived out all his days in Babylon, and the same applies to R. Joshua b. Levi's Halakha quoted in the Babylonian Talmud (*Sanhedrin* 14a): 'There is no ordination outside of Eretz-Israel', even where the authority wishing to confer the ordination had himself been ordained by a Sage in Eretz-Israel (as the Talmud itself understands, *ibid.*). Yet this passage itself contradicts this Halakha for, according to that same tradition, Rav was ordained by R. Ḥiyya, and the continuation of that passage teaches that Rabbi ordained him directly (testimony that is in essence substantiated by the Palestinian Talmud, *Ḥagiga* i, 76c; *Nedarim* x, 42b).[99] Hence this doubtful evidence is unreliable.

It is nevertheless a reasonable conclusion that, as a whole, the records telling of Rabbis ordaining their disciples are trustworthy. First the practice allowed certain circles among the Sages to give expression to their disposition to preserve their individual freedom as against the tendency to centralization which had become increasingly prevalent in the entire world of the Sages in the form of authorization by the Sanhedrin and Patriarchate. Just as we find evidence in the remaining areas (Halakha and Halakhic decisions) of this rivalry between the aim to subordinate the Sages to the authority of the leadership and the demand for complete independence on the part of the Halakhists, so can the vestiges of these traditions furnish evidence of the striving on the part of some of the Sages to retain their individual independence in the area of jurisdiction. Secondly, in practice non-ordained Sages tried lawsuits and even held permanent appointments in this area in certain cities. Furthermore the Patriarch himself (and the Bet Din) was accustomed to send non-ordained judges to the smaller cities.[100] What those judges (permanent or oc-

99 Albeck (*op. cit.*, p. 90) seeks to resolve this last contradiction in a manner that, to me, seems far-fetched. (It is not in place here to delve into the subject in all its details.) The entire substance of the passage in *Sanhedrin* is a 'composite', its elements being drawn from divergent sources (Cf. Ṣori's attempt at an analysis, *op. cit.*, pp. 184 ff).

100 Levi, who was delegated by Rabbi to serve as lecturer and judge, etc. in Simonia (*T.P. Yevamot* ii, 13a, and the parallels in the Midrashim; the tradition in *T.B. Yevamot* 105a probably does not give adequate mention to the circumstances surrounding the event) was never ordained. The same would apparently apply to the 'Babylonian' sent by Resh Laqish and R. Joḥanan to Basra. It is to be assumed that discharging juridical functions without ordination entailed, in principle, non-participation in the Sanhedrin, and, in

easional) were in practice required to possess was sufficient knowledge to judge in accordance with the prescriptions of the Torah, which would be attested to by the Rabbi (and could be regarded as something similar to 'ordination'), but their authority in law cases was inferior to that of the ordained Sages.

Furthermore, the consolidation of the ordination procedure was dependent first of all on the organizing and strengthening of Jewish jurisprudence as a whole, and even more upon the growing supremacy and control of the central authority over the population of Eretz-Israel. These two prerequisites were not automatically equally guaranteed in all generations and localities. Sometimes the knowledge of law had become weakened even when the period was not one of forcible conversion; nor did the control of the central authority over the population increase in strength all at once, and probably also not in all localities simultaneously. Under these circumstances 'a free judiciary of Sages' based on their specialized knowledge could well find a place for itself, by freeing itself from the mastery and rulership of the supreme leadership. Especially from the time of Rabbi onwards, however, the general development moved in the direction of strengthening the power of the centre and particularly the Patriarchate, and the improvement of its position and influence in the settled areas. Concomitant with this development, ordination became increasingly crystallized as an authorization granted by those who wielded supreme control: the Patriarch and the Bet Din.

The principal powers delegated to the ordained were: (a) To offer theoretical public instruction in the House of Study and the community (the discourse);[101] (b) to issue practical Halakhic rulings to

practice, lesser independence and authority than was enjoyed by the ordained (although we are unable to prove this from actual events).

101 In *Sifre*, Pineḥas cxl (ed. Horowitz, p. 186) and *Sifre Deuteronomy* §cccv: 'Give Joshua a *Meturgeman* who will question, expound and deliver Halakhic rulings' etc. Since Tannaim had expounded that Moses' 'ordination' of Joshua was of the same nature as the ordination of the Sages, this passage furnishes us with evidence for our topic. (In his above-mentioned article, Albeck has stated his view that every appointment entailed being assigned to head a minor Academy. Hence he has cited this passage as evidence for his approach. Yet even if such an implication can be read into the text before us — for ordination in general did entail the heading of an Academy in addition, as was explained above — in this article as it is, the *Derasha Barabbim* is taken to include public discourses as well, and not to refer to the studying with groups only. As for interpreting 'sitting at the head' as 'heading a House of Study', see our article itself, above, for another approach.

individuals; and (c) to try lawsuits. In all of these instances, ordination generally signified nothing more than the granting of absolute, recognized authority, but in practice authority was not denied to the non-ordained to deal with these matters by withdrawing from them the preferential rights accorded to the ordained. Now when the first element ceased appearing in the ordination formulas in the Talmudic sources, the trying of lawsuits became instead the chief feature of ordination.

Even though the giving of practical Halakhic decisions was a less significant feature of ordination than the power to adjudicate, it is not to be excluded to the extent that scholars are accustomed to assert (especially in the time before Rabbi). It is known that the tradition of the Palestinian Talmud testifies of Rabbi that he was the first to institute 'that no student render Halakhic decisions'. What is referred to here is undoubtedly the obtaining of authority from the central administration (the Patriarch) in the form of ordination, and not as the Babylonian tradition has it: from the disciple's rabbi.[102] From here it would seem to follow that until the days of Rabbi, the giving of Halakhic decisions was not dependent upon ordination, as many of the most recent scholars presume. Yet, even though the sources show that 'disciples' were accustomed to issue such rulings in the Jabneh period,[103] certainly there is no proof from here of the lack of any official, preferred status for ordained Sages even in the area of Halakhic decisions. For non-ordained Sages were not in practice precluded from adjudicating law suits, although they were regarded as not completely competent to try such cases.

Yet several items of evidence prove that (complete) authority to decide questions of law was dependent upon ordination in the generation of Jabneh. So we learn in a Baraita: 'Distinguished disciples like Simeon b. Azzai are fit to decide matters of law.'[104] This teaches that legal decisions did not lie within the province of any and all disciples, but of Sages. Furthermore, R. Judah b. Bava testified fo himself: 'I am one of those capable of deciding points of law' etc.[105]

102 *T.P. Shevi'it* vi, 36c; *Gittin* i, 39c; *T.B. Sanhedrin* 5b.

103 *Tosefta Kil'ayim* i, 3–4.

104 *Tosefta Horayot* i, 1 and the parallels in the Talmudim. Even though the Halakha speaks here of dependence on the Great Bet Din in Jerusalem, nevertheless this no longer applied to the post-Destruction usage and reality.

105 *Tosefta Terumot* v, 10. In my opinion 'those fit to render decisions' denotes a special level, some kind of permanence among the Sages. The topic deserves a study of its own, which is not in place here.

Here, too, presumably complete authority to render such decisions was confined to the 'Sages', while in *practice* even the non-ordained who possessed sufficient scholarship to be able to render decisions were considered fit and permitted to do so. Our assertion may be deduced with some certitude from *M. Bekhorot* (iv, 4), where R. Akiba said to R. Ṭarfon, who had erroneously declared a firstborn permissible: 'You are absolved, since you are an expert (*Mumḥe*), and whoever is an expert for the Bet Din is absolved from reparation.'[106] It follows, then, that there is a distinction between the expert and non-expert (not-ordained) in rendering legal decisions, just as there is in law suits.[107] Perforce, then, deciding points of law also constituted an element of ordination, even before Rabbi's day. In practice, however, even the non-ordained would give rulings and at times the boundary between the decision of a 'disciple' and of a Sage was effaced, till Rabbi arose and categorically denied disciples the right to render decisions.[108] Nevertheless, the essential distinction of ordination became restricted to the area of jurisdiction, since it is there that full public authority becomes requisite in order to oblige and compel the litigants to comply with the verdict. This is not so in respect of giving legal decisions which generally remain optional and dependent upon the attitude of the individual.

Essentially, ordination did not signify the assignment of any concrete functions in practice, but merely the competence to perform them. Hence ordained Sages are found studiously avoiding judicial functions,[109] and recommending 'withdrawal from litigation'. Their motive was either the realization of the excessive liability entailed in

106 From Rabbi's generation onwards, however, we find that the granting of authority to rule firstborn animals permissible was the exclusive prerogative of the Patriarchs and they were extremely particular in granting it to Sages alone.

107 To what extent serious limitations were imposed in the field of rendering decisions during the days of R. Gamaliel may be seen from the incident involving R. Joshua's nephew, Ḥanania, who gave a ruling. R. Gamaliel objected and sought to punish him, until it became apparent that the author of the ruling had been R. Joshua, *T.B. Nidda* 24b.

108 That Rabbi's regulation was not maintained in its original form subsequent to his time is apparently indicated by R. Abba's statement, as well as R. Abbahu's in the name of R. Huna and Rav (*Soṭa* 22a), who speak of 'students who are qualified to rule and do not' and 'disciples who are not, and do'. (It stands to reason that being qualified to rule does not imply ordination, but represents a status similar to 'those who are fit to rule'.)

109 *Tanḥuma*, Mishpatim 2.

rendering legal judgement or else the desire, in general, to avoid becoming preoccupied with communal needs — which would distract them from Torah study.[110] Sages confined their world to the study and dissemination of Torah and regarded any connection with public affairs as lying outside their purview and duty.[111] Moreover, the 'judge' was permitted to excuse himself from judging a case even after the trial had begun, in such cases where he might possibly suffer physical hurt at the hands of a violent litigant, were the latter to lose the case.[112]

Yet, presumably, ordination was often tied up directly with the assignment of official duties to the person on whom it was conferred. This is proved, ostensibly, by the recurring formula found among Tannaim, 'appointed over the community', or 'the Bet Din appointed him over the community' (*Deuteronomy Rabba* i, 3: 'An Israelite who has been appointed Sage or judge of the community'),[113] which

110 R. Ishmael b. R. Jose in *M. Avot* iv, 7. See also *Avot de-R. Nathan*, version II, xxxiv; ed. Schechter xxxviii, 2. Even the remark of R. Simeon in *T.P. Sanhedrin* i, 18a: 'Blessed be the Allpresent that I do not know how to judge' must not be taken as pertaining to the earlier tradition, 'In the days of R. Simeon b. Joḥai monetary cases were taken away from Israel', and so implying that R. Simeon had studiously avoided becoming appointed by the Roman government to try cases according to their law, once the Jewish legal system had been proscribed, as recent scholars have averred. The remark signifies instead that the Tanna in question (who is renowned for demanding that the life of the moment, including the performance of *mitzvot* and good deeds, be set aside in favour of a complete communion with Torah learning, the 'eternal' life) praises himself as not being expert in (practical) laws, and hence is exempt from the obligation to become preoccupied with judicial functions for the benefit of the community. (His observation is in no way connected with the previous tradition, except insofar as the name is the same: R. Simeon b. Joḥai).

111 The sources are many, and Dinaburg has already adduced several in his above-mentioned study. The subject, however, requires systematic treatment on its own. Insofar as the exercise of judicial functions is concerned, however, attention deserves to be drawn further to *Tanḥuma* (Mishpatim) where the disciples of R. Assi comfort and praise him for his deeds, since he 'kept himself far removed from judging' 'and did not allow himself to be appointed over the public' and he replied: 'Perhaps I shall have to render account for having been fit to try Jewish lawsuits', etc. Cf. *Exodus Rabba* xxx.

112 *Tosefta Sanhedrin* i, 7 and the parallels in the Talmudim (the recension appearing in the body of the article being the correct one).

113 *Tosefta Ta'aniyot* i, 50, and the parallels in the Talmudim; *Tosefta Bava Qamma* vii, 13; *Sifre Deuteronomy* §306. These 'Parnassim' were not the heads of cities and communities but spiritual leaders (as opposed to the view of Dinaburg, *op. cit.*, p. 85 on Sages who occupied permanent, civil

signifies ordination. The same would apply to those testimonies in the sources which prove that appointments brought wealth and a livelihood in their train.[114] Certainly no fixed salary or remuneration is referred to. Instead, the remark is to be understood in terms of the communal practice of providing the Sage living and officiating in the community with greater or lesser material support. The statement in *Exodus Rabba* xxvi, 9 bears this out: 'R. Neḥemiah said: . . .As long as one is but an ordinary scholar (*ḥaver*), he has no concern with the community and is not punished on their account. Once he is appointed as their head and dons the cloak of leadership he shall not say: I live for my own benefit; I do not care about the community. Instead the whole burden of the community is on his shoulders. If he sees anyone acting violently against his neighbour or committing a transgression, and does not try to prevent him, he is held punishable.'[115]

It seems that the communal and local implications of ordination which had become current began spreading and crystallizing from the time of Rabbi onwards.[116]

Were the appointments dependent upon the ratification of the community? We apparently possess the answer to this question. In *Sifre Deuteronomy* § 13 (ed. Finkelstein, p. 23) we find: ' "And I shall make them heads over you" — you might think that if you appoint them they are appointed, and if not, not. Scripture teaches: "And I shall make them heads over you." If I appoint them they are appointed, and if not, not. . .' This homily on Moses' appointments certainly reflects the opinion of the expositors towards the appointment of 'Elders' in their time.[117] Yet, at all events, to the extent that

administrative posts). Cf. Ginzberg, *Perushim*, etc., Introduction, pp. lxiii–lxiv; *ibid.* I, pp. 403–406. (His view that, in the Palestinian sources, 'Parnas' signified 'a secular appointment' only is inaccurate.)

114 *Sifre Deuteronomy* §81; *T.B. Soṭa* 40a; *Horayot* 10a–b.

115 In the parallel, *Midrash Pss.*, ed., Buber, however, it is not clearly so.

116 Certainly in the Babylonian tradition already R. Eleazar Ḥisma and R. Joḥanan b. Gudgada had received emoluments for heading the Academy. In Sifre, however, the whole discussion between R. Joshua and R. Gamaliel concerning R. Joshua's poverty is missing. The same applies to R. Neḥemiah's above-mentioned statement in *Exodus Rabba* which the Tanna need not necessarily have made verbatim in that form.

117 In his *Legends of the Jews*, Vol. III, p. 72; Vol. VI, n. 164, Ginzberg writes that, in contradistinction to this tradition, it is to be inferred from Josephus, *Ant.* iii, 4, 1 (which speaks of the qualities of the judges Jethro advised Moses to appoint) that 'the people had to ratify the appointments made by Moses'. Where he deduced this from is not clear to me. Apparently he derived it from

ordination in practice entailed appointment to public office, there was some reason for it. Apparently, the sources portray divergent opinions, for we read so in the Palestinian Talmud (*Taʿaniyot* iv, 68a) of the testament of Rabbi to Rabban Gamaliel, his son: ' "And appoint R. Ḥanina b. Ḥamma its head." And why did he himself not make the appointment? Said R. Derusai: "Since the people of Sepphoris cried out against him (in Sepphoris)." And because of a (vain) protest, we do (as they wish)? Said R. Eliezer b. Jose: "Because he raised an argument against him (Rabbi) in public".' The first Amora lays down, then, that because of the opposition of the inhabitants of Sepphoris, appointment was withheld from R. Ḥanina, who should automatically have served as *Parnas* (leader) of the community in that city (as he did after Rabbi's death). Yet the anonymous tradition in the Palestinian Talmud questions this supposition and rejects it.[118]

The need for the populace to assent to the appointment of Sages in their own localities, however, is indirectly substantiated also by R. Isaac's dictum (*T.B. Berakhot* 55a): 'A leader is not appointed over a community without it being consulted.' Similarly, we read in the tradition preserved in *Midrash Hagadol* (Leviticus, ed. Rabinowitz, p. 168): ' "And gather all the congregation. . ." and furthermore all

the passage: οἳ δὲ δοκιμασθέντες ὑπὸ τοῦ πλήθους παντὸς εἶναι ἀγαθοὶ καὶ δίκαιοι κτλ ('known amongst the entire people as good and righteous'). This, however, has nothing to do with the selection of judges but with their reputation as fit and faithful men.

118 That ratification by the populace was a prerequisite may perhaps be derived from the tradition in *Sifre Zuṭa* (ed. Horowitz, p. 321): ' "And you shall place him before Eleazar the priest and before all the congregation" — that he should be [acknowledged] a *Mumḥe* by Eleazar, the priest, and all the congregation' (as is well known, everything pertaining to ordination was deduced from Joshua). An allusion to this may perhaps be found in the remark in *Sifre* Behaʿalotekha §92 (and similarly in *Sifre Deuteronomy* x): 'It teaches that one does not occupy a seat in the Academy beneath. . . till people talk favourably of him and say: "That particular man is fit and righteous and deserves to be a Sage".' (As for the preceding Midrash: ' "Whom you know to be the Elders of the people and officers over them" — you have to know if they are selected before Me,' it is reasonable to adopt the reading of R. Meir Ish Shalom, 'Before the people', as is found in the *Yalkut*. If so, we have a Halakhic tradition before us teaching that at least tacit consent on the part of the public is required.) As for the communal activities of the Patriarchs and Sanhedrin in general, the texts of the Baraita in the *Tosefta Sanhedrin* ii, 10: 'The year is not intercalated nor public action undertaken except on condition that they are acceptable to the majority of the public' should be contrasted with the divergent recension in the Talmudim.

communal office is only (conferred) in the presence of the entire congregation.'

What may be decisive here is the tradition of the Palestinian Talmud, *Yevamot* xii, 13a concerning Levi b. Sisi, whom Rabbi 'gave' to the inhabitants of Simonia to serve them as lecturer and judge, etc., for they dismissed him immediately on their own authority and did not at all require the consent of the Patriarch[119] (Levi, however, was not ordained).

It therefore appears that although, in principle, the right to appoint to office rested with the Patriarch (and the Sanhedrin), in practice the ordained Sages would not serve as judges in the cities without the consent of the inhabitants.[120]

119 Indeed, exactly as in the manner that the men of Terbanat had dismissed the scribe of their city, since he had been accustomed to read the Ten Commandments in conformity with the Halakha and prohibitions laid down by R. Ḥanina, and not with the view of the members of the community (*T.P. Megilla* iv, 75b).

According to Klein, however (*MGWJ*, 1934, pp. 170–171), Levi was at first only taken on trial in Simonia. The questions posed to him by the local inhabitants were for the purpose of testing him. The view, however, which maintains that the candidate for Sage-judge was tested by his 'discourse' during the Talmudic epoch is not substantiated by other sources and is not supported even by the tradition of the episode before us. Had they 'constructed a large platform and placed him on it' in order to test whether he was suitable to be a judge or not, Levi would not have been able to offer the excuse for having forgotten his learning at that time to Rabbi 'that his spirit had become proud', for then 'dread of the public' (stage fright) rather than pride would have been the cause.

120 Courts composed of Sages and *hedyoṭot* (commoners or non-ordained Sages) combined did in fact exist. This state of affairs was considered Halakhically valid on account of the requirement that even an ordained Sage abstain from being a sole judge, even according to those who considered him fit to do so in principle (see *T.P. Sanhedrin* i, 18a–b). Hence, R. Ḥiyya coopted 'one disciple' when he conducted a trial (*T.P. ibid.*, b). This is to be learnt from R. Ishmael b. R. Jose's remark in *M. Avot* (iv, 8): 'Do not be a sole judge for none may judge alone except One; do not say, "Accept my view", for they are entitled to, but not you.' This Mishna presents the case of a Sage sitting together with two unqualified judges trying a lawsuit, and warns of the rights of the other two judges in determining the verdict. Some of the Rishonim give a similar interpretation. It may be possible, perhaps, to follow Gulak (*Yesode Hamishpat Ha'ivri*, IV, p. 33) in deriving the competence of such a composite Bet Din to try monetary cases by comparison (*hekesh*) with the procedure in the annulment of vows, which, according to R. Judah (*T.B. Bekhorot* 37a) is dispensed by three [judges], only one of whom is required to be an ordained Sage. (This requires further

The arbitrators. All the information we possess concerning the institution of arbitration is contained in a single Halakha in Mishna and Baraita dating from the time of R. Meir and his colleagues. Furthermore, the text of the Mishna seems to prove that arbitration was the sole authorized procedure in lawsuits, for so we find in the Mishna: 'Monetary cases are to be tried by three. Each litigant chooses one...' This tradition, then, knows of no other method of conducting law suits except by arbitration. These facts led more recent scholars to propound the view that the institution of arbitration only became established in the generation following the Bar Kokhba rebellion because the Roman government had proscribed the trying of law suits by Jews. At that time, when the regular courts had been forcibly abolished, the Jews found a loophole, namely private, occasional jurisdiction.[121]

This view cannot, it seems, be sustained. First we read of R. Joḥanan already making statements (*T.P. Mo'ed Qatan* ii, 82a) which ostensibly attest to the existence of arbitrators even in his days.[122] Furthermore, R. Meir himself and the Sages of our Mishna and Baraitot speak of judges 'qualified for the Bet Din', that is to say they were aware of the existence of the courts of the Sanhedrin in their time. Certainly, we could posit that arbitration first came into existence at the time when the permanent courts were in abeyance but that its existence persisted even after the regular courts were reinstated.

Nevertheless it is far-fetched to make arbitration in Israel dependent on adverse circumstances alone. This institution existed among many ancient (and modern) peoples, side by side with the central and local,

study.) The following tradition, however, forces us, apparently, to assume that the Sages rebelled against such a state of affairs. For, in practice, this constituted a compromise between the jurisdiction of the Sages and that of the 'commoners', one that resulted from the struggle between the competing judiciaries. In *Tanḥuma* Shofetim, ed. Buber (p. 30), we read: 'Another explanation: "You shall not pervert judgement" — this is an admonition to the Sage not to let sit next to him someone unfit to judge. If he did seat such a one, it is tantamount to his having planted an *Ashera*...' Here then is a protest against Sage-judges who co-opted actual 'commoners', couched in the same language used by those opposing the Patriarchs for appointing ignoramuses as judges.

121 Gulak, *op. cit.*, IV, pp. 30–32. Cf. the miscellany, *Hamishpat Ha'ivri* (1936), p. 199 for the debate on this issue between the Sages of Jerusalem.

122 The very words of R. Jeremiah b. Abba in *T.B. Bava Meṣi'a* 20a; *Bava Batra* 168a.

established judiciaries, and there is no reason to deny its existence among Jews in normal times. Yet the explicit assertion of the Mishna cannot lightly be set aside, and it recognizes the existence of arbitrators alone, a state of affairs which cannot possibly be ascribed to the entire Talmudic epoch.[123] Nevertheless no deduction may be drawn from one Mishna. The Halakha clearly sets down 'each party chooses one' etc. as the exposition, so to say, of the Halakha, 'Monetary cases are to be tried by three', a statement transcribed from the first Mishna, as if in order to explicate it. 'How is this? Each (litigant) chooses one (judge)...' We sometimes, however, do find dicta in the Mishna directly attached to earlier Halakhic generalizations apparently as their complete elucidation, and opening with, 'How is this?' — whilst in fact this is only a method of tying in traditions which deal with one or more specific details related to the general Halakhot themselves. The Mishna attaches them to the earlier tradition because they contain something novel or some dispute.[124] This then is a device of literary editorship and not a really, but only an apparently, exhaustive exposition of the generalization. Here, too, in our Mishna, the same relationship obtains between the 'explication' and the basic Halakha. The general rule, 'Monetary cases are to be tried by three judges' is not exhaustively explained, but a tradition is appended to it which sets down the differing opinions of Tannaim concerning one of the forms assumed by a three-judge court, i.e. how this court is constituted. This tradition knew of no discussion or doubt on the part of the Sages pertaining to the permanent courts.

The juridical authority of the non-ordained, as contrasted with the ordained, Sages. It is found that the very Halakha in which the existence of courts of non-ordained is accepted as such discriminates between the authority of the non-ordained as compared with the

123 Indeed scholars are to be found who have the view that no permanent courts of the three judges ever existed in the Talmudic epoch, but only courts of arbitration instead (Ginzberg, *MGWJ*, 1912, pp. 303–304. See Frankel, *Der gerichtliche Beweis*, p. 89. Similarly, Fassel, *Das rabbinische Gerichtserfahren*, par. 235. Cf. M. Bloch, *Die Civilrechtprozessordnung*, p. 11, n. 13; Sidon, *Magazin*, 17, 207).

124 Such as *M. Gittin* v, 6: 'There was no *sicaricon* in Judea for those killed in the war; from (the termination of) the killing of war there has been *sicaricon*. How is this? If one bought from the *sicaricon*, and then bought it over again from the owner, his purchase is void' etc. Here there is no direct comprehensive explication of the law of *sicaricon* but the selection of an example of a specific problematic detail of that Halakha.

ordained Sages, and restricts the juridical functions of the former. And there are divergent views.

The classical tradition,[125] as is known, withdrew the adjudication of 'penalty cases' (where the amounts to be paid are punitive and do not coincide with the value of the loss sustained) from the jurisdiction of non-ordained judges, since these cases require the authority to enforce the judgements, and this was withdrawn from those without ordination by order of the Patriarch or Sanhedrin. Yet it also happened that the fields denied to the non-expert were extended to cover even 'robbery and assault suits', including damages (or certain classes thereof) and only the adjudication of money disputes arising from business relations (obligations between the parties) were left to the judicial authority of the non-ordained.[126] Furthermore, in principle, the current Halakhic tradition even removed the right from these courts to try cases of 'admissions and loans', and only allowed them to judge these cases in practice on the general (assumption) that these judges were 'acting as the agents' of the ordained judges (that is to say, theirs was only a delegated authority granted by the highest body in law, the Sages or the Sanhedrin or Patriarch).[127]

Did these Halakhot and their like constitute the real factors in the judicial functioning of the local administrations? Or were they stated as requirements only? It stands to reason that originally these courts did not restrict their judicial authority. Just as there were Sages who intended to deprive them of all authority in all fields, so, too, were there public figures in the cities, who completely divested themselves of any dependence whatsoever on the jurisdiction of the Sages and Sanhedrin. It was possible, however, in the course of time, for that very conflict caused by the existence of two parallel judiciaries in the settlements to have produced some proposal for the defining of the boundaries between them. Such an equilibrium could only have been conditional upon an upsurge of power among the Sages, and even more so upon the strengthening of the Patriarchate, and an increase in its influence in the social life-patterns of the settlements of Eretz-Israel.

125 *T.B. Sanhedrin* 14a, 13b, 8a, and all passages which deny the right to judge penalty cases outside Eretz-Israel (since the diaspora judges are *hedyoṭot*, unqualified).

126 *T.B. Sanhedrin* 2b; *Bava Qamma* 84a–b.

127 *Bava Qamma, ibid.*; *Giṭṭin* 88b (from their stance against the judges in Babylon, we learn of their attitude to the 'unqualified' in Eretz-Israel).

The Halakhic sources afford a clear insight into the rights of the litigants to choose judicial tribunals or the judges of which these were composed. A dispute among Amoraim is mentioned in the Babylonian Talmud (*Sanhedrin* 23a). It first interprets the statement in the Mishna, 'Each party chooses one', etc., to refer to the choice of court — as to whether the parties have the right to object to a court proposed by the other side only when it is composed of non-expert judges or even when it is composed of experts. The tradition does acknowledge the distinction in question between the judicatures (even though our Mishna is definitely dealing with the composition of a court of arbitrators, as the conclusion of the passage shows).[128] Yet even the Palestinian Talmud (*Sanhedrin* iii, 21a) records a difference of opinion among Amoraim on the subject. For so Resh Laqish expresses himself: 'They said this of the (Gentile) courts of Syria, but not of Torah lawsuits.' R. Joḥanan (is of the opinion): 'even in Torah lawsuits'. This dispute is identical with the first in the Babylonian Talmud: In Resh Laqish's view, once he is summoned, the defendant has no right to demand that he be tried by another court, except where the court consists solely of non-experts. In R. Joḥanan's view he may object even where ordained judges alone comprise the court.[129]

Tannaim had, however, differed on this point earlier. For so we are taught: 'Each party may reject the judge of the other — this is R. Meir's view. But the Sages say: When? — At the time that he adduces proof that they are relatives or unfit, but if they were recognized as experts (*Mumḥin*) by the Bet Din he may not disqualify

128 The Babylonian Talmud's explication of the first Halakha as referring to the selection of courts can only have resulted, it seems to me, from the proper reference of a tradition associated with our Mishna having become forgotten — and this was the second Halakha. (T.P. immediately proceeds to expound 'This party chooses one for itself' in its plain sense.)

129 That this is the significance of the divergent opinions of Resh Laqish and R. Joḥanan is also substantiated by the continuation of the discussion 'How? They said: Two men had a lawsuit in Antioch...' Here the Talmud adduces an example of the preference of one of the litigants for a court outside the city. (R. Joḥanan denied him this right, since he would force ['tear away'] his opponent to travel afar. See R. Joḥanan's remarks in *T.B. Sanhedrin* 30b on the tradition of R. Safra.) The preceding passage, 'So is the Mishna: This one may disqualify... but not his judge', which is obscure and has puzzled the commentators, may perhaps be based on the Halakha which speaks of the disqualification of the arbitrating judge. Yet even so this does not constitute any substantiation of the discussion that follows.

them'. The commentators explain our Mishna as tied to the preceding Halakha: 'Each party may choose one'. Hence, here too the Tannaim would be differing as to whether, in their opinion, each litigant may reject the arbitrator chosen by the other side. It seems that this explanation cannot be sustained. First, such a right would contradict the first Halakha: 'Each side may choose one.' Furthermore, we are taught in a parallel Baraita (*T.B. Sanhedrin* 23a): 'One may go on rejecting judges until he undertakes that the case be tried before a Bet Din publicly recognized as expert.' The selection of courts must then be referred to. The wording of our Mishna, too, 'at the time when he adduces proof that they are relatives, unfit, fit, *Mumḥin*', teaches, apparently, that judges are the subject of discussion, that is to say: a college of judges and not individual arbitrators proposed by the litigants.[130] Hence it stands to reason that R. Meir and the Sages also differ in regard to the right of the litigants to choose their judicial tribunals. But our Mishna does not explicitly draw any distinction between unqualified judges and Sages.

However, an examination of the parallel Baraitot (and the Mishna itself) leads us to discover this difference. What is surprising first of all is the wording of the Mishna: 'But if they were fit, or recognized by the Bet Din as qualified', for if one is unable to reject the unqualified (when they are neither related nor unfit), is it necessary to state that one may not reject the qualified? Now we read in a Tosefta (and also in the parallel in the Babylonian Talmud), *ibid.*: 'It is not in his power to disqualify the recognized, expert judge' (the 'fit' is not mentioned), which teaches that the Sages concede that he has the right to reject non-ordained judges. Secondly, we read in another Baraita in the Talmud: 'He may go on rejecting until he accepts upon himself a publicly recognized, qualified Bet Din, so the words

130 It is certainly possible to advance the forced explanation that the wording refers to repeated disqualifying, in the manner of the Baraita in the Babylonian Talmud: 'Indeed he may continue to disqualify. . .', which is not stated in the Mishna as such. The Talmud, apparently, gives this explanation, since it proceeds to raise the query: 'Has he then the power to disqualify judges?' Now if our Mishna is taken to be dealing with arbitrators nominated by the litigants then what is surprising? The same applies to the answer given by R. Joḥanan: 'This was taught of Syrian lawcourts', which signifies permanent courts (of unqualified judges) but not arbitrators. As to single judges, see above n. 131. The disqualification of a proposed court, however, could result from the rejection of one of its judges. The conflicting opinions of those Tannaim on the rejection of witnesses makes the interpretation of this Halakha as referring to arbitrators appear even more far-fetched.

of R. Meir.' According to this tradition, then, even R. Meir agrees that qualified judges may not be rejected. Perforce, then, there must have been conflicting traditions in the Academies of other Tannaim in respect of the dispute between R. Meir and the Sages. One of these traditions takes the dispute to refer to unqualified judges alone: R. Meir upholds the right to disqualify them, and the Sages deny it. According to the other, these Tannaim differed in respect of qualified judges, and R. Meir upholds the right to reject even them. The first being the main tradition ('when he adduces proof that they are relatives or unfit, but if they are fit...'), the Mishna nevertheless finally concludes by inserting the later tradition as an addition, 'or qualified'.[131] So it follows that the Sages adopted conflicting attitudes. Some denied the right of choice even where the courts consisted of unqualified judges, and others upheld it in this instance, while others extended this right even to courts of ordained judges. (In the days of the Amoraim, the Halakha was finally established that the litigants did possess this right. They [the Amoraim] differed, however, concerning the courts of the Sages. In this instance Resh Laqish denied, while R. Joḥanan upheld the right).[132]

131 As is known, the Halakha distinguishes between unqualified (*hedyoṭot*) and ordained, qualified (*Mumḥin*) judges, even in judging singly, although the Sages of Eretz-Israel (in part) were still protesting against judges conducting lawsuits singly at the end of the third century. Gulak (*op. cit.*, IV, p. 36), however, holds the view that the Halakha which recognizes the right of *Mumḥin* to judge singly first appeared only at the beginning of the era of the Amoraim. Yet R. Ishmael b. R. Jose's admonition in *M. Avot*, 'Do not judge alone' tells of a previously existing situation (or at least, an existing custom in practice). The same applies to the evidence of R. Simeon the flax merchant in the *Tosefta* (*Bava Qamma* viii, 14 and the parallels in the Talmudim) on 'my father's house which was destroyed because they judged monetary cases singly' (hence even prior to Bar Kokhba, and it seems that there is mention of it dating back to Temple times). So we must assume that the institution of single judges trying cases may have possibly stemmed from an ancient tradition.

132 I refrain from making any comparisons between the structures and mutual relations of the judicial authorities in Eretz-Israel prior and subsequent to the Talmudic epoch, and also of the diaspora judicial authorities (especially Babylon) in the same era, since these demand a study on their own. We still lack a complete and trustworthy presentation of the subject. It would similarly have been fitting to make comparisons with the judiciaries of other peoples (especially those of the Ptolemies, since the papyri certainly furnish us with considerable source material) but this task must be undertaken on its own.

It is in place now, perhaps, to sum up some of the topics we have dealt with so far, to a lesser or greater extent.

We have seen that, already during the generation of Jabneh there was a dispute among the Sages concerning the jurisdiction of unqualified (judges of the wealthy classes and parentage). Those who upheld this right, who esteemed the abilities of these classes because of their economic standing in conducting public affairs, regarded them as fit to judge, while others denied their competence on the grounds of their lack of Torah knowledge. Even though our sources complain against 'corrupt judges' of that generation,[133] the main opposition of the Sages to these 'Israelitish judges' was not on account of their socio-moral turpitude but because of their ignorance. The Tannaitic traditions, which should be ascribed to the latter half of the second century, on the other hand, frequently denounce judges for unethical conduct, for perverting justice, and for corrupting the entire generation.

These complaints reveal a social situation which arose especially and reached its peak of intensity after the Bar Kokhba rebellion. The collapse of the central authority, the enfeebled Patriarchate and Sanhedrin, which failed to regain their previous strength (of Jabneh days) until Rabbi's days, greatly reduced the juridical powers of the Sages (their influence on the general life of the population also declined considerably in that period). On the other hand, the political conditions that arose after the war paved the way for the ascendance and seizure of power by certain elements among the wealthy and pedigreed in the country. Certainly through them and among them, those circles ('collaborators') arose on whom the government could rely for its own purposes and so give them the authority over the population in the communities. These tax-gatherers and (great) treasurers, which the sources of the generation following Bar Kokhba mention a great deal, certainly stemmed from these circles, and they gave their support to the ruling power in the cities of the land. Even the prolonged economic impoverishment of the country from the time of the Antonines, which helped to weaken the traditional social structure of the settlements and their institutions as well, was able to serve as a factor in strengthening the above-mentioned circles and increasing their power in the communities.[134]

133 In *Esther Rabba*, Petiḥta 9 and *Midrash Abba Gorion* (*initio*), it is ascribed to Rabban Gamaliel.

134 I shall revert to this in my Article, *Qavvim* [never written — ed.].

The Tannaim, who censured these judges-leaders for their moral depravity, certainly uncovered much of the grave state of affairs of their times. By striking out against the judicial functioning of these uppermost classes, the Sages were also attacking them for their conduct of public life in general, which at all events brought evil and harm upon the community. Yet it stands to reason that these accusations, as true as they may have been, nevertheless are tied up with the rivalry between the Sages and the power-wielding classes in Eretz-Israel for influence on public life, a situation first drawn to our attention by the late Dr. Büchler.[135] We may therefore justifiably assert that the generalizations indulged in by the Tannaim do not completely reflect the true state of affairs. Certainly the rich also had their noble individuals who were solicitous of the welfare of the community and who helped shore up the beaches after the Rebellion. The same applies to the Sages: It cannot be asserted that all of them categorically denied the right of these circles to assume communal leadership and judicial functions, even though that generation evinced a negative attitude towards them on the whole.

This socio-ethical consideration ought not to blind us to the antagonism among the ranks of the Sages to the 'unqualified' officiating as judges, since the Sages aimed at a uniform jurisprudence based exclusively on the law of the Torah. There were some, however, who approved the existence of such judicatures and accorded them recognition to a greater or lesser extent. This fact enabled the emergence of a set of accepted rulings, for the purpose of regulating relationships between the courts of the non-expert judges and of the qualified, and which inclined towards giving preferential treatment to the latter, and establishing some balance of power between the various judicatures in the country.

In the judicial world of the Sages, a rivalry obtained between the two combined and competing central elements, the Patriarchate and the Sanhedrin, in respect of the authority in making appointments. This rivalry, which was merely one manifestation of the constant struggle of these two elements for control of the supreme leadership, was decided once and for all at the end of the second and the beginning of the third century (the time of Rabbi) in favour of the Patriarchate. Yet that outcome did not, most probably, eliminate the power of the Sages completely, nor still the desire of the Sages once again

135 See also Dinaburg in his above-mentioned study, p. 89, although I am unable to concur with all his remarks.

to lay claim to a position of strength *vis-à-vis* the Patriarchate. Consequently the practice finally came into being which aimed at creating a balance between the Sanhedrin and the Patriarchate, by awarding the right of ordination to either party with the consent of the other.

To revert to the first topic. The appointment of non-qualified judges on the part of the Patriarchs first of all meant that the problem of recognition for judiciaries in the settlements and of a civil legal system for 'commoners' had finally been solved. We have seen before that, from the time of the Sages of Jabneh and onwards, the attitudes of the Tannaitic world toward the standing of these courts had become polarized; some upheld, while others denied, their authority. In awarding these judges 'ordination' the Patriarchs were only confirming the existence of an ancient social tradition, even though it had elicited protests from many of the Torah scholars.[136] Secondly the elevation of local judges to the level of the ordained was likely to abolish the rivalry between the one judicial authority and the other in regard to their respective realms of authority. From now on, the courts of the 'commoners' were equal to those of the Sages, and were able to try all civil cases (including penalties, etc.). This fact meant the removal of a complicated and quarrelsome factor from urban Jewish life.

This recognition afforded by the Patriarchs is significant mainly for its regulation and strengthening of the 'democratic' tradition in the judicial world, the granting of power to civil judicatures. In actual practice, however, these appointments were mainly allotted to the ruling classes in the cities, i.e. the country aristocracy. The opposition of the Sages to the appointment of such judges was also a link in the chain of their rivalry with the powerful classes in the cities of Eretz-Israel for influence in (and control of) the settlements.

Granting 'ordination' to city judges drawn from the ruling strata meant, on the other hand — together with the imposition of organizational supervision over the local, civil courts on the part of the central administration — the inclusion of the country aristocracy, the governing circles in the settled areas, in the social and national structure, which became increasingly stabilized during the course of

136 We find objections raised against unworthy appointments already at the end of the second century. *Midrash Tannaim*, p. 8: 'R. Simeon b. Eleazar says: There is not a single Academy, no member of which will go to Gehinnom, but the last Academy will all go to Gehinnom' etc. Did some similar situation exist to some extent as early as in Rabbi's days?

generations in Eretz-Israel, with the Patriarch at the head,[137] for recognition of this judicial authority entailed obedience to the supreme leadership, and cooperation with it in reinforcing its rule over the nation (as well as its standing with the Roman government).

What led to this act was the prevailing historical situation, the development that occurred especially during the days of the Severan emperors. We discern the tendency of the Patriarchate already in Rabbi's days to base its strength on the economically powerful classes in the country.[138] Such conduct on the part of the Patriarch certainly

137 We have no substantial information on the relations between the Patriarchate, Sanhedrin and municipal authorities in respect of the subordination of the latter to the central authority, in the area either of adjudication or administration, prior to the end of the second century. Logically, we may well assume as almost certain that the control of the central body did not extend over the settlements in these areas. (We are unable to deal in this article with the subject of the relationship obtaining between the city judges and the local administration on the one hand and the supreme authority of the nation on the other during the days of the Second Temple.) One tradition, however, is capable of teaching us apparently that the Patriarchs had the power to depose heads of cities (or communities) in the generation subsequent to the Destruction. So we learn in a Baraita (*Rosh Ha-Shana* 22a; *T.P. ibid.*, i, 57b) of Rabban Gamaliel that he removed the head of Gader from office. (There are still scholars who retain the reading in this form, thereby identifying the locality as Gader in Transjordan. So, Klein *'Ever Hayarden Hayehudi*, pp. 30–31; *Sefer Hayishuv*, s.v. *Gader*. This, however, is impossible, since the Sabbath is not set aside for witnesses coming to give evidence on having seen the new moon, except from a 'walking [distance] of a night and a day', and Gader is farther than this from Jabneh. Horowitz [p. 92] has previously rejected this view. He, however, takes it to be the Gederah mentioned in Joshua xv, 36. To me, it appears that the locality is Gezer, and we have already found Greek sources substituting Gader for Gezer Γάζαρα, Γάδαρα, see Schürer, *Geschichte*⁴, I, p. 339. In MS Leyden the Palestinian Talmud has גר and above it a letter that, in my mind, is only to be read as ז. Other references in our sources also testify to the existence of a Jewish settlement in Gezer after the Destruction.) This 'head' was certainly a leader of the community and so these functionaries were obviously subordinate to the Patriarch. Although the tradition in the Mishna repudiates this testimony, yet in many respects, the authority of the centre, which gained in strength from the days of Rabbi onwards over the settlements, existed already in the time of the Patriarchate of R. Gamaliel and disappeared afterwards, till it was reinstated at the end of the second century and thereafter.

138 *T.B. Eruvin* 85b: 'The son of Bonyin once visited Rabbi. He said to them: Make room for the owner of 100 maneh. Another person came. He said: Make room for the owner of 200 maneh. R. Ishmael b. Jose said before him: This one's father owns a thousand ships at sea and also judges a thousand

did not merely arise from personal predilection. These classes had produced from among themselves an elite (the most 'patriotic'), the instrument for promoting social life in the communities of the country. Support of public institutions, provision of funds for public needs, was derived in abundant measure from them. In the days of the Antonines, after the Bar Kokhba rebellion, Jewish Palestine was crushed, populationwise, economically and socially. Public institutions, such as community schools, synagogues, etc. had disappeared altogether or become enfeebled. With the beginning of the Severan dynasty, economic conditions began to improve. The restoration of public life to normalcy, however, was only made possible by the support of the wealthy classes. They served, then, as a necessary basis for the rehabilitation process of the Jewish population.[139]

Yet another factor also operated here. In the period under discussion, the process of the consolidation of the ruling status of the wealthy elements in the cities of the Roman Empire reached its culmination. Henceforth the State granted them additional legal rights in the colonies (which had become transformed in the course of time into legally endorsed hereditary rights of these families). There came into being that defined, crystallised class of βουλευται, *curiales*, as opposed to the plebs, who had lost the right to participate in city government. Burdensome responsibilities and obligations, however, were also forcibly thrust upon these classes. The Bouleute were compelled to assume the responsibility for the administrative and financial obligations of the populations of the cities and their environs. The combination of additional privileges and heavy responsibilities led to the centralization of communal supervision and caused the administration of the cities to fall into the hands of the above-mentioned class.

Certainly, in theory, this development only pertained to communities organized in the form of the πόλεις. Three 'cities' of this type were added in Eretz-Israel during the rule of the Severan dynasty,

towns on land. He said to him: When you come to his father, say to him: Do not send him in such clothes to Rabbi, since Rabbi respects the rich, while R. Jacob respects the saintly.' (This is the recension of the Geonim, as the tradition itself testifies, and this is apparent from the discussion, *ibid.* 86a — that honour was bestowed on them because they brought benefit to the public by supplying its needs. See Koenigsberger, *Haqedem*, II, p. 153.) Cf. the evidence of Ben El'asa's son-in-law's wealth.

139 To clarify this matter requires a detailed study, which would not be in place here.

most (or a large minority) of the populations of these cities being Jews (Lod – Diospolis; Emmaus – Nicopolis; Bet Guvrin – Eleutheropolis). Moreover, the continuation of the process must be assumed to have occurred even in the larger settlements, which had obtained a broad measure of autonomy, although they did not rank officially as πόλεις (cities). This situation most likely helped to make the rich elements of the settlements the basis of the organized national structure in Eretz-Israel.[140]

On the other hand, Rabbi also instituted a number of regulations designed to consolidate the realm of the Sages.[141] Although these actions of his led to the enforcement of the mastery of the Patriarchs and some denial of the freedom of the former,[142] nevertheless it was he who facilitated the increase of their influence in the cities, their appointment as communal leaders and the consolidation of their rights.

The reinforcement of the communal status of the Sages, however, brought about an intensified religious educational endeavour on their part in the towns (in cooperation with and under the supervision of the Patriarchate) in Torah study which became immeasurably intensified. There ensued a certain saturation of spiritual influence within the broad strata of the nation, a rejuvenation as it were, effected by the Torah scholars (and stimulated by the Patriarch).[143] All these

140 This does not detract from the deeds of the Patriarchs directed at times at depriving the leadership of these elements in the diaspora communities of any permanence, according to the evidence of Palladius, p. 381 above.

141 We do not hear of the Sages being exempted from taxes (only the occasional?) until his day, in the manner that they had been exempted from the Coronation Tax by the Patriarch (*Bava Batra* 8a).

142 For instance, the ordinance: 'A student shall not give Halakhic decisions', or his decree that the Sages should not give instruction to their disciples in the market place (but in the House of Study instead; *T.B. Mo'ed Qaṭan* 16a), and 'the high-handed conduct of the Patriarch and casting bitterness among the disciples' in general which he commanded to his son.

143 There are conclusive proofs testifying to the widespread teaching of Torah in the settlements by Sages despatched there by the Patriarchs, from the days of Rabbi onwards, concomitant with the upsurge of Torah study in the world of the Sages themselves during that period. One need only recall all the traditions referring to the Sages 'who went out to the towns' (which began in the reign of the Severan dynasty and continued) or 'who were sent to traverse' the cities of the land. Perhaps it is in place here to consider Origen's evidence. He reiterates in several places that he saw 'many Jews who study Torah constantly, from infancy to old age', and uses similar expressions.

efforts enhanced the power of the Sages and prepared the way for their powerful position in the future, both *vis-à-vis* the 'secularized' wealthy elements and the Patriarchate itself.

Rabbi's practice of including those circles in the organizational structure of the nation was continued by the succeeding Patriarchs. From now onwards, the Bouleute and the *Ḥaverim*[144] (or 'heads' or 'Elders') constituted the two bodies assuming the leadership of the communities in the settlements. Each of its field (civil and spiritual) was joined with the Patriarchate and operated under its supervision.[145]

144 See, e.g., *T.P. Nedarim*, vi, 40a, and *Sanhedrin* i, 19a, and the parallels in Midrashim: ' "The craftsmen and smiths a thousand" — R. Berekhia said in the name of R. Ḥelbo: These are the associates (Sages), while the Rabbis say: These are the Bouleute.' The passage reveals the duality existing in public administration in the view of these Amoraim (cf. *Massekhet Soferim* xix, 9–10: Associations of Elders and Bouleute; the 'good men' of the city and the associates), just as other statements deal with the comparison of the rights of 'those who help the public', the monied (and the 'performers of *mitzvot*') with the rights of the 'Torah scholars' and with the question as to who is the more important (see, for instance, *Sifre Deuteronomy* §47, ed. Finkelstein, p. 106 in reference to the charity treasurers and the Elders). Cf. for the rivalry between the Bouleute and the Sages for superiority in the Patriarchal House, *T.P. Shabbat* xii, 13c; *Horayot* iii, 48c (Büchler, *Manhige Ṣippori*, p. 135. Cf. also Baron, *The Jewish Community*, I, p. 119).

145 Here, too the sources reveal the separate realms and the problem of which of the two was superior. In *T.P. Horayot*, iii, 48b we read: 'R. Joshua b. Levi said: [As between] the head and the Elder, the Elder takes precedence, for if there is no Elder there can be no head' etc. The nature of the 'head' is not explained properly here (the continuation of the passage is not sufficiently clear for our purposes). Further on, however, *ibid.* c, 'R. Joshua of Sikhnin in the name of R. Levi: Because Moses foresaw by means of the Holy Spirit that Israel would become entangled (*sic*) in the kingdoms, and their heads would stand by them, he gave the heads priority over the Elders.' Hence the functions of the 'heads' were social and political. The same conclusion emerges from the statement in *Midrash Tannaim*, ed. Hoffman, p. 213: ' "Heads of. . ." — Scripture tells us that when the heads enter to take counsel below, they sustain the Kingdom of Heaven above, as it is said, "Heads of. . .", and these are none other than great men' (the great men of the city, the civic leaders). This, however, is the recension of the Geonim (*Halakhot Gedolot*, Warsaw, 124b; *ibid.*, Berlin, and *Teshuvot Hageonim*, ed. Koronel, Nos. 117 and 703; Lyck, No. 2) and the *Seride Yerushalmi*, p. 286: 'The head and the Elder — the head takes priority over an Elder who is not a head.' This recension might likely support the view held by scholars that ordinary Sages served as leaders of the communities. However, our recension seems to be the correct version. For so we read in *Midrash Tanḥuma*, ed. Buber, end of *Shemot* (p. 17): 'Hah! They indeed consult with the Elders. So Moses "called to the Elders of the people" and afterwards "to

The opposition of the Sages to the appointment of ignorant judges also brought about the first clash between the two elements in civil leadership, perhaps more violently at first. This was occasioned by the growing power of the wealthy classes and the increased strength of the Sages, who sought to prevent the former from interfering in what they considered exclusively their province. Yet it is feasible to regard this protest, too, as an expression of the opposition to the Patriarchate itself, for the manner in which it had assumed control by basing itself upon the power-wielding classes. Certainly moral and religious-social self-assertion was involved here as well. It was only right for the Sages to protest against the 'secularization' likely to ensue from the assignment of judicial functions to 'commoners' drawn from among the heads of the settlements, and against the corruption existing in that world, both of which were liable to lead to the perversion of justice. The Patriarchs, however, who were alive to the needs of the nation at the time, who, more than most of the Sages, grasped the full compass of public affairs and who, more than the latter, were capable of sensing and adapting themselves to the requirements and circumstances of the hour, were also mindful of the discharge of their own function: The inclusion and balancing of the ruling elements and their subordination to the supreme leadership, and their involvement in the government of the nation.[146]

What results emerged from this development? It seems that the

the heads and judges": When does Israel have heads? — When they have Elders.' Our Midrash which serves as a parallel to the passage in the Palestinian Talmud undoubtedly supports the recension we have before us (which draws a distinction between the authority of the heads and that of the Elders), which is explained after the manner of the commentators: 'Who is not a head' — that is to say that Israel cannot attain to orderly and effective political and civil administration unless it has Elders, although Ginzberg, *Perushim* etc., III, p. 113, takes 'Heads' to mean Sages, and identical with Elders (the tradition ascribed to R. Akiba in the Talmud, *Pesaḥim* 112a, and Rabbi, *Pirqe Rabbenu Hakadosh*, see ed. Higger, *Ḥoreb*, V, p. 133: That a person should not reside in a city, the Head of which is a *Talmid Ḥakham* — reveals the same duality and the same attitude of withdrawal from all preoccupation with public affairs evinced by some of the Sages).

146 There can be no reasonable doubt that the dependence of the Sages on the supremacy of the Patriarchs also increased the power of their own realm, by ensuring consolidation and order. It seems, indeed, that this is the meaning conveyed by R. Mana's remark in *T.P. Pesaḥim* vi, 33a: 'I heard from R. Yudan and all the rabbis: Why are the courts below (the House of the Patriarch) accustomed to insist on honour? So that disputes should not proliferate in Israel.' Such disputes were certainly liable to erupt too frequently in the realm of the Sages. (The question and answer before us con-

actions of the Patriarch were vindicated. The power of the central authority continued to increase. The joining of the 'heads of the cities' to the rule of the Patriarchate enhanced its authority, but in like manner helped to stimulate the process of the penetration of the influence of the Torah scholars among the local population and with it the stabilization of the religious-spiritual world of the masses.[147] Yet it seems that, in practice, the appointment of unqualified judges by the Patriarchate encouraged the predominance of Torah lawsuits — i.e. the judgement by the Sages. Through their dependence on the supremacy of the Patriarchate the two authorities came closer to one another and proceeded towards integration.[148]

Quite possibly, too, this unification of the judicial systems, which the Patriarchs endeavoured to bring about in Eretz-Israel, also helped, in

cerning the reason for the Patriarchate insisting on being honoured also implies the negation, in principle, of any assumption of power and privilege by the Patriarchate. It teaches that their control did not stem from the fact of power or by right, but was exercised for the benefit of the public alone, and only endured because of the endorsement of the Sages at such time as they alone deemed fit.)

147 Just as we find Rabbi himself appointing officials (Parnassim), so do we find the Sages making appointments, *T.P. Pe'a*, viii, 20a, here, too, presumably with the assent of the Patriarch — Bacher, *Die Aggada der Palaestiner Amoraim*, II, p. 153. (We read of R. Ḥiyya b. Abba, among others, appointing archons. According to Lieberman's opinion, *Tarbiz*, II, ii, p. 235; *JQR*, 1943/44, p. 230, n. 20, the heads of the diaspora communities are intended here. This may be possible and even probable. R. Ḥiyya tarried in many diaspora communities, perhaps as an emissary of the Patriarch. Nevertheless, Lieberman's proof, based on the fact that we do not find archons in the sense of heads of communities in our sources except in reference to diaspora communities alone, is not conclusive. For so we read in *Midrash Yelammedenu*, as quoted in *Arukh*, s.v. "*Erekh Alef*', *Sefer Halikkutim*, ed. Grünhut, Numbers xix, 1: ' "And he saw the heads of the people" — [teaches] that he came to each single group and took remuneration for the Parnassim separately and for the archons separately.' It is far-fetched to assert that by using the term archon, the observation was directed especially at the diaspora population. It should further be noted that the name *'arkhuna* among the Samaritans is commonly used to designate the head of the community.) After the abolition of the Patriarchate, however, we find the 'Sanhedrins of the two Palestines' appointing 'great men' in the cities of the land (C. Th. 16, 8, 9).

148 The attempts of the 'ignorant judges' to deliver public discourses and to clothe themselves in the 'garment' certainly arises from the fact that the ordained Sages were accustomed to behave in this manner. Our method of inquiry, however, leads us to learn from here of the inclination of the ignorant to approach more closely to the world of the Sages and to combine Torah knowledge with judicial functions.

some measure, to bring about the acknowledgement of the suzerainty of Eretz-Israel in the area of jurisdiction, which took the form of subservience to the judicial authority of the Patriarchate on the part of the diaspora communities of the Roman Empire and which was initiated and continued progressively during the third and fourth centuries.[149]

What, then, is meant by 'taking money from the appointees'? We certainly recall the 'selling of office' which received wide mention in the tradition of the Roman Empire (and so too in our sources in reference to the High Priesthood at the end of the Second Temple period).[150] We should by no means absolve the Patriarchs from all social and moral taint (social developments in general in the Roman Empire at the end of the third and during the fourth century were likely to encourage the rise of arbitrary rule and despotism in the world of the Patriarchate). It is probable, however, that the above-mentioned practice in itself is based on a tradition of urban life. It is known that immediately prior to the period under discussion Greek citizens were accustomed, on being elevated to 'honorary office' (ἀρχαί) in their cities or to other positions of prestige, to pay sums of money to the city treasury for public needs (*summa honorari*). It is, accordingly, not at all far-fetched to assume that a similar practice existed in at least some of the cities of Jewish Eretz-Israel. From the time the 'appointments' became the prerogative of the Patriarchs, however, these sums, which had previously been contributed to the local treasury by city inhabitants upon their being appointed 'judges' in their localities, were now by right handed over to the central authority which had made the appointment, i.e. to the general treasury controlled by the Patriarchs.[151]

Here, too, the polemical language used by the Sages opposed to the appointment of unqualified judges was likely to obscure the tradition underlying the conduct of the Patriarchs and to obliterate its social background and organizational significance, thus unfairly to deprive the Patriarchs of the justification for their conduct.

149 The dependence of the diaspora judiciaries on the Patriarch's establishment of their supremacy is tied up with their control of the administration of the communities as a whole, a fact which is found in Roman legal sources and in the literary sources cited in this article.

150 Cf. above, pp. 65 ff.

151 The same applies to the contributions of the leaders of the diaspora communities under Roman suzerainty which were transmitted to the Patriarch, according to the evidence of Palladius.

Appendix

ON DIOCLETIAN'S RESCRIPT, C. J. III, 13, 3.

We have dealt above with the continuing struggle between the Patriarchate and the Sages on the appointment of judges, even after the 'compromise' reached between them, a matter stressed by Dinaburg as well. That scholar, however, wanted to infer from Diocletian's Rescript written to 'Judah' that this controversy had become so intense that the struggle of the Patriarch against Sages appointing judges without his consent led to the intervention of the Roman government, with the Emperor pronouncing his verdict against the Sages. For many reasons, it is difficult to sustain Dinaburg's conjecture. Even if the argument raised by scholars against the commentators who wished to regard our document as relating to the Jewish lawcourts is discarded — viz. the absence of any mention of Jews in the text — it still remains doubtful whether the Emperor could speak of *qui judicio praeest*, of someone, anonymous, as possessing official power, if he had Jewish judges (authorised by the Patriarch and not by him) in mind, and whom the government had not endowed with judicial authority (except over Jews). Moreover, if this document refers to the conflict between the Patriarchate and the Sages on the right to appoint judges, how can it refer without qualification to those appointed by the Sages (the Bet Din) as chosen by the consent of private persons as axiomatic, for the entire issue (submitted, according to Dinaburg, by the Patriarch to the government) was: Who are to be the judges considered authorised and duly appointed — those appointed by the Patriarch or those ordained by the Bet Din? It follows, then, that the main point at issue is missing from the Emperor's reply. It is also somewhat far-fetched to give the expression *consensu privatorum* the interpretation suggested by Dinaburg: 'with the consent of other people' (i.e. the Sages). Its plain sense, it seems to me, is similar to *consensus partium*, of the parties to the trial. This is, it appears, substantiated especially by the clause, *qui nulli praeest judicio*. For if the reference is to the appointment of overall judges by the Sages (without the authorization of the Patriarch), is it possible to say that prior to their appointment they did not possess the status of heads of lawcourts? It is accordingly much more reasonable to interpret this document as dealing with courts of arbitration chosen by the litigants from amongst the unqualified who do not judge by consent of the government and has nothing at all to do with the Jews.

True, the name, Judah, ostensibly inclines one to assume that we are dealing here with a Jew. Nevertheless, I see no difficulty in Juster's assumption that he was a Christian governor in one of the Hyparchies. For we learn from many sources of Christian governors, officers and court officials in Diocletian's day, all the time until he began persecuting them. At all events it may be worthwhile to dwell on the inscription published by L. Wickert, in his article, *Vorbemerkungen zu einem Supplementum Ostiense des Corpus Inscriptionum Latinarum* in *Sitzungsberichte der Preussischen Akademie usw.*, 1928. This inscription was written by *Ordo Augustalium* of Ostia and here is its text: *M. Aurel[io] f. Ter. p. a. sui - - - Scythop[oli] p[an] tomim[o sui] temporis] primo in O[riente - - -] to approbato a[b impp. Valeriano e]t Gal... ex provincia e[- - - ..post] mortem patr[is s]ui Jud[ae; item de] curioni civitat[iu]m Ascalo[nito]narum et Damascen[or]um. Huic s...ndus ordo Augustalium non propter memoriam pat[ri]s eius, sed et propter plenam [ipsius per] itiam postul[antibus omnibus pariter civibus...*

The reconstructed text *Jud[ae; item de] curioni* was taken over by the author from Wilken (who mentions Judah, the chronographer of the days of Septimus Severus known from Eusebius' *Ecclesiastical History*). While another reconstruction suggested itself first to him at the time, he finally rejected it (see *ibid.* p. 41, n. 3). Now, first of all, it is necessary to examine whether it is reasonable to assume that M. Aurelius, the Pantomime, son of Judah, was a Jew. Certainly we do find a Jewish mime in the time of Nero (Josephus, *Life* 3). Yet that a Jewish Pantomime should have risen in the third century (the inscription most certainly is to be dated between 253–260; see *ibid.* p. 40), to serve honorarily, because of his preeminence as an artist, as a member of the municipal council of Ashkelon (which hated Jews) and of Damascus is much too far-fetched. Nor, for the same reason can he be regarded as a Christian.

The inscription, however, also clearly informs us that Judah the father as well served in a capacity similar to that of the son, and that the latter went from Beisan to Ostia to replace his own father, who had died (hence the honour of the father is alluded to first), as the author explains (p. 42). Perhaps the conjecture is not far-fetched that the father was the *citharoedus* praised in the inscription at Dessau (ILS No. 5233) for his accomplishments in *Sebasia aput Damascum III, Actia aput Bo[s]tram II, Pithia Karthaginis*, etc. It is almost definite that this Judah could not be regarded as Jewish. Yet there is nothing strange, in my mind, in a non-Jew (Semitic), a native of Beisan being called by a name inherited from Jews in that city and its surroundings (or perhaps he was an apostate?).

So we do have some support in our hands for regarding the Judah of Diocletian's Rescript as a pagan Gentile.

Dinaburg, however, also relies for his conjecture upon the document in *Codex Theodosianus* II, 1, 10, which speaks of Jewish judication, *apud Judaeos vel patriarchas* (among the Jews or Patriarchs). This scholar accordingly discerns two distinct types of courts in Eretz-Israel (in the eyes of the authority): Those officially recognized ('among the Patriarchs') and those not officially recognized ('among the Jews'), and assigns the beginnings of these two authorities to the same document of Diocletian, whose above-mentioned decision was responsible for the rise, from then onwards, of courts not appointed by the Patriarchs and regarded by the Empire as 'private'. It seems, however, that we cannot assume any rivalry existing between the courts of the Patriarchs and the Sages elsewhere than in Eretz-Israel. We have not heard as yet that the rivalry extended into the diaspora, and had gained ground there, becoming a permanent reality, till it became necessary for it to be mentioned in Roman legislation (the order under discussion does not elaborate and speaks generally of Jews in the Empire).

The principal substance of our document makes it reasonable to assert that only one type of court existed among Diaspora Jewry, and this consisted generally of the heads of the community, but that it went by several names. Some referred to it (in Gentile language, and chiefly in the Empire) as being *apud Judaeos* ('among the Jews') and some called it after the judges, 'of the Patriarchs' (i.e. minor patriarchs, the heads of the communities. That such courts existed is in my mind incontrovertible[1]). In our document, the combining of the two names by the conjunction '*vel*' into a single term is not surprising (or perhaps the reference is to the Bet Din of the members of the community, 'commoners', side by side with the leaders of the community?).

1 The *interpretatio* gives this version of our passage: *Sane si apud maiores legis consentientes ambae partes* etc., which is identical with 'the law-court of the heads of the communities'.

THE SONS OF THE SAGES

There are Tannaitic and Amoraic sources which mention the 'Sons of the Sages' side by side with the 'Sages' and 'disciples' themselves, thereby indicating some sort of special stratum, intermediate between the other two, and closer to the latter. Like the disciples, the 'sons' are entitled to certain privileges reserved for Sages and are adjudged as possessing the right to succeed their parents in status, in teaching and in public service.

This fact affords us evidence of a process of consolidation, as it were, of a 'Sages' class' which incorporates within itself a heritage of scholarship and dignity, some sort of spiritual and professional aristocracy.

At first sight this must seem surprising,[1] since innumerable Tannaitic dicta point up and emphasise that everyone has a right to Torah, which is the heritage of all Israel, and that all in the nation are equal in respect of the study of Torah.[2] A discriminating investi-

1 Büchler wrote (*Der galiläischer 'Am Ha-'aretz*, p. 174; *The Social and Political Leaders*... p. 15, n. 1) that administrative offices alone were hereditary, but not those in the realm of Torah. Similarly, Louis Ginzberg, *Perushim Ve-Ḥiddushim Biyerushalmi*, I, p. 405: 'And it is self-understood that it never occurred to them (the Sages of the Halakha) to assert that a son should inherit his father, succeeding him in the Yeshiva of Bet Din, where the appointments depended upon merit (lit. 'wisdom') and not on family pedigree. And it is obvious that, in respect to the Jewish Parnasim (whose sons did succeed them), they only had communal leaders like the Patriarch in mind, whose pre-eminence passed on by inheritance from father to son.'

2 In Sifre, *Bamidbar* § cxix (ed. Horowitz, p. 144): 'There are three crowns: the crown of Torah, of Priesthood and of Royalty. Aaron attained the crown of Priesthood... but the crown of Torah is set down...' See also R. Simeon in *Avot de-R. Nahtan*, Version I, xli: 'Whoever wishes to take up the crown of the Torah, may come and take it.' It is taught in the Mekhilta, too, Jethro, *Baḥodesh*, end of v (ed. Horowitz, p. 222): 'The Torah was given [in the presence of] three things: The desert, fire and water. Just as these are free to all men, so are the words of Torah free to all men on earth.' The Mishna, *Horayot* iii, 8 is well known: 'A bastard who is a scholar takes precedence

gation of what took place in practice, insofar as we are able to study the sources, teaches us that in general the realm of the Torah and Sages was free of all restriction of dynastic privilege in the days following the Destruction.[3] Needless to say, that same freedom dominated the world of the Pharisaic Sages during the Temple period. Indeed, this characteristic, the popular nature, and the absence of any real signs of any class consolidation or of the rise of any pedigreed rulership contributed to the preeminence and extensive influence of the Pharisaic 'teachers' on the nation, which outweighed the power of the other elements competing with them for public leadership: the priesthood and the moneyed aristocracy.

Before, however, we proceed to try and explain the fact under discussion itself, it is necessary to examine it in the sources, for the scholars have apparently failed altogether to apprise us of it until now.

We learn in the Tosefta (*Sanhedrin* vii, 8–9; *T.B. Horayot* 13b): 'At the time when the public needs them, the sons of the Sages and the scholars may even tread on the heads of the people. Even though they have said that it is no praise of the disciple that he should enter last, he goes out for his needs and reenters and sits in his place. The sons of the Sages and the Sages when they have the knowledge to understand turn their faces towards their fathers; when they do not have the knowledge to understand, they turn their faces towards

over a High Priest who is an ignoramus' (see the parallel Baraitot in the Tosefta and Talmuds).

Similarly, there is the Baraita ascribed in the Talmud (*Bava Qamma* 38a and the textual variants) to R. Meir: 'that even a gentile who occupies himself with the study of Torah is like a High Priest' (however, in the parallel in Sifre, *Aḥare Mot*, vi, 1, the reading is: 'R. Jeremiah said: From where [do we learn] that even a gentile who does the Torah ...', i.e. 'who fulfils it', a text the originality of which is proved even by the substance of the Baraita in the Talmud, for the Tanna derives it by expounding the Scriptural passage: 'that man shall do and live'.) See below in the body of the essay.

3 For there were many Tannaim who were not "Sons of the Sages" — for instance, R. Akiva, R. Meir etc., although these may be contrasted with the families of R. Ḥalafta (himself, his son, R. Jose and the latter's sons) and R. Judah b. Ile'ai (himself, his son, R. Jose, and the latter's sons). Certainly R. Gamaliel sought to exclude from his great Academy disciples 'whose character did not correspond to their exterior' (and the Sages frustrated his design). Nevertheless even in this instance, the criterion was personal and moral and nothing else.

the people. R. Eliezer b. Zadok says: In the house of feasting, they are treated as attached [to their fathers].'[4]

We see then that the Sons of the Sages are mentioned side by side with the disciples as a separate group, sitting together with the latter in the House of Study, serving the people, and sharing the honour conferred on their fathers both there and in the house of feasting.

The tradition of the Babylonian Talmud (*Giṭṭin* 59b–60a) gives evidence of the existence of this state of affairs at the end of the third century: 'The Galileans sent to R. Ḥelbo: Who are entitled to read after them? He had no answer. He came and asked of R. Isaac Nappaḥa. He said to him: The Sages who are appointed as Parnasim on the public read after them; the disciples of the Sages who are qualified to be appointed Parnasim over the community after them; the sons of the disciples of the Sages, whose fathers are appointed Parnas over the public after them, and the heads of the synagogue and everyone else after them.'

Here, too, the status of the Sons of the Sages is held to confer privilege and universal respect, more than is accorded to the heads of the synagogues but close to that of the disciples of the Sages. This same fact is even taught in the supplement to the Mishna[5] in *Soṭa* ix, 15 (according to Ms. Kaufman which seems to have the correct text): 'R. Pinḥas b. Ya'ir says: When the Temple was destroyed, the *ḥaverim* and the sons of *ḥaverim* (חֲבֵרִים, so vowelled in the Ms.; in *Shilte Ha-gibborim*, 'and sons of free men' חורין) were ashamed and covered their heads; men of good deeds were disregarded and the strong-armed grew powerful . . .' It is reasonable to assume that this is the original text, for the Tanna does not speak of 'nobles and pedigreed' but of Sages and righteous men as opposed to the strong-armed and the persuasive. Accordingly, the 'sons of the *ḥaverim*' are none other than the 'Sons of the Sages'.

This distinction certainly applied to inheritance rights, the son inheriting the standing and status of his father. We learn this ex-

4 Variants in the traditions of the Baraita in the Tosefta and of the Talmud are to be found which involve certain expressions; but we are not obliged to deal with them here, since the subject under discussion, the grouping, 'Sons of the Sages', as distinct from the disciples of the Sages, emerges clearly from the two. The combining of the honour due the Sages in their seat in the Bet Midrash with the honour due them in the house of feasting is repeated in R. Ami's dictum (*T.B. Bava Batra* 120a): 'At the session (*Yeshiva*) go according to wisdom; at the feast, according to age.'

5 See J. N. Epstein, *Mevo Le-nusaḥ Ha-Mishna*, p. 976.

plicitly from the tradition (in *Sifre Zuta*) found in the *Yalkut* on the Torah, Deuteronomy x, 416: 'This can be illustrated by the case of an Av Bet Din who had many children. While (the rest) were ignorant, the oldest was educated (lit. a *Ben Torah*). He willed each his portion . . . He said to the eldest: For you it is enough to take my place.'

This Av Bet Din is only some 'elder' (*zaqen*) or Sage, and not the Patriarch's deputy.[6] We learn, then, that it was customary for the eldest (the first-born) sons of great Sages to succeed their fathers in learning and in status.[7]

The evidence is substantiated by Origen in the first half of the third century. He also portrays the 'son of the Sages' as a common phenomenon in Eretz-Israel. In his reply to Africanus (*PG*, vol. XI, col. 61–64), he writes:

> Μέμνημαι μὲν τοί γε φιλομαθεῖ Ἐβραίῳ καὶ χρηματιζοντι παρ'αὐτοῖς σοφοῦ υἱῷ, ανατραφέντι ἐπί το διαδέξασθαι τὸν πατέρα, συμμίξας περὶ πλειόνων κτλ.
> ('I remember that I discussed with much directness with a certain Hebrew, a lover of knowledge, that it was accepted by them [the Jews], that the son of a Sage would be raised to succeed his father . . .')[8]

In the light of these evidences, the incident of the son of R. Eleazar b. R. Simeon related in the Babylonian Talmud (*Bava Mesiʿa* 85a) becomes abundantly clear: 'Rabbi chanced to visit the town of R. Eleazar b. R. Simeon. He asked: Did that saintly man have a son? He answered: He has a son, and every harlot that is hired for two hires him for four.[9] He had him brought to him and ordained him a Rabbi and entrusted him to Simeon b. Jose b. Laqonia, his mother's

6 That the younger sons of the Av Bet Din were ignoramuses was no accident, since the eldest was due to succeed him.

7 See above, p. 385, n. 37.

8 It is evident from the Greek that the Church Father was familiar with the title, 'Son of a Sage', as established and current among Jews in Eretz-Israel. (The letter was written about 240 C.E., however, while he was living temporarily in Nicomedia, Bithynia, after he had first settled in Eretz-Israel and had lived there for many years. See Bardenhewer, *Geschichte der altkirchlichen Literatur*, II, p. 178.

9 This is the correct wording, as it is in the *Midrash Ha-gadol* (Ms.), and Gaster, *Maʿaseh Buch*, p. 87. The version we have was combined from the first and second halves of another version: 'If she would hire herself for four, she would hire him for eight.'

brother. Every day he would say: I am going back to my town. He said to him: The Sages have made you, have spread a gold cloak over you, and called you Rabbi, and you say: I am going back to my city? He said to him: I swear (*mumi*) this is ugly for me.[10] When he grew up he came and sat in the Academy of Rabbi. He heard his voice. He said: The voice resembles the voice of R. Eleazar b. R. Simeon. They said to him: He is his son. He replied to him: "The fruit of the righteous is a tree of life" — this refers to R. Jose b. R. Eleazar b. R. Simeon; and "he that wins souls is wise" is R. Simeon b. R. Jose b. Laqonia.'

Accordingly the son of R. Eleazar b. R. Simeon was initially a licentious youth, devoid of Torah learning, casting it contemptuously aside. Nevertheless Rabbi ordained him and covered him in a scholar's cloak. Only afterwards did Rabbi force him to sit down and study Torah. Clearly it was the merit of his father that was responsible for this, for as a 'Son of a Sage' he would be appointed a Sage *in potentia* in his youth, since he was destined to be ordained in actuality when he matured in Torah scholarship.

Certainly, this fact does not merely impart information concerning the incident as such, since it conforms to the practice found, at times, in the Roman Empire during the third and fourth centuries, namely that the sons of the leaders of communities were appointed in their youth and childhood as μελλογραμματεῖς (archon designatus) μελλάρχοντες and the heads of congregations were also appointed similarly.[11]

Corroborative evidence for the existence of the practice under discussion emerges from the following Baraita. In *Avot de-R. Nathan*, Version I, iii (ed. Schechter, pp. 14–15), we are taught: ' "And raise up many disciples" — for Bet Shammai say: One should only teach someone who is wise, humble and the son of (distinguished) ancestry and rich;[12] and Bet Hillel say: One should teach everybody, for

10 The meaning of the language is apparently: 'By an oath, it is ugly' (*T.B. Qiddushin* 9b, etc.), that is to say, 'It is difficult for me to occupy myself with Torah.' (The original reading, it is reasonable to assume, was: עזיבא, in Aramaic 'ugly', and as Yallon has shown in his *Quntresim*, II, pp. 52 ff., the verb *'azav* has this connotation in the language of the Talmudic Sages.

11 See above, p. 381, n. 25.

12 Reifman, *Bet Talmud*, iv, p. 48 has sensed that the wording we have ועשיר is incorrect, and suggests the reading: וכשר, 'and fit'. Certainly, no conclusive proof can be deduced from Bet Hillel's omitting to mention 'wealth' in their reply (for neither did they mention 'Sons of Sages'). It is even more

there were many sinners in Israel that came close to Torah, and righteous, saintly and worthy men were descended from them.' *Avot de-R. Nathan*, Version II, iv, is similar: 'Bet Shammai say: Only the worthy sons of (distinguished) fathers and the sons of the sons of (distinguished) fathers are to be taught; and Bet Hillel say: Everyone. They gave an illustration: What is this like? — To a woman who set a hen on eggs. From the many she hatches out few, and from the few she hatches out none.'

What the nature of these 'Sons of the Sages' might be is not adequately elucidated. The simplest signification of the expression would seem to be 'the sons and grandsons of Sages'.[13] We learn, then, that there were circles among the Sages who sought to confine and restrict the study of Torah to the realm of the 'Torah-educated families' alone, although this tradition gives no evidence of any family-pedigree having crystallised in actuality. The Baraita, however, requires precise investigation. From Bet Hillel's reply we learn that the main point at issue with Bet Shammai was the ethical character of the student alone. According to the latter, the morally debased were not, because of their wickedness, to be drawn to Torah study, while the former held the opinion that Torah study would impel them to mend their ways. According to the tradition in Version II, they differ on the issue of whether, from the pedagogic-economic standpoint, the dissemination of Torah was to be broadened or narrowed. Bet Hillel urged the removal of all barriers to learning, lest Torah instruction decline in consequence of the attraction of worthy students alone. Consequently the qualification that students be descended from the families of Sages only pertained to the distinction drawn above. That is to say: The presumption was that sons of Sages were *ipso facto*

incorrect to draw conclusions from the wording of the Rishonim (R. Jonah, R. Simeon b. Zemaḥ, et al.), since they did not transcribe the Baraita verbatim. Since, however, even in Version II, the word 'rich' does not appear in Bet Shammai's statement, it is reasonable to assume that the text is not original. On the subject itself, see the traditions cited below, which prove that a certain tendency did exist among the Sages to require their students to be wealthy.

13 The same applies to בר אבהן = 'the son of fathers', which is found in the Talmud (*Menaḥot* 53a) in a remark made by a Palestinian Sage, and is joined on to בר אוריין = 'a Torah scholar'. Freund's interpretation (the *Schwarz Jubilee Volume* [1917], p. 183) of בר אבהן as 'one of noble ancestry' (*ein Mann der vornehmer*), and his regarding of this Talmudic passage as support for his contention that noble ancestry was superseded by the honour of the Torah — is without foundation.

worthy and virtuous.[14] This presumption was probably borne out by the prevailing social and spiritual situation. There is substantiating evidence in the Talmudic sources which reveal that moral defects and a certain religious lawlessness went hand in hand with the neglect of Torah study among certain types of *ʿamme ha-ʾareṣ*.

Nevertheless our Baraita does not seem to be of one complete unit. In its primary element Bet Shammai and Bet Hillel only differ in respect of the 'worthy, the humble' and the like. The last Tanna, however, to teach it inserted 'the sons of the fathers' in the text, a situation that emerged later, after the above-mentioned Houses of Study had ceased to exist.[15]

How powerful the process of aristocratic and professional consolidation in the world of the Sages had become is perhaps proved by the many traditions which assert that all Israel are free and equal in relation to Torah, in studying and inheriting it, for their wording proves that the dicta were intended as a protest against an actual situation that had spread to a noticeable extent.

In *Sifre Deuteronomy* § xlviii (ed. Finkelstein, p. 112), we find: 'You might say: Let the sons of the elders study; let the sons of the great study; let the sons of the prophets study. — Scripture therefore teaches: "But you shall surely observe all this commandment." Scripture teaches that all are equal in relation to Torah, and so it says: "Moses commanded the Torah to us, it is the inheritance of the congregation of Jacob," instead. And so it says: "You are standing this day, all of you, before the Lord your God; your heads, your tribes, your elders and your officers, even all the men of Israel".'

The *Midrash Tannaim* states it with even greater clarity (pp. 212–213): '*Morasha* and not *yerusha* — that the son of an ignoramus should not say: Since my father is no disciple of the Sages, what will it profit me if I learn Torah? — Instead "water shall flow from *dolav*" — from the *dallin* ("the poor") among them.'

It would seem that the following Baraita (*Tosefta Bava Meṣʿia*, iii, 25) also contains some similar protest. We learn: 'If one saw a pros-

14 This requirement first arises in connection with Rabban Gamliel (see n. 3), and in the words of R. Simeon b. Joḥai in *T.P. Avoda Zara*, ii, 41d: 'You are not permitted to impart (שקע lit. 'to sink') the words of Torah except to men who are fit', and similarly in other dicta, which it is unnecessary to enumerate.

15 So the existence of these 'Sons of Fathers' cannot be ascribed to the days of Bet Shammai and Bet Hillel, even if we accept the substance of the tradition below as authentic.

elyte coming to study Torah, one must not say: See who has come to study Torah? Someone who had eaten carcasses and carrion, insects and reptiles. And so it says: "And one man of the same place answered and said: And who is their father?" — Now does Torah have a father? Has it not been said before: "What is his name and what is his son's name, if you know?" And it says: "House and wealth are the inheritance of the fathers; but a prudent wife is from the Lord".'

Even though the substance of the tradition refers to oppressing a proselyte verbally and preventing him from studying Torah because he lacks the 'merit of the fathers' of an Israelite,[16] nevertheless it is apparent that the last remark which intends essentially to exclude 'patrimony' and the 'inheritance of the fathers' from the realm of Torah study in general is directed essentially at the situation mentioned above which existed in the world of the Sages.

The same would apply to the famous passage in *T.B. Nedarim* 81a: 'And why is it unusual for scholars to beget sons who become scholars? — Said R. Joseph: That it might not be said, that the Torah is their heritage.' It may reasonably be assumed that the passage is aimed at those who wished to make Torah learning hereditary and to confine it within the boundaries of the 'heritage of the fathers.'[17]

We have discerned two facts in the sources: First, the making of Torah learning and status, as well as the privileges these conferred, hereditary among the families of the Sages, through the medium of the 'Sons of the Sages' who constituted the candidates to inherit the advantages of their parents, and who formed some permanent stratum of their own, somewhere below the 'Sages' themselves, and similarly among the 'disciples'. Secondly, the existence of the tendency in the world of the Sages to restrict Torah study to their own circles by preventing the ignorant from raising up 'Sages' within the nation.[18]

16 We see that some found it necessary to deduce the right of the proselyte to study Torah from the Hagiographa (*Midrash Tehillim*, ed., Buber, ix, 2; *Num. Rabba*, xiii, 16).

17 Is something similar alluded to in R. Jose's dictum in *Avot*, ii, 12: 'And make yourself qualified to study Torah, for it does not come to you by inheritance'?

18 See *T.B. Sanhedrin* 96a: 'For R. Judah b. Bathyra sent from Nisibis... and take heed to [honour] the sons of the ignorant, for from them shall Torah go forth... They wrote on a scroll and sent it to Babylon. Certainly it is doubtful whether this tradition can correctly be ascribed to R. Judah b. Bathyra. (It is a variant Sugya as compared with *T.B. Berakhot* 8b, cf.

Now, before we proceed to explain this fact, we shall attempt as far as is possible, to determine the time when it emerged. We have seen that the situation definitely existed in the days of Rabbi (i.e., at the end, or close to the end, of his life), although 'Sons of Sages' are already found and described in the days of R. Eleazar b. Zadok. The reference here, however, appears to be to the latter R. Eleazar b. Zadok, an older contemporary of Rabbi. Accordingly, the earliest sources yielding evidence of the existence of this situation appear after the middle of the second century. At the other extreme, no evidence is available of its having endured beyond the middle of the fourth century.

It is my opinion that we are not entitled to regard this situation existing as a social reality either before or after the limits we have delineated, although some beginnings, possibly and probably, existed even beforehand and afterwards, and its consequences possibly survived to a greater or lesser extent.

What causes promoted the perpetuation of this phenomenon? It would seem to me that two factors were primarily responsible, their main influence being facilitated by circumstances operating in the latter half of the second century.

From the end of the second century onward the world of the Sages contained two elements of status and public function: First, the teaching of Torah to disciples — the Sage being the master-craftsman imparting specialised knowledge to those who sought instruction from him, and secondly, his serving as Parnas or spiritual leader, judge and decisor in many areas of public affairs.[19]

Historical development, at the beginning of the period under discussion, brought about the permanent and broad consolidation of these two social functions in Eretz-Israel.

ibid., where the tradition is ascribed to R. Joshua b. Levi), and Büchler, too, (pp. 19–20, n. 3) has doubted its accuracy, although his contention that R. Judah b. Ezekiel is the correct reading is neither conclusive nor even probably correct.

In *Pirqe de-Rabbenu Ha-Kadosh* (ed. Schoenblum 20b; see also Jellinek, *Bet Ha-Midrash, Ḥeder Bet*, p. 95; Higger, *Ḥoreb*, Vol. VI): 'R. Judah b. Bava commanded seven things to his disciples . . . Write a scroll and send to Babylon and say to them: . . . And take heed of the *'amme ha-'areṣ* for from them shall Torah go forth [to Israel].' Certainly here is a protest against those who would deny instruction to the sons of the *'amme ha-'areṣ*.

19 The direct influence of the Sages in the civic leadership of the settlements is evidenced especially by our finding Sages (at the end of the third century and during the first half of the fourth century) setting up Parnasim in the settlements (*T.P. Pe'a*, viii, 21a: [R. Jose, R. Ḥaggai, R. Ḥiyya b. Abba]).

In the generation of Usha, 'Torah study diminished' among the population and the glory of Torah and Torah scholars declined. The general collapse that befell Eretz-Israel after the Bar Kokhba rebellion, the political and economic depression, as well as the social and spiritual transformations, deliberately or unwittingly, prevented the masses from having contact with Torah study and teachers of Torah, and similarly deprived them of the ability to study or to spend time attending to their spiritual needs in general. Towards the end of the Antonine dynasty the economic situation improved somewhat; also the 'great accomplishments' of the Sages of Usha of the earlier time had also given a spiritual mold to the world of the masses. It was in this period that Rabbi began his patriarchate.

With the inception of the reign of the House of Severus, however, the economic situation became even more stabilised. Politically, too, the position of Jews in Eretz-Israel (and the diaspora as well) improved greatly. All these factors encouraged the intensification of the contact on the part of the masses with the 'national culture'— with Torah. From then onwards the numbers of those 'going to learn Torah' increased, just like those 'going to learn a trade', and became a common feature of the land.[20] The increase of the number preoccupied with Torah study was related to the preferential and secure social status accorded the Sages of those days in the settlements, something we shall deal with later.

In our period, then, teaching attained the level of a craft and had assumed all the conspicuous features of all the crafts.[21]

Now, the sources indicate that during our period, crafts were concentrated within the bounds of the family, and were passed on from father to son as an inheritance, a fact that had existed in Israel even earlier, just as it was current among other peoples in various ages.

Perhaps it would be worthwhile to examine the evidences. Few as the sources happen to be, they are sufficient to yield up the main substance of the subject. R. Joḥanan's dictum (*'Arakhin* 16b) is well known: 'One should never change his own or his father's craft.'

Even more cogent are the following illustrative stories. We read in *Midrash Samuel* xiii (ed. Buber, pp. 84–85): 'This may be compared

20 See for instance, *Tosefta Bava Batra* vi, 4: 'Brothers, one of whom took 200 zuz and went to study Torah or to learn a trade . . .'

21 I intend to return at some opportune time to deal with the subject of the economic, social and religious class in Eretz-Israel, in particular during the period under discussion.

to a certain fuller[22] who died and left an only son. His mother would take him to some craft, and he would run away. She brought him to the synagogue, and he ran away. She said: The only way to remedy the situation is to teach him his father's occupation. She went and brought him to a friend of his father. She said to him: Here, teach him his father's occupation . . .'[23]

Similarly, in *Pesiqta de-R. Kahana*, *Vayehi beshallaḥ* (ed. Buber, pp. 92–93): 'R. Eleazar b. R. Simeon was appointed superintendent of forced public labour . . .[24] Once Elijah of blessed memory appeared to him in the form of an old man . . . He said to him: All this trouble[25] has come upon you because it was not good enough for you to take up[26] the occupation of your fathers.'[27]

22 The 'fuller' is a familiar character in the Aggada of the Sages. Here is one of the 'fuller parables'.

23 In accordance with our method, we learn from this fascinating anecdote how widowed mothers struggled to elevate their sons above the lowly occupations of their fathers — but were unsuccessful and, in addition, how the craftsmen themselves were opposed to youths seeking to rise above their own station.

24 אנגרבטוס — ἀγγαρεύτης. The person in charge of, and appointed over, the forced labour service of the government. The expression occurs frequently in Egyptian papyri of the Imperial and Byzantine periods. It seems to me that the ascription of this office to R. Eleazar b. R. Simeon by this Aggada, is tied up with the fact that this same Aggada (see *ibid.* 91b) attributes the exercise of the office of chief of police to him and as I have suggested earlier, in *Yedi'ot Ha-Ḥevra La-Ḥakirat Ereṣ Israel Va-Atiqoteha* XIV, (1947), 12–14, the name ἀρχιριπάριος, head of the *riparii*, should be taken to mean head of the city police, since the 'ριπάριοι appear frequently in this sense in the papyri of the fourth–sixth centuries. See the Hebrew edition of this work, Vol. I, pp. 88 ff.

Indeed, in the papyri (fifth century) we find, once or twice, that the same persons who exercised the office of *riparii* at the same time fulfilled the function of ἀγγαρεύται. It is reasonable to conclude, then, that it was customary in later times to combine both functions in practice at times.

25 The expression טרופתא has not been elucidated by scholars. It seems possible that it is indeed θλίψις which signifies distress, trouble, difficulty.

26 תופס = take hold of, take up.

27 See also *T.P. Rosh Ha-Shana*, i, 57b: 'And the Rabbis say: To a doctor who had a bag of medicines. When his son grew up, he gave it to him.' Cf. Kraus, *Talmudische Archäeologie*, Vol. II, pp. 254–255. On the concentration of certain occupations in the families of the craftsmen's societies, as a matter of inheritance, in the Roman Orient during the Empire, see Rostowzew, *Gesellschaft und Wirtschaft*, II. As for the monopolisation of certain skills connected with the Temple, when it stood, cf. the action of the house of Garmu and of Abtinas 'who would not teach' others their skills, which they regarded as a family inheritance. (See Appendix.)

The nature of the Sages' instruction as a specialised craft made it more readily absorbable in the 'secondary education' of the 'study houses' for boys, which almost definitely existed after the Bar Kokhba rebellion.[28] Although the instruction imparted by the Sages (especially the greatest among them) was for the most part given to adult disciples in the domain of the *Bet Ha-Midrash* (or else to elderly individuals) and to *ḥaverim*, there were also Sages who served as Mishna teachers in the House of Learning (these, too, being sometimes referred to as *Bate Midrash*).[29] Now, for teaching to assume the character of a craft was made possible to a great extent by the practice of charging fees which made its appearance for the first time at approximately the beginning of the period under discussion. Taking fees must certainly have been more prevalent in the 'Learning Houses', there being much evidence of this practice, which took the form of a fixed salary paid by the city or else of individuals making the payments.

There is no room for any doubt, however, that even for instruction on the highest level, teachers took fees directly from their pupils. We learn in *T.B. Bekhorot* 29a: ' "Even as the Lord, my God commanded" — just as I teach gratuitously, so shall you teach gratuitously. And from where is it deduced that if one cannot find someone to teach him gratuitously, he must pay for learning? — It states, "Buy truth." And from where do we derive that one should not say: Just as I paid to learn Torah, so will I take a fee for teaching it? — It states: "And do not sell".' It follows logically that here the reference is to an individual adult being taught by a great scholar and not to a youth being educated in a House of Learning.

28 *T.P. Ḥagiga* i, 76c: 'R. Simeon b. Joḥai taught: If you see towns that have been removed from their sites in Eretz Israel, know that this is in consequence of their not keeping up the wages of the scribes and Mishna teachers (see the parallels in the Midrashim). As for the Aggada of the 'four hundred and eight' houses of scribes and of 'Talmud' which stood in Jerusalem up till the Destruction (R. Pinḥas in the name of R. Osha'ya) — *T.P. Megilla* iii, 73d ('Three hundred and ninety' — in *T.B. Ketubbot* 105a, *Bate Midrashot* instead of *Bate Talmud*) — no conclusions may be inferred from it.

29 See end of preceding note. Other such instances are found elsewhere. See *Gen. Rabba* lxiii, ed. Theodor-Albeck, p. 693. As for the Sages, of whom many were outstanding and who served in the Talmud Houses, cf. Levi who was appointed 'lecturer, superintendent, Bible and Mishna teacher' in Simonia (*T.P. Yevamot* xii, 13a). The same applies to the Babylonian who was dispatched to Baṣra by Resh Laqish and R. Joḥanan, according to the Midrashic tradition (*Deut. Rabba*, ed. Lieberman, pp. 60–61).

The same is evident from the Baraita in *Avot de-R. Nathan* (Version I, xvii; ed. Schechter, p. 65): 'R. Jose says: "Let the property of your friend be as precious to you as your own" . . . How so? . . . Another explanation: How so? At the time when the disciple of the wise comes in to you, if you are capable of teaching him, teach him; if not, dismiss him forthwith and do not take his money from him . . .'[30]

The practice did not, however, spread to any appreciable extent, and there were some who objected to it, a result indirectly related to the opposition of the Sages to making Torah teaching a profession, and to the very idea of Torah learning being hereditary, a subject to which we shall revert below.

As to the other role of the Sage, his serving as communal leader and spiritual Parnas, although this did not usually entail local office, this could also promote (or make prevalent) the practice of inheritance in the world of the Sages. Yet, here too, it was only after the days of Rabbi and onward, that permanent status in communal leadership in the settlements, proved by the recurrent title among Tannaim, 'appointed over the public' in conjunction with ordination by the Sages, became, it seems reasonable to assert, widespread or entrenched.[31] In both areas, then, circumstances prevailing at the

30 Although the passage 'And do not take money from him' is missing from the Ms. commentary on *Avot*, it is clear that this is the correct reading, since the entire dictum is aimed at elucidating R. Jose's warning: 'Let your friend's property be as dear to you as your own.'

The image of the teacher that emerges from the passage below is of a person renowned as erudite in knowledge of the Torah who comes to another city (or who lives in his city to whom someone from another city comes in order to acquire wisdom), but does possess sufficient learning to disseminate to others. So he devises schemes to conceal this fact, while he nevertheless continues to take his salary. This characterisation calls the Sophists to mind, 'who go from city to city' to teach their doctrines to the sons of the rich who seek wisdom, as we know from Plato's works.

Perhaps the tradition in *Midrash Tehillim* (ed. Buber, p. 59b) gives proof that the practice of taking pay for teaching had become widespread, since it sets Hillel and Shammai apart as not teaching Torah for pay.

The Sages sought to make the acceptance of remuneration for teaching Mishna permissible in the end, by stating that 'they take wages for remaining unemployed' (*T.P. Nedarim* iv, 38c and in several instances in Midrashim. Here Mishna teachers are spoken of), just as they finally permitted the *dayyan* to accept 'wages for remaining unemployed' (*T.P. Sanhedrin* i, 18b). This is essentially a forced dispensation for a practice that had become increasingly widespread by force of circumstances.

31 See above pp. 413, 428–30.

time caused the situation to arise,[32] for the practice of inheriting spiritual leadership among the Sages was bound up with the hereditary rights to public office among the city Parnasim in the settlements, a subject we must examine briefly as it affects the subject under discussion.

Several Tannaitic traditions mention the Halakha pertaining to hereditary office, for so we learn from *Sifre Deuteronomy* (§162; ed. Finkelstein, pp. 212–213): ' "He and his sons" — if he dies, his son succeeds him. I only deduce this; from where is it inferred that the sons of all Jewish Parnasim succeed their fathers? — Scripture states: "He and his sons in the midst of Israel".'[33] Similarly, we learn from *Tosefta Sheqalim* ii, 17: 'Whoever has a son, the son takes precedence; a brother — he takes precedence; whoever takes precedence in inheritance takes precedence in holding office, if only he behaves like his father.' We learn here of precedence (not as a complete right) as it affects the heirs of office-holders. The Baraita, however, speaks of Parnasim in the Temple. True, the Halakha first lays down that Priests, Levites and Israelites are eligible to become treasurers and trustees. It is clear, however, that in practice the Priests arrogated these offices to themselves.[34] And it is reasonable to assume

32 Origen (*Homilide*, Num. xxii, 4) testifies to bishops in his days who had willed their positions to their sons and relatives. This, it may be inferred, was also connected with the consolidation of the monarchial bishopry during the course of the second century.

33 We read in *Midrash Tannaim*, p. 106: 'Just as the monarchy is inherited by sons so is the High Priesthood inherited by sons, as is said: "And the priest anointed in his stead", and so in regard to all hereditary offices and appointments, from father to son, to grandson, etc.' The language of the passage proves, however, that it is no more than a paraphrase of Maimonides' Code, Laws of Kings, i, 7.

34 *Tosefta Menaḥot*, xiii, 21 (*T.B. Pesahim* 57a): 'Abba Saul and Abba Jose b. Joḥanan, the man of Jerusalem, would say: Woe is me because of the house of Boethius . . . for they are High Priests and their sons, treasurers, and their sons-in-law, trustees' (the sons-in-law too, were presumably priests, since in practice the priests were accustomed to marry within their own tribe). In *T.P. Horayot*, iii, 48b, we learn: 'The head of the father's house takes precedence over the trustee, and the trustee takes precedence over the treasurer, and the treasurer takes precedence over an ordinary priest,' etc., which teaches you that even the trustee and treasurer were priests. Similarly the Baraita in Sifre, *Deuteronomy* § cxvi (ed. Horowitz, p. 131): ' "And they shall escort you and serve you" — in their service. Appoint treasurers and trustees from among them . . .' which teaches that these were to be Levites and not Israelites (and similarly, it is proved by I Chron. 28–29; II Chron. xxxi, 11–19, that Levites functioned in the area of the financial supervision

that among 'the great personalities of the Priesthood' the practice of inheriting office was more likely to become entrenched than in other areas.[35]

In Sifra, however, we learn (*Behar* § ii; ed. Weiss 107a) concerning the Hebrew slave who goes free in the Jubilee year: 'Another explanation: "And you shall return every man unto his possession, and you shall return every man unto his family" — he returns to what is presumed to be his family, the words of R. Meir; R. Judah says: He returns "to his possession and unto his family" but not to reassume any office he had held, and he says so of the exile as well.'

What the Sifra alludes to here is elucidated in a Baraita in the Babylonian Talmud (*Makkot* 13a): 'And so in reference to the exile, as is taught in a Baraita: "The murderer shall return to the land of his possession" — he returns to the "land of his possession" but not to what (office) his father had held. These are the words of R. Meir. R. Judah says: He also returns to what his fathers had held.'[36]

Accordingly, an ordinary office-holder acquires a proprietary right to it from his 'fathers', as a family inheritance.[37] This last tradition is, in our eyes, more conclusive since it quite innocently testifies to some actually existing situation, unlike the first Baraitot which merely teach laws.

This same evidence is corroborated by the Mishna, *Avot* ii, 2: 'Rabban Gamaliel b. R. Judah the Prince said: Torah study combined with some earthly occupation is good, for the exertion involved in the two of them makes sin be forgotten . . . and let all employed with the public act with them for the sake of Heaven, for the merit of

of the Temple). See Büchler, *Die Priester und der Cultus*, etc. pp. 94–97; Schürer, *Geschichte*[4] II, p. 326; Jeremias, *Jerusalem zur Zeit Jesu*, II, pp. 23–32. These observations should be added to their remarks.

35 Here the passage in Sifra, *Shemini* (ed. Weiss, 47a; *Pesiqta de-R. Kahana*, ed. Buber, p. 173b; *Lev. Rabba* xx, 11) is pertinent: 'Had Nadab and Abihu had children they would have taken precedence over Eleazar and Ittamar, for whoever takes precedence in inheritance takes precedence in honour.' (According to Midrashic tradition, Nadab and Abihu were, as is known 'Deputy Priests').

36 See also Sifre, *Num.* §160 (ed. Horowitz, p. 220).

37 It may be assumed that the Tannaim did not differ on the fact itself, but on the restoration of the slave and exile to their former office, just as Amoraim differed on whether great persons who had sinned were to be restored to their former station after they had been deposed and punished, or not. See, for instance, *T.P. Sanhedrin* ii, 19d. Or do they, perhaps, differ on the preemptive rights of families altogether?

their fathers sustains them and their righteousness endures for ever.'[38]

Certainly the fathers' merits only apply to those who were employed with the public, as some of the Rishonim have explained,[39] and not the 'merit of the fathers' of the entire community. This teaches, then, that communal leaders as such were 'sons of fathers', that is to say, the sons of the Parnasim.[40]

There still remains the evidence of Epiphanius. He wrote:

> Ὡς δὲ ἐν τούτοις κατετρίβετο ἁδρύνεται ὁ παῖς ὁ καταλεφθεὶς ὑπὸ Ἑλλὴλ εἰς πατριαρχίαν τρεφόμενος. οὐδεὶς γὰρ ἁρπάζει τὰς ἀρχὰς παρὰ τοῖς Ἰουδαίοις, ἀλλὰ υἱὸς πατέρα διαδέχεται. (Panarion, *haeres.* 30, 7, 1; ed. Holl I, 341–342; ed. Dindorfius II 97). ('Those days when [Joseph] was involved in these difficulties, the son that was left by Hillel [when he died] and had been raised to succeed to the Patriarchate became of age; since one does not confer office on his own among Jews; instead the son succeeds his father.')

Apparently, the Church Father referred to the Jewish practice of offices being hereditary. The main purpose of the passage, however, is to explain the fact that the son of the Patriarch succeeds his father. So it is doubtful whether his generalisation is reliable. As is known, Epiphanius is not generally considered accurate in respect of the Sages. It is possible, then, that he was expressing his own opinion, and not writing from actual knowledge, when he broadened the application of the practice of inheritance from that of the Patriarchate to include all other offices as well.

From the sum of the sources we have transcribed, however, we learn that transmitting office by inheritance was practiced in Tannaitic times. To what extent was this a continuation of an earlier tradition existing from the time of the Second Temple onwards? This is difficult to determine, although it would not be far-fetched to fix a certain limit by conjecture.[41]

38 In *Avot de-R. Natan*, Version II, xxxii: 'R. Gamliel (Beribi) says: Those who hold sway over the public do not in truth toil with them, for the covenant of their fathers helps them.'

39 Zuri, *The Rule of the Patriarchate and Council* (Hebrew), I, 3, p. 168.

40 Like 'the sprinkler the son of a sprinkler' (*T.B. Berakhot* 28a; *T.P. ibid.* iv, 7d; *Ta'anit*, iv, 67d). This requires a separate study, which is out of place here.

41 The assumption (Funk, *MGWJ*, 1911, p. 706) that membership in the Sanhedrin passed on from father to son during the existence of the Temple

Yet that earlier existing situation was capable of increasing in strength and becoming more widespread on account of certain general socio-historical factors. From the days of the House of Severus and onwards, the position of the *Bouleutai*, who assumed public leadership in the settlements, continued to become more firmly entrenched in the cities organised after the pattern of the Greek πόλεις. This process was also current in Palestinian cities populated by Jews, the autonomous rule of which was in Jewish hands. In the course of time, that ruling class confined the right to leadership to certain families by means of inheritance rights which had their basis in government laws.[42]

This general development was certainly not restricted to those settlements organised after the pattern of the polis, and it is logical to assume that it penetrated to the rest of the settlements in the land.[43]

When we come to deal finally, however, with the extent to which it was in force and the duration of its existence, we become obliged to turn once more to the practice of hereditary office, to determine to what extent it was prevalent in our period. For even the law of inheritance (or precedence in inheritance) in holding office was undoubtedly no established, widespread practice, entrenched in the nation in the days with which we are dealing, although it was a recognisable fact and served as the sign of powerful social trends. Several considerations will make the assumption more acceptable, that a tradition of freedom did exist in Eretz-Israel and the diaspora, and that

is unfounded. Were we able to rely on the Mishna, *Sanhedrin* iv, 4, we would infer that this was not so. The same applies to the tradition of R. Jose (*Tosefta Ḥagiga* ii, 2; *Sanhedrin* vii, 1; *T.B. Sanhedrin* 88b; *T.P. ibid.* i, 19c) concerning Sages who were appointed to the Sanhedrin. 'They would send and investigate whoever was wise and humble . . . and would bring him up and seat him on the Temple Mount' etc. But there is no mention of 'sons of fathers'.

Certainly, the headship of Zimri, the founder of the colony of Bathyra in Transjordan, passed over to his son (Jacimus) and his grandson (Philip), *Ant.* xvii, 2, 3. In respect of the office of Chief Parnas however, that practice continued even after the Destruction. Moreover, this was essentially a family colony, the original settlers being members of a single family. The same applied to leadership in the first Judeo-Christian community in Jerusalem, which passed over to James, Jesus' brother, and afterwards to Calops, also of the same family. For here, too, this was the top leadership.

42 Presumably from the beginning of the third century. See Rostowzew. *Gesellschaft und Wirtschaft*, II, p. 143; Abbott and Johnson, *The Municipal Administration in the Roman Empire*, p. 113.

43 See above, p. 428.

the populace did wield influence in the appointment of their leaders, a tradition which increased in strength as opposition to it developed.[44] And the Halakha itself testifies to this.

We have learned from *Torat Kohanim* (*Ṣav*, v; ed. Weiss, 31b; *T.B. Yoma* 72b–73a; *T.P. ibid.*, i, 38d; *Horayot*, iii, 47d): 'One might assume that even the Anointed for Battle should be included (he, too, having to offer a tenth of an Ephah, like the High Priest), Scripture therefore teaches: "Seven days shall the son that is priest in his stead dress in them, even he who comes into the Tent of Meeting to serve in holiness" — the one who comes into the tent to serve in holiness is the son who comes in his place. This excludes the Anointed for Battle who does not come into the tent of meeting to serve in holiness.'

The Anointed for Battle is second in rank to the High Priest (as we have been taught by the Tosefta, *Horayot* ii, 10): 'The anointed with oil takes precedence over the Wearer of the many garments, and the Wearer of the many garments takes precedence over the Anointed for Battle, and the Anointed for Battle takes precedence over the Deputy, etc.).[45] Nevertheless, he was deprived of any heredi-

44 See above, p. 387, n. 42; p. 414. To what extent the Sages opposed the appointment of the pedigreed and nobly born as Parnasim can be inferred from the remarks of R. Joḥanan in the name of R. Simeon b. R. Jehoṣadaq in *T.B. Yoma* 22b: 'One should not be appointed *Parnas* of a community unless he has a basket of reptiles on his back, so that if he become arrogant, one could tell him: Turn around.'

45 In the Baraita in *T.B. Ta'anit* 31a, however, we learn: 'The daughter of the High Priest borrows from the daughter of the Deputy, and the daughter of the Deputy borrows from the daughter of the Anointed for Battle' etc., which teaches that the Deputy takes precedence over the Anointed for Battle. The traditions contradict one another.

The Baraita in *T.P. Horayot* iii, 48a, however, teaches: 'The King takes precedence over the High Priest; the High Priest takes precedence over the prophet; the prophet takes precedence over the Anointed for War; the Anointed for War takes precedence over the head of the Guard; the head of the Guard takes precedence over the [head of] the father's house; the [head of the] father's house over the trustee; the trustee takes precedence over the treasurer,' etc. Here, then, after the High Priest and prophet, the Anointed for Battle takes precedence over all degrees of the priesthood. We can learn more about this from the *Book of Maccabees* i, 3, 56 which deals with Judah officiating as Anointed for Battle. (*II Maccabees* ii, 8, 23 makes it appear that his brother, Eleazar, performed this function.)

Essentially, it is clear, however, from the Baraita in *Torat Kohanim* under discussion that, with the exception of the High Priesthood, heredity played no part in the priesthood, as opposed to the Baraita in Sifre, *Deuteronomy*,

tary right and this applies with even greater force to the ordinary priests,[46] and even more so to office-holding in Israel.

The opposition to hereditary office grew stronger in the world of the Tannaim, and the controversy might well be regarded as a reflection of an actual struggle in public life.[47]

We have already dealt with the evidence of the widespread opposition to hereditary rights on the part of the Sages, which became increasingly crystallised, and additional proofs of this are available.[48]

which extends the application of the law of inheritance to all offices and in every location.

46 For even in the area of degrees and offices in the Temple, the appointment of priests and Levites was in some way dependent upon public consent (how the appointments were made is not clear, and perhaps the 'public' was merely all the priests in general), as we learn from the Mishna, *Sheqalim* v, 3: 'There were no less than seven trustees . . . except for Aḥija who was over intestinal illness and Eleazar who was over the veil, for the majority had accepted them over themselves.' In practice, heredity was not absolutely entrenched even in the High Priesthood (see above, p. 59). Even the zealots who had chosen Phanni of the village of Aphthia by lot 'and had based this evil practice on law' (*Wars* iv, 3, 8) did not do so in completely arbitrary fashion. (Even in our sources no objection was raised against choosing this person by lot, *Tosefta Yoma* i, 6, and the parallels.)

47 From the remarks of R. Huna (the second, in Eretz-Israel) it follows that anyone could obtain an appointment as Parnas when he so desired (*Lev. Rabba* xxv, 1): 'If a man falls into sin and incurs the death penalty by Heaven, what shall he do to live? If he was accustomed to study one folio, he should study two folios . . . if he is not accustomed to read Scripture or study Mishna, what shall he do to live? Let him go and become a Parnas of the public and a charity treasurer and live.'

48 The allusions in the sources to the existence of the tendency among Sages to restrict Torah to the world of the rich and 'great' should be examined in connection with our topic. *Avot de-R. Natan* Version I, xl, ascribes the tradition to R. Gamliel the Elder: 'R. Gamliel expounded four things in reference to disciples: A ritually impure fish and a ritually pure fish . . . What constitutes an impure fish? A son of poor (parents) who studied Scripture, Mishna, Halakhot and Aggadot and has no understanding. What constitutes a pure fish? This is the son of rich (parents) who studied Scripture, Mishna, Halakhot and Aggadot,' etc.

Proof is also furnished by the following Baraita, which presumably raises its objection to this tendency, as it appears in Sifre, *Deuteronomy* §345: 'From "an inheritance of the congregation of Jacob" I infer that the sons of kings (of the nobility, the wealthy and pedigreed) inherit. From where, that the sons of the small (the common people) inherit? Scripture teaches: "You are standing this day, all of you" ("all the men of Israel").'

The same emerges from the statement (*T.B. Nedarim* 85a): 'Take heed of the children of the poor for from them shall Torah go forth.' (See also the remark in *Pirqe de-Rabbenu Ha-Kadosh*, mentioned above, n. 19). Although

From the absence of any signs in the sources of the persistence of this situation beyond the fourth century,[49] we are entitled to conclude that the tendency for an aristocratic and professional class to crystallise in the world of the Sages gradually disappeared. The first cause of this was the dissemination of Torah in all its aspects among the broad strata of the population, something which detracted very much from the uniqueness of the appointed, ordained Sage. The proliferation of non-ordained Sages, who held no permanent position in public leadership, but, nevertheless, sporadically discharged public functions, also had the effect of detracting indirectly from the pre-eminent status of the appointees. This is how it came about that the leadership status of the Sages was not very firmly grounded. Furthermore, the very increase in the number of the educated automatically pressed against and finally burst the confines of the 'sons of fathers'.[50] And it should be mentioned here that from the second to the fourth centuries, scholars and disciples immigrating to Eretz-Israel from Babylon and other diaspora communities kept increasing in number. Many of them received 'appointments' and became communal leaders. These immigrants helped in great measure to undermine the dynastic restrictions on Torah spiritual-leadership — for heredity could only have been the privilege of families residing in the locality for generations, and not of recently arrived foreigners.

the tendency should be ascribed to powerful circles among the Sages, this is connected, in my opinion, with the social class that became entrenched as communal leaders among the Sages as a whole. Distinguished ancestry and privileged economic status strengthened their ability to obtain the office of Parnas, especially under the prevailing social circumstances which developed in Palestine and the Roman world generally from the fourth to the sixth centuries. This is what the author of the statement in *Avot de-R. Nathan* had in mind (he should not be regarded, indeed, as R. Gamliel the Elder, since this work ascribes many dicta of later origin to the ancients). 'A son of wealthy parents who has understanding' signifies one who has the understanding of life requisite for dealing with people and for preoccupation with public affairs. ('Every scholar who has no understanding . . .')

49 The statement, 'the son of a Sage is half a Sage', transcribed in *Midrash Ha-Gadol, Gen.*, ed. Schechter, p. 310, and in *Yalkut Shim'oni* on the Torah, *Vayera* §95 from *Pirqe de-R. Eliezer* (it is not found in our editions, *ibid.*) is not relevant to our discussion, because its substance is that the son of a Sage also possesses some understanding in deducing one thing from another in worldly affairs. See the episode recorded in *Pirqe de-R. Eliezer*, xxx.

50 On the growth and spread of Torah learning among the population at the beginning of the third century, see p. 428, n. 143.

Opposition to professional exclusiveness did not cease at any time among the Sages. The tradition of earlier generations, which considered teaching Torah a privilege and a Divine commandment, and recoiled from imputing the nature of a craft to it, persisted among many of the Sages and their disciples even in later generations. What aided them in their stand was, first, that many were accustomed to 'benefit scholars, who generally lived in poverty, from their estate'. Moreover, the contributions which were collected in the diaspora and remitted for the needs of the Sages (either directly or through the Patriarchs) also helped to make the Sages independent, not having to accept remuneration for their Torah. Needless to say, the religious duty of engaging in manual labour as such as the means by which to escape from making the teaching of Torah a gainful occupation, a commandment which many scholars fulfilled in practice, was also a contributing factor in restricting the process of professionalization in the world of the Sages. The combination of these factors contributed, then, to the maintenance of the popular nature of, and freedom in, the realm of Torah and prevented the rise and consolidation of a spiritual aristocracy, a process which had extended over generations and was impelled by powerful forces from within and without.[51]

51 This last topic which I have not dealt with extensively, requires broad clarification, which is not in place in these lines. It is worthwhile noting, however, that even with the spread of hereditary office in the diaspora, the democratic tradition in the appointment of Parnasim was not abolished. This conclusion is to be drawn from the *Historia Augusta*, Severus Al. 45 (ed. Hohl I, p. 287), which speaks of the Emperor being accustomed to publicize the names of the candidates to serve as rulers of hyparchies and to ask the populace to voice their objections to the proposed individuals, after the manner of the Jews and Christians — 'in praedicandis sacerdo tibus, qui ordinandi sunt' ('in proclaiming [informing] the priests who had to be appointed'). Certainly, the view is widely held by recent scholars that this is a later work, dating from the days of Julian (*HTLR*, 1934, p. 176). In *Antiquité Classique*, Mattingly (1946, pp. 213–215) wants to fix the time of its composition at about 350 C.E. Needless to say, it is doubtful whether the entire substance of the information belongs to the days of Severus Alexander (Geffcken, *Hermes*, 1920, p. 286). At all events, the evidence cannot be dismissed out of hand. Indeed, it was customary in many communities to have the populace participate in the appointment of their administrators. It is likely that a triple approach existed, and grew steadily stronger, in the appointment of the heads of communities and settlements (in the diaspora and in Eretz-Israel itself): (i) Inheritance on the part of the pedigreed, (ii) appointment by the Patriarch, (iii) election by the communities.

Appendix

Inheritance in teaching is also to be found among Jewish Christian 'instructors of the Law' in Eretz-Israel in the second century, as we learn from the Epistle of Peter appended at the beginning of Clement's *Homiliae* (*Patrologia Graeca,* vol II, col. 32) where the teacher sent through him to 'my brother, the master' (Jacob) undertakes by oath that should he go to some other locality, he would not take the books with him, but deposit them with the Bishop, etc.

Εἴ δὲ καὶ τύχοι με νοσῆσαι καὶ τὸν θάνατον ὑποπτεῦσαι, ἐὰν ἄτεκνος ὁμοίως ποιήσω. 'Αλλ εἰ καὶ τελευτῶ, τέκνον ἔχων οὐκ ἄξιον ἢ μηδέπω δυνάμενον, ὁμοίως ποιήσω. Τῷ γὰρ ἐπισκόπῳ μου παρακαταθήσομαι, ἵνα εἰ μὲν τύχοι ἐφ' ἡλικίας γενόμενος ἄξιος εἶναι τῆς πιστεως ὡς πατρῴαν παρακαταθήκην τῷ τέκνῳ ἀποδώσῃ κατὰ τὸν τῆς διαμαρτυρίας λόγον. ('If I become ill and likely to die childless, I shall do likewise. Should I die and leave a son unfit to [teach] or not yet ready for this [on account of his age], I shall do so again, for I will deposit them [the above-mentioned books], with my Bishop with the stipulation that he restore them to him [the son] as his patrimony when he becomes of age and is worthy of trust'.)

These Jewish Christian teachers took no part in the leadership of their communities. Their sole function was to 'teach the Law'. Possibly, then, the practice of inheritance in their domain applied to the passing on of an occupation from father to son.

The very assumption, however, that we have an ancient Jewish 'heretical' source here is not certain. It is known that most contemporary scholars have held the opinion that a common source underlies Clement's two works, the *Homiliae* and the *Recognitiones* (and it, too, is a combination of other elements). The Epistle of Peter also belongs, according to this view, to a Jewish-Christian element in the second century. Recently, however, E. Schwarz has rejected the entire substance of this theory. He believes that these works are late, and flimsy figments of the imagination, without any substantive tradition. Nevertheless, he does not seem to have succeeded in refuting the view currently held by scholars, nor has he submitted any concrete substantiation of his view.

THE 'STRATEGOI' IN THE PALESTINIAN CITIES DURING THE ROMAN EPOCH*

Asher Gulack devoted his last research studies to the field of the socio-legal history of Jewry in Palestine during the period of the Roman Empire. In one of these studies,[1] the last to be published in its original form during his lifetime, the scholar dealt with the following two sources (which are really one), which pertain to the history of the administration of Eretz-Israel during that period, and the remittance of taxes to the government by the Jewish population in Palestine in respect of the autonomy that had been conferred on it.

T.P. Yoma i, 39a: 'Like this. The Bule and the Strategoi (אס[ט]רטגי) had a lawsuit. The case came before Rabbi, and he said: Is Bule not included in Strategoi? For what matter did it state: Bule and Strategoi? So he said: These shall give half and those shall give half.'

T.B. Bava Batra 143a: 'When R. Isaac b. Joseph came, he said: There was that *kalila* (aurum coronarium) which the Imperial government (דבי מלכא; var. lec.: דבי קיסרי) imposed on the Bule (אאבולי; Ms. אבולי) and the Strategoi (אאיסטרוגי; Ms. אאיסטרטיגי). Rabbi said: Bule shall give half and the Strategoi (איסטרוגי; Ms. איסטרטיגי) shall give half.'

After rightfully rejecting the dictionary definition of *strategoi* in its usual sense of 'military officers', Gulack puts forward the following suggestion, that the word in question should be read as איסטרטיגיא = στρατηγία, and taken to have the same connotation as is found in the Egyptian papyri: district administrators (νομός). The scholar presumes that in those days the same administrative order prevailed in Eretz-Israel as in Egypt, that is to say that the chief city (μητρόπολις) of the district had a Bule which was in charge of collecting government taxes within the city boundary alone, while

* In tribute to the memory of my late teacher, Prof. Asher Gulack, on the third anniversary of his death.

1 *Tarbiz*, 1940, pp. 119–122.

the remittance of the taxes from the rural settlements of the district was handled by the στρατηγός, the head of the district appointed by the government. Yet, even the Bule was under the supervision of the Strategos in its administering the tax collections. So the system operated and persisted till the fourth century, at which time the Strategos lost his authority and the entire district became incorporated in the territory of the city, which, through the Bule, henceforth conducted the tax collections in the villages and towns as well. According to this scholar's view, then, the case brought before Rabbi involved the following issue: The order of the government had levied the *kalila* (στέφανος, aurum coronarium) on the Bule and Strategoi without specifying what share each was to bear. Consequently the Bule became involved in litigation with the inhabitants of the towns and villages of the district, where taxes had previously been directly collected by the Strategos, on how the payment was to be divided. Rabbi ruled that each should pay half, since he relied upon the text of the order which spoke of Bule and Strategoi, for, indeed, the Bule were under the supervision of the Strategos. Had the order mentioned Strategia alone, then the Strategos would certainly have included the Bule of his district and exacted payment from the urban inhabitants as well.[2] Since, however, the order mentioned the two together, it followed that the intention of the document was that payment be divided equally between the city inhabitants and the villagers.

Further on, Gulack transcribes the reply of the Gemara to the explanation of Rabbi's verdict: 'There, previously when they wrote, they directed it to the Bule, and the Strategoi assisted them, and the government was aware that they were assisting. Why did it now

2 There is some reason for the standing of the Bule in Egypt (during the course of the third century), *vis-à-vis* the district — it enjoyed a certain authority even in the area of tax and finance in the area as a whole and it would choose many of the government officials in these matters. See Wilcken, *Chrestomathie*, 1_1, p. 38; Jones, *Cities of the Eastern Roman Empire*, pp. 311–312; Jouget, *La Vie municipale dans l'Egypt Romaine*, p. 461; Jones, *The Greek City* etc. (1940), I, p. 79; Oertel, *Die Liturgie*, p. 379; Rostowzew, *Social and Political History of the Roman Empire*, p. 379; Abbott and Johnson, *Municipal Administration* etc., p. 135. It is therefore possible to describe the administration of the Egyptian district in the period under discussion as some sort of Diarchy (Jones, *Cities* etc., p. 337). Furthermore the responsibility for collecting the taxes of the entire district was placed on the Bule (Abbott and Johnson, *op. cit.*, pp. 83, 134–135). This being so, it is doubtful whether the Strategoi was accustomed to interpret it as his function alone to encompass and include the Bule as well as a matter of course.

direct the order to both Bule and Strategoi? — Only to indicate that these should give half and those should give half. From this tradition, Gulack infers that the Bule was no longer included in the Strategia, but had assumed the principal role, while the Strategos only assisted. Having fixed the date of this tradition as the fourth century, he explains it against the background of the new situation that had arisen in Egypt in that period. In those days the Strategos had ceased functioning in that country, and the district had become incorporated within the territory of the city. It is to be presumed, then, in his view, that these administrative changes (or their like) had occurred simultaneously in Eretz-Israel as well, and so the Talmud could correctly give evidence that the Bule had now taken over the main role in collecting taxes, while the Strategia had become secondary.

Before we begin a detailed examination of this view, it would be worthwhile first to consider another interpretation, close to Gulack's view in its main substance, and which was first submitted by two other scholars, and then to examine both together.

In Frank Tenney's *Survey of Economic History of Ancient Rome*, XIV (1938), p. 234, Heichelheim also examines the noun איסטרוגי = στρατηγία (he relies solely on the tradition of the Babylonian Talmud), and explains it in the sense of 'the district' as such, that is to say: the aurum coronarium was imposed upon the city and the district (the rural settlements) and the prominent rural and urban inhabitants disagreed on how the payments were to be shared. This view is similar to Gulack's.

So, too, in his *Political and Social Leaders of the Jewish Community of* Sepphoris, p. 39, Büchler speaks of two sections of the population being responsible for tax collections: the wealthy citizens and the rich landowners. He also adopts the reading: στρατηγία.

Let us now examine these views together.

(1) Contrary to both interpretations, the districts in Eretz-Israel were never called by this name, but toparchies (τοπαρχίαι) instead, as we learn from Pliny and Josephus, as well as from *I Maccabees*.[3]

(2) The practice prevailing in the Roman provinces never recognized the existence of a πόλις unless it possessed a *territorium* which

3 In *I Maccabees*, however, the name νομός appears as well (as in Egypt). I have in mind to deal with the Strategoi in Eretz-Israel during the Second Temple period (including the στρατηγός τοῦ ἱεροῦ) and the districts (*pelakhim*) after the Destruction (in such places where no city government had been established).

was enclosed within the general periphery of the district. Generally speaking, wherever a polis was to be found, there was never any Strategia (or toparchy, or their like) and wherever a Strategia was to be found, there was no city. True, some isolated instances of this kind were to be found in Tracheae and Cappadocia; but even there, these were no longer in existence in the days of Trajan and Hadrian, at the time when the process of urbanisation had intensified in the provinces, which had declined socially and administratively, and the provincial districts had become the 'territories' of the cities.[4] Indeed, Jones presumes that even Sepphoris and Tiberias (in one of which, the previously mentioned incident had occurred, as we shall see below) did not at first rule over their districts. Even if we do accept the far-fetched thesis, however, Jones himself concedes that from Hadrian's time onwards, the districts became incorporated within the boundaries of those cities.[5]

(3) The administrative patterns and socio-economic conditions in Egypt during the Roman period differed in many fundamental respects from those prevailing generally in the rest of the provinces. Consequently we are not entitled to draw any analogies between what was practised there and the administrative situation in any other provinces. This distinction is especially relevant to our topic. For it is known that no Bule whatsoever was to be found in Egypt (it being unique in this respect among the countries of the Roman Empire) until Septimius Severus instituted it in Alexandria and the capital cities (μετροπόλεις) of the districts (νομοί). Yet the system described by Gulack was a mere passing phase even in Egypt, and lasted only until the end of the third century (202–297 C.E.); [that is to say], when Septimius Severus had decided to organise the methods of tax-collection and public service in Egypt on the lines obtaining in the Roman Empire as a whole (the Bule had demonstrated their efficiency in tax-collecting, and especially at the time when collective responsibility had been imposed on them for remitting the taxes of their cities[6]), for fiscal reasons he sought to avoid eradicating altogether the particular situation prevailing in the province. Hence, this can only be regarded as a prolonged transition from one system to another, arising out of the special conditions of that country. We apparently have no reason to exclude Eretz-Israel from the rest of

4 Jones, *The Greek City*, pp. 83, 10, 15, 178.
5 Jones, *The Cities*, p. 279.
6 Abbott and Johnson, *op. cit.*, p. 135.

the provinces in general, and to ascribe to it the anomaly which existed in Egypt during some specific period.

(4) According to the view of these scholars we would have to emend the word אוסטרטגי (איסטרוגי) in seven instances (in the Babylonian and Palestinian Talmuds), and read instead אסטרטגיא.

(5) The following, too, requires investigation, although, certainly, it is not sufficient to decide the issue. The passages in both Talmuds deal with an Halakhic problem: A fiscal obligation (or sum of money) had been levied on two bodies, the one consisting of numerous individuals, the other only of one or a few. Was the obligation to be divided equally per capita, or half and half between the two bodies? We are certainly not entitled to deduce or presume that the tax-paying inhabitants of Tiberias or Sepphoris were much fewer than the land-owners of the surrounding districts.

Consequently, it appears to me that the interpretations neither of Gulack nor of the other scholars are satisfactory.

It is my opinion that the name in question should be read as it is: אסטרטגי = στρατηνοί. These Strategoi were none other than the members of the executive authority of the autonomous city, similar to the archontes (ἄρχοντες). The argument mentioned in the sources occurred between the Bouleute — the Bule who constituted the legislative and consultative body of the city — and the Strategoi — the members of the executive, over the division of the payments levied on the city (alone) for the *kalila*, in respect of the decree which had certainly been formulated in the usual manner: στρατηγοῖς καὶ βουλῇ — ἄρχουσι κ. βουλῇ (καὶ δήμῳ) κτλ. We have, however, to verify the assumption, that Strategoi in this sense did in fact exist in Tiberias (or Sepphoris).[7]

That Strategoi in this sense did exist in the Roman period is well known both from the literature and inscriptions, especially *vis-à-vis* Asia Minor (and Greece).[8] As for the other provinces, we can only garner some scattered items of information, some of them doubtful, but at all events when considered together they prove that this

7 Since the Palestinian Talmud does not specify where the incident occurred, it should naturally be assumed to have been Tiberias, and since the other incident involving the crown tax (*T.B. Bava Batra* 8a) also occurred in that province; nevertheless it cannot be ruled out that the incident might have happened in Rabbi's city (Sepphoris, in that period).

8 Chapot, *La Province romaine proconsolaire d'Asie*, pp. 240 ff. See also Isidor Levi, *REG*, 1895, p. 210, et al.

situation did exist in the countries adjacent to Eretz-Israel and in Eretz-Israel itself.

(A) SYRIA (Mesopotamia)

(1) PALMYRA (Tadmor), CIS, No. 3932.

'The statue of יוליס אורליס זבדלא בר מלכו ברמלכו נשום who was the אסטרטג (Strategos) of Colonia (Palmyra) when Alexander (Severus) came . . . and he is רב שוק (the price controller) of the market . . ., the year 554 (242–243),' and in the Greek version of the inscription: στρατηγήσαντα — ἀγορανομήσαντα.

The civic-administrative function of the Strategos accordingly is shown to be the same as that of the *agoranomos*, the capacity in which that person served.

Ibid. No. 3934: 'The Bule and Demos of יוליס אורליס and גא — called סלוקוס בר עבינו [בר] עבינו who served them להון and was accepted over them as Strategos (function) . . . the year 566 (253–254).' Here then it is certainly unnecessary to say that this Strategos function is indeed municipal service (שיש ושפר להון 'to them' = to the people of the city, who had appointed him).

Ibid. No. 3939. The inscription tells of a statue erected in honour of Septimius Varod (son of Odinat) by the Strategos of the Colonia, and its Greek text has στρατηγὸς τῆς λαμπροτάτης κολωνείας.

Ibid. No. 3942, Greek. A statue erected in honour of the Septimius Varod mentioned above. λαμπρῶς στὸατηγήσαντα καὶ αγορανομήσαντα τῆς αὐτῆς μητροκολωνείας, Here, too, the Strategos serving as *agoranomos* is certainly a municipal appointee.

(2) EDESSA (Orhai).

In a deed of sale (of a slavewoman) written in Syriac in Edessa in 243 C.E. and found in the excavations at Dura-Europos[10] we find the signature: העמרותא (?) דמרקוס אורליס אנטיוכס הפוס רהומס (ἱππεὺς Ῥωμαῖος) בר בלשן ובאסטרטגותא דמרכוס אורלוס אבגר הפוס רהומס בר מענו בר אגא, ודאבגר בר חפסי בר ברכמר דתרתין זבנין. Torrey, who first published the document in *Zeitschrift für Semitistik*, X, pp. 36–37, translates the word אסטרטגותא as 'military command'. Now, first, what has 'military command' to do with the subordinate role mentioned after עמרותא? Furthermore, Torrey took no account of the last two words, דתרתין זבנין, which must certainly mean: '. . . in

9 'Who served in exemplary manner as Strategos and *agoranomos* of that Mother Colonia.'

10 See *Excavations* etc. (1936), p. 435.

Avgar bar Ḥofsi's second term as Strategos, for generally speaking the city Strategoi would serve for one year only (in all municipal offices of the polis). At that time, the two Strategoi served in Edessa (Marcus Aurelius and Avgar bar Ḥofsi). And Wells, too, *YCS*, Vol. V (1935), interpreted the text correctly.

The following source, however, can very likely prove that municipal Strategoi were common in the (later) Roman period in Syria as a whole.

The Syrio-Roman compilation of laws (end of the fifth century), ed. Bruns-Sachau, Ms. London, par. 8 (p. 6; Ms. Paris, p. 42) deals with someone who had died intestate and left a widow, and she refused to act as guardian or curator of the orphans. It concludes with: 'אן דין אפלא אנתתא דתסב טענא דבניה יתמא، נמוסא פקד לאסטרטיגא דמדינתא דאיתיהון רשנא דאנון נשלמון להון אסטרופא אן קורטור'. And these scholars translate the last part of the text as follows: '*So befieblt das Gesetz dem Strategos der Provinz* . . .' They took the word אסטרטגא to mean the governor of the province, but overlooked the continuation of the text which definitely excludes any such interpretation. Clearly, however, the words דאיתיהון רשנא are in apposition to, and explanatory of אסטרטגא, which has no specific connotation, and these רשנא are none other than πρώτοι τῆς πόλεως, the title indicating that they were members of the municipal administration. Land understood this correctly even earlier. He was the first to publish this compilation (*Anecdota Syriaca*, Vol. I, p. 131), and he translated: magistratus municipales (Urbis ατρατηγούς), i.e. principes lex jubet, etc.[11]

(B) BASHAN, HAURON, TRACHONITIS

Some inscriptions found in these areas testify to the existence of Strategoi in the villages, generally one Strategos for each settlement.[12] The following inscription found in Sha'ara in Trachonitis speaks of a body of Strategoi in that village: ὑπὲρ σωτηρίας Αὐτοκρατορος M. Αὐρηλίου Αντωνείνου καὶ Αὐρηλίου Οὐηρου, Πρόκλος Γερμανοῦ καὶ Σαῖος Σοβαίδου καὶ Ἄλεος Αβάδου ατρατηγοὶ ανέθηκαν ('Dedicated to the wellbeing of the Autocrat Marcus Aurelius Antoninus and Aurelius, by Proculus, son of Germanus and Saius son of Sobaidos and Aleos son of Abados the Strategos').[13]

11 Sachau himself retracted and later explained it correctly, *Syrische Rechtsbücher*, I.

12 These inscriptions are to be found in Lebas-Waddington and Enno Littmann.

13 Waddington, No. 2520; Littmann, No. 803.

The fact that a college of Strategoi existed in a single village dispenses with the assumption by Jones, *Cities of the Eastern Roman Empire*, p. 255, that these constituted some sort of survival of the earlier phylarches (φύλαρχοι heads of tribes), who ruled their tribe in the name of the Government. The implication would be that after a permanent rural regime had been instituted among these Arabs, the earlier name survived but in a different denotation, for the phylarchoi were always individuals. Consequently, once one encounters a body of Strategoi, one is compelled to conclude that these constituted some sort of municipal administration, modelled on the Strategoi of the cities. The substance of the matter may be explained in accordance with Harper's view, *YCS*, Vol. I, 1928, p. 112, that these villages (since they were located in vast areas where there were few cities) preserved their independence *vis-à-vis* the cities, and were even accorded some form of municipal organisation. Indeed, we do find other municipal institutions, such as σύνδικοι and ἔκδικοι, and even βουλευταί among them.[14] It must follow then, that the city Strategoi, who furnished the example for the village Strategoi, were common in that province.

(C) GERASA

Inscription No. 62, Kraeling, *Gerasa*, p. 404, middle of the third century: [Φλ(άουιος) Μου]νάτιος Φλ(αουίου) Μουνατίου (εκατοντάρχου) υἱὸς ἱππικὸς βουλ(ευτὴς) ἱερασ(αμενος) [ἁ]γνὸς ατρατη[γὸς] [τὸ πρὸ]ναιον τῆς κυρίας Αρτέμ[ιδ]ος ἐκ τῶν ἰδίων ἐψηφοθετη[σ]εν. ('Flavius Munatius son of Flavius Munatius the centurion of the equestrian order, member of the Bule, who served as pure priest and Strategos has erected the pronaeon of the lady Artemis out of his own funds'.)

As against the presumption (see Kraeling, *ibid.*) that here Strategos is used in its usual sense — as a Roman praetor (of Arabia) — one must first counter that this person also served as Bouleute and priest (in the city, in the temple of Artemis); and there is no room for doubting that his officiating as Strategos was the exercise of a municipal function. Moreover, the title ἁγνὸς στρατηγός, certainly indicates the same function, since this title which designates functions performed by the municipal governments in religious rites is found in connection with the governments of the cities.

Ibid. No. 191 (p. 442, middle of the third century). Φλ(άουιον) 'Αγριππεῖνο[ν] Φλ(αουίου) Εὐμένους ἐκ γένους εὐγ[ενοῦς] στρατηγὸν

14 Harper, *op. cit.*, pp. 143–145; Jalabert, *JGL*, vol. II, p. 352.

κα[ὶ πά]τρωνα τῆς κ[ολω]νείας Γ(αίος) 'Ιούλι[ος] Φίλιππος ὁ κ[αὶ] Σιμπλίκις τι[μῶν] τὸν ἑαυτοῦ πά[τρω]να εὐνοίας κ(αί) στοργῆς χάρ[ιν].

This person, Flavius Agrippinus Eumenus, is mentioned in another inscription as well (No. 159). There he is designated as serving in the capacity of ἐπιμελητής of the city. It is clear then that his serving as Strategos also indicates some municipal function.

Even though scholars cast doubt on it,[15] in connection with the matter under discussion, the following inscription, too, almost certainly shows that here, as well, the word does not signify anything more than in the above-mentioned inscriptions.

Ibid. No. 161 (p. 431, the fourth century). Αὐτοκράτορα Καίσαρα Φλ(αουιον) υ. υ. Οὐαλ(ήριον) Κωνστάντιον τὸν επιφανέστατον Καίσαρα Αὐρ(ήλιος) Τοργόνιος ὁ διασημότατος ἡγούμε[ν]ος τῆς ἐπαρχείου διὰ τῶν ἀπὸ στατηγιῶν.

It is most likely that the last-named were none other than a group of men who had first served in the capacity of Strategos in the city of Gerasa (and it was they who had erected the stone pillar in honour of Constantius on behalf of the governor of Arabia).

(D) GAZA

In his *Ecclesiastical History*, v, 3, Sozomen speaks of Miomes (the port of Gaza) which succeeded in liberating itself from dependence upon Gaza (a city, the majority of its inhabitants, Hellenists) through Constantius and organising itself as an independent city with the name of Κωνστάντια (Constantia) (all the inhabitants of this small city were Christians). Julian restored the previous situation. He annexed this settlement to the territory of Gaza, making the two one city — κοινοὶ δὲ αὐταῖς πολιτικοὶ ἄρχοντες καὶ στρατηγοί καὶ τὰ δημόσια πράγματα.

The archons and Strategoi here are certainly none other than the municipal executive of Gaza, and were called by both names together; and Sozomen's evidence is especially reliable, as far as we are concerned, because he was a native of that vicinity.

Now, as it appears, our sources, too, mention these Strategoi. Although they are mentioned without any qualification, nevertheless the authors of the Palestinian Aggada were, evidently, quite familiar with them.

Genesis Rabba, lvii; ed. Theodor, p. 625: 'R. Isaac said: It is written, "he was sitting" — they had appointed him arch-Strategos that day, so that a great man should not buy from an insignificant in-

15 See also Jones, *JRS*.

dividual.' Theodor interprets 'arch-Strategos' as 'Chief of the army officers'.

Obviously, in its Scriptural interpretations, the Aggada adopts the usage of its own days. Now it would be impossible to state of any city in the Roman Empire, that it had appointed any chief of its armed forces. This apart, his very appointment was only for the purpose of conducting negotiations with Abraham, the alien, who had come to purchase a burial plot there. It therefore seems certain that what we have here is the same title under discussion. Although we do not find 'arch-Strategos' elsewhere, nevertheless, the head of the council of archons-Strategoi was most probably named thus (and perhaps he was the Eponimus) similarly to the Pretonis. In the parallel in *Exodus Rabba*, xxxi, 17, however, the name appears in its usual form: 'Thereupon, they (the people of Hebron) went and appointed him אסטרטיגוס over them.'

Deuteronomy Rabba, iii, 3: 'R. Levi said: This may be compared to the friend of a king who had deposited some article with him. The king's friend died. His son came and claimed the article. The king said to him: Go, bring me two Strategoi and twelve Bouleute, and through them I will give you the article . . .' The combination of Strategos and Bouleute proves that here we are dealing with none other than the governing body of the city, and these certainly are the members of the municipal executive, as in the sources cited above[16] (so here, too, we find the Strategoi connected with the Bouleute, as we have seen in the passage of the Babylonian and Palestine Talmuds dealt with above).

These sources, it seems to me, provide a firm basis for our assumption that even in the countries near Eretz-Israel, as well as in Eretz-

16 Two Strategoi and twelve Bule were enumerated here because of the reference (Moses and Aaron and the Twelve Tribes). At all events we have already encountered two Strategoi in Edessa (and as has been noted, the city was a colonia then, with two heads, after the manner of the duoviri of the Roman cities). We read in *Massekhet Soferim*, xix, 7: 'On Rosh Ḥodesh the councils of Elders and Bouleute hold session . . .' (Such combinations of Elders and Bouleute, the spiritual and secular leaders, is found in *T.P. Sanhedrin*, i, 18c, and in the parallels: ' "And the craftsmen and the smiths a thousand" — R. Berekhia in the name of Rabbi: These are the associates (*ḥaverim*); and the Rabbis say: These are the Bouleute' etc.). And *ibid.* viii: 'And when he praises him, he praises him with the twelve nobles of the city and twelve *ḥaverim*' etc. It would appear that the *ḥaverim* are the Elders mentioned above, while the 'nobles of the city' are the Bouleute mentioned above. So there were actual localities (at the end of the sixth century) where twelve Bouleute served in the cities.

Israel itself, Strategoi, in the sense of municipal executives functioned in the cities (organised upon the lines of the Greek polis).[17]

We return to the exposition of the sources under discussion, but must first deal briefly with the person mentioned here and the time when the incident occurred. It is certainly possible to assume this 'Rabbi' to be R. Judah Nesi'a, for he is so designated in certain instances. Yet, apart from the fact that Rabbi generally signifies R. Judah the Prince, the two Talmuds tie this incident to the Halakha mentioned in Rabbi's name in the Tosefta, *Yoma* i, 5, and the Talmuds concerning the High Priest taking half (or five loaves). Now since the title 'Rabbi' is only rarely found in Tannaitic sources as designating R. Judah Nesi'a, we should not follow the few instances but assume with the Talmuds that this 'Rabbi' is, as usual, R. Judah the Prince.

As for the time when the incident occurred, this would depend upon the chronology of Rabbi's life. It is known that scholars differ on this score. Some place his life earlier and have it end in the last days of Commodus, while others place it later. The main problem hinges on the identity of Antoninus, Rabbi's companion. Who was he? (Here the scholars differ. They consider all the emperors, beginning with Antoninus Pius and ending with Alexander Severus, as possibilities). Yet it appears that we should adopt the view of the scholars who take Antoninus to be Caraccala. (It is out of place here to enumerate all the arguments in favour of this assumption; and it is possible to adduce an additional proof to those advanced by the scholars, one which they have overlooked). Even the sources under discussion support this view.

It is reasonable, then, to fix the date of this lawsuit in the days of Caraccala, for the evidence of Dio Cassius, that he repeatedly levied the aurum coronarium and strictly enforced its payment, is well known.[18] Indeed we find a similar event occurring in Rabbi's days.

17 Maximinus' letter (on the persecution of the Christians) as it is transcribed by Eusebius, *De mart. Palaest.*, ed. Schwartz, p. 928 gives evidence of the extent to which city Strategoi were common (at the beginning of the fourth century): ἀθρόως δ'οὖν ἀυθὶς Μαξιμίνου διαφοιτᾷ καθ' ἡμῶν πανταχοῦ γράμματα... τοὺς ἐν ἁπάσαις πόλεμσι λογισταις (= curatores) ἅμα στρατηγοῖς (Cf. his *Ecclesiastical History*, ix, i, 8, ed. Schwartz, p. 804, a variant version, line 24). The expression σαρτηγοῖς is rendered into Latin (by the translator of *De mart. Palaest.*) as *Civitatis magistratus* (Violet, *Die Palaestinischen Märtyrer des Eusebius von Cäsarea*, Texte und Untersuchungen, XIV).

18 This is the excerpt from Dio Cassius (LXXVII, 9), ed. Dindorf, Vol. IV, pp. 286–287. χωρὶς γὰρ τῶν στεφάνων τῶν χρυσῶν οὓς ὡς καὶ πολεμίους

The aurum coronarium levied on Tiberias was so difficult to meet that 'all' the inhabitants of the city fled.[19]

And now we have to elucidate the incident under discussion. The Bule (apparently of Tiberias) and the Strategoi, that is the ruling executive of the (autonomous) city[20] were ordered to remit the crown tax to the government. The Strategoi were few in number, as were all members of the municipal administrations of cities in general.[21] On the other hand, the members of the Bule were numerous.[22] Consequently the Strategoi (they were, for the most part at least, Jews, just as the Bule of Tiberias and Sepphoris consisted mostly of Jews) appealed and argued that each individual Strategos should be required to contribute the same sum as each of the Bouleute, who also did so as individuals. Against them, the Bouleute argued that since the decree of the authority (the governor of Caesaria) had enumerated the two bodies separately, each should pay half. Rabbi rendered his verdict independently, ruling that the institutions and not their constituent individuals were determinant. To decide how this tax levelled on the municipal governments was to be paid was not easy. Two approaches are open: one, to explain it in accordance with the sources taken at face value, that essentially this 'contribution' was levied on the Bule and Strategoi themselves, and not on the

τινὰς ἀεὶ πολλάκις ᾔτει, λέγω δὲ οὐκ αὐτὸ τοῦτο τὸ τῶν στεφάνων ποίημα... ἀλλά τὸ τῶν χρημάτων πλῆθος τῶν ἐπ' ὀνόματι αὐτοῦ διδομένων, οἷς στεφανοῦν αἱ πόλεις τοὺς αὐτοκράτορας εἰώθασι κτλ.

19 I see that Kraus (*Synagogale Altertümer*, p. 183) sensed that the Strategos mentioned in *T.P. Yoma* have some connexion with the heads of the cities, but he erred astonishingly in his exposition of the passage in the Palestinian Talmud (see *ibid.*, n. 5. He imagines that the reference to Aaron and his sons is only metaphorical, and he explains יתנון פלגא to mean: 'They manage half the affairs of the city.' He even maintains that Rabbi laid down a rule affecting the High, and the common, priests, 'the Bule-priests are not included in the Strategos High Priests', rendering it a statement rather than a question! That is to say that Rabbi was merely dealing with an Halakha involving High Priests and ordinary priests, and he applied the metaphor of Bule and Strategos to them, but not that an actual lawsuit was submitted to him!).

20 This is the incident concerning the levying of the crown tax in Tiberias (*T.B. Bava Batra* 8a). Yet the possibility that the two incidents are one and the same is not positively excluded. We, however, find ourselves unable to reconcile them, since the traditions in their present form differ from one another.

21 We find councils of Strategoi comprising from two to ten members.

22 Sometimes the Bouleute numbered as many as hundreds (even in cities in Eretz-Israel, like Tiberias and Gaza).

entire citizenry. Although this interpretation closely follows the language of the tradition, it can only be upheld historically with difficulty (see below). Or else: that here we are dealing with the *responsibility* imposed on municipal governments to pay the taxes on which the debtors, the citizens at large, had defaulted.

Now it is known that Septimius Severus was the first to establish that the city authorities were responsible to the government for the royal debts of citizens who had defaulted.[23] Consequently, to set the time of the incident under discussion (in the days of Caraccala, Septimius' son) fits the historical-legal situation which had recently come into being and was established close to those days.

We now proceed to elucidate Rabbi's reasoning as it is set down in the tradition of the Palestinian Talmud and stated by himself: 'Is Bule not included in the Strategoi? — Then for what reason did it state: Bule and Strategoi? — This is what it says: These shall give half and those shall give half.'

The tradition under discussion may be further elucidated by reference to the later structure of municipal government as it last existed in the Roman Empire. At first, a meeting of the citizenry would select an executive for the city. After the conclusion of their term of office, these individuals would enter the Bule (composed for the most part of former members of the city executive). Later, the executive was appointed by the Bule and its members and drawn from the Bouleute, so that the members of the municipal executive were always members of the Bule (decuriones).

In the light of this situation, the passage under discussion, should, in my opinion, be explained in slightly emended form. Instead of 'Is not Bule included in the Strategoi?', the reading should be, 'Are not the Strategoi included in Bule?' — that is to say that the Strategoi, being always selected from among the Bouleute, are *ipso facto* included in the Bule and participate on equal terms with the rest of all the Bouleute in being responsible for remitting the royal taxes. Now, therefore, if the government explicitly mentioned 'Bule and Strategoi', it did not of course refer to that responsibility which the Strategoi bore as Bouleute, but to something more than that, to making them responsible as a second institution.

Now it is evident from the sources that the heads of municipal governments did have a responsibility, distinct from and over and

23 Rostowzew, *op. cit.*, p. 358.

above that of the Bule.[24] But it is a reasonable assumption that Rabbi also rendered his ruling in accordance with his appraisal of the actual situation, for the members of the executive authority were especially wealthy (since they would appoint — under the surveillance of and through the persuasion of the government — such people from among the large property owners as would be required to provide for municipal services out of their own funds, especially insofar as the responsibility affected the administrative needs of the provincial governor and the army).[25]

Once again, however, we have to attend to dates. Kuhn was the first to raise the same important and difficult question: When did the decisive change occur? For, on the one hand, we still find the earlier practice in force — namely election of the city administration by the assembled citizenry, who were not of the curiales — in the days of Pius. On the other hand, at the beginning of the third century (especially during the reign of Alexander Severus) the later practice was in force and established in law. When, then, did the event occur which changed the structure of the city (and of society as a whole) in the Roman Empire?

It seems that we are entitled to assume (along with other scholars) that this decisive innovation took place in the days of Septimius Severus, who promulgated it and gave it legal status and permanence.[26] This Emperor had made the municipal administrations responsible for the royal taxes. He founded 'cities' in Egypt for fiscal and financial ends. He reorganised the craftsmen's guilds and made them subservient to the government.[27] And he also consolidated the status of the Bouleute, and handed over to them (to their detriment rather than to their advantage) the control over and responsibility for their cities.[28] It is especially probable, then, that it was Severus

24 Wilcken, *op. cit.*, p. 38; Oertel, *op. cit.*, p. 347.

25 *Die städtische und bürgerliche Verfassung des römischen Reiches*, I, pp. 231–242.

26 Although the citizen's assemblies had begun to decline already in the days of the Antonines (Isidor Levi, *op. cit.*, p. 209).

27 Rostowtzew, *op. cit.*, p. 359; *Real Enz.*, VII, p. 422. With the assistance of experts, he had compiled a complete legal system of the city *liturgiae* (Rostowtzew, *op. cit.*, p. 358).

28 The same consolidation of the wealthy classes had already received its definitive expression in the law of inheritance (the sons inheriting the rights and debts of the fathers in serving as curiales) at the beginning of the third century (Abbott and Johnson, *op. cit.*, p. 113). We find that in Sepphoris. in about the middle of the third century, the בולבטייא 'Bouleutiae' and the

who carried out (or reinforced) that basic change which we have mentioned. Now we no longer have to reject the traditions as they were transmitted and assert that Rabbi's explanatory remarks are an elaboration inserted in later times (in itself, not difficult to assume, since the Babylonian Talmud does not include the remarks in the actual report of the incident), since at the time of the case, this state of affairs was already permanently established. But it appears to me that even the remarks at the conclusion of the Babylonian Talmud constitute Rabbi's own reasoning, as is stated in the Palestinian Talmud. The passage reads: 'There, when an order was issued on previous occasions it was directed to the Bule, and Strategoi contributed together with them, and the Government knew that they were assisting. Why, then, did they now direct the order to both Bule and Strategoi? To indicate that these should give half and those half?' This could not be a merely theoretical, reasoned rejection of the argument, since conditions prevalent in Babylon, in the Persian Empire, did not fit in with the situation which the Talmud speaks of. It must, perforce, be a tradition emanating from Eretz-Israel.

It is also reasonable to assume that R. Isaac b. Joseph, who stated the tradition quoted it in its essential form. This 'help' which the Strategoi gave the Bule, however, can only be interpreted conveniently as the participation (individually) with the rest of the members of the Bule, as Bouleute, in the payment of the crown tax. This would entail their contributing a smaller share (since the Bouleute were many). The two traditions, then, give evidence that the Government began, in those days, to give greater prominence to the Strategoi (the municipal executive) as responsible for the remittance of the royal taxes. The assumption itself, however, that the tradition only deals with the *responsibility* of the Bouleute and Strategoi for the payment of the aurum coronarium, although probable, is not altogether compelling, for we learn from the Codices (fourth century) that this tax was only levelled on the decuriones. Yet we do not hear of the rest of the citizenry (the plebs) being exempt from this obligation except in reference to 'the beginning of the fourth century at the latest'.[29] At all events, there was nothing to have prevented this last practice from having begun earlier. Even if the first practice had survived in certain localities, nevertheless this innovation (which fits into the general development of the social situation in Rome) may

פגניא 'plebs' had crystallised permanently into two classes (*T.P. Shabbat* xii, 13c; *Horayot* iii, 48c).

29 E. Stein, *Geschichte des spätrömischen Reiches*, I, p. 176.

possibly have its roots in the 'military monarchy'. It seems that Septimius Severus' last actions in the area of organising and consolidating classes and economic occupations should render the view reasonable that he was responsible for this innovation as well. (This would follow the general trend of his actions: to divide the financial burden of debt and services of the province, and to concentrate the financial obligation within the realm of the wealthy classes especially, who controlled the city administration.[30]) If we adopt this assumption, we shall have to interpret the remarks of the tradition in the Talmuds somewhat differently from their apparently plain meaning, which seem to speak of the payment of the crown tax which had been imposed from the outset on the Bouleute (curiales).

In his study, Gulack notes the fact that a case affecting the payment of the crown tax had been submitted to Rabbi for his verdict, and claims that here is proof of the large measure of autonomy conferred on the Jews by the Government in the area of taxation, since it did not interfere in the distribution of the obligation, and it was the Patriarch who rendered the decision. This would teach, then, how great was the authority exercised by the Patriarchs in allocating the royal taxes and in the methods of its collection. His remarks lead one to infer that this scholar tends to hold the view that the Patriarchs were responsible for remitting the taxes collected from the Jewish settlements in Eretz-Israel. Indeed, Zucker[31] held the view as well (his source?), that this function of the Patriarch, the remittance of the taxes collected in the name of the inhabitants of Eretz-Israel, provided the Patriarch with one of his main sources of revenue.

The entire substance of this conjecture, however, is without foun-

30 From Lampridius, *Scriptores Historiae Augustae, Al. Sever.* 32 we learn that in the days of this Emperor an artisans' tax was already in force (aurum negotiatorium et coronarium Romae remittit). Now since we know of the relationship between the *kalila* and the tax mentioned above (on craftsmen and merchants), which were collected once every five years (or at their end, every four years), and that the latter was levied on the plebs of the city — just as the first (in later times) was levied on the decuriones alone, we can, it appears, infer that this division was in force even before Alexander Severus — the Bouleute paid the coronation tax, while the rest of the citizens paid the trading and artisans taxes (כריסרגירון). It apparently stands to reason that this change leading to class distinction and consolidation should be attributed to Septimius Severus (see Abbott and Johnson, *op. cit.*, who note that the tax on artisans was in effect already in the days of Alexander Severus, and was levied once every five years during his reign).

31 *Studien zur jüdischen Selbstverwaltung*, p. 159.

dation. No single source, even in an allusion, supports it. Certainly Jewish taxes were paid according to the 'cities' in which they lived through the local authorities; and where there was no 'city', the Government would collect the taxes directly from all the inhabitants individually. Now, if it is at all possible to speak of the responsibility of the Patriarch in the area in question, this would only apply to the 'half-shekel' (the traces of which are recognisable until the middle of the third century, approximately). Yet, even here there is no basis for the exclusion of the direct collection by the *Procuratores Fisci Judaici*. And if any argument is needed in order to prove the contrary, this is furnished by these many sources (Tannaitic and Amoraic) which refer to 'tax collectors' in derogatory terms. It is impossible for these individuals to have been under the aegis of the Patriarch (for if it were he who 'remitted the taxes' to the Imperial Government, he would have appointed his tax-collectors himself, and in accordance with the practice prevailing [in the 'cities']). And if it was stated that 'a *ḥaver* who becomes a Gabbai (tax-collector) is expelled from his association', we can infer that the latter did not belong in the company of the *ḥaverim* (and the Patriarch along with them).

Essentially, then, we are dealing with Jewish individuals who came before the Patriarch to have him decide their case concerning some particular matter (for as is known, the Government took no interest, generally, in how the liability for the sums it had levelled on the communities was allocated among the taxpayers. Rabbi only acted as a judge, deciding a point of law, here. Just as ordinary Sages, not Patriarchs, have been found to arrange payments to the government by allocating and imposing the obligations on individual citizens,[32] so are similar instances to be found even in Babylon in Amoraic times.[33]

32 Such as *T.P. Mo'ed Qatan*, iii, 81d: 'In the days of R. Jeremiah trouble befell Tiberias. He sent and asked for a silver candelabra of R. Jacob b. R. Bun', etc.

33 *T.B. Bava Batra* 8a on the subject of capitation tax.

The tradition discussed here cannot, then, be taken as providing the peg on which to hang the view that seeks to regard the Patriarchs as appointed by the Government to tax the Jews of Eretz-Israel on its behalf, and as the controllers in practice of one of the main areas of public finance.[34]

34 Several papyri reveal that in the course of the third century the aurum coronarium was collected even from the village landowners; see, for instance, *PO* XVI, 1659. Apart from the fact, however, that generally speaking the situation in Egypt was different from all the other provinces of the Roman Empire, in respect of taxes and other payments to the crown, as well as in respect of its administrative structure, the Bule in Egypt (in the century mentioned above) functioned only partially, as we have seen. It is reasonable to conclude, then, that in that country, the Bouleute did not constitute an entrenched class, as did their counterparts in other lands. And apart from this we cannot assume that a uniform practice obtained in all the provinces of the Empire in the period with which we are dealing. Even in respect of other affairs (municipal administration, taxes) there were differences between one province and another in that period.

As for the aurum coronarium that was levied on Tiberias, even after we have discarded the Aggadic elements in the tradition in *T.B. Bava Batra* 8a (such as the instance of the 'fuller', a character appearing frequently especially in Aggadot recounting Rabbi's deeds), we still have no reason to assume that *all* the men of the city fled on account of the crown tax for which they had become liable. All we can say by right is that the decree affected the dignitaries of the city, that is to say, the Bouleute, who tried to save themselves by flight (and even the 'rabbis' among them belonged to the same class). The whole incident, however, requires further study.

INDICES*

I. Sources

* Edited by Yehoshua Schwartz.

E. Tosefta

F. Palestinian Talmud

H. Midrashim

J. New Testament

II. Persons

III. Places

IV. Topics